Please remember that this is a library book,
and that it belongs only temporarily to each
person who uses it. Be considerate. Do
not write in this, or any, library book.

Under the editorship of

LEONARD CARMICHAEL

SOCIAL BEHAVIOR:
A FUNCTIONAL ANALYSIS

Elliott McGinnies

UNIVERSITY OF MARYLAND

Houghton Mifflin Company • *Boston*

NEW YORK   ATLANTA   GENEVA, ILL.   DALLAS   PALO ALTO

TO MY MOTHER AND THE
MEMORY OF MY FATHER

Editor's Introduction

Today social psychology is recognized as a well organized and important sub-science that is basic in a modern understanding of much of human nature and human culture. The increasing pressures of our ever more crowded world make it clear that a knowledge of the way groups behave and how groups influence individuals and how individuals influence groups is essential if we are to have a viable and advancing society.

This new book is an original, factual, and carefully constructed introduction to this vital contemporary field of scholarship. It presents a good cross-section of salient results of modern research in social psychology in such a clear way that its chapters cannot help being of immediate interest to every serious student. It demonstrates the fact that modern science can clarify the nature of the processes involved as individuals and groups interact. This new knowledge makes possible an understanding of the way in which the dynamics of collective behavior operate in our urban-dominated world.

The student who approaches social psychology through these pages will learn not only what the major problems of this field are but also how science goes about solving them. The analysis that is presented makes it clear that many complex social questions can be understood in terms of the simpler processes that are now described in general scientific psychology. For example, this book shows how the reinforcement of units of behavior by the positive and negative rewards present in an organism's environment lead to the strengthening of specific social responses. It is made very clear that appropriate or inappropriate patterns of reinforcement are all-important in creating effective or pathological human social behavior.

To an unusual extent the theoretical position of this volume is a reflection of its author's particular constellation of capabilities. He began his academic work as a student of philosophy and psychology at the University of Buffalo. Next he did graduate work at Brown University, where he learned the importance of a knowledge of the solid facts of a psychology that is grounded in biological science. In his studies while taking the Ph.D. degree at Harvard, he carried over this natural-science attitude in constructing his understanding of the nature of personality and of social psychology in general. This broad educational background started him on a research career that so far has resulted in the publication of over forty scholarly papers emphasizing such topics as persuasion and attitude change.

But Dr. McGinnies is not merely a gifted research man and publisher of papers. He has also won recognition as an outstanding teacher. The practiced hand of the real educator can be clearly seen in every chapter of this book.

There is one other point in the career of Dr. McGinnies that has been of especial importance to him in developing his understanding of the relationship between national culture and everyday social life. He has not only had an active university career in teaching and research in the United States, but he has also conducted studies in Japan and Taiwan on the reactions of university students to various modes of persuasion. This significant part of his professional work has led him to publish a series of articles bearing on some cross-cultural aspects of communication and attitude change.

The editor cannot resist saying that he has enjoyed in a very special way the privilege of assisting in the preparation of this book for publication. It became increasingly clear to him that this volume will be an important one. It has much to say that is urgently relevant to the modern businessman, lawyer, physician, educator, and even the present-day parent.

This book also has a special lesson for university students in this period of unrest and turmoil. It clearly shows that a modern scientific understanding of human social psychology can help provide a useful frame of reference for any person who wishes to achieve a free and yet constructive life in our still all-too-imperfect democratic society.

Leonard Carmichael

Preface

It is my conviction, after many years of teaching courses in social psychology, that students become restive at having to acquire a new vocabulary to deal with social behavior. They often conclude, with justification, that social psychology has little in common with general experimental psychology, that the first is rather loose and speculative, whereas the latter is relatively well organized and disciplined. They frequently complete the course with the feeling that social psychology suffers from a surfeit of unrelated and often inconsistent research findings. We need not be surprised at this appraisal if we pause to consider that social psychologists themselves are often at odds about both theory and methodology.

One of my intentions in writing this book has been to strip away some of the more elaborate theoretical trappings that characteristically grace the pages of our professional journals. These may intrigue professionals in the field, but they serve only to mystify and frustrate the student. In striving for a unified and parsimonious theory of social behavior, I have adopted what I hope will be received as a modern and somewhat broadened version of functional behaviorism. This point of view makes sense to students. It does not require the introduction of a host of essentially mentalistic and teleological concepts that never seem quite at home among the elaborate experimental designs and statistical strategems of current research.

More important, a discussion of social behavior in terms of reinforcement principles provides the student with a consistent and generally applicable vocabulary with which to analyze the subject matter. What he may lose by being immersed in a somewhat parochial viewpoint, he more than gains by acquiring a systematic theoretical stance. He is the master of a small island rather than the confused surveyor of a vast, uncharted domain.

It is my additional hope that the approach of this book, while being provocative to the student, will not grate too harshly upon the instructor who does not subscribe to reinforcement theory. The critical lecturer can always draw bead on those interpretations with which he disagrees, in which case the book may serve as a foil for discussion and debate. The theoretical posture that I have adopted has not prevented me from covering what I have judged to be some of the basic, or classic, studies in social psychology. At the same time, I have attempted to range from the early research in any given area to some of the more current and interesting findings. The degree of selectivity that has been necessary reflects not only my own major interests but also what I feel to be topics that will hold the attention of the reader. The book, as far as I am concerned, will stand or fall on how it is received by the interested student.

Elliott McGinnies

Acknowledgments

Writing a book is, as an author friend of mine has observed, largely a matter of applying one's bottom to the seat of a chair for long periods of time. Having friends with good advice is also important, and I have been fortunate in this respect. I should like to acknowledge here their support and assistance.

Leonard Carmichael has been a source of advice and encouragement throughout the preparation of this book. His kind and astute editing was crucial to the completion of the manuscript, and I gained much from our association. Robert Rooney, of Houghton Mifflin, patiently awaited the outcome of my efforts while applying occasional deserved prods.

During the early stages of the writing, I received many valuable suggestions from William S. Verplanck; his contributions to the theoretical development of the book got me started. Various colleagues gave generously of their time in reading and criticizing chapters falling in their areas of interest, and for their valuable suggestions I extend my thanks to Irwin Altman, Lee Becker, Willard Larkin, and Harold Vetter.

I am particularly grateful to Charles Ferster, an outstanding behavioral scientist, for working closely with me on the entire book. He deserves much of the credit for any meritorious qualities that the book may have, and he will recognize many of his ideas, and even his words, among the pages. The treatment is probably not quite as behavioral as Dr. Ferster would have liked, and he is not to be held responsible for any flights into mentalism that I may have taken.

Finally, I appreciate greatly the careful and professional editing of Mrs. Diane Faissler, whose efforts eliminated many errors and trimmed the rough edges off the finished product.

Elliott McGinnies

Contents

1

Background

and Concepts

It would not be an exaggeration to say that virtually all human behavior reveals the products of social influence. Even those laboratory experiments where individuals are studied in relative isolation involve an interaction between subject and experimenter. The effects of this interaction on the subject's performance may, in fact, be considerable. Nor are we likely to overstate the practical necessity of increasing our store of knowledge about human relationships in a world that has seen scientific progress in the social sciences outstripped by that in the physical sciences.

The study of social behavior invites us to apply to human interaction those principles from general experimental psychology that seem to be most firmly established. There will be areas in which we shall make only slow and difficult headway because our understanding of fundamental behavioral principles is still incomplete. But this need not deter us from comprehending social behavior in terms of what we know about individual learning and performance. We already possess much of the information that we need to build a science of social behavior, and research in this area is burgeoning. Although we must approach our subject matter with caution, the fact that we have at least a modest understanding of behavioral principles allows us to muster confidence.

Let us propose a brief and simple definition: *social behavior is evidenced whenever two or more organisms, either directly or indirectly, serve both to prompt and to reinforce one another's performances.* Such interaction may occur within or between species. A man interacts socially with his wife, but he also interacts with his dog. Animals have complex social relationships with one another, and domesticated animals also interact socially with humans. Although we are primarily interested in human social behavior, we shall refer to instances of social interaction among animals

1

whenever these throw light upon some general behavior pattern that is common across species.

The reactions of each participant to a behavioral exchange are understood in terms of (a) the genetic endowment of the participant, (b) his prior learning and performance history, and (c) those features of the immediate situation that prompt his performance. In analyzing the relative contributions of these three sets of factors, we begin with as complete a description of each individual's performance as we can achieve. We then look to the stimulus features of the situation that were antecedent to the behavioral sequence and to the effects that the behavior of each person has on the other as well as on the environment. This functional approach to a behavioral exchange provides us with a key both to understanding the behavior in terms of stimulus-response relationships and to predicting the course of future interactions.

What we have outlined here, of course, is the mere skeleton of the theoretical framework upon which we shall attempt to amass a body of experimental data. In the next chapter, we shall consider in some detail the meaning of *reinforcement* and the other technical terms that will be used throughout the book. Now, however, we turn to a brief review of the historical and philosophical background of modern social psychology and to a brief consideration of social behavior as it is expressed by other species.

Concepts of Human Nature

Notions of Causality

The question most frequently asked in connection with human behavior is "Why?" Social behavior, like all other natural phenomena, is assumed to be lawful and predictable. Without digressing into the concept of causality, we can probably agree that all events serve to initiate other events, so that searching for a cause reduces to specifying the events that have been necessary precursors to the one whose origins we seek. Thus, if I strike a blow on a person's patellar tendon, his foot kicks out. This response is said to result from the stimulus that has been applied. We could bring about a similar reaction by asking the subject to kick. Either stimulus can be said to have caused the response, and we have effectively answered the question of "why" the response occurred. One stimulus elicited a reflex, whereas the other was the occasion for a learned reaction to verbal instruction. Not only do we understand both instances of behavior in terms of their antecedents, but we can produce them at will, given a healthy and willing subject.

Although behavior is considered to be the lawful consequence of antecedent stimulation, the nature of the controlling stimulus events frequently is not known. As a result, we may not understand why people behave as

they do, and we may be attracted by simplistic theories that attribute behavior to such unitary principles as hedonism, gregariousness, imitation,
or suggestion (Allport, 1968). Why, when a controversial political figure
is introduced to an audience, do some members "boo" and "hiss," while
others applaud? Referring these contrasting behaviors to the operation of
"hostility" or "suggestion" is not helpful. We might invoke the concept
of "attitude," with the understanding that the respective performances
must still be understood in terms of certain prior learning experiences that
have led to these varied reactions.

We have said that social behavior is largely the product of past experience or learning. To be sure, genetic factors set limits to what the individual is able to learn, and they may even determine to some extent the
reactions that others will have to him. For example, the very tall person
or the very short person is likely to be singled out for the type of attention
that a person of average height would not receive. This will inevitably
influence the way that person reacts to others. A beautiful girl is destined
to receive compliments and other forms of social approbation that a plain
girl will never experience. One could cite many instances of the role that
genetically determined characteristics play in the individual's social
learning experiences. The Negro, of course, is an outstanding example of
the effect that skin color alone may have on the behavior of other persons,
and the behavioral development of Negroes can scarcely be understood
without taking this fact into consideration. But the contribution of genetic
variables to behavior has often been extended far beyond what we have
suggested as being legitimate. It has been asserted that some attitudes
and beliefs are innate, or inborn. It has been argued at times that man has
a "natural" affinity for certain religious convictions, that man is "innately"
aggressive, or that man instinctively prefers his "own kind." Persons who
would not for a moment suggest that individuals are born with a preference
for the Republican or Democratic party will unhesitatingly agree that
many other behavioral dispositions are rooted in "human nature." How
did the concept of human nature evolve, and what status does it enjoy in
current psychological theory?

The Early Greek Philosophers

Theories about human nature are probably as old as man himself. Regardless of their conceptual differences, most of them reduce to a matter
of attributing man's essentially human characteristics either to heredity or
to learning. Some observers, as we have noted, have decided that certain
behavioral dispositions are transmitted through the germ plasm, that is,
genetically. According to this line of reasoning, an individual might inherit tendencies toward aggressiveness, submissiveness, honesty, crimi-
nality, or even psychosis. Almost any objective description of human
behavior could be suspected, from this viewpoint, of defining an innate

predisposition. We shall examine this contention later in some detail, but it should be pointed out that two of the earliest and most astute of the Western philosophers, Plato and Aristotle, considered human conduct to result from the interaction of innate proclivities with the educational forces of society.

Writing over 2,000 years ago, Plato, in *The Republic*, described individuals as essentially the products of their culture. Although he believed that some persons were more fitted at birth to be leaders and others to be followers, Plato did not overlook the importance of education in fitting each individual into his place in the State. He said, for example: "There will be discovered to be some natures who ought to study philosophy and to be leaders in the State; and others who are not born to be philosophers and are meant to be followers rather than leaders." In appraising the importance of training in producing virtuous citizens for his ideal State, Plato said: "Education and admonition commence in the first years of childhood and last to the very end of life."

Plato's pupil, Aristotle, also wrote at length about society and the ideal community. He, like Plato, viewed men as being endowed from birth with different talents and capacities. From this consideration he reasoned, as Plato had, that not everyone is suited to a position of leadership: "For he who has the 'practical reason' to foresee (what should be done) is suited by nature to be lord and master, while he who is endowed with the bodily power to carry out (such plans) is by nature a subject and a slave."

However, Aristotle did not, as some writers mistakenly interpret him, view society as merely the product of innate human nature. He recognized, as much as Plato did, the critical roles of training and education in molding human social behavior. It is true that he believed man has an innately gregarious tendency, beginning with the procreative instinct. This "natural instinct in all men toward community living," as Aristotle phrased it, merely established the basis for a societal framework within which education could operate. In *The Nichomachean Ethics*, he states: "The virtues, then, are not engendered in us either by nature or in opposition to nature; rather nature gives us the capacity for receiving them, and this capacity is developed through habit." Aristotle, incidentally, devoted considerable attention to developing the philosophy of a liberal education. He recommended pursuit of the arts, for example, because they lead to the cultivated enjoyment of leisure and not simply because of any practical utility they might have.

Despite a number of rather extreme and unusual viewpoints that arose in the interim, the similarity between the modern view of human nature and that of Plato and Aristotle is rather striking. We do not, of course, support Aristotle's notion that some men are born to be slaves, nor do we feel, with Plato, that the State should dictate the functions of its individual members. But the significant roles of education and experience in producing the patterns of behavior that characterize each person are commonly recognized. We might even do well to heed Aristotle's admonition:

> For as man when perfected is the noblest of animals, so apart from law and justice he is the worst of all; because injustice is most dangerous when it is armed, and man is equipped at birth with weapons intended to serve the cause of moral intelligence and virtue but capable of being put to opposite uses. Hence, where man is without virtue he is the most unscrupulous and bestial of animals, outdoing all the rest in lust and gluttony.

Although these early Greek philosophers laid the groundwork for understanding social interaction, they did not possess the methods of investigation that might have enabled them to specify more clearly the relative contributions of genetic and experiential factors to human behavior. Later in this chapter we shall attempt a clarification of this problem.

Certain other historical landmarks are of interest in providing us with an orientation through which to analyze the current status of social psychology. It must be remembered that man's progress toward understanding his own behavior has been slow and tortuous, much more so than his progress in understanding the external world. We are, of course, part of the physical world, but we have difficulty in scrutinizing ourselves with the same detachment and objectivity with which we study other aspects of nature. One of the functions of this book will be to provide an analytic framework within which such an objective appraisal of our social behavior can be attained.

Modern Philosophical Views

The man who enjoys the reputation of being the first social scientist, Auguste Comte, proposed in 1848 a philosophical position which he believed would lead to a dispassionate analysis of man such as we are attempting. Comte argued that mankind passes progressively through three stages of development. These are (a) the *theological stage*, in which knowledge is derived from revelation and belief in the supernatural, (b) the *metaphysical stage,* in which man attempts to reach understanding through reason and logic, and (c) the *positive stage,* in which the scientific method replaces both revelation and speculation as the principal source of human knowledge. Comte's position, in fact, is known as *positivism.* A positivist, therefore, is one who scorns "revealed" truth and supernatural explanations of events and relies, instead, upon objective observations and experiments, that is, upon the outcome of scientific research. Most scientists today are positivists of one sort or another in their own fields.

Why should Comte have scorned theology as a source of knowledge? Probably he was cognizant of some of the logical dilemmas in which theologians had trapped themselves during the Middle Ages in attempting to solve the problem of good and evil in human behavior. Basically, theologians of the medieval period recognized the problem of accounting for the existence of behavior that they deemed undesirable or sinful. It seemed illogical to assume that a benevolent supreme being would countenance the existence of evil if he were able to prevent it. It followed, therefore, that such a being could not be both beneficent and omnipotent. To deny either alternative, however, would be damaging to the conception of a supreme being as both all good and all powerful. This dilemma was resolved theologically by postulating a force opposed to God known as Satan, or the Devil, and assuming that man was given the prerogative of choosing freely between good and evil. Since it was assumed that man is free to choose between these alternatives, he could be held culpable for taking the wrong path and was liable, therefore, to punishment in this world as well as the next. Heaven and hell were thus postulated as alternative destinies for man, who could freely elect his own fate. This general theological position leans heavily on the doctrine of *free will.*

This point of view was subjected to critical analysis by the British empiricists, from Francis Bacon through John Stuart Mill. During this period of philosophical development, attention was focused on the notions of *cause* and *effect,* particularly in the writings of David Hume. The empiricists took the position that certain events are regularly conjoined with other events and do not occur capriciously. Perhaps the clearest statement of this was made by Hume in 1748: "It is universally allowed that matter, in all its operations, is actuated by a necessary force, and that every natural effect is so precisely determined by the energy of its cause that no other effect, in such particular circumstances, could possibly have resulted from it."

What Hume said, in essence, was that every cause has one, and only one, effect. This basic postulate underlies the general theory of *determinism* and is directly contradictory to the doctrine of free will in its application to human behavior. Man's behavior must be lawful and predictable, according to the principle of causality, or it must vary unpredictably in accordance with freedom of the will. Obviously, acceptance of the latter alternative would make the scientific study of behavior impossible. Whether they recognize the fact or not, most scientists behave in a way consistent with the deterministic viewpoint. Since man is a part of the physical world, there is no reason to assume that he behaves other than in accordance with the same laws that govern other natural phenomena. To be sure, human behavior is not as predictable as events that transpire in the physics, chemistry, and biology laboratories. The greater degree of uncertainty in our predictions of human behavior, however, means only that we have not yet delineated all the antecedent conditions for the many behavioral phenomena that interest us. In fact, Hume recognized this problem:

> We must not, however, expect that this uniformity of human actions should be carried to such a length as that all men, in the same circumstances, will always act precisely in the same manner, without making any allowance for

the diversity of characters, prejudices, and opinions. Such a uniformity is found in no part of nature. On the contrary, from observing the variety of conduct in different men, we are enabled to form a greater variety of maxims, which still suppose a degree of uniformity and regularity (in Burtt, 1939, p. 637).

Hume also introduced the concept of *multiple causation,* which, when recognized, elucidates many of the thorny problems in current experimental research. In modern guise this concept goes under the terms confounding variables or extraneous variables. In many experiments, particularly where social behavior is involved, we may attribute an experimental finding to the operation of a particular independent variable, or cause, that we have purposely introduced, only to discover that some uncontrolled factor has actually contributed to the observed result. The effects of a drug on performance, for example, invariably represent the concomitant operation of the physiological effects induced by the drug together with the effects of suggestion, induced by the subject's knowledge that he is being given medicine. The use of placebos with control subjects does not always solve this problem. As Orne (1962) has found, many subjects will behave in terms of hypotheses that they have formed about the nature and purpose of the experiment. They are responding not just to the independent variables introduced by the experimenter, but also to what they perceive as the "demand characteristics" of the total situation.

We arrive, then, at the inescapable conclusion that behavior must be viewed as essentially lawful and determined. To conclude otherwise would make a science of behavior pointless, if not impossible. The causes of behavior, of course, are many, and psychologists generally observe caution in conducting experiments so that uncontrolled or confounding variables do not lead them to erroneous conclusions about cause-effect relationships. Actually, most psychologists prefer to sidestep the philosophical problems posed by the terms *cause* and *effect* and refer, instead, to *antecedent* and *consequent* conditions in behavioral research. We shall discuss these concepts in later chapters.

Instinct Theory

The early philosophers, of course, did not derive their ideas from experimentation. They were astute observers of human behavior, and they resorted to logical analysis in attempting to understand the problems of human nature. Much of their effort was directed toward problems of morality, justice, and ethics. Questions of this type could be approached empirically, since they involve the learning of various performances, but they have been largely neglected by experimental psychology. Many of the problems entertained by the philosophers have implications for psychological theories of human behavior and are susceptible to analysis by modern research techniques. These include the questions to which Plato and Aristotle turned their attention, concerning the essential nature of man. No less a figure than William McDougall, the most prominent social psychologist in the United States a half century ago, revived certain features of Aristotelian thinking by emphasizing instinct as a factor in human behavior. Writing in 1923, McDougall explicated the concept of instinct as follows:

> We may . . . define an instinct as an inherited or innate psychophysical disposition which determines its possessor to perceive and to pay attention to objects of a certain class, to experience an emotional excitement of a particular quality upon perceiving such an object, and to act in regard to it in a particular manner, or, at least, to experience an impulse to such action (p. 30).

McDougall, in developing his theory, proposed that man has seven principal instincts, each with its associated emotion:

Instinct	Emotion
flight	fear
repulsion	disgust
curiosity	wonder
pugnacity	anger
self-abasement	subjection
self-assertion	elation
parental	tenderness

McDougall describes these paired relationships in colorful fashion. With reference to the instinct of repulsion and the emotion of disgust, he states:

> The one impulse of repulsion is to reject from the mouth substances that excite the instinct in virtue of their odor or taste, substances which in the main are noxious and evil-tasting; its biological utility is obvious. The other impulse of repulsion seems to be excited by the contact of slimy and slippery substances with the skin, and to express itself as a shrinking of the whole body, accompanied by a forward throwing of the hands. The common shrinking from slimy creatures with a "creepy" shudder seems to be the expression of this impulse (p. 58).

We cannot but admire McDougall's engaging description of the reactions elicited by certain classes of objects, described as "noxious" or "slimy." But a problem arises in connection with his contention that the reactions he describes are innate or "instinctive." For example, McDougall argues that while the instinct of repulsion is displayed by some children in the first year of life, it appears much later in others, so that ". . . the child that has handled worms, frogs, and slugs with delight suddenly evinces an unconquerable aversion to contact with them" (p. 58).

It is axiomatic in the scientific approach that a parsimonious, or simple, explanation is always preferred to a more complex one. This is because the simpler explanation involves fewer assumptions about unknown and perhaps unobservable factors. In line with this scientific tenet, we prefer to explain social behavior whenever possible in terms of stimulus-response relationships rather than by recourse to a doctrine of inherited traits that is based largely on assumptions that are difficult to support. If, in fact, nearly everyone in a particular society displays repugnance in the presence of certain objects, as McDougall suggests is true, an explanation in terms of learning would be more parsimonious than one employing the notion of instinct. The "sudden, unconquerable aversion" to which McDougall refers is in all likelihood the product of a single traumatic learning experience. We may not have witnessed it, but we can duplicate such an experience, if we desire to, through straightforward procedures.

Perhaps what McDougall really was suggesting is that the basic mechanism of escape and avoidance is innate, and that the individual has the capability of acquiring behaviors that are instrumental in terminating or escaping from an aversive stimulus. In brief, we can accept the position that each individual has an ontogenetic (individual) history which is responsible for the form and existence of certain behaviors and a phylogenetic (racial) history which determines the particular stimuli that are effective. In some species more behavior can be accounted for ontogenetically than phylogenetically, while in others the reverse is true.

Hebb (1958), for example, has reported intense fear responses in chimpanzees at the sight of a model of either a chimpanzee head or a human head. Since the animals under observation had had no opportunities to acquire these specific fears, it seems probable that their reactions depended upon an innate, or unlearned, aversion to certain classes of objects. In this instance, Hebb suggests that a conflict exists between the effects of the immediate sensory input and the reaction patterns set up by past experience. It must be admitted, in general, that as yet we know little about the genetic control of certain types of behavior. When the possibility of prior learning has been ruled out, we must conclude that certain species-specific behaviors may have their origins in the orderly development of sensory-neural mechanisms.

A re-examination of the usefulness of the concept of instinct has been urged by Breland and Breland (1961) as a result of their years of experience training animals in complex behavior repertoires. They cite several interesting examples of what they have termed "instinctive drift," which means the interruption of certain well-learned behaviors by what seem to be species-specific responses that actually interfere with or delay the animal's reward. They describe, for example, the behavior of a grown Bantam chicken that has learned a routine that might be called "What makes Sammy dance?":

> In the exhibit in which this occurred, the casual observer sees a grown Bantam chicken emerge from a retaining compartment when the door automatically opens. The chicken walks over about three feet, pulls a rubber

loop on a small box which starts a repeated auditory stimulus pattern (a four-note tune). The chicken then steps up onto an 18-inch, slightly raised disc, thereby closing a timer switch, and scratches vigorously, round and round, over the disc for fifteen seconds, at the rate of about two scratches per second, until the automatic feeder fires in the retaining compartment. The chicken goes into the compartment to eat, thereby automatically shutting the door. The popular interpretation of this behavior pattern is that the chicken has turned on the "juke box" and "dances" (p. 681).

Actually, as the authors point out, the development of this particular exhibit was quite unplanned, since they had originally required that the chicken simply stand still on the platform for about fifteen seconds. However, they found that over 50 per cent of their animals scratched vigorously at the platform, scratching more persistently the longer they stood there. The experimenters simply made use of this natural tendency of the chicken in developing a pattern of behavior they called "dancing."

Two other misadventures, involving a raccoon and a pig, illustrate their point further. The raccoon, whose manipulatory ability is similar to that of the primates, was trained to pick up coins and drop them in a toy bank, for which he received a reward of food. A pig also was trained to pick up large wooden coins and deposit them (where else?) in a "piggy bank." The animals learned these habits readily. However, after a short time they both began to exhibit interfering responses. The investigators describe the raccoon's behavior as follows:

> Not only could he not let go of the coins, but he spent seconds, even minutes, rubbing them together (in a most miserly fashion), and dipping them into the container. He carried on this behavior to such an extent that the practical application we had in mind — a display featuring a raccoon putting money in a piggy bank — simply was not feasible. The rubbing behavior became worse and worse as time went on, in spite of non-reinforcement (p. 682).

The pig, after having learned the same pattern of behavior — depositing coins in a piggy bank — became increasingly slower at performing this trick. He would pick up the dollar, but instead of immediately depositing it in the bank as he had previously done, ". . . he would repeatedly drop it, root it, drop it again, root it along the way, pick it up, toss it up in the air, drop it, root it some more, and so on" (p. 683).

The authors cite some other examples of competing behaviors which suddenly emerged in the middle of conditioned sequences of complex manipulatory responses. They suggest, by way of interpretation, that the dancing chicken is exhibiting a scratch pattern which, in nature, often precedes the ingestion of food. The raccoon has suddenly reverted to what has been termed "washing behavior." This would have the practical utility, for a wild raccoon, of removing the exoskeleton, or shell, of a crayfish. The rooting and shaking behavior of the pig represents behavior, typical for this species, that ordinarily is necessary in digging food out of the ground. The authors conclude that these animals are trapped by strong instinctive behaviors that are prepotent over any behavior patterns that have been conditioned. They go even further, conceding that the notion of instinct is indispensable in their analysis of animal behavior. "When behaviorism tossed out instinct," the Brelands state, "it is our feeling that some of its power of prediction and control were lost with it. . . . After 14 years with continuous conditioning and observation of thousands of animals, it is our reluctant conclusion that the behavior of any species cannot be adequately understood, predicted, or controlled without knowledge of its instinctive patterns, evolutionary history, and ecological niche" (p. 684).

We have taken time to examine instinct theory in some detail because recourse to this type of explanation is by no means rare in current thought. Nor, as the Brelands point out, can we assume that this concept has no scientific value. Misuse of the term instinct can be avoided, however, by recognition of these facts: (a) at the present time, the concept of instinct has descriptive rather than explanatory value; and (b) many behaviors that initially seem to result from an "innate" tendency or disposition turn out to be dependent upon specific kinds of experiences that are common to members of the species. Perhaps a basic problem here is that psychologists frequently fail to take sufficient account of the fact that there are wide individual differences or variations in performance. Such variations cannot always be ascribed to differences in learning histories. Populations, as Hirsch (1962) has argued, vary widely in both form and other biological characteristics, and these differences are reflected in behavior. He even suggests that different behavioral laws may be found for different subjects, and that all subjects should be screened and classified prior to experimentation.

The Environmental Position

Probably the most vigorous proponent of the environmental viewpoint was John B. Watson, known generally as the founder of that theoretical position in psychology known as behaviorism. Watson was unwilling to grant any great significance to heredity as the source of individual behavior patterns. He argued that behavior was molded by environmental factors and that biological differences among normal individuals play a minor role in their behavioral differences. Watson expressed this viewpoint quite unequivocally:

> Give me a dozen, healthy infants, well-formed, and my own specific world to bring them up in and I'll guarantee to take any one at random and train him to become any type of specialist I might select — doctor, lawyer, artist,

merchant-chief, and yes, even beggar-man and thief, regardless of his talents, penchants, abilities, vocations, and race of his ancestors (1930, p. 104).

It is interesting to note in this statement that Watson did not deny the existence of individual differences in what he called "penchants, abilities, vocations." He apparently felt, however, that these variations in "innate" capacities were of minor importance compared to the overriding power of the environment to influence the individual's behavior. As we shall see in the next section, few psychologists at the present time would be so bold as to agree with Watson that any "well formed" individual can be turned into a doctor or artist regardless of whatever native capacities or talents he might have. A notion similar to that expressed by Watson can be found in Aldous Huxley's *Brave New World* (1962). This is a rather frightening projection of a future society in which each person is trained, through Pavlovian conditioning procedures, to accept a specified place in society. One of the scenes described by Huxley depicts the process by which such conditioning is accomplished:*

"Infant Nurseries. Neo-Pavlovian Conditioning Rooms," announced the notice board.

The Director opened a door. They were in a large, bare room, very bright and sunny; for the whole of the southern wall was a single window. Half a dozen nurses, trousered and jacketed in the regulation white viscose-linen uniform, their hair aseptically hidden under white caps, were engaged in setting out bowls of roses in a long row across the floor. Big bowls, packed tight with blossoms. Thousands of petals, ripe-blown and silkily smooth, like the cheeks of innumerable little cherubs, but of cherubs, in that bright light, not exclusively Aryan, but also luminously Chinese, also Mexican, also apoplectic with too much blowing of celestial trumpets, also pale as death, pale with the posthumous whiteness of marble.

The nurses stiffened to attention as the D.H.C. came in.

"Set out the books," he said curtly.

In silence the nurses obeyed his command. Between the rose bowls the books were duly set out — a row of nursery quartos opened invitingly each at some gaily coloured image of beast or fish or bird.

"Now bring in the children."

They hurried out of the room and returned in a minute or two, each pushing a kind of tall dumb-waiter laden, on all its four wire-netted shelves, with eight-month-old babies, all exactly alike (a Bokanovsky Group, it was evident) and all (since their caste was Delta) dressed in khaki.

"Put them down on the floor."

The infants were unloaded.

"Now turn them so that they can see the flowers and books."

Turned, the babies at once fell silent, then began to crawl towards those clusters of sleek colours, those shapes so gay and brilliant on the white pages.

* From *Brave New World*, by Aldous Huxley (New York: Harper, 1960). Copyright, 1932, 1960 by Aldous Huxley. Reprinted by permission of Harper and Row, Publishers, Mrs. Laura Huxley, and Chatto and Windus Ltd.

As they approached, the sun came out of a momentary eclipse behind a cloud. The roses flamed up as though with a sudden passion from within; a new and profound significance seemed to suffuse the shining pages of the books. From the ranks of the crawling babies came little squeals of excitement, gurgles and twitterings of pleasure.

The Director rubbed his hands. "Excellent!," he said. "It might almost have been done on purpose."

The swiftest crawlers were already at their goal. Small hands reached out uncertainly, touched, grasped, unpetaling the transfigured roses, crumpling the illuminated pages of the books. The Director waited until all were happily busy. Then, "Watch carefully," he said. And, lifting his hand, he gave the signal.

The Head Nurse, who was standing by a switchboard at the other end of the room, pressed down a little lever.

There was a violent explosion. Shriller and ever shriller, a siren shrieked. Alarm bells maddeningly sounded.

The children started, screamed; their faces were distorted with terror.

"And now," the Director shouted (for the noise was deafening), "now we proceed to rub in the lesson with a mild electric shock."

He waved his hand again, and the Head Nurse pressed a second lever. The screaming of the babies suddenly changed its tone. There was something desperate, almost insane, about the sharp spasmodic yelps to which they now gave utterance. Their little bodies twitched and stiffened; their limbs moved jerkily as if to the tug of unseen wires.

"We can electrify that whole strip of floor," bawled the Director in explanation. "But that's enough," he signalled to the nurse.

The explosions ceased, the bells stopped ringing, the shriek of the siren died down from tone to tone into silence. The stiffly twitching bodies relaxed, and what had become the sob and yelp of infant maniacs broadened out once more into a normal howl of ordinary terror.

"Offer them the flowers and the books again."

The nurses obeyed; but at the approach of the roses, at the mere sight of those gaily coloured images of pussy, and cock-a-doodle-doo and baa-baa black sheep, the infants shrank away in horror; the volume of their howling suddenly increased.

"Observe," said the Director triumphantly, "observe."

Books and loud noises, flowers and electric shocks — already in the infant mind these couples were compromisingly linked; and after two hundred repetitions of the same or a similar lesson would be wedded indissolubly (1960, pp. 20–22).

Huxley's colorful description requires little comment except to note that the scene he depicts is not beyond the realm of possibility. Indeed, we should not be too hard-pressed to find analogous examples of attitude formation in our society at the present time. Children, for example, are conditioned to avoid objects and situations that are related to cultural taboos. These include excremental activities and sex. Each society probably conditions its members to respond negatively to situations that are deemed "wicked," "sinful," or "dirty." Nor does it take two hundred repetitions to accomplish these results. The fear responses described by Huxley could be learned in less than half a dozen trials.

Current Viewpoints

The Search for Motives

McDougall's list of instincts contains several that have begun to enjoy renewed popularity. But now they are referred to as drives and are suspected of having a genetic basis. However, it is only the general *pattern* of the behavior that is considered to be genetically determined. The particular eliciting stimuli must acquire control over the behavior through experience. One method of approaching this general problem is illustrated by the recent research of Harlow (1953) and his associates on curiosity. They have found that monkeys will learn certain instrumental acts which have as a consequence nothing more than the presentation of a visual display. Why should a monkey operate a wheel to open a window in his cage when the only reward is an opportunity to look outside? Harlow postulates an innate drive of curiosity which, when appropriately reinforced, can provide a basis for learning.

Research on exploratory behavior by Montgomery and Segall (1955) also provides some tangible basis for taking a fresh look at what McDougall called the curiosity instinct. These investigators found that rats will learn a black-white discrimination when the only reward is an opportunity to explore a large, Dashiell-type maze for one minute. At the human level, we might view the nearly universal curiosity of children as suggesting a genetic basis for both manipulative and exploratory behavior. The fact that human infants will spontaneously play with toys provided by their parents, this activity apparently being an end in itself, suggests that behavior of this type may be independent of prior learning. Montgomery (1954) argues for such a point of view by asserting that the introduction of novel external stimulation into an animal's environment is sufficient to evoke exploratory behavior. If exploration does, in fact, represent an unlearned class of behaviors, then one might speculate as to whether this disposition is shared by all humans to the same extent or whether some individuals show more innate curiosity than others.

McDougall's instincts self-abasement and self-assertion have appeared in different guise in Murray's (1938) system for personality description and analysis, where we find abasement and dominance on the list of acquired needs. In many instances these dispositions can probably be traced to earlier life experiences where the individual has achieved certain rewards or satisfactions from behaving either assertively or submissively. A convincing argument for the genetic basis of such general behavioral traits as these, however, is achieved most easily in the case of animals other than man. Different breeds of dogs, in fact, have been shown to exhibit characteristically different temperaments. Whether or not individual humans are hereditarily disposed to either passive or dominant behavior remains a matter of conjecture.

Finally, pugnacity as a basic human tendency has been re-examined in the research of Dollard and his coworkers (1939). They redefine it as "aggression" and argue that an invariant relationship exists between aggressive behavior and antecedent states of frustration. This generalization, however, is open to question, since reactions other than aggression occur to frustration. In a recent analysis, Scott (1958) suggests that, "On the whole it is best to assume that any human being has the capacity to develop a fair amount of aggressiveness, but that his need to express it will depend upon his training and the amount of stimulation in his environment" (p. 131).

Some recent research has focused on the matter of an innate or genetically determined basis for certain aversions that organisms have. Hunt and Quay (1961) have reported that rats reared in a vibrating cage from before birth to fifty-six days of age pressed a bar less frequently to stop the vibration than did control animals that were reared normally. In other words, the experimental animals appeared to have been somewhat habituated to a sensation that rats normally strive to avoid. At the same time, these animals did not press the bar to start vibration more often than did the controls. In short, they had not acquired, during the prenatal and postnatal habituation period of vibration, a "need" to live under this unusual condition. The authors suggest that merely becoming accustomed to stimulation which is innately aversive does not necessarily render it positively reinforcing. In similar fashion, Warren and Pfaffmann (1958) demonstrated that guinea pigs raised to drink only a bitter solution were less rejecting of this liquid than control animals when later given an option of choosing pure water; however, even these habituated animals still preferred ordinary water. Still other researchers have reported that mice reared with a flashing light will, when given the opportunity to change, prefer an environment that has constant illumination.

Certain other stimuli seem to have positive reinforcing qualities that are independent of learning. Human infants have been observed to fixate longer on the colors blue and green than on red. Infants also show a tendency to prefer certain flavors over others, as indicated either by sucking and licking or by turning away. Finally, infant monkeys show a preference for artificial mothers (mother surrogates) that are padded over mothers made of wire, even when they have been fed by the latter. The reinforcing qualities of the padded mother surrogate are apparently prepotent over those of the wire model that has been paired with feeding. Interestingly enough, these experiments with infant monkeys and mother surrogates also revealed that monkeys that were denied contact even with a wire mother during infancy never learned to "love" either a real or an artificial mother when they grew older. Harlow (1958), who reports these effects, suggests that those individuals that do not learn to love as infants may never learn to love at all.

Nature and Nurture Revisited

Intelligence. All of these investigations and viewpoints relate to the differences between what Ewer (1961) has called *endogenous* and *experience-conditioned* patterns of behavior. These terms are the current equivalents of the older concepts of nature and nurture, or environment and heredity. The term *endogenous* means "produced from within" or "originating from internal causes," while the term *experience-conditioned* refers simply to learning. These two categories are not mutually exclusive; that is, any specific instance of behavior cannot be assigned merely to one or the other. As Ewer puts it, "the two 'categories' are rather complementary aspects of central nervous activity which are integrated to produce adaptive ways of behaving" (p. 258). He states further that ". . . learning can take place only on the basis of self-differentiating endogenous responses, and an endogenous pattern may show modification as it matures" (p. 258).

Perhaps the best example of this principle is language. Speech is a characteristically human performance, and all normal children are endowed with the capacity to acquire this skill. In this sense, speech is an endogenous human response. But all humans do not speak the same language, so this endogenous pattern is highly variable and develops differently depending upon the society in which one is raised. The same is true of many other human behavior variables. Probably all persons are capable of the types of behavior just discussed — curiosity, assertion, abasement, aggressiveness — but these behavioral dispositions develop differently in different individuals according to the environmental conditions that they encounter.

Where general intelligence is concerned, some slight disagreement among psychologists is encountered concerning the extent to which the maximum level of development is fixed by heredity and the extent to which an individual's intellectual level can be changed by social and other environmental factors. In general, it is apparent that each person inherits a certain capacity for learning, and that this capacity is modifiable only within limits. An impoverished physical and social environment can depress the individual's level of intellectual functioning, and this will show up in his performance on intelligence tests. A favorable environment, on the other hand, one that provides superior cultural and educational opportunities, is capable of raising the individual's tested intelligence to some extent. Changes of twenty I.Q. points have been reported in certain dramatic cases. However, the average person operates within a certain predetermined range of intelligent behavior that is susceptible to only limited modification by his physical and social environment. No amount of training and encouragement will turn John Doe into an Einstein if his basic I.Q. is 100. Conversely, even a total lack of educational and cultural stimulation will not reduce him to the level of a moron — although disease can do so. Goodenough and Tyler (1959) have commented as follows:

> The search for general ways of increasing the rate of mental growth in children has been unsuccessful. Under special circumstances of deprivation, providing the needed medication or stimulation has produced beneficial results. But under normal favorable circumstances, the individual's mental development proceeds at its own natural pace and is not much affected by attempts to speed it up (p. 305).

Talent. While most authorities agree on the essentially endogenous nature of intelligence, less consensus is exhibited concerning the innateness of special talents or abilities. We refer here not to capacities based on physique or health but, rather, to capacities for learning particular kinds of skills. The most obvious examples of learned behavior that probably reflect inherent talent are musical skill, aesthetic sensitivity, and athletic prowess. Given apparently equal desire, instruction, and practice, some individuals reveal an aptitude for playing musical instruments, while others display virtually none. The same seems to be true for skill in the areas of painting, sculpture, and the performing arts. In all of these instances, of course, environmental influences cannot be completely discounted. The children of musicians and other artists are exposed to a considerable amount of stimulation designed to elicit behavior similar to that of their parents. Any expression of interest in the artistic endeavors of the parent is strongly reinforced. It is not surprising, therefore, that children frequently exhibit interests and abilities similar to those characterizing their parents. Furthermore, the fact that the children of talented parents are not always talented themselves leads to a suspicion that the particular capacities involved are not necessarily transmitted by the genes. So far as the other side of the coin is concerned, it is a matter of common observation that the children of untalented parents can be subjected to years of intensive training in one of the performing arts with little salutary effect upon their skill. This situation is generally a source of considerable frustration to both parent and child.

In his analysis of the social psychology of music, Farnsworth (1958) summarizes the results of his inquiry into the problems of the inheritance of musical aptitude:

> . . . an ability is always the resultant of the interplay of heredity and environment. The organism limits or facilitates achievement in many ways. The environment likewise aids or inhibits. From these two sets of interacting limitations and facilitations abilities develop. Musical abilities seem in general no more nor less inherited than abilities in many other areas (p. 186).

Although avoiding a direct commitment to the proposition that musical aptitude, or the lack of it, is inherited, Farnsworth seems to concede that talent for various forms of artistic expression apparently depends upon hereditary factors. Judging merely from naturalistic observation, we may surmise that such a relationship also appears to hold with regard to athletic aptitudes of various sorts.

Temperament. We mentioned previously the possible innate basis of a general temperamental disposition. We do not suggest that tendencies toward any specific patterns of temperamental reactivity are present at birth. However, it is conceivable that such broad characterizations of behavior as placidity or excitability might have an innate basis. Wenger (1941) has shown that some persons react physiologically through the sympathetic branch of the autonomic nervous system, whereas others show a predominance of parasympathetic activity. In other words, the characteristic reaction of some individuals to stress involves an increase in blood pressure, heart rate, and amount of perspiration. Others seem to respond to stress with a suppression of these functions. The investigator felt that the stability of individuals' reactions suggested a constitutional, or genetic, factor which was modifiable through experience. Lacey (1950) has reported that individuals are characterized by the particular organ systems that they use in reacting to stress. He measured such reactions as blood pressure, pulse pressure, palmar conductance, and heart rate and discovered that individuals show unique patterns of response to stress when these several organ systems are involved. One person may perspire more than another. A different person may respond to stress most characteristically with increased heart rate. These various patterns of autonomic activity, together with the verbal and other overt reactions that accompany them, comprise a part of what we have termed temperament. In the absence of clear evidence that different patterns of temperamental, or emotional, reaction are learned, it is tempting to suggest that they are part of the individual's constitutional equipment at birth. Since persons obviously inherit their physical structure and appearance, it is not illogical to suppose that they may also inherit certain unique and consistent patterns of emotional response to stress and frustration. If this assumption is eventually verified, then we shall have to conclude that these genetically determined temperamental dispositions place a further constraint on the behavior that an individual may acquire through experience.

Genetically determined dispositions to characteristically underreact or overreact to the environment could conceivably form a basis for the later development of psychosis. A genetic link for schizophrenia has, in fact, been suggested by Kallmann (1953). He showed not only that schizophrenia present in both parents was related to a high incidence of schizophrenia in their offspring, but also that identical twins share this disorder more often than either nonidentical twins or other siblings. Since environmental factors are inextricably confounded with heredity in most cases of this sort, it is not possible to conclude that individual differences in susceptibility to personality disturbance have been conclusively demonstrated. However, the possibility that physiological or enzyme factors underlie the individual's dispositions at birth remains an interesting problem for study. Some evidence certainly points in this direction.

An appraisal. Even if all the human potentialities just discussed actually were determined at birth, the individual, as he developed, would be quite unprepared to respond in any consistent or adaptive ways to the complex environment surrounding him. His physiological needs would go unsatisfied unless he eventually acquired behaviors instrumental in securing access to food, water, and sex objects. Any talents that he might have for acquiring particular skills would be unrealized unless the environment provided him with opportunities to develop and express them. Finally, any temperamental bias that might have been furnished him, either genetically or through prenatal influences, would influence his behavior only in conjunction with other environmental factors that limited or widened the scope of his behavioral potentialities. As Verplanck (1955) puts it, "The laws of learning operate within limits determined by the genetic characteristics of the animal" (p. 142). We must conclude that the individual's behavior results from the joint operation of these endogenous and experiential variables.

Both the physical and the social environment contribute support to those behaviors that are characteristically human. Certainly the small amount of evidence available on the effects of deprivation of a normal human environment indicates that children who have been abandoned to nature at an early age cannot later become socialized. The Wild Boy of Aveyron, described by Itard, was captured in France in 1799. He was eleven at the time, and it was estimated that he must have lived in isolation from the age of four. Despite years of patient effort, Itard was unsuccessful in training this child to completely adopt the habits of a normal, civilized person. He reasoned that anyone spending his early years without human companionship would be essentially nonhuman in behavior. Other, similar cases have been reported from India, with substantially the same results as those reported by Itard. These accidental instances of individuals growing up in a nonhuman environment certainly provide little more than circumstantial evidence bearing on the question of innate human nature, particularly in view of the fact that the children may have been mentally retarded. But since experimentation in this area is scarcely feasible, we can only conclude from the information available that the socialized human is made, not born. The process of becoming a socialized human being, therefore, necessarily requires interaction with other humans. Social psychology attempts to understand the nature of these interactions and their effects upon the behavior of individuals, both singly and collectively.

Comparative Approaches

Rather than discuss the social behavior of animals as a separate topic, we will introduce parallels between the social aspects of human and animal behavior as appropriate at various points in the book. It is interesting to note, however, that our earlier discussion of the relative contributions of genetic and experiential factors to behavior is illuminated by data gathered by ethologists. Because the behavior of animals is less subject to artificial controls than that of humans, the emergence of certain species-specific dispositions is more readily observed. Among humans, any such dispositions are too readily contaminated by a cultural overlay that makes isolation of the innate and acquired components exceedingly difficult.

We do not imply, however, that social variables are any less important in animal behavior than among humans. A leading animal behaviorist, John P. Scott (1960) has asserted that all animals are social to some degree, and that the effects of social factors on behavior often outweigh those coming from the physical and biological environments. Any animal that is capable of behavior, he asserts, will show some degree of social interaction. The fact that we tend to perceive most easily the social behavior of mammals such as the primates, who are most like ourselves, is due to the nutritional dependency of their young upon the mother. Even species very dissimilar to man, however, may show social relationships of great complexity, including the formation of families and larger social groups differentiated as to role and status. Social interaction, in fact, appears to be essential to the optimal development of the individual. As Scott points out, any mammal reared in isolation shows adult behavior which is quite abnormal for its species. Furthermore, the individual ant or bee — insects whose social behavior is so complex as to seem a caricature of the human — cannot survive independent of its group.

Aggression. Several species of lower animals have been studied rather intensively in an effort to discover the types of dominance hierarchies that develop. Following the early work of Schjelderup-Ebbe (1935), Guhl (1953) describes the establishment of a pecking order among hens. Whenever two strange hens meet, they first investigate one another and then engage in mutual attack until one is driven off. On subsequent meetings, the hen that has been "outpecked" becomes less and less aggressive, until finally she is completely submissive to her opponent. Some flocks of hens establish a straight-line pecking order, in which the most aggressive, or dominant, hen pecks all those lower in the order. Each hen, in turn, pecks only those less dominant than herself. One is reminded here of the hierarchical dominance relationships that exist in military organizations, as well as in many industrial and educational settings. Social relationships based on rank are formed at all levels of the animal world, including the human.

Fighting, as Scott (1958) points out, is one kind of response to a stimulus. The question that comes to mind almost immediately is whether fighting, or aggression, is the inevitable reaction to certain stimuli. It appears that it is in many subhuman species, where the controlling stimuli are often quite specific. For example, mice will struggle over food if they can pick it up but not if it is fixed in one place. Dogs will battle over a receptive female, and male deer, buffalo, and mountain sheep fight fiercely during the rutting season. As a result of his laboratory investigation, Scott reached the conclusion that the technique for training a mouse to become a "fighter" was basically one of providing it with a series of easy victories. Because aggressive behavior was thus rewarded, or reinforced, it became more frequent and more effective. Scott was also able to raise both mice and dogs that had been trained not to fight by placing them in circumstances where aggressive behavior was least likely to occur.

It is well established that the males of most species are innately more aggressive than the females. This fact seems to be understood largely in terms of the physiological effects of the sex hormones. As Scott reminds us, "Stock breeders have long known that aggressive tendencies can be decreased by castration, and the difference in behavior between the plodding ox and the ferocious bull is obvious to anyone. In horses it is the common practice to castrate or geld most of the males, which then become more manageable" (p. 70). Among humans, boys are nearly always found to be more aggressive than girls, beginning as young as two years. This could be a matter of early socialization, but the evidence is against this explanation. Among dogs, where genetic factors can be controlled more readily than with humans, it is known that certain breeds are much more aggressive than others. James (1951) put beagles (which are larger) and terriers in competition for both food and females. Not only did the terriers dominate the beagles in obtaining a single bone or dish of food, they also monopolized the females and sired all the offspring. The evidence for a genetic basis for aggressiveness in both animals and man does not mean that such behavior is destined to occur without support from the environment. Among animals, aggressive behavior, and other behaviors, appears only in the presence of a particular stimulus called a *releaser*. It appears this is not true among humans, where social learning determines to a great extent the conditions under which certain species-specific behaviors, such as language, will occur.

Communication. One of the most fascinating examples of communication among animals is the manner in which foraging bees indicate to other members of the hive the direction and distance of honey used as bait. They accomplish this by engaging in a "dance." As described by von Frisch (1954), this consists of a circular movement that is reversed after each complete cycle and goes on for about half a minute when the food is less than one hundred meters from the hive. If the food is at a distance greater than one hundred meters, the bee executes a more complicated routine, in which it describes roughly a figure-eight pattern. The direction of a straight run in the center of the figure-eight indicates the location of the food with respect to the sun. Investigations of communicative performances of this sort are being extended to many other species, and it now seems probable that even fish communicate with one another through underwater sounds.

No animals, however, possess the capacity for detailed vocalization found in man.

The highest degree of social organization among invertebrates is found in insects. According to Scott (1960), these societies are primarily characterized by great emphasis on care-dependency and mutual-care relationships. Termites, ants, bees, and wasps display the most elaborately organized societies. Differentiation of individuals in the group into queens, workers, and soldiers has been observed, and members of other species may even be introduced as slaves. These functions apparently are determined primitively and do not necessarily reflect what might be termed "intelligent" social organization. We shall consider some of the comparative aspects of communicative behavior in further detail in Chapter 8.

Territoriality. As a final illustration of behavior that finds parallels in both animals and humans we consider briefly the phenomenon of territoriality. Contrary to popular belief, songbirds perform not out of sheer ebullience or desire to welcome the new day but, rather, as a device to warn away other birds that might intrude on their territory (Wynne-Edwards, 1962). Although by no means universal among animals, territoriality has been observed in the gibbon (Carpenter, 1940), in fish (Tinbergen, 1953), and among dogs (Scott, 1958). Bands of gibbons will roam the forest until they begin to encroach upon the home territory of another group. Both sides then display threat behavior, with the gibbons nearest their own territory usually prevailing. Signals from rival fish, usually chemical or visual, release fighting behavior in a fish that is within its own territory. Frequently, the resident is able to intimidate the intruder by means of a threatening display. Similarly, a prairie dog seldom molests an intruder unless he crosses the line that demarcates the territory. Most territorial disputes between animals are resolved without actual fighting.

Tinbergen suggests that one function of territoriality is to bring about a spacing-out of individuals, thus providing the members of a species with the space necessary for reproduction. Too many individuals in the same area would result in low rations. This theory is also endorsed by Roger Brown (1965), who observes that birds ordinarily resist invasion of their territory only by other birds of the same species, which have similar food requirements. The biological utility of such dispersion is obvious, and it appears to be a species-specific reaction that is under the control of certain environmental stimuli, or releasers.

The exclusive use and defense of territory is also commonly observed among humans. This phenomenon, according to Altman (1968), should become increasingly interesting to social psychologists as a result of the population explosion, unplanned use of space by community developers, urban deterioration, and increased longevity. Territoriality among humans, unlike that among animals, involves the acquisition of "things" as well as space. An individual may resent lending his fountain pen as much as he resists intrusions onto his property.

Each of us manifests territorial behavior in a variety of circumstances, often without being aware that we are doing so. Sommer (1966) reports that individuals whom he interrogated often selected seats at a library table in such a manner as to discourage others from taking adjacent seats or to avoid those who might do so. In the first instance, the person selected the middle seat, while in the second instance he took an end seat. How many of us have observed at repeated meetings of a group that the members gravitate to the same seats; a person who finds his accustomed place occupied is apt to reveal obvious signs of disturbance. These reactions occur in exaggerated form under conditions of social isolation. Altman and Haythorn (1967) observed the behavior of pairs of Navy volunteers who were experimentally isolated in a small room for a ten-day period. As compared with control pairs not subjected to complete isolation, the isolated pairs showed earlier development of patterns of territoriality. That is, they rather promptly appropriated beds and chairs and gravitated to the same seats around a table. Incompatible pairs were especially prone to exhibit territorial behavior of this sort.

How shall we account for this rather remarkable similarity between animals and man with respect to territoriality? One investigator, Ardrey (1966), has ventured to suggest that territoriality in humans, as in animals, is an innate disposition that has developed through evolution. At present, it is difficult to see how this proposition can be put to an empirical test. We should perhaps be more concerned with establishing the conditions under which territorial behavior occurs in humans and with identifying the stimuli that control this behavior and the reinforcers that maintain it.

Everyone becomes "socialized" in one way or another. Some persons become prison wardens, while others end up as inmates. Some become psychiatrists, others their patients. Obviously, in such extreme cases, the socialization process follows different lines, that is, the individuals concerned acquire different habitual ways of responding to their environments. To understand the acquisition of social behavior, therefore, we shall look first to the learning process. Then we will examine the conditions that either maintain or decrease the frequency of such behavior once it has been learned. Many of the basic principles of learning have been enunciated in psychological laboratories, and techniques for prompting, sustaining, and extinguishing human performances have been described. We shall find that these processes are neither mysterious nor impervious to scientific examination; moreover, they are evident in both individual and social behavior.

Summary   In this chapter we have traced some of the historical landmarks in the development of theories about human nature. Some of these viewpoints have focused on the problem of the relative contributions of environmental and genetic factors to human behavior.

Among the early Greek philosophers, Plato and Aristotle believed that men possess different innate capacities which are shaped by the educational forces of society. This point of view has found its modern counterpart in the writings of psychologists such as McDougall, who postulated a number of instincts, or innate behavioral dispositions, that he thought characterized all men. Although the notion of instinct as an inherited pattern of behavior has not been accepted by most contemporary social scientists, recent research has indicated that man may, indeed, possess certain genetically determined behavioral dispositions. Several of these are analogous to McDougall's "instincts," and they include curiosity, manipulative behavior, and aggressiveness, as well as such broad temperamental dispositions as excitability and placidity.

During the intervening period between ancient and modern times, several other important developments occurred in philosophical thought. Two of the most important of these for our purposes involved the notions of *determinism* and *causality*. It has become generally accepted that human behavior is not random and capricious but lawfully determined. Our task, as psychologists, is to discover the natural laws that govern human conduct. At the same time, we recognize that behavior cannot generally be traced to simple causes, and that social behavior in particular is subject to multiple causation. This is simply a more precise way of saying that an individual's actions are under the control of many stimuli, only some of which are known to us.

Since the behavioral dispositions that the individual receives at conception are at best general and diffuse, we have adopted the position that social behavior is largely the product of learning and experience. In the next chapter we shall outline some principles of an objective behavior theory that will form the basis of our subsequent discussion. A functional analysis using these principles promises us considerable success in understanding the many complex aspects of social interaction.

References

ALLPORT, G. W. The historical background of modern social psychology. In G. Lindzey and E. Aronson (Eds.), *Handbook of Social Psychology* (2nd ed.). Vol. 1. Reading, Mass.: Addison-Wesley, 1968.

ALTMAN, I. Territorial behavior in humans: An analysis of the concept. Paper presented at *Conference on Explorations of Spatial-Behavioral Relationships as Related to Older People*, Institute of Gerontology, University of Michigan, May 1968.

ALTMAN, I., and HAYTHORN, W. W. The ecology of isolated groups. *Behavioral Science*, 1967, *12*, 169–182.

ARDREY, R. *The territorial imperative*. New York: Atheneum, 1966.

BRELAND, K., and BRELAND, M. The misbehavior of organisms. *American Psychologist*, 1961, *16*, 681–684.

BROWN, R. *Social psychology.* New York: The Free Press, 1965.

CARPENTER, C. R. A field study in Siam of the behavior and social relations of the gibbon. *Comparative Psychology Monographs*, 1940, No. 84, 1–212.

COMTE, A. *A general view of positivism* (trans. by J. H. Bridges). Stanford, Calif.: Academic Reprints, 1848.

DOLLARD, J., DOOB, L. W., MILLER, N. E., MOWRER, O. H., and SEARS, R. R. *Frustration and aggression.* New Haven: Yale University Press, 1939.

EWER, R. F. Further observation on suckling behavior in kittens, together with some general considerations of the interrelations of innate and acquired responses. *Behavior*, 1961, *17*, 247–260.

FARNSWORTH, P. R. *The social psychology of music.* New York: Dryden Press, 1958.

FRISCH, K. VON *Bees: Their vision, chemical senses, and languages.* Ithaca, N.Y.: Cornell University Press, 1950.

GOODENOUGH, FLORENCE L., and TYLER, LEONA E. *Developmental psychology.* New York: Appleton-Century-Crofts, 1959.

GUHL, A. M. Social behavior of the domestic fowl. *Kansas State College Agricultural Experimental Station Technical Bulletin*, 1953, No. 73.

HARLOW, H. F. Mice, monkeys, men and motives. *Psychological Review*, 1953, *60*, 23–32.

HARLOW, H. F. The nature of love. *American Psychologist*, 1958, *13*, 673–685.

HEBB, D. O. *A textbook of psychology.* Philadelphia: W. B. Saunders, 1958.

HIRSCH, J. Individual differences in behavior and their genetic basis. In E. L. Bliss (Ed.), *Roots of behavior.* New York: Harper, 1962.

HUME, D. An essay concerning human understanding. In E. A. Burtt (Ed.), *The English philosophers from Bacon to Mill.* New York: Modern Library, 1939.

HUNT, J. McV., and QUAY, H. C. Early vibratory experience and the question of innate reinforcement value of vibration and other stimuli: A limitation on the discrepancy (burnt soup) principle in motivation. *Psychological Review*, 1961, *68*, 149–156.

HUXLEY, A. *Brave new world.* New York: Harper, 1960.

JAMES, W. T. Social organization among dogs of different temperaments, terriers and beagles, reared together. *Journal of Comparative and Physiological Psychology*, 1951, *44*, 71–77.

KALLMANN, F. J. *Heredity in health and mental disorder.* New York: W. W. Norton, 1953.

LACEY, J. I. Individual differences in somatic response patterns. *Journal of Comparative and Physiological Psychology*, 1950, *43*, 338–350.

McDOUGALL, W. *An introduction to social psychology.* Boston: John Luce, 1923.

MONTGOMERY, K. C. The role of the exploratory drive in learning. *Journal of Comparative and Physiological Psychology*, 1954, *47*, 60–64.

MONTGOMERY, K. C., and SEGALL, M. Discrimination learning based upon the exploratory drive. *Journal of Comparative and Physiological Psychology*, 1955, *48*, 225–228.

MURRAY, H. A. *Explorations in personality.* New York: Oxford University Press, 1938.

ORNE, M. T.   On the social psychology of the psychological experiment. *American Psychologist*, 1962, *17*, 776–783.

SCHJELDERUP-EBBE, T.   Social behavior of birds. In C. A. Murchison (Ed.), *Handbook of social psychology.* Worcester, Mass.: Clark University Press, 1935.

SCOTT, J. P.   *Aggression.* Chicago: University of Chicago Press, 1958.

SCOTT, J. P.   Comparative social psychology. In R. H. Waters, D. A. Rethling-shafer, and W. E. Caldwell (Eds.), *Principles of comparative psychology.* New York: McGraw-Hill, 1960.

SOMMER, R.   The ecology of privacy. *The Library Quarterly*, 1966, *36*, 234–248.

TINBERGEN, N.   *Social behavior in animals.* London: Methuen, 1953.

VERPLANCK, W. S.   Since learned behavior is innate and vice versa, what now? *Psychological Review*, 1955, *62*, 139–144.

WARREN, R. D., and PFAFFMANN, C.   Early experience and taste aversion. *Journal of Comparative and Physiological Psychology*, 1959, *52*, 263–266.

WATSON, J. B.   *Behaviorism* (rev. ed.). New York: W. W. Norton, 1930.

WENGER, M. A.   The measurement of individual differences in autonomic balance. *Psychosomatic Medicine*, 1941, *3*, 427–434.

WYNNE-EDWARDS, V. C.   *Animal dispersion in relation to social behavior.* Edinburgh and London: Oliver and Boyd, 1962.

2

Some Principles
of Behavior

Students frequently comment on the apparent discrepancy between the experiments that many psychologists perform and the realities of everyday life that we all experience. There is a very common tendency, even for psychologists, to talk about social behavior in terms different from those that are used in textbooks. In this chapter we shall attempt to rectify this situation by reviewing some of the more firmly established principles of modern behavior theory as these apply to social interaction. It will be important to remember that certain well established principles explaining the behavior of animals in laboratory experiments can be very useful in describing more complex human situations. An appeal to fundamental behavior processes is essential in describing and analyzing complex social phenomena.

In order to better understand how individuals acquire those patterns of behavior that mark them as social beings, then, we shall first review some basic principles of learning and performance. Most of these will be familiar to the student who has previously studied psychology. This recapitulation should be helpful, however, in setting the course that we will follow in attempting systematically to explain certain aspects of social behavior. Let us consider briefly some of the terms and assumptions of modern behavior theory as these might be applied to social processes.

Basic Concepts in Learning

Responses may be classified as *elicited* or as *emitted*. Elicited responses, also called *respondents*, have been described as follows by F. S. Keller:

Respondent (reflex) behavior takes in all those responses of human beings, and many other organisms, that are *elicited* ("drawn out") by special stimulus changes in their environments. It is shown whenever the pupils of your eyes contract or dilate in response to changes in the lighting of a room; whenever your mouth waters at the taste of some choice bit of food; whenever a gust of cold air raises goose flesh on the surface of your skin; whenever you shed tears while peeling onions; whenever you gasp at an unexpected dash of water in your face; and in many other ways . . . (1954, p. 2).

Emitted responses, better called *acts* or *performances,* have no readily identifiable stimulus the first time they occur. It is not always easy to specify the stimulus that caused you to look at your watch, reach for a book, speak to your friend, or hum a tune, or to emit any number of other behaviors. On the other hand, a person familiar with your habits can increase the probability of some of these performances by supplying an appropriate stimulus, for example, by asking the time. Since there is no guarantee that your act will be the predicted one, it should be noted that the stimulus does not elicit the behavior in question. Emitted performances constitute our chief interest, and we will have much to say about them later. Let us first, however, turn our attention to some of the more important features of respondent behavior.

Respondent Learning

Most students will be familiar with the now classic research of Ivan Pavlov, the Russian physiologist who in the early years of the present century described the basic learning process now called classical or *respondent conditioning* (Pavlov, 1927). In its simplest terms, respondent conditioning refers to a sequence of events by which a reflex response is brought under the control of a new, or conditioned, stimulus. While studying certain aspects of the digestive processes, Pavlov discovered that the salivary response in a dog could be elicited by a tone from a tuning fork, provided the tone had previously been paired several times with food. This learning situation can be shown diagrammatically.

$$N\ [S^c\ +\ S^{uc} \longrightarrow R^{uc}]\ \dashrightarrow [S^c \longrightarrow R^c]$$

| Tone | Food | Salivating, chewing, swallowing | Tone | Salivating |

In the above representation, S^{uc} stands for *unconditioned stimulus* and S^c for *conditioned stimulus.* In Pavlov's experimental procedure, the tone and the food were presented to the animal simultaneously a number of times, indicated by the letter N before the brackets. Gradually, the tone acquired the capacity to evoke a salivary response in the dog. When salivation occurred in response to the tone, it was termed the *conditioned re-*

sponse. Prior to this, of course, the dog had pricked up its ears or responded in some other way at the sound of the tone. This behavior was gradually replaced by the response of salivating. As in nearly all classical conditioning procedures, the conditioned response that emerges is a part, or fractional component, of the original unconditioned behavior; it is closely related but not identical to it. This fact is indicated in the diagram by labeling the R^c as salivating, which is one of the components of eating behavior. The exact relationship between any given S^{uc} and S^c can be determined only by experimentation.

As another illustration of classical conditioning, we have the work of Bechterev, a contemporary of Pavlov, who trained dogs to withdraw a paw to a variety of stimuli, using electric shock as the unconditioned stimulus.

$$N [S^c + S^{uc} \longrightarrow R^{uc}] ------ \rightarrow [S^c \longrightarrow R^c]$$

| Tone | Shock | Paw withdrawal, struggling, barking | Tone | Paw withdrawal |

Again, we see that the tone, by being paired with an electric shock, acquires the power to evoke a fractional component of the unconditioned reaction to shock. The dog eventually ceases to struggle and learns merely to lift his paw when the tone is sounded. Both examples can be viewed as processes of *stimulus substitution* in which S^c comes to serve as a substitute for a S^{uc}. The experimental procedure results in the animal responding to the tone in a manner derived from its original response to either food or shock.

In each of the situations just described, presentation of the unconditioned stimulus provides *reinforcement* of the conditioned response. Successful conditioning is indicated by the fact that the animal responds to the tone in the absence of either food or shock. If, on subsequent trials, these reinforcers are regularly omitted, the magnitude of the conditioned response gradually diminishes until it no longer occurs when the conditioned stimulus is presented. This process, known as *extinction* of the conditioned response, results when reinforcement is not given. Reinforcement is thus seen to be necessary in many situations for both the acquisition and the maintenance of behavior.

Emotional reactions. Where human social behavior is concerned, classical conditioning may have its greatest relevance in providing a basis for "emotional" reactions. It has been shown by Liddell (1942) that foot withdrawal in animals as a conditioned response to aversive (unpleasant) stimulation is accompanied by changes in both heart rate and breathing and that these internal reactions are conditioned at the same time as the withdrawal response. The same phenomenon is found in man. Notterman,

Schoenfeld, and Bersh (1952), as well as others, have found that individuals exposed to tone-with-electric-shock conditioning develop a conditioned heart response to the tone when presented alone. Real life examples of this process are not difficult to find. If we have received bad news over the telephone on several occasions, the next ring of the phone may arouse in us reactions similar to those we experienced after receiving unpleasant information.

Emotion has traditionally been conceived as representing a category of behaviors distinguished by unique manifestations at the levels of cognition, body physiology, and overt behavior. Although a case can be made for defining emotion in these terms, a difficulty arises in the fact that other response patterns not ordinarily considered as emotional can be similarly analyzed. It is perhaps more useful to think of emotion as a reaction that disrupts or interferes with an organism's ongoing behavior (Brady, 1957). A typical situation illustrating the effects of a conditioned "anxiety" response upon the lever-pressing performance of albino rats is described by Brady:

> Briefly, thirsty animals initially are trained in lever pressing for a continuous and then for a periodic water reward. When their lever pressing output has stabilized they receive a series of conditioning trials, each consisting of the presentation of a clicking noise (the conditioned stimulus) followed by a pain shock to the feet (the unconditioned stimulus). . . . The clicking noise continues for three minutes and is terminated contiguously with the shock. Within a few trials, the anticipatory response to the clicker begins to appear as a perturbation in the lever pressing curve, accompanied by crouching, immobility and, usually, dejection (pp. 20, 22).

The foregoing analysis of a relatively simple emotional reaction can be extended to the complex emotions of humans, provided we recognize the limitations on our capacity to specify all the conditioned stimuli in a given situation. Many cases, as Skinner (1953) points out, are familiar. A sudden loud noise is usually sufficient to induce fear. Physical restraint or other interference with behavior may generate rage. Failure to receive an accustomed reinforcement due to any of a variety of factors results in a kind of rage called frustration. The emission of behavior that has been punished in the past may be accompanied by embarrasment. Most emotional reactions cannot, of course, be described so simply, and their specific manifestations may vary widely depending upon the circumstances in which they are elicited. A more subtle emotion, such as loneliness, is described by Skinner as a "mild form of frustration due to the interruption of an established sequence of responses which have been positively reinforced by the special environment. The lonely man has no one to talk to (1953, p. 165).

We will have occasion to refer to emotional reactions, but in so doing we will emphasize the effects of the reaction on other ongoing behavior and will attempt to specify the conditions which produce the emotional behavior. Certain features of emotional behavior may be both public and dramatic, as in the case of excitement or depression. Other aspects of an emotional reaction include such automatic responses as changes in perspiration, blood pressure, and heart rate, which can be recorded directly using appropriate apparatus. These responses are typically acquired in situations that contain all the important elements of experimentally produced conditioned responses. Like their laboratory counterparts, they exhibit the phenomena of extinction, spontaneous recovery, generalization, and discrimination. Conditioned emotional reactions seem to be prominent components of attitudes, those generalized response dispositions that characterize much of our social behavior.

The prompting of attitude-related behavior, such as that involving politics or religion, tends also to activate the individual's autonomic nervous system. The autonomic system has primary control over such vital physiological processes as heart rate, blood pressure, and breathing. The fact that these internal reactions may be conditioned to social stimuli is of considerable importance to an understanding of the emotional nature of much social interaction. Think in your own experience of some of the occasions on which you became emotionally aroused in the course of a discussion that began quite amicably. One's normal verbal processes frequently are disrupted under conditions of strong emotion, and the discussion may degenerate to insult and invective. The explanation for this phenomenon must be sought in the individual's past history, where words have become the conditioned stimuli for emotional reactions. In some instances, the early learning experiences that have led to conditioned emotional reactions have been repressed (to borrow a concept from Freud), or driven from consciousness. Psychoanalysis is one method by which recovery of such repressed experiences is attempted.

Operant Learning

Let us now consider a different type of learning situation, one that is not easily understood in terms of classical conditioning. If an albino rat is placed in a cage containing a lever, a feeding tube, and a food dish, its behavior for some time can best be described as exploratory, or simply curious. Eventually, in the course of its exploration, the rat will strike the lever, thus delivering a pellet of food to the dish. The response of moving the lever, the first time it occurs, must be considered as purely adventitious in regard to feeding; that is, we cannot predict when the rat will do it, nor can we make him do it. We may try to expedite the learning process by creating conditions that favor the lever-pressing response; for example, we can smear some food on the lever so as to attract the rat's notice. In attempting to eat the food, the animal will usually exert enough force on the lever to move it and cause a pellet of food to be delivered to the feeding dish. The animal, in effect, *operates* on the environment by moving the lever, thus producing food. This particular response, lever-pressing, is extremely low in the hierarchy of behaviors that we may expect the rat to emit spontaneously. Many other responses will precede it, and they are said to have higher probabilities of occurrence in this particular situation.

We may diagram this state of affairs as follows, using R (with subscript) to indicate the approximate order of frequency of the many potential responses that the rat may make.

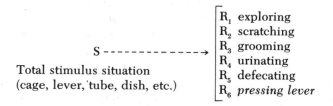

$$
S \dashrightarrow
\begin{bmatrix}
R_1 & \text{exploring} \\
R_2 & \text{scratching} \\
R_3 & \text{grooming} \\
R_4 & \text{urinating} \\
R_5 & \text{defecating} \\
R_6 & \textit{pressing lever}
\end{bmatrix}
$$

Total stimulus situation
(cage, lever, tube, dish, etc.)

Exploratory behavior, in particular, is characteristic of rats in a strange environment. As described by Bindra (1959): "Exploration is generally quantified in such terms as the frequency of approaching and sniffing a novel object, orientation movements of the head, the extent of perambulation, and time spent in looking at or manipulating (novel) stimulus objects" (p. 33).

Of course, the various units of behavior that we have listed are controlled by the makeup of the rat's nervous system and by stimuli impinging upon the animal from many sources, only a few of which are known to us. By depriving the rat of food, we can insure that some of these stimuli will be internal (and probably aversive), and that they will be relieved only when the animal has made the response that will secure food. Assume in the present instance that the rat has been deprived of food for twenty-four hours and that it will therefore eat after it has pressed the lever and secured a pellet. Because the response of lever-pressing has an initially low probability of occurrence, the rat will not immediately solve the problem. When the rat finally does strike the lever, a food pellet will be delivered atuomatically to the feeding dish and will be promptly consumed by the hungry animal. It can then be observed that the animal spends more time in the vicinity of the lever and the feeding dish until, in due course, it again hits the lever and receives another pellet. The lever-

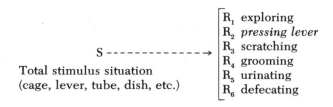

$$
S \dashrightarrow
\begin{bmatrix}
R_1 & \text{exploring} \\
R_2 & \textit{pressing lever} \\
R_3 & \text{scratching} \\
R_4 & \text{grooming} \\
R_5 & \text{urinating} \\
R_6 & \text{defecating}
\end{bmatrix}
$$

Total stimulus situation
(cage, lever, tube, dish, etc.)

pressing response now has moved well up in the animal's hierarchy of behavior and takes precedence over everything but a residual of exploratory behavior.

Following long periods of food deprivation, lever-pressing will quickly become the rat's most frequent response, and it will occur on subsequent occasions almost as soon as the rat is placed in the cage. (Typically, the rat still explores its surroundings first.) Lever-pressing behavior is now highly probable under conditions of food deprivation. Theoretically, the rat has always had the potential of emitting this type of response. By arranging conditions so that the probability of this behavior is increased, as by making the rat hungry and then feeding it when it presses the bar, we have, in effect, taught the animal to do regularly something that it was unlikely to do previously. The animal has learned to press the lever, and when it is hungry and the lever is present, it will keep busy pressing it.

Can we say that the rat has acquired a conditioned response? It should be immediately apparent that the events we have just described do not fit the classical conditioning paradigm. For one thing, the behavior to be learned, lever-pressing, bears no resemblance to the reinforcing response of eating. Another difference is the fact that food (the unconditioned stimulus in classical conditioning) is not presented to the animal until *after* the instrumental response of lever-pressing has occurred. In classical conditioning, the animal is reinforced from the first learning trial, and the reinforcement does not depend upon the appearance of the conditioned response.

In a situation where the learned response (lever-pressing) is instrumental in producing the reinforcing stimulus (food), the entire sequence of events is known as operant conditioning. The term *operant,* as Skinner (1953) has pointed out, emphasizes the fact that the behavior operates upon or modifies the environment to generate consequences. Reinforcement, the delivery of food, is contingent upon the animal's emitting a given operant, in this instance lever-pressing. As in the case of classical conditioning, the process can be represented with a diagram.

$$S^D \longrightarrow R^{op} \longrightarrow S^{rein} \longrightarrow R^{rein}$$

Lever,	Pressing	Food	Eating
cage,	lever		
etc.			

We have modified the symbols somewhat in order to provide a further distinction between operant conditioning and the type of classical conditioning discussed earlier. Following Skinner (1938, 1957), we shall refer to *discriminative stimuli* (S^D) as those which, with training, gain control of behavior. Several of these can be identified in this situation; they are symbolized S^D. It is understood, of course, that a variety of stimuli control behavior in a given situation. Relevant controlling stimuli for the rat include internal stimuli resulting from food deprivation and external stimuli provided by the lever, the cage, and other features of the immediate environment.

The behavior of pressing the lever, since it bears no resemblance to the unconditioned behavior of eating, is represented as R^{op}, standing for *operant response*. This term will also be used in reference to social behavior, where performances will be considered as generally instrumental in effecting some change in the environment. Finally, following Skinner, we shall refer to the *reinforcing stimulus* (S^{rein}), rather than to the unconditioned stimulus. This notation includes those many social reinforcements that are themselves the products of experience and hence may not properly be referred to as "unconditioned." Although few social responses to reinforcing stimuli are of the unconditioned variety, like eating, we shall refer instead to a *reinforcing response* (R^{rein}) wherever appropriate.

In man, unlike many infrahuman forms, many instrumental performances, both simple and complex, can be learned rapidly because of man's capacity for imitation and communication. Very few animals below the level of the primates are able to learn by imitating another animal; consequently, they must acquire new behavior through the sometimes lengthy and uncertain process just described. Trainers frequently abbreviate this process by the technique of "putting through." A dog, for example, can be taught to roll over if one physically turns him over and then immediately rewards him with food. This is a crude but effective means of communicating to the animal what one wants him to do. Technically, we would say that we have established some new S^Ds by which to control the dog's behavior. Fortunately for parents, it is not necessary to put children through all the behaviors that one expects them to learn. Once the child has acquired speech, he can respond to verbal instructions when attempting to learn new patterns of response. In a sense, new behavior must still be emitted, but the probability of its occurrence can be increased through the mediation of verbal admonition. It is obviously not possible to draw a direct parallel between the behavior of a rat learning to press a lever and a child learning to tie his shoelaces. The basic principles of acquisition, however, seem to be the same; that is, they follow the sequence (a) *discriminative stimulus* (lever, shoelace), (b) *operant response* (pressing bar, tying shoelace), (c) *reinforcement* (food, praise).

It may be that "satisfaction" is sufficient reinforcement for a child who is attempting gradually to master his environment. Obviously, the concept of self-reinforcement implied here requires closer analysis. But this problem can be reserved until later. The point is that the basic elements in learning seem to be continuous from animals to man and that these can quite appropriately be extended to include social interaction as well as individual behavior.

Primary Reinforcement

The exact nature of reinforcement in learning has been a troublesome theoretical problem, although there is no doubt of its effectiveness in controlling behavior. In a sense, Skinner (1953) has bypassed these difficulties by taking the position that reinforcers cannot be identified apart from their effects on a particular organism: ". . . the only defining characteristic of a reinforcing stimulus is that it reinforces" (p. 72). How do we find out whether something will act as a reinforcer? We do so, says Skinner, by first observing the frequency of a response, then making some event contingent upon the response and observing any change in frequency. Specifically, we might observe how frequently a rat presses a lever when there are no consequences other than a click. After establishing a baseline for the rat's performance, we then alter the situation so that every movement of the lever is followed by delivery of a food pellet. If the frequency of lever-pressing increases, then the food pellets are considered to have acted as reinforcers.

The consequences of behavior fall into two broad categories, *reinforcing* and *aversive*. As we have noted, a positive reinforcer is identified by the fact that it increases the frequency of any behavior upon which its presentation is made contingent. On the other hand, a stimulus that decreases the frequency of the behavior that produces it is said to be aversive. For example, any behavior of laboratory animals that is followed by the presentation of food, water, or a sex object tends to become more frequent than behavior not followed by these agreeable, or positively reinforcing, consequences. Behavior followed by such things as electric shock or harsh sounds tends to become less probable, and these consequences are termed aversive. Behavior that accomplishes either the removal or the avoidance of an aversive state of affairs tends to increase in frequency and is said to be *negatively reinforced*.

Many learning theorists like to think of behavior as *motivated* and of a reinforcer as having the effect of reducing a *drive* or *need*. Because of the difficulties of adequately defining the term motivation, we shall avoid using it. It is sufficient for a scientific analysis of behavior that we be able to identify the stimuli that control a performance and the consequences that either maintain or suppress it. It is obvious, of course, that the effectiveness of reinforcing stimuli can be varied by appropriate manipulation of certain antecedent conditions. As Goldiamond (1962) has pointed out, "the thirst drive can be increased, or *water can be made an effective reinforcer,* by depriving the organism of water, by feeding salt, by exercise in the sun, by administering a diuretic, by appropriate brain stimulation or ablation, by paying the subject to drink, by showing Sahara travelogues, and so on" (p. 294). All these procedures have in common the fact that they make a particular reinforcement effective, thereby influencing the establishment and maintenance of discriminative behavior.

Similarly, we might analyze a *need for affiliation* in terms of those antecedent conditions that have made association with other individuals reinforcing. Thus, a person who displays this "need" may have just emerged from isolation, may have been assigned to write a report about a social gathering, may be trying to meet prospective clients, may be out picking pockets, or may be watching a football game along with 20,000 other people. We accomplish little in the way of explanation by appealing to motives or needs, and we do stand a chance of finding an explanation if we look instead to the antecedents and the consequences of the behavior.

Conditioned Reinforcement

Reward. It is obvious that human behavior is maintained by circumstances of much broader scope than those represented by primary reinforcement. People act in ways that will insure their social acceptability, that will evoke affectionate responses from others, and that will enhance their self-esteem. These behaviors are maintained not by primary reinforcement but by consequences that have acquired conditioned reinforcing properties. In view of the fact that the great bulk of social behavior is maintained by conditioned reinforcers, we shall attempt to identify these in a variety of social situations.

The principle of conditioned reinforcement was first described by Pavlov, whose classical conditioning procedures we have already described. You will recall that a conditioned response (R^c), salivating, was obtained from a dog when the conditioned stimulus (S^c), a tone, was sounded regularly about two seconds before the unconditioned stimulus (S^{uc}), food, was presented. A coworker of Pavlov's, named Frolov, extended this procedure so as to provide still another conditioned stimulus with the capacity to elicit salivating in the dog. A description of this technique was provided by Pavlov and has been reported, with some elaboration, by Hull (1943):

> Dr. Frolov experimented with a dog one of whose salivary glands had been diverted surgically so that the saliva discharged through a fistula in the side of the animal's face instead of flowing into its mouth. Suitable apparatus was provided for the precise determination of the number of drops secreted within a given time interval. When hungry this dog would be presented with the ticking of a metronome for a minute or so, and after 30 seconds meat powder would (presumably) be blown into its mouth; the meat would then be eaten by the dog, a considerable amount of saliva evoked by the incidental gustatory stimulation and chewing activity at the same time flowing from the fistula. After numerous reinforcements of this kind it was found that the metronome acting alone for 30 seconds evoked 13.5 drops of saliva; this is an ordinary or "first-order" conditioned reflex. The above account presents a fairly typical picture of conditioned-reflex learning by the Pavlovian technique.
>
> Next, a black square was presented in the dog's line of vision for the first time; no saliva flowed from the fistula during the stimulation. Following this

test the black square was held in front of the dog for 10 seconds, and after an interval of 15 seconds the metronome was sounded for 30 seconds, no food being given. The tenth presentation of the black square (alone) lasted 25 seconds; during this period 5.5 drops of saliva were secreted. This is an example of "higher-order" conditioned reflex (p. 85).

In Frolov's experiment, the visual stimulus of a black square acquired the capacity to evoke salivary secretion independent of stimulation by the metronome, the original S^c. Since the presentation and consumption of food did not immediately follow salivating to the square, this response was reinforced by the metronome. The metronome, accordingly, is said to be a conditioned reinforcing agent.

We have included this rather detailed description of Frolov's procedure because the principle of conditioned reinforcement is important in understanding much of social behavior. A clear example of a conditioned reinforcer for humans is money, which by itself does not provide nourishment, warmth, comfort, or shelter, but it can be exchanged for these commodities. The process by which money acquires reinforcing value is described by analogy in an experiment performed by Cowles (1937). Two chimpanzees were trained to insert colored discs, or tokens, into a slot machine (a Chimpomat) which delivered a raisin for each disc. This simple instrumental sequence can be diagrammed as follows:

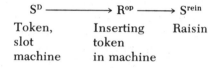

$$S^D \longrightarrow R^{op} \longrightarrow S^{rein}$$

Token,	Inserting	Raisin
slot	token	
machine	in machine	

After this habit had been learned, the animals were given the task of discovering which one of five covered boxes contained a token. The chimps had to complete twenty learning trials in this new situation before they were permitted to exchange the tokens for raisins; the only reinforcement for solving the problem was the acquisition of tokens, as diagrammed below:

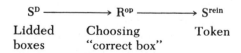

$$S^D \longrightarrow R^{op} \longrightarrow S^{rein}$$

| Lidded | Choosing | Token |
| boxes | "correct box" | |

Through setting the occasion a number of times for presentation of a primary reinforcer (food), the tokens acquired the capacity to reinforce problem-solving behavior, thereby functioning as conditioned reinforcers. One might say that they represented money to the chimps, because they could be exchanged for objects (raisins) that had primary reinforcing value.

The distinction we made earlier between respondent and operant conditioning also applies to the phenomena of higher-order conditioning. In fact, higher-order conditioning of the respondent type is very difficult to obtain. Razran (1955) reports that of 347 Russian reports on classical conditioning of dogs and monkeys he could find only eight that described any degree of successful second-order conditioning. Operant techniques, on the other hand, have been used to establish long *chains* of responses, with only the final response instrumental in securing primary reinforcement.

One of the basic problems in research on conditioned reinforcement has been determining whether or not the establishment of a discriminative stimulus is a necessary and sufficient condition for establishment of the stimulus as a conditioned reinforcer (Kelleher and Gollub, 1962). In simpler terms, we may ask whether a stimulus must be associated with a response that is reinforced in order to acquire reinforcing properties.

An answer to this problem may have been provided by Olds and Milner (1954), who perfected a technique for implanting electrodes in the brains of rats and thus were able to deliver electrical stimulation directly to various brain centers. When delivery of a mild electric shock to the midbrain was made contingent upon bar-pressing, rats would emit as many as two thousand bar-presses per hour for as long as twenty-four hours. More recently, Olds (1958) has shown that behavior reinforced in this fashion does not show satiation in the manner of consummatory responses, such as eating and drinking. Some of his animals pressed a bar to obtain electric shock in certain areas of the brain for as long as forty-eight hours without any reduction in the rate of response. When other areas are stimulated, the rat will press a lever that terminates the stimulus.

Reinforcement may be viewed, then, as fundamentally a pattern of events in the brain that is ordinarily achieved through direct sensory stimulation or feedback from various skeletal responses. It is unnecessary that we be able to identify an overt or consummatory performance as the vehicle of reinforcement, although some acts, such as eating, are obvious. There is evidence that stimuli associated temporally with a reinforcing stimulus may themselves become reinforcing. For example, Stein (1958) presented rats with a tone just before brain stimulation of the type just described. The rats were subsequently observed to engage in bar-pressing when it produced the tone; the tone had become a conditioned reinforcer. Because brain stimulation had not been made contingent upon any operant response, the tone had not become a discriminative stimulus. A stimulus need not, therefore, be a discriminative stimulus in order to become a conditioned reinforcer. Contiguity with an established reinforcer seems to be sufficient for this purpose.

How may these rather technical concepts in learning theory be extended to social behavior? Let us hazard an illustration. It is common practice for politicians when campaigning for votes to "drape themselves in the flag," as the expression goes. Political oratory is frequently ornamented with

references to God, mother, the home, and the American Way of Life, concepts that evoke favorable reactions in a listener and may, therefore, be
regarded as positively reinforcing. We need not here delve into the learning experiences that have conferred positive connotations upon these
terms, but they probably reflect attitudes that have prevailed in the home
and family. An individual who associates himself with these comfortable
expressions, then, takes on some of their reinforcing characteristics. Consider another example. It is often observed that a person frequently comes
to like those persons with whom he has shared enjoyable experiences.
Engaged couples doubtless tend to enhance their mutual endearment by
engaging in pleasurable activities together. We may suppose that the reinforcing value of each person is enhanced through contiguity with such
familiar positive reinforcements as music, moonlight, and entertainment.
That marriage may provide less frequent occasions for these experiences is
seldom considered during courtship.

A good grade in school is positively reinforcing because it has been
followed in the past by other reinforcers, such as praise and attention.
As conditioned reinforcers, satisfactory grades help to maintain study
behavior. Poor grades, on the other hand, by failing to reinforce efforts
at learning may result in discouragement and withdrawal from academic
pursuits. To someone who is reinforced more by the acquisition of knowledge than by grades, the latter may be a matter of relative indifference.
In the public school system as presently conceived, however, grades are
powerful conditioned reinforcers.

Incentives. We shall have occasion to refer to the role of incentives in
instigating and maintaining certain performances. The implication of
incentives for behavior theory is that an organism can in some way anticipate reinforcement and that such anticipation facilitates instrumental
behavior (Bolles, 1967). A man who is told he can achieve a salary raise
by increasing his productivity has, in general terms, been offered an incentive for improved performance. He has been placed under additional
stimulus control.

Bindra (1968), in discussing the properties of conditioned reinforcers,
distinguishes between those that are presented at the *end* of an instrumental performance and those that are presented *prior* to initiation of the
performance. The former are ordinarily called reinforcers, and the latter
are termed incentives. To act as an incentive, however, a stimulus must
have functioned at some time as a reinforcer, or it must resemble a reinforcer sufficiently so that the subject can generalize his response to it.
Of course, such a stimulus cannot be an effective incentive to prompt behavior which is not in the individual's repertoire.

Money is a powerful incentive because it makes possible many other behaviors that are reinforced, such as eating, drinking, driving an automobile,
or buying books. In behavioral language, an incentive is simply a stimulus

that increases the frequency of some behavior that is already in the person's repertoire. In this sense, an incentive has many of the properties of a discriminative stimulus that controls specified instrumental, or operant, performances. Unlike a discriminative stimulus, an incentive tends to control a variety of behaviors. Money, for example, may be the incentive for going to college, for writing a book, for managing a newspaper route, or for stealing hubcaps. Other factors will determine which of these behaviors occur. Among humans, incentives are frequently represented by words — in the form of offers, promises, or prospects.

Those verbal stimuli that fall into the category of *threats* might be called negative incentives, since they have the effect of decreasing the frequency of certain performances that otherwise might be expected to occur. An individual whose behavior is under the simultaneous control of both incentives and threats is said to be in *conflict*. This occurs when the consequences of a given course of action will be reinforcing in some respects and aversive in others. Visiting the dentist is an item of common experience that seems to fit this pattern. Arriving at a decision to marry places many persons in conflict, because they are able to envisage both the reinforcing and aversive consequences that this action will entail. The attainment of a stable source of sexual gratification must be measured against a certain loss of personal freedom; the comforts of home life must be balanced against an increase in financial and other responsibilities. Because human behavior is nearly always under such multiple stimulus control, the outcomes are not easy to predict. One goal of the science of psychology is to arrive at a better understanding of the factors that control behavior so that more accurate predictions can be made.

Conditioned aversive stimuli. Neutral stimuli, by occurring in contiguity with aversive stimuli, may acquire conditioned aversive qualities. This phenomenon has been well established experimentally. Schoenfeld (1950) notes that "if the occurrence of an operant response is followed by the removal or reduction of a stimulus associated in the past with a noxious stimulus, the strength of the response will increase" (p. 82). Unconditioned aversive stimuli, such as pain, intense heat or cold, and verbal abuse, arouse emotional reactions in addition to overt attempts to escape, and these emotional responses become conditioned to other cues present at the time of the aversive event. For example, a light that signals the onset of an electric shock will become a conditioned stimulus (S^c) for a conditioned response (R^c) of anxiety. This Pavlovian or classical conditioning procedure is necessary to establish the light as an effective stimulus to some of the behavior that ensues when the shock is applied. If an organism can now *avoid* the shock by pressing a bar in the presence of the light, the light has become a discriminative stimulus (S^D) to an instrumental response (R^{op}). This type of learning, as Mowrer (1947) has pointed out, involves two processes: classical conditioning and instrumental learning. The dilemma that learning theorists have faced is that of explaining how avoidance of the unconditioned stimulus (shock) can be reinforcing. This dilemma is resolved if we recognize that the light serves as a cue not only to "fright" behavior but also to emotional reactions that provide a source of aversive stimuli. Any behavior that avoids the shock also terminates these aversive internal stimuli, and is thereby negatively reinforced.

A conditioned aversive stimulus is developed by pairing a neutral stimulus with punishment and then observing subsequent behavior in the presence of this new stimulus. Brown and Jacobs (1949) confined rats to one compartment of a shuttle box and then electrified the floor of the box while sounding a tone paired with a light. Twenty-two such experiences were provided for the animals over a two-day period. The shock was then discontinued, the door separating the two compartments was raised, and the tone-light stimulation was presented alone. If the rat jumped into the other compartment, the stimulus was terminated. During the ensuing twenty trials, the rats promptly jumped over a hurdle into the other compartment at the presentation of the now aversive tone-light combination. This finding illustrates the point we made earlier — that a neutral stimulus (in this case, tone-light) may acquire aversive qualities by association with an aversive stimulus (shock), even when it has never served as a discriminative stimulus for an avoidance response. A stimulus upon which aversive qualities have been conferred is called a *conditioned aversive stimulus* or *preaversive stimulus*.

With little effort, we could probably identify many persons, situations, and events that have acquired conditioned aversive properties by contiguity with other aversive stimuli. Teachers are aversive to some students because they have been associated with study. Some people find policemen aversive because they are associated with arrest and punishment. Driving a car may gradually become aversive to someone who is bothered by traffic congestion and exhaust fumes. Even words may, by association with punishment, become aversive; this seems to be what happens with words considered obscene. A series of conditioned reactions at successively higher levels of abstraction must underlie an aversion to verbal events, but we as yet have little understanding of this process.

Avoidance Behavior

As Dinsmoor (1954) points out, "The punished response is not an isolated incident, *in vacuo*, but a member of some sequence or chain of responses which is linked together by a series of discriminative, and thereby secondary reinforcing, stimuli" (p. 44). If the termination of a particular chain is an aversive event, then, as Dinsmoor suggests, the individual may make responses that are incompatible with the next member of the chain and serve as digressions from the sequence. "Even a slight delay in the completion of the chain," he says, "may to some extent be reinforced, and a certain amount of seemingly pointless 'boondoggling' may be expected, like the dilatory behavior of a small child heading for bed" (p. 44). In short, individuals learn to anticipate certain unpleasant or unwelcome events toward which circumstances are impelling them and in some cases to forestall or postpone them by appropriate reactions.

If an unconditioned aversive stimulus is discontinued, avoidance behavior weakens and eventually ceases. Thus, an animal that has been running in an activity wheel to avoid shock will respond less quickly on successive trials until, by delaying too long, it is once again shocked (Sheffield, 1948). In the case of *traumatic avoidance learning,* however, instrumental avoidance responses may continue almost indefinitely. Solomon and Wynne (1953, 1954) suggest that the emotional reaction attached to a traumatic stimulus actually never diminishes below a certain level, even with the passage of time. In a series of experiments concerned with the effects of punishment on behavior, these investigators found that dogs would respond to a conditioned stimulus by jumping a hurdle in order to avoid an intense electric shock. After only a few such shocks, some dogs continued jumping *without further shock* for as many as 650 trials. The most obvious explanation of this finding is that the animal was responding to a conditioned response of *fear* and that termination of this aversive emotional reaction reinforced (negatively) the avoidance behavior. Solomon and Wynne point out, however, that jumping occurred within one or two seconds after presentation of the S^c, a period of time too short for the autonomic nervous system to mediate a fear response. Only if the animal delayed responding could fear develop. As these investigators explain, ". . . the subject is responding so quickly in the presence of the danger signal that he removes himself from its presence before he can become upset by it" (1954, p. 359). However, any delay in the avoidance reaction allowed time for a fear response to develop and serve as the stimulus for jumping. There are certain unresolved dilemmas posed by these findings that we need not go into here. It is sufficient for us to recognize that avoidance behaviors do not necessarily decrease in frequency, particularly if their execution avoids a severely punishing stimulus. Perhaps it will not do violence to our behavioristic orientation to suggest that people (and dogs) *remember* to avoid things that have been very painful.

Noncontingent punishment. We should mention here an additional type of avoidance behavior, one in which no discriminative stimulus is provided as a warning of impending punishment (Sidman, 1953). A rat is confined in a cage containing only a lever, and electric shocks are delivered to the animal on a regular schedule until it presses the lever. By pressing the lever it postpones delivery of the next shock for, say, fifteen or twenty seconds. Continued pressing will postpone the shock indefinitely. The situation is described by Millenson (1967):

> Consider the behavior of the rat early in training, prior to the development of efficient avoidance behavior. Shocks are being delivered frequently; occasionally, an operant-level lever press is emitted, thus postponing the shock.

Let us turn our attention to what the rat is doing at the moment it is shocked. It may be poking its nose in the corners of the cage, investigating the walls of the box, resting motionless, and so forth. Although we cannot say with any certainty exactly what the animal will have just done when it receives a shock, we can say with great certainty what it will *not* have just done. It will not have just pressed the lever. If it had, it would not be getting the shocks (p. 425).

Effectively, any part of the animal's behavior except lever-pressing can in time be paired with shock. The effect is to make large portions of the rat's behavior take on conditioned aversive properties. Only bar-pressing is safe, and by responding frequently enough the rat avoids further shock. What stimuli control the bar-pressing, and what stimuli reinforce it? Anger (1963) suggests that long intervals of time tend to become aversive because they are more apt to be followed by shock than short intervals. The effective S^D in Sidman avoidance responding, then, is some interoceptive consequence of not having responded recently. To be consistent with the research findings that we have already discussed, let us say that these interoceptive stimuli are registered at the cognitive level as fear or anxiety. These emotional reactions are aversive, and they strengthen by negative reinforcement the response that terminates them. This interpretation is consistent with that offered by Mowrer and Keehn (1958) and is supported by data from Bolles and Popp (1964). Finally, it should be emphasized that aversive stimuli, whether primary or conditioned, can effectively control behavior only when the animal is required to make a response which is already part of its innate defensive repertoire (Bolles, 1967).

When individuals live under constant threat of aversive stimulation, their usual performances may be almost totally disrupted. A noted psychiatrist who spent a year in the German concentration camps at Dachau and Buchenwald during World War II reports that the inmates, almost without exception, reverted to infantile patterns of behavior (Bettelheim, 1943). This general reaction was mutually reinforced among the prisoners because it constituted a type of behavior that was least likely to evoke further cruel treatment from the guards. In more technical terms we might say that the regressive behavior described by Bettelheim represented a generalized pattern of avoidance characterized by nearly total disruption of the usual adult repertoire.

Other, less dramatic, examples of avoidance behavior are readily found. Some students seem to develop effective study habits as a result of the positive reinforcements they receive in the form of good grades and parental approval. We may say that their behavior with respect to scholarly activities is under positive control. Other students, however, seem to study only to avoid the aversive consequences of low grades and parental disapproval. In the case of male students, an unusual dedication to their studies may be occasioned by the alternative (aversive) consequence of being drafted for military service. It is unnecessary to postulate motivational factors governing these two different patterns of behavior; it is sufficient to recognize that academic performance may come under either positive or aversive control depending upon the individual's history of reinforcement. Both may operate to keep the student at his books, but, as in most activities, behavior under the control of positive reinforcement is more durable and dependable.

Superstitious avoidance behavior has the effect of terminating conditioned feelings of anxiety that would otherwise persist in response to walking under a ladder, checking into a room on the thirteenth floor of a hotel, breaking a mirror, or boasting about one's good fortune ("knock on wood"). Consider, also, someone who has just left his home and driven off, only to reflect that he may not have locked the door. If he continues on his way, he will experience increasing apprehension about the possibility of burglary should his suspicions be true. He can terminate these aversive thoughts by returning home and checking the door. This behavior is reinforced not because it achieves a reward but because it terminates apprehension. The situation just described is much more complex than that of a rat avoiding electric shock, because the human responds to ideas and images as well as to external cues. Modern behaviorism can readily accommodate such cognitive concepts as these, and Mowrer (1960), for one, does not hesitate to suggest that stimuli can effectively signal fear, disappointment, relief, and hope.

Escape and avoidance compared. The stimuli for escape behavior are ordinarily external and include such things as loud noises, noxious odors, excesses of temperature, or bad company. One also learns ways of escaping from aversive *internal stimuli,* such as those arising from indigestion or a headache. Such instrumental acts as taking medicine either increase or decrease in frequency depending upon their effectiveness in eliminating the aversive sensations. Those paliative measures that achieve termination of the pain are strengthened by negative reinforcement.

Avoidance behavior is explained in essentially the same way as escape behavior, since negative reinforcement is again involved. As in escape behavior, the preaversive stimuli may be internal or external or both. If, while arguing with someone, I observe that he is becoming angry, I may avoid an unpleasant incident by making some placating remark. I am then responding to cues that through past experience I have come to associate with an imminent outburst of hostility. The preaversive stimuli may not themselves be aversive, so my behavior is better described as avoidance than as escape. Yet, in another sense, I am escaping from a *potentially* unpleasant situation, and my behavior is triggered not just by the other person's behavior but by my own reactions of anxiety or apprehension at his darkening countenance and threatening tone. My own reactions thus constitute a source of aversive stimuli, and I terminate them by behaving in a concilliatory fashion.

The point of this discussion is that it may not be necessary to postulate separate mechanisms of escape and avoidance. As we have indicated, it is possible to consider all instances of avoidance as behavior that has the effect of terminating conditioned aversive stimulation — in short, escape (Kamin, 1956, 1959). There is another possibility, however, and that is that avoidance and escape behaviors, if we choose to maintain the distinction, are both strengthened by positive reinforcement. This contention has been advanced by Schoenfeld (1950), who says: "The proprioceptive stimuli produced by the avoidance response may, because they are correlated with the termination of noxious stimuli, become secondary positive reinforcers and hence strengthen the tendency to make the response which generates them" (p. 88). This view is offered as an alternative to the use of such expressions as emotion, fear, and anxiety in describing avoidance learning. The difficulty in identifying a particular class of internal, or proprioceptive, stimuli which regularly follows avoidance behavior makes this a less appealing explanation for the data at hand then the concept of negative reinforcement.

Generalized Reinforcers

Certain social consequences, such as attention and praise, are *generalized conditioned reinforcers* because they support a great variety of performances (Skinner, 1953). For example, it is necessary to gain the attention of someone before speaking to him will evoke a reply; frequently you may observe that if you shift your gaze away from someone who is speaking to you, he will stop speaking. The child says "Mom" several times, with rising inflection, until Mom says, "Yes, what do you want?" This is analyzed as a chain of behaviors in which the parent's attention is the generalized conditioned reinforcer. A dog is trained initially by praising him at the same time that one gives him food. Praise thus becomes a generalized conditioned reinforcer and is used to maintain other behaviors, such as walking to heel, coming when called, and jumping over obstacles.

Because it maintains a wide variety of behaviors (i.e., working, stealing, lying) money is a generalized conditioned reinforcer. As a result of experience, money becomes associated with entertainment, warmth, food, sexual opportunities, and so forth. The possession of money makes it possible for other responses to occur, each having its own distinct reinforcer (Millenson, 1967). Generalized conditioned reinforcers have not been extensively studied in the laboratory, and the explanatory value of this particular concept should perhaps be deferred until more evidence is available.

Schedules of Reinforcement

Thus far, we have viewed reinforcement as some event that has the effect of increasing the probability of occurrence of the response that precedes it. When each occurrence of a response is reinforced, the process is termed *continuous reinforcement*. Several interesting examples of continuous reinforcement have been described by Aldis (1961), who observes that in parts of Asia and Africa workers are often paid on the spot for each wheel-barrow load of dirt that they have transported. When Sir Hillary climbed Mt. Everest, he carried extra baggage in the form of sacks of coin so that the native bearers could be paid at the end of each day's climb. Without this immediate reinforcement for their labors, they might have refused to continue. A device familiar to all of us that provides immediate and certain reinforcement whenever we insert coins in it is the vending machine. In most actual life situations, however, reinforcers seldom accompany every occasion of a response but, rather, follow one of several patterns. Ferster and Skinner (1957) have studied four basic *schedules of reinforcement,* which we shall describe briefly.

First, there is the *fixed interval,* or FI, schedule. In this condition, the individual is reinforced only after a fixed interval of time has elapsed since the previous reinforcement, provided only that he has made at least one appropriate response during that interval. For example, a pigeon may be given food every sixty seconds if it has pecked at an illuminated disc even once before this amount of time expired. Another example of reinforcement on a fixed interval schedule is seen when a teacher tells the children in her class that they have ten minutes in which to complete an arithmetic problem; at the end of this time, if they have completed the problem, they may engage in some recreational activity of their own choosing; however, every child must work on the assigned task for at least ten minutes. As a result, many of the children will delay working on their solutions until the time has partly expired, since finishing early will only result in their having to wait. Productivity under this type of schedule obviously will be low, since many individuals are capable of completing more than the assigned material during the allotted interval. Furthermore, if reinforcement ceases to be forthcoming at the termination of such an interval, extinction of the behavior is rapid; if a worker fails to receive one or more of his weekly paychecks, he may soon stop working.

The second type of reinforcement schedule is known as a *variable interval,* or VI, schedule. Here the performing organism is rewarded at irregular and unpredictable times. For instance, we might say that a pigeon must peck at a disc at least once during successive intervals of 10, 60, 90, 40, and 50 seconds in order to be fed, that is once every 50 seconds on the average. Obviously, the animal's behavior will proceed at a fairly high rate on this type of schedule, since reinforcement will be missed if responses are not made during the shorter intervals. More important, the rate of response is steady, and there is no last-minute spurt just before the reinforcement is due. Examples of variable interval reinforcement in human social behavior are not too common, although several can be observed. A teacher, for example, may walk about the classroom praising the work of randomly selected children. Reinforcement of any one student obviously occurs at unpredictable intervals, and work output is continuous at a stable, fairly high level with this schedule. Surprise inspections, such as those conducted at military installations, also have the characteristics of variable interval reinforcement. Since the consequences, in the form of either approval or censure, will be contingent upon the satisfactory appearance and operation of the facility, efficiency is apt to remain at a high level under this system. The loss of behavior that has been maintained under VI reinforcement is very slow because responses have been conditioned to the nonreinforced trials as well as to the reinforced trials. The human subject, who can verbalize the situation, has no way of knowing whether reinforcements have ceased altogether or whether he is simply in the middle of an unusually long interval. A girl who behaves affectionately toward her boyfriend at random intervals, not contingent upon his behavior, keeps him in a state of continuous anticipation and will probably receive his attention long after she has decided that she will no longer reinforce him at all.

When reinforcements are supplied only after a fixed number of responses have been made by the organism, we say that performance is on a *fixed ratio*, or FR, schedule. Thus, a pigeon may be rewarded for every ten pecks at a disc. The animal's work output is extremely high on this schedule, since the higher his rate of responding, the more reinforcements he gets. Factory workers who are paid according to the number of units they produce are effectively on a fixed ratio schedule. This is known as piece work, and piece-rate pay is not always well received by members of labor unions. As Aldis (1961) has pointed out, the objections to this system are frequently justified, since technological innovations may increase worker efficiency in some parts of a plant and not in others, thus creating inequities in the piece-rate pay of workers in different situations. Another example of behavior on an FR schedule is the child who learns that the more frequently he raises his hand in class, the more often he is called upon. The rate of response in this case, as every teacher knows, may constitute a nuisance.

Finally, we have reinforcements that are contingent upon varying amounts of specified behavior by an organism, yielding a *variable ratio*, or VR, schedule of reinforcement. A pigeon that is rewarded after, say, 10, 20, 5, 30, and 25 pecks is on a VR schedule. Reinforcement depends upon how much work the organism does, but the amount of work required for each reinforcement varies. Probably the best and most dramatic example of this at the human level is gambling. Consider the behavior of a person operating a slot machine, or "one-armed bandit." Reinforcement, in the form of coins returned, is not contingent upon the intervals at which he pulls the handle, nor does it follow any fixed number of responses. He is on a variable ratio schedule; that is, the more often he pulls the handle, the more times he gets money from the machine. That he puts in more money than he gets out is for all practical purposes irrelevant, as anyone who has a chronic gambler in the family knows ("I know the dice are crooked, but it's the only game in town"). In both animals and humans, extinction of behavior acquired on this schedule of reinforcement is very slow. A pigeon will continue to make as many as five thousand unrein-forced pecks at a disc after having learned the habit with variable ratio reinforcement. In like manner, the gambler continues to try his luck even after a long period of nonreinforcement, in the conviction — produced by the VR schedule — that "next time" he will hit the jackpot.

Chaining

The idea of chaining, to which we have already alluded, was introduced by Skinner (1938), who argued that "the response of one reflex may con-stitute or produce the eliciting or discriminative stimulus of another" (p. 32). Thus, a rat may be placed in a cage arranged so that a click briefly precedes delivery of a food pellet into the feeding dish. After several such presentations, the rat will approach the food dish at the sound of the click and will consume the food pellet when it appears. The click serves as a discriminative stimulus that controls the operant response of approaching the feeding dish; it is also an eliciting stimulus for respondents such as salivating (Shapiro, 1960). This distinction is important because in every-day behavior humans are guided by stimuli that not only control operant behavior but also elicit conditioned emotional reactions that influence subsequent behaviors in complex ways. For example, if one has to leap back (R^{op}) from a speeding car (S^D), he immediately experiences a condi-tioned emotional reaction (R^c) that may disrupt the ongoing chain of be-haviors for several minutes.

A simple illustration of chaining is provided by rats that learn a rather complex sequence of responses before they are finally reinforced. Of course, they must first be reinforced for every response in the series. Once they have acquired the discrete responses required for the chain, reinforce-ment can be withheld until all of the component responses have been executed. Keller (1954) describes the behavior of an accomplished rat at the University of Minnesota named Pliny:

> Pliny's accomplishment amounted to this. He would first pull a string that hung from the top of his cage. This pull would cause a marble to be released from an overhead rack. When the marble fell to the floor, he would pick it up on his forepaws and carry it across the cage to a small tube that projected vertically two inches above the floor. He would then lift the marble to the top of the tube and drop it inside, whereupon, a pellet of food was auto-matically discharged into a nearby tray. Pliny would then approach the tray, seize the pellet, eat it, and turn again to repeat the sequence of acts. In this way, he earned his living, day after day (p. 24).

The events that occur in chaining may be diagrammed as follows:

$$S^{D_1} \longrightarrow R^{op_1} + S^{D_2} \longrightarrow R^{op_2} + S^{D_3} \longrightarrow R^{op_3} \longrightarrow S^{rein}$$

In the sequence shown opposite, ever S^D except the first one is produced by the immediately preceding response. These are sometimes referred to as response-produced cues. The capacity to learn long S-R chains increases as one ascends the phylogenetic scale from animals to man. Rats ordinarily can learn only a limited sequence of S-R events before being reinforced. Man, on the other hand, chains together exceedingly long sequences of stimuli and responses.

Consider an individual who on Election Day presses a lever in a voting booth. How might this act be analyzed in terms of stimuli, responses, and reinforcers? Unlike the rat who presses a lever and obtains food, the human who presses the lever to record a vote does not receive a primary reinforcer. We shall assume that the consequences of voting involve conditioned reinforcement and are effective in maintaining a long sequence of preceding acts. Conceivably, one could trace the conditioned reinforcing properties of the voting performance to other stimuli that are either concurrent with it or anticipated. Such a procedure would be not only tedious and speculative but unnecessary for the purpose of understanding the sequence of events that led to the behavior. Although it is difficult, if not impossible, to identify the first response in the chain, let us arbitrarily start with the individual being reminded by the morning paper that it is Election Day. This information sets the occasion for the person telling himself, "I had better vote before lunch." Other events will now initiate chains of behavior that are unrelated to voting, such as eating breakfast, driving to work, and engaging in certain tasks. Our subject will probably dwell no further on his voting intentions until another relevant stimulus is presented, perhaps the indication by his wristwatch that noon has arrived. From this point, his locomotion to the polling place will be controlled by a number of factors. His intention was to vote before eating, but a friend may appear with an invitation to eat at once, and our subject may accede to this proposal with the revised intention of voting after lunch. Following lunch, and barring additional intrusions, he enters his car, drives in a particular pattern according to habit and the constraints of traffic, and arrives at the polling place. Here again, certain features of the situation will influence his behavior. For example, if there are long lines of people at the voting booths, he may avoid the aversiveness of waiting by leaving. He may "rationalize" this decision to leave without voting by telling himself that it is more important that he return to work on time, that with so many people voting his own vote is not important, or the like. Or, if a booth is immediately available, he will enter, move the lever in a particular manner, and return to work. This particular chain of behaviors is completed.

Suppose we return to the beginning of this sequence of performance and ask whether we could have predicted any of the subject's behaviors. We have identified a number of the stimuli to which he responded, we have described some of his behaviors, and we have identified some of the consequences. For example, the friend who dissuades him from voting until after lunch may be someone with whom he has enjoyed eating on several past occasions. The friend, therefore, may be viewed both as an agent of positive conditioned reinforcement and as a discriminative stimulus for the response of saying, "Okay, let's go to lunch." The initial chain of behaviors that otherwise would have terminated with voting has been interrupted by a new chain that leads to eating. Each act in the sequence of "going to lunch" is part of a familiar and well practiced chain (with minor variations), and primary reinforcement in the form of food combines with a number of conditioned social reinforcers to maintain the preceding behaviors in the chain. If we had known in advance that this particular friend would appear at the lunch hour, and that such encounters had previously been reinforcing, then we could have predicted with some degree of confidence that our subject would delay going to the polls until after lunch.

If we ask why our subject voted for Candidate X rather than Candidate Y, we open up a whole new area of inquiry. His performance in the voting booth is probably part of a class of performances, mostly verbal, that have in common a consistent orientation with respect to certain social and economic issues. We are sometimes able to sample such behaviors, as by obtaining the individual's verbal responses to questions on an opinion poll. Or we may have witnessed on occasion other verbal performances from which we infer a general behavioral disposition, or attitude, that makes certain specific acts more probable than others. In short, to predict voting behavior we would have to know a great deal about the individual's past history of reinforcement in those kinds of situations to which the act of voting is related. In undertaking such an analysis, it is possible to take into consideration all the factors that have been identified by social psychologists as useful in predicting behavior, for example, beliefs, attitudes, prejudices, and group affiliations, without forsaking the use of behavioral terms and concepts.

Generalization

Two additional concepts that will be indispensable in our analysis of social behavior are *generalization* and *discrimination*. The student may already be familiar with these terms from his introductory course, but a brief review at this point will be helpful. Generalization is said to occur when the organism gives a response, originally conditioned to one stimulus, to other stimuli having properties in common with the conditioned stimulus (Schoenfeld and Cumming, 1963). Such stimuli acquire partial control over the original conditioned or instrumental behavior. Let us consider two laboratory examples, one a classic case of auditory generalization in rats, and the second a case of visual spatial generalization in humans.

As described by Hull (1943), a rat conditioned to jump at the sound of a 1000-cycle tone that has been followed by an electric shock (escape behavior) will also jump when tones of 900 and 1100 cycles are sounded. The strength of this behavior decreases as the test stimuli become less similar to the training stimulus; thus, a 500-cycle tone may produce only tensing and quivering. A tone of 100 cycles will probably elicit no response at all, as its frequency is too far removed from that of the original tone to produce generalization.

More recently, Harleston (1961) has demonstrated spatial generalization in human subjects. His apparatus consisted of a horizontal row of eleven lamps, uniformly spaced. The center lamp, number 6, was the training lamp, while those on either side were used to test generalization. After thirty training trials on the center lamp, in which the subjects were required to press a key every time the lamp went on, the test lamps on either side were lit at random intervals interspersed with lighting of the center lamp. As expected, the subjects generalized their responses to the test lamps, but generalization decreased as a function of the distance from the test lamp to the training lamp. Lamps 1 and 11 were responded to fewer times than Lamps 3 and 9, and these in turn elicited fewer false responses than Lamps 5 and 7, which were adjacent to the training lamp, number 6. An additional finding of interest was that subjects who were under pressure from the experimenter to respond made more errors than those who were allowed to respond at their own pace.

This tendency of behavior to generalize from the reinforced stimulus to similar stimuli provides a basis for understanding a variety of social responses. An individual who has had even one unpleasant experience with a member of a minority ethnic group, say a Scotchman, a Negro, or a Jew, may generalize his resulting antagonistic behavior to all members of these groups. A child who has been bitten by a large black dog may come to fear all dogs, regardless of their size or color. Children who learn polite manners at home will usually generalize this behavior to a variety of social situations; it is not necessary for them to learn politeness in each new setting. Finally, an individual who is hostile toward his father frequently behaves in a hostile manner toward any person who in some way resembles his father. The hostility may even generalize to all persons in authority because they represent the father. In this connection, we might note that some forms of psychotherapy involve helping the patient to verbalize the basis for the generalized responses he is making and which are inimical to his establishing satisfactory relationships with other people. For example, a person who responds to all authority figures as if they were dominating fathers is bound to have difficulty in working effectively with them. By recognizing the nature and basis of his generalizations, he is often able to learn new and more adaptive behavior.

Osgood (1953) has emphasized an important educational principle embodied in the concept of generalization: "The more closely a training situation resembles that in which the training is to be used, the more effective will be the training" (p. 351). This principle has been successfully employed in a number of training situations. Infantrymen who learn to advance under a stream of real bullets in training camps are less likely to panic under battle conditions, where they are faced with a similar but more dangerous situation. Individuals who will require skill in speaking a foreign language are better advised to take courses in conversation than courses which would concentrate their efforts on learning to read and write the language.

Discrimination

The obverse of generalization, of course, is discrimination. Here the training situation is arranged so that the organism will restrict his response to a narrow range of stimuli and not generalize beyond this range. If we wish to limit the jumping response of a rat to a tone of 1000 cycles, we must provide a learning situation in which only a performance in the presence of this tone is reinforced. In other words, we want the animal to make an escape response to the training tone and not to others. Shocking the rat when this tone is presented and never shocking him when other tones are sounded will eventually result in his jumping only to the reinforced tone. Jumping responses to tones of other frequencies gradually become less frequent because they are never reinforced. A history of differential reinforcement is the basis of most of our discriminations. In the experiment previously described, in which human subjects generalized their responses to lamps on either side of a training lamp, we may assume that with continued training the subjects would have learned to respond only to the center lamp.

Differential reinforcement also underlies much of our social behavior. Children are not only positively reinforced for saying things that are truthful, they also experience the aversive consequences of saying truthful things that embarrass or offend others. The child learns to discriminate between social situations where honesty is appropriate and those where it is not. These and other discriminations will be learned, however, only if adults and peers provide differential reinforcement in consistent fashion.

One of the best illustrations of the principles of generalization and discrimination at the level of human social behavior is provided by cultural, racial, and ethnic prejudice. As we have noted, responses that are prejudicial to an entire class of individuals provide a clear example of generalization. The individual who responds to members of minority groups as *individuals* and not simply as representatives of a class has acquired a habit of discrimination in an important social context.

Stimulus Control of Behavior

When a cue, or discriminative stimulus, becomes the occasion on which a particular performance occurs, it can be said to control that performance. Let us consider for a moment the concept of discriminative stimuli in simple learning situations. By reinforcing a desired response, we place this behavior under experimental control, so that only specific stimuli come to produce it. It is possible, in fact, to train an animal to respond only in the presence of a particular signal, say a light. This type of learning has been demonstrated with rats, pigeons, and other animals, as well as man. Pigeons have been trained to peck at an illuminated disc by reinforcing pecking only under this condition. If the bird pecks at a dark disc, it receives no food. The disc has become the discriminative stimulus that controls the pecking behavior. Unless the organism performs differentially, much of its behavior will go unreinforced.

This fact is of critical importance in understanding human social behavior, where appropriate, or reinforcing, responses depend upon selective discrimination of the relevant controlling stimuli. In an argument, for example, each adversary must be able to discriminate the signs (facial, vocal, etc.) which indicate that his opponent is becoming angry to the point of overt hostility. He may then respond to these cues, or discriminative stimuli, either by further aggravating his antagonist or by attempting to placate him. In more technical language, we may say that certain aversive stimuli, such as those represented by expressions of anger, may come to control a person's behavior. The result is an increase in the frequency of negatively reinforced operants, that is, behavior that is followed by withdrawal of threat.

Social Learning

Social reinforcers are scarcely ever as simple and direct as food, and it is sometimes difficult to trace the events through which social consequences have acquired reinforcing value. We can, however, describe and understand a great deal of social behavior in terms of the principles just discussed. They provide a systematic and parsimonious description of many seemingly complex social responses. A particularly good illustration of this is the acquisition of language. As some recent research by Rheingold, Gewirtz, and Ross (1959) has indicated, the frequency of vocalization by infants can be increased if vocalization is reinforced by smiling or tickling from an adult. Failure to reinforce these operants results in a decrease in the frequency of vocal behavior. In learning to use words, the child first emits reasonable facsimiles of them, and these responses become an occasion for reinforcing behavior from an adult.

Consider, for example, the behavior acquired by a child when he learns to say "How do you do?" and extend his hand on the occasion of meeting someone. Unlike the rat in a lever-pressing situation, he has previously acquired a degree of verbal facility, which gives him the capacity to respond to verbal cues. The learning process can thus be abbreviated and need not depend to a great extent upon the initial operant strength of the behavior. For one thing, the child has learned that behaving in a manner consistent with his parents' verbal injunctions is likely to be followed by agreeable consequences, whereas behaving otherwise produces aversive consequences. Consequently, he can generally be expected to do what the parents tell him, provided that the required behavior is within his capabilities. Whether or not he emits the appropriate behavior on subsequent relevant occasions depends upon the reinforcement contingencies that are established. The controlling stimuli in the "meeting someone" situation consist of the parent's saying, "I want you to meet so-and-so," combined with the presence of the other person. If the child responds by extending his hand and saying, "How do you do," he is making an instrumental, or operant, response that will be followed by certain reinforcing events, namely, expressions of approval from the other persons present.

Such a social learning situation might be diagrammatically represented as follows:

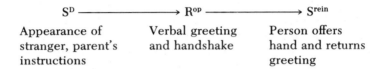

$$S^D \longrightarrow R^{op} \longrightarrow S^{rein}$$

| Appearance of stranger, parent's instructions | Verbal greeting and handshake | Person offers hand and returns greeting |

This example is intended to show that learning in a social setting is no different in principle from the learning of a simple instrumental motor act by a laboratory animal. Additional theoretical constructs may be needed to describe more complex examples of social behavior, but these need not be invoked until our supply of basic principles is no longer adequate to the task.

Cognitive Factors in Behavior

So far, we have leaned rather heavily upon examples of learning and performance borrowed from experiments with infrahumans, such as rats and pigeons. The reason for this is simply that the fundamental principles of behavior are more easily demonstrated in these organisms than in man, where we find the picture vastly complicated by man's great capacity for symbolic activity. By symbolic activity we mean such complex processes as imagery, verbalization, concept formation, and reasoning. These capacities, of course, are possessed to a more limited extent by animals lower than man in the phylogenetic scale. It has been amply demonstrated that laboratory rats are capable of an elementary form of reasoning in learning to solve simple problems. Bees are able to remember and communicate the location of food to other bees through a pattern of body movement. Chimpanzees have even learned to utter two or three words in apparently meaningful fashion. But these examples represent only the barest beginnings of the higher mental capacities that have evolved in the human species.

Consider the behaviors of an individual playing chess, a mathematician solving a problem, or a violinist performing a concerto. The behavior that we are able to observe in each of these three instances is largely manual. The chess player manipulates pieces on a board, the mathematician moves a pencil over a sheet of paper, and the violinist fingers the strings of his instrument with one hand while bowing with the other. Each of these chains of motor activities is assumed to be correlated with a complex chain of symbolic or "mental" processes, the exact nature of which can only be the subject of speculation at present. Chess players, according to introspective accounts, engage in a great deal of implicit trial and error before they commit themselves to an actual move. In similar fashion, the mathematician may work out a problem "in his head," without ever putting pencil to paper. The violinist has probably "imagined" many times how he would interpret a particular composition, but his interpretation is shared by a listener only when it leads to manipulation of an instrument. These various *covert* behaviors may be viewed as occasions that control certain *overt* performances.

Behavioral scientists, of course, can deal only with data derived from observation of an individual's public behavior. We assume that others have private experiences, as we ourselves do, but we can know about these only by inference from overt behavior. Researchers have attempted persistently to penetrate the shell of private behavior and to devise techniques for recording those neural and psyiological activities that underlie them. We attempt to probe the autonomic basis of emotional experience, for example, by measuring changes in blood pressure, blood chemistry, heart rate, breathing, and perspiration. Although the emotional experience is not identical with these physiological processes, it is assumed to be related to them. An even deeper penetration of the physiological basis of symbolic behavior has been made through techniques of introducing electrodes into the brain at various levels in an attempt to stimulate the nerve centers that control specific responses. The effects of electrical stimulation of a "pleasure center" was described earlier in this chapter. These procedures were originally developed with animals, but they have recently been used with humans during brain surgery (Penfield and Rasmussen, 1950).

There are several levels at which performances may be observed and studied. Reductionism to the level of neurophysiology is not the goal of the social psychologist, who generally confines his attention to the relatively gross aspects of behavior of an individual as he interacts with other persons. We cannot be entirely unconcerned with physiological processes, however, particularly those involving the autonomic nervous system, because these are intimately involved in so much of everyday behavior. Nor can we disregard the possibility that conscious or volitional factors may mediate the effects of reinforcement on response selection (Dulany, 1967). It is very possible that thought processes do not depend for their maintenance upon the kinds of reinforcement contingencies that seem to control overt behavior. "Thinking" is undoubtedly lawful, but we do not yet have an adequate theory to explain events at this level of complexity.

In the chapters that follow we shall direct our attention primarily to those aspects of social behavior that are both public and measurable. There is one area of cognition, however, that does seem to be of rather unusual significance in our understanding of social behavior. That is perception. Defined briefly, perception refers to that meaningful organization of sensory impressions (colors, sounds, textures, distances, and groupings) that constitutes one's immediate awareness of his environment. We rarely, for example, perceive elementary sensations such as redness or loudness; these are nearly always identified as attributes of objects or situations.

An interesting question arises here: Do we all perceive the world in the same way? Evidence is accumulating to show that our individual perceptions are determined to a significant extent not just by an inborn genetic code but by past experience and certain deprivation operations. Even our perception of other persons is a complex and highly individual process that has only recently been a subject of study. The importance of perception and cognitive organization in learning, of course, has been emphasized for many years by Tolman (1932) and his students. The role of cognitive and perceptual factors in social behavior has been analyzed in detail by Krech and Crutchfield (1948) and Krech, Crutchfield, and Ballachey (1962). We will take the position that our perceptions of the environment are influenced by social reinforcements in much the same way that our overt behavior is shaped by its consequences. This is because we are able to make our perceptual responses public by communicating them to other persons, who in turn communicate their perceptions to us. Through verbal and other reinforcements, we come, in many instances, to acquire those perceptual responses that have a likelihood of being positively reinforced when we express them publicly. If most of our associates describe a particular form of art as "ugly" or "beautiful," then we will in all probability come to describe it in similar fashion; this means simply that we have all attached the same verbal label to an item of common experience. We generally infer from this concordance of verbal labeling that our perceptions are also similar. Evidence for this is sometimes difficult to obtain. We shall examine relevant research findings in Chapter 5.

Summary   In this chapter we have reviewed some basic principles of learning and behavior that will be useful in understanding social interaction. One of the simplest forms of learning, classical conditioning, probably underlies many of the emotional responses that individuals exhibit in social situations. This occurs when a conditioned stimulus (S^c) has been followed repeatedly by an unconditioned stimulus (S^{uc}). Part of the behavior elicited by the S^{uc} becomes attached to the S^c

and will occur in response to it so long as occasional reinforcement is provided by presenting the S^{uc}.

Most social learning seems to follow an instrumental, or operant, learning paradigm. Behavior emitted by the individual increases in frequency if it is reinforced and decreases in frequency if it is not reinforced. A stimulus that has the effect of increasing the frequency of any behavior upon which its presentation is contingent is called a positive reinforcer (S^{rein}). On the other hand, if a given behavior serves either to terminate or to avoid a particular stimulus, that stimulus is said to be aversive (S^{av}), and the behavior is said to be maintained through negative reinforcement ($S^{neg\ rein}$). Stimuli that immediately precede reinforced behavior and thereby acquire a capacity to control the behavior are called discriminative stimuli (S^{D}). Most behavior involves chaining, in which each response produces the stimulus for the next in a series.

Much behavior involves chaining, a process in which each response produces the stimulus for the next in a series. Many complex behavioral repertoires are developed through the chaining of discrete components. Each act in the series serves both as a reinforcer for the act immediately preceding it and as a discriminative stimulus for the act to follow. In many instances, the chain terminates with some behavior that is followed by primary reinforcement. A stimulus may become a *conditioned reinforcer* if its presentation is the occasion on which the next act in an instrumental chain can occur.

Aversive stimuli, both primary and conditioned, may be internal or external to the individual. A stomachache is aversive and has its locus in the digestive tract. Emotional reactions also provide stimuli to which the individual responds. Behavior that reduces or terminates aversive stimulation will be strengthened through negative reinforcement. In daily life, we engage in many behaviors that have the effect of reducing such unpleasant feelings as fear and anxiety.

The reinforcements which strengthen a habit, that is, increase its probability of occurrence, may be delivered at fixed or variable intervals or in fixed or variable ratio to the number of responses made. These various reinforcement contingencies are known as schedules of reinforcement, and they lead to different rates of response and different levels of resistance to extinction.

We have reviewed briefly the concepts of generalization and discrimination. Generalization means responding to a range of stimuli lying along the same sensory continuum as the stimulus that has been reinforced. Discrimination is learned when reinforcements are provided only in the presence of the S^{D}. Both generalization and discrimination play important parts in everyday social interactions. Group or ethnic prejudice, for example, illustrates generalization of avoidance or hostility to an entire group of persons. Discrimination would be illustrated by a person reacting to other persons as individuals rather than as representatives of a group.

Finally, the role of cognitive factors in behavior has been considered. The implicit responses of thinking and feeling must be taken into account in any comprehensive theory of behavior. These concepts are given meaning through the operations by which they are made public. Making explicit the relationships between cognitions and overt behavior poses one of the more challenging problems for social psychology.

References

ALDIS, O. Of pigeons and men. *Harvard Business Review*, July–August, 1961, 59–63.

ANGER, D. The role of temporal discrimination in the reinforcement of Sidman avoidance behavior. *Journal of the Experimental Analysis of Behavior*, 1963, 6, 477–506.

BETTELHEIM, B. Individual and mass behavior in extreme situations. *Journal of Abnormal and Social Psychology*, 1943, 38, 417–452.

BINDRA, D. *Motivation: A systematic reinterpretation*. New York: Ronald Press, 1959.

BINDRA, D. Neuropsychological interpretation of the effects of drive and incentive motivation on general activity and instrumental behavior. *Psychological Review*, 1968, 75, 1–22.

BOLLES, R. C. *Theory of motivation*. New York: Harper and Row, 1967.

BOLLES, R. C., and POPP, R. J., JR. Parameters affecting the acquisition of Sidman avoidance. *Journal of the Experimental Analysis of Behavior*, 1964, 7, 315–321.

BRADY, J. V. A comparative approach to the experimental analysis of emotional behavior. In P. H. Hoch and J. Zubin (Eds.), *Experimental psychopathology*. New York: Grune and Stratton, 1957.

BROWN, J. S., and JACOBS, A. The role of fear in the motivation and acquisition of responses. *Journal of Experimental Psychology*, 1949, 39, 747–759.

COWLES, J. T. Food tokens as incentives for learning by chimpanzees. *Comparative Psychology Monographs*, 1937, *14*, Whole No. 71.

DINSMOOR, J. A. Punishment: I. The avoidance hypothesis. *Psychological Review*, 1954, *61*, 34–46.

DULANY, D. E. Awareness, rules, and propositional control: A confrontation with S-R behavior theory. In T. R. Dixon and D. L. Horton (Eds.), *Verbal behavior and general behavior theory*. Englewood Cliffs, N. J.: Prentice-Hall, 1968.

FERSTER, C. B., and SKINNER, B. F. *Schedules of reinforcement*. New York: Appleton-Century-Crofts, 1957.

GOLDIAMOND, I. Perception. In A. Bachrach (Eds.), *Experimental foundations of clinical psychology*. New York: Basic Books, 1962.

HARLESTON, B. W. The effect of speed-up on spatial stimulus generalization. *Journal of Experimental Psychology*, 1961, *61*, 242–244.

HULL, C. L. *Principles of Behavior.* New York: Appleton-Century-Crofts, 1943.

KAMIN, L. J. The effects of termination of the CS and avoidance of the US on avoidance learning. *Journal of Comparative and Physiological Psychology,* 1956, *49,* 420–424.

KAMIN, L. J. CS-termination as a factor in the emergence of anticipatory avoidance. *Psychological Reports,* 1959, 5, 455–456.

KELLEHER, R. T., and GOLLUB, L. R. A review of positive conditioned reinforcement. *Journal of the Experimental Analysis of Behavior,* 1962, 5, 543–597.

KELLER, F. S. *Learning: Reinforcement theory.* New York: Random House, 1954.

KRECH, D., and CRUTCHFIELD, R. S. *Theory and problems of social psychology.* New York: McGraw-Hill, 1948.

KRECH, D., and CRUTCHFIELD, R. S., and BALLACHEY, E. L. *Individual in society.* New York: McGraw-Hill, 1962.

LIDDELL, H. S. The conditioned reflex. Chapter 8 in F. A. Moss (Ed.), *Comparative psychology.* New York: Prentice-Hall, 1942.

MILLENSON, J. R. *Principles of behavioral analysis.* New York: Macmillan, 1967.

MOWRER, O. H. On the dual nature of learning: A reinterpretation of "conditioning" and "problem-solving." *Harvard Educational Review,* 1947, *17,* 102–148.

MOWRER, O. H. *Learning theory and behavior.* New York: Wiley, 1960.

MOWRER, O. H., and KEEHN, J. D. How are intertrial "avoidance" responses reinforced? *Psychological Review,* 1958, 65, 209–221.

NOTTERMAN, J. M., SCHOENFELD, W. N., and BERSH, P. J. Conditioned heart rate response in human beings during experimental anxiety. *Journal of Comparative and Physiological Psychology,* 1952, 45, 1–8.

OLDS, J. Satiation effects in self-stimulation of the brain. *Journal of Comparative and Physiological Psychology,* 1958, *51,* 675–679.

OLDS, J., and MILNER, P. Positive reinforcement produced by electrical stimulation of septal area and other regions of rat brain. *Journal of Comparative and Physiological Psychology,* 1954, *47,* 419–427.

OSGOOD, C. E. *Method and theory in experimental psychology.* New York: Oxford University Press, 1953.

PAVLOV, I. P. *Conditioned reflexes* (tr. by G. V. Anrep). London: Oxford University Press, 1927.

PENFIELD, W., and RASMUSSEN, T. *The cerebral cortex of man: A clinical study of localization of function.* New York: Macmillan, 1950.

RAZRAN, G. A note on second-order conditioning — and secondary reinforcement. *Psychological Review,* 1955, 62, 327–332.

RHEINGOLD, H., GEWIRTZ, J., and ROSS, H. Social conditioning of vocalizations in the infant. *Journal of Comparative and Physiological Psychology,* 1959, 52, 68–73.

SCHOENFELD, W. N. An experimental approach to anxiety, escape, and avoidance behavior. In P. H. Hoch and J. Zubin (Eds.), *Anxiety.* New York: Grune and Stratton, 1950, pp. 70–99.

SCHOENFELD, W. N., and CUMMING, W. W.   Behavior and perception. In S. Koch (Ed.), *Psychology: A study of a science.* Vol. 5. New York: McGraw-Hill, 1963, pp. 213–252.

SHAPIRO, M. M.   Respondent salivary conditioning during operant lever pressing in dogs. *Science,* 1960, *132,* 619–620.

SHEFFIELD, F. D.   Avoidance training and the contiguity principle. *Journal of Comparative and Physiological Psychology,* 1948, *41,* 165–177.

SIDMAN, M.   Two temporal parameters of the maintenance of avoidance behavior by the white rat. *Journal of Comparative and Physiological Psychology,* 1953, *46,* 253–261.

SKINNER, B. F.   *The behavior of organisms: An experimental analysis.* New York: Appleton-Century, 1938.

SKINNER, B. F.   *Science and human behavior.* New York: Macmillan, 1953.

SKINNER, B. F.   *Verbal behavior.* New York: Appleton-Century-Crofts, 1957.

SOLOMON, R. L., and WYNNE, L. C.   Traumatic avoidance learning: Acquisition in normal dogs. *Psychological Monographs,* 1953, 67, No. 354, 1–19.

SOLOMON, R. L., and WYNNE, L. C.   Traumatic avoidance learning: The principles of anxiety conservation and partial irreversibility. *Psychological Review,* 1954, *61,* 353–385.

STEIN, L.   Secondary reinforcement established with subcortical stimulation. *Science,* 1958, *127,* 466–467.

TOLMAN, E. C.   *Purposive behavior in animals and men.* New York: Appleton-Century-Crofts, 1932.

3

Behavior Shaping and Socialization

The behavior of a human infant bears only the crudest resemblance to that of the surrounding adults. Unheedful of even the most elementary social customs and amenities, the newborn faces many years of learning to behave in ways that not only will insure its survival but will be acceptable to other persons. This process is called *socialization*, a shorthand way of referring to those kinds of learning experiences that have particular relevance for shaping the individual's behavior in ways that are characteristic of the adult members of his community.

Primary and Acquired Behaviors

About all that the individual possesses in the way of a behavior repertoire at birth is a set of reflexes that will help to maintain his existence in an environment that provides adequate nourishment and protection. Other species-specific behaviors, such as walking and talking, will appear later as a result of maturational processes, and these will be elaborately shaped through the intervention of interested adults. It will be useful for us to make a distinction between *primary behaviors*, which are common in one form or another to all humans, and *acquired behaviors*, which may be absent in some individuals because they were never learned, and which may show wide differences in expression among those individuals who do exhibit them. An example of a primary behavior is eating, and an example of an acquired behavior is stamp collecting. Other distinctions between the two classes of behavior will become apparent in our discussion.

G. A. Miller (1962) asks an interesting question: "How lazy can a man get?" He goes on to say:

The absolute limits, of course, are imposed by his body: At the very least he must obtain and consume food and drink; he will occasionally have to move out of harm's way; he must deposit his wastes at some distance from his place of repose; he will have to cover himself when it gets too hot; and while this is not vital in quite the same sense, he will one day surely advertise to attract the attentions of a mate. Yet in a friendly, nurturant environment these minimal demands of biology will fill only a fraction of his waking hours. From all we might learn in a textbook of physiology, a man could dare to be very lazy indeed" (p. 248).

Miller's fanciful question suggests that we can usefully distinguish between those kinds of minimal activities that will ensure continued survival and those more elaborate behaviors that make life interesting. Eating, drinking, breathing, eliminating, sleeping, and copulating are examples of species-specific behaviors that characterize humans in all societies. We have referred to these as *primary* or *unconditioned behaviors* and have designated their environmental supports as *primary* or *unconditioned reinforcers*. In some cases, the reinforcers are environmental commodities, such as food and water; in other cases, the reinforcers are activities that restore the organism to a state of balance or *homeostasis*. The eliminative functions of urinating and defecating, for example, prevent the accumulation in the body of substances that would eventually have a toxic effect. A constant body temperature of 98.6 degrees is maintained by self-regulatory neural mechanisms that control, among other things, sweating, activity level, and the tonus of the peripheral blood vessels. Sleeping occurs as a natural response to fatigue or boredom. All of these vital activities occur periodically and spontaneously if they are not interfered with by disease, trauma, or volition. Some of them are not under voluntary control; an individual may refuse to take food or drink, but he cannot stop breathing, eliminating, or sleeping. As we shall show in this chapter, all of these primary or unconditioned behaviors eventually come under social control; that is, they are expressed, or shaped, in accordance with the social reinforcement contingencies that characterize a given place and time.

Because those social stimuli that we can identify as reinforcers do not themselves have the capacity to restore homeostatic imbalances, they are assumed to have acquired their reinforcing potential through prior association with primary reinforcers. Therefore, they are referred to as *secondary* or *conditioned reinforcers*, terms that were introduced in the last chapter. As Bolles (1967) points out, conditioned reinforcement is a useful concept only if we can identify the stimuli, responses, and reinforcements that are involved in the behavior being explained. It is often difficult to meet these criteria in the case of social behavior, but we shall find the attempt challenging and instructive.

Let us begin with a functional analysis of those primary behaviors that are designed either to support life or to perpetuate the species. Our purpose will be to determine how they are shaped and maintained by their social consequences. Stated in somewhat more technical language, our problem is understanding how certain behavior repertoires common to all members of a particular society are shaped through the patterns of social reinforcement characteristic of that society. We shall employ the symbolic representations introduced in the previous chapter as useful devices for understanding the reciprocal reinforcement of behavior that occurs whenever two individuals interact.

Food ingestion. Consider first the manifestations of the need for food, one of the earliest forms of behavior to come under social control. The physiological factors that take part in evoking eating behavior in the presence of food need not concern us. It is sufficient for our purposes to know, as Bindra (1959) has pointed out, that stimuli communicated to the nervous system from the stomach, as well as from other organs affected by blood changes following food deprivation, exert some control over eating behavior. The times and places of eating, the kinds of foods eaten, and the manner in which one eats all come under social control early in life.

The earliest eating responses of infants are largely instigated by internal stimuli arising after a period of food deprivation. When food is supplied by a parent, the parent becomes a discriminative stimulus (S^D) for anticipatory feeding responses by the child. If food is not presented, the child is likely to respond with crying, a species-specific expression of distress. If the parent produces food, the crying behavior is reinforced and may be expected to occur more frequently following periods of food deprivation. This situation can be diagrammed as follows:

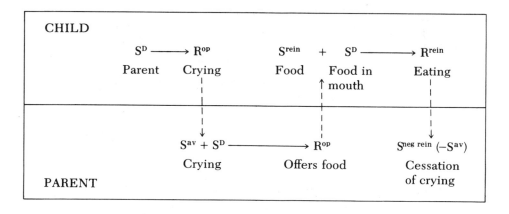

Eventually, the process of feeding the infant whenever it cries becomes aversive to the parent because it interrupts other activities in which he or she may be engaged. As a result, the parent initiates a schedule of feeding the child only at regular mealtimes. If this routine is adhered to, crying at other times will go unreinforced and will be extinguished. The occasional reinforcement of crying, however, will maintain this behavior at a fairly high level of frequency and will make extinction a long, difficult process. Assuming that the parent does adhere rigorously to the new schedule, the child will learn to cry only when it is not fed at the scheduled time, since this is the only time it will be reinforced. The parent avoids additional effort, annoyance, and the interruption of other activities and so is reinforced for not feeding the child between meals. In this way, the repertoires of both parent and child are modified to conform to the prevailing cultural patterns, and the child has effectively been shifted from a variable ratio to a fixed interval schedule of feeding. Most children will also be differentially reinforced for chewing with their mouths closed instead of open, using eating utensils instead of their fingers, eating certain types of foods in preference to others, and exhibiting acceptable deportment at the dinner table. When the child does not emit these socially sanctioned behaviors, the consequences are frequently aversive, in the form of criticism or ridicule. Punishment may simply suppress an undesirable behavior in the presence of the parents, without necessarily altering its probability of occurrence in other situations. Reinforcement of the desired behavior, as Skinner (1948) has suggested, is a more effective method of control.

The various instrumental acts that become part of the child's feeding repertoire constitute one small part of what is termed the "socialization" process. Factors indigenous to the culture determine the particular kind of shaping that takes place. Food preferences, for example, are more appropriately explained by reference to learning principles than by reference to notions of innate preferences or aversions. Most Americans find the idea of eating raw fish repugnant because they have not been given opportunities to acquire a taste for fish prepared in this manner. Many visitors to Japan, however, learn to relish raw fish, or *sashimi*, due in part to the social reinforcement they receive for sampling it. In some countries, smacking one's lips audibly while eating is an indication that one enjoys the food. This behavior is reinforced by others, who interpret it as a sign of appreciation. If a middle- or upper-class American eats noisily, however, he is quite likely to experience aversive reactions from others. Eating for most persons is an occasion for social interaction, and the social consequences of the instrumental acts used to achieve food ingestion are what shape the eating behavior.

Sex behavior. Sexual expression probably undergoes the most complex shaping of any of the primary behaviors. To be sure, not all human societies have developed the elaborate set of rituals and taboos with respect to sex that characterizes Western society, where the social control of sex behavior begins in early childhood and persists throughout the individual's life. The operant strength of sexual behavior seems to be quite high, which probably explains why its control has been the subject of so much attention. As Kinsey, Pomeroy, and Martin (1948) have shown, specific sexual practices vary according to such variables as age, marital status, religious background, and social level. Each of these factors identifies circumstances in which certain sexual practices are reinforced and others are punished. Most persons are not exposed to a consistent series of learning experiences in this important area of human conduct. Because the reinforcement contingencies associated with sexual behavior frequently are unpredictable, such behavior has become a source of considerable personal conflict for many individuals, who may be punished on one occasion and rewarded on another for the same act. Another way of looking at this situation is to say that approach and withdrawal tendencies with respect to sex may occur with almost equal frequency in many persons.

As has been known for some time, the sexual impulse does not appear full-blown at puberty but is manifest during early childhood. Very young children have been observed to gain satisfaction through masturbation (Kinsey *et al.*, 1948), and sex play between children is commonly engaged in until it comes under parental injunction. There seems to be little doubt that manipulation of the genitalia and other erotic behavior is innately reinforcing. Since masturbatory behavior is common not only among humans in all cultures but also among many animal species (Ford and Beach, 1951), it can provide us with a paradigm for the early acquisition of sexually oriented behavior:

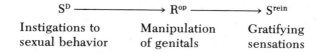

$$S^D \longrightarrow R^{op} \longrightarrow S^{rein}$$

| Instigations to sexual behavior | Manipulation of genitals | Gratifying sensations |

We have chosen this example not only because it represents a prototype for the later, more elaborate shaping of sexual behavior but also because it demonstrates further the endogenous character of manipulatory and exploratory behavior as discussed in Chapter 1. It is reasonable to assume that the child's initial manipulation of his genitals is no different from his exploratory handling of other parts of his body, such as his toes and his ears. The genitalia, however, are provided with sensory end-organs that lead ultimately to centers in the brain that are responsible for "voluptuous" feelings. Certain sensory inputs such as these must be viewed as positively reinforcing, whether they originate in peripheral stimulation or from direct electrical stimulation of midbrain centers (Olds and Milner, 1954). If no other factors entered the situation, the behavior would probably continue as a source of gratification. In fact, in many human societies children are not punished for engaging in masturbation or other forms of sex play (Ford and Beach, 1951).

In Western countries, however, most parents tend to take a less permissive view of erotic behavior in children. We cannot go into the reasons for this negative attitude, except to say that it is based, in part, on a host of misconceptions concerning such allegedly harmful effects as nervousness, insanity, and weakening of the spinal cord. Needless to say, these allegations have been shown to be false. Nevertheless, a case of reciprocal learning generally occurs in which the child is induced through punishment to cease practices that are abhorrent to the parent. The parents, by punishing the behavior, prevent its recurrence (in their presence, at least) and thus terminate an aversive situation.

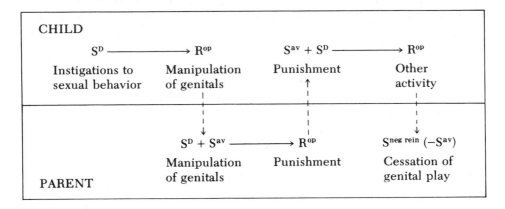

This model, of course, oversimplifies what is obviously a rather complex social situation. Left unexplained is the question of why the child's sexual behavior is aversive to the parents in the first place. However, we may assume that the parents underwent similar learning experiences when they were young, and as a result any display of sexuality by their own children acts as a conditioned aversive stimulus. The entire situation is tailor-made for generating conflict. When the child initially emits some form of sexually oriented behavior, the resultant sensations are positively reinforcing; we know this because without interference the behavior tends to be repeated. After one or more punishing experiences at the hands of an adult, however, the discriminative stimuli associated with genital play become associated with reactions of shame and guilt as well as with pleasure. As the individual alternately either engages in sex play or suppresses this response tendency, he experiences the reinforcing consequences associated with each course of action. This conflict situation may be diagrammed as follows:

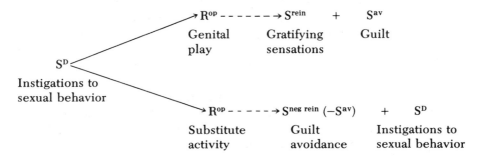

As indicated in the diagram, the individual's behavior is controlled by stimuli that have been associated both with incompatible responses and with different consequences. If he indulges himself, he achieves pleasure at the cost of experiencing guilt, while if he suppresses the tendency to engage in genital play, he avoids guilt but is denied pleasure. In the latter instance, however, he continues to be controlled by the provocative stimuli to which satiation has not yet rendered him insensitive or inattentive. The individual frequently alternates between these two behavior patterns depending upon situational features of the moment. By a straightforward process of stimulus generalization, some persons who were punished for sex play as children later display avoidance tendencies for many sexual activities as adults. The occasions for sexual behavior that they encounter in their later years are similar to those that preceded punishment when they were children, and the conditioned emotional reactions may persist for some time.

We have discussed the shaping through social reinforcement of two important classes of primary behavior. Without going into as much detail, we may now consider the manner in which several other primary behaviors are brought under social control.

Fluid ingestion. Drinking behavior is not subjected to as elaborate a program of social control as is eating. In general, the folkways do not constrain individuals to the ingestion of liquids at specified times or in specified places. Like eating, however, drinking may be quite unrelated to antecedent states of deprivation or satiation. The consumption of various liquids, particularly those with alcoholic content, has become a ritualistic aspect of many cultures and is only occasionally related to any physiological deficit. How many times during the day does the average person drink because he is thirsty? Exercise and elevated body temperature are occasions for drinking, but ordinarily the routine consumption of beverages both at meals and between meals prevents acute thirst sensations from ever arising. Coffee breaks, coke breaks, beer stops, and cocktail hours are all reinforced more by their social consequences than by relief of a fluid deficit. The ingestion of these several commodities is maintained through conditioned reinforcement and sets the occasion for social interactions. Following our instrumental learning paradigm, the events typical to one situation might be represented as shown on page 68.

In this example, the serving of cocktails creates an occasion on which conversation can be initiated without being preceded by formal introduction of the participants. Social interaction is seen to emerge from two independent chains of behavior. In addition, the alcoholic content of the cocktails serves to depress those cortical centers that control the inhibition of verbal and other behaviors in a new or unfamiliar social situation. This has the effect of facilitating social interaction, at least to a point.

Probably the only type of drinking behavior that sometimes leads to

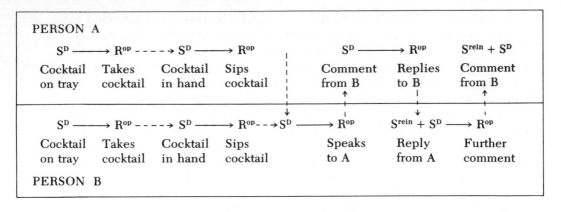

aversive social consequences is that involving alcohol. In part, this is because the behavior exhibited by inebriated individuals is frequently aversive to others. (The offensiveness of some individuals following excessive drinking, however, is not the only basis for the social control of alcohol consumption. Taxation as a means of control reinforces the governmental agencies that benefit from the revenue.) Drinking may also be considered aversive when it is inconsistent with other behaviors deemed more desirable, such as appearing at work on time. In 1918, when social disapproval of the consumption of hard liquor was widespread, the 18th Amendment, prohibiting the manufacture and sale of alcoholic beverages, was adopted. In 1933, this action was reversed as a result of change in public attitudes toward drinking. History frequently reveals the transient nature of many of our social taboos. There is, of course, no clear evidence of the extent to which the Prohibition Act actually changed the drinking habits of the nation, but available data indicate that not only did widespread drinking continue but vast bootlegging empires flourished as a direct result of the Act. In fact, an increased public disregard for laws in general has been partially attributed to behavior generalized from the Prohibition era. Today, social drinking is reinforced on a variety of occasions and is punished only when it leads to public intoxication or other offenses. The reinforcing consequences of solitary and social drinking are probably quite different, and inadequate understanding of these has so far been a stumbling block in devising a "cure" for chronic alcoholism.

Elimination. A primary behavior that presents a very interesting picture of social shaping of behavior is elimination. By this term, we mean specifically the body functions of urination and defecation. These responses, which are stimulated by pressures in the bladder and bowel, are subjected early in life to a program of shaping by one's parents. Freud contended that nearly everyone in Western society has repressed (driven from consciousness) memory of those early occasions on which eliminative responses were punished. It is significant in this respect that attitudes toward elimination in Western culture frequently are wedded to attitudes toward sex; both are often referred to as "dirty" or "nasty." What types of learning situations have brought about this state of affairs?

Left to their own devices, children would probably relieve themselves rather indiscriminately. After the first two years, however, they are introduced to a training regime designed by their parents to confine their excretory behavior to the facilities provided for this purpose. Relieving oneself publicly, or even announcing publicly the need to urinate or defecate, is discouraged. Both praise for the desired behavior and reproof for undesirable behavior are used by adults to produce the desired results in their children.

The initial unrestrained and exhibitionistic behavior of the child with respect to urination and defecation, therefore, is gradually replaced with socially appropriate behavior. Elimination continues to be reinforcing, since it involves pleasurable sensations as well as reduction of unpleasant tensions in the bladder and bowel. But the individual learns that these matters are not suitable for public discussion, nor are the actual performances to be engaged in openly or conspicuously. Again, we must recognize that the social taboos with which we have surrounded these functions are not universal in all cultures. In some European and Asiatic countries, men and women share common toilet facilities, and it is not an uncommon sight to see men and women relieve themselves outdoors in the sight of passersby. It would be inappropriate to label this behavior "shameful" or "exhibitionistic," since in these cultures the eliminative functions simply do not have the aversive connotations that they have elsewhere. Certain practical considerations also enter the picture, in that not all societies are able to afford the luxury of modern plumbing facilities provided separately for males and females.

The association of "dirtiness' and "nastiness" with both sex and elimination is probably not coincidental. We cannot with certainty identify the genesis of this symbolic connection, but we may conjecture that the anatomical proximity of the external genitalia and the orifices of elimination is partially responsible. More probably, these negative attitudes are simply learned from one's parents and peers. In any case, it is interesting to note that cultures which view elimination as a natural function having no particular aversive qualities frequently take a more tolerant or permissive attitude toward sex as well.

Temperature maintenance. A constant body temperature of 98.6 degrees Fahrenheit is maintained in part by brain mechanisms that respond to changes in the external temperature by inducing appropriate muscular and vascular responses. Excessive heat causes more blood to be circulated near the surface of the body, where it can be cooled by evaporation of moisture from the skin. A drop in temperature, on the other hand, induces shivering and peripheral vasoconstriction. These responses serve to create body heat and to reroute blood to the interior of the body, where it does not cool so rapidly. Humans manage to interfere in various ways with these adjustive processes, principally through wearing clothing that is inappropriate to the temperature, and thereby experience more discomfort than is necessary in conditions of extreme heat or cold. In the winter, for example, women tend to dress in a manner designed more to enhance their appearance than to help retain body heat. Fortunately, their summer apparel is generally more appropriate to the climate. Men's fashions, on the other hand, permit them to dress more warmly in winter, but in the summer many social occasions demand accessories such as jackets and ties that serve to confound the body's cooling mechanisms. Until fairly recently, most men would not carry an unbrella in the rain lest they be considered "soft." In certain age groups and localities boys dare not wear hats in cold weather for the same reason. On those social occasions when the requirements of either fashion or tradition determine that an individual dress in a manner not appropriate to the weather, we see clearly the results of a learning process in which social reinforcements have triumphed over the body's homeostatic mechanisms.

Culture and Personality

The socialization process that we have described in relation to certain primary, or biologically prepotent, behaviors extends, of course, to a much wider range of performances having little or nothing to do with biological requirements. We refer here to what are commonly termed the *customs* of a society. But it must be remembered that social customs are manifested in the behavior of the members of a society; they are not entities that exist in the abstract. In fact, Whiting (1954) suggests that a custom is simply a special case of a habit, adding: "Thus, the psychological principles which apply to habits should, by this definition, apply to customs. To be more explicit, a custom may be thought to refer to the behavior of a typical individual in a given society" (p. 526).

It follows from these considerations that customs develop as the collective representation of similar behaviors exhibited by a substantial number of the individuals in a society. It is customary, for example, for an American man to wear a shirt and trousers as part of his basic apparel, and there are virtually no exceptions to this practice. It is less common for American men to wear beards, although some do. In any society certain customs are virtually universal, whereas others characterize the behavior of limited segments of the population.

Modal Personality

It has been suggested that the shared behaviors of the members of a society can be referred to as "national character." More specifically, Linton (1945) has conceived of national character as a *modal personality structure,* or configuration that appears with considerable frequency in a society. He has also referred to a *basic personality type* as "that personality configuration which is shared by the bulk of the society's members as a result of the early experiences which they have in common" (1945, p. viii). These two notions are very similar, and we will use them interchangeably. Linton recognized the fact that individuals display different personality configurations and that several modal types may exist together in a society. Identification of such modal behavior configurations makes it possible to arrive at certain generalizations about any given society and to describe more succinctly the differences between one society and another. At the same time, we must recognize that such generalizations are likely to conceal the vast individual differences that are found among the members of any group. With caution, however, it is possible to view both the forest and the trees in this respect.

There is a wealth of evidence indicating that behavioral tendencies common to many members of a society develop because of certain child-rearing practices prevalent in that society. Paraphrasing Linton, we may hypothesize that: (a) the members of any given society will have many elements of early experience in common; (b) as a result of this, they will learn similar behaviors; (c) because the early experience of individuals differs from one society to another, many of the behavior patterns common to the individuals in one society will differ from those found in other societies.

Child-Rearing Practices

The fact that most adults are reinforced by social acceptance and approval may have its genesis in the tendency of infants to thrive in circumstances where they are the recipients of love and affection. The absence of affectional stimuli from adults may even cause infants to suffer mental and physical retardation (Ribble, 1944; Spitz, 1945). An excess of indulgence and overprotection, particularly by the mother, may produce highly dependent children (Levy, 1943; Heathers, 1953). Among the Dakota and Hopi Indians, for example, generosity is one of the cardinal virtues, and this trait is inculcated in children as young as five and six. Other groups, such as the Iroquois, are reported to have encouraged aggressive behavior in children because it was necessary for the development of adult warriors (Klineberg, 1954).

The anthropological literature is replete with descriptions of child-rearing practices that are readily seen as the precursors of behavior patterns that prevail among adults in the society. DuBois (1944) has studied in depth the behavior of the people of Alor, a small island in the Netherlands East Indies. The culture of this area is generally Indonesian, but the subjects of this research were oceanic negroid in type, living a rather isolated existence in the mountains. We will take note of merely one small

part of the findings regarding these people, namely, the mother's treatment of her children. This has been summarized by Kardiner (1945) as
follows:

> Temper tantrums are prominent in the child's behavior. The commonest
> cause is the mother's daily desertion. At first the child may try to follow his
> mother; then, as she outstrips him, he may roll over on the ground and beat
> his head on the earth. The mother is not consistent; once she comforts, an-
> other time ignores, and still another time she may beat him. Promises of
> reward for good behavior are rarely made, and never kept. Older siblings
> who care for the child are not more dependable. The child may be placated
> and fed, or struck and deserted for the same provocation. Tantrums are
> commonest before five, but occasionally occur up to seven (p. 134).

Obviously, the child cannot, in these circumstances, emit any behavior
that is consistently reinforced or consistently punished. What type of an
adult develops from this type of learning situation? Kardiner comments
as follows:

> The basic personality in Alor is anxious, suspicious, mistrustful, lacking in
> confidence, with no interest in the outer world. There is no capacity to ideal-
> ize parental image or deity. The personality is devoid of enterprise, is filled
> with repressed hatred and free floating aggression over which constant vigi-
> lance must be exercised. The personality is devoid of high aspirations and
> has no basis for the internalization of discipline. Individuals so constituted
> must spend most of their energy protecting themselves against each others'
> hostility. Cooperation must be at a low level and a tenuous social cohesion
> can be achieved only by dominance–submission attitudes, not by affection
> and mutual trust (p. 170).

In contrast to the type of socializing experiences just described, consider
the early treatment of children in a small American farming community,
located "somewhere in the Midwest." A detailed description of life in
Plainville, U.S.A. has been provided by West (1945), from which we may
summarize a few child-rearing practices for comparison with those of Alor.
A great variety of techniques are used by the parents of Plainville to induce
and maintain desired forms of behavior in their children. According to
West, techniques for securing obedience include whipping, spanking,
shaming, teasing, scolding, nagging, threats, privations, rewards, en-
couragements, demonstrativeness, and affection. He notes that teasing,
kidding, and shaming, alone or in combination, are the most effective
means of controlling a child's behavior. Disobedience is most commonly
punished by keeping the child indoors, where he cannot play with other
children, or by depriving him of something desirable, such as a favorite
food or a trip to town. Other social groups outside the family, such as the
school, church, peers, and other adults, also play an important role in the
socialization process. The physical needs of the child are carefully attended to, and he experiences no serious or prolonged deprivations or

periods of rejection. He is the recipient of a great deal of affection, especially from the mother.

What kinds of behavior generally emerge from this constellation of early
social influences? According to Kardiner, the child learns to depend upon
a resourceful and powerful parent.

> As a result the child's acquaintance with his environment is facilitated, the
> traumatic influence of that environment is diminished, and a foundation is
> laid for the development or stimulation of curiosity, investigative manipula-
> tion of objects in the outer world, and some confidence in handling them. A
> foundation is also laid for the idealization of the parent, especially the mother
> and the functions associated with her, an idealization which in our culture
> sometimes becomes maudlin (p. 347).

Finally, and perhaps most important, is the fact that discipline in Plainville is consistent. The child comes to know what is expected of him;
approval and disapproval, reward and punishment, are clearly defined.
Because of the specific situations in which these alternative consequences
are experienced, certain attitudes and behaviors come to characterize the
adults of Plainville. There is a general conviction that pleasure in itself
is not a legitimate goal, that free sexual expression (particularly in females)
is undesirable, and that "progress" is to be viewed cautiously. The overall
picture is one of a conservative, Midwestern community in which security
and comfort, having served as reinforcers throughout childhood, control
a large measure of adult behavior.

A wide variety of techniques have been used by anthropologists and
others in attempting to determine what modal behaviors characterize
individuals in various societies. These, as summarized by Inkeles and
Levinson (1954), include the use of projective techniques, personality
inventories, clinical interviews, case histories, and analysis of such cultural products as folklore and drama. Perhaps the most valuable approach
to an understanding of patterns of adult behavior is through study of child-
rearing practices, such as those that we have briefly described. For, without doubt, those behavior repertoires designated as habits, attitudes, beliefs, values, and other dimensions of adult behavior have their origins in
early learning. These behaviors and behavioral dispositions are developed
and maintained through their consequences to the individual, and they
may be understood in terms of the stimuli that come to control them and
the reinforcements that are provided by both the physical environment
and the social community.

The reinforcers supporting the child's behavior shift gradually from the
home to the outside environment. A brief description of this process is
provided by Ferster (1963):

> This shift occurs first as the child plays with other children. Then it occurs
> as the various institutions of society, the church, governmental agencies, boy
> scouts, local clubs, or gangs, acquire control. Hobbies develop, such as col-

lecting stamps, building models, hiking, hunting, fishing, swimming, and various other sports and activities. Direct reinforcers of a less social nature emerge, mediated less by other individuals than, for example, by books, movies, or television (p. 320).

Perhaps the best way to examine the manner in which these various social and socially derived controls of behavior develop is to review some of the experimental work that has been done. It is well to remember that in the natural social environment the socializing process must always be carried out through some individual who selectively reinforces one performance rather than another, selectively punishes various types of behavior, and extinguishes, by nonreinforcement, segments of the child's repertoire.

Experimental Control of Early Behavior

Positive Control

The nature of reinforcement. What kinds of events constitute reinforcers and punishers for both children and adults? Given man's inherent sensory equipment, motor capabilities, and complex nervous system, it follows that certain classes of stimuli will be reinforcing and others aversive to the average individual. You will recall that we have defined positive and aversive consequences according to whether they strengthen or weaken the behavior that preceded them. Because behavior that is instrumental in securing food for a deprived individual tends to occur more frequently and dependably, food is classified as a positive reinforcer. When behavior that is instrumental in avoiding or escaping from certain stimuli tends to become more probable on subsequent occasions, such stimuli are classified as aversive. Not all reinforcers derive their reinforcing characteristics from a prior state of deprivation; some seem to be innately rewarding. And, as we have seen, behavior can also be reinforced by stimuli that have been paired with such primary reinforcers as food, water, shelter, and sex objects.

To what consequences or reinforcing events shall we attribute the gradual increase in a child's mastery over his environment: his acquisition of motor skill, his success in school, his development of athletic ability? There is evidence that changes in sensory stimulation may be sufficiently reinforcing to maintain the behavior that produces them. If such behavior is essentially manipulative or exploratory, it will generalize to other situations and provide for the acquisition of other, more complex behaviors that are reinforced primarily by sensory feedback from the environment. An illustration of the process by which such early learning might occur has been provided by Rheingold, Stanley, and Cooley (1962). These investigators devised an instrument-equipped crib in which infants as young as four months could control the frequency of presentation of a visual display by manipulating a stainless steel sphere, four inches in diameter, located within easy reach. This interesting apparatus is pictured in Figure 3.1.

Those infants who could, by handling the sphere, produce a motion picture of brightly colored geometric figures on a screen in front of them moved the sphere more frequently than infants whose manipulation of the sphere produced no projected images. These findings were confirmed and extended with twenty-five children from two to five years of age in a later

Figure 3.1

Experimental crib: a, seat; b, manipulandum (sphere); c, screen; d, projection opening; e, sound source; f, projector; g, control room; h, ventilator; i, rocker; j, intercom; k, crib lights; l, microphone; m, television camera; n, doors of crib; o, window. (After Rheingold, Stanley, and Cooley, 1962; copyright © 1962 by the American Association for the Advancement of Science)

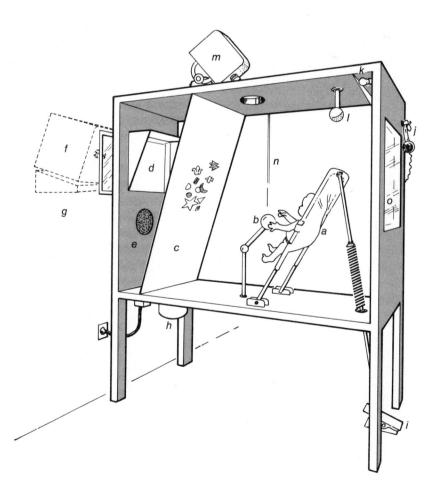

experiment in which auditory stimuli were also used as reinforcers (Rheingold, Stanley, and Doyle, 1964). Commenting on these reports, Bijou and Baer (1967) state: "Apparently, a changing pattern of light and sound can be enough of a stimulus consequence of a young infant's response to affect the future strength of that response. . . . A wealth of other reinforcing stimuli in the infant's environment may teach him a corresponding wealth of skills" (p. 16). The significance of these experiments is clear, namely, that the *consequences* of a performance increase or decrease the probability that the performance will be repeated. By observing the kinds of consequences, or reinforcement contingencies, that come to control the behavior of naive organisms, we gain information about the general classes of stimuli that can be expected to act as reinforcers or as deterrents.

A great deal of the infant's behavior in any society is followed by social stimulation, so that social reinforcement serves to increase or decrease the frequency with which many performances will be repeated. A laboratory demonstration of the social control of vocalizations in infants has been reported by Rheingold, Gewirtz, and Ross (1959). Two parallel experiments were performed, each divided into three phases. During the first phase, a female experimenter leaned over the infant's crib and looked at him with an expressionless face for three minutes. An observer tallied any vocalizations made by the infant during this time. Nine three-minute periods were scheduled in a single day, and the results were used to establish a *baseline* of normal vocalization for each of twenty-one infants, all of whom were residents of an institution. During the second, or *conditioning*, phase of the experiment, the experimenter behaved as before, except that now she responded to vocalizations from the infant by (a) smiling broadly, (b) saying "Tsk, tsk, tsk," and (c) tickling the infant's abdomen. Finally, during an *extinction* phase, the experimenter behaved as she had at first, registering no change in expression when the infant vocalized.

The unit of analysis was the number of vocalizations produced by the infant within each of the three-minute periods, averaging over the nine periods for each reinforcement condition. The results in the two experiments were virtually identical, and the curves drawn in Figure 3.2 represent the overall findings.

The data indicate rather convincingly that an infant's vocal behavior in a social situation can be brought under experimental control. The reinforcing stimuli in this case took the form of facial, vocal, and touching behavior by an adult. Anyone familiar with the behavior of infants and young children is aware of the extent to which their behavior can be modified by the manner in which adults respond to them, and the experiment just described makes this process explicit in terms of the learning principles we have discussed.

Incidental learning. It is likely that those behaviors that are common to most individuals in a society result as much from examples set by parents

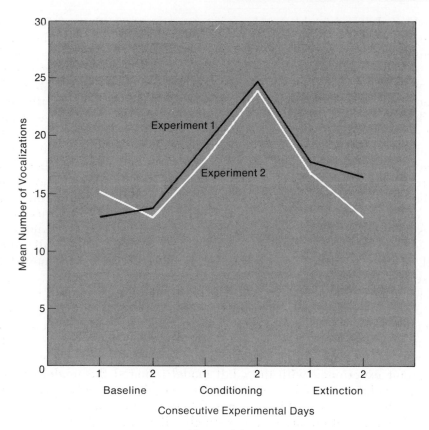

Figure 3.2

Mean number of infants' vocalizations during three experimental phases. (After Rheingold, Gewirtz, and Ross, 1959)

and adults as by actual reinforcement of specific behaviors and nonreinforcement of others. This may be a case of what McGeoch and Irion (1952) have called incidental learning. More often than we may suspect, the child learns something that was not intended by the parent. Thus, when the parent punishes a child physically for having aggressed toward another child, the intended outcome is that the child desist from such behavior. At the same time, however, the child is being provided with an example of the very behavior that the parent is trying to discourage, and this incidental learning, rather than the intended learning, may guide the child's later behavior.

An example of incidental learning is provided by Bandura and Huston (1961), who performed an experiment to demonstrate that nursery school children would, while learning a two-choice discrimination problem, also learn to imitate certain of the experimenter's behaviors that were quite irrelevant to the assigned task. However, this was expected to occur only after the adult had established herself as a source of positive reinforcement. One of the investigators, a young woman, brought each child to the experimental room fifteen minutes before the task was to start. With twenty of the subjects, she interacted in a warm, friendly fashion, sitting close to them on the floor and helping them play with toys. Toward the other twenty subjects, she was aloof and impersonal, busying herself with paperwork at a desk in a far corner of the room while the child played alone. Following this experience, each child was told by the experimenter that he and the young woman would play a game in which they were to guess which of two boxes held a prize, a small colored picture, to be placed there by the experimenter. The adult always made the first choice, and if the child made the same choice, he was rewarded by finding the prize. On each trial, the adult performed certain stereotyped behaviors as follows: She said "Here I go" marched slowly toward the box containing the picture repeating "March, march, march," knocked a small rubber doll off the lid of the box, exclaimed "Open the box," and removed the prize.

The experimenters were interested in discovering the extent to which the children would imitate the adult's behavior while solving the problem. Remember that half of them had previously enjoyed a period of enjoyable interaction with the adult, whereas the others had been ignored for the same period of time. Fifteen of the twenty children who had enjoyed the nurturant experience with the adult model imitated the model's nonaggressive behaviors, such as marching and vocalizing. Only seven of the twenty children who had been exposed to the nonnurturant condition displayed this type of imitation. Interestingly, all twenty of the first group and sixteen of the second group imitated the model's aggressive behavior of knocking the doll off the box. In contrast, none of the children in a control group, where no adult model was present, marched or verbalized while solving the problem. Thus, the predicted effect of prior social reinforcement on imitative behavior was confirmed, with the children emulating the friendly adult to a significant extent and failing to imitate the adult who was cold and distant.

These findings are consistent with the general theoretical statement that adults acquire conditioned reinforcing properties to the extent that they provide children with such positive reinforcers as attention and affection. On occasions when the behavior of an adult is positively reinforcing to a child, the child attempts to reproduce these reinforcing consequences by imitating the adult. In other words, since the adult has become a conditioned reinforcer to the child, almost any performance of the adult that can be imitated has reinforcing value. This is essentially what is meant by the *identification* of children with their parents or other adults. Identifying with someone else frequently involves imitating that person. The imitative behavior is maintained by virtue of its properties as a conditioned reinforcer.

There is considerable experimental evidence in support of this generalization. Mussen and Distler (1959), using doll play techniques, found that boys who perceived their fathers as sympathetic and rewarding behaved in a more masculine fashion than boys who perceived their fathers as punitive and threatening. These findings were later replicated by Mussen and Rutherford (1963), who found that girls reacted in a similar fashion to their mothers; that is, in comparison with girls who scored low on femininity in doll play tests, the more feminine girls described their mothers as significantly warmer, more affectionate, and more gratifying. The mothers of these girls, in turn, reported warmer relationships with their daughters and more interest in them than did the mothers of the less feminine, or less strongly sex-typed, girls.

A similar experiment was performed by Mussen and Parker (1965), but in this case five-year-old girls solved a maze problem under the tutelage of their mothers, who had previously been rated on the basis of interviews as being nurturant (warm, concerned) or nonnurturant (cool, unconcerned) toward their daughters. Each mother was instructed to engage in certain behaviors that were irrelevant to solving the problem, and the investigators were interested in the extent to which the daughters would imitate these irrelevant behaviors. They found no differences in the problem solving behavior of the daughters of the two types of mothers, but they did discover that the girls with nurturant mothers imitated the task-irrelevant behaviors to a much greater extent than did the girls with nonnurturant mothers.

Anticipation of reinforcement. Rotter (1954) suggests that the probability of occurrence of a particular behavior is a joint function of (a) the subjectively held probability, or expectancy, that the behavior will be reinforced, and (b) the value of the reinforcer to the individual. The value of a reinforcer, of course, can only be determined empirically, that is, by observing the kind and amount of instrumental behavior the individual will engage in to attain it. An "expectancy" is not so readily defined, although a number of theories have addressed themselves to this problem. For our purposes, we may say that it is represented by an individual saying to himself, perhaps not in so many words, "If I do thus and so, then such and such will result." However, this process need not necessarily be verbalized. Expectancies, or anticipations, or subjective probabilities, must, of course, derive from experience. Certain expectancies are formed with regard to the probable occurrence of events over which one may have no control, as in predicting the weather. Confirmation of an expectancy is rewarding; nonconfirmation is nonrewarding. Some incorrect probability estimates may even have aversive consequences, as in erroneously predicting the course of the stock market.

One aspect of expectancy of reinforcement involves interacting with someone from whom future rewards and punishments may or may not be anticipated. Children are more apt to be influenced by their parents and friends than by strangers from whom they expect little in the way of further interaction. A temporary agent of reinforcement is less likely to influence behavior than one with a more permanent status. An experimental demonstration of this generalization has been provided by Mischel and Grusec (1966) with nursery school children. Fourteen children were assigned to each of four treatment groups: (a) *High reward, high future control.* An adult female played enthusiastically with the child for twenty minutes and informed him that she would be his new teacher. (b) *High reward, low future control.* The adult played with the child as before, but told him that she was just a visiting teacher and would not see him again. (c) *Low reward, high future control.* The adult left the child to play by himself for twenty minutes, but established herself as his new teacher. (d) *Low reward, low future control.* The adult ignored the child while he played and also identified herself as only a temporary teacher.

Following these initial play periods, to establish the immediate as well as the long-term reinforcing value of the adult, the child played a game in which certain of his responses in operating a toy cash register were punished verbally by the adult. In all cases, the model engaged in certain neutral, incidental behaviors, such as walking around the table saying "March, march, march." Next, the child was allowed to play by himself, and the experimenters observed whether he enacted any of the model's performances, either neutral or aversive. The results are shown in Figure 3.3.

Inspection of Figure 3.3 reveals the following: Those children who had enjoyed a preliminary period of enjoyable play with the nurturant adult reproduced more of her behavior, both neutral and aversive, than did the children who had not been reinforced in this fashion. The rewarding adult, in other words, was imitated to a greater extent than the nonrewarding adult, even when she dispensed aversive stimuli. She was also imitated more often after she had told the child that she would be his new teacher. The low reward, low future control condition produced the least frequent incidents of imitative behavior. (A subsequent phase of the experiment in which the children were given an opportunity to *transmit* the model's behavior to someone else were somewhat inconclusive, and we will not consider them here.)

The most interesting feature of the findings just reported is that children not only will apparently reproduce without reinforcement certain incidental behaviors of an adult but also will rehearse punishing behavior — provided that the model has previously established herself both as an effective agent of reinforcement and as one who is going to exercise control in the future. If either of these contingencies is lacking, then the incidence of modeled behavior will probably be low. If one has reason to expect continued interaction with an effective agent of reinforcement, then some identification with that person may occur. Lack of expectation of future control makes identification unlikely. The results of this study help

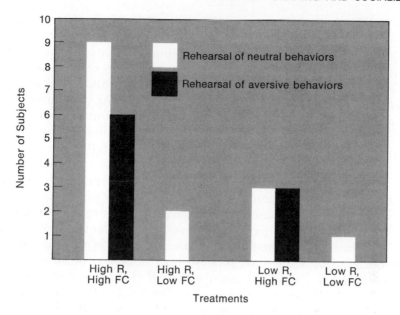

Figure 3.3

Number of subjects rehearsing neutral and aversive behaviors as a function of the model's reward value (R) and amount of "future control" (FC). (After Mischel and Grusec, 1966)

us to understand why children model their behavior even after someone who occasionally punishes them. They may even incorporate certain of the punishing performances into their own repertoire, thus establishing the basis for self-discipline.

The reinforcing agent. Analysis of the effective social reinforcers for children would have to include such variables as the age, sex, and relationship of the person who is the source of the reinforcing stimuli. It is obvious that the parents are in a position to provide the greatest number and variety of reinforcers, both social and nonsocial, at least during early childhood. Later, during puberty and adolescence, other individuals are the sources of behavior that is either rewarding or aversive to the individual. Chief among these extrafamilial agents of social reinforcement are the individual's peers. This not infrequently distresses parents, who find themselves no longer the principal agents controlling their children's behavior. Why this particular evolution occurs we are not able to say with certainty. Maturational factors are certainly involved, as are certain other inevitabilities of the growth process. After all, a teen-age girl has certain unique and undeniable capacities to reinforce behavior in a teen-age boy.

Sigmund Freud (1949) is generally credited with the theory that children tend to develop a strong affective attachment to the parent of the opposite sex. This Oedipal phenomenon, if true, would suggest that the opposite-sex parent either is biologically a more potent reinforcer to the child than the same-sex parent or provides more reinforcements for the child's behavior, hence, is preferred. We cannot know which of these alternatives is a better explanation of the observed effect, but there is evidence that women do provide more effective reinforcement for the performance of boys and that men have a greater effect on the performance of girls (Gewirtz, 1954; Gewirtz and Baer, 1958a). Taking Freudian theory as a point of departure, Stevenson (1961) has speculated that through her role in satisfying the child's basic needs the mother becomes a generalized reinforcer for a variety of behaviors. The child's response to the mother generalizes to other women. But as the girl grows older and enters the Oedipal period, a shift in preference from the mother to the father is manifested. During this same period, however, the boy not only continues to prefer the mother but may even show antagonism toward the father. Theoretically, as the Oedipal relationships decrease in strength during later childhood, girls should again establish close ties with the mother, and the boy should come to appreciate the father. Between the ages of seven and eleven, therefore, women should be more effective reinforcing agents for the behavior of girls than of boys, and men should now be able to reinforce the behavior of boys more effectively than that of girls.

Stevenson attempted to test these predictions using a "game" in which male and female children at three different age levels took colored marbles from one bin and dropped them into another through small holes in a covering plate. Their performance in this task was observed during (a) a nonreinforced period during which the base rate of response was established, and (b) a reinforced period in which various supportive remarks such as "You're doing very well" and "That's fine" were made at fixed intervals by either a male or a female experimenter. The base rate was subtracted from the number of marbles inserted during each of five successive minutes, and the mean of these five difference scores was used as an index of the effectiveness of the social reinforcement in modifying the child's rate of response. The results are shown in Figure 3.4.

The data presented in the chart may be summarized as follows: Verbal reinforcements delivered by a woman were significantly more effective than those from a man for both boys and girls at the 3–4 year level. Although it had been predicted that women would be more effective reinforcers of boys at the 6–7 year level and that men would be more effective in reinforcing girls, the data did not bear this out; the differences were in the predicted direction but were not statistically significant. Finally, the prediction that boys 9–10 years old would be more influenced by men and girls at this age more influenced by women was not supported. There was an overall tendency for men to become more effective agents of reinforcement with increasing age of the children and for women to have about the same level of effectiveness across age levels. Gewirtz and Baer (1958b)

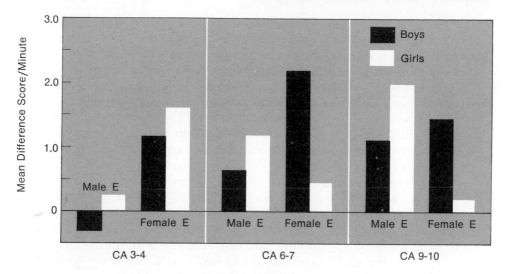

Figure 3.4

Average difference score obtained for each minute of the game according to age and sex of subjects and sex of experimenter. (After Stevenson, 1961)

had shown previously that the effectiveness of social reinforcement is increased by social deprivation. If a child is relatively deprived of contact with adults of the opposite sex, then individuals of that sex will become more effective dispensers of social approval than the parent of the same sex, with whom the child has been more frequently associated. Stevenson argues that due to social emphasis on the child's adopting the appropriate "sex role," boys are relatively more deprived of contact with females than with males, and girls are relatively more deprived of contact with males. Because of this deprivation, the effectiveness of women as reinforcing agents for boys in the 9–10 age group increases, as does the effectiveness of men as reinforcers for girls in the same age group.

Modeling. Demonstration of the effectiveness of adult models in shaping the behavior of children has been provided by Bandura and McDonald (1963). In a procedure borrowed from Piaget (1948), they presented 165 children aged five to eleven with pairs of stories, each of which described a well-intentioned act that resulted in considerable material damage. For example, in one story John unwittingly opens a door to a dining room and breaks fifteen cups that are on a chair behind the door. In the companion story, Henry breaks a cup while climbing on a chair to reach a cookie jar. The child is asked to judge "Who did the naughtier thing?" and to provide a reason for his choice. In some cases, an adult "model" participated in the procedure, giving his answer first and being reinforced by the experimenter's saying "That's good" or "That's fine." The child was then similarly reinforced if he or she made the same type of judgment as the model.

In other cases, the model was reinforced, but the child was not reinforced when his answer matched that of the model. In a third situation, the model was not present, and the child was reinforced whenever he gave a particular kind of response selected in advance by the experimenter.

The most effective behavior shaping occurred when both the model and the child were reinforced or when the model alone was reinforced. The least effective procedure was reinforcement of the child with the model absent. Perhaps the most important conclusion from this study is that operant conditioning procedures are not particularly effective in reshaping behavior when strong dominant response tendencies are present and the desired alternative responses are either weakly developed or absent. In other words, a response cannot be strengthened through reinforcement until it occurs, and it is unlikely to occur when competing responses are already in the individual's repertoire. However, when a model who emits the desired behavior is provided, and this behavior is reinforced, there is a tendency for the child to imitate the behavior *whether or not he is also reinforced.* This was shown by the fact that the children who were present with the reinforced model imitated his behavior to nearly as great an extent as those children who were reinforced alone for making the desired response. As suggested earlier by Bandura (1962), it may be that reinforcement functions primarily as a performance-related variable and response acquisition is based simply on perceived contiguity of events. Seeing someone do something and hearing him praised for it, in short, may effectively teach an observer how to achieve the same result. But the observer will not consistently behave in a similar manner until he can anticipate being reinforced himself.

There is evidence that while *positively reinforced* behaviors may be imitated, *punished* behaviors are learned but not imitated. In support of this contention, Bandura (1965) showed that imitation by children of aggressive behavior in adults was readily acquired through observation alone; however, performance by the child of similar aggressive behavior depended upon whether or not the adult model was observed to have been punished. Three different groups of children watched a film in which the model was rewarded or was punished or experienced no consequences for aggression. Children in all three conditions were later able to reproduce the aggressive behavior when promised a reward for so doing. But immediately after seeing the film, those children who had observed the model being punished emitted the smallest number of aggressive responses when given an opportunity to do so. The children who had witnessed the model being rewarded for aggression were somewhat more inclined to imitate this behavior than the children who saw aggression occur with no consequences. The hypothesis that children may learn by observing others but will not necessarily behave in a similar fashion themselves without being placed on a schedule of reinforcement seems to be tenable in view of the available evidence.

These several experimental findings all bear on the general phenomenon of observational learning or matching behavior as an essential part of the socialization process. The terms imitation and identification, as Bandura and Walters (1963) point out, "encompass the same behavioral phenomena, namely the tendency for a person to reproduce the actions, attitudes, or emotional responses exhibited by real-life or symbolized models" (p. 89). There is considerable evidence, then, that the principles of reinforcement can account for the acquisition and maintenance of a considerable portion of the child's behavior repertoire. Many components of this repertoire seem to be acquired by the child's observation of the behavior of adults who have been the sources of reinforcements for other behaviors. Adults who are associated either with nonreinforcement or with punishment are less likely to be effective models for the child's behavior.

How may the several kinds of observational learning just described be understood in terms of a functional analysis? What is reinforcing about imitating someone else's behavior? Must the occurrence of imitative behavior be ascribed to some innate proclivity on the part of children, or can it be referred to the operation of those learning variables with which we have become familiar? A partial answer to these questions is provided in an experiment reported by Baer and Sherman (1964). As a model for imitation they used an animated talking puppet dressed as a cowboy and capable of moving his head, talking (by means of a loudspeaker that carried the experimenter's voice), and pressing a bar located beside his chair. The subjects in the experiment were children in a day-care nursery, who were seated individually in front of the puppet.

The investigators were interested in determining whether the children would imitate bar-pressing responses made by the model but never reinforced. Other responses, also imitative of the model, were controlled by reinforcement operations. They reasoned that reinforcement serves to strengthen not only those acts that are directly reinforced but also the entire *class of responses* that may be termed imitative. In other words, when a child is reinforced for modeling some performance after that of an adult, he generalizes this modeling tendency to many other behaviors as well. Baer and Sherman arranged the situation so that during an initial period, lasting from ten to twenty minutes, the puppet would talk to the child and, at the same time, press his bar frequently. This was to establish the child's operant level of bar-pressing, that is, the rate at which the child would imitate the puppet's bar-pressing without being specifically reinforced for doing so. Then, during a second time period, the puppet stopped bar-pressing and began making other responses, prefacing each one with the question to the child, "Can you do this?" These responses included nodding, opening and closing his mouth, and uttering such statements as "One, two, three, four" or "Red robins run rapidly." If the child imitated any of these behaviors, the puppet said "Very good" or "Fine." Almost without exception, the children imitated virtually every response that was presented in this way, and after a few reinforcements the puppet no longer said "Can you do this?" before each act. When the children were consistently making the reinforced responses, the puppet resumed bar-pressing, at the same time emitting and reinforcing imitation of nodding, mouthing, and verbalizing. Although bar-pressing was never directly reinforced, any increase in the child's frequency of bar-pressing over the operant level would suggest that *similarity of responding* was being learned, rather than responding in specific ways that had been reinforced by vocal approval.

Of the eleven children studied, seven showed varying degrees of increase in bar-pressing during the period when nodding, mouthing, and verbal imitation were being reinforced. Two of the four who did not show an increase in frequency of bar-pressing during this time had already developed a high level of bar-pressing during the operant period. Extinction was accomplished with two children after a stable rate of imitative bar-pressing had been established by having the puppet stop giving reinforcements for the other behaviors. Then reinforcement was resumed for another brief period. The results with one of these children are shown in Figure 3.5.

The most important point to remember from this experiment is that nonreinforced behaviors may be acquired through cbservation of someone else, provided that other imitated behaviors have previously been reinforced. Apparently, what is learned is a generalized tendency to imitate. It is altogether possible that children develop complex repertoires of behavior through the operation of this principle.

Extinction procedures. In Figure 3.5, we saw a decrease in the rate at which a previously reinforced response was made when reinforcement was temporarily discontinued. This procedure, known as extinction, also plays an important role in the socialization process. It can result in the elimination of certain behaviors from the individual's repertoire, or it may

Figure 3.5

Acquisition and extinction (time out) of generalized imitative bar-pressing in a child.   (After Baer and Sherman, 1964)

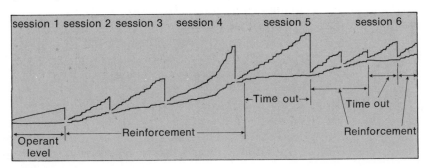

be used in conjunction with the reinforcement of other responses to effect some change in the individual's behavior. Certain beliefs acquired during childhood, for example, may be replaced by other, perhaps even contradictory beliefs in later life simply because the verbal statements embodying the old beliefs no longer receive social approval, whereas the vocal expression of new convictions is reinforced. The same may be said of attitudes, a subject to which we will devote a later chapter. As the individual moves from one group to another and his life experiences change, certain of his characteristic behaviors undergo alteration. We do not know the degree to which the behaviors and attitudes that develop as a result of the child's early socialization are stable over long periods of time. As Mussen (1967) has observed,

> When the child emerges into the broader community and has contacts with peers, teachers, books, television, and movies, he encounters new and attractive models and identifies with some of them. Moreover, these agents teach the child a great deal by rewarding and punishing various responses. To what extent do later identifications with extrafamilial models and learning outside the home reinforce and strengthen what the child has assimilated from the parents? To what extent do later identifications modify earlier developed ones? Under what conditions are early identifications and learning, and their products, so firmly established that they strongly resist changes? (p. 104).

Although we are not yet able on the basis of available evidence to answer these several questions posed by Mussen, we have seen how many behavioral dispositions can be strengthened by experimental manipulation of the reinforcement contingencies. Extinction as a method of eliminating certain behaviors has also been a subject of study. In one such experiment, Williams (1959) was able to treat tyrant-like tantrum behavior in a male child successfully by removing reinforcement. The subject, who was twenty-one months old, had been ill for many of his first eighteen months and, because of the special care and attention he had been given, had developed the habit of screaming and crying at bedtime unless a parent remained in the room with him until he fell asleep, which often required as long as two hours.

After it had been determined that the child was medically sound, a new procedure was instituted in line with the learning principle that behavior that is not reinforced will decrease in frequency. Until this time, the interaction between parent and child had been such as to reinforce both the child's crying and the parent's subservience. However, staying with the child until he slept also was aversive to the parent, hence measures designed to eliminate the necessity for this behavior were even more strongly reinforced over the long run.

After putting the child to bed, the parent left the room, closed the door, and did not return despite the ensuing outcry. The duration of the child's tantrum was recorded from the time the door was closed. By the tenth day, the child no longer whimpered or cried when the parent left the room. About a week later, however, crying occurred again, and an aunt returned to the room until the child went to sleep. This, of course, reinforced the undesirable behavior, and the extinction procedure had to be repeated. Figure 3.6 shows both extinction curves.

The data obtained by Williams (1959) are virtually self-explanatory and illustrate clearly the effectiveness of nonreinforcement in eliminating a class of behaviors that had been maintained inadvertently by the parents. This general technique has been used to control a number of undesirable behaviors among nursery school children, such as crying episodes, excessively isolated play behavior, excessive passivity, and regressed crawling. The shaping procedures, as reported by Harris, Wolf, and Baer (1964), involved giving attention to the children when they exhibited desired behavior and withholding attention when they behaved in an undesirable manner. Obviously, adult attention must have acquired generalized reinforcing properties for the child in order for it to be effective as a controlling device. Similar data have been reported by a number of investigators, and it seems well established that much of the behavior of young children is susceptible to management by the straightforward use of reinforcement principles.

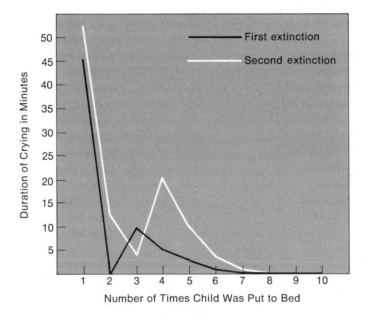

Figure 3.6
Length of crying in two extinction series as a function of number of times child was put to bed without further attention. (After Williams, 1959)

Aversive Control

There is considerable evidence that aversive social stimuli are more effective than positive social reinforcers in achieving prompt control over behavior. In fact, it is likely that a great deal of the socialization process with children involves the use of aversive control. Adults, in some situations, are equally susceptible to management by this means. Anyone who has served with the military forces can testify to the effectiveness of punishment in bringing about at least outward conformity to regulations.

A home in which punishment is used more often than reinforcement to govern the child's behavior can be described as a punitive home. Similarly, an entire culture might be characterized as punitive if aversive consequences play a primary role in shaping behavior. Such appears to be the case in Algeria, where the usual form of punishment for children is beating, administered by a dominating father (DeVos and Miner, 1958). In other cultural groups, such as the Hopi Indians, corporal punishment is rarely if ever used with children, and the father relies instead on precept, example, and admonition (Klineberg, 1953). It has generally been found that while punishment is frequently effective in suppressing certain behaviors, it may also serve as a stimulus to emotional reactions that are undesirable (Church, 1963). With this later consideration in mind, Patterson (1965) conducted an experiment in which children played a game of dropping marbles into a box. The child was permitted to select the marbles from a bin and drop them one at a time through either of two small holes. During the course of one hundred responses, the experimenter recorded the child's choices of holes so that the preferred hole could be identified. Following this operant baseline procedure, one of the child's parents was seated near the child and equipped with earphones so that he or she could hear instructions from the experimenter. The parent had been instructed to respond on signal by making one of several aversive utterances, i.e., "Not too good," or "No, that's not right," following certain responses by the child. The parent's aversive comments were programed by the experimenter so as to occur each time the child dropped a marble into the preferred hole. After the child had made ten responses to the preferred hole, he received twenty additional aversive stimuli on a 4:11 variable ratio schedule. Finally, the parent was instructed to make positively reinforcing comments on signal from the experimenter to counteract the long period of disapproval.

Patterson reports that the aversive stimuli supplied by the parent were highly effective in changing the child's choice behavior. The nonpreferred response began to occur more frequently after the child began experiencing the aversive consequences of dropping the marble into the preferred hole. Some additional findings from this experiment are of interest. For one thing, boys from punitive-restrictive homes were more responsive to the experimental manipulations than boys from supportive-permissive homes. They were also described by their parents as "immature." We might say that those boys whose learning experiences characteristically involved aversive control responded out of habit to negative remarks from a parent by changing from the preferred to the nonpreferred response. Just the opposite seemed to be true of the girls in the experiment; that is, those from nonpunitive homes were more responsive to disapproval. The investigator offers no immediate explanation of this apparent difference between the boys and girls. He does suggest, referring to earlier research, that children who are regarded as maladjusted have been socialized more by the use of aversive control than control through positive reinforcement. The children reveal this by being relatively more responsive to social disapproval in an experimental situation (Patterson, Littman, and Hinsey, 1964).

These experimental findings are consistent with much that we know about the effects of child-rearing practices on later behavior. Harsh treatment of the child as a means of shaping his behavior seems generally to have unfortunate side effects, including some impairment of his capacity for adjusting to other persons. We need to know a great deal more about this subject, however, before we can make definitive statements concerning the causal relationship between early learning experiences and adult behavior.

Another approach to the comparison of positive and aversive control of behavior has been through assessing the influence of various types of interaction between an experimenter and a subject on the experimenter's later effectiveness as an agent of reinforcement (Berkowitz, 1964). It has been suggested that a period of being deprived of social reinforcement is followed by an increased effectiveness of such reinforcement, in much the same way that food deprivation increases the reinforcing value of food (Gewirtz and Baer, 1958a, 1958b). It follows that someone who has effectively been satiated with social interaction will be less influenced in a subsequent task situation where social reinforcement is used to maintain performance. McCoy and Zigler (1965), however, have introduced evidence to show that a preliminary period of warm interaction between experimenter and child enhances, rather than reduces, the experimenter's effectiveness as a reinforcer. Satiation theory would predict otherwise. Can these two apparently opposing viewpoints be reconciled? One important methodological difference has been detected in such experiments regarding the time elapsed between the initial interaction and the later role of the experimenter as a reinforcer. Satiation might occur if the experimenter attempted to reinforce a child's performance immediately following a period of pleasant interaction. On the other hand, if a week or so is allowed to elapse before the reinforced performance is measured, any satiation effects will have dissipated, and the experimenter's effectiveness will be a function of whatever prior impression he left with the child. If his previous behavior was acceptable, then he will function as a positive reinforcer; if his behavior was neutral, or aversive, then his effectiveness as a reinforcer will have been diminished.

This hypothesis found support in data collected by Berkowitz and Zigler (1965), who played a "criterion" game with children either one week after or immediately after having interacted with them in another game situation in a positive (reinforcing) or negative (aversive) manner. A control group in which the members had experienced no earlier interaction with the experimenters was also observed. The measure of the experimenter's effectiveness as a social reinforcer was the amount of time the children were willing to continue playing the criterion game, which consisted of dropping marbles into holes. The results of this experiment are shown in Figure 3.7.

We can see in Figure 3.7 that those children who had enjoyed a generally pleasant interaction with the experimenter a week earlier chose to play the criterion game longer than the children who had been told a week earlier while playing a different game, "You're not doing very well," or "You aren't getting any right." Such aversive reactions from the experimenter depressed to a significant extent the children's interest in playing the criterion game a week later. The playing time for the control group was longer than for the group that experienced the negative interaction with the experimenter but shorter than the playing time for the reinforced children. As seen at the right of Figure 3.7, playing time when the criterion game was introduced immediately after the period of interaction was longest for those children who had experienced criticism for their previous performance. This apparently paradoxical finding is attributed by the investigators to a "contrast effect," in which positive reinforcers acquire a greater reinforcing value for the child immediately after negative social contact. Further research by Berkowitz, Butterfield, and Zigler (1965) yielded substantially the same result. Perhaps the child develops an "attitude" toward the adult

Figure 3.7

Mean time the "criterion game" was played by each group. (After Berkowitz and Zigler, 1965)

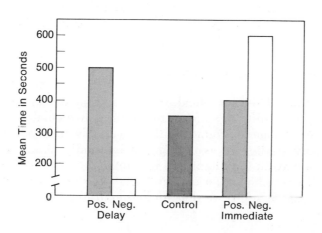

during the delay period, so that approval received later from that adult is perceived as less rewarding than it would have been immediately following a negative interaction. This is clearly an area in which we need more information.

Despite the obvious effectiveness of punishment in suppressing certain performances, it can also be maintained that many of the ills of human society are derived from aversive control (Ferster, 1968). This point of view has also been affirmed in some detail by Skinner (1948), who describes in his *Walden Two* a mythical society in which order and stability are maintained by positive reinforcement, without the use of aversive consequences for undesirable behavior. Although the control of behavior through positive reinforcement alone may represent an ideal state of affairs, is not punishment sometimes necessary to suppress behavior that might be harmful to the individual? Most parents, for example, would consider it more desirable to punish their child for running into the street than to permit this behavior to continue at the risk of the child's safety. Indeed, aversive control is widely used because it produces an immediate change in behavior. The change may benefit the subject of the aversive control only at some future time, a fact which explains his immediate reaction of resentment.

Application of aversive control in the case of mentally disturbed children who are self-destructive has been described by Lovaas and his co-workers (1964). Painful electric shocks contingent upon head and arm banging effectively suppressed these acts within minutes in the two children who were studied, and this effect lasted for eleven months. Self-destructive behaviors can also be eliminated by extinction, that is, by removal of the attention and sympathy ordinarily evoked from adults by the child's self-destructive acts (Lovaas *et al.*, 1965). Simultaneous reinforcement of competing behavior, such as singing or bar-pressing, was also found to be an effective means of behavior control. Placing the child on extinction, as the investigators point out, exposes him to continued danger from his own behavior because of the slowness of the extinction process. Suppression of the behavior through the use of aversive stimuli not only is more rapid but permits other, more desirable behaviors to be learned.

Internal and External Stimulus Control

Self-regulation. The theoretical orientation that we have adopted does not deny the possibility of self-controlled, or self-regulated, behavior. In fact, there are substantial grounds both in everyday observation and in data from laboratory studies for assuming that internally monitored reinforcement systems play an important role in human performance. Bandura and Perloff (1967) have shown, for example, that children will perform as well under conditions of self-reward as under conditions of external reinforcement. They argue that "Unlike rats or chimpanzees, persons typically set themselves certain standards of behavior, and generate self-rewarding or self-punishing consequences depending upon how their behavior compares to their self-prescribed demands" (p. 111).

Four groups of children, ranging in age from seven to ten years, participated in an experiment designed to test the validity of this proposition. All of the children engaged in the task of turning a small wheel that caused different scores to be registered on a display panel. Some of the children were allowed to set their own performance standards, in terms of how many turns of the wheel they would accomplish before rewarding themselves. For each eight turns of the wheel, they received 5 points. This constituted a fixed ratio schedule of 8:1, so that a total of thirty-two wheel turns would be required to achieve the maximum of 20 points shown on the display. Some of the children were allowed to reward themselves with one or more plastic tokens that were dispensed by the apparatus at the press of a button. These children made up the *self-monitored reinforcement* condition. The members of a second group were rewarded automatically by the experimenter and were yoked with those in the self-monitoring group with respect to the number of tokens received. That is, if a child in the self-reward condition treated himself to two tokens for a particular performance, his counterpart in the *external reinforcement* condition also received two tokens.

Two additional groups were set up in this experiment. In one of these, called the *incentive control* group, the children were given at the beginning of the experiment the same number of tokens that had been acquired by their "partners" in the self-reward condition. Finally, a *control* group performed the task with no tokens, so that an estimate could be made of the intrinsic capacity of the task to maintain behavior in the absence of reward. The results are shown in Figure 3.8, on page 94.

Several conclusions stand out in this experiment. First, the performances of those children who received either self-administered or externally administered reinforcements were superior to those of the children who either received their reward in advance or were not rewarded at all. Girls were about equally responsive to reinforcement, whether received from themselves or the experimenter. The boys, however, appeared to perform better under the condition of external reinforcement. The fact that the boys worked harder at turning the wheel when frequency of reinforcement was externally controlled suggests that males in American culture learn to depend more upon external controlling agencies than females. Perhaps one of the most interesting findings was that none of the children in the self-monitoring condition chose the lowest ratio schedule, and about half of them chose to turn the wheel the maximum of thirty-two times before claiming their reward. This finding, according to the authors, is at variance with reward-cost theories, which predict that the individual generally tries to achieve a maximum reward for a minimum effort.

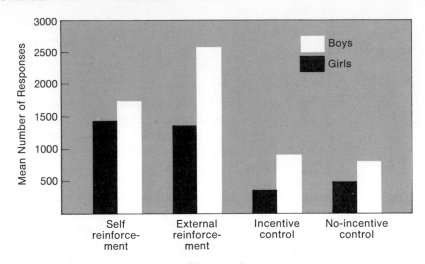

Figure 3.8

Mean number of responses emitted as a function of sex of subject and method of reinforcement. (After Bandura and Perloff, 1967)

Reinforcement history. Because of their greater use of symbolic processes, humans are undoubtedly less constrained in their behavior by the immediate features of a situation than are pigeons or chimpanzees. Once we remove the limitation of predicting behavior only from the external stimuli that are immediately present, we greatly increase the power of reinforcement theory to handle complex social situations. In order to take into account the mediating processes of a subject that determine the particular manner in which he will respond to a situation, therefore, we must learn something about his past learning experiences. One way to do this is simply to ask him some questions. For example, we can determine to some extent how a person might react to the members of a particular minority ethnic group by having him respond to the items on the California Ethnocentrism Scale. Or we might determine the extent to which he has undergone frustration or aversive control by obtaining his responses to the Test Anxiety Scale. From his performance on questionnaires such as these, we say either that he tends to be a "prejudiced" person or that he is "anxious" in certain situations. With this information in hand, we can then predict how he will perform on occasions where these particular dispositions are relevant. In discussing with others a motion picture film that depicts racial prejudice as a "communicable disease," the person who has scored high on the E Scale, for example, volunteers a number of comments that can be evaluated as clearly indicative of prejudice (Mitnick and Mc-Ginnies, 1958). In a task requiring the learning of difficult words, high school sophomores who score low in test anxiety are superior to those who are either moderately or highly anxious in situations of this sort (Sarason and Harmatz, 1965).

In short, a person carries his learning history around with him. The countless habits and dispositions that he has acquired, together with his innate capacities, talents, or disabilities, make up what we call his personality. Because both his genetic background and his particular experiences have been unique, his reactions to situations will seldom, if ever, be identical with anyone else's. This is true even with laboratory animals, such as rats and pigeons, although their behavioral variations are more attributable to genetic differences than to prior learning. In considering the effects of particular reinforcement contingencies on the performance of human subjects, therefore, it is necessary for us to recognize that they come to the experimental situation with highly developed and varied behavior repertoires. Cues, or discriminative stimuli, provided by the experimenter cannot be expected, therefore, to control precisely the same performance in each subject. This is because similar stimuli have in the past been the occasions for different patterns of reinforcement for each individual. Psychologists frequently try to devise situations that will be relatively unfamiliar to their subjects for just this reason. However, it is unlikely that human subjects in psychological experiments are ever as naive as laboratory animals, whose prior experiences can be fairly rigidly controlled.

As just one example of the manner in which individual differences determine the effectiveness of reinforcement, we may take an experiment reported by Rotter and Mulry (1965). These investigators first measured, by means of a questionnaire, the extent to which sixty-one female and fifty-nine male college students believed that their fates were controlled more by chance or by their own efforts. Two sample items from this questionnaire, called the Internal-External Control Scale, are as follows:

(a) In my case getting what I want has little or nothing to do with luck.
(b) Many times we might just as well decide what to do by flipping a coin.

Those who scored below the median (midpoint) of the group were designated as *internals*, that is, persons who perceive reinforcement in a variety of social situations to be contingent upon their own behavior or personal characteristics. Those scoring above the median were classified as *externals*, or persons who perceive reinforcement as representing the operation of luck or chance. Internals, in other words, may be described as believing that they have some control over the consequences of their behavior, whereas externals tend to think that rewards and punishments are largely beyond their personal control.

The subjects were randomly assigned to either "chance" or "skill" groups. All faced the task of matching a standard angle (drawn on a four-by-four-inch card) with one of four comparison angles. The sample angles all resembled the standard closely, but a "correct match" was not possible. The experimenter arbitrarily said "right" or "wrong" on certain trials, and the subjects did not dispute his judgments. The subjects in one condition were told that "some people have a special skill at this and do consistently better than others." The remaining subjects were informed that "under these conditions success is entirely a matter of chance." Because they had all been assigned randomly to these two conditions, it turned out that each set of instructions was given to some "internals" and some "externals."

The experimenters had postulated that those subjects who believed they controlled their fates would exercise more care in judging the angles under the skill instructions than under the chance instructions. Conversely, the subjects who believed that chance governed the probability of their being reinforced should give no more attention to the task under the skill than under the chance condition.

The mean number of seconds taken by the subjects to reach a decision about the best match of angles was greatest for "internals" in the skill condition (37.74 seconds). The shortest decision times were evidenced by "internals" when they were instructed that a correct choice could be made only by chance (24.65 seconds). Decision times of the "externals" were intermediate and showed little difference between the chance and skill conditions. The authors make several interesting suggestions as a result of these findings. They speculate that differences in achievement behavior across cultures might reflect the extent to which the members of different cultural groups perceive chance, fate, or powerful others as controlling their destinies. Those who view control as external would be less inclined to develop skills and other techniques for achievement than would those who perceive themselves as largely controlling the outcome of their own performances. The authors also suggest a testable hypothesis: "Internals may tend to select activities in which they can demonstrate skill, and externals activities in which they can demonstrate luck." Presumably, "externals" would tend to be more superstitious and more attracted to gambling than "internals."

The fact that they express beliefs in chance or fate as determiners of reward or punishment suggests that "externals" have come more under the control of noncontingent, or accidental, reinforcement. Persons who perceive a link between their own actions and the possibility of reinforcement, on the other hand, have probably experienced contingent reinforcement more often. Skinner (1953) describes the behavior resulting from the adventitious connection between a response and the appearance of a reinforcer as "superstitious." Someone whose behavior has been shaped to a significant extent by noncontingent reinforcers would tend to ascribe reinforcement more to chance than to his own performances. Perhaps it is because of such differences as these in their reinforcement histories that some persons come to establish higher goals than others and some persons come to believe more in the workings of fate than in self-determined consequences.

Summary   In this chapter we introduced a distinction between *primary behaviors*, those that relate to biological requirements and are common to all humans, and *acquired behaviors*, those that depend upon learning and show wide individual differences in both occurrence and expression. Stimuli that increase the frequency of primary behaviors are called *primary reinforcers*, whereas those that maintain acquired behaviors are called *conditioned reinforcers*.

Although the primary behaviors are innately determined, the specific instrumental acts by which they are expressed are shaped by society. Eating behavior and sexual practices are examples of primary behaviors that are shaped in accordance with social customs and traditions. The fact that the expressions of the primary behaviors, as well as those of many acquired behaviors, are shared by most members of a society has led to the concept of a *modal personality*. The basis for modal behavior patterns in any society is to be found in child-rearing practices common to the society or to groups within the society. Certain characteristics of the adults in different cultures are traceable to child-rearing practices that are distinctive to that culture.

Psychologists and others have reported a number of situations in which the behavior of children has been manipulated by adults through the appropriate control of reinforcements. It seems likely that much of what we call socialization is achieved by various methods of *behavior shaping*, that is, the selective reinforcement of performances that approach some socially acceptable standard. Children learn to model their behavior after that of certain adult members of their society. Parents generally control much of the child's early behavior, but other individuals and social agencies (such as the mass media) exert a gradually increasing influence. The most effective adult models for the child have usually been agents of positive reinforcement, and children are sometimes said to have *identified* with those adults whose behavior they tend to emulate most frequently. Modeling behavior, because it serves as a cue to reinforcers that have been either experienced directly or observed, acquires conditioned reinforcing properties. It is not necessary that the observer be directly reinforced for such imitative behavior; but it is necessary that he have witnessed some contingency between the model's performance and a particular consequence.

Aversive stimuli are effective in accomplishing immediate changes in behavior. However, some theorists have argued that the undesirable emotional and other side effects of aversive control make it a less attractive technique for socializing the child than the use of positive reinforcement. Many undesirable behaviors will decrease in frequency if they are simply not reinforced. A large measure of social control over the individual's behavior is accomplished when his performances become *self-regulated*. This occurs when certain self-administered consequences serve either as rewards or punishments and thus have the effect of increasing or decreasing the frequencies of the behaviors upon which they are contingent. Thus, a person with a "guilty conscience" is effectively punishing himself for some action that has been the occasion for either directly or indirectly experienced aversive consequences in the past.

Because some persons probably have been the objects of adventitious reinforcement, they do not behave as though they perceived a relationship between their own efforts and the possibilities of reward or nonreward. Their behavior has been described as revealing belief in the *external control* of reinforcement. Persons who have experienced a more orderly relationship between their behavior and its consequences come to believe in the *internal control* of reinforcement. These relationships, if confirmed by further research, may help us to understand why some individuals seem to rely more upon skill to achieve success, while others tend to leave things to chance.

References

BAER, D. M., and SHERMAN, J. A.   Reinforcement control of generalized imitation in young children. *Journal of Experimental Child Psychology*, 1964, *1*, 37–49.

BANDURA, A.   Social learning through imitation. In M. R. Jones (Ed.), *Nebraska symposium on motivation.* Lincoln, Neb.: University of Nebraska Press, 1962.

BANDURA, A.   Behavioral modification through modeling procedures. In L. Krasner and L. P. Ullmann (Eds.), *Research in behavior modification.* New York: Holt, Rinehart and Winston, 1965.

BANDURA, A., and HUSTON, A. C.   Identification as a process of incidental learning. *Journal of Abnormal and Social Psychology*, 1961, 63, 311–318.

BANDURA, A., and MCDONALD, F. J.   The influence of social reinforcement and the behavior of models in shaping children's moral judgments. *Journal of Abnormal and Social Psychology*, 1963, 67, 274–281.

BANDURA, A., and PERLOFF, B.   Relative efficacy of self-monitored and externally imposed reinforcement systems. *Journal of Personality and Social Psychology*, 1967, 7, 111–116.

BANDURA, A., and WALTERS, R. H.   *Social learning and personality development.* New York: Holt, Rinehart and Winston, 1963.

BERKOWITZ, H.   Effects of prior experimenter-subject relationships on reinforced reaction time of schizophrenics and normals. *Journal of Abnormal and Social Psychology*, 1964, 69, 522–530.

BERKOWITZ, H., BUTTERFIELD, E. C., and ZIGLER, E.   The effectiveness of social reinforcers on persistence and learning tasks following positive and negative social interactions. *Journal of Personality and Social Psychology*, 1965, 2, 706–714.

BERKOWITZ, H., and ZIGLER, E.   Effects of preliminary positive and negative interactions and delay conditions on children's responsiveness to social reinforcement. *Journal of Personality and Social Psychology*, 1965, 2, 500–505.

BIJOU, S. W., and BAER, D. M. *Child development: Readings in experimental analysis.* New York: Appleton-Century-Crofts, 1967.

BINDRA, D. *Motivation: A systematic reinterpretation.* New York: Ronald Press, 1959.

BOLLES, R. C. *Theory of motivation.* New York: Harper and Row, 1967.

CHURCH, R. M. The varied effects of punishment on behavior. *Psychological Review*, 1963, *70*, 369–402.

DEVOS, G., and MINER, H. Algerian culture and personality in change. *Sociometry*, 1958, *21*, 255–268.

DUBOIS, C. *The people of Alor.* Minneapolis: University of Minnesota Press, 1944.

FERSTER, C. B. Essentials of a science of behavior. In J. I. Nurnberger, C. B. Ferster, and J. P. Brady, *An introduction to the science of human behavior.* New York: Appleton-Century-Crofts, 1963.

FERSTER, C. B. Arbitrary and natural reinforcement. *Psychological Record*, 1967, *17*, 341–347.

FORD, C., and BEACH, F. *Patterns of sexual behavior.* New York: Harper, 1951.

FREUD, S. *An Outline of psychoanalysis.* New York: W. W. Norton, 1949.

GEWIRTZ, J. L. Three determinants of attention-seeking in young children. *Monographs of the Society for Research in Child development*, 1954, *19* (2), No. 59.

GEWIRTZ, J. L., and BAER, D. M. The effect of brief social deprivation on behaviors for a social reinforcer. *Journal of Abnormal and Social Psychology*, 1958a, *56*, 49–56.

GEWIRTZ, J. L., and BAER, D. M. Deprivation and satiation of social reinforcers as drive conditions. *Journal of Abnormal and Social Psychology*, 1958b, *57*, 165–172.

HARRIS, F. R., WOLF, M. M., and BAER, D. M. Effects of adult social reinforcement on child behavior. *Young Children*, 1964, *20*, No. 1.

HEATHERS, G. Emotional dependence and independence in a physical threat situation. *Child Development*, 1953, *24*, 169–179.

INKELES, A., and LEVINSON, D. J. National character: The study of modal personality and sociocultural systems. Chapter 26 in G. Lindzey (Ed.), *Handbook of social psychology.* Reading, Mass.: Addison-Wesley, 1954.

KARDINER, A. *The psychological frontiers of society.* New York: Columbia University Press, 1945.

KINSEY, A., POMEROY, W., and MARTIN, C. *Sexual behavior in the human male.* Philadelphia: W. B. Saunders, 1948.

KLINEBERG, O. Cultural factors in personality adjustment of children. *American Journal of Orthopsychiatry*, 1953, *23*, 465–471.

KLINEBERG, O. *Social psychology.* New York: Henry Holt, 1954.

LEVY, D. M. *Maternal overprotection.* New York: Columbia University Press, 1943.

LINTON, R. Foreword. In A. Kardiner, *The psychological frontiers of society.* New York: Columbia University Press, 1945.

LOVAAS, O. I., FREITAG, G., GOLD, VIVIAN J., and KASSORLA, IRENE C. Experimental studies in childhood schizophrenia. I. Analysis of self-destructive behavior. *Journal of Experimental Child Psychology,* 1965, *2,* 67–84.

LOVAAS, O. I., FREITAG, G., KINDER, M. I., RUBENSTEIN, D. B., SCHAEFFER, B., and SIMMONS, J. B. Experimental studies in childhood schizophrenia: Developing social behavior using electric shock. Paper read at American Psychological Association meetings, September, 1964.

McCOY, N., and ZIGLER, E. Social reinforcer effectiveness as a function of the relationship between child and adult. *Journal of Personality and Social Psychology,* 1965, *1,* 604–612.

McGEOCH, J. A., and IRION, A. L. *The psychology of human learning.* New York: Longmans, Green, 1952.

MILLER, G. A. *Psychology: The study of mental life.* New York: Harper and Row, 1962.

MISCHEL, W., and GRUSEC, JOAN. Determinants of the rehearsal and transmission of neutral and aversive behaviors. *Journal of Personality and Social Psychology,* 1966, *3,* 197–205.

MITNICK, L. L., and McGINNIES, E. Influencing ethnocentrism in small discussion groups through a film communication. *Journal of Abnormal and Social Psychology,* 1958, 56, 82–90.

MUSSEN, P. Early socialization: Learning and identification. Chapter 2 in G. Mandler, P. Mussen, N. Kagan, and M. A. Wallach, *New Directions in psychology, III.* New York: Holt, Rinehart and Winston, 1967.

MUSSEN, P., and DISTLER, L. Masculinity, identification, and father-son relationships. *Journal of Abnormal and Social Psychology,* 1959, 59, 350–356.

MUSSEN, P., and PARKER, A. Mother nurturance and girls' incidental imitative learning. *Journal of Personality and Social Psychology,* 1965, *2,* 94–97.

MUSSEN, P., and RUTHERFORD, E. Parent-child relations and parental personality in relation to young children's sex-role preferences. *Child Development,* 1963, *34,* 589–607.

OLDS, J., and MILNER, P. Positive reinforcement produced by electrical stimulation of septal area and other regions of the rat's brain. *Journal of Comparative and Physiological Psychology,* 1954, 47, 419–427.

PATTERSON, G. R. Parents as dispensers of aversive stimuli. *Journal of Personality and Social Psychology,* 1965, *2,* 844–851.

PATTERSON, G. R., LITTMAN, R., and HINSEY, C. Parents as reinforcers. *Journal of Personality,* 1964, *32,* 182–199.

PIAGET, J. *The moral judgment of the child.* Glencoe, Ill.: Free Press, 1948.

RHEINGOLD, H. L., GEWIRTZ, J. L., and ROSS, H. W. Social conditioning of vocalizations in the infant. *Journal of Comparative and Physiological Psychology,* 1959, 52, 68–73.

RHEINGOLD, H. L., STANLEY, W. C., and COOLEY, J. A. Method for studying exploratory behavior in infants. *Science,* 1962, *136,* 1054–1055.

RHEINGOLD, H. L., STANLEY, W. C., and DOYLE, G. A. Visual and auditory reinforcement of a manipulatory response in a young child. *Journal of Experimental Child Psychology,* 1964, *1,* 316–326.

RIBBLE, M. A. Infantile experience in relation to personality development. Chapter 20 in J. McV. Hunt (Ed.), *Personality and the behavior disorders.* New York: Ronald Press, 1944.

ROTTER, J. B. *Social learning and clinical psychology.* Englewood Cliffs, N.J.: Prentice-Hall, 1954.

ROTTER, J. B., and MULRY, R. C. Internal versus external control of reinforcement and decision time. *Journal of Personality and Social Psychology,* 1965, *2,* 598–604.

SARASON, I. G., and HARMATZ, M. G. Test anxiety and experimental conditions. *Journal of Personality and Social Psychology,* 1965, *1,* 499–505.

SKINNER, B. F. *Walden two.* New York: Macmillan, 1948.

SKINNER, B. F. *Science and human behavior.* New York: Macmillan, 1953.

SPITZ, R. Hospitalism. In A. Freud, H. Hartmann, and E. Kris (Eds.), *The psychoanalytic study of the child,* I, 1945, 53–74; II, 1946, 113–117.

STEVENSON, H. W. Social reinforcement with children as a function of C. A., sex of E, and sex of S. *Journal of Abnormal and Social Psychology,* 1961, *63,* 147–154.

WEST, J. *Plainville, U.S.A.* New York: Columbia University Press, 1945.

WHITING, J. W. M. The cross-cultural method. Chapter 14 in G. Lindzey (Ed.), *Handbook of social psychology.* Reading, Mass.: Addison-Wesley, 1954.

WILLIAMS, C. D. The elimination of tantrum behavior by extinction procedures. *Journal of Abnormal and Social Psychology,* 1959, *59,* 269.

Social Influence
and Conformity

A signal feature of human societies is the fact that most of the members exhibit remarkable similarities of behavior. For example, virtually all males in Western countries wear shirts, trousers, and shoes. On formal occasions, all wear neckties. In other parts of the world, the prevailing fashions for males (or females) may be quite different. People also generally avoid behaviors that could have aversive consequences in a particular community. Very few women in Western society are seen nursing their infants in public, although this is practiced in Eastern countries. We could cite numerous examples of behavior patterns that are common to members of any given culture. Such similarities of response may be said to reflect the prevailing customs or practices of a society, and they represent one product of the socialization process.

General Theory

When an individual behaves generally in ways that are consistent with the modal behavior patterns of his community, we say that he is *conforming* to these standards. When his behavior is dissimilar to these modal patterns, we describe him as *deviating* from the established norms. From a theoretical position consistent with the one that we have adopted, Bachrach, Candland, and Gibson (1961) define conformity as a situation in which reinforcement provided by a group is adequate to produce and maintain the behavior of an individual; the individual's behavior, in turn, is reinforcing to the group. Deviation is represented as a situation in which reinforcement from the group is not adequate to produce and maintain the same behavior by the individual, who, consequently, will not perform in ways that are reinforcing to the group.

In instances of deviancy it is probable that another group is providing the reinforcements for the individual. Deviation thus becomes in part a matter of conformity to the norms prevailing in a different group. Other instances of nonconformity will occur when a particular activity, even though it is idiosyncratic, is intrinsically very rewarding, and when punishment for deviancy is improbable.

A similar theoretical position is taken by Campbell (1961), who has analyzed in some detail the ways in which individual behavioral dispositions are formed. Campbell argues that behavior is acquired (a) individually, through trial-and-error learning and perceptual learning, or (b) socially, through imitation, observation of another's trial-and-error learning, or verbal instruction. The individual modes of acquisition, presumably, would not necessarily lead to conformity, whereas the social modes of acquisition inevitably do so. Apparent conformity, as Hollander and Willis (1967) have observed, may be due to similarity of nonsocial circumstances, as when a coat is worn in the winter not because others do so but because it is cold. Environmental stimuli control a great deal of our behavior, and a distinctive environment will inevitably bring about certain commonalities in the behavior of the inhabitants. Of more interest to us, however, are those instances in which behavior is controlled by the reactions of other individuals. For example, a child may with a minimum of instruction and largely through trial and error learn to convey food from a dish to his mouth. His eating performance, however, will not conform to the rules of etiquette prevailing in his social group until it has been shaped through the intervention of others, who will selectively reinforce certain components and punish others. It is probably safe to say that the bulk of our behavior is shaped socially and that relatively few performances achieve their final form either through sheer trial and error or entirely through insight. Conformity to the behaviors that are selectively reinforced in one's community is to be expected in most instances.

Sherif and Sherif (1964) observed small groups of adolescent boys over periods of five to seven months in their natural environments. As expected, each group developed normative behavior patterns appropriate to the ecological backgrounds of the members. Especially significant was the fact that collective praise from peers for conforming to these norms was more frequent than negative sanctions for deviation. Adult observers concluded — to put it in plain terms — that the boys complied with the norms of their groups out of a sense of loyalty and responsibility. We may assume that the standards of the various groups provided guidelines for behaviors that were mutually reinforcing and served to discourage behaviors that would have been mutually aversive. This is, after all, the major function of group norms.

Some norms are adhered to more in precept than in practice. That is, certain verbalizations may persist ritualistically long after the related nonverbal performances have been extinguished. This contingency, sometimes called cultural lag, is likely to arise when certain norms outlive the individuals and circumstances that gave rise to them. Every society has its *folkways* and *mores*, the origins of which frequently are obscure. When these are codified as part of a society's formal system of jurisprudence, they may be invoked to coerce or to punish individuals who behave in ways that are offensive to their fellows. More frequently than not, violations of these taboos go unpunished provided the deviant individuals are not too public, or obvious, in their nonconformity. Research by Kinsey and his colleagues (1948, 1953) provides illustrations of this in the striking disparities that were noted between the sexual mores of American society and the actual sexual behavior of many persons. In fact, these investigators observed that if all the individuals who had engaged in sexual activities proscribed by law were punished accordingly, ten per cent of the population would be standing guard over an imprisoned ninety per cent. This fanciful situation gains significance if we recall our discussion of behavioral conflict in Chapter 3. It seems clear that conflict is generated in situations where the reinforcement contingencies are not consistent, that is, where the same class of behaviors is rewarded on one occasion and punished on another, or where the consequences of a performance may be immediately reinforcing but ultimately aversive.

In such instances, the individual's behavior appears to be controlled by short-term rather than long-term consequences. Because the reinforcement for sexual activity is immediate, even those acts that are not sanctioned tend to occur despite the probability that they will ultimately have such aversive consequences as guilt, anxiety, or social ostracism. Whenever we discover instances of individuals behaving in ways that appear to be self-damaging, it is well to remember that the *immediate* consequences of the behavior are usually rewarding and that the stimuli controlling the behavior have preceded these rather than any later aversive effects. Furthermore, as shown by Logan (1960), partial punishment is less effective than continuous punishment in suppressing a performance. Rats running down an alley were slowed more by punishment delivered on every trial than by punishment given on only half of the trials. Azrin, Holz, and Hake (1963) found that the number of times a rat would press a bar to obtain food was reduced in proportion to the number of responses that had been punished by electric shock. These and similar findings taken together suggest that the relatively high incidence of various kinds of nonconformity, which ordinarily should produce aversive reactions from others, is attributable to the irregularity with which such behavior is actually punished. For example, the reinforcements for criminal behavior (money, property, revenge) are generally prompt and continuous, whereas the negative sanctions (fines, imprisonment) are invoked only at some later time, if at all.

Imitative Behavior

How have those modal behavior patterns that are characteristic of different societies developed? Certain of the early sociologists, such as Bagehot, Durkheim, and Tarde, saw in the concept of *imitation* a simple explanation for all conformity behavior. Unfortunately, the term imitation does little more than name an event that we can all observe, namely, behavior by one individual modeled after that of another. Left unanswered is the question of what situational features control emission of the imitative performance and what stimuli occur as a consequence. A behavioral analysis requires that we specify the functional antecedents of the behavior as well as the reinforcers that maintain it.

Positive Control

Comparative approaches. Miller and Dollard (1941) were among the first to demonstrate the importance of differential reinforcement in imitative behavior. They trained hungry albino rats to turn either right or left at the choice point of a T-maze in order to secure reward. A black card was placed at the end of the runway containing food, and a white card was placed at the end of the other arm. The positions of the two cards were shifted randomly on successive trials so that the animal had to make a correct visual discrimination rather than learn a simple position habit. After the "leaders" had learned to make the correct discrimination, naive "followers" were placed directly behind them at the start of the maze. If a "follower" made the same response as the "leader," it was rewarded with food. If it responded differently, it was picked up and removed from the maze until the next trial. Another group of animals was trained *not* to imitate. If a rat in this condition turned in the same direction as the leader, it received no food. Only when these animals turned in the direction opposite that taken by the leader were they rewarded. Figure 4.1 shows the learning curves for eight animals that were reinforced for imitative behavior and eight animals that were reinforced for nonimitative behavior.

Similar findings have been reported by Church (1957), who trained six rats to follow leader rats along an elevated maze to obtain water. The leaders were responding consistently with respect to incidental cues provided by lights over the runway. When tested alone after one hundred trials of following these leaders, the followers were able 77 per cent of the time to go to the arm of the maze marked by the cue to which the leader had responded. The imitative performance in this case clearly was controlled not only by the behavior of the model but also by other relevant environmental features to which the model had been responding.

Miller and Dollard extended their investigations to include other variables that might be crucial to the acquisition of imitative behavior. They discovered that rats that had learned to follow an albino leader to obtain food would also follow a black leader that had previously been trained in the same problem. There was also some tendency for rats that had learned to imitate another rat in the T-maze to imitate a leader in a situation requiring jumping from a center platform to one of four surrounding platforms. Transfer of imitative behavior to this new situation, however,

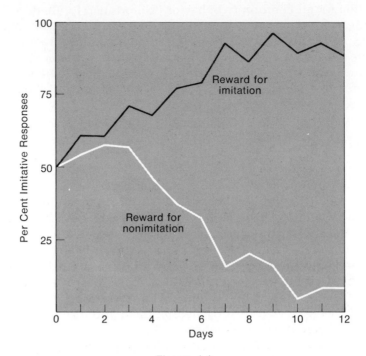

Figure 4.1
Learning of imitation and nonimitation by rats.
(After Miller and Dollard, 1941)

occurred only about 40 per cent of the time. Inasmuch as imitation would have occurred by chance on 25 per cent of the trials, the evidence for generalization of imitation to a new environment was not conclusive.

Imitative behavior does not necessarily occur with greater than chance expectancy until it has been strengthened through reinforcement. This seems to be true of both animals and humans. Miller and Dollard arranged an experiment in which two children were to select one of two boxes in order to secure a piece of candy. One of the children, designated as the leader, had previously been told by the experimenter which box contained the candy, and he was allowed to choose first. The second child was told merely that his turn to find the candy would come second. As a control, another group of children was also run in pairs, but one piece of candy was placed in each of the two boxes so that only nonimitative behavior would be rewarded. On the first trial, 20 per cent of the "imitators" and 25 per cent of the "nonimitators" chose the same box as the leader. On subsequent trials, all of the imitators and none of the nonimitators chose the same box as the leader. Clearly, the dependent members of the pairs had learned when to imitate and when not to imitate in order to secure a piece of candy.

A variation of these procedures was devised by McDavid (1962) to determine the degree to which imitative behavior is controlled by the performance of a model and by cues from the environment. Social cues for the subjects, who were children, were provided by an adult; nonsocial cues included color and position of a glass panel that was a component in a discrimination learning problem. For some of the children the model's behavior in a button-pressing task involving three choices was associated 100 per cent of the time with a particular color, for others 67 per cent, and for the remaining subjects only 33 per cent. Imitative behavior occurred most frequently when the social and nonsocial cues were associated 100 per cent of the time and least frequently when cues from the model and from the environment were associated only partially, that is, 67 per cent of the time. Under random association (33 per cent) between the two sets of controlling stimuli, the subjects disregarded the color cues and simply imitated the leader.

Observational learning. A programmatic approach to this general problem has been undertaken by Bandura and Walters (1963), who view imitation as an indispensable aspect of learning. They reject Miller and Dollard's conception of imitation as a form of instrumental conditioning on the grounds that it does not account for *observational learning,* in which the observer reproduces the model's behavior some time after it is actually witnessed. Direct reinforcement of imitation, therefore, seldom occurs; instead, the observer is *vicariously reinforced* by merely observing the consequences of the model's behavior. Children develop a generalized tendency to match the performances of successful models, that is, models whose reinforcement they have observed. Their continued imitation of a particular performance must, of course, be maintained by some schedule of direct reinforcement. Social learning through imitation, then, is explained by Bandura and Walters in terms of the combined influence of models and differential reinforcement. In the previous chapter, we reviewed some of the experimental findings that support this general position.

For example, Bandura, Ross, and Ross (1964) have found that new social responses may be acquired, or existing behavior may be modified, when one person merely observes the behavior of others and its consequences. It may not be necessary for an individual to be reinforced directly for imitative behavior; he may learn vicariously, that is, by observation. These investigators observed the play behavior of nursery school children who had watched a five-minute movie in which aggressive behavior by one adult toward another was either rewarded or punished. They report that in a subsequent play situation children who had witnessed the aggressive model rewarded displayed more imitative aggression than did children who had witnessed the aggressive model punished. It seems that both imitation and conformity may be learned as a result of merely observing the consequences of various types of behavior. There are probably wide individual differences in this respect, however, with some persons more prone to learn through first-hand experience and others by observation. The important point is that the behavior is maintained by its consequences, whether such consequences are experienced directly or vicariously.

In nearly all cultures, parents make use of *exemplary models*, which may range, according to Bandura and Walters, from national heroes or villains to members of the family or the children of neighbors. These exemplary models often typify the norms of the community and are held up to the child as examples of desirable or appropriate conduct. Positive models are those whom the parents would like the child to emulate, whereas negative models are presented as object lessons for the child to avoid. How are these cognitive representations translated into behavior? Bandura (1965) argues that an observer acquires (a) retrievable images of the events he has witnessed, and (b) verbal labels that serve as equivalents of the model's behavior. Either or both of these can serve as discriminative stimuli that control instrumental performances in the same way environmental events do. "It is likewise assumed," writes Bandura, "that symbolic matching responses possess cue-producing properties that are capable of eliciting, some time after observation, overt responses corresponding to those that were modeled" (p. 11). Perhaps the most significant feature of this theory, and the experimental data that support it, is that an individual may, through imitation, display performances that were not previously within his behavior repertoire. For example, swinging a golf club involves a series of movements that would rarely occur fortuitously and that depend upon observation of someone who has already attained skill at this activity. The operant strength of this particular performance is negligible, but it can be acquired through imitation and maintained by subsequent reinforcement of the correct manner of execution. Because skill at this particular sport necessitates learning a highly stylized pattern of muscular responses, successful "nonconformers" to this modal response topography are rare.

As Bandura points out, the behavior repertoires that constitute an enduring aspect of a culture are transmitted largely on the basis of behavior displayed by social models. We may conveniently refer to this process as imitation, with the understanding that it follows the principles of learning and behavior that were developed in Chapter 2. Another way of looking at this situation is to say that imitation of an observed performance occurs through a process of *representational mediation* (Berger, 1968). It has been demonstrated in a number of situations that an observer responds with covert representations of the model's behavior. In other words, images, ideas, and words that are the responses of someone who is merely watching another's behavior can serve as the stimuli to some subsequent performance of the observer. These cognitive events thus mediate between observation and subsequent imitation; they serve as implicit discriminative stimuli for the modeled performance. To the extent that individuals imitate what they see and hear on television, for example, an explanation in these terms is applicable.

Aversive Control

Conformity behavior can be increased in frequency by both positive and negative reinforcement. The usual consequences of conformity are social approval and acceptance, and most individuals learn to behave in ways that will elicit these reactions from others. The learning process is straightforward and can be demonstrated in a variety of situations. But conformity behavior is also instrumental in avoiding or escaping from the anxiety that a person may experience when he begins to deviate from established social norms.

Negative reinforcement. Miller (1948) gave a white rat a number of electric shocks while the animal was confined in a white compartment. On later trials, the rat could escape into a black compartment and avoid the shock by making the instrumental response of rotating a wheel. Subsequently, whenever the animal was placed in the white compartment it promptly turned the wheel with its forepaws, thereby escaping into the black compartment. We would say that the white compartment had become a conditioned aversive stimulus as a result of being paired with the primary aversive stimulus of electric shock. Termination of this aversive stimulus was accomplished by the wheel-turning behavior. Any behavior that removes conditioned aversive stimulation, in this case that provided by the white compartment, will be reinforced. This is referred to as negative reinforcement.

Following Mowrer (1960), we have defined fear and anxiety as emotions that become conditioned to response-correlated stimuli. Emotions are basically reflexive, and when elicited by some environmental circumstance they may serve as cues, or S^Ds, that control certain instrumental acts. Thus, the anxiety aroused when one is stopped by a traffic policeman may cause one to be unusually polite. Such an operant performance has the effects of terminating the anxiety and of avoiding some further aversive occurrence. Beyond this, however, it appears that the punishing value of social disapproval is derived as much from its being paired with the removal of reinforcing events as with the onset of an aversive event (Logan and Wagner, 1965). In other words, performances that deviate from an established norm not only fail to be reinforced but preempt the time during which reinforced behavior might have occurred. A period of time during which previously rewarded responses are no longer rewarded, in fact, has been shown by Ferster (1957) to be aversive. The net effect of such punishing consequences on deviant behavior is to increase the frequency of conformity, even when the conformity is not specifically reinforced. So it is not necessary that we be able to identify the reinforcers for every instance of conformity behavior in order to understand how it is maintained. The fact that conformity prevents the aversive effects of nonconformity is sufficient in many instances to explain its occurrence.

How do these principles apply specifically to conformity behavior in society? Let us assume that most persons at one time or another have behaved in ways that were aversive to their fellows. Such behavior may have consisted of simply being "different," for example, having poor table manners, going unshaven, wearing outlandish clothes, or voicing unpopular opinions. Depending upon the situation, these and other unusual behaviors will be the occasions for a variety of aversive reactions from others. Behavior that conforms to the standards prevailing in a particular social group, on the other hand, will be positively reinforced in a number of ways. Having experienced the aversive consequences of being too obviously "different" in social situations, as well as the rewarding consequences of being "one of the crowd," the individual comes to perform more frequently in ways that for the most part are modeled after the behavior of those with whom he associates. Different situations, of course, provide different reinforcement contingencies; hence, similar behaviors may be rewarded in one setting but punished in another. The manner of dress of a laborer on his way home from work would not strike anyone as unusual, but if the same individual were to enter an expensive restaurant dressed in his working clothes he would be unwelcome. Men may exchange bawdy stories and use profane language during an all-male "bull session," but similar behavior would not be acceptable at a church social. Most persons learn the appropriate discriminations; in one sense, we can say that they assume the "role" that is most likely to be reinforced in a given set of circumstances.

Situational Factors in Conformity

The Presence of Others

What we call conformity behavior, then, is behavior that is controlled largely by the reactions of others in particular social situations. A demonstration of this in a natural setting is provided in an experiment by Blake, Mouton, and Hain (1956), who manipulated certain features of a social situation so as to produce either conforming or nonconforming performances by subjects. College students were asked to sign a petition on a relatively neutral matter in the presence of a confederate of the experimenter who either signed or refused to sign the petition. In some instances, the subjects were shown a petition that already contained a long list of names, while in other cases the petition contained only a few names. As anticipated, more of the naive subjects signed the petition when the confederate also signed and when a large number of names were already appended to it. Social support in the form of either written material or the behavior of another person apparently was an inducement to conformity. The critical stimuli controlling the individual's actions in this instance were derived from the modal behavior exhibited by others in the same situations.

Blake (1958) asked male students at the University of Texas to sign a petition asking that illumination be provided for a fountain located on the campus. The request for endorsement was made in three different ways: (a) "Would you read and sign this petition, please?" (A pencil was offered the student.) (b) "Would you read and sign the petition?" (No pencil was offered, but one was attached to the clipboard with the petition.) (c) "You don't want to sign this petition do you?" (No pencil was in view.) In addition to these modes of request, the situation was further varied by having a confederate either sign the petition in the presence of the naive respondent or refuse to sign the petition. The results were as expected, namely, a higher frequency of endorsement following the strongest request in conjunction with the presence of another person signing the petition. Endorsement was secured least often with the negatively-worded request accompanied by refusal of the confederate to sign.

In another experiment reported by Blake (1958), it was predicted that disobeying a traffic signal by naive individuals would occur more frequently when they were able to observe a person of high-status committing a violation than when they perceived a person of lower status in similar violation. An accomplice of the experimenter either obeyed or disobeyed the "wait" signal at a pedestrian crossing in Austin, Texas. Half the time, the accomplice, by his manner of dress, appeared as a person of high status. On the remaining occasions he was poorly dressed in order to convey an impression of lower status. An observer stationed a short distance away recorded the number of persons who were apparently influenced by the accomplice to cross the street before the "walk" light flashed on. Comparisons were made between those times when the accomplice appeared in high status attire and in low status attire, and when he was absent from the location.

Blake reports the results as follows: "Violation by the accomplice, dressed either in high or low status clothing, increased significantly the pedestrian violation rate. When he violated in the low status attire, a small percentage of the pedestrians violated, whereas when he violated in high status attire, the pedestrian violation rate increased dramatically" (p. 234). The data showed that significantly more persons were influenced by the accomplice to violate the traffic signal when he dressed in high status attire than when he dressed in low status attire. "Here, perhaps, is one of the reasons we live in a status-conscious society," concludes Blake. "Status is power!" (p. 234).

Raven (1959) presented groups of subjects with material describing the case history of a juvenile delinquent. The task of the subjects was to decide whether harsh or lenient treatment was merited in that particular case. Although the subjects actually tended to favor lenient handling of the case, the experimenter reported a false consensus advocating harsh treatment. Following this experimental manipulation, each subject was asked to write a description of the case, which some of the subjects were told would be passed around for the others to read. The remaining subjects were told that their essays would remain private. Finally, the subjects were again asked for a recommendation of treatment for the offender. This time, 39 per cent of the subjects whose essays had been made public changed their judgments in the direction of the group norm, while only 26 per cent of the subjects whose descriptions were privileged moved toward this norm. Public commitment on an issue apparently disposes some individuals to express viewpoints that conform to what they perceive to be the majority position.

One might ask why the subjects in these several experiments were influenced by their knowledge of the reactions of others when there was no indication that their own actions would have tangible consequences. Theoretically, there are several concurring explanations for the persistence of imitative or conformity behavior in situations where no direct reinforcement can be identified. For one thing, conformity behavior is generally acquired on a schedule of intermittent reinforcement. As we have seen, behavior acquired on a variable interval or variable ratio contingency is very resistant to extinction. This means that a number of unreinforced occurrences of a previously acquired performance will not necessarily decrease its frequency, and that occasional reinforcement of normative social performances is sufficient to maintain them. Another critical factor in these findings is the individual's perception of new situations as having similarities to those he has encountered in the past, where certain of his behaviors were rewarded and others either went unrewarded or were punished. In short, individuals tend to behave consistently in situations having certain features in common. One's perception of conformity by other persons becomes the occasion on which he also conforms. This has sometimes been referred to as a "bandwagon effect."

Conforming behavior seems to follow a generalization gradient in situations that bear varying degrees of resemblance to those in which the behavior was acquired. Teen-age gatherings are occasions on which a teenager will conform to what he sees his peers doing. Adult gatherings are occasions on which he will conform to what he has learned are adult expectations. Occasions not readily identified as falling to either category, such as a mixed age group, may result in awkwardness and uncertainty on the part of all concerned. Typical teen-age behavior would be described as conformity in a group of teenagers but would be classed as deviant in a group of adults. We shall have more to say later on the subject of deviant behavior.

Attraction to the Group

Back's experiment. Several factors determine the extent of conformity that occurs in a group. One of these is the attractiveness of the group to the members, a feature that has been termed "group cohesiveness." An experiment by Back (1951) was designed to measure the effects of cohesiveness on social influence in two-person discussion groups. In this experiment, subjects first answered a questionnaire asking them to describe the type of person with whom they would most like to work. They were then assigned partners in accordance with three different sets of instructions. In one condition, each subject was told that he had been teamed either with someone who fit his description "almost exactly," or with a partner who did not "fit the description exactly." These two pairs were presumed to be strongly or weakly cohesive on the basis of *personal attraction*. In a second condition, the members of the pairs were told either that their performance on the task would be judged in comparison with that of students at other universities or simply that the task tested the way people use their imaginations. These pairs were designated as strongly or weakly cohesive on the basis of *task direction*. (It should be noted that the "strongly cohesive" pairs in this condition were also offered the prospect of a $5.00 reward if they performed well.) In a third condition, the subjects in each pair were told either that they had been selected because it was thought that they would be especially good at the assigned task or simply that they would be good material for a work group. These two sets of instructions tended to induce strong or weak cohesiveness on the basis of *group prestige.*

The actual instructions were longer than this, of course, and in all of the strongly cohesive pairs mention was made of the compatibility of the partners. In the weakly cohesive conditions, a probable lack of congeniality was emphasized. It is Back's contention that individuals seek membership in a group because (a) they like the other members, (b) belonging to the group is something of an honor, or (c) the group mediates goals that are important for the members. He attempted experimentally to establish these three bases for membership in his task groups. Unfortunately, the personal attraction factor was confounded with the other two variables, making it difficult to interpret his results.

The task of each subject was to examine a set of three photographs showing two seated individuals, write a story connecting the three pictures, discuss the story with his partner, then write a final, improved version of his story. A number of measures were made of each subject's performance, based on observer ratings. For example, the stories were broken down into units (unspecified) and the amount of change in a person's story in the direction of his partner's story was determined. During the discussion one observer "noted all the communication," using an observation blank containing twenty categories. A second observer "noted only the attempts to influence," taking the sentence as a unit and classifying these into seventeen categories, such as "assertion, hypothetical example, rhetorical question, and exhortation." These attempts to influence were also rated on a four point scale of intensity, and these ratings were reported to be reliably similar when made independently by different observers.

Finally, the two observers classified each discussion as following an *active* pattern or a *withdrawal* pattern. Each subject also filled out a socio metric scale indicating the extent to which he would enjoy further inter-action with his partner. We may summarize briefly some of Back's findings:

(a) Sixteen strongly cohesive pairs showed an "active pattern" of dis-cussion, while eleven showed a "withdrawing pattern." Three pairs could not be classified. Nineteen weakly cohesive pairs showed a "withdrawing pattern," and seven showed an "active pattern." Four of these pairs could not be categorized. Cohesiveness was judged to be related significantly to degree of discussion activity.

(b) In the more cohesive pairs, there was more argumentation and more serious consideration by each partner of the other's position than in the less cohesive pairs.

(c) In the more cohesive pairs, the partners changed more toward one another's positions than in the less cohesive pairs.

(d) Time devoted to discussion was greater in the strongly cohesive groups based on personal attraction and group prestige than in the strongly cohesive groups based on task direction.

Interpretation. An appraisal of Back's experiment in behavioral language leads us to conclude, first, that instructions given to subjects required to perform in pairs will lead to detectable differences in their subsequent dis-cussion behavior. It is not possible to identify in Back's data the effects of any specific differential reinforcement contingencies that could account for the results. However, on theoretical grounds, we assume that the frequency of a performance is raised above some operant level by the reinforcers that operate in a particular setting. Both the verbal and the nonverbal events that occur in discussion serve to reinforce the participants and, thus, to maintain verbal behavior at a certain level. Whether this level is high or low depends in part upon what is said; that is, rewarding as well as aversive comments serve to stimulate active rejoinder among the par-ticipants. One aspect of a discussion that has positive reinforcing proper-ties is a relatively high verbal output by the participants. A person is reinforced in conversation by both the frequency and the content of the replies that he elicits from others. This explanation presupposes that each participant will verbalize at a sufficiently high initial operant level to pro-vide the occasions on which reinforcement can occur. Enhancement of the operant level may be achieved by instructions designed to increase favorable personal impressions among a group of discussion participants. An active discussion, once joined, thus tends to become self-maintaining. Such an interpretation might account for the fact that Back's strongly co-hesive groups, with one exception, talked longer than the weakly cohesive groups. The exception occurred in the groups where the importance of the task had been stressed and where a monetary reward had been offered for good performance. In this case, we may conjecture that more rapid completion of the assigned task was due to increased effort stimulated by an incentive. A leisurely discussion under these circumstances would have delayed attainment of the incentive, hence would have been aversive.

Anticipation of reinforcement from a congenial partner seems the most straightforward interpretation of the fact that the strongly cohesive pairs were more "active" as well as more argumentative in discussion. One learns that at least occasional assent to another's viewpoints will induce reciprocation. Verplanck (1955), for example, has demonstrated that expression of agreement with another's opinions brings about an increase in the frequency with which such opinions are offered. Repeating or paraphrasing what another person has said amounts to incorporating part of the other's verbal repertoire into one's own speech. A convergence of verbal patterns may then occur, to a point where the verbal performances of two individuals are highly redundant. This is probably what takes place when one individual is said to have influenced another in discussion.

One manifestation of conformity, then, occurs as a redundancy in the verbal performances of two individuals as a result of their having been "set" both to verbalize at a fairly high level of output and to reinforce (agree with) one another. Agreement, defined as a high incidence of common elements in their respective verbal productions, enhances the flow of conversation, thus providing more occasions on which concurrence of opinion may occur.

Cohesiveness and conformity. Because one is reinforced more frequently by his close associates than by strangers, it follows that conformity should be induced more readily among the members of existing groups than in newly formed groups. Such an effect, in fact, was found by Thibaut and Strickland (1956), who compared social influence effects in groups of fraternity pledges and in groups of strangers. The task assigned to six-man groups composed in this fashion was one of judging the "degree of friendliness" represented by abstract patterns of dots representing persons. The group members exchanged written ballots until unanimity was reached. Actually, in a typical bit of deception, the experimenter intercepted the ballots and substituted others that showed each subject deviating from the judgments of the other members. Some members of the groups were told that achieving *cooperation* was of principal importance in their efforts, whereas others were told that judgmental *accuracy* was most important. Not surprisingly, more individuals were influenced by the bogus ballots when given a cooperative set than when given a task set (60 per cent vs. 30 per cent). Induced conformity also was greater among those groups where the members had enjoyed previous acquaintance.

Festinger and Thibaut (1951) found that the members of highly cohesive discussion groups directed 70 to 90 per cent of their remarks toward individuals whose opinions deviated from those held by most of the group members. This effect can be seen as shaping the behavior of the deviant members along lines more acceptable to the majority. Deviant behavior is probably aversive to the conforming members of cohesive groups because it interferes with other activities that are reinforcing. In weakly cohesive groups, on the other hand, most of the members are probably not engaged in strongly reinforced performances, so deviant behavior by a few is not necessarily perceived as aversive.

It has been suggested that with increased attractiveness of a group to its members, less group pressure is required for conformity (Thibaut and Strickland, 1956). In many situations, it is desirable for practical reasons to generate a high degree of group cohesiveness and thus minimize non-conformity. For example, many inductees into military service have only a nominal identification with their units. One function of training and indoctrination is to generate a high degree of group cohesiveness, or *esprit,* so that conformity and obedience will be maintained by the trainees themselves, and deviant behavior will be reduced in frequency. This is accomplished through an intensive program of both positive and aversive control, in which the shaping of appropriate verbal repertoires is especially important. Acceptable verbal performances are those that glorify the group and its mission and that stress the value of loyalty, comradeship, and mutual support.

Deviation and Rejection

Schachter's experiment. An experiment designed to examine the consequences for an individual deviating from the group has been reported by Schachter (1951). Because it illustrates rather well the problems and procedures of many social-psychological experiments, we will review it in some detail. However, we will interpret the results in different terms than Schachter did, referring, where possible, to the operation of reinforcement variables. The subjects, students in several economics classes at the University of Michigan, were invited to become members of one of four social clubs dedicated, ostensibly, to activities concerned with criminology, journalism, motion pictures, and radio programming. Interested students indicated on a four-point scale the extent of their interest in each club. The criminology and movie clubs were then formed from students who had shown something between "moderate" and "extreme" interest in them. In view of their expressed interest in these two clubs, and the implied attractiveness of the clubs to them, the members of these groups were designated as *high in cohesiveness.*

The journalism and radio clubs, on the other hand, were made up of students who had rated them as being of "little" or "no" interest. Because of the implied lack of attractiveness of these clubs to their members, they were designated as *low in cohesiveness.* Another independent variable, *task relevance,* was also manipulated by the experimenter. All of the groups, during their first (and only) meeting, were presented with a case history of Johnny Rocco, a juvenile delinquent whose misadventures were described sympathetically. Discussion of this case was considered to be relevant to the purposes of the criminology and journalism clubs but irrelevant to the functions of the movie and radio clubs.

After discussing the problems of Johnny Rocco, each of the group members was asked to indicate the type of corrective treatment he should receive. Judgments were rendered along a seven-point scale on which Position 1 represented extreme leniency and Position 7 represented extreme punitiveness. Each member, after reading the case, announced aloud which position on the scale he had chosen as a rating. Unknown to the subjects, each group of five to seven members also contained three paid participants who were confederates of the experimenter. One of the paid participants, the "deviate," took a very punitive stand; another, the "mode," took a rather lenient position; the third, the "slider," initially took a very punitive (deviant) position but gradually moved toward the modal point during the ensuing discussion. In all of the groups, the naive members chose scale position ranging from 2 to 4, thus revealing a preference for leniency, whereas the paid deviate always took Position 7, representing extreme punitiveness.

Following a forty-five-minute discussion of Johnny Rocco, the group members filled out the questionnaires designed to measure (a) their interest in continuing in the group, (b) their nominations for membership on three committees, and (c) their ranked preferences for the other members on the criterion of congeniality. These responses constituted the dependent variables of the experiment.

Schachter had made several predictions about the reactions of the subjects in the thirty-two groups he observed. In general, he assumed that within any social group there are pressures on the members to adopt uniform attitudes. The strength of these pressures will vary with the *cohesiveness* of the group as well as with the relevance of the issue to the group. If there is a deviate within the group, the other members will exert pressure to change the individual. Such pressure should be greater in high- than in low-cohesive groups, and it should be greater where relevant issues are concerned. Failure to bring a deviate into conformity with the other members should result in his being rejected. Inasmuch as the deviate in each of the experimental groups was instructed not to give any evidence of modifying his initial stand, it was predicted that he would be *rejected* by the group. Indications of rejection would be low sociometric ranking and nomination to the least desirable committee (in this case, the Correspondence Committee rather than the Executive or Steering Committee).

Schachter's results with respect to the interactive effects of cohesiveness and relevance on sociometric choice are shown in Table 4.1, page 118. A lower ranking (higher number) indicates rejection.

After statistical evaluation, Schachter drew the following conclusions from the data presented: (a) Paid participants in the *mode* and *slider* roles were not rejected, but as *deviates*, they were definitely rejected. (b) There was greater rejection of the deviate in high- than in low-cohesive groups. Relevance of the issue did not appear to have influenced degree of rejection of the deviate. Schachter also reports that in three of the four condi-

Table 4.1
Mean sociometric rankings of the paid participants.
(Based on Schachter, 1951, Table 3, p. 198)

Group	Deviate	Mode	Slider
Hi-Co/Rel	6.44	4.65	5.02
Lo-Co/Rel	5.83	4.70	4.56
Hi-Co/Irrel	6.51	4.68	4.44
Lo-Co/Irrel	5.67	3.83	5.03

tions, the deviate was overnominated for the Correspondence Committee and undernominated for the Executive Committee. Not only was the deviate considered relatively undesirable as a fellow club member, he was also judged least capable of handling an important committee assignment.

Interpretation. This is what appears to have occurred in Schachter's experiment. The members of a discussion group encounter a situation in which one individual adheres tenaciously to a viewpoint not shared by the others. The behavior of this person is aversive to them, particularly if they are attracted to the group, and they make some attempt to modify his stand by addressing more remarks to him. When this strategy fails to change his behavior, the group members express relatively little interest in having the offending individual continue as a member of the group. In the event that he does remain in the group, he is punished by being relegated to the least desirable committee. Participants who either conform to the group from the start or exhibit conforming behavior by the end of the discussion are not treated in this fashion.

Behaviorally, the results may be interpreted as follows: (a) Deviant behavior by one individual is more aversive in a group where the members anticipate positive reinforcement than in a group where positive reinforcement is not anticipated. (b) Termination of the aversive behavior of a deviate is accomplished by rejecting him from the group; he is also punished with negative evaluations and undesirable assignments. (c) Individuals whose behavior is reinforcing to the other members of the group are rewarded by being accorded both positive evaluations and nominations to desirable assignments.

Individual Variations in Conformity

Status and Competence

It would appear from Schachter's experiment that a person who fails to conform to the modal behavior in a group is rather summarily rejected by the other members. If this were always so, however, very little innovation would ever occur in groups, and a kind of institutional *rigor mortis* would set in. Actually, an individual may under some circumstances deviate with impunity from the norms established by a group. Such an individual may thereby influence the other members of the group in such a way as to bring about a change in the normal, or modal, frequency of certain of their performances. His behavior is perceived by the other members as innovative or imaginative, rather than simply deviant or nonconforming. The innovative person, however, can safely behave in this manner only if he has demonstrated both competence in the work of the group and some prior conformity to the standards adhered to by the other members.

These assumptions were taken by Hollander (1960) as the basis for an experiment in which a confederate of the experimenter, by demonstrating competence in a group task, was later able not only to behave deviantly but to influence the other members to follow his lead. Twelve groups, each composed of four male subjects, were enlisted by the experimenter in the solution of a task that required a consensus of the individuals on every trial. The subjects in each group were identified by numbers and were seated out of sight of one another, communicating only by means of microphones and headsets. Each was given a sheet of instructions and a page containing a problem matrix. This matrix contained seven rows, identified by code names for the letters of the alphabet, and seven columns, headed by the names of colors. The cells of the matrix contained positive and negative values indicating the number of pennies that the group could win or lose in any trial. A portion of the matrix is shown below to clarify further description of the experiment:

	Green	Red	Blue
Able	−1	−12	+5
Baker	+10	−1	−2
Charlie	−5	+5	−3

The task of the subjects was to decide which row they should select on each trial as having the greatest chance of paying off. After they had designated a row, the experimenter announced which *column* was "paying off" on that trial. The number lying at the intersection of row and column indicated how many pennies that group had won or lost. Thus, if on a given trial the group decided to choose row Baker and the experimenter announced column Green, the group would have won ten cents; if the experimenter had announced column Blue, the group would have lost two cents.

Each group was given a "bank" of two hundred pennies, so that the subjects were not gambling with their own money. They were told that the payoffs involved a system, and they were invited to discuss the strategy they wished to employ before announcing their collective choices. The individuals accepted certain rules of procedure. They agreed to offer suggestions according to their assigned numbers and to accept a majority decision on each trial. The experimenter's accomplice operated as the fifth member of each group and normally reported his own opinion about the strategy to be followed after the others had already spoken. By pre-arrangement, the accomplice always suggested a correct solution on eleven of the fifteen trials, scattered randomly. His behavior thus appeared to the others as highly *competent*. However, as far as conformity was concerned, the accomplice behaved differently in each of three blocks of five trials. These variations were nonconformity (a) for all fifteen trials, (b) for the first ten trials, (c) for the first five trials, (d) for the last ten trials, and (e) for the last five trials. In a control condition, the confederate conformed on all trials to the rules adopted by the group. Nonconformity consisted mainly of speaking out of turn and questioning the agreement about majority rule. Hollander's principal manipulation was the timing of such deviant behavior; it could occur early or late in the series of trials or not at all.

Influence effected by the accomplice was measured as the number of trials on which his recommended solution to the problem was adopted by the group. Analysis of the results showed that more of the accomplice's suggestions were accepted in the later trials, as his competence in the task became increasingly evident. Furthermore, his solutions were accepted more often following a series of five trials in which he had conformed. This finding was consistent with Hollander's hypothesis that past conformity is essential to the wielding of influence in a group.

We may interpret Hollander's findings in essentially the same way that we did Schachter's. An individual who performs in a manner consistent with that of the other members of a group reinforces those with whom he interacts. If he deviates from what others are doing, he disrupts or disturbs their ongoing behaviors and thereby becomes a source of aversive stimulation. He will subsequently be responded to in kind; his suggestions will not be accepted. If, on the other hand, he has demonstrated competence at the task, his instrumental value to the other members will more than offset the aversive effects of his nonconformity. And if he has demonstrated both competence and conformity in the group, his behavior will in general have become positively reinforcing, including actions that might otherwise have been perceived as deviant and aversive. In short, nonconformity will be aversive only when it has no value or utility to the group. When nonconformity by an individual is instrumental in assisting the other members to behave in ways that are positively reinforced, the nonconformity may be perceived as innovation and be welcomed.

Not too surprisingly, a number of investigators have found that individuals who have reason to believe they possess greater than average competence in a task are less susceptible to social influence than those who are not convinced of their own ability. This has been demonstrated primarily in situations where judgments voiced by the other members of a group are at variance with certain objective features of the stimulus. A naïve subject in these circumstances will be less apt to bend to majority pressure if he has been given evidence of his own competence in responding to the requirements of the task.

In one experiment concerned with this problem, Samuelson (1957) arranged to convey to certain of his subjects the impression that their performances in identifying tachistoscopically presented nonsense syllables demonstrated superior visual acuity. When making similar attempts at recognition in a group situation, these subjects conformed less to guesses made by others in the group than subjects who had not been convinced of their superior vision. Fagen (1963) also found that subjects who were given evidence of their ability at a task were less inclined to conform to others performing the same task. We would attribute these findings to the fact that reinforcement of behavior that is primarily under the control of task stimuli will increase the frequency with which these features of the situation control future performances. That is, the individual whose responses have been reinforced by the experimenter following attention to certain dimensions of a task will tend to be guided more by these dimensions than by the performance of others. The obverse of this would also be expected, namely, that reinforcement for patterning one's behavior after that of others would tend to reduce the frequency with which responses are controlled by the nonsocial features of a situation.

Merely witnessing another person's successful performance on a task may cause an individual to conform to that person's behavior rather than to the behavior of someone else who has been observed failing (Mausner, 1954). This would seem to be a relatively straightforward case of behavior coming under the control of stimuli that have been paired with reward rather than with punishment. Past experience in similar situations would have tended to reinforce the observer for emulating successful rather than unsuccessful models and to increase the frequency of this behavior in the future.

Personality Factors

A systematic program of investigation into the basis for individual differences in conformity behavior has been undertaken by Crutchfield (1955). In order to avoid using an actual group situation to study conformity, Crutchfield devised an interesting and economical procedure for simulating group interaction. Five subjects are seated in booths separated by partitions. Displayed before each subject are four signal lights, one for each of the other subjects. Each subject also has several switches by means of which he can indicate his responses to stimuli presented on a screen visible to all members of the group. The signal lights tell him how the other members of the group have responded to the stimulus.

In reality, all of the signal lights are controlled by the experimenter, who is stationed at a master control panel out of sight of the subjects. Thus, the same pattern of lights can be displayed in each of the booths, regardless of how the subjects have actually responded. Furthermore, each subject can be led to think he is the last to respond, so his behavior will be influenced by his knowledge of how the other group members have "responded."

In one experiment, Crutchfield presented his subjects with a display consisting of a standard line and five comparison lines from which the subject must choose one equal in length to the standard. The experimenter controlled the information given to the subjects so that each thought the others had judged Line 5 to be correct. Actually, Line 4 matched the standard, and this fact must have been apparent to many of the subjects. Nevertheless, out of fifty male subjects fifteen (30 per cent) responded in conformity to the false judgments ostensibly rendered by the other four members of the group. The remaining thirty-five subjects reported correctly despite the fact that their responses were at variance with those of the other subjects. When judging whether a circle or a star presented together had the greater area, 46 per cent of the subjects conformed to the information that the others had judged the star as larger. (Actually, the circle was about one third larger in area.) In general, Crutchfield found that conformity behavior was more frequent when the stimulus figures were less well structured. One such task involved the completion of a number series, for which there was actually no logically correct solution. Faced with this problem, 79 per cent of the subjects conformed to a spurious group consensus which fixed upon an arbitrary and irrational answer.

Responses required of the subjects ranged from simple dimensional judgments to choices involving attitudes and personal preferences. When each subject was asked to indicate which of two simple line drawings he preferred, only one man out of fifty agreed with a spurious group consensus on what was obviously the inferior of the two figures. In some of the other situations, there were wide individual differences among the subjects in susceptibility to influence by consensus. One subject's judgments were influenced on seventeen of the twenty-one experimental items, whereas several others conformed on only one or two occasions. These differences in generalized conformity behavior appeared to be correlated with certain personality traits. When evaluated on the basis of a battery of standardized personality assessment procedures, those subjects who tended to conform to the group norm in a variety of tasks could be described as follows (Crutchfield, 1955):

Submissive, compliant, and overly accepting of authority
Narrow range of interests
Inhibited and overcontrolled
Unable to make decisions without vacillation or delay
Confused, disorganized, and unadaptive under stress
Lacks insight into his own behavior

On the other hand, those subjects who exhibited extreme independence in the various situations had the following characteristics:

An effective leader
Ascendant rather than submissive in relations with others
Skillful at persuasion

Active and vigorous
Seeks and enjoys aesthetic and sensuous experiences
Efficient and capable

No differences were found between "conformers" and "nonconformers" on scales designed to detect "neuroticism." However, conformers tended to describe their parents in more highly idealized, less critical fashion than nonconformers. In addition, the nonconformers more frequently reported a personal history of broken homes or an unstable home environment than did the conformers. Two measures of intellectual competence yielded higher scores for the nonconformers.

In still other experiments with college students and adult females, Crutchfield found some interesting examples of conformity in certain controversial matters. For example, subjects were asked to express agreement or disagreement with the following statement: "Free speech being a privilege rather than a right, it is proper for a society to suspend free speech whenever it feels threatened." Only 19 per cent of a group of control (uninfluenced) subjects agreed with this viewpoint. Among experimental subjects who were led to believe that the other members of their groups had unanimously agreed with the statement, 58 per cent expressed agreement. Another item offered the subjects a choice of five alternatives in response to the following question: "Which of the following do you feel is the most important problem facing our country today: (a) economic recession, (b) educational facilities, (c) subversive activities, (d) mental health, (e) crime and corruption?" Only 12 per cent of control subjects chose "subversive activities" as the most important problem. But when given the spurious information that their group had unanimously picked "subversive activities," 48 per cent of the experimental subjects made this choice. Crutchfield concludes, ". . . here we have evidence of the operation of powerful conformity influences in the expression of opinion on matters of critical social controversy" (1955, p. 197).

The power of the group to influence individual judgments was increased when the experimenter announced his concurrence with the group consensus on those trials involving such objectively scorable items as perceptual judgments, logical solutions, and vocabulary matching. Apparently, the prestige of the experimenter provided an additional measure of social reinforcement for conformity by the subjects.

When the individual is informed about the nature of a group consensus, as in Crutchfield's experiments, his behavior is partially controlled by this knowledge. The probability that he will actually conform to this consensus is obviously determined by a number of factors. These include the individual's history of reinforcement in similar situations and the extent to which the occasion allows for alternative judgments or interpretations. It is amply clear that simulated consensus in situations like those studied by Crutchfield does not control the behavior of all subjects. Conformity in the face of consensus is obviously predictable only when we know a great deal about both the individual and the occasion. Despite certain artificialities inherent in a laboratory setting, it can be seen that the situational features that support conformity behavior are susceptible to a degree of control and manipulation.

There remains, then, some doubt as to whether conformity is a generalized personality disposition that is manifested in a variety of social situations. Back and Davis (1965) adopted Crutchfield's technique in determining the extent to which subjects would conform in a perceptual judgment situation. They next obtained self-reports from the subjects indicating their degree of acceptance of peer group norms as well as acceptance of authority pressures. The investigators report a small but consistent trend for persons who conformed in one situation to report conformity in the others as well. Vaughan (1964) evaluated conforming behavior in four tasks designed to measure conformity behavior as a function of social acquiescence, direct command, normative pressure, and group pressure. His subjects were sixty-four female college undergraduates. Conformity to both group pressure and normative pressure were significantly correlated, but correlations between the other variables were low. Vaughan concludes that individuals cannot in general be described as behaving consistently in a conforming or nonconforming manner. Situational factors and the manner in which an individual perceives the situation are seen as the major variables that determine whether conformity will occur. This problem obviously deserves further study. At present we can conclude only that conformity may be a generalized disposition in some individuals, but for other persons it is specific to the situation.

Age, Sex, and Birth Order

Crutchfield (1955) reported that female students exhibited conformity significantly more frequently in a variety of situations than did males. A similar finding is reported by Whittaker (1965). Tuddenham (1961) found not only that females conformed more than males but that children conformed more than adults. Lest we imply agreement with the popular notion that women are more compliant and submissive than men, it should be pointed out that females may show greater evidence of conformity only in situations that they perceive as having primarily masculine relevance. McDavid (1965) pretested a number of statements to determine which ones would be judged as having reference to male or female interests. Later, thirty-four male and thirty-four female subjects participated in a Crutchfield-type situation, where the degree of compliance with simulated majority agreement was determined. The female subjects conformed no more often than the males on items of either feminine or neutral interest. But they did agree more frequently with statements they regarded as having more relevance for males when group consensus accepted these statements.

Several studies have found that firstborns are more susceptible to social influence than laterborns (Dittes, 1961; Schachter, 1964). In an earlier investigation, Schachter (1959) discovered that female students who had been told they were about to participate in an experiment involving painful electric shocks more frequently chose to be with other girls during a waiting period than did subjects who had been given no such information. Further analysis of these data revealed that firstborn and only children were prominent among those who made this affiliative choice. Anticipation of a stressful or unpleasant experience appears to enhance the reinforcing value of other persons, especially if the other persons are in similar jeopardy. Having established that the girls preferred to wait with others who were also anticipating a painful experience, Schachter concluded, "Misery doesn't love just any kind of company, it loves only miserable company" (1959, p. 24).

Why should firstborns exhibit this type of behavior to a greater extent than laterborns, and how does this fact help explain their apparently greater tendency to conform in many situations? The most probable explanation lies in the different types of parent-child interactions that have occurred in the case of firstborn or only children. In a comprehensive study of child-rearing practices by the mothers of five-year-olds, Sears, Maccoby, and Levin (1957) were able to distinguish between two broadly different approaches: love-oriented techniques and object-oriented techniques. Both make use of positive and aversive controls over the child's behavior, but a love-oriented pattern is distinguished by the expression or withholding of parental affection and approval, whereas the object-oriented pattern utilizes more tangible reinforcers, such as candy, toys, or physical punishment. The only child, because he does not have to share his attention with a sibling, interacts more frequently with his parents; consequently, he is more apt to be love-oriented than object-oriented. As McDavid and Harari (1968) point out, parents are likely to be more permissive and more solicitous of their firstborn and to spend more time interacting with him. As a result, these children will tend to acquire a larger repertoire of behaviors that are under the control of social stimuli and are maintained by social reinforcement.

An interesting bit of confirmatory evidence for this is found in the fact that firstborns are more likely than laterborns to be among the volunteers for psychological experiments (Capra and Dittes, 1962). However, Ward (1964) failed to replicate these findings, and later work has revealed that the relationship between birth order and affiliative behavior is more complex than first imagined. Both Becker and Carroll (1962) and Sampson (1962) did find that firstborn males were more sensitive to conformity pressures than laterborn. In a study in which the conditions of recruitment were manipulated so as to provide opportunity for participation in a group, individual, or isolation experiment, Wolf and Weiss (1965) found that firstborn males volunteered more often for the group experiment, but only when they were under some pressure to do so. Females do not follow this pattern, and additional research will be needed to disclose differences in the socialization patterns of males and females that lead them to react differently to requests for volunteers in psychological experiments.

Carrigan and Julian (1966) asked sixth-grade students to pick one of four brief stories that best fitted a picture projected on a screen. The pictures were taken from a projective device called the Thematic Apperception Test. While being shown the pictures, some of the students were told which story had been selected by the previous year's class as being the most appropriate. Conformity was indicated by concurrence with this choice. Analysis of the results showed that firstborns were more readily influenced than laterborns, and that females conformed more readily to suggestion than males. It has also been reported by Smart (1965) that firstborn males in a sample of 370 college students were proportionately more affiliated with social clubs. Altogether, there is substantial evidence to support the contention that birth order affects the frequency with which the individual acquires performances as a result of "social" rather than "object" reinforcement. The more he comes to depend upon social reinforcement, the more he will tend to exhibit conforming behavior. "Acceptance of an individual by other members of a social group," as McDavid and Harari (1968) point out, "is ordinarily directly contingent upon his behaving in accordance with the collective standards and conventions of the group" (p. 87).

Birth order as a determinant of the frequency with which an individual would emit reinforcements to a speaker was examined by Weiss (1966). Specifically, it was predicted that firstborn and only children, because of their greater sensitivity to affiliative cues, would be more responsive to a speaker than laterborns. Each of seventeen male and twelve female subjects listened to a tape-recorded speech and pressed a button whenever they felt impelled to make a rejoinder that would help to "maintain rapport." Significantly more firstborn or only-child subjects fell above the 50th percentile in terms of number of reinforcements emitted to the speaker. So it appears that birth order may lead to learning experiences that cause one to be more reinforcing to others in addition to being more susceptible himself to social influence.

Public versus Private Conformity

A question that inevitably arises in connection with conformity behavior is whether the performance in question reflects a stable or simply a transitory social influence effect. Does the behavior persist beyond the group situation in which it is produced? This general problem is reviewed by Allen (1965), who suggests that four different combinations of conformity are possible: (a) public conformity and private agreement, (b) public conformity and private disagreement, (c) public nonconformity and public disagreement, (d) public nonconformity and private agreement.

In two of these instances, there is a correspondence between public and private response (a and c), while in the remaining two instances there is a lack of such correspondence (b and d).

The apparent discrepancies that Allen describes between public behavior and private conviction are resolved by reformulation of the problem. By dealing with the concepts "public" and "private" we obscure the nature of the variables that control the behavior in which we are interested. A functional analysis requires that we consider any behavior designated "conformity" as an operant performance controlled by two kinds of stimuli, those that precede it (discriminative) and those that follow it (reinforcing). Obviously, certain stimuli set the occasion for behavior that conforms to some modal pattern of a group, whereas other stimuli do not. Accordingly, the individual's behavior is more or less conforming, that is to say, more or less invariant, depending upon the situation. The matter of "public" versus "private" reduces to a concern with the particular discriminative stimuli governing the occurrence of a performance that by comparison with the behavior of others is regarded as conforming or deviant. Another way of looking at this problem is to say that when an individual performs similarly both in the presence and in the absence of a group, his behavior is under relatively broad or diffuse stimulus control. On the other hand, if he performs differently when alone than when in a group, his behavior is under relatively narrow or precise stimulus control.

Conformity behavior, then, apparently will generalize to situations having elements in common with occasions on which such behavior has been socially reinforced. The critical elements, as we have suggested, are other individuals behaving in some normative fashion; when these individuals are not present, conformity to the norms that they have established will not necessarily appear.

Forced compliance. Festinger (1957), has described what he calls "forced compliance," a procedure by which an individual "... may come to privately accept the opinions and standards which his neighbors have" (p. 98). He cites as examples a child who accepts practicing on the piano after initially having been coerced into this behavior, or a person who comes to accept the gardening standards of a new neighborhood after first adopting these standards under the impact of community opinion.

In an experimental situation, a desirable set of conditions for bringing about such a change in behavior, according to Festinger, would be either a reward incentive for compliance or the threat of punishment for noncompliance. These specifications are, of course, quite consistent with the postulates of reinforcement theory. Festinger illustrates this procedure with data from two unpublished experiments (Burdick, 1955; McBride, 1954). High school students were organized into discussion groups of five to seven members. At the outset of the experiment, they were asked to indicate in writing by "yes" or "no" whether they thought a curfew should be lifted on the nights of high school athletic contests. A fictitious tally of these votes was given to each student to convey the impression that everyone else in the group disagreed with him. The subjects were then asked to discuss the matter by exchanging notes. Actually, the experimenter, who handled the exchange, substituted prepared notes urging each participant to change his opinion. After fifteen minutes of this written "discussion," the subjects in each group again indicated publicly their opinions about the curfew issue. Following this procedure, a final, *anonymous* vote was taken on the curfew.

The control subjects (N = 116) were treated as described above. Two groups of experimental subjects were either offered a reward for changing their opinion (N = 135) or threatened with loss of a privilege if they did not change their opinion (N = 124). Each of these contingencies was communicated by notes prepared in advance by the experimenter but appearing to have come from the other members. The results showed that only 14 per cent of the subjects who were offered an incentive and 12 per cent of those who were threatened with punishment changed their answers on the second administration of the questionnaire immediately following the "exchange" of notes. All of these subjects reverted to their initial opinions on the final, anonymous questionnaire. Their conformity to majority opinion was apparently public rather than private. In contrast, only 3 per cent of the control subjects complied with majority influence in the absence of either incentive or threat.

An average of 12 per cent of the subjects in all three conditions (incentive, threat, and control) revealed private opinion change at the final interrogation. Rather surprisingly, more of the control subjects (11 per cent) displayed change when reporting anonymously than when reporting publicly. The reason for this is not entirely clear, but Festinger leans to the interpretation that the discomfiture of perceiving themselves in disagreement with so many of their fellows led the control subjects to change their opinions privately, even though they did not reveal publicly the impact of either an incentive or a threat.

We shall consider this general problem in greater detail in Chapter 11 in relation to research on persuasion and attitude change.

Because of the ubiquitous nature of learning to conform, much of our behavior can be controlled through such relatively simple devices as advice, admonition, or instruction. These have been followed sufficiently more often by satisfactory than by aversive consequences to give them control over a wide range of performances. In fact, some of the early sociologists considered conformity in its most dramatic forms — leadership, fashions, crowd behavior — to be simply manifestations of suggestion (Asch, 1961). Instruction, or suggestion, is often delivered in such a way as to conceal its function in effecting conformity to some norm or standard. There is even a possibility that subtle social influence is more effective than direct influence, since it circumvents what Brehm (1966) has called "reactance" or negativism.

Manipulation of Reinforcement

Walker and Heyns (1962) report several interesting experiments in which reinforcement contingencies were manipulated in such a way as to conceal the nature of the influence process. In one study, eighty-two subjects were invited to participate in a test of extrasensory perception. Their assignment was to guess what someone in another room was thinking. Small groups of the students were first taken to a room occupied by the "sender." This individual had before him a control panel by means of which he could signal the subjects' room, located some distance away. When the subjects returned to their room, they were shown a panel containing lights that corresponded to the buttons on the "sender's" panel. On signal from the experimenter, who was seated with the subjects, the "sender" was to start thinking about which button he intended to press. At the same time, each subject tried to "receive" this message. The subjects then reported their guesses aloud. These were recorded by the experimenter, who then signaled the "sender" to press the button about which he had been thinking so that the corresponding light on the subjects' panel would be illuminated.

Actually, the "sender" played no part in the experiment, except to deceive the subjects about the procedure. Another experimenter in an adjacent room made note of the guesses voiced by the subjects and then activated the light that corresponded to either a majority or a minority guess. The subjects responded in a different order on each of the twenty trials, so that position effects alone would not influence their choices. A maximum of conformity would be evidenced if all the subjects responded in the same manner as the first one who reported on each trial. Nonconformity would be represented by a highly varied pattern of responses by the subjects.

Some of the groups were reinforced for conformity behavior, other groups were reinforced for nonconformity. This was accomplished by the hidden experimenter, who turned on the signal light that had been chosen either by many or by few of the subjects. Thus, the subjects were rewarded either for imitating one another or for behaving independently. It should be noted that the first subject to report his guess had to choose a light not previously chosen. The second subject could make the same choice as the first subject, and thus conform, or he could react independently. When conformity was reinforced, there was a tendency on later trials for the subjects to begin to imitate one another, with the result that fewer lights were chosen. Reinforcement of nonconformity resulted in less imitation of one another's choices, with the result that more lights were chosen as the trials progressed. The results with eight lights and seven subjects in each group are shown in Figure 4.2, page 130.

Walker and Heyns summarize their findings as follows:

> These experiments seem to demonstrate that groups can be made to appear as "individualists" or "conformists" almost at will through subtle but never-

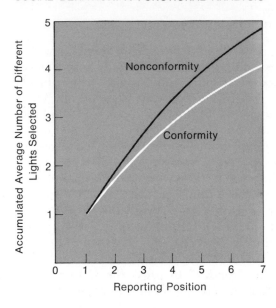

Figure 4.2
*Conformity and nonconformity
behavior under conditions of
differential social reinforcement.* (After Walker and Heyns,
1962)

theless effective differential reward for the two forms of behavior. Furthermore, these effects can be produced without those involved being in any
sense aware either of the effort made to control their behavior or of the
direction which they are being induced to take (1962, p. 75).

That the experience of prior success is sufficiently reinforcing to maintain a particular class of behavior was demonstrated by Kidd and Campbell
(1955). Their subjects first worked on a group anagram task under conditions of success, partial success, and failure. Following this experience,
they estimated the number of times a light flickered during a five-second
period. After each trial, the experimenter reported an "average estimate"
for each three-person group. Conformity on subsequent trials was measured as a shift away from the individual's original judgments and toward
this reported estimate. Such shifts in reported judgments occurred only
among subjects who had enjoyed success in the anagram task. Those who
had experienced either partial success or failure did not show evidence of
conformity. It would appear that the experience of positive reinforcement
in a group situation might lead the individual to expect similar reinforcement in the same group on a different problem. Approval was rendered in
each instance by the experimenter, so the subjects may have simply generalized to the second task their experiences of success or relative failure
on the first task. That is, those who had been positively reinforced for a
"group effort" in the anagram task conformed to feedback information in
the judgmental situation. Those who had found their experience in the
first task either nonrewarding (partial success) or aversive (failure) did not
acquire a disposition to perform in a manner that was consistent with information provided by the experimenter.

Research on Deviancy

Freedman and Doob (1968) carried out an experimental program to discover how the self-perception of deviancy influences behavior and how persons who do not share this self-concept differ from those who do. Rather than attempting to identify deviants in society, these investigators tried to manipulate deviancy experimentally. Subjects took a series of personality tests, after which they were shown their composite scores in comparison to those of four or five other persons who had been tested at the same time. These "feedback sheets" showed the subjects either as being deviant, by scoring near the end of the distribution, or as standing near the mean of the group.

Having thus suggested to the subject that he was either similar or dissimilar to the other members of his group with respect to certain personality traits, the experimenters introduced additional procedures designed to measure the effects of this evaluation on other performances. Among other findings, they report that (a) deviant subjects prefer to associate more with other deviants than do nondeviants, (b) deviants prefer others who are deviant in the same respects as themselves rather than those who deviate in different ways, and (c) nondeviants prefer to punish rather than to reward deviants, whereas deviants choose for other deviants reward instead of punishment.

There was some evidence that subjects who were led to believe they were deviant were more compliant with social influence than those not so informed. However, several qualifications must be placed upon this finding. Freedman and Doob conclude:

> When the situation involves little direct confrontation of the subject and the source of the pressure, deviants conform, change their attitudes, and comply no more or sometimes less than nondeviants. When the subject is confronted directly by the person making the request, deviants comply more than nondeviants, and this difference is particularly strong when the request is being made by a nondeviant (p. 146).

As these investigators admit, their manipulations induced a very specialized and limited type of deviancy. Whether or not their results can be generalized to nonexperimental situations, therefore, is open to question. Assuming that their results are generally valid, it is not difficult to restate them in terms of controlling and reinforcing stimuli. For example, it is the common experience of most individuals that nonconformity, or deviancy, either fails to be reinforced or is punished. The aversive consequences of deviancy are usually administered by nondeviants, hence a deviant could reasonably anticipate more favorable reactions from someone like himself. The finding that nondeviants tend to punish rather than reward deviancy is of course consistent with other experimental findings.

An increase in the degree of compliance by deviants in face-to-face confrontation with those whom they believe to be nondeviants would be interpreted as behavior that is instrumental in avoiding the aversive reactions that a deviant anticipates, particularly from a nondeviant. It is also possible that the emotional reaction to being told that they had deviant personalities made the subjects less cooperative than they might have been otherwise. Tangential evidence for this interpretation comes from a mail survey conducted by Freedman and Doob, in which there were fewer returns from respondents who were approached as having households "very different" from others in the area than from those who were told their households were "very similar" to others in the area. Apparently, there is something aversive about being informed that one is "different," and the behaviors under this type of verbal control are not the same as those controlled by knowledge that one is average, or typical. One hesitates to venture further into theoretical speculations on these matters until more data are available.

Many instances of apparent nonconformity may be understood if we recall that behavior is not always under the control of its long-term consequences. Of greater importance in shaping the behavior of some nonconformists are the immediately reinforcing effects. Thus, many "criminal" acts are committed because the immediate consequences are reinforcing to the offender, and he either discounts or fails to contemplate the eventual aversive consequences of his actions. One can cite countless instances where the behavior of individuals is uneconomic in the long run but produces immediate reinforcers, hence is maintained. Overeating, smoking, or reckless driving are all examples of this. To understand certain extremes of behavior, whether these involve dress, manner, or abiding by the law, one must look to the immediate consequences of these behaviors in the subcultures with which the individual is in contact. His conduct in these groups is not unusual, and no other groups really can be said to control his behavior.

Summary   One consequence of social interaction is that most of the individuals in a stable group exhibit very marked similarities of behavior. They are said to *conform* to certain standards or modal patterns of behavior that are reinforced by the other members. Individuals whose performances are at variance with a particular group norm are said to *deviate* from that norm, although the behavior in question may conform to the pattern prevailing in some other group.

Imitative behavior has been demonstrated with both animals and children. In one type of imitation, a leader's performance provides the cues, or discriminative stimuli, to control the performance of a follower, which is subsequently reinforced. Imitation by observation occurs in children, who will learn to perform in a manner similar to that of a model whom they have seen rewarded. This is called *vicarious reinforcement,* and the follower's behavior is assumed to be under the control of either images or verbal processes that were generated during observation of the model. To the extent that a leader, or model, is behaving in accordance with some social norm, the effect of his influence on others will be in the direction of increased conformity. But, of course, deviant behavior can also be acquired by imitation, provided that it finds some measure of social support.

Conformity is maintained by both positive and negative reinforcement; that is, modal performances may be instrumental in either achieving reinforcement or avoiding punishment. Simply being "different" from others in dress or deportment frequently generates aversive consequences. Unless the nonconformity is reinforced in some manner, it will tend to diminish in frequency. Actually, the rather widespread occurrence of what the majority considers to be deviant patterns of behavior may be due to the fact that such behaviors are intermittently reinforced, hence are quite resistant to extinction.

By and large, individuals are influenced more by the modal performances of individuals in groups to which they are attracted than by those of individuals in groups that they find unattractive. Because deviant individuals interfere with the opportunities for reinforcement that others derive from a group activity, attempts are made to bring such persons "back into line." If they do not respond favorably to persuasion, they are derogated by the other members and rejected by the group. In other words, aversive nonconforming behavior tends to be punished.

An individual may deviate with impunity from group standards only if he has *status* in the group, that is, if he has demonstrated both competence and some degree of prior conformity. We would say that his behavior must have become positively reinforcing to the other members of a group if it is to become a model for their performances.

The rather broad spectrum of individual differences in conformity behavior may possibly be explained in terms of personality differences or variations in the dispositions that individuals have acquired to model their behavior after that of others. However, situational factors relating to the past reinforcement history of the individual seem to be the principal determinants of conformity and nonconformity.

When we say that a person conforms publicly but deviates privately from a group norm, we mean that his behavior is controlled by different stimulus variables when alone and in the presence of others. Identification of these critical stimuli enables us to predict the occurrence of behavior that is either congruent with or at variance with some standard. In general, the most likely performance will be one that has a history of positive or negative reinforcement under similar circumstances.

References

ALLEN, V. L.   Situational factors in conformity. In L. Berkowitz (Ed.), *Advances in experimental social psychology.* New York: Academic Press, 1965.

ASCH, S. E.   Issues in the study of social influences on judgment. In I. A. Berg and B. M. Bass (Eds.), *Conformity and deviation.* New York: Harper, 1961.

AZRIN, N. H., HOLZ, W. C., and HAKE, D. F.   Fixed-ratio punishment. *Journal of the Experimental Analysis of Behavior,* 1963, *6,* 141–148.

BACHRACH, A. J., CANDLAND, D. K., and GIBSON, J. T.   Group reinforcement of individual response experiments in verbal behavior. In I. A. Berg and B. M. Bass (Eds.), *Conformity and deviation.* New York: Harper, 1961.

BACK, K.   Influence through social communication. *Journal of Abnormal and Social Psychology,* 1951, *46,* 9–23.

BACK, K. W., and DAVIS, K. E.   Some personal and situational factors relevant to the consistency and prediction of conformity behavior. *Sociometry,* 1965, *28,* 227–240.

BANDURA, A.   Vicarious processes: A case of no-trial learning. In L. Berkowitz (Ed.), *Advances in experimental social psychology.* New York: Academic Press, 1965.

BANDURA, A., ROSS, DOROTHEA, and ROSS, SHEILA A.   Vicarious reinforcement and imitative learning. In A. W. Staats (Ed.), *Human learning.* New York: Holt, Rinehart and Winston, 1964.

BANDURA, A., and WALTERS, R. H.   *Social learning and personality development.* New York: Holt, Rinehart and Winston, 1963.

BECKER, S. W., and CARROLL, J.   Ordinal position and conformity. *Journal of Abnormal and Social Psychology,* 1962, *65,* 129–131.

BERGER, S. M.   Vicarious aspects of matched-dependent behavior. In E. C. Simmel, R. A. Hoppe, and G. A. Milton (Eds.), *Social facilitation and imitative behavior.* Boston: Allyn and Bacon, 1968.

BLAKE, R. R.   The other person in the situation. In R. Taguiri and L. Petrullo (Eds.), *Person perception and interpersonal behavior.* Stanford, Calif.: Stanford University Press, 1958.

BLAKE, R. R., MOUTON, JANE S., and HAIN, J. D.   Social forces in petition-signing. *Southwestern Social Science Quarterly,* 1956, *36,* 385–390.

BREHM, J. W.   *A theory of psychological reactance.* New York: Academic Press, 1966.

BURDICK, H.   The compliant behavior of deviates under conditions of threat. Unpublished Ph.D. dissertation, University of Minnesota, 1955.

CAMPBELL, D. T.   Conformity in psychology's theories of acquired behavioral dispositions. In I. A. Berg and B. M. Bass (Eds.), *Conformity and deviation.* New York: Harper, 1961.

CAPRA, P. C., and DITTES, J. E.   Birth order as a selective factor among volunteer subjects. *Journal of Abnormal and Social Psychology,* 1962, *64,* 302.

CARRIGAN, W. C., and JULIAN, J. W.   Sex and birth order differences in conformity as a function of need affiliation arousal. *Journal of Personality and Social Psychology,* 1966, *3,* 479–483.

CHURCH, R. M. Transmission of learned behavior between rats. *Journal of Abnormal and Social Psychology*, 1957, *54*, 163–165.

CRUTCHFIELD, R. S. Conformity and character. *American Psychologist*, 1955, *10*, 191–198.

DITTES, J. E. Birth order and vulnerability to differences in acceptance. *American Psychologist*, 1961, *16*, 358.

FAGEN, S. A. The effects of real and experimentally reported ability on confidence and conformity. *American Psychologist*, 1963, *18*, 357–358 (Abst.).

FERSTER, C. B. Withdrawal of positive reinforcement as punishment. *Science*, 1957, *126*, 509.

FESTINGER, L. *A theory of cognitive dissonance.* Evanston, Ill.: Row, Peterson, 1957.

FESTINGER, L., and THIBAUT, J. Interpersonal communication in small groups. *Journal of Abnormal and Social Psychology*, 1951, *46*, 92–99.

FREEDMAN, J. L., and DOOB, A. N. *Deviancy: The psychology of being different.* New York: Academic Press, 1968.

HOLLANDER, E. P. Competence and conformity in the acceptance of influence. *Journal of Abnormal and Social Psychology*, 1960, *61*, 365–369.

HOLLANDER, E. P., and WILLIS, R. H. Some current issues in the psychology of conformity and nonconformity. *Psychological Bulletin*, 1967, *68*, 62–76.

KIDD, J., and CAMPBELL, D. Conformity to groups as a function of group success. *Journal of Abnormal and Social Psychology*, 1955, *51*, 390–393.

KINSEY, A. C., POMEROY, W. B., and MARTIN, C. E. *Sexual behavior in the human male.* Philadelphia: W. B. Saunders, 1948.

KINSEY, A. C., POMEROY, W. B., MARTIN, C. E., and GEBHARD, P. H. *Sexual behavior in the human female.* Philadelphia: W. B. Saunders, 1953.

LOGAN, F. A. *Incentive: How the conditions of reinforcement affect the performance of rats.* New Haven: Yale University Press, 1960.

LOGAN, F. A., and WAGNER, A. R. *Reward and punishment.* Boston: Allyn and Bacon, 1965.

MAUSNER, B. The effect of one partner's success in a relevant task on the interaction of observer pairs. *Journal of Abnormal and Social Psychology*, 1954, *49*, 557–560.

MCBRIDE, E. The effects of public and private changes of opinion on intragroup communication. Unpublished Ph.D. dissertation, University of Minnesota, 1954.

MCDAVID, J. W. Effects of ambiguity of environmental cues upon learning to imitate. *Journal of Abnormal and Social Psychology*, 1962, *65*, 381–386.

MCDAVID, J. W. The sex variables in conforming behavior. Technical Report No. 8, Office of Naval Research Contract, 1965.

MCDAVID, J. W., and HARARI, H. *Social psychology: Individuals, groups, societies.* New York: Harper and Row, 1968.

MILLER, N. E. Studies of fear as an acquirable drive. I: Fear as motivation and fear reduction as reinforcement in the learning of new responses. *Journal of Experimental Psychology*, 1948, *38*, 89–101.

MILLER, N. E., and DOLLARD, J. *Social learning and imitation.* New Haven: Yale University Press, 1941.

MOWRER, O. H. *Learning theory and behavior.* New York: Wiley, 1960.

RAVEN, B. H. Social influence on opinions and the communication of related content. *Journal of Abnormal and Social Psychology,* 1959, 58, 119–128.

SAMPSON, E. E. Birth order, need achievement, and conformity. *Journal of Abnormal and Social Psychology,* 1962, 64, 155–159.

SAMUELSON, F. Conforming behavior under two conditions of conflict in the cognitive field. *Journal of Abnormal and Social Psychology,* 1957, 55, 181–187.

SCHACHTER, S. Deviation, rejection, and communication. *Journal of Abnormal and Social Psychology,* 1951, 46, 190–207. Copyright 1951 by the American Psychological Association. Data in Table 4.1 of this book reprinted by permission.

SCHACHTER, S. *The psychology of affiliation.* Stanford, Calif.: Stanford University Press, 1959.

SCHACHTER, S. Birth order and sociometric choice. *Journal of Abnormal and Social Psychology,* 1964, 68, 453–456.

SEARS, R. R., MACCOBY, ELEANOR E., and LEVIN, H. *Patterns of child rearing.* New York: Harper and Row, 1957.

SHERIF, M., and SHERIF, CAROLYN. *Reference groups: Exploration into conformity and deviation of adolescents.* New York: Harper and Row, 1964.

SMART, R. G. Social group membership, leadership, and birth order. *Journal of Social Psychology,* 1965, 67, 221–225.

THIBAUT, J., and STRICKLAND, L. Psychological set and social conformity. *Journal of Personality,* 1956, 25, 115–129.

TUDDENHAM, R. D. Studies in conformity and yielding: A summary and interpretation. Final report. Office of Naval Research Contract, 1961.

VAUGHAN, G. M. The trans-situational aspect of conforming behavior. *Journal of Personality,* 1964, 32, 335–354.

VERPLANCK, W. S. The control of the content of conversation: Reinforcement of statements of opinion. *Journal of Abnormal and Social Psychology,* 1955, 51, 668–676.

WALKER, E. L., and HEYNS, R. W. *An anatomy for conformity.* Englewood Cliffs, N.J.: Prentice-Hall, 1962.

WARD, C. D. A further examination of birth order as a selective factor among volunteer subjects. *Journal of Abnormal and Social Psychology,* 1964, 69, 311–313.

WEISS, R. L. Some determinants of emitted reinforcing behavior: Listener reinforcement and birth order. *Journal of Personality and Social Psychology,* 1966, 3, 489–492.

WHITTAKER, J. O. Sex differences and susceptibility to interpersonal persuasion. *Journal of Social Psychology,* 1965, 66, 91–96.

WOLF, A., and WEISS, J. H. Birth order, recruitment conditions, and volunteering preferences. *Journal of Personality and Social Psychology,* 1965, 2, 269–273.

Social Factors in

Perception and Judgment

Writing in 1913, for the benefit of his students, E. B. Titchener observed that "Stable objects and substantial things belong, not to the world of science, physical or psychological, but only to the world of common sense" (p. 16). The world of common sense, as Titchener was well aware, does not always correspond to the physical world. Perhaps the most straightforward example of this is afforded by those experiences that we term illusions. Consider the lines in Figure 5.1, for example. Which is longer, the vertical or the horizontal line?

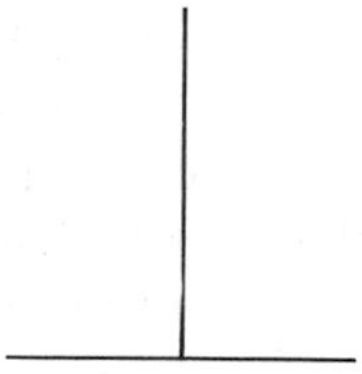

Figure 5.1
An example of a discrepancy between actual and perceived length.

This illusion, familiar to most students in psychology, illustrates the core problem in studying those responses that we term perceptual. In this case, there appear to be two stages to the response process: one private and the other public. First we make a judgment based on what we perceive, or on experience, and then we report which of the two lines is longer. Does one's verbal report always match his private judgment? Suppose one is in a room with three other persons, each of whom reports in turn that the horizontal line is clearly longer. What will he report? No experiment has been done using this particular stimulus configuration, but the problem we have posed has been attacked in other ways by a number of investigators, and we will consider these shortly.

Just what is the scientific status of such postulated events as perceptions and judgments? Admittedly, these terms refer to private experiences that are immediately accessible only by introspection. Titchener recognized this problem sixty years ago and asked, "How can psychology be anything more than a body of personal beliefs and individual opinions?" In answer, he reasoned that fundamental agreements in the reports of different observers provide a basis for establishing the scientific validity of the events upon which their observations focus. This viewpoint has undergone considerable refinement, and its evolution has led, in its currently most acceptable form, to the general proposition that perception refers to a class of stimulus-response functions, where responses are observed as dependent upon systematic changes in certain dimensions of the stimulus (Graham, 1958). Titchener's use of introspective data, however, would not begin to meet Graham's criterion that responses be restricted to clearly defined alternatives having scalar properties.

Some Operational Definitions

"Whatever the word perception may or may not mean," assert Schoenfeld and Cumming (1963), "one thing must be true if it is to be of any use whatever to a natural science of behavior; it must show up, or evidence itself, in observable behavior" (p. 215). Because those phenomena that we call perceptual are not adequately covered by the $S \rightarrow R$ formula, these writers suggest that another representation be used, namely, $S \rightarrow R_1R_2$. In this restatement of the familiar stimulus-response paradigm, it is suggested that R_1 is an initial response to S and that R_2 is conditional upon the occurrence of R_1. If we apply this symbolic notation to a situation in which someone is asked, "Do you recognize that man over there?" and the answer is "No," we have designated the question as S, the reporting response as R_2, and the perceptual event as R_1. Study and analysis of R_1, the perceptual response, is legitimate and informative, so long as we anchor it to S and R_2. This definition of perception is consistent with the position taken by Postman (1963): "The term *perceptual* . . . denotes a disposition or process inferred on the basis of observed stimulus-response relationships" (p. 41).

Another avenue to the definition of the terms perception and judgment is by way of the operations through which they are studied. If I give verbal labels to two figures having different geometric properties, as for example O and X (calling them *oh* and *ex*), I can determine whether or not you perceive any difference by instructing you to press a key when I show you O but not when I show you X. Even at very brief exposure durations, say 1/100 second, you probably will discriminate between these figures with a high degree of accuracy, as evidenced by the fact that you always press the correct key. Now, if I make the discrimination somewhat more difficult, say by presenting you with the figures O and Q (called *oh* and *kew*), it is likely that you will press the key not just when O is shown but occasionally also when Q is shown, particularly at 1/100-second exposures. We shall assume that your key-pressing behavior is dependent upon some prior perceptual discrimination that you have made. The fact that you press the key on some trials and not on others suggests that your perceptions differ. If I observe that twenty subjects never fail to discriminate correctly between O and X, but occasionally confuse O and Q, then I have learned something about their perceptual capacities as well as something about the discriminability of the figures. I also conclude that we (the subjects and I) probably perceive these figures in the same way, although I can never have any direct evidence of this based on an actual sharing of perceptual experiences.

To repeat, we make assumptions about the perceptions of other individuals on the basis of observable behaviors. Why not just limit our concern to behavior and not worry about perception? This question has, in fact, been asked quite seriously by some psychologists. So far as predicting behavior is concerned, it is probably not necessary that we make inferences about private events to which we can never have direct access. But it certainly is a matter of psychological interest to know how our fellow men perceive the world; the fact that our inferences about their perceptions must be based on their behavior does not make the topic of perception any less intriguing. For the clinical psychologist, the problem of individual idiosyncrasies in perception is of obvious importance. The paranoid individual, for example, may taste "poison" in his food, see "spies" following him, and hear "people talking about him," when in reality none of these things is occurring. It may be possible to predict the behavioral consequences of his delusions simply by recording the circumstances in which bizarre reactions are observed. But for a more adequate understanding of his problem one would have to appreciate the fact that his perceptual world is quite different from that of nearly everyone else.

What about judgment? How does judgment differ from perception, and what are the operations by which it is rendered public? Rendering a judgment involves making a *discriminated response* in accordance with some instruction. For example, the figures O and o are perceived as different, and one can perceive the difference without necessarily verbalizing the basis for it. If instructed to indicate which is the *larger* of the two, then a judgment or decision must be made, in this instance a judgment with respect to size. If one is instructed to indicate which is more elliptical, then a different judgment is involved, one involving shape. Note that judgments about either size or shape may be indicated by the same overt response, in this case, pointing. The act, or operation, of pointing does not by itself tell us which of the two judgments has been made. Rather, we infer this from the instructions that were given. In short, the perception of a difference can lead to specific judgments which, in turn, are communicated by some instrumental response, such as pointing or verbalizing.

A music lover may listen to a concert for the sheer sensuous pleasure that he experiences. His enjoyment, indeed, may depend to a large extent upon his ability to perceive nuances in pitch, loudness, and rhythm; but it is doubtful that he meditates upon these discriminable aspects of the musical pattern while he is enjoying them. The music critic, on the other hand, behaves under a different set of "instructions." He attends to the tonal qualities, phrasing, pace, and other attributes of the music and makes judgments relative to the excellence of the performance in comparison with certain standards that he has acquired from past experience. The devotee relaxes in enjoyment of the auditory experience, while the critic is busy judging the conductor and the musicians in terms of specified criteria. Here, in a complex real-life situation, is the difference between perception and judgment. The two are closely related, but they may be studied separately by employing different operations.

Now let us turn our attention from these everyday situations to the laboratory and see what psychologists have learned about the impact of social variables on perception and judgment. Most of the experimental work in this area has been done in the past thirty years, and a great deal of controversy has developed with regard to both theory and methodology.

Judgmental Processes

Autokinetic Movement

An interesting visual phenomenon that has been known for a long time is the apparent movement of a point of light against an otherwise dark background. This can be experienced in the night sky by looking at a single star or, better, in the laboratory by looking at one small light source in a totally dark room. The light will appear to move despite efforts by the observer to "hold" it stationary, and this effect is called *autokinetic movement*. In the early 1930's a psychologist named Muzafer Sherif became interested in the autokinetic phenomenon as a means of demonstrating the formation of social norms (Sherif, 1966). One of the key findings in social psychology is that individuals often tend to behave in rather similar fashion when they are in groups. This trend toward uniformity of response in some circumstances can be referred to as the development of a social norm.

Why should Sherif have used autokinetic movement in his experiments on social norms? For one thing, social influences on perception can be detected most readily in situations where the controlling stimuli are not too clearly structured. It is quite unlikely that I will perceive a street light moving about, even if two or three other persons report such movement. More likely I will judge the other individuals as either deluded or inebriated. Nearly everyone, however, perceives movement of a pinpoint of light in the dark, even though the light is stationary. Under these conditions, it is possible for social influence to operate, because one's perceptual experience is not so strongly determined by the external stimulus.

Sherif's experiments. Sherif's first objective was to determine the manner in which his individual subjects perceived the autokinetic effect. The subjects were male students at Columbia University and New York University. Each was seated at a table with a telegraph key about five meters from the light source, which was projected through a small hole in a metal box by means of a shutter operated by the experimenter. The following instructions were given in written form: "When the room is completely dark, I shall give you the signal *Ready,* and then show you a point of light. After a short time the light will start to move. As soon as you see it move press the key. A few seconds later the light will disappear. Then tell me the distance it moved. Try to make your estimates as accurate as possible."

Each of the nineteen subjects who participated was observed to establish his own individual range of perceived movement. These preliminary results established the fact that autokinetic movement is responsive to individual differences and that such differences can be described quantitatively. Sherif's next step was to determine whether these individual patterns of perception would change in a group situation. Using forty additional subjects, he had some students view the light first by themselves and then in groups of two or three; other subjects observed the effect first in a group situation and then individually. The results were quite interesting. Those subjects who first reported the extent of autokinetic movement by themselves, converged toward a group norm when making their judgments in the presence of one or two other persons. Figure 5.2, taken from Sherif's report, shows this converging effect for individuals in two groups, one containing two persons and the other three persons.

Figure 5.2

The converging reports of groups of two and three individuals observing autokinetic movement. (After Sherif, 1966)

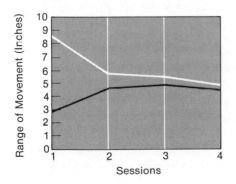 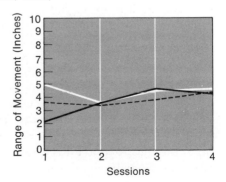

Sherif also discovered that those subjects who first viewed the light in groups of two or three established a group norm that persisted during the individual sessions that followed. It appeared, therefore, that the perception of apparent movement in this type of situation was influenced by the way other observers reported their perceptions.

Would the same results have been obtained had the light actually moved? In this case, each observer would have had an objective standard against which to test his own judgments as well as those of the other members of his group. To answer this question, Schonbar (1945) devised an apparatus by which she could actually move the point source of light. Ten subjects judged the extent of the movement first alone, then in pairs, then alone again. Individual differences in ranges of reported movement appeared even in this more clearly structured situation. Yet, when making judgments in groups of two, the subjects tended to converge, as had Sherif's subjects. When later reporting on the autokinetic effect by themselves, the individuals gave responses which resembled those established in the group situation more closely than those established originally during isolated viewing. Apparently the behavior of another person is an influence that, in some situations, can override evidence supplied by an external stimulus.

We may, of course, quite properly ask whether the *perceptions* of the subjects in these experiments were being influenced or whether their *verbal reports* were simply being modified in the direction of greater agreement. As we have noted, perceptual experience is not susceptible to direct observation. We must, therefore, entertain the possibility that experiments of the kind just reviewed demonstrate the effects of group factors upon *verbal behavior* rather than upon *perception*. There is no way to answer this question from the data just described.

Follow-up studies. Subsequent research on the autokinetic effect has largely confirmed Sherif's original findings and has emphasized the role of social reinforcement in the formation of a group perceptual norm. Telling the subject that his judgments of the extent of autokinetic movement are correct tends to increase the frequency of such judgments (Kelman, 1950). Perhaps even more to the point is the fact that a *previous history* of reinforcement can be shown to determine the extent to which the judgments of paired observers will converge or remain independent. Mausner (1954) manipulated experimentally the number of times subjects were either reinforced or punished for reporting the lengths of lines. Some subjects were consistently told they were "right" on 82 per cent of the trials, while others were told they were "wrong" 82 per cent of the time, regardless of the accuracy of their judgments. Individuals whose judgments during this time showed little or no overlap were then paired in the same task. This time they were not told whether their responses were right or wrong. Some of the pairs consisted of subjects both of whom had been positively reinforced during the training period, some pairs contained one subject who had been rewarded and one who had been punished, while others contained two previously punished subjects.

Convergence of judgments did *not* occur when both subjects had previously been reinforced for independent behavior. Convergence *did* occur when both subjects had previously been punished or when one had been punished and one rewarded. The results for one pair of each type are shown in Figure 5.3, page 144.

The effects of several different schedules of reinforcement on conditioning of the autokinetic effect have been investigated by Spivak and Papajohn (1957). They found that a variable interval schedule resulted in increased resistance to extinction as compared with continuous reinforcement of a particular range of reported movement. Although the verbal report of the subjects thus was clearly manipulated by reinforcement from the experimenter, can we assume that the perceptual experiences of the subjects were similarly controlled? This is the conclusion that has been reached by other investigators who have successfully controlled the extent of reported movement by selectively reinforcing their subjects (Solley and Murphy, 1960; Jacobs and Campbell, 1961).

If the experimenter says "Right" when the subject reports movement exceeding a certain amount, responses come to be concentrated in this range. Furthermore, reinforcement of a particular pattern of responses is superior to mere practice in rendering the behavior resistant to extinction, as shown by Stone (1967). This investigator further concluded that the judging-with-others effect can be duplicated by the delivery of verbal reinforcement to solitary respondents. Whether or not we agree that perception has been influenced in such experiments, it seems clear that norms for verbal reports can be established and manipulated by reinforcement (Schoenfeld and Cumming, 1963).

Estimates of Length

A distinguishing feature of Sherif's experiments was the complete ambiguity of the stimulus — a stationary light, the apparent movement of which is attributable to characteristics of the observer's sensory-neural structures. What will happen in circumstances where the evidence from the individual's senses is contradicted by judgments from other persons? Such a situation presumes a reasonably well structured stimulus, so that we might expect a number of individuals not under any social pressure to render identical, accurate judgments.

Asch's experiments. Solomon Asch devised a procedure not only to measure the accuracy with which subjects make certain comparative judgments but also to determine the effects of group influence on such judgments. More precisely, Asch was concerned with the conditions in which individuals either resist or yield to group pressure when the group

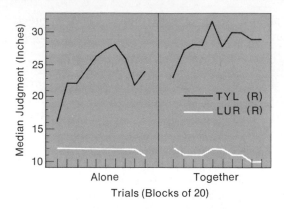

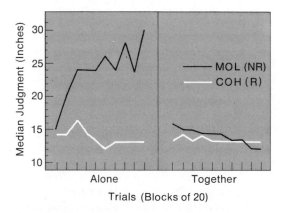

Figure 5.3
*Judgments of lengths of lines
by pairs of subjects who had
been previously reinforced (R)
or punished (NR). (After Mausner, 1954)*

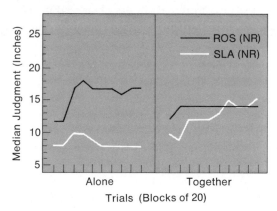

judgment is *contrary to fact*. The subjects' task was to match a given line
with one of three lines of different lengths. The procedure is as follows:

A group of seven to nine individuals, all college students, are gathered in a
classroom. The experimenter explains that they will be shown lines differing in length and that their task will be to match lines of equal length. The

setting is that of a perceptual test. The experimenter places on the black-board in front of the room two white cardboards on which are pasted vertical black lines. On the card at the left is a single line, the standard. The card on the right has three lines differing in length, one of which is equal to the standard line at the left. The task is to select from among the three lines the one equal to the standard line (1952a, p. 451).

While observing the lines, as pictured in Figure 5.4, each subject in turn called out which of the comparison lines (1, 2, or 3) was equal to the standard. After all the subjects had responded, the cards were removed and replaced by a new set. Twelve sets of standard and comparison lines were used by Asch, with the position of the equal comparison line varied randomly from trial to trial.

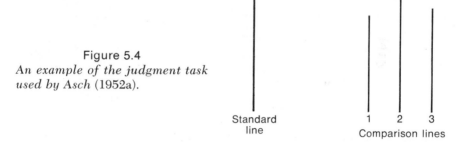

Figure 5.4
*An example of the judgment task
used by Asch* (1952a).

Standard line

1 2 3
Comparison lines

Ordinarily, one would have little difficulty in making a correct match. However, in Asch's procedure a subject frequently rendered a judgment that was different from that reported by other group members. As he found himself in repeated disagreement with his peers, this individual showed signs of nervousness or diffidence as he made his report. In fact, unknown to this subject, he was the only naive member of the group. The other members were confederates of the experimenter who had been instructed to give incorrect judgments on certain trials. Seating arrangements had been contrived so that the naive subject was always the last to voice his judgment, thus maximizing the group influence effect.

The experimental situation was designed to measure the effects of majority opinion upon the behavior of minorities of one. How did the naive subjects respond? The subjects who were confederates of the experimenter had been instructed to give false reports on twelve of the eighteen trials. The number of naive subjects who yielded to majority pressure on each trial is shown in Table 5.1. There were fifty naive subjects, and each could make a maximum of twelve errors if he went along with the majority on every critical trial. You may judge for yourself the extent to which these individuals were influenced by the incorrect judgments reported by the seven "instructed" subjects.

As evidenced by the data in Table 5.1, page 146, there were extreme individual differences among the naive subjects. About one fourth rendered

Table 5.1

Frequency distribution showing the number of naive subjects who yielded from zero to twelve times on the critical trials. (After Asch, 1952b, p. 5)

Number of Errors	Number of Naive Subjects Committing Errors
0	13
1	4
2	5
3	6
4	3
5	4
6	1
7	2
8	5
9	3
10	3
11	1
12	0
	Total 50

correct judgments on all of the trials, despite the fact that they were in disagreement with every other member of the group. If displacement of estimates toward the majority position on half or more of the trials is taken as the criterion of influence, then one third of the naive subjects could be considered as having yielded to majority pressure. This means approximately half the naive subjects were influenced on fewer than half the trials.

We remarked earlier, in connection with Sherif's experiments, that it was impossible to determine whether the formation of a group norm reflected a converging of perceptual experiences or simply a consensus of verbal report. The same question might be asked of Asch's data, and Asch did, in fact, consider these two alternatives. To obtain information that would bear upon this problem he interviewed his subjects at the conclusion of the experiment. After explaining the real purpose of the research, he attempted to ascertain the subject's reasons for responding as he did. Among the *yielding* subjects, Asch discovered three distinct categories of reaction. These were: (1) *distortion of perception,* in which the subjects were not aware that their estimates had been displaced, or distorted, by the majority; (2) *distortion of judgment,* in which the subjects began to doubt their own perceptions and believed that the majority must be correct; (3) *distortion of action,* in which the subjects did not doubt their own perceptions but simply went along with the majority report. The majority of the yielders, it should be noted, fell into the second category. Those subjects classified as independent, on the other hand, apparently had confidence in their own judgments, even though some of them felt tense and uncomfortable in their roles as dissident minorities of one.

Asch also introduced several variations into his basic procedure. One of these involved providing the naive subject with a "partner," that is, another naive individual. Majority pressure in this condition thus was only six to two instead of seven to one, and the frequency of errors made by the naive subjects fell from the previous level of 32 per cent to only 10 per cent. When the partner was instructed always to make correct judgments, errors by the naive subject fell to 5.5 per cent. Sudden abandonment by the partner caused errors by the naive subject to rise to 28.5 per cent. It is obvious that even minimal social support may be sufficient to free a dissenting individual from majority influence.

Follow-up studies. Deutsch and Gerard (1955) replicated and extended the procedures developed by Asch. One of the variations they introduced was having the subjects render their judgments first while the lines were present and then again after the lines had been removed. To control for possible order effects, approximately half of the subjects were given the visual series first and the rest were given the memory series first. In what the investigators called the "anonymous situation," the subjects were separated from one another by partitions, and they responded by pressing buttons. A panel of bulbs before each subject informed him of how the other subjects had responded; actually, the experimenter controlled these signals, so that apparent group unanimity in a wrong judgment could be communicated to each subject on certain designated trials. As in Asch's experiments, this occurred on twelve of the eighteen trials.

The results of these experimental manipulations are given in Table 5.2. The numbers represent the mean numbers of trials on which subjects' judgments conformed to incorrect estimates made by three other persons, reported either vocally in a face-to-face situation or simulated on a visual display viewed by each subject in isolation.

Table 5.2

Mean number of socially influenced errors in individual judgment in anonymous and face-to-face situations. (Based on Deutsch and Gerard, 1955, Table 2, p. 632)

Situation	Visual Series	Memory Series	Total
Face-to-face (N = 13)	3.00	4.08	7.08
Anonymous (N = 13)	2.77	3.15	5.92

Statistical evaluation of differences among these several measures revealed that significantly more socially influenced errors occurred in the face-to-face than in the anonymous situation. In addition, the memory series, where judgments could not be checked against the actual stimulus figures, resulted in a greater social influence effect.

In another experimental manipulation, using only the anonymous reporting arrangement, Deutsch and Gerard instructed some of the subjects that if they made more accurate judgments than the other participating groups, they would be rewarded with tickets to a Broadway play. It was assumed that the subjects who were so instructed would consider themselves more a part of a "group" than would uninstructed subjects, who would function merely as an aggregation. The results of this manipulation are shown in Table 5.3. The authors concluded from these data that "nor-

Table 5.3

Mean number of socially influenced errors in individual judgment in group and nongroup situations. (Based on Deutsch and Gerard, 1955, Table 1, p. 632)

Experimental Treatment	Visual Series	Memory Series	Total
Group (N = 15)	5.60	6.87	12.47
Nongroup (N = 13)	2.77	3.15	5.92

mative social influence upon individual judgments will be greater among individuals forming a group than among individuals who do not compose a group. The average member of the group made more than twice as many errors as the comparable individual who did not participate in the task as a member of a group" (p. 632).

How may we interpret this "normative process" in terms of behavioral variables? In order to generate a "group situation," it will be recalled, Deutsch and Gerard offered the subjects incentives for accurate group performance. This clearly established a condition in which reinforcements could be anticipated by the individuals involved, and it is not surprising that they tended to agree with one another's judgments in order to avoid individual "error," which, according to the experimenter's instructions, would count against the group score. Agreement would be interpreted by each member as confirmation of accuracy, hence reinforced. The data in Table 5.3, of course, clearly supported the prediction that agreement with errors would be greater in the group situation than in the nongroup situation. The memory series, because it deprived the naive subjects of a visible standard against which to check their judgments, resulted in a greater social influence effect.

Asch suspected that some of his subjects had not experienced distortions of judgment but had simply tailored their verbal reports so as to appear in agreement with the group. Post-experimental interrogation of his subjects supported this hypothesis. Can the same be said of the findings of Deutsch and Gerard? Some of these subjects were requested to write down their judgments before they were exposed to the responses of the others in the group. It was found that subsequent verbal reports by these individuals rarely conformed to the mistaken estimates rendered by the other group members. On the average, *less than one error* was made by these "committed" subjects during the twelve trials on which they received information that the other subjects had unanimously reported a comparison line which was incorrect.

We have already asked whether perceptual experience or verbal report is being influenced in experiments such as those of Sherif and Asch. Linton (1954) concluded that judgment rather than visual experience is manipulated in such settings, a conclusion that Asch (1951) had previously reached with regard to a majority of his subjects. In social influence experiments that employ judgmental tasks, therefore, it is probable that many of the subjects are simply displaying outward conformity. Considerable evidence has been accumulated by some investigators to indicate that what we consider to be conformity behavior is actually under fairly precise stimulus control; namely, it occurs in the presence of other individuals who are performing in a uniform manner. For example, Luchins and Luchins (1955) found that subjects who had agreed with the other members of a group in judging the length of the Asch lines no longer rendered incorrect judgments when later performing alone. When subjects who had previously shown the effects of majority influence made the same judgments individually but in the presence of the confederates, they persisted in their conforming behavior. However, when tested alone only one day later, they made no errors.

We now seem to have an answer to the question of whether perceptual experience or verbal report has been manipulated in these experiments. In situations such as those contrived by Sherif and by Asch, some individuals apparently come to perceive a stimulus event in a manner similar to that reported by other individuals. Such a reaction, however, is rare. More frequently, an individual who finds himself in disagreement with others behaves publicly in a manner that does not set him apart from others in his group. Whether he actually perceives and judges the stimulus situation in a manner similar to that of the other group members must be seriously doubted. Even the reporting responses of the subjects in these two experiments show evidence of a conformity effect no more than half the time, in circumstances most favorable to group influence.

Wide individual differences in susceptibility to a majority pressures can probably be expected in most situations. Some further evidence on this effect has been reported by Weiner and McGinnies (1961), who presented groups of three subjects, two of whom were confederates, with schematic representations of the human face showing only the mouth. On one of the faces the mouth was a perfectly straight line, while on two others the mouth curved slightly up or down. The stimulus figures are shown in Figure 5.5.

Figure 5.5
The three "faces" used in an experiment by Weiner and
McGinnies (1961).

The stimulus figures were projected singly on a screen in random order for twenty-seven trials. Two of the three subjects were instructed to answer either "smiling" or "frowning" on certain trials when the face with the *straight* line was shown. In this Asch-type situation, it was hypothesized that the third (naive) subject would be influenced by this majority report of the ambiguous figure. In order to increase the ambiguity of the stimulus, and thus impart greater stimulus value to the reactions of the confederates, the faces were exposed for only a fraction of a second. It was found that the forty naive subjects agreed with the confederates significantly more often than they disagreed on the critical trials. Interestingly, the investigators report that in a pilot study in which the confederates were instructed to voice a judgment that was in obvious contradiction to the stimulus figure (that is, saying "frowning" for the upturned mouth or "smiling" for the downturned mouth), not even one of eight naive subjects was influenced. Other investigators (Coffin, 1941; Luchins, 1945) have similarly reported that suggestion effects are relatively ineffective unless the stimulus is somehow made unclear or ambiguous.

A Functional Analysis

The experiments we have just described are fairly typical of those dealing with group influences on perception and judgment. What variables can we identify that will account for the fact that some individuals are susceptible to majority suggestion while some apparently are not. In Chapter 2, where we considered several experiments in which behavior was maintained by stimuli that had been associated with primary reinforcers, we introduced the concept of conditioned reinforcement. Can this principle contribute to our understanding of individual differences in response to social influence in such situations as we have described here? Suppose we consider one possibility. Because he has frequently been reinforced for crossing the street on a green light instead of a red, swinging at a pitch that crosses the plate instead of one that is outside or inside, and judging correctly the heights of steps so as not to stumble, the average person tends to make discriminations that are fairly consistent with events in the external world. He has acquired a generalized disposition, in short, to categorize objects and events in certain ways, such as longer or shorter, higher or lower, louder or softer, and so forth. Confirmation of these judgments is reinforcing because confirmed expectancies have generally accompanied successful instrumental acts. The mere act of making a judgment and having it confirmed, then, is maintained through conditioned reinforcement.

Disconfirmation of a judgment is aversive for several reasons. First, errors in judgment frequently are followed by failures of those instrumental acts to which they have been a prelude. For example, if a center fielder misjudges the flight of a baseball, he is apt to drop it, surely an aversive consequence. If I miscalculate my chance of running a traffic light that has just turned red and I am hit broadside by another car, my error in judgment is painfully aversive. Experiences of this sort, either direct or vicarious, have the effect of conferring aversive qualities upon judgments that do not conform to outward reality.

Another way in which inaccurate judgments become aversive is through the reactions of other persons. This process generally begins in childhood, when trial-and-error behaviors often elicit either praise or reproof from both adults and peers. Examples of this include learning to grasp and manipulate objects, learning to avoid danger, and acquiring skill at games and other competitions. All of these activities require that judgmental ability be developed. Formal education in the schools, of course, provides countless occasions on which "correct" judgments are rewarded and "incorrect" judgments are either extinguished or suppressed. These occasions provide ample opportunity for the disconfirmation of judgments to acquire conditioned aversive properties. In those experiments that have dealt with group influences on perception and judgment, the individual is placed in conflict on certain trials. In the Asch situation, for example, the subject makes a private judgment that is confirmed by visual inspection of the stimulus figures. The reports of the other subjects, however, provide disconfirmation of his self-report. What does he now report verbally: his original judgment, or one that will be consistent with those of the other group members? It is obvious from Asch's data that different individuals do different things. Since the situation is basically the same for the yielding as for the independent subjects, the basis for individual differences in reaction must reside in their respective reinforcement histories.

Let us assume that those subjects who maintain independence by reporting their judgments without regard to what the others have said are more habituated to respond adequately to a task than to behave in a manner that will be agreeable to others. Let us further assume that those subjects who yield to majority pressure have more often been reinforced for behaving in a "socially acceptable" fashion than for maintaining consistency between their private impressions and their public behavior. The behavior of both the conforming and the nonconforming subjects then becomes understandable. Each is positively reinforced for whatever he does, and the effective reinforcement is the one that has most frequently been contingent upon his behavior in similar past situations.

The nonconforming subject enjoys the satisfaction of having responded consistently to the task, but he will also experience some discomfort as a result of his obvious deviation from the modal group response. If his previous experiences have included frequent praise for responding adequately to assigned tasks, then the positive reinforcement deriving from response consistency will outweigh the aversive consequences of being different from the others. Similarly, the positive reinforcement that the conforming subject experiences by agreeing with the group outweighs any aversiveness that attaches to his having behaved inconsistently with respect to the task. In the case of some individuals, conflict seems to be avoided by the technique of *perceptual distortion*, by which inconsistent modes of responding never become conscious alternatives. By analyzing the behavior of the subjects in this fashion, we do more than just describe what happens in the situation. We relate individual differences to prior reinforcement histories and, thus, are able to theorize in the realm of well-established behavior principles. In order to predict individual differences in response, of course, we would have to have more detailed information about the reinforcement histories of those concerned. Direct information of this sort is difficult to obtain, and so we often make inferences about an individual's response dispositions from his scores on attitude scales, interest inventories, and questionnaires dealing with personal values and beliefs. We turn now to some of the experimental work that has utilized this general approach.

Perceptual Selection

At any given moment, we are presented with a near infinitude of potential stimulus events. Given both limited receptor capacities and a limited span of attention, an observer cannot possibly attend to more than a small fraction of these energies. He must select *spatially* as well as *temporally*. One cannot, for example, perceive what is outside one's field of vision; that is, there are spatial limitations on the perceptual field. Even within the range of visible, audible, or tactile stimulus events, one's attention can be captured by only a few stimuli, and there is evidence that attention tends to fluctuate among stimuli rather than to encompass several at once.

If one selects from a number of stimulus events that are available only briefly for inspection, then selection occurs within the limitations of both time and space. Soldiers, for example, often learn to recognize various types of aircraft at very brief exposure intervals. Learning to make accurate discriminations usually occurs with practice. The observer is trained to look for certain unique characteristics, such as wing or tail configurations, that will distinguish the aircraft as friendly or hostile. And he must do this in the brief interval of time during which the aircraft is in sight.

Word Recognition

In everyday situations, we are ordinarily under no such duress in making perceptual discriminations. Nevertheless, we still tend to select from the perceptible environment those objects and events that have significance to us. This assumes, of course, that all are equally available in terms of extent, intensity, and duration and that it is not possible to perceive all at once. We have argued that certain percepts come to have reinforcing characteristics, while others become aversive. This is true, in particular, with regard to verbal stimuli. There are many words in the English language — indeed in every language — that have the capacity to elicit either positive or negative affect in a reader or listener. As a result of learning, words like "mother" and "patriotism" evoke positive reactions in most people; the notorious four-letter words generally elicit negative reactions, at least in polite company. The perception of such words thus becomes a matter not just of the physical dimensions of the stimulus but also of certain reactions that have been conditioned in the perceiver. F. H. Allport (1955) has referred to a *central directive state* that includes "needs, tensions, values, defenses, and emotions of the individual, and of course his past experience generally" (p. 305). Directive state theory has generated a large number of empirical studies, from which we will select for analysis some relating to the recognition of words.

Since the 1940's, a great number of experiments have been performed on the problem of recognition thresholds for various types of stimuli, both verbal and pictorial. One group of experiments has dealt with *perceptual* selection, that is, the tendency of individuals to report (R_2) with greater alacrity perceptual responses (R_1) that are either associated with certain personality variables or have had a particular history of reinforcement in the individual. The exact nature of the behavioral variables that lead to facilitation or inhibition of recognition has, as we shall see, been a matter of dispute. Whether the perceptual response or the reporting response is being measured has also been a troublesome question. In addition, some of the experiments in this area have been criticized for allowing confounding variables, such as word frequency or response suppression, to compromise the results. In general, the principal assumption underlying these experiments is that perceptual response can be either facilitated or inhibited by factors other than the psychophysical characteristics of the stimulus. Goldiamond (1962) comments, "Differences in operant responses can reflect differences in conditioning history, effects of reinforcement, state variables, and other experimental conditions rather than differences in discrimination or sensory thresholds inferred from them" (p. 295). The perceptual responses, he argues, are subject to control by the same variables that govern other operant responses.

Personal values. One of the earliest and most often cited experiments dealing with perceptual selection was that reported by Postman, Bruner, and McGinnies (1948). These investigators reasoned that the basic values or interests of an individual should be related to his perception of verbal stimuli representing these values. More specifically, they assumed that a person's thresholds of recognition, measured in hundredths of a second, would be lower for words symbolizing positive values and higher for words symbolizing negative values. Low threshold means that a word flashed on a screen is recognized at a very short duration of exposure, whereas high threshold means that the word requires a relatively longer exposure before it is recognized. If preferences and aversions played no role in perception, one would predict that words of the same length and of the same degree of familiarity would be recognized with equal ease. Postman, Bruner, and McGinnies sought to discover whether personal values, which describe certain aspects of a person's reinforcement history, would predict differences in the readiness with which subjects recognized words representing these values.

They first determined the value orientations of twenty-five Harvard and Radcliffe students by means of a questionnaire called the *Study of Values* (Allport, Vernon, and Lindzey, 1951). This instrument is based on a theory of personality proposed by a German philosopher named Spranger (1928). It was Spranger's theory that persons can be categorized as *theoretical, aesthetic, economic, social, political,* or *religious* types. A person dominated by theoretical interests, for example, values truth above all else, whereas the economically inclined person judges people and things in terms of their utility, or usefulness. The political man is principally concerned with power, the aesthetic man with beauty, the social man with sympathy, and the religious man with the significance of life. These brief descriptions do an injustice to Spranger's theory, which is developed in great detail, but they will suffice to convey the flavor of the typology that he propounded.

After they had answered the items on the questionnaire, the subjects were seated before a tachistoscope (a laboratory device for exposing visual stimuli at controlled, short durations, usually a tenth of a second or less). Six words were selected as representative of each of the six value areas, and these were exposed one at a time for increasingly longer intervals until the subjects reported each word correctly. Thus, the word "kindly" (social value) was exposed at durations of .01, .02, .03 second, and so on, until the subject saw it clearly enough to report it. The average duration thresholds for the most-valued to the least-valued words for each subject were then computed and plotted as a function of these ranked values. Figure 5.6 shows the results of this analysis.

It is apparent that the average duration of exposure necessary for correct report of value-related words increases as value rank declines. Assuming that the subjects reported each word as soon as they recognized it one may conclude that the thresholds of recognition of the words were indeed influenced by their relative positions in the subjects' hierarchies of values.

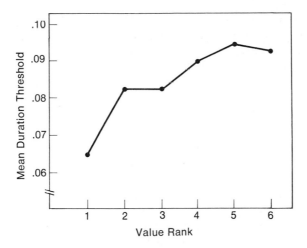

Figure 5.6

Thresholds of recognition as a function of value rank of the stimulus words. (After Postman, Bruner, and McGinnies, 1948)

As might have been anticipated, this interpretation of the results did not go unchallenged. Howes and Solomon (1951) discovered that the ease with which subjects are able to correctly report words presented to them tachistoscopically can be predicted from the frequency with which the words occur in printed English. Estimates of the frequency of occurrence of words in a sample of books and magazines are available in lists compiled by Thorndike and Lorge (1944). The relationship described by Howes and Solomon is shown in Figure 5.7, where duration thresholds of recognition are plotted as a function of the Thorndike-Lorge word frequency counts.

Note that as frequency of occurrence increases, recognition threshold decreases. Other investigators (McGinnies, Comer, and Lacey, 1952) have reported a similar relationship, and there seems to be little doubt that a person recognizes more readily those words with which he has come into contact more frequently. What does this finding have to do with the previous experiment relating recognition to personal values? Solomon and

Figure 5.7

The relationship between the logarithm of word frequency and threshold of recognition (mean duration of stimulus). (After Howes and Solomon, 1951)

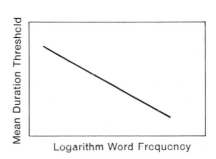

Howes (1951) maintain that a religious individual, for example, deals more with words symbolizing religion than does a person who places highest value on some other area of endeavor. A political type of person tends both to use and to encounter words that connote power and prestige more than, say, a person whose major value is theoretical. Different individuals thus bring to the experimental situation varying degrees of familiarity with words representing the six value areas. If familiarity with different words operates in a personal, or idiosyncratic, way to determine recognition thresholds, then selectivity in terms of personality dispositions, such as values, need not be invoked to explain the relationship reported by Postman, Bruner, and McGinnies.

Although an explanation of differential recognition thresholds in terms of sheer frequency of exposure to different words is appealing because of its greater parsimony, later experiments have generated results that are not readily handled by the frequency concept. Postman and Schneider (1951) selected words representative of the Spranger values in such a way that some words had high frequency counts, while others, representing the same values, occurred with much lower frequency. For the common, or high frequency, words, value orientation of the subjects did not differentially predict recognition thresholds, thus apparently confirming the Solomon-Howes hypothesis. Ease in recognizing the less frequent words, however, was, as Postman, Bruner, and McGinnies had found, related to the personal value profiles of the subjects. Perceptual selection, therefore, seems to be revealed in recognition thresholds only when the stimulus is somewhat ambiguous. Ambiguity in this case was represented by the relatively low probability of occurrence of one list of value-related words.

This particular controversy might be resolved if we could determine whether a person who scores high in, say, economic value actually uses or is exposed to more frequently words symbolic of this value. Some evidence bearing on this question was obtained by Sachidanandan (1960), who asked subjects to associate for a period of sixty seconds to words symbolizing the Spranger values. If value orientation measures familiarity with value-related words, then one would expect the subjects to have acquired more associations to words representing their preferred values. Such apparently is not the case, because the subjects in this experiment gave as many associations to low-value words as to high-value words. Although this issue cannot be considered fully resolved, the weight of evidence seems to favor the position that perceptual selection in terms of values and interests may occur without necessarily being mediated by sheer frequency of prior usage. This position, of necessity, implies that seeing words which are consistent with one's personal value orientation is more reinforcing than seeing words which are not consistent with one's values.

Perceptual avoidance. A more dramatic and focused attack upon the role of affective, or attitudinal, factors in perceptual selectivity was made by

McGinnies (1949), who postulated that perceptual thresholds would be raised for words that were embarrassing or threatening to the individual. This research led to a host of what some observers have referred to, tongue in cheek, as the "dirty word" experiments. Typically, the procedure here is to devise a list of stimulus words containing some that are offensive or threatening and some that are innocuous. (Of course, words that might have caused embarrassment if uttered in mixed company twenty years ago do not necessarily evoke the same reaction today.) The words used by McGinnies were classified as either "neutral" or "taboo" and were presented one at a time for gradually increasing durations until eight male and eight female subjects could report them correctly. He found that the subjects required on the average significantly longer exposure durations before they reported *raped, belly, whore, kotex, penis, filth,* and *bitch* as compared with the durations necessary for the correct reporting of *apple, dance, child, glass, river, sleep, broom, stove, music, trade,* and *clear.* An additional finding of importance was that the galvanic skin responses of the subjects were higher immediately following prerecognition presentations of the taboo words than those of the neutral words.

The interpretation of these findings given by McGinnies was that a taboo word elicits a conditioned autonomic reaction from the observer before he can correctly identify the word. The autonomic response, having a lower threshold than the recognition response, provides stimuli which lead to avoidance of recognition of the disturbing word. This avoidance behavior is negatively reinforced because it delays the more aversive consequences of, first, saying the taboo word to oneself, and second, reporting it aloud. Sooner or later, of course, with increasing exposure durations, a threshold of veridical recognition is reached, and the subject reports the word aloud in accordance with the experimenter's instructions. At some stage in this process, the subject is probably in conflict about whether to say the word or not, an interpretation that has been advanced by Howes and Solomon (1950).

In fact, Howes and Solomon challenged on several counts an interpretation of McGinnies' findings in terms of "perceptual defense." First, they argued that the higher recognition thresholds of the taboo words could be accounted for by the lower frequency of occurrence of these words in the printed language. Second, they suggested that the subjects probably did not report the taboo words as soon as they recognized them because of the conflict that we have already mentioned. These criticisms have merit but they are inconsistent. If the subjects recognized the taboo words as readily as the neutral words but delayed reporting them, then word frequency obviously did not determine recognition thresholds. And if word frequency alone determined threshold, then where was the source of conflict? (McGinnies, 1950). So the most logical alternative to an interpretation in terms of perceptual avoidance is one that assumes verbal response bias, or the tendency of subjects to report certain words more frequently than others.

Such an interpretation is favored by Goldiamond (1958, 1962), who found evidence for response bias, that is, the tendency of subjects to respond with common or familiar items even when the tachistoscope presented "blanks." His results were replicated by Goldstein (1962), who used both blank and stimulus presentations and found response probability to be higher for neutral than for taboo words.

Postman (1951), in modifying his earlier position, has come to support a "hypothesis interpretation" of the so-called perceptual defense data. This is best presented in his words:

> Under conditions of highly reduced stimulation (e.g., very rapid tachisto-scopic exposure) a small amount of appropriate stimulus information is fed into the organism. Other things being equal, that specific hypothesis is aroused which has been confirmed most frequently in the past in the presence of this type of stimulus information. Further input of appropriate stimulus information then serves to confirm the hypothesis. . . . Only under conditions of partial information are there degrees of freedom in the arousal of alternative hypotheses. . . . What appears to be perceptual defense results from the dominance of strong alternative hypotheses rather than from active repression of the inimical or dangerous. In the presence of partial information, strong hypotheses incompatible with the threatening stimulus may be evoked (pp. 252, 256).

In a somewhat altered version of McGinnies' 1949 experiment, Postman, Bronson, and Gropper (1953) reported that their subjects actually recognized taboo words at lower intensities of illumination than neutral words. They concede that this rather surprising result may have stemmed from the fact that the neutral words, selected on the basis of having frequencies of occurrence in print no greater than those of the taboo words, may actually have been less familiar to the subjects. For example, words such as *capon*, *tiara*, and *bathe* are not necessarily encountered as frequently as the taboo words listed earlier in connection with the McGinnies experiment. It is not inconceivable that subjects would have heard, read, or used the taboo words more frequently than the neutral words used by Postman and his associates. However, as these investigators point out ". . . the invocation of an hypothetical effect (i.e., perceptual defense), which is obscured by the operation of a known variable (i.e., word frequencies), would carry little conviction" (p. 222).

Individual differences. In a critical review of this area of research, J. S. Brown (1961) observes that because "randomly chosen subjects may not exhibit defense, particularly when frequency of prior experience with the stimuli has been controlled, does not mean that *some* individuals might not exhibit the effect" (p. 323). If some individuals are *selective* and some are *defensive* with regard to threatening stimuli, then such distinctive modes of reacting by randomly chosen subjects would be concealed by the process of averaging.

Several investigators have, in fact, reported systematic relationships between personality characteristics and the perception of material that could be described as taboo or threatening. Eriksen (1954) in particular has argued that manifestations of selectivity in perceptual response are idiosyncratic rather than typical reactions to threat. Some individuals are more "defensive" than others in a threatening, or anxiety-provoking, situation. For example, in one experiment subjects were differentiated on the same basis of whether they responded to incomplete sentences with sexual or aggressive conclusions. Those subjects who gave sexual solutions and were classified as "expressive" with respect to sex were later able to hear sentences containing sexual content as well as nonsexual sentences. Subjects who either blocked or gave inappropriate conclusions to the incomplete sexual sentences, however, experienced difficulty in hearing the sexual statements (Lazarus, Eriksen, and Fonda, 1951). Even in the several experiments where recognition thresholds for value-related words have been obtained, some subjects show a consistent tendency to perceive low-value words more readily than high-value words (Postman, Bruner, and McGinnies, 1948; Vanderplas and Blake, 1949).

Brown's curvilinear hypothesis. If one accepts the evidence for the differential discriminability of words as a function of their conditioning histories, then there seems to be a critical degree of emotional arousal beyond which recognition thresholds of the provocative stimuli begin to fall. This was first reported by Chodorkoff (1956) and later elaborated upon by W. P. Brown (1961), who hypothesizes: "Recognition thresholds at first rise with increases in stimulus emotionality, but reach a peak, and subsequently fall with further increases in stimulus emotionality" (p. 39). This relationship is pictured in Figure 5.8.

Confirmation of this trend has also been reported by Dorfman, Grossberg, and Kroeker (1965). It is awkward for either the response suppression

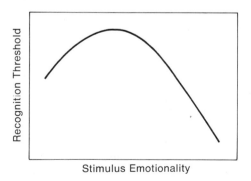

Stimulus Emotionality

Figure 5.8

The theoretical function relating stimulus emotionality to recognition threshold. (After Brown, 1961)

hypothesis or the response bias hypothesis to explain why highly emotional stimuli should lead to lower thresholds of report than stimuli that have only a moderate capacity to elicit an emotional response. Recent research supports the interpretation that the elevated report thresholds for emotion-arousing words are, in fact, due to higher *recognition* thresholds for these words and are not explained away simply as reluctance to utter the word (Mathews and Wertheimer, 1958; Minard, 1965; Minard, Bailey, and Wertheimer, 1965). The best technique for selecting emotional words seems to be that of first asking subjects to associate freely to a larger number of words. Those words having the longest association times and accompanied by other signs of emotional arousal such as stuttering, blushing, or perspiring are judged to be emotionally arousing. These are presented tachistoscopically along with neutral words, and a correction is made for response bias by either (a) having the subject indicate on a card containing all the stimuli which word is being shown, or (b) including in the list words that were not expected by the subject and noting whether he always tends to guess a nonemotional word. These and other devices that have been used for minimizing or detecting response bias have shown rather convincingly that delay of recognition does occur as an avoidance response to unpleasant words, even though distortion or suppression of the reporting response may also occur.

Goldstein (1962, 1964) has adduced further evidence that differential thresholds of emotion-arousing and non-emotion-arousing words are not due merely to verbal response bias. Although he failed to confirm the finding by Dorfman and others (1965) that defense changes to vigilance with increasing exposure duration of the stimulus word, Goldstein (1966) did find the subjects had greater difficulty recognizing threatening words than neutral words only on the first of several experimental sessions. During two succeeding experimental periods, the subjects were more accurate at recognizing the threat words than the neutral word. This result is interpreted as a shift from "defense" to "vigilance," but it occurs as a function of repeated response to the stimulus materials rather than as a result of an increase in exposure time of the threat and nonthreat words.

Commentary.   Where does this discussion bring us in our consideration of selective factors in perception? Although we have examined only one aspect of this problem, the perception of words, there seems to be sufficient evidence to support the conclusion that the selection and organization of perceptions is controlled at least in part by the same kinds of reinforcement contingencies as those that govern overt behavior. Perceiving the world may be conceived as an instrumental act on the part of the observer rather than as simply a passive response to stimulation. To be sure, we cannot literally perceive the world as we might like it to be. But when some degree of ambiguity is introduced into the stimulus situation, as, for example, through vagueness or brevity, then the individual tends to perceive selectively in accordance with certain habits and expectancies that he has acquired. Certain words, in particular, have come to have affective, or emotional, significance. Those words that elicit negative affect are likely to be recognized either more or less readily than neutral words. Although a reluctance to breach the social amenities may cause some subjects to delay reporting taboo words in perceptual experiences, there is convincing evidence that a delay in recognition contributes significantly to the higher report thresholds for such words. Research will doubtless continue in this perplexing area, and we may expect to learn much more about the ways in which an individual's perception of the world is structured by his previous reinforcement history in a variety of situations.

Person Perception

A related area of investigation involves individual and selective factors in the perception of persons. Experiments in this area have dealt with the role of such factors as values, interests, and personal idiosyncrasies in the judgment of others. "Person perception," as Secord and Backman (1964) have observed, "focuses on the process by which impressions, opinions or feelings about other persons are formed" (p. 91). Variables that influence one's perceptions of others include the amount of information available to him, the nature of the situation in which the interaction occurs, and his past history in forming impressions of others. One of the most firmly established generalizations in the area of person perception is that individuals tend to perceive others whom they like or admire as similar to themselves. Persons whom one dislikes, or who are threatening, frequently are perceived as unlike oneself. The learning experiences that lead to consistent modes of perception assume additional importance when one considers that the stimulus for person perception is frequently ambiguous. How many of us could give an objective and insightful description of ourselves, much less of another person? Yet, despite the difficulty of specifying the stimuli upon which the perception of persons is based, we do seek to understand how such impressions are formed and how they influence our social interactions.

Early research. Suppose we begin by seeing how research in person perception has developed. It was necessary, first, to establish whether or not there is sufficient consistency in the expressive acts of individuals to support reliable impressions. Our perceptions of other persons would be tentative and fleeting if their posture, facial expressions, handshake, gait, and speech did not possess some unifying dimensions that lend a degree of consistency to these expressive behaviors. An experimental assessment of expressive movements was made in 1933 by Allport and Vernon. They report, for example, that a group of judges was able to match, with considerable success, samples of handwriting and recordings of handwriting pros sure with brief personality descriptions of the writers. In addition, these investigators found that virtually none of the measurements from four selected individuals contradicted the subjective impressions that one would have of these persons. The indices included speed and fluency of speech, forcefulness, freedom of movement, neatness, and voice intensity. A vocational counselor, an artist, a college sophomore, and a college junior possessing strikingly different personalities all yielded different measures on the various indices of expressive movement. Judges experienced no difficulty, however, in matching brief personality sketches of these individuals with their ratings on the various expressive measures. Allport and Vernon concluded that "insofar as personality is organized, expressive movement is harmonious and self consistent" (p. 182). An individual apparently presents a fairly stable configuration of behavioral characteristics as a stimulus for social perception.

Perception of another, as we have emphasized, is determined not only by that individual's appearance and movements but also by the momentary set and long-term habits of the perceiver. Bruner and Tagiuri (1954) have suggested that we tend to judge others within the framework of certain naive, implicit theories of personality. That is, we have acquired certain preconceptions of what kinds of personality traits go together, and we frequently form a global impression of someone on the basis of little evidence. Thorndike (1920) referred to this tendency by the term *halo effect*, which means that judges tend to rate others on a variety of characteristics in terms of a general impression of "goodness" or "badness."

Characteristics of the Perceiver

An individual's own personality has been shown by several investigators to influence his judgments of others. Personality can be described in many different ways, and one of these involves the concepts of *concreteness* and *abstractness* (Harvey, Hunt, and Schroder, 1961). The "concrete" person tends to view the world in extremes of good-bad, right-wrong, black-white. He finds it difficult to cope with ambiguous situations, depends upon precedent and authority in making decisions, and is incapable of empathic identification with others. In contrast, the abstract individual recognizes graded distinctions in judging the world, is not uncomfortable in ambiguous situations, and does not rely to as great an extent upon external authority as guidelines for his behavior. In several respects this method of categorizing persons resembles that by which the concept of the *authoritarian personality* was developed (Adorno, Frenkel-Brunswik, Levinson, and Sanford, 1950). Those who are more rigid, or concrete, in their perceptual habits tend to perceive others in more stereotyped, simplified fashion than persons whose perceptual expectancies allow for inconsistency and ambiguity.

For example, it has been found that prejudiced individuals are more prone to identify other persons as the targets of their antipathy than are tolerant individuals. Allport and Kramer (1946), in an experiment conducted with Harvard undergraduates, discovered that those students who scored high in anti-Semitism on an attitude questionnaire identified more facial photographs of Jews and gentiles as Jewish than did nonprejudiced subjects. Furthermore, the prejudiced subjects were more often correct in their judgments. This study was replicated in its essential aspects by Scodel and Austrin (1957), who report that the anti-Semitic subjects tended to label most of the photographs indiscriminately as "Jewish." This finding appeared to cast doubt on the assumption that prejudiced persons are more accurate in identifying the objects of their prejudice by showing that they made such identifications with greater frequency than those who are less prejudiced and should therefore more often be correct.

A further examination of this possibility was made by Pulos and Spilka (1961), who presented matched photographs from a college yearbook of Jewish and non-Jewish males in cap and gown to forty high scorers and forty low scorers on an anti-Semitism scale. The photographs were selected from a large number that had been rated by judges for distinctiveness of Jewish or non-Jewish appearance, and the easily distinguished ones were discarded. However, even when presented with a reasonably homogeneous set of photographs, the high anti-Semitic subjects were more accurate than the low anti-Semitic subjects in identifying the Jewish photographs. Their increased accuracy was manifest even when their tendency to label more of the photographs as Jewish was taken into account.

We would conclude from these findings that certain behavioral dispositions, such as attitudes, render the individual more sensitive to discriminative stimuli that have a reinforcement history related to the attitude. It must be assumed that the accurate identification of other persons with respect to religion or ethnic background has been more frequently reinforced in the prejudiced than in the nonprejudiced individual. Confirmation of these perceptual identifications serves to maintain them and to bolster the attitudes from which they are derived.

Characteristics of the Target Person

Nearly everyone is influenced to some extent in his perception of others by certain sailent traits or characteristics that seem to generate a halo effect. Asch (1946) was one of the first to demonstrate this by distinguishing between those qualities that are the "key" to a person and those that are peripheral, or subsidiary. In one of his experiments, Asch read a list of character traits to two groups of subjects. The lists were identical for both groups with the exception of one term, *warm*, which was replaced with the term *cold* for one of the groups. The following words were used: intelligent, skillful, industrious, *warm*, determined, practical, cautious. The subjects, after having heard one of the two lists of descriptive adjectives, wrote a brief personality sketch of the person described and then selected from eighteen pairs of different adjectives the one of each pair that they thought best described the individual. Asch reports that the two experimental groups differed considerably both in the way they described the person and in their choice of descriptive adjectives. The "warm" group wrote more positive sketches than the "cold" group. In addition, the "warm" subjects selected adjectives such as wise, humorous, popular, and imaginative, whereas the "cold" subjects tended to select opposite attributes. Other traits (reliability, honesty, and physical attractiveness) were selected equally often by both groups, showing that the warm-cold effect did not generalize to all descriptive choices. The halo effect, in other words, was limited. Moreover, such key words as *polite* and *blunt* did not markedly influence the subjects' choices of other adjectives in describing the person to whom the critical traits were attributed (Asch, 1952a).

An impression of a fictitious individual formed on the basis of adjectives is one thing, but the perception of a real person may be something else (Luchins, 1948). Recognizing this fact, Kelley (1950) devised an experiment to test some of Asch's conclusions in a different social setting. Three classes of male students at the Massachusetts Institute of Technology took part. The stimulus person was also a male and he was unknown to any of the subjects before the experimental period. He was introduced by the experimenter as a substitute instructor for the day. Prior to this, the experimenter had told the class that this would be an opportunity to obtain some data about student impressions of an instructor. Each student was given the following short description of the substitute instructor before he appeared:

> Mr. _____ is a graduate student in the Department of Economics and Social Science here at M.I.T. He had three semesters of teaching experience in psychology at another college. This is his first semester teaching Ec. 70. He is 26 years old, a veteran, and married. People who know him consider him to be a rather cold person, industrious, critical, practical and determined.

Half of the students received the above note, while the other half received a note that was identical except that the expression "rather cold" had been replaced with "rather warm." None of the subjects was aware that two different kinds of information were being provided. The stimulus person then appeared and led the class in a twenty-minute discussion. Following this experience, the stimulus person left the room, and the students were asked to write a free description of him and to rate him on a set of fifteen scales dealing with such traits as knowledge, consideration, intelligence, and temperament. Kelley's findings were similar in all important respects to those of Asch, that is, more favorable descriptions and ratings were made by those subjects who had been given the term "warm" in the introductory note.

The terms "warm" and "cold" seem to convey a number of meanings, with those suggested by "warm" being more positive, or acceptable, than those suggested by "cold." The expectations that one has of interacting with a warm person apparently are more positive than those he has of interacting with a cold person. The mere "set" to perceive an individual as possessing either one of these qualities probably influences the additional impressions that are formed through direct interaction. This set or expectancy may, in fact, determine the nature and extent of the interactions that will take place. For example, Kelley reports that 56 per cent of the subjects who were given the "warm" preinformation participated in the discussion, whereas only 32 per cent of the "cold" subjects took part. This is consistent with our hypothesis that the anticipation of positive reinforcement is greater when we interact with "warm" persons than when we interact with "cold" persons.

This same type of selectivity is obvious in other situations where the perception of persons is involved. Fensterheim and Tresselt (1953) obtained scores from subjects on the *Study of Values*. The subjects were then given a list of traits appropriate to the six value areas and were asked to match these traits with a series of photographs and to indicate their preferences for the various photographs. The experimenters report that the subjects preferred those photographs onto which they had projected a value system similar to their own. Here again, we may assume that a favorable judgment of a person is more readily maintained when the person is perceived as having characteristics similar to oneself.

Interpersonal Effects

Authoritarianism. The role of social interaction in person perception is perhaps best illustrated by several experiments in which the trait of authoritarianism has been related to judgments of personality traits. The authoritarian person is described as rigid in his thinking, conforming in his behavior, stereotyped in his judgments, and intolerant of ambiguity. Nonauthoritarian, or egalitarian, persons are seen as contrasted to each of these characteristics. Scodel and Mussen (1953) investigated the accuracy with which authoritarian and nonauthoritarian individuals were able to estimate each other's real attitudes. They first determined the degree of authoritarianism of their subjects by having them respond to the California F Scale, a questionnaire that measures this particular configuration of attitudes. Twenty-seven high scorers were then paired with an equal number of low scorers of the same sex and were asked to carry on a twenty-minute discussion of radio, television, and the movies. At the termination of this conversation, each subject was taken to a separate room and asked to answer the questionnaire again, this time as he thought the subject with whom he had just conversed would respond to it. Each subject thus responded to the F Scale twice, once as he himself felt and once as he thought his discussion partner would feel. The authors of this study report that authoritarians inaccurately perceived the nonauthoritarians as having high scores on the F Scale. The nonauthoritarians accurately perceived the authoritarians as having higher scores than themselves, but did not see them as being as high as they actually were. Some variations on this procedure were introduced by later investigators, who formed dyads in which members were either alike or different with respect to authoritarian attitudes (Scodel and Freedman, 1956; Crockett and Meidinger, 1956). The results of these experiments, in general, confirmed the conclusions just reported.

Lipetz (1960) made use of recorded interviews that were heard by both low-F and high-F subjects, who then rated the person interviewed with respect to six personality characteristics. The subjects had previously rated themselves on the same six traits. Lipetz found that the authoritarian subjects perceived the person in the interview as more like themselves than did the nonauthoritarians, and he suggests that authoritarian persons have a need to perceive others as like themselves. This particular disposition, stemming presumably from feelings of insecurity, did not characterize the nonauthoritarians.

These various experimental findings, of course, are open to alternative explanations. First, it might be argued that individuals who score low in authoritarianism are more accurate in discerning the authoritarian tendencies of others than are persons who score high. For example, high authoritarians frequently perceive lows as being like themselves, whereas low authoritarians seldom make this error. Alternatively, it has been suggested that because nonselected individuals expect to encounter more authoritarians than nonauthoritarians, they ascribe more authoritarian traits to both real and fictitious stimulus persons (Rabinowitz, 1956). One way of resolving these questions is to devise a situation in which the participants evaluate one another on traits that are directly related to the nature of their interactions. By having more relevant information on the dispositions of his fellows, each individual is less likely to form impressions that are simply probabilistic estimates based on past contacts.

Ethnocentrism. Such an experiment was performed by Altman and McGinnies (1960). Subjects classified according to their degree of ethnocentrism (intolerance of minorities) discussed a film dealing with group prejudice. Each discussion group contained six members, and five different types of groups were formed according to subjects' scores on the E (Ethnocentrism) Scale. Two groups were balanced; that is, they each contained three high E's (prejudiced persons) and three low E's (tolerant persons). Two more groups were composed uniformly of either high-E or low-E individuals. Finally, two unbalanced groups were formed containing either four high E's and two low E's, or four low E's and two high E's. Each of the groups viewed a film advocating tolerance of ethnic minorities and then discussed this general problem for half an hour. Various measures of the discussion process were taken, and several questionnaires were distributed to the group members at the end of the discussion.

Among the questions asked of the discussion group members, one was concerned with their perceptions of the opinions of the other participants. They were asked to indicate which of the other individuals in the group appeared to have opinions similar to or different from their own. In general, the low E's were more accurate in correctly identifying the attitudes held by other members of their group. Their judgments were more often correct when they were in either a majority or a minority position, and they were also more active in discussion in these conditions. The balanced groups showed the least amount of verbal activity. In the unbalanced conditions, the tolerant individuals interacted more with their fellow discussants and, as a result, had more information on which to base judgments of the others' attitudes. When asked which group members they liked best, they selected those whose attitudes they had perceived as being most like their own.

These findings of Altman and McGinnies are consistent with those reported by investigators who have studied the role of *authoritarian* attitudes in person perception. Of course, a relationship exists between authoritarian attitudes and ethnocentrism: both high-F and high-E persons tend to be intolerant of minority groups. It seems probable, then, that the past experiences of the authoritarian, or prejudiced, individual have been such as to render him relatively imperceptive of the actual attitudes of others; that is, he judges others to be like himself even when they actually hold different views.

Situational Factors

Leader-follower relations. The importance of the situation in person perception was demonstrated in several experiments by Fiedler (1958), in which certain measures of interpersonal perception were related to the effectiveness with which a work group functioned. As measures, Fiedler used both sociometric data (statements of preferences for other persons) and *assumed similarity* (ASo) scores. Although there are a variety of ways of obtaining ASo scores, the measure is taken to indicate the degree to which one person perceives another as similar either to himself or to a third person. For example, someone might be asked to describe himself by answering the questions on a standard personality inventory and then to describe another person using the same inventory. If the subject describes the other person in essentially the same terms as he uses to describe himself, this is evidence for an "assumed similarity" between himself and the other individual. This may be found to differ from "real similarity" when one compares the self-descriptions of the two individuals. It may also differ from "predictive accuracy," where an individual tries to answer the personality inventory the same way he thinks another person might answer it.

In one study, Fiedler attempted to determine the relationship between the effectiveness of a number of high school basketball teams and the ways in which the team members perceived one another. Before they had played their first game of the season, the players on fourteen teams were asked to name one person with whom they played best and one with whom they played least well. They were also asked to describe their most preferred and least preferred teammates. These two procedures enabled the investigators to determine both sociometric choices and assumed similarity scores. The criterion for team effectiveness was the proportion of games won by midseason. Although it had been expected that congenial relationships among team members would be related to success on the basketball court, such was not the case. As Fiedler describes his results, "The ASo scores of the team's most preferred co-worker — that is, the team's informal leader — were negatively related to team effectiveness. The better teams chose relatively distant, reserved persons as leaders, poorer teams chose the more accepting persons as informal leaders" (p. 248). Other studies involving air crews and industrial workers served to verify further the general finding that a person who leads a task group should be a "psychologically distant" individual. This means that he should be preceived by his subordinates as emotionally detached from them. Perception of the leader as just "one of the boys" frequently is inimical to the maintenance of discipline and effective working relationships.

Most attacks on the variable of "assumed similarity" in person perception have yielded findings indicating that individuals perceive those whom they like as more similar to themselves than those whom they dislike. One problem in interpreting these findings lies in the fact that certain traits or characteristics are considered more socially desirable than other traits. Intelligence and honesty, for example, are thought to be more desirable attributes than stupidity and dishonesty. One tends to attribute more desirable characteristics to both himself and his friends. Consequently, it is not surprising to find that one's friends are described in generally the same terms as one uses to describe himself. Any similarity in the ascribed traits, therefore, may be due simply to a *social desirability* effect rather than to some basic principle of interpersonal perception. It is possible to make a correction, or allowance, for this factor, and Secord (1964) has concluded that an assumed similarity effect exists over and above the operation of social desirability. He demonstrated this, in part, by showing that individuals also tend to attribute more often to liked than to disliked persons the *undesirable* traits that they perceive in themselves.

Expectancies of the perceiver. Inasmuch as each party to a behavioral exchange serves both as a stimulus and as a source of reinforcement to the other, a critical setting in which to assess the determinants of person perception is one in which the "perceiver" is able to interpret the actor's behavior as having some consequences for him. Situations that provide clearly specified contingencies, either positive or aversive, for the perceiver have not been studied to any great extent. One investigation, that of Jones and deCharms (1958), did make use of a contrived situation in which the perceiver could be deprived of a reward as a result of certain performances by the stimulus person. The situation was arranged so that the stimulus person would be seen as having failed a problem either through lack of application or through lack of aptitude. In either case, the perceiver was deprived of a reward. When subsequently given an opportunity to rate the stimulus person on a variety of traits, the perceiver assigned more undesirable traits only in those cases where the other person was seen as having failed through lack of effort. The fact of being punished as a result of the actions of another was not a sufficient basis for causing an unflattering appraisal of the other person unless the other person was perceived as culpable.

Gerard and Greenbaum (1962) used an Asch-type situation to manipulate the point in an experimental session at which a "partner" began to agree with a naive subject who had previously found his judgments to be at variance with those of a unanimous majority. When there are four individuals in such a group, the naive subject, who is Number Three, apparently perceives One as the leader, Two as the follower, and Four as a *persona non gratis* because he agrees with One and Two instead of with Three. Gerard and Greenbaum guessed that the naive subject's evaluation of Four would change, depending upon when Four began to agree with him rather than with One and Two. Specifically, they postulated that Four would be perceived more favorably the later he joined the naive subject in his judgments of the lengths of lines. They reasoned that a late rather than an early appearance of Four as a "partner" would reduce the subject's uncertainty more, hence would be more reinforcing. (In some respects, we may suggest, this resembles a deprivation operation.)

To test this hypothesis, they manipulated the point in a series of eighteen trials at which the fourth member of a group appeared to switch his judgments of the Asch lines to agree with the subject. All of the responses, of course, including those by subjects One and Two were actually controlled by the experimenter. The predictions were confirmed only for the later trials in the series, where the subjects ranked Four as more attractive than the other group members. Inconsistencies among the earlier ratings suggest that a problem still remains in establishing the conditions under which a person whose behavior changes from aversive to rewarding will be perceived more favorably.

This general problem has been approached by Jones and Davis (1965) with a view to determining how a perceiver evaluates the "intentions" of another person in a particular situation. Preferably, one might simply ask in what manner the cues that control a perceiver's interpretations of an actor's dispositions have arisen. We know that in an experimental situation this information may simply be supplied by the experimenter. In nonexperimental situations, it may be a matter of individual discernment. In any case, such inferences belong to the behavior of the perceiver and do not necessarily describe the behavior of the person being judged.

There is little doubt, of course, that any additional information possessed by a perceiver will influence his judgments, and that experimental manipulation of such information can drastically alter the perceiver's appraisal of another person. For example, Jones and others (1959) devised a situation in which a female student could "overhear" derogatory remarks being made about her by one of two female students in an adjacent room. She and a companion, who also overheard the remarks, had previously been informed that one of the overheard students was personally maladjusted. The situation was designed so that some subjects were derogated by the "well adjusted" member of the overheard pair and some were derogated by the "maladjusted" person. When the derogator was "well adjusted," the target of her derogation judged her much less favorably than did the bystander. When the derogator was thought to be "maladjusted," on the other hand, she was not judged any more harshly by the target subject than by her companion. Apparently the factor of personal maladjustment was considered in evaluating the source of the overheard invective.

This experiment, and others like it, serve to re-emphasize the fact that the total stimulus complex upon which one bases his judgments of another person includes not only that person's actual behavior but also any beliefs that one has about that person's traits or dispositions. Perhaps most important among such inferential determinants of person perception is the assumed relevance of that person's behavior to the perceiver. As Jones and Davis suggest, a very important feature of many person perception settings is that the behavior of the actor has significant rewarding or punishing implications for the perceiver. Of course, the extent to which the actor's behavior is either reinforcing or aversive will be a function of the context within which it occurs. An important feature of this context is the *expectancy* that we have of the actor. If the actor behaves in a manner that is inimical to our interests, but we had anticipated this behavior, the result frequently is less aversive than if we had expected some positive response from him. For example, an anti-American diatribe is likely to be less aversive if it issues from the mouth of a Soviet diplomat than if it is delivered by a British statesman.

One's perceptions and judgments of others are also a function of the extent to which his own behavior has been socially reinforced. Strickland, Jones, and Smith (1960) found that an individual who perceived his ideas as having group support was more likely to react negatively toward a stimulus person who criticized him than when he perceived himself as lacking such support. In the absence of reinforcement from others, individuals will be more inclined to react to criticism with self-doubt than to display hostility toward the critic. Apparently derogation of a critic is a more probable reaction when the criticized person feels his own position is secure. A similar process seems to operate in the case of ethnic prejudice, where social reinforcement for prejudicial judgments seems essential to both the development and the maintenance of such judgments. Individuals who for any reason begin to interact in groups where ethnic prejudice is not acceptable behavior are likely not only to suppress overt expressions of prejudice but actually to undergo a change in attitude. We will consider some evidence for this in later chapters.

Frequency of interaction. It is common knowledge that individuals tend to associate with and to like those persons with whom opportunity for personal contact is favored by propinquity. Homans (1950) has asserted that "if the frequency of interaction between two or more persons increases, the degree of their liking for one another will increase" (p. 112). Why should this necessarily be so? Newcomb (1956) has argued that when two persons interact, the reward-punishment ratio more often than not will be reinforcing. While this is not always so, it is probably true that if individuals continue to interact it is because they have found their interactions to be more rewarding than punishing. A high incidence of aversive behavior from either party to the interaction would soon discourage approach tendencies from the other person, and the relationship would terminate. It is probably safe to say, therefore, that any prolonged relationship between two individuals involves more reciprocal rewards, as Newcomb suggests, than reciprocal punishments. This, in turn, leads to more favorable assessment of each person by the other.

In situations where two or more individuals cannot readily terminate a relationship, it often happens that mutually reinforcing behavior occurs more frequently than mutually aversive behavior. In an extensive series of experiments dealing with the behavior and interpersonal perceptions of male students in a rooming house, Newcomb reports that even those roommates who had been preselected on the basis of minimal attraction came to like one another better than did nonroommate pairs. We may conjecture that individuals who have relatively little in common initially when brought face to face will learn through trial and error to engage in behaviors that maximize the frequency of pleasant interactions and minimize the frequency of unpleasant exchanges. Theoretically, we might argue that the occurrence of mutually irritating interactions will be self-limiting by virtue of the aversive consequences to each party. Alternative modes of interacting, having more rewarding consequences, will tend to increase. As Newcomb puts it ". . . the likelihood of being continually rewarded by a given person varies with the frequency with which that person is in turn rewarded" (p. 576). Mutually favorable impressions are readily seen as correlated with mutually reinforcing behavior.

There are obvious exceptions to this general principle; perhaps the most notable is the current high incidence of marital discord, a situation in which frequency of interaction between the two protagonists is assured. We cannot discover an explanation of this particular problem in a roominghouse situation such as that studied by Newcomb. Certainly there seem to be many situations where each party to a behavioral exchange acts in such a way as to exacerbate any frictions and conflicts that arise. We can only surmise that each person has somehow come to react to the other with attempts at aversive rather than positive control. The heightened emotionality engendered in each partner as a result of the general aversiveness of the situation interferes with the development of new behavior that might break this cycle and generate the results foreseen by Newcomb.

Summary   The data of psychology are based on measurable aspects of behavior. Nevertheless, many overt performances are presumed to have been mediated by implicit processes. Among these processes are those that involve perceptual organization and judgment. These cognitive events are revealed in behavior, and they are legitimate objects of scientific inquiry to the extent that the operations by which they are made public can be clearly specified. Recording the verbal behavior of an experimental subject is the most common operation by which data concerning cognitive processes are obtained.

Reinforcement principles seem to apply as well to analysis of aspects of perception and judgment as to analysis of overt behavior. It seems well established that individuals frequently perceive an ambiguous situation in terms of whatever information they have about the reactions of others in the same situation. Where the stimulus configuration is relatively well structured, the role of social factors in perception is considerably diminished. Ambiguity may be introduced by impoverishing the stimulus in various ways, such as making it unclear or presenting it only briefly. There is evidence that in such conditions personal attitudes and dispositions determine to some extent the readiness and accuracy with which stimuli relevant to these dispositions are perceived and reported. This effect has been referred to as selective perception. The readiness with which one recognizes words, for example, varies with the frequency with which they have been encountered as well as in accordance with certain attitudinal sets of the perceiver. Socially acquired dispositions, therefore, are seen as having some influence on perceptual processes that once were thought to depend solely upon invariant relationships between the properties of the stimulus and the receptor characteristics of the perceiver.

The perception and judgment of other persons is similarly influenced by dispositions acquired in a social context. But because a person presents a much more complex stimulus pattern than a visual display of words or pictures, it is more difficult to determine the exact nature of the variables that control person perception. It does seem to be established that a subject may be given a set, or expectancy, that will influence his subsequent perception of someone else. It also seems probable that we judge more favorably persons whom we perceive as similar to ourselves. Finally, there is evidence that individuals with certain personality dispositions, for example, authoritarianism, are less accurate in their judgments of others than those characterized by some other personality structure.

One of the major difficulties in interpreting the results of experiments dealing with social and personality factors in perception and judgment has been that of appropriately allocating the observed effects to cognitive variables and to response variables. In brief, a person may not always report exactly what he sees, or he may not report it promptly. For this reason, some investigators would prefer to deal only with overt performances and not engage in speculation about mediating cognitive events. For those who believe that behavior cannot be adequately understood without analysis of the underlying cognitive processes, however, the problems that we have considered in this chapter will present a continuing challenge.

References

ADORNO, T. W., FRENKEL-BRUNSWIK, ELSE, LEVINSON, D. J., and SANFORD, S. N. *The authoritarian personality.* New York: Harper and Row, 1950.

ALLPORT, F. H.   *Theories of perception and the concept of structure.* New York: Wiley, 1955.

ALLPORT, G. W., and KRAMER, B. M.   Some roots of prejudice. *Journal of Psychology*, 1946, *22*, 9–39.

ALLPORT, G. W., and VERNON, P. E.   *Studies in expressive movement.* New York: Macmillan, 1933.

ALLPORT, G. W., VERNON, P. E., and LINDZEY, G.   *Study of values.* Boston: Houghton Mifflin, 1951.

ALTMAN, I., and McGINNIES, E.   Interpersonal perception and communication in discussion groups of varied attitudinal composition. *Journal of Abnormal and Social Psychology*, 1960, *60*, 390–395.

ASCH, S. E.   Forming impressions of personality. *Journal of Abnormal and Social Psychology*, 1946, *41*, 258–290.

ASCH, S. E.   Effects of group pressure upon the modification and distortion of judgments. In H. Guetzkow (Ed.), *Groups, leadership and men.* Pittsburgh: Carnegie Press, 1951.

ASCH, S. E.   *Social Psychology.* Englewood Cliffs, N.J.: Prentice-Hall, 1952a.

ASCH, S. E.   Effects of group pressure upon the modification and distortion of judgments. In G. E. Swanson, T. M. Newcomb, and E. L. Hartley (Eds.), *Readings in social psychology* (rev. ed.). New York: Holt, Rinehart and Winston, 1952b.

BROWN, J. S.   *The motivation of behavior.* New York: McGraw-Hill, 1961.

BROWN, W. P.   Conceptions of perceptual defense. *British Journal of Psychology: Monograph Supplement*, Cambridge: The University Press, 1961.

BRUNER, J. S., and TAGIURI, R.   The perception of people. In G. Lindzey (Ed.), *Handbook of social psychology.* Vol. 2. Reading, Mass.: Addison-Wesley, 1954.

CHODORKOFF, B.   Anxiety, threat, and defensive reactions. *Journal of General Psychology*, 1956, *54*, 191–196.

COFFIN, T. E.   Some conditions of suggestion and suggestibility: A study of some attitudinal and situational factors influencing the process of suggestion. *Psychological Monographs*, 1941, No. 241.

CROCKETT, W. H., and MEIDINGER, T.   Authoritarianism and interpersonal perception. *Journal of Abnormal and Social Psychology*, 1956, 53, 378–380.

DEUTSCH, M., and GERARD, H.   A study of normative and informational social influences upon individual judgment. *Journal of Abnormal and Social Psychology*, 1955, *51*, 629–636. Copyright 1955 by the American Psychological Association. Data in tables 5.2 and 5.3 of this book reprinted by permission.

DORFMAN, D. D., GROSSBERG, J. M., and KROEKER, L.   Recognition of taboo stimuli as a function of exposure time. *Journal of Personality and Social Psychology*, 1965, 2, 552–562.

ERIKSEN, C. W.   The case for perceptual defense. *Psychological Review*, 1954, 61, 175–182.

FENSTERHEIM, H., and TRESSELT, M. E.   The influence of value systems on the perception of people. *Journal of Abnormal and Social Psychology*, 1953, 48, 93–98.

FIEDLER, F. E.   Interpersonal perception and group effectiveness. In R. Tagiuri and L. Petrullo (Eds.), *Person perception and interpersonal behavior*. Stanford, Calif.: Stanford University Press, 1958.

GERARD, H. B., and GREENBAUM, C. W.   Attitudes toward an agent of uncertainty reduction. *Journal of Personality*, 1962, 30, 485–495.

GOLDIAMOND, I.   Indicators of perception. I. Subliminal perception, subception, unconscious perception: An analysis in terms of psychophysical indicator methodology. *Psychological Bulletin*, 1958, 55, 373–411.

GOLDIAMOND, I.   Perception. In A. Bachrach (Ed.), *Experimental foundations of clinical psychology*. New York: Basic Books, 1962.

GOLDSTEIN, M. J.   A test of the response probability theory of perceptual defense. *Journal of Experimental Psychology*, 1962, 63, 23–28.

GOLDSTEIN, M. J.   Perceptual reactions to threat under varying conditions of measurement. *Journal of Abnormal and Social Psychology*, 1964, 69, 563–567.

GOLDSTEIN, M. J.   Relationship between perceptual defense and exposure duration. *Journal of Personality and Social Psychology*, 1966, 3, 608–610.

GRAHAM, C.   Sensation and perception in an objective psychology. *Psychological Review*, 1958, 65, 65–76.

HARVEY, O. J., HUNT, D. E., and SCHRODER, H. M.   *Conceptual systems and personality organization*. New York: Wiley, 1961.

HOMANS, G. C.   *The human group*. New York: Harcourt, Brace and World, 1950.

HOWES, D., and SOLOMON, R. L.   A note on McGinnies' "Emotionality and perceptual defense." *Psychological Review*, 1950, 57, 229–234.

HOWES, D., and SOLOMON, R. L.   Visual duration thresholds as a function of word probability. *Journal of Experimental Psychology*, 1951, 41, 401–410.

JACOBS, R. D., and CAMPBELL, D. T.   The perpetuation of an arbitrary tradition through several generations of a laboratory microculture. *Journal of Abnormal and Social Psychology*, 1961, 62, 649–658.

JONES, E. E., and DAVIS, K. E.   From acts to dispositions: The attribution process in person perception. In L. Berkowitz (Ed.), *Advances in experimental social psychology.* Vol. 2. New York: Academic Press, 1965.

JONES, E. E., and DECHARMS, R.   The organizing function of interaction roles in person perception. *Journal of Abnormal and Social Psychology,* 1958, 57, 155–164.

JONES, E. E., HESTER, S. L., FARINA, A., and DAVIS, K. E.   Reactions to unfavorable personal evaluations as a function of the evaluator's perceived adjustment. *Journal of Abnormal and Social Psychology,* 1959, 59, 363–370.

KELLEY, H. H.   The warm-cold variable in first impressions of persons. *Journal of Personality,* 1950, *18,* 431–439.

KELMAN, H. C.   Effects of success and failure on "suggestibility" in the autokinetic situation. *Journal of Abnormal and Social Psychology,* 1950, 45, 267–285.

LAZARUS, R. S., ERIKSEN, C. W., and FONDA, C. P.   Personality dynamics and auditory perceptual recognition. *Journal of Personality,* 1951, *19,* 471–482.

LINTON, H. B.   Autokinetic judgment as a measure of influence. *Journal of Abnormal and Social Psychology,* 1954, 49, 464–466.

LIPETZ, M. E.   The effects of information on the assessment of attitudes by authoritarians and nonauthoritarians. *Journal of Abnormal and Social Psychology,* 1960, 60, 95–99.

LUCHINS, A. S.   Social influences on perception of complex drawings. *Journal of Social Psychology,* 1945, *21,* 257–273.

LUCHINS, A. S.   Forming impressions of personality: A critique. *Journal of Abnormal and Social Psychology,* 1948, 43, 318–325.

LUCHINS, A. S., and LUCHINS, E. H.   On conforming with true and false communications. *Journal of Social Psychology,* 1955, *42,* 283–303.

MATHEWS, ANNE, and WERTHEIMER, M.   A "pure" measure of perceptual defense uncontaminated by response suppression. *Journal of Abnormal and Social Psychology,* 1958, 57, 373–376.

MAUSNER, B.   The effect of prior reinforcement on the interaction of observer pairs. *Journal of Abnormal and Social Psychology,* 1954, 49, 65–68.

McGINNIES, E.   Emotionality and perceptual defense. *Psychological Review,* 1949, 56, 244–251.

McGINNIES, E.   Discussion of Howes and Solomon's note on "Emotionality and perceptual defense." *Psychological Review,* 1950, 57, 235–240.

McGINNIES, E., COMER, P. B., and LACEY, O. L.   Visual recognition thresholds as a function of word length and word frequency. *Journal of Experimental Psychology,* 1952, *44,* 65–69.

MINARD, J. G.   Response-bias interpretation of "perceptual defense": A selective. review and evaluation of recent research. *Psychological Review,* 1965, 72, 74–88.

MINARD, J. G., BAILEY, D. E., and WERTHEIMER, M.   Measurement and conditioning of perceptual defense, response bias, and emotionally biased recognition. *Journal of Personality and Social Psychology,* 1965, 2, 661–668.

NEWCOMB, T. M.   The prediction of interpersonal attraction. *American Psychologist,* 1956, *11,* 575–586.

POSTMAN, L.   Toward a general theory of cognition. In J. H. Rohrer and M. Sherif (Eds.), *Social psychology at the crossroads.* New York: Harper, 1951.

POSTMAN, L.   Perception and learning. In S. Koch (Ed.), *Psychology: A study of a science.* Vol. 5. New York: McGraw-Hill, 1963.

POSTMAN. L., BRONSON, WANDA C., and GROPPER, G. L.   Is there a mechanism of perceptual defense? *Journal of Abnormal and Social Psychology,* 1953, *48,* 215–224.

POSTMAN, L., BRUNER, J. S., and McGINNIES, E.   Personal values as selective factors in perception. *Journal of Abnormal and Social Psychology,* 1948, *43,* 142–154.

POSTMAN, L., and SCHNEIDER, B.   Personal values, visual recognition, and recall. *Psychological Review,* 1951, *58,* 271–284.

PULOS, L., and SPILKA, B.   Perceptual selectivity, memory, and anti-Semitism. *Journal of Abnormal and Social Psychology,* 1961, *62,* 690–692.

RABINOWITZ, W.   A note on the social perceptions of authoritarians and non-authoritarians. *Journal of Abnormal and Social Psychology,* 1956, *53,* 384–386.

RAVEN, B. H.   Social influence on opinions and the communication of related content. *Journal of Abnormal and Social Psychology,* 1959, *58,* 119–128.

SACHIDANANDAN, G. S.   Verbal association as a function of personal values. M.A. thesis submitted to the University of Maryland, 1960.

SCHOENFELD, W. N., and CUMMING, W. W.   Behavior and perception. In S. Koch (Ed.), *Psychology: A study of a science.* Vol. 5. New York: McGraw-Hill, 1963.

SCHONBAR, R. A.   The interaction of observer pairs in judging visual extent and movement: The formation of social norms in "structured" situations. *Archives of Psychology,* 1945, No. 299.

SCODEL, A., and AUSTRIN, H.   The perception of Jewish photographs by non-Jews and Jews. *Journal of Abnormal and Social Psychology,* 1957, *54,* 278–280.

SCODEL, A., and FREEDMAN, MARIA L.   Additional observations on the social perceptions of authoritarians and nonauthoritarians. *Journal of Abnormal and Social Psychology,* 1956, *52,* 92–95.

SCODEL, A., and MUSSEN, P.   Social perceptions of authoritarians and nonauthoritarians. *Journal of Abnormal and Social Psychology,* 1953, *48,* 181–184.

SECORD, P. F.   Perception of similarity between self and alter. Reported in P. F. Secord and C. W. Backman, *Social Psychology.* New York: McGraw-Hill, 1964.

SECORD, P. F., and BACKMAN, C. W.   Interpersonal congruency, perceived similarity and friendship. *Sociometry,* 1964, *27,* 115–127.

SHERIF, M.   *The psychology of social norms.* New York: Harper and Row Torch-books, 1966. Originally published in *Archives of Psychology,* 1935, No. 187, under the title, "A study of some social factors in perception."

SOLLEY, C. M., and MURPHY, G.   *Development of the perceptual world.* New York: Basic Books, 1960.

SOLOMON, R. L., and HOWES, D.   Word frequency, personal values, and visual duration thresholds. *Psychological Review,* 1951, *58,* 256–270.

SPIVAK, M., and PAPAJOHN, J.   The effect of the schedule of reinforcement on operant conditioning of a verbal response in the autokinetic situation. *Journal of Abnormal and Social Psychology,* 1957, *54,* 213–217.

SPRANGER, E. *Types of men.* Halle: Max Niemeyer, 1928.

STONE, W. F. Autokinetic norms: An experimental analysis. *Journal of Personality, and Social Psychology,* 1967, 5, 76–81.

STRICKLAND, L. H., JONES, E. E., and SMITH, W. P. Effects of group support on the evaluation of an antagonist. *Journal of Abnormal and Social Psychology,* 1960, *61,* 73–81.

THORNDIKE, E. L. A constant error in psychological ratings. *Journal of Applied Psychology,* 1920, *4,* 25–29.

THORNDIKE, E. L., and LORGE, I. *The teacher's word book of 30,000 words.* New York: Columbia University Press, 1944.

TITCHENER, E. B. *A textbook of psychology.* New York: Macmillan, 1913.

VANDERPLAS, J. M., and BLAKE, R. R. Selective sensitization in auditory perception. *Journal of Personality,* 1949, *18,* 252–266.

WEINER, H., and McGINNIES, E. Authoritarianism, conformity, and confidence in a perceptual judgment situation. *Journal of Social Psychology,* 1961, 55, 77–84.

6

Behavior in
Small Groups

In considering the manner in which perceptions and judgments are influenced by social variables, particularly in a group setting, we focused our attention on the individual. But the group itself is also a legitimate object of study, and there is evidence that the products of group interaction cannot necessarily be predicted from the performance of the individuals outside the group situation. Experiments on group behavior frequently are designed to permit observation of the effects of social interaction on all of the members, not just the effects on one person selected for study. Both the composition and the behavior history of a group are determinants of its effective stimuli for the individual members. The group also determines the nature and pattern of the reinforcements the members receive in the course of their interactions with one another. Group composition and other salient features of the situation can be manipulated in the social-psychological laboratory, and we shall examine some of the studies of small groups in which this has been done.

Primary and Secondary Groups

Group influences are most apparent in face-to-face situations where communication between individuals is immediate and direct. But everyone reveals his past history of interaction in groups, even when he is alone. The behaviors that have been acquired in group situations become habitual, so that in a real sense each of us is the product of a number of social groups. To be sure, the behavior of some persons seems to reflect group influence more than the behavior of others; that is, they behave more in accordance with the prevailing norms of their society. The striking differences that can be observed among individuals in matters of opinion and attitude can be traced to affiliation with different groups and consequent differences in histories of social reinforcement.

Individuals seek different kinds of group memberships depending upon their particular habits and attitudes. These behavioral dispositions, in turn, have derived from earlier social interactions, the most important of which involved the family. Parents are not only the most important stimulus figures for the child, they also provide the reinforcements that shape his behavior. Behavior acquired at this early stage, with minor changes, frequently characterizes the individual for the rest of his life. Certainly most of our important attitudes dealing with such matters as religion, morals, and political philosophy are learned in the family. A group such as the family, where the members have intimate and immediate access to one another, is called a *primary group*. A group in which the members, due to geographical or other circumstances, may only occasionally engage in face-to-face interaction, is called a *secondary group*. This is a classic distinction derived from German sociology, in which the terms *Gemeinschaft* and *Gesellschaft* are used to distinguish between a smaller community and a larger society.

The distinction between a primary and a secondary group is sometimes tenuous and arbitrary. As the children in a family grow older, they increasingly interact with individuals outside this primary group. They join with their peers to form new primary groups, in which the members share interests relating to politics, education, religion, work, or recreation, to mention just a few possibilities. These primary groups may, in turn, be parts of a larger, secondary group, such as a political party or a church organization. The resources of secondary groups generally exceed those of primary groups, and membership in a secondary group frequently enables the individual to extend his behavior repertoire in ways that cannot be supported by a smaller, primary group. Joining a political party, for example, provides one with a greater opportunity to effect social change than he would have when acting either entirely by himself or in concert with others in a small group. The members of a political group are held together not just by certain commonalities of interest and intent but also by long-term expectancies of reward for their efforts.

Reference Groups

The term reference group is sometimes used to denote that primary or secondary group from which an individual has acquired certain attitudes or certain behavior patterns. Because most persons belong to a number of different groups, both primary and secondary, i.e., the family, church, labor union, fraternal or civic organization, their behavior often can be understood in terms of those groups in which it was acquired. What happens when different groups reinforce incompatible behaviors? Consider a college freshman who comes from a family where drinking alcoholic beverages is disapproved but who joins a fraternity in which a certain amount of alcohol consumption is not only tolerated but encouraged. He may behave discriminatively by drinking when with his companions and abstaining when at home. In this manner, he is positively reinforced for his behavior in both groups. Or he may attempt to demonstrate his newfound independence and striving for maturity by drinking both in college and at home. Inasmuch as he will experience aversive consequences in the home situation, we must assume that his behavior is controlled more by the immediate consequences of drinking than by his family's reactions. What he does when not in the presence of either his family or his fraternity brothers will depend upon which of these two reference groups has more effectively reinforced his behavior of drinking or not drinking.

An illustration of the role of reference groups in social behavior is provided by some observations made at Bennington College in the 1930's by Theodore Newcomb. Questionnaires measuring political-economic progressivism were given to members of the student body each year to determine how these attitudes might change over four years of college experience. A steady decrease in conservatism, with a concomitant increase in progressivism, was found in students as they advanced from the freshman through the senior years. For example, significant differences existed among these four groups in support for the conservative Republican presidential candidate of 1936, Alfred Landon. Sixty-two per cent of the freshmen, 43 per cent of the sophomores, 15 per cent of the juniors, and 15 per cent of the seniors favored Landon. Interestingly, 66 per cent of the parents of the students favored Landon, a figure most closely approximating that of the freshmen. It was apparent that political-economic attitudes became increasingly divorced from parental attitudes as the students proceeded from freshman class to senior class. An additional finding was that the more popular students scored more often as progressives than as conservatives on the attitude measure (Newcomb, 1943).

Charters and Newcomb (1958) asked students from a large psychology class who had identified themselves as members of the Roman Catholic Church to participate in an experiment ostensibly designed to construct an attitude scale. The students were divided into two groups. Members of a control group were given no special instructions other than to respond to the items on the scale. The members of the experimental group, however, were reminded of their membership in the Catholic Church, after which they discussed certain basic assumptions of the Church. Following this procedure, which was designed to emphasize their religious affiliation, they responded to the items on the attitude scale. Certain items were worded so that they could be answered not only from a Catholic point of view but from other points of view as well. It was found that the students in the experimental group, for whom membership in the Catholic Church had been made salient, responded to the critical items in a more orthodox Catholic fashion than did the students in the control group.

Both of the experiments just cited demonstrate that behavior often can be predicted from information about a person's history of affiliation with different social groups. An individual can be said to behave in accordance with his identification with certain reference groups which are important and significant to him. Or he can be said to have adopted a typical performance, or *role*, that is appropriate to the group situation in which he finds himself. Although the concepts of role and reference group are useful as descriptive devices, it will suit our purposes better to view the behavior as reflecting an acquired capacity of the individual to make discriminations that maximize his chances of being positively reinforced in a particular social situation. Consider the Bennington students studied by Newcomb. Many of the freshmen undoubtedly found themselves in a conflict situation. Certain verbal responses (attitudes) that had been positively reinforced within the family failed to evoke similar approval from those they recognized as campus leaders. As they progressed from freshman class to senior class standing, these students must occasionally have made utterances on political and economic issues that were not in accord with the attitudes they had acquired in their families. These utterances, we may assume, were promptly reinforced, and the probability that they would be repeated was thus increased. Because the sources of reinforcement were fellow students, including upperclassmen with more liberal attitudes, the attitudes of the freshmen were gradually modified in the direction of conformity to those prevailing in the college community.

The results obtained by Charters and Newcomb may be explained in a similar manner if we are willing to make several additional assumptions. The verbal habits in this situation were probably acquired in large part through prior education in Catholic ideology. Why did those subjects for whom membership in the Catholic Church was made salient respond in a more typically Catholic fashion than those who were not reminded of this particular group affiliation? The simplest explanation of this is that the instructions altered the stimulus characteristics of the situation so as to make the s^Ds similar to those associated with previously reinforced, pro-Catholic verbalizations. In other words, if I am reminded of the fact that I am a Catholic in a group of fellow Catholics and then am asked to respond to questions that allow for a doctrinal interpretation, I will tend to make those responses that have been reinforced in similar situations in the past. In short, my behavior will generalize to this new situation. If, on the other hand, I am not made aware of the special nature of the group, then my behavior is controlled by a different set of stimuli, and I will not necessarily emit characteristically Catholic responses. Identifying a group as having certain properties relevant to an individual's attitudes gives a unique structure to the situation and highlights the discriminative stimuli to which he will respond. The *behavior most likely to occur in a new situation is that which has a history of positive reinforcement in similar prior situations.*

Even the selectivity of perception may in some instances be attributed to the influence of reference groups. As Shibutani (1961) points out, a prostitute and a social worker walking through a slum area probably notice different things. Differences in taste concerning art, music, and decor reflect the influence of the social groups to which one has belonged. These groups provided the occasions on which certain behaviors were learned and from which responses will generalize to new situations that contain some of the same stimulus elements.

Audience Effects on Task Performance

Floyd Allport (1920) has taken the position that an individual's motivational state is altered in the context of a group. The effect on behavior is generally one of enhancement, or *social facilitation.* Allport studied groups composed of three to five students at Harvard and Radcliffe colleges. The task of all the subjects in the groups was to write associations to stimulus words such as "building" and "laboratory." Their responses were compared with those of other subjects who formed associations working alone instead of in a group. The results, according to Allport, showed that the presence of a coworking group had the effect of speeding up the process of free association. To be sure, individual differences were manifested; some subjects were distracted in the group situation and were less productive of verbal associations. In general, however, Allport's experiment revealed the operation of a subtle social influence on behavior that had traditionally been studied only with single individuals. In work groups, this facilitation effect is sometimes manifested as greater quantity but poorer quality of output.

Social Facilitation

We may consider it an established principle, then, that being in a group has unique stimulus value for the individual. Can the group situation be shown to influence behavior more complex than that involving simple discriminations or judgments? For example, do individuals perform skilled tasks better alone or in a group? An early attempt to answer this question was made by Travis (1925), who trained twenty-two college undergraduates to perform fairly skillfully on a pursuit rotor. This device resembles a phonograph turntable near the edge of which is mounted a small metal disc about the size of a nickel. The subject's task is to keep a flexible pointer in contact with this target while the turntable revolves at 60 R.P.M. After the students had practiced on this task until their performances had reached a stable level, they were asked to do the same thing in front of a small "audience" consisting of other students. The average time on target for the subjects when performing before their peers was somewhat longer than when they had performed alone, indicating an apparent group influence on accuracy in a simple task involving motor skill. Other early demonstrations of this sort included the discovery that individuals solved simple multiplication problems more rapidly and produced more associations to words when in the presence of passive spectators than when working alone (Dashiell, 1930).

Taylor and Faust (1952) also obtained evidence that the performance of individuals in a group may be superior in some respects to their individual efforts. They recorded the number of questions asked as well as the time required by individuals alone and in groups to guess the correct answer in a game of Twenty Questions. The groups, composed of either two or four individuals, required on the average fewer questions and less time to solve the problems than did individuals. Size of the group, within these limits, was not an important variable. The authors point out, however, that in terms of man-minutes required for solution, the performance of individuals was superior to that of groups and the performance of groups of two was superior to that of groups of four. Two persons, however, did not solve a given problem in less than half the time required by one person, as would be necessary to demonstrate group superiority. These experimental results suggest that the performance of individuals in a group is indeed likely to be different from their performance alone, but not necessarily more efficient.

A vigilance problem. More recently, Bergum and Lehr (1963) recorded the performances of twenty National Guard trainees who were required to sit in isolated booths and observe a panel on which twenty red lights were mounted in a circle. The lights were lit up in sequence, and this circular pattern was repeated every five seconds. During an hour, however, there were twenty-four instances of a light failing to go on in its proper sequence. It was the task of the subjects to monitor the display and press a button whenever such an interruption in the sequence occurred. After twenty minutes of training, followed by a ten-minute rest, the subjects performed alone on this vigilance task for two hours and fifteen minutes. Twenty additional subjects, similarly trained, were told that from time to time during the test period their booths would be visited by a Lieutenant Colonel or a Master Sergeant. Four such visits were actually made to each subject. The mean performance of these "supervised" subjects was then compared with that of the "unsupervised" subjects over five successive twenty-seven minute intervals. The results are shown in Figure 6.1.

As a result of fatigue, the performance of both the groups shown in Figure 6.1 deteriorated with time. But the subjects who were subjected to unannounced visits by their superiors maintained a distinctly higher level of performance than those who monitored the light panel unsupervised. The occasional visits by a military superior placed these subjects on a variable interval schedule of reinforcement, and their performances — aside from fatigue decrement — were typical of those found with this type of schedule.

Decision-making. A different type of task, devised by Banta and Nelson (1964), required college students to judge the reactions of a hypothetical

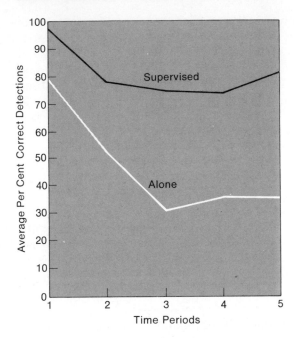

Figure 6.1
Accuracy on a vigilance task performed alone and under supervision. (After Bergum and Lehr, 1963)

individual to a list of attitude statements after first being told the person's reaction to five similar statements. Dyads (two-person groups) were formed to work on this task, and the partners were told that they must agree on a decision, then record their action by pressing a signal button. A light was flashed by the experimenter whenever the decision favored by a previously designated member of each pair was adopted. Control groups performed the same task under noncontingent reinforcement. The probability that the reinforced partner would have his opinions reported out of the dyad rose with successive trials. The nonreinforced subjects, on the other hand, made fewer and fewer proposals for a solution, and their partners began to dominate the decision-making process. This experimental result has its counterpart in committee processes, where those members whose proposals are consistently adopted are often seen to play an increasingly dominant role in the group's deliberations. Nonreinforcement, through repeated failure to have their suggestions acted on by the group, causes some individuals to virtually withdraw from debate in favor of those whose contributions are rewarded. As we shall see later in this chapter, it is possible by selective manipulation of the reinforcement contingencies to encourage the performance of the more reticent members of a group and to depress that of the more aggressive individuals.

Social Inhibition

Social interaction may also have an inhibiting rather than a facilitating effect. Allport (1920) reported, for example, that individuals who free associated to words in the presence of others gave more common and fewer uncommon responses. Idiosyncratic associations, in other words, seem to be inhibited, or suppressed, in a group situation. This observation is consistent with the findings of Sherif (1966) and Asch (1952), discussed in Chapter 5. These investigators, as you will recall, observed a trend toward development of a group norm in situations where individuals re- ported their perceptions of either the movement of a point of light or the length of a line. The giving of more "common" associations to stimulus words in a group situation reveals the operation of a similar movement toward established norms. The general principle that seems to emerge from these experiments is that individual behavior in a group situation is modified in accordance with the particular stimulus features that charac- terize the group. Differences in the prior experiences of the individual group members determine whether task performance will be facilitated or inhibited in any single case.

Zajonc (1966) has argued that a distinction should be made between situa- tions where individuals are performing tasks in the mere *presence of others* and those where several persons are *simultaneously engaged in* the same activity. We might add a third category, where a task can be solved only through the *joint or combined efforts* of several individuals. This last situation involves a special sort of social interaction, called cooperation, and may be deferred for later discussion. Consider for a moment just those situations where a person performs in the company of others or where several persons perform simultaneously but independently. Although we have focused our attention on results that indicated a *facilitation effect* in both of these instances, several investigators have reported just the oppo- site. Pessin (1933) found that subjects who memorized lists of nonsense syllables in the presence of spectators required more repetitions and made more errors than when they learned equivalent materials alone. Pre- viously, Husband (1931) had reported that finger-maze learning was slower in the presence of an observer. As we have already noted, there is evidence that both the quality and originality of performance may suffer in a group situation. Apparently, a social context for individual task performance does not provide unalloyed advantages.

Learning vs. performance. Zajonc, (1966), after reviewing this general problem, suggests that "learning is impaired and performance facilitated by the presence of an audience" (p. 14). *Learning,* Zajonc points out, refers to the acquisition of new responses, while *performance* refers to the emis- sion of previously learned responses. He argues that in any learning situa- tion the subject tends at first to make a great many incorrect responses. When performing a previously learned task, however, an individual emits more correct than incorrect responses. An audience has the effect of en- hancing the emission of *dominant responses*, and these are predominantly incorrect during learning and predominantly correct during performance.

Although Zajonc offers an explanation of this effect in terms of increased motivation and arousal in the presence of an audience, let us suggest an alternative interpretation. First, as pointed out, individuals tend to make a great many errors during learning. As a consequence of previous experiences in performing before a group, the individual comes to anticipate reactions of disparagement when he commits blunders. He is likely to generalize this expectancy to a learning situation in which other persons are present. In other words, his behavior is controlled not only by stimuli representing the task but also by stimuli provided by the audience; and the latter have been the occasions for ridicule contingent upon the commission of blunders. Consequently, every error he makes during learning serves as a conditioned stimulus for the anxiety occasioned by public disparagement, whether or not such a reaction is actually forthcoming from the present audience. Because he makes more incorrect than correct responses during the early phases of learning, the emotional reactions that have been conditioned to public ineptness interfere with both his attention and his coordination. The individual, therefore, does not acquire new response patterns as readily when he is in a situation that has the potentiality of becoming aversive whenever he makes a mistake.

Consider, on the other hand, the behavior of a person who is engaged before an audience in a previously learned, well-practiced task. If he has any degree of competence in the task, he will make more correct than incorrect responses. Previous experience has taught him that a competent performance will earn the plaudits of onlookers. Insofar as the correct responses are already within his repertoire, he will be reinforced by the sheer presence of an audience whenever they occur. Incorrect responses, although they will be more aversive in the presence of a group, will occur less frequently, and the attendant emotional reactions will not be as disruptive of the total performance as those that would occur during learning under similar circumstances. Whether or not the presence of others facilitates or inhibits performance, then, is seen to depend upon the overall level of task competence that the individual has attained. His operant level of correct responses must exceed that of incorrect responses in order for reinforcing consequences to occur more frequently than aversive consequences. We need not look far in everyday experience to find examples of this principle. The amateur performer in any field — entertainment, sports, public speaking — finds his behavior progressively deteriorating as soon as he commences to fumble and blunder before an audience. The task that was incompletely mastered when practiced alone becomes a nightmare in the presence of a group, the very existence of which is aversive when one performs inadequately. To the skilled professional, on the other hand, an audience serves as an additional source of reinforcement, adding to the satisfaction that the performer experiences when he practices competently alone.

Reasoning from everyday observation, however, is not an adequate substitute for experimental data. Fortunately, several studies have been reported that bear upon the adequacy of this analysis. Cottrell, Rittle, and Wack (1967) examined both the difficulty of the task and the degree of competence of their subjects in relation to speed of learning either alone or in the presence of an audience. Their subjects were 102 male undergraduates confronted with the task of learning lists of paired associates. This is a situation in which the subject views pairs of words, presented one pair at a time on a memory drum. On successive trials, he must try to name correctly the *second* word of each pair upon presentation of the first word. Items typical of such pairs would be *barren-fruitless, arid-grouchy,* and *desert-leading.* These particular pairs, in fact, were part of a difficult list used by these investigators. The difficulty lies in the fact that there are few within-pair associations and many strong associations between members of different pairs, for example, *barren, arid,* and *desert.* This means that a subject is apt to respond to the first word of a pair with its associate from another pair. In an easier task, the words in each pair had strong associations, and there were few associations between members of different pairs. Thus, the correct responses in the case of pairs such as *adept-skillful* and *barren-fruitless* would be learned more readily than those in the pairs previously mentioned.

The subjects were divided into slow, medium, and fast learners on the basis of the number of trials required for them to learn a practice list. The numbers of errors they made in learning the test lists were then computed as a function of the presence and the absence of a two-person audience watching the subject attentively while he learned. When the subjects learned the easy lists, it apparently made little difference whether the two observers were present or not. Nor did differences in learning skill of the subjects appear to affect their reactions markedly in the presence of an audience. In the case of the difficult list, however, the presence of an audience had the effect of causing the less able learners to commit more errors. The fast learners made slightly fewer errors when their performance was being observed. These results are shown graphically in Figure 6.2.

Attentive vs. inattentive audiences. Zajonc's view that the mere presence of other persons increases the subject's "motivation" to perform suggests that it should make little difference whether or not the audience members are attending to what the subject is doing. If, as we have suggested, the potential of other individuals as agents of reinforcement is critical in their effect upon a performer, then it should matter whether they are merely physically present or are present as spectators. Cottrell and his colleagues (1968) examined the possibility that subjects engaged in a recognition task would perform differently in the presence of an audience and in the presence of others who did not constitute an audi-

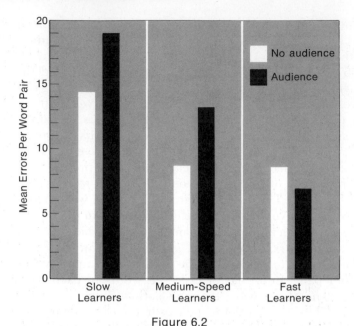

Figure 6.2

Errors in learning paired associates as a function of skill and presence of an audience. (Adapted from Cottrell, Rittle, and Wack, 1967)

ence. Forty-five male college students first practiced pronouncing ten nonsense words like *afworbu* and *biwonji*. Two words were assigned to each of five training frequencies: 1, 2, 5, 10, and 25. Thus, the subjects read and repeated some of the words twenty-five times and others only once. This procedure established certain of these new verbal habits as more dominant than others. Dominant responses, remember, have been found to occur more readily than weaker responses in the presence of an audience.

The subjects were then assigned to one of three test conditions. They attempted to recognize the words they had just practiced when the words were projected at very short durations on a screen seven feet away. Some of the subjects did this alone, others were observed by two spectators, and still others performed in the presence of two *blindfolded* individuals, who were ostensibly becoming dark-adapted for another experiment. Out of 160 flashes on the screen, 120 constituted pseudo-recognition trials; that is, the stimulus was one of the training words but presented in a reversed position and thereby rendered unreadable. Inasmuch as the subjects were instructed to guess on every trial, the experimenters could determine the extent to which they would emit responses that had been made more or less dominant during training. And they could relate these differences to the particular conditions in which the subjects found themselves. The results of this experiment are shown in Figure 6.3.

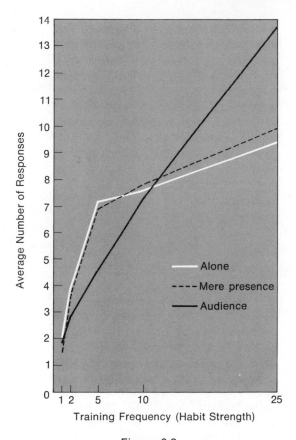

Figure 6.3

*Number of responses of different training frequency classes (habit
strength) emitted on the pseudo-recognition trials, averaged over subjects and over trial blocks.* (From Cottrell, Sekerak, Wack, and Rittle,
1968)

The data revealed that the presence of an audience enhances the emission of dominant responses in preference to subordinate responses. The
mere presence of other persons, however, produces no such effect upon
performance; that is, the subjects guessed as many of the high frequency
training words when alone as they did in the presence of two blindfolded
students. In reconsidering these and related findings, Cottrell (1968) suggests what amounts to a reinforcement interpretation. He observes that if
performance before an audience usually results in positive or negative
outcomes for the individual, he will come to anticipate such outcomes
when placed in an audience situation. Although Cottrell goes further and
speaks of a learned source of drive, it is not necessary to do so. The nonsense words that were practiced less frequently by the subjects may be
viewed as having the status of potentially "incorrect" responses during the

guessing phase, while those that were frequently practiced are analogous to "correct" responses. As we have previously suggested, an audience provides cues for the emission of performances having the greatest likelihood of being positively reinforced. Responses that are most likely to be correct ordinarily are those that have been practiced most frequently. Individuals who are present but are not able to observe what one is doing do not provide the same cues to potential consequences as an audience does. Performance in these circumstances is not likely to differ from performance when alone. This analysis proceeds from a consideration of the individual's history of reinforcement in situations similar to the one in which he now finds himself. No inferences about drive states are needed, and none are made. We can make fairly accurate predictions about how an individual will perform if we know something about his level of skill, his past experience in similar situations, and the nature of the occasion on which he is currently being required to demonstrate his proficiency.

The Role of Incentives

One way of facilitating task performance is to offer incentives for increased competence. The most generally effective incentive seems to be money, but money will serve this function only in situations where its potential as a reinforcer will not be offset by other, aversive consequences. An experiment conducted in the late 1920's (Roethlisberger and Dickson, 1947) illustrates this point. As one of a series of studies done at Western Electric's Hawthorne plant in Chicago, the experiment involved workers who attached and soldered banks of wires to a telephone switchboard component. Fourteen workers and one observer were placed in a special room, and various wage incentives were introduced in an attempt by the management to discover which ones would most facilitate production.

Taken at face value, this experiment would seem to represent a straightforward manipulation of amount of anticipated monetary reinforcement to discover the effect on productivity. The results, however, were disappointing. Level of productivity remained relatively constant despite variations in the wage incentives that were offered. The apparent explanation for this failure to increase production through wage incentives is one of those that seems obvious after the fact. Each worker feared that if output were increased, management would maintain its current level of expenses by decreasing the payment for each unit produced. Management did not, of course, threaten any such readjustment of incentives in the event of an increase in output, but the workers apparently assumed that this might happen. Olmstead (1959) summarizes the situation in the vernacular of the participants: "A good guy won't be a chiseler: he'll do his share and not expect others to 'carry' him (except in certain circumstances). Thirdly, he won't be a squealer; he will protect the group code against outside interference. Finally, he won't put on airs or be a snob, that is, he will manifest in his non-work behavior his 'democratic' submission to group ideals" (p. 29).

This classic study illustrates the danger of attempting to define a reinforcer independent of its effects upon behavior. Money, in this instance, was rendered ineffective as an incentive because of the way in which the workers interpreted the situation. This interpretation was reinforced by the group, and deviant behavior by an individual member in the form of increased productivity would probably have had aversive consequences to that individual. In fact, Coch and French (1948) observed a clothespresser who was "scapegoated" by her coworkers because her efficiency rating had climbed above the average for the group.

Field Theory

Many of the earlier experiments on the behavior of individuals in groups reflected a viewpoint expressed by Floyd Allport in 1924, namely, that there is no psychology of groups which is not essentially a psychology of individuals. There is, however, another conceptual approach to group behavior that sees the group as an entity possessing emergent qualities that cannot be discovered through analysis of the behavior of the individuals comprising the group. Probably the most articulate spokesman for this theoretical approach was Kurt Lewin, who, writing in 1951, stated: "Instead of picking out one or more isolated elements within a situation, the importance of which cannot be judged without consideration of the situation as a whole, field theory finds it advantageous, as a rule, to start with a characterization of the situation as a whole" (p. 63).

Lewin took the position, characteristic of gestalt psychology, that an individual's subjective perception of the world is more important to an understanding of his behavior than what we might define as "objective reality" (Shepherd, 1964). The proper subject matter for the social psychologist, according to this view, is the *psychological field* or *life space*. The individual is seen as being attracted to certain persons or objects within his life space and being repelled by others. Those situations that attract him are said to have positive valence, while those that repel him have negative valence. In its simplest form, this type of descriptive system lends itself to the following form of schematic representation.

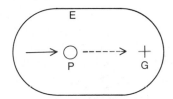

The psychological field is presented as a space (E) within which a person (P) moves (dashed arrow) toward a positive goal (G) in accordance with certain field forces (represented by vectors, such as arrow at left). A negative object or goal G(−) would repel rather than attract the individual. Analysis of behavior using these types of constructs involves the basic assumption, stated by J. F. Brown (1936), that ". . . any attempted isolation of the individual from the group or consideration of the group as independent of the individuals composing it is impossible" (p. 67). For example, the psychological field is critically altered if more than one person is present, and the resulting field forces cannot be predicted from knowledge of the vectors that govern the behavior of each single individual.

The full flavor of Lewin's theory can only be appreciated when it is recognized that his concept of *field* took into account not only the objective environment but also the psychological environment of the individual. Thus, a given objective environment provides the substrate for several different psychological environments experienced by different persons. The same object, in other words, can be either attractive or repulsive, depending upon the dispositions of different observers. Lewin's theoretical system is complicated, however, by the fact that he uses the term "person" in different ways, referring sometimes to an entity moving in the psychological field and sometimes to a differentiated region representing an individual's life space (Deutsch, 1968).

Field theory, as Lewin elaborated it, has little current vitality and is of interest mainly because of the impact it has had on the directions taken by social-psychological research. Both *group dynamics* and *action research* have stemmed from Lewin's writings and from his personal influence on his students (McGrath and Altman, 1966). His major contributions to social psychology, apart from his theoretical work, have been summed up by Deutsch: "He believed . . . that the attempt to bring about change in a process is the most fruitful way to investigate it; that important social-psychological phenomena can be studied experimentally; that the scientist should have a social conscience and should be active in making the world a better place to live in; and that a good theory is valuable for social action as well as for science" (1968, p. 478).

Lewin deserves much credit for being the first social psychologist to bring together effectively theory, real-life problems, and experimental methodology. We will not attempt to detail further this particular theoretical approach, except to note that it employs a vocabulary that is likely to mystify more than it enlightens. Nevertheless, field theory has generated concern with the patterns of interactions among individuals in groups — what is more commonly known as *group dynamics*. We turn now to several areas in which the manipulation of situational variables has been shown to influence the course of individual behavior in small group settings.

Verbal Interaction

Social situations can take almost infinite numbers of forms, and the behavior exhibited by individuals in these situations is so varied and complex as to almost defy analysis. Because we can seldom, if ever, specify all of the variables that control behavior in social situations, we must content ourselves with identifying those that are most frequently encountered. Social psychologists have devised several ingenious procedures for manipulating one class of variables, namely, verbal interaction in small groups. Since communication is itself a potent form of social behavior, it is important that we understand something about the key variables that control the communicative process. For example, several factors operate to determine the direction and fluidity of communication among the members of groups. One of these, as Steinzor (1950) discovered, is the spatial position of the individual in a group. He found that in a circular seating arrangement the participants in a group discussion interacted more frequently with those sitting some distance from themselves than with individuals seated closer. Steinzor hypothesized: "If a person happens to be in a spatial position which increases the chances of his being more completely observed, the stimulus value of his ideas and statements increases by virtue of that very factor of his greater physical and expressive impact on others. People sitting next to each other in a circle will probably not observe each other as fully as those sitting further away" (p. 552). This amounts to saying that an individual is more likely to engage in mutually reinforcing behavior with others when his spatial position *vis-à-vis* these others makes him a more effective stimulus. Hare and Bales (1963) obtained similar results with five-man discussion groups seated around three sides of a rectangular table. More recently, Ward (1968), using a circular seating arrangement with five subjects, found that individuals who faced several others did more talking and were more likely to be perceived by the other members as leaders.

Communication Networks

Another factor of obvious importance in group behavior is the number and pattern of avenues, or channels, of communication available to the members. In an open discussion, such as Steinzor employed, there is little opportunity for the experimenter to exert control over the direction or type of communication that takes place. Bavelas (1950) and his coworkers have devised techniques for controlling the flow of communication in a group and observing the effects of different communication patterns on productivity, emergence of leadership, and member satisfaction. One way of doing this is to seat subjects around a table, separated by partitions, so that they can communicate only by passing notes through slots. This type of arrangement prevents facial expressions from influencing communication and allows the experimenters to control both the direction and the amount of interchange that takes place. Another technique for accomplishing these same purposes is to have the subjects isolated in booths and able to communicate only by pressing buttons that cause one or more signal lights to go on in the adjacent booths. With this arrangement, the experimenter can also control the content of the communication by simply operating all of the signal lights from a central panel. The subjects can be led to think that they are receiving messages from one another when actually the messages are being transmitted by the experimenter. Devious techniques such as these are sometimes necessary to give the experimenter fuller control over the independent variables in which he is interested.

Efficiency. An interesting and frequently cited experiment involving manipulation of communication channels was done by Leavitt (1951), who studied five-man groups using written communications and a simple task. Figure 6.4 shows the seating arrangement he used.

A five-layered, pentagonal box in the center of the table permitted any pattern of communication between the various members of the group. Each shelf was designated for one individual, so that messages could be exchanged in any direction. By opening or closing various of these slots, the experimenter could vary the communication network. Six symbols printed on cards were used in the task assigned to the subjects. These are pictured below.

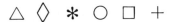

Each subject was given a card containing only five of the symbols, and each card had a different symbol lacking. Thus, the cards held by the subjects contained only one symbol in common. The problem was for the subjects to discover this common symbol. To accomplish this, they passed written messages to one another through the slots at the intersection of the partitions shown in Figure 6.4. When all five subjects indicated that they knew the common symbol, the trial was ended and another was begun using a different set of cards with a new common symbol. Four possible networks of communication were set up by the experimenter, as shown below.

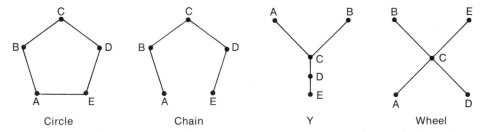

| Circle | Chain | Y | Wheel |

In the circle, for example, each member of the group could communicate only with the person on either side. In the chain, messages could go in one direction only, starting with either A or E. In the Y, all messages eventually went to C, who had complete decision-making authority. The wheel also gave C the most central position in the communication network.

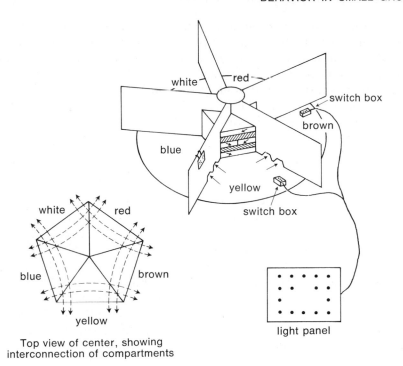

Top view of center, showing
interconnection of compartments

Figure 6.4

*Apparatus used to permit five-way communication by means of written
notes.* (After Leavitt, 1951)

Although Leavitt analyzed his results in considerable detail, we shall
mention only a few of the more prominent findings. Questionnaires administered after each experimental session allowed the subjects an opportunity to indicate their perceptions of any leadership behavior that emerged
in the group and to express their reactions to the group's performance.
Several reasonably unambiguous findings emerged: (a) Taking the shortest
single trial (solution of one problem) as a criterion, the wheel yielded the
fastest performance, with the chain, Y, and circle following, in that order.
(b) The Y pattern made the fewest errors, and the circle made the most,
with the chain and the wheel falling in between. (c) Members' expressed
satisfaction with the various patterns followed this order: circle, chain, Y,
wheel. Leavitt comments, "The circle, one extreme, is active, leaderless,
unorganized, erratic, and yet is enjoyed by its members. The wheel,
at the other extreme, is less active, has a distinct leader, is well and stably
organized, is less erratic, and yet is unsatisfying to most of its members"
(p. 46).

Durability. We shall consider briefly one more experiment in which the
channels of communication available to the members of small problem-

solving groups were experimentally manipulated. Heise and Miller (1951) studied the performance of three-person groups in three different tasks. The subjects sat in adjoining rooms and communicated by means of microphones, an amplifier, and earphones. By switching the various microphones on or off, the experimenters were able to control the directions in which communication could occur. Five different communication nets were studied, as pictured below.

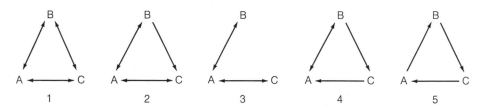

Net 1, it can be seen, is similar to Leavitt's circle. Net 3 is analogous to the wheel, because Individual A is in a central position and thus becomes the coordinator for the group. Net 5 is a closed chain; and there was no arrangement in this experiment comparable to Leavitt's Y. Three intensities of white noise (a hissing sound) were introduced into the sound system so that the experimenters could determine which network was the most resistant to this type of interference for the different tasks.

The simplest of the three problems required the subjects to reconstruct a list of words from the partial list that each possessed. The way in which the subjects could communicate with one another was standardized. Each subject had to say, "You will write . . . [one of the words on his list]." When each subject had compiled a twenty-five-word list, the problem was solved. A second task required the group members to construct a sentence. Each subject had a portion of the words, listed in the order in which they occurred in the sentence. This was a more interesting task and one that allowed for more initiative. Performance measures were (a) accuracy of the completed lists, (b) the time required to complete the task, and (c) the total number of words spoken in completing the task.

The main effect of different levels of white noise interference was to exaggerate differences in efficiency between the several communication nets. Figure 6.5 shows the time required by the subjects in the five communication nets to finish the word list task and the sentence completion task under the condition of maximum noise interference (lowest signal-to-noise ratio).

As the graphs show, group efficiency in each of these tasks was related to the communication pattern that was used. For the word list problem, a closed chain (Net 5), which allowed only one-way communication between any two persons, was the least efficient. A closed chain that permitted two-way communication among all of the group members (Net 1) was the most efficient. For the sentence completion problem, the closed chain per-

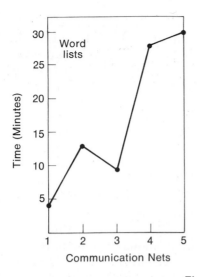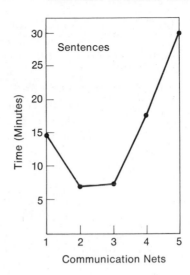

Figure 6.5

*Performances of the five communication nets on the word list problem
and the sentence completion task under maximum noise interference.*
(Adapted from Heise and Miller, 1951)

mitting only one-way communication (Net 5) again was the least efficient.
However, the open chain (Net 3), which had one man in a central coor-
dinating position, replaced the two-way closed chain (Net 1) as the most
efficient. The relative durability of the several communication nets under
stressful conditions depended upon the kind of problem the group was
trying to solve.

We have considered these two experiments in some detail because they
illustrate the manner in which social psychologists have studied communication in small groups under relatively well controlled conditions. Both
investigations involved independent manipulation of the channels of
communication available to the group members as well as control over the
type of problem solving in which the members engaged. In each experiment, the subjects obviously were disposed to cooperate with the experimenter and to behave in accordance with his instructions. Deference to
teachers and supervisors has frequently been reinforced in the course of
one's progress through the educational system, and it is not surprising to
find that this behavior generalizes to many experimental situations. Although no extrinsic incentives were provided in the experiments just discussed, we may assume that the achievement of a solution to the problems
was sufficiently rewarding to maintain the behavior on successive trials.

Satisfaction. In fact, it has been shown that an intangible reaction
termed satisfaction is related to knowledge of the success of one's group
in solving a problem. A group of investigators (Collins, Davis, Myers, and

Silk, 1964) studied the circle form of communication network by placing experimental subjects in a *relayer* position. The subjects thus were not able to solve any of the problems submitted to the five-man groups of which they were members, but when they relayed messages to a particular member of the group, they were told that their group had solved the problem. Following the experimental sessions, questionnaires designed to measure satisfaction with the task were given to these subjects, and it was found that expressions of satisfaction were related to the number of times they had been informed of the success of their group. In a society such as ours, where the successful solution of various kinds of problems is socially reinforced, it is not surprising to find that information denoting success can serve as a reinforcer or that expressions of subjective satisfaction with one's performance are related to such information.

We may conclude that communication nets do vary in the degree to which they facilitate exchange of information among the members of small, problem-solving groups. However, the relative effectiveness of a particular net seems to depend upon the type of problem being attacked. Because an exchange of information frequently establishes conditions in which other reinforced performances may occur, the act of communicating acquires generalized conditioned reinforcing properties for many people. In the experiments that we have just described, the successful outcome of a group task was related to the efficiency with which certain communication channels were utilized. Success in solving the problem, in turn, determined the extent to which the participants experienced satisfaction (i.e., were reinforced) for their performance.

Using a variation of the Bavelas situation, Butler and Miller (1965a) studied five-man groups in which messages were exchanged on strips of cardboard, with the content not seen by the sender. The subjects were separated by partitions, and they could communicate only by means of one hundred such "messages" bearing the letter A or B on the back. The message cards were color-coded, so that each subject knew from whom a message had come.

The subjects were told to try to collect as many "A messages" as they could. Inasmuch as the experimenter had allocated different numbers of "A messages" to the several participants, a given person's "power" to reinforce another was predetermined according to one of five schedules. For example, in Group 1, the distribution of "A messages" was as follows: 50, 90, 90, 90, 90. In Group 11, the distribution was 10, 10, 10, 10, 50. Different proportions of "rewarding" messages were assigned in three other experimental groups, so that some subjects had more power, in this respect, than others. The results, reduced to their simplest form, showed that the number of "A messages" received was a direct function of the number an individual was able to disburse. That is, those individuals with a greater initial capacity to reinforce others in the group were the recipients of more communications as well as the recipients of more of the rewarding "A messages." In a subsequent attempt to extend these findings, Butler and Miller (1965B) found that a subject's reward power was more effective than punishment power in controlling the punishments that were addressed to him. Mild punishment was judged an ineffective method of interpersonal control. This finding is consistent with our earlier conclusion that the control of behavior through positive reinforcement is preferable, generally speaking, to aversive control.

Reinforcement effects. One shortcoming of most of the experiments on communication nets is that they have failed to provide any meaningful consequences to the participants for their performances. Burgess (1968) overcame this procedural deficiency by offering his subjects — students who were participating in the experiment in lieu of writing a term paper — the incentive of having to devote less than the required ten hours to the tasks if they worked quickly. The four members of each group sat in individual compartments facing panels containing the same five letters of the alphabet. Each letter had a small light next to it, and a different light was illuminated on each person's panel. The task of the subjects was to discover, by passing one another notes through slots in the partition (see Figure 6.4), which light was not illuminated on any of the panels.

Without any reinforcement contingencies in effect, the wheel network produced a higher solution rate than the circle. This is consistent with earlier findings, and it seems clear that the problem of developing an adequate relay system in the circle impedes the problem-solving efficiency of the members. They work more quickly when they can relay messages through a common individual, as in the case of the wheel. However, Burgess discovered that the introduction of reinforcement eliminated differences in solution rates between the two networks. This effect is shown in Figure 6.6, page 200, where the performance curve for one group is shown under the two different network conditions, with reinforcement introduced during the last twenty minutes of the hour's activity.

Working with groups that were required to solve as many as one thousand problems, Burgess found that ". . . once a steady state has been reached *and* contingencies of reinforcement are in operation, there are no significant differences between the two networks with regard to the solution rate" (p. 331). It appears, then, that the reported differences in the relative efficiency of different communication networks may have resulted in part from the fact that no tangible reinforcers were made contingent upon the members' outputs. In a practical sense, this suggests that in situations where there are incentives to either speed or accuracy of group problem solving, the members may be able to overcome any limitations inherent in the particular pattern of communication channels open to them. However, as Shaw (1964) has pointed out the effects of various

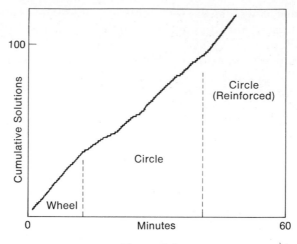

Figure 6.6

Rates of problem solution of a group under three experimental conditions, the wheel net, the circle net, and reinforcement under the circle net. (After Burgess, 1968)

schedules, magnitudes, and kinds of reinforcers upon performance in different communication networks in relation to different kinds of tasks remain to be investigated.

Group Discussion Behavior

Interaction process analysis. Ordinarily, the members of groups are not as constrained in communicating with one another as in the experimental settings we have just described. In fact, perhaps the single most notable characteristic of a group is the diversity of verbal interaction that takes place. At first glance, the sheer complexity of these verbal exchanges would seem to preclude either categorization or analysis. Actually, quite a number of classification systems have been proposed as frameworks within which to systematize and quantify verbal interaction. Perhaps the best known of these is the one described by Bales (1950). To better understand the problems of observing and categorizing verbal behavior in groups, let us imagine for a moment what happens in a group discussion. For one thing, certain individuals are apt to dominate the conversation. Others, who speak less, may actually have more information to offer. Still others may be characteristically negative and sarcastic, in contrast to some who are helpful and sympathetic. We might continue at length describing the various kinds of verbal behaviors that are encountered in group situations. Obviously, these behaviors cannot be dealt with systematically until they can be adequately categorized and enumerated. What is needed is a set of general categories into which the almost limitless variety of verbal responses may be ordered.

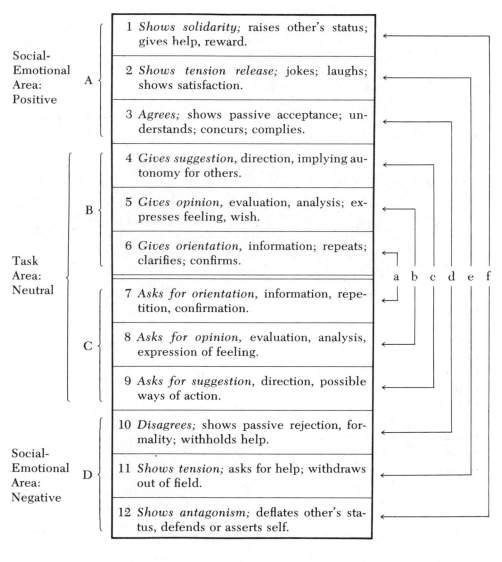

Social-
Emotional
Area:
Positive

A

1 *Shows solidarity;* raises other's status; gives help, reward.

2 *Shows tension release;* jokes; laughs; shows satisfaction.

3 *Agrees;* shows passive acceptance; understands; concurs; complies.

Task
Area:
Neutral

B

4 *Gives suggestion,* direction, implying autonomy for others.

5 *Gives opinion,* evaluation, analysis; expresses feeling, wish.

6 *Gives orientation,* information; repeats; clarifies; confirms.

C

7 *Asks for orientation,* information, repetition, confirmation.

8 *Asks for opinion,* evaluation, analysis, expression of feeling.

9 *Asks for suggestion,* direction, possible ways of action.

Social-
Emotional
Area:
Negative

D

10 *Disagrees;* shows passive rejection, formality; withholds help.

11 *Shows tension;* asks for help; withdraws out of field.

12 *Shows antagonism;* deflates other's status, defends or asserts self.

a b c d e f

A Positive reactions
B Attempted answers
C Questions
D Negative reactions

a Problems of communication
b Problems of evaluation
c Problems of control
d Problems of decision
e Problems of tension reduction
f Problems of reintegration

Figure 6.7
Bales' system of observational categories. (From Bales, 1950)

Bales' system of *interaction process analysis* provides a set of twelve such categories. One or more observers is stationed behind a one-way vision screen where he can see and hear what takes place in a group without being seen himself. He is provided with a form listing the twelve categories of interaction, and he records the occurrence of each type of response on a moving tape, where the time of the response is automatically indicated. Considerable skill is needed for an observer to make prompt and accurate categorizations of what is said. With practice, however, a high degree of interobserver reliability can be attained using this system. Figure 6.7 presents the twelve categories of verbal response developed by Bales.

The categories listed represent the final distillation of nearly ninety different kinds of responses that Bales originally recorded. That many categories, however, would be unwieldy, and the twelve that are listed represent the number that can be used with reasonable precision by a trained observer. There is one rather serious flaw in the system, a flaw that is present in most systems of this type. What constitutes a response in discussion behavior? Does the observer record a word, a phrase, a sentence, or an entire speech utterance? Bales' definition of the *unit* of behavior to be recorded is unclear. This absence of a clearly defined metric, however, has not prevented raters from achieving a fairly high degree of reliability in their observations.

How useful is interaction process analysis? The tabulated responses can be plotted in the form of a profile that shows their relative frequencies of occurrence. Profiles generated by different groups, or by the same group under different conditions, thus can be compared. The profiles reflect certain dimensions of verbal interaction in groups, and the type of interaction is obviously determined both by the characteristics of the individuals in the groups and by the circumstances of the discussion. The author used Bales' system to analyze the behavior of small groups that were discussing a previously shown film dealing with problems of mental illness. Figure 6.8 shows the profile obtained with one of these groups.

The group for which this profile was drawn had been instructed to voice their opinions about the film, and the profile indicates that this was what they did. Because the group was composed of youngish, upper-middle-class housewives, meeting voluntarily on a topic of mutual interest, there were few expressions of negative feeling toward other members of the group. Differently constituted groups, or groups meeting for a different purpose, might be expected to generate different profiles. Changes in the attitudes of the group members over several discussion periods would be revealed to some extent in changing interaction of profiles. This technique is just one method of describing and quantifying behavior in a group situation and of relating the behavior to selected antecedent conditions.

Contentless measures. Some indices of discussion behavior may be essentially "contentless" (Heyns and Lippitt, 1954), that is, they may re-

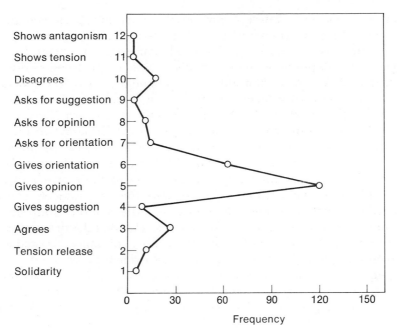

Figure 6.8
Interaction profile for a group discussing the film "Angry Boy."

flect such aspects of a discussion as frequency and duration of verbal behavior rather than what is said. McGinnies and Altman (1959) studied tape
recordings of discussions held by students who were either very prejudiced, very tolerant, or indifferent toward ethnic minorities. Each group,
composed of nine high school students, first viewed and then discussed
a sound film that diagnosed the irrational bases of prejudice. Five quantitative measures of discussion behavior were found to differentiate effectively among the three conditions of ethnocentrism. Those students who
were more tolerant and who, therefore, were more sympathetic toward
the position advocated by the film differed from the prejudiced subjects
in the following respects: (a) They emitted more words during the discussion. (b) They responded more frequently. (c) They became more
animated as the discussion progressed. (d) They responded more often
without prompting from the discussion leader. (e) More of them participated in the discussion. The prior attitudes of the subjects thus were
shown to predict certain aspects of their discussion behavior, given a
particular kind of social situation and a particular topic for discussion.

The same investigators later manipulated the majority-minority composition of six-person discussion groups, the members of which were either
very prejudiced or very tolerant toward minority groups (Altman and
McGinnies, 1960). Some of the groups contained three prejudiced and
three tolerant members. Others were of imbalanced composition, that is,
four to two in both directions, while still others were composed uniformly

of six prejudiced or six tolerant individuals. Each group viewed and then discussed a film concerned with the elimination of group prejudice. Analysis of the discussions disclosed that the balanced groups were less spontaneous (more dependent upon the discussion leader) and had a lower overall rate of response than either the homogeneous or the unbalanced groups. The tolerant subjects, regardless of which group they were in, participated the most in discussion. Doubtless this was because their viewpoints were reinforced by the content of the film. When they were in a minority, they talked to one another as much as to the members with whom they disagreed. Again, we would interpret this as behavior having the effect of eliciting support and confirmation of their own views from those holding similar opinions. Finally, the tolerant subjects expressed greater liking for their discussion groups, regardless of the group structure, than did the prejudiced subjects. We may assume that the discussion situation, oriented as it was about a film advocating tolerance, was somewhat aversive to the prejudiced participants. Their reaction was a lowered rate of response as well as a failure to be attracted to the group, except when they were in a majority position. The effects of the initial attitudes of the subjects on their rates of verbal response during discussion of the film are shown in Figure 6.9.

Despite its complexity, group discussion behavior when observed under laboratory conditions is susceptible to analysis using quantitative measures like those used in conventional laboratory experiments on learning and performance.

Reinforcement effects. The effect of a nonverbal stimulus on the rate of verbalization in an eighteen-person discussion group was observed by

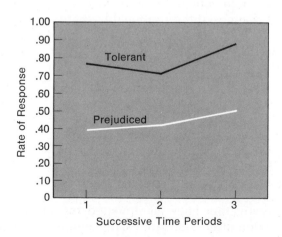

Figure 6.9

Rates of response of tolerant and prejudiced subjects in discussing a film that advocated elimination of group prejudice. (Adapted from Altman and McGinnies, 1960)

McNair (1957). The subjects were shown pictures depicting interpersonal situations and were instructed to talk about them. A bell was sounded on a prearranged variable interval schedule (but was never presented when no one was talking). The subjects had been told that the bell signaled approval of the discussion. It was found that the higher the rate of reinforcement, the higher the rate of verbalization in the group. A similar result was obtained by Cieutat (1959), who first determined which two persons in a four-man discussion group participated the least. He and a colleague then attended subsequent discussions of these same groups and selectively paid rather obvious attention to any comment made by these two persons, while pointedly ignoring remarks made by the two who had previously been most active. As a result of this procedure, the rates of verbal response of the two selectively reinforced participants rose sharply, while those of the nonreinforced participants declined.

These general findings have been confirmed in later experiments by Aiken (1965a), who used a flashing light to signal approval of what a student said during a discussion with three of his peers. After analyzing the discussion protocols in terms of Bales' interaction categories, he discovered that reinforcing an originally submissive individual resulted in that person's making more comments in the "opinion giving" and "orientation providing" categories. But the reinforced individual also showed evidence of increases in "tension showing" and "tension release" behaviors. In another experiment, Aiken (1965b) investigated the effects of rewarding a given individual during a discussion on how that person was perceived by the other members of the group, who were punished for their comments. The reinforced individuals were rated by the punished members as higher in leadership, participation, quality of ideas, and self-confidence after the reinforcement manipulations. So it appears that the direct administration of symbolic rewards and punishments to the members of discussion groups can influence not only the rate at which the individuals participate but can also the kinds of interpersonal ratings they give one another. In a practical situation, this suggests that a teacher who selectively reinforces the verbal responses of certain pupils not only will encourage them to volunteer comments even more frequently but also will tend to enhance their status in the judgments of their peers. Conversely, a student who, by being ignored or criticized, is discouraged from participating may also suffer a loss of status in his group. The social effects of selective reinforcement in group discussion undoubtedly have wide ramifications and implications for the future behavior of the individuals concerned.

Some other studies have also dealt directly with the effects of manipulated reinforcement on discussion behavior. In one of these, Oakes (1962a) formed twenty-four discussion groups of introductory psychology students. The subjects, four in each group, were seated at a table with diagonal screens placed so that they were unable to see one another. Each subject had before him a signal light that was controlled by the experimenter. A psychiatric case history was to be discussed, and the subjects were told that a person's signal light would flash whenever he made a statement that showed psychological insight into the patient's behavior. Actually, the experimenter reinforced in this fashion all responses falling into one or another of the Bales categories. Two groups were assigned to each of the twelve categories.

To determine whether the experimental manipulations had been effective, transcripts of the discussions in each group were evaluated by another experimenter, who did not know with which group he was dealing and, therefore, could not be biased in his scoring. A significant effect was discovered only in the two groups that were reinforced for making remarks falling in Bales' Category 5, described as "giving opinion, evaluation, analysis." That is, after the experimenter began flashing the subjects' lights every time a remark of this type was made, the number of reinforced comments rose significantly. A similar effect was not evident when the group members were reinforced for comments falling into any of the other eleven categories. It turned out that Category 5 contained the greatest number of responses, whether reinforced or not, so that remarks of this type had the greatest opportunity to be reinforced in the two groups where such reinforcement was provided. Categories 1, 4, 9, 11, and 12 had very low operant rates, which is to say that relatively few remarks of these types were made even before reinforcement by the experimenter was begun. As we know, behavior must first be emitted before it can be strengthened by reinforcement. It should also be pointed out that the *situation* places constraints upon the kinds of behavior that individuals will display. In the present instance, for example, the subjects were informed that they would be signaled when they made "insightful" contributions to the discussion. Assuming that their behavior was influenced by these instructions, one may question whether remarks falling into the categories having initially low operant rates would be used by the participants, even when reinforced. That is, one would scarcely make remarks that "showed solidarity," "asked for suggestions," or "showed antagonism" while under instruction to "demonstrate insight." Some reinforcers, as Oakes suggests, may be specific to a particular response class; or, we might say that an individual who is behaving in terms of a particular set or disposition will effectively be reinforced only by events that relate logically to that disposition. If I am making some remarks with serious intent, I am not reinforced by laughter from an audience; under different circumstances, if humor is my intent, laughter might well function as a reinforcer. The consequences of my behavior must bear a certain correspondence to my intentions or expectancies before they can function as positive reinforcers. Events that disconfirm an expectancy or that frustrate an intention are aversive almost by definition.

Evidence for this contention has been obtained by Oakes, Droge, and August, (1960), who arranged an experimental situation similar to that just described. In this case, however, two members of the four-man discussion groups were informed that the signal light would flash whenever one of them made a statement exhibiting "psychological insight," while the other two were told that the light would flash whenever one of them said something revealing "lack of psychological insight." The number of words emitted by the subjects during successive ten-minute periods in these two reinforcement conditions were tallied and compared. The results are shown in Figure 6.10.

The data in Figure 6.10 show rather convincingly that individual productivity during a discussion can be controlled by the appropriate administration of stimuli that the discussants identify as rewarding or punishing. Additional evidence confirming this type of relationship between fluency in discussion and social feedback can be adduced from common experience. How often have we heard the expression "to squelch" someone, which is generally interpreted to mean to respond to him in such a manner as to discourage him from further comment. The skillful teacher uses selective reinforcement to encourage the less verbal pupils to participate in class discussion. Concurrent nonreinforcement of the more talkative pupils may also be necessary in order to decrease their rate of response and thus permit the reticent ones an opportunity for participation. The situation is not altogether unlike that of a rat pressing a lever to obtain a pellet of food, except that in this case the subjects are children (or adults), and the pellets are encouraging replies from a teacher or other discussion leader. The individual who never volunteers a comment, of course, cannot be reinforced; there must be some minimum operant level which can be raised by appropriate reinforcement.

Additional research in the area of group discussion by Oakes, Droge, and August (1961), using the techniques described above, showed that dis-

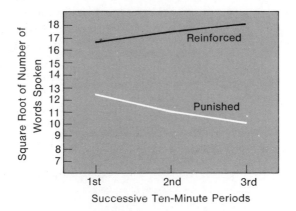

Figure 6.10

Number of words emitted during a discussion as a function of reinforcement and punishment. (Adapted from Oakes, Droge, and August, 1960; reprinted with the permission of authors and publisher)

cussants could, by reinforcement, be led to reach a predetermined solution to a problem. Identifying the source of reinforcement was found by Oakes (1962b) to differentially influence participation in discussion. That is, individuals who thought that approval was being dispensed by a group of professionals were more influenced than those who thought the feedback was coming from their peers; the latter in turn participated more than those who thought that laymen were reacting to their remarks. We have known for some time that not all reinforcing stimuli are equivalent in altering the response rates of animals. It seems equally true that social reinforcers differ in the effectiveness with which they may come to maintain behavior.

One additional experiment is worthy of our attention because it represents an attempt to manipulate reinforcement contingencies in a group situation involving controlled channels of communication. Bavelas and his colleagues (1965) used a type of situation described earlier, where four subjects sit around a table and engage in discussion of a selected topic. The experimenter signals approval or disapproval of each subjects' comments by causing a green or red light to flash, visible only to the subject in question. Essentially, this experiment examined the matter of whether an individual who was initially rated low in participation could be encouraged, by appropriate shaping procedures, to participate more actively. This "target person" was identified as the one lowest in participation during a practice period in which the discussants received no feedback on the quality of their comments; that is, during the practice period the signal lights were not activated by the experimenter. We might refer to this as the operant baseline for the subjects.

The experimental manipulation consisted of flashing the target person's green light (reward) whenever he made statements of fact or opinion and flashing the other three participants' red lights if they made similar comments. To further change the target person's behavior, his red light (punishment) was flashed occasionally when he remained silent, and the other individuals were rewarded with a green light when they interacted or agreed with him.

These procedures were clearly effective in altering the distribution of verbal outputs in the discussion groups. In every case, the target person talked more following reinforcement than he had during the initial discussion, when his spontaneous discussion participation had been low. The investigators concluded that the most effective procedure for generating results of this kind is to both reward the target person for appropriate remarks and simultaneously depress the verbal outputs of the other group members.

Cooperation and Competition

Manipulation by instruction. The design of experiments on small group behavior requires that the investigator select as his dependent variables behaviors that are both significant and measurable. This may involve behavior not commonly exhibited by individuals in isolation. Kelley and Thibaut (1954) make the point that group problem solving involves much more than just individual problem solving. The "extra" factor derives from the unique array of stimulus conditions presented by a group situation. For example, two very important types of social interaction— cooperation and competition—can be studied only if the subjects are aware that other persons are involved. To be sure, a person may behave competitively in private, as when studying for an exam or producing an article that will eventually compete in the open market with other wares. More commonly, cooperative and competitive behaviors occur in groups. In order to control some of the conditions that are antecedent to cooperative or competitive behavior, investigators have devised various kinds of situations in which these behaviors can be induced.

An experiment that illustrates the manner in which cooperation and competition can be studied in the laboratory was done by Morton Deutsch (1949). Although Deutsch was working at the time with Lewin and, consequently, describes his procedures in field theory terminology, we will attempt to report his methods and findings using behavioral concepts. Deutsch's insightful analysis of the general problem led him to observe that few, if any, real-life situations are purely cooperative or purely competitive. The members of a basketball team, he noted, may cooperate with one another to win a game, but each may also compete to become the "star" of the team. This amounts to saying that individuals may alternately cooperate and compete with one another within the context of an extended behavior episode. In some situations, such as a team sport, both cooperation and competition may be reinforced. On the other hand, competitive behavior sometimes hampers the performance of the other members of a group and is punished. This consequence increases the likelihood that each person will behave cooperatively.

Deutsch's experiment involved situations in which subjects could be induced, by instruction, to behave either cooperatively or competitively. The subjects were students in an industrial relations course at the Massachusetts Institute of Technology. Ten groups of five students each met once a week for a period of five weeks to solve two types of problems, logical puzzles and problems in human relations. Five of the groups were given instructions designed to make them cooperate in solving the two types of problems, and five were given instructions designed to make the members compete with one another for better individual scores. Specifically, the members of half the groups were offered incentives for superior *group* performance, while members of the other five groups were offered incentives for superior *individual* performance.

Deutsch found that the cooperative groups did, indeed, solve the puzzles more rapidly than the competitive groups. Individual productivity also tended to be greater in the cooperative groups. In solving the human

relations problem, the cooperative groups produced longer recommendations, and these were judged to be of higher quality than those prepared
by the competitive groups. Observers also recorded a greater proportion
of encouraging or rewarding remarks in the cooperative groups and a significantly larger proportion of aggressive remarks in the competitive groups
during discussions of the human relations problem. The puzzle-solving
situation presented less of an opportunity for either friendly or unfriendly
exchanges, and no differences were found in this respect between the cooperative and competitive groups. The nature of the task is clearly a
determinant of the type of interaction that is likely to occur among cooperating or competing individuals. Discussion of a human relations
problem provides a context within which the probability of personal remarks is increased. A more impersonal task, such as puzzle solving, is not
an appropriate background for *ad hominem* comments. The conclusions
to be reached from this experiment are fairly straightforward. If reinforcement is contingent upon the joint efforts of the members of a group, then
cooperative behavior is more effective than competitive behavior. On the
other hand, if individual performances are selectively reinforced, then
task-oriented behavior tends to be displaced by competitive behavior,
and a group product is less readily achieved.

It should be emphasized that problem-solving behavior can be maintained in both cooperative and competitive groups. But experimental
data, such as those obtained by Deutsch, give evidence that cooperative
behavior is more productive. In the competitive group situation, a problem-solving response by any one individual has the potential effect of
depressing someone else in the final rank-ordering of performances. If
ranking is to be the basis for assignment of rewards, superior individual
performance is less likely to be positively reinforced by the other group
members. In such a situation, any progress made by one person toward a
goal that cannot be shared by all is probably aversive to the other members.
Among cooperating individuals, on the other hand, a process of reciprocal
reinforcement serves to maintain the frequency of problem-solving behavior by each person at a high level.

The basis for cooperation in a dyad is, as Cohen (1962) has suggested,
that both individuals are involved and both are reinforced. Competition
involves behavior in which both individuals are involved and only one is
reinforced. Extending this definition to larger groups, we see cooperation
as involving behavior that is followed by reinforcement for all of the participants and competition as involving behavior in which some of the
participants will go unrewarded. Consistent nonreward will eventually
lead to extinction of the behavior. The fact that reinforcement for competitive behavior is often on a variable interval or variable ratio schedule,
however, means that the behavior may persist for a long time even when it
is seldom reinforced. A baseball team that anchors the bottom of the
second division occasionally wins a game, and the golfer who shoots 100+

occasionally pars a hole. These intermittent reinforcements are sufficient to maintain the behavior at a stable rate. Even chronic losers will continue to compete so long as they are on a partial reinforcement schedule. And if competition is the only means by which a person can survive, physically or psychologically, he will continue to compete even for small and infrequent rewards. The vigor of his efforts will be determined not so much by his occasional successes as by the challenge of those with whom he must compete. Such is the nature of a competitive system.

Manipulation by reinforcement. Is it necessary for cooperation and competition in groups to be instigated by instructions from an overseer, such as an experimenter? Cats and rats can learn to cooperate with one another in solving a problem simply by virtue of the fact that only cooperative behavior will be followed by presentation of food (Tsai, 1953). There is evidence in an experiment by Azrin and Lindsley (1956) that cooperation between children can also be developed, maintained, and extinguished by manipulating the contingency between reinforcing stimuli and cooperative behavior. Twenty children, aged seven to twelve years, were organized into ten teams of two children each. Seven teams were boys, and three were girls. The experimental situation was very simple. Each pair of children sat facing one another across a small table, divided in the center by a wire screen (see Figure 6.11).

The surface of the table in front of each child contained three small holes, and each child held a stylus that was wired to an electronic recording device. The children were told merely that the "sticks" (styli) could be put into each of the three holes, and that occasionally some jelly beans

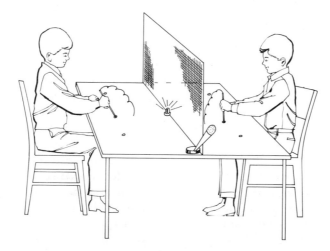

Figure 6.11
Apparatus used for the reinforcement of cooperation between children.
(After Azrin and Lindsley, 1956)

would drop into a cup accessible to both of them. The experimenter than left the room after telling the children that they could play any game they wished. If the children placed the styli in corresponding holes within .04 second of each other, a red light flashed on the table (conditioned reinforcing stimulus) and a jelly bean (reinforcing stimulus) fell into the cup. Cooperative responses were recorded automatically by counters in an adjoining room. Every cooperative response was reinforced over a fifteen-minute period or until five minutes had passed with no marked change in the rate of cooperation. An extinction period followed, in which cooperative responses were not reinforced for a period of at least fifteen minutes or until a steady response rate for at least five minutes was recorded. During a second reinforcement period, cooperative responses were again reinforced until a stable rate was achieved for at least three minutes. The results of these procedures are shown in Table 6.1.

Table 6.1
Cooperative responses during the critical experimental periods.
(Based on Azrin and Lindsley, 1956, Table 1, p. 101)

	Number of Cooperative Responses Per Minute			
	First 3 minutes of first reinforcement period	Last 3 minutes of first reinforcement period	Last 3 minutes of extinction period	Last 3 minutes of second reinforcement period
Median	5.5	17.5	1.5	17.5
Range	1–26	6–26	0–7	6–27

As may be seen in the table, cooperative responses increased in frequency when reinforced and decreased in frequency when not reinforced. Reinforcement following extinction restored the rate of cooperation to its pre-existing value. The investigators also observed that leader-follower relations developed in most of the pairs and that in eight pairs the candy was eventually divided in some equitable fashion. In the remaining two pairs, one member took all the candy until the other member refused to cooperate. We have little reason to doubt that cooperation and competition are developed and maintained in a manner analogous to this in a host of social situations.

A laboratory setting that provides what has been termed a "minimal social situation" has been described by Sidowski, Wyckoff, and Tabory (1956). The distinguishing feature of this arrangement is that neither of two subjects, who are performing simultaneously, knows that certain reinforcing and aversive stimuli that he will experience are under the control of another person. How can such a situation be termed "social"? An answer to this question is provided by the principal assumption underlying the several experiments in this series, namely, that awareness of the existence of a cooperative situation is not necessary for the development of cooperative behavior. Although Azrin and Lindsley did not instruct their subjects that cooperative effort would secure rewards, it is conceivable that some of the children reached this conclusion, particularly since they performed in full view of one another. Sidowski and his colleagues, on the other hand, stationed their subjects in separate cubicles, so that each was unaware of the other's presence. Each subject was provided with two pushbuttons that could be pressed in any sequence to obtain points indicated on a scoring counter. The subjects also had electrodes attached to their left hands through which they could receive electric shocks. If Subject A, quite unaware of the consequences, pressed the right-hand button, Subject B received a shock; if he pressed the left-hand button, B scored a point. Similar control over A's fate was enjoyed by B, who also was unaware of this fact. Each person, it turned out, assumed that their rewards (points) and punishments (shocks) were being administered by some automatically programed device. Under these circumstances, did they come through trial and error to make only those responses that would minimize the number of shocks that each received?

Suppose we try to analyze what is happening. Four possible combinations of responses are possible between the two subjects. While either A or B presses the right-hand button (r), the other person can be pressing the right (r) or left (l) button, hence, the possible combinations are A(r) + B(r); A(r) + B(l); A(l) + B(r); A(l) + B(l). Only one of these combinations, A(l) + B(l), reinforces both subjects. In the course of emitting one or the other response, both subjects, under the aversive control of electric shock and the positive control of point scores, quickly adjusted to the correct combination without necessarily being aware of the true nature of the situation. In a later experiment, Sidowski (1957) informed half of his groups that their rewards and punishments were under one another's control. This information did not hasten learning among these subjects as compared with uninformed groups; thus, his contention that learning was not necessarily mediated by cognitive factors apparently was supported.

This interesting experiment was repeated with some variations by Kelley, Thibaut, Radloff, and Mundy (1962), who used only positive reinforcement, in the form of points scored, rather than both positive and aversive consequences. They also required the subjects to respond simultaneously on cue so as to control response rate, something that Sidowski had not done. Their results in general confirmed those obtained earlier and, in addition, lent weight to the hypothesis that the "correct" response combinations emerge from initially random behavior as a result of selective reinforcement. One important difference was found, however. Those pairs who were carefully and explicitly informed about the manner in which they controlled each other's fate learned more rapidly than those who were not so informed. This finding confirms what one would expect in this type of situation and leads us to question whether or not Sidowski's informed subjects fully comprehended the extent of their mutual dependence. Certainly, knowledge of the fact that cooperative behavior can achieve the solution to a problem should yield faster learning than would result from sheer trial and error. It is also important to note that some uninformed pairs never did solve the problem. They simply never emitted the appropriate pattern of responses and, consequently, were not reinforced. Behavior, when it must occur fortuitously, may require a long time before it is shaped by selective reinforcement. Perhaps this is why some individuals never seem to hit upon the mutual patterning of behaviors that will achieve a cooperative solution to a problem. Cooperative progress toward a goal seems to be more rapid when at least one member of a pair is aware of the reinforcement contingencies through which the other person's behavior may be manipulated. In these circumstances, the likelihood of cooperation is not left to chance (Rabinowitz, Kelley, and Rosenblatt, 1966).

A series of experiments derived from the general assumption that reinforcing events are essential components in the development and maintenance of cooperative behavior have been conducted by Rosenberg and his associates (Rosenberg and Hall, 1958; Rosenberg, 1959; 1960; 1963). A typical situation studied is one in which two individuals sit in adjacent booths and each turns a small concealed knob to adjust a pointer on a scale he cannot see. Feedback, in the form of knowledge of results, is provided only upon completion of a trial. Cooperative behavior occurs when both subjects manipulate their control knobs so as to achieve positive reinforcement in the form of an accurate positioning of the pointer. This type of arrangement is similar to the "minimal social situation" studied by Sidowski, and Rosenberg has been able not only to produce behavior that is essentially "cooperative" but to develop systematic relationships between cooperative behavior and different reward systems. Although the details of his results are presented in a manner that is too technical to include here, we mention them because they represent one more avenue of experimental attack upon a complex social situation.

We should not conclude this discussion of the reinforcement of cooperation without acknowledging that some studies have been designed to demonstrate the effects of reinforcing disagreement. In naturalistic settings, of course, cooperation is not always the rule, and there are circumstances in which dissension seems to be quite effectively maintained. A demonstration of the effects of encouraging disagreement in a small group has been reported by Shapiro (1963). This study was based on previous research, where it had been established that the order in which individuals participated in a conversation could be manipulated by selective reinforcement (Levin and Shapiro, 1962). To promote disagreement, Shapiro simply made success in achieving a group decision contingent upon this type of interaction. A "game" was contrived in which a group of three women sit around a table on which is placed a panel of colored lights. There problem is to try to guess the name of a color contained in a list held by the experimenter in another room. When all three have reached agreement, they stop talking and press one of several response keys that correspond to the colors discussed. Appropriate behavior by the subjects (R^{op}) causes the display panel in the center of the table to be illuminated. After five seconds, a tone (S^{rein}) is sounded if the subjects guessed correctly. A buzzer (S^{av}) sounds if they have guessed incorrectly.

Disagreement was defined as the naming of different colors by at least two of the three subjects before a final decision was reached. Two schedules of reinforcement were used. One was contingent reinforcement, in which the group was given the signal for being "right" only when disagreement had occurred during a trial. The other was noncontingent reinforcement, in which "right" and "wrong" signals were delivered randomly, regardless of how the group members had behaved. Performance during the period of noncontingent reinforcement provided a baseline with which behavior during reinforcement of disagreement could be compared. Since there is a tendency for individuals to agree with one another increasingly in a task situation, the effect of reinforcing group decisions following disagreement was to offset this trend and, in some of the groups, actually to increase the frequency of disagreement. This is obviously a highly complex situation in which some persons are reinforced for agreeing and others for disagreeing. Furthermore, two or more persons may agree with one another yet, at the same time, find themselves in disagreement with another faction. We are only at the threshold of being able to identify the stimuli that control these alternative classes of behavior and the consequences that maintain or terminate them. The fact that certain individuals acquire skill at manipulating cooperation and dissension in a group situation suggests that they have achieved some measure of control over the types of reinforcement contingencies that we have described.

Groups in Isolation

An intriguing program of research in the social psychology of small groups of men in confining quarters over varying periods of time has been conducted at the U. S. Naval Medical Research Institute. Space voyages of extended duration will present small groups of astronauts with an unusual set of social as well as physical circumstances. They will have to contend with the personal and interpersonal stresses that derive from close contact in an extremely small living space. Manned spacecraft are not, of course, the only potential sources of such problems. A great deal of current research is concerned with similar problems confronting the crews assigned to undersea ventures such as Sealab and other deep submergence systems. Whether man can survive in space or in a marine habitat will depend in large measure upon his ability to interact effectively with his companions in these ventures.

Four principal sources of stress have been identified in these types of closed ecological systems. They are described by Haythorn (1967) as resulting from (a) stimulus reduction, (b) social isolation, (c) confinement, and (d) interpersonal friction. Data from such isolated social situations as those existing in submarines, Antarctic weather stations, and Arctic radar stations suggest that these four sources of stress impair human performance in several ways.

Discussing these factors in greater detail, Haythorn and Altman (1967) point out that the first *stimulus, reduction,* has been shown to induce such behavior as anxiety, hallucinations, delusions, apathy, and fear of losing one's sanity. Humans seem to require a minimum level of stimulation in order to behave "normally." Men are also accustomed to a large number of social interactions, and being deprived of these through *social isolation* creates a situation for which appropriate behaviors may not have been developed. The sheer fact of *confinement* generates its own specific problems, among which is the tendency for individuals to demand the exclusive use of particular chairs, beds, or sides of a table (Altman and Haythorn, 1967). This phenomenon, known technically as *territoriality,* has been observed in many animal species, and when disturbed by over-crowding or restriction of movement, they may show behavior pathology as well as physiological malfunctioning. Finally, *interpersonal friction* is likely to increase when two or three individuals are confined together for more than just a few hours. These psychosocial hazards are seen as posing as great a threat to the cooperative functioning of groups in isolation as do the more obvious stresses of increased pressure, exotic gas atmospheres, and loss of gravity.

In several experiments, subjects have been confined to small rooms in complete darkness and silence for as long as seven days. In one such study, nineteen of forty stimulus-deprived subjects were unable to complete the seven-day confinement period as compared with only one of twenty control subjects who asked to be taken off the experiment. During the period of isolation, various measures of emotionality and subjective stress were obtained. For example, both experimental and control subjects were allowed to listen at will to a monotonous recording of an old stock market report. They could obtain this form of stimulation through the instrumental act of pulling continuously on a spring-loaded lever. By the last day of con-finement, the stimulus-deprived subjects were listening to the recording for more than two thirds of the time during which it was available. By contrast, the control subjects, who had access to such customary sources of stimulation as lights, television, and recorded music, were pulling the lever very little (Haythorn, 1967). The results are reminiscent of those of Gewirtz and Baer (1958), who found that nursery school children who had been deprived of social interaction for a brief period subsequently emitted more socially reinforced responses than children who had not been so deprived. The reinforcing value of even the dullest form of social stimulation is apparently enhanced following a period of deprivation.

Altman, Haythorn, and their collaborators have also studied the reactions of pairs of young men — sailors in basic training — to long periods of isolation. Of nine two-man crews isolated in a 12-foot × 12-foot room for ten days, two pairs were unable to complete the assignment. The others performed regularly scheduled tasks and had virtually no contact with the outside world. Nonisolated control pairs performed the same tasks in identical rooms but were permitted normal freedom of movement when not on duty. Haythorn reports that the members of the isolated pairs who stuck out the assignment performed cooperative tasks better than the controls. We would be inclined to interpret this as a further example of the effect of social deprivation in enhancing the value of those social reinforcements that are available. Each individual in this unusual situation was probably a more effective reinforcer for the other in cooperative tasks because of the lack of other sources of stimulation. Presumably, the members of the control pairs were relatively more satiated with respect to social reinforcement and, hence, did not as effectively maintain one another's behavior in tasks demanding cooperation.

These investigations have also thrown considerable light on the role of personality factors in the adjustment of men to such situations as we have described. Haythorn and Altman (1967) identified thirty-six subjects whose behavior could be characterized on the basis of personality tests as showing more or less *achievement, dominance, affiliation,* and *dogmatism*. (An achieving individual is one who describes himself as concerned with the successful completion of tasks and the successful attainment of goals. A dominant person characteristically tries to control others. Individuals who frequently seek companionship are scored high in affiliation. Inability to tolerate dissent from others in controversial matters defines the dogmatic individual.) Pairs were formed so that in one third both men were high on each of these traits, in another third both were low, and in the final third one was high and one low. The experimental pairs lived and worked in a small (12-foot × 12-foot) room, while the control pairs were free to leave the room between tasks and to pursue their usual activities.

The design of this experiment was such that compatibility under stressful conditions could be measured as a function of certain salient behavioral characteristics of the individuals involved. What would we expect the result to be in terms of reinforcement concepts? In general, we would predict that the most congenial pairs would be those in which each member was disposed to reinforce the behaviors that were characteristic of his partner. An effective living and working relationship would depend upon the extent to which each member of a pair provided reinforcing stimuli for the other. For example, we would hardly expect two dominant individuals to be compatible when confined together for seven days. Domination, by definition, requires subservience; that is, a person becomes dominant because he has been reinforced with submission by others. He is not so apt to be reinforced by another dominant person, whose behavior, in fact, frequently will tend to be aversive. That such is the case was evidenced by the fact that of the four groups that had the most trouble, including arguments and fighting, the members of three pairs were both high in dominance.

When a person high in achievement was paired with one low in achievement, difficulties also arose. In theoretical terms, we would say that a person who is striving to successfully complete a series of tasks that requires the cooperation of someone else is rewarded when that person behaves similarly and that he is punished when the other person is not particularly task- or work-oriented. Similarly, a person whose repertoire includes relatively little that could be termed achievement probably resents close contact with someone who is busy and ambitious.

Two persons who are both highly affiliative will reinforce one another's social overtures and, hence, should be compatible. On the other hand, two dogmatic persons would frequently find themselves in contention, a situation that would soon become aversive. Both of these relationships were found by Haythorn and Altman, who caution, however, that such conclusions are specific to the isolation situation. Among the control pairs, where the members were not solely dependent upon one another for social stimulation, incompatible individuals frequently performed better than those who were compatible.

It is obvious that predictions about the impact of personality variables on social interaction in small groups must be qualified according to the nature of the situation. Where the stresses of isolation are involved, the positive as well as the aversive impact of one person's behavior on that of another becomes intensified. Not only does each individual's customary behavior repertoire suffer disruption, but the operant level of those few performances that are possible under the special circumstances of isolation must be maintained socially by only one person. Each partner's potential as an agent of reward or punishment thus becomes enhanced.

Summary   Most of our significant social interactions probably occur in small groups, the most important of which is the family. When the members of a group enjoy frequent face-to-face interaction, it is called a primary group. Larger aggregates, the members of which come into contact only infrequently, if ever, are termed secondary groups. Many of the social groups to which an individual belongs serve as reference groups for his behavior in other situations. That is, people frequently generalize certain behaviors from those situations in which the behaviors were originally reinforced to new circumstances that are in some way similar. Thus, an individual who is reminded of his religious or political affiliation is placed partially under the control of stimuli that have previously led to reinforced behavior.

There is a great deal of experimental data to indicate that task performance by individuals in groups is measurably different from performance on the same tasks in isolation. Either facilitation or inhibition of performance may occur depending upon the exact circumstances. As a general rule, the learning of new performances seems to suffer in the presence of a group, whereas performances of responses that are already in the individual's repertoire are facilitated. In other words, groups can be sources of conditioned reinforcement for the maintenance of previously learned behavior, but they can also serve as potential sources of aversive stimuli and so impede new learning.

In free discussion situations, those persons who occupy spatial positions in a group that make them more salient stimuli for the other members tend to engage in more interactions. They are also more likely to be perceived as leaders. Experiments in which the flow of communications among the members of small groups has been manipulated have yielded results suggesting that problem solving is dependent, in part, upon the type of communication net available to the participants. Those individuals who are able, through access to more channels of communication, to reinforce more frequently the responses of others are themselves the recipients of more messages.

It is possible, using a system of response categories, to characterize rather concisely the types of remarks that are made in the course of a group discussion. An increase in the frequency of comments of a given type can be brought about by selective reinforcement. Individuals can also be singled out for support and their rates of participation increased as a function of the number of reinforcements they receive.

Cooperation in groups depends upon the extent to which individual performances are mutually reinforcing. Cooperation is most likely to occur when individual rewards are made contingent upon a certain level of group performance rather than some criterion of individual performance. When individual rather than group performance is rewarded, the members are more likely to behave competitively. It is not necessary that the individual members of a group be aware of the reinforcement contingencies for cooperative behavior to develop. It is essential, however, that cooperative responses be reinforced and that noncooperative behavior either be extinguished through nonreinforcement or suppressed by punishment.

Research on the behavior of small groups living and working in relative isolation has emphasized the role of social reinforcers in both task behavior and interpersonal adjustment. Where individuals are confined together, they exercise an unusual amount of stimulus control over one another's behavior. Incompatibilities are thus magnified, as are the opportunities for cooperation among compatible persons.

References

AIKEN, E. G.   Interaction process analysis changes accompanying operant conditioning of verbal frequency in small groups. *Perceptual and Motor Skills,* 1965a, *21,* 52–54.

AIKEN, E. G.   Changes in interpersonal descriptions accompanying the operant conditioning of verbal frequency in groups. *Journal of Verbal Learning and Verbal Behavior,* 1965b, *4,* 243–247.

ALLPORT, F. H.   The influence of the group upon association and thought. *Journal of Experimental Psychology,* 1920, *3,* 159–182.

ALLPORT, F. H.   *Social psychology.* Boston: Houghton Mifflin, 1924.

ALTMAN, I., and HAYTHORN, W. W.   The ecology of isolated groups. *Behavioral Science,* 1967, *12,* 169–182.

ALTMAN, I., and MCGINNIES, E.   Interpersonal perception and communication in discussion groups of varied attitudinal composition. *Journal of Abnormal and Social Psychology,* 1960, *60,* 390–395.

ASCH, S. E.   Effects of group pressure upon the modification and distortion of judgments. In G. E. Swanson, T. M. Newcomb, and E. L. Hartley (Eds.), *Readings in social psychology* (rev. ed.). New York: Holt, Rinehart and Winston, 1952.

AZRIN, N. H., and LINDSLEY, O. R.   The reinforcement of cooperation between children. *Journal of Abnormal and Social Psychology,* 1956, 52, 100–102. Copyright 1956 by the American Psychological Association. Data in Table 6.1 of this book reprinted by permission.

BALES, R. F.   *Interaction process analysis.* Reading, Mass.: Addison-Wesley, 1950.

BANTA, T. J., and NELSON, C.   Experimental analysis of resource location in problem solving groups. *Sociometry,* 1964, *27,* 488–501.

BAVELAS, A.   Communication patterns in task oriented groups. *Journal of the Acoustical Society of America,* 1950, *22,* 725–730.

BAVELAS, A., HASTORF, R. H., GROSS, A. E., and KITE, W. R.   Experiments on the alteration of group structure. *Journal of Experimental Social Psychology,* 1965, *1,* 55–70.

BERGUM, B. O., and LEHR, D. J.   Effects of authoritarianism on vigilance performance. *Journal of Applied Psychology,* 1963, *47,* 75–77.

BROWN, J. F.   *Psychology and the social order.* New York: McGraw-Hill, 1936.

BURGESS, R. L.   Communication networks: An experimental reevaluation. *Journal of Experimental Social Psychology,* 1968, *4,* 324–337.

BUTLER, D. C., and MILLER, N.   "Power to reinforce" as a determinant of communication. *Psychological Reports,* 1965a, *16,* 705–709.

BUTLER, D. C., and MILLER, N.   Power to reward and punish in social interaction. *Journal of Experimental Social Psychology,* 1965b, *1,* 311–322.

CHARTERS, W. W., and NEWCOMB, T. M.   Some attitudinal effects of experimentally increased salience of a membership group. In E. E. Maccoby, T. M. Newcomb, and E. L. Hartley (Eds.), *Readings in social psychology* (3rd ed.). New York: Holt, Rinehart and Winston, 1958, pp. 276–280.

CIEUTAT, J. J. Surreptitious modification of verbal behavior during class discussion. *Psychological Reports,* 1959, 5, 648.

COCH, L., and FRENCH, J. R. P., JR. Overcoming resistance to change. *Human Relations,* 1948, *1,* 512–532.

COHEN, D. J. Justin and his peers: An experimental analysis of a child's social world. *Child Development,* 1962, 23, 697–717.

COLLINS, B. E., DAVIS, H. L., MYERS, J. G., and SILK, A. J. An experimental study of reinforcement and participant satisfaction. *Journal of Abnormal and Social Psychology,* 1964, 68, 463–467.

COTTRELL, N. B. Performance in the presence of other human beings: Mere presence, audience, and affiliation effects. In E. C. Simmel, R. A. Hoppe, and G. A. Milton (Eds.), *Social facilitation and imitative behavior.* Boston: Allyn and Bacon, 1968.

COTTRELL, N. B., RITTLE, R. H., and WACK, D. L. Presence of an audience and list type (competitional or noncompetitional) as joint determinants of performance in paired associates learning. *Journal of Personality,* 1967, 35, 425–434.

COTTRELL, N. B., SEKERAK, G. J., WACK, D. L., and RITTLE, R. H. Social facilitation of dominant responses by the presence of an audience and the mere presence of others. *Journal of Personality and Social Psychology,* 1968, 9, 245–250.

DASHIELL, J. F. An experimental analysis of some group effects. *Journal of Abnormal and Social Psychology,* 1930, 25, 190–199.

DEUTSCH, M. An experimental study of the effects of cooperation and competition upon group process. *Human Relations,* 1949, 2, 129–152, 199–231.

DEUTSCH, M. Field theory in social psychology. In G. Lindzey and E. Aronson (Eds.), *Handbook of social psychology* (2nd ed.). Reading, Mass.: Addison-Wesley, 1968.

GEWIRTZ, J. L., and BAER, D. M. The effect of brief social deprivation on behaviors for a social reinforcer. *Journal of Abnormal and Social Psychology,* 1958, 56, 49–56.

HARE, A. P., and BALES, R. F. Seating position and small group interaction. *Sociometry,* 1963, 26, 480–486.

HAYTHORN, W. W. Project Argus: A program of isolation and confinement research. *Naval Research Reviews,* December 1967, 1–8.

HAYTHORN, W. W., and ALTMAN, I. Together in isolation. *Trans-Action,* January/February 1967.

HEISE, G. A., and MILLER, G. A. Problem solving by small groups using various communication nets. *Journal of Abnormal and Social Psychology,* 1951, 46, 327–336.

HEYNS, R. W., and LIPPITT, R. Systematic observational techniques. In G. Lindzey (Ed.), *Handbook of social psychology.* Reading, Mass.: Addison-Wesley, 1954.

HUSBAND, R. W. Analysis of methods in human maze learning. *Journal of Genetic Psychology,* 1931, 39, 258–277.

KELLEY, H. H., and THIBAUT, J. W. Experimental studies of group problem solving and process. In G. Lindzey (Ed.), *Handbook of social psychology.* Vol. 2. Reading, Mass.: Addison-Wesley, 1954.

KELLEY, H. H., THIBAUT, J. W., RADLOFF, R., and MUNDY, D.   The development of cooperation in a "minimal social situation." *Psychological Monographs*, 1962, *76*, No. 19.

KRECH, D., and CRUTCHFIELD, R. S.   *Theory and problems of social psychology.* New York: McGraw-Hill, 1948.

LEAVITT, H. J.   Some effects of certain communication patterns on group performance. *Journal of Abnormal and Social Psychology*, 1951, *46*, 38–50.

LEVIN, G., and SHAPIRO, D.   The operant conditioning of conversation. *Journal of the Experimental Analysis of Behavior*, 1962, *5*, 309–316.

LEWIN, K.   *Field theory in social science.* New York: Harper and Row, 1951.

MCGINNIES, E., and ALTMAN, I.   Discussion as a function of attitudes and content of a persuasive communication. *Journal of Applied Psychology*, 1959, *43*, 53–59.

MCGRATH, J. E., and ALTMAN, I.   *Small group research.* New York: Holt, Rinehart and Winston, 1966.

MCNAIR, D. M.   Reinforcement of verbal behavior. *Journal of Experimental Psychology*, 1957, *53*, 40–46.

NEWCOMB, T. M.   *Personality and social change.* New York: Dryden Press, 1943.

OAKES, W. F.   Reinforcement of Bales' categories in group discussion. *Psychological Reports*, 1962a, *11*, 427–435.

OAKES, W. F.   Effectiveness of signal light reinforcers given various meanings on participation in group discussion. *Psychological Reports*, 1962b, *11*, 469–470.

OAKES, W. F., DROGE, A. E., and AUGUST, B.   Reinforcement effects on participation in group discussion. *Psychological Reports*, 1960, *7*, 503–514.

OAKES, W. F., DROGE, A. E., and AUGUST, B.   Reinforcement effects on conclusions reached in group discussions. *Psychological Reports*, 1961, *9*, 27–34.

OLMSTEAD, M. S.   *The small group.* New York: Random House, 1959.

PESSIN, J.   The comparative effects of social and mechanical stimulation on memorizing. *American Journal of Psychology*, 1933, *45*, 263–270.

RABINOWITZ, L., KELLEY, H. H., and ROSENBLATT, R. M.   Effects of different types of interdependence and response conditions in the minimal social situation. *Journal of Experimental Social Psychology*, 1966, *2*, 169–197.

ROETHLISBERGER, F. J., and DICKSON, W. J.   *Management and the worker.* Cambridge, Mass.: Harvard University Press, 1947.

ROSENBERG, S.   The maintenance of a learned response in controlled interpersonal conditions. *Sociometry*, 1959, *22*, 124–138.

ROSENBERG, S.   Cooperative behavior in dyads as a function of reinforcement parameters. *Journal of Abnormal and Social Psychology*, 1960, *60*, 318–333.

ROSENBERG, S.   Influence and reward in structured two-person interactions. *Journal of Abnormal and Social Psychology*, 1963, *67*, 379–387.

ROSENBERG, S., and HALL, R. L.   The effects of different social feedback conditions upon performance in dyadic teams. *Journal of Abnormal and Social Psychology*, 1958, *57*, 271–277.

SHAPIRO, D.   The reinforcement of disagreement in a small group. *Behavior Research and Therapy*, 1963, *1*, 267–272.

SHAW, M. E.   Communication networks. In L. Berkowitz (Ed.), *Advances in experimental psychology*. Vol. I. New York: Academic Press, 1964.

SHEPHERD, C. R.   *Small groups: Some sociological perspectives*. San Francisco: Chandler, 1964.

SHERIF, M.   *The psychology of social norms*. New York: Harper and Row Torchbooks, 1966. Originally published in the *Archives of Psychology*, 1935, No. 187, under the title "A study of some social factors in perception."

SHIBUTANI, S.   *Society and personality*. Englewood Cliffs, N. J.: Prentice-Hall, 1961.

SIDOWSKI, J. B.   Reward and punishment in a minimal social situation. *Journal of Experimental Psychology*, 1957, 54, 318–326.

SIDOWSKI, J. B., WYCKOFF, L. B., and TABORY, L.   The influence of reinforcement and punishment in a minimal social situation. *Journal of Abnormal and Social Psychology*, 1956, 52, 115–119.

STEINZOR, B.   The spatial factor in face-to-face discussion groups. *Journal of Abnormal and Social Psychology*, 1950, 45, 552–555.

TAYLOR, D. W., and FAUST, W. L.   Twenty questions: Efficiency in problem solving as a function of size of group. *Journal of Experimental Psychology*, 1952, 44, 360–368.

TRAVIS, L. E.   The effect of a small audience upon eye-hand coordination. *Journal of Abnormal and Social Psychology*, 1925, 20, 142–146.

TSAI, L. T.   Cited in O. Koehler, Team arbeit bei ratten. *Orion*, 1953, 8, 5.

WARD, C. D.   Seating arrangement and leadership emergence in small discussion groups. *Journal of Social Psychology*, 1968, 74, 83–90.

ZAJONC, R. B.   *Social psychology: An experimental approach*. Belmont, Calif.: Wadsworth, 1966.

7 *Leaders and Followers*

Nearly every social group contains one or more individuals whose behavior constitutes a powerful controlling stimulus for the behavior of the other members. We call such persons leaders, as distintinguished from the other group members, who are termed followers. Some commentators on man's history have argued that the course of human events is determined by the lives of history's great men. Other observers of the human scene have taken the position that leaders are merely thrust into prominence by the unfolding of significant historical events. We need not explore this controversy, nor take sides in it, to reach the conclusion that leaders, whatever their origins, do play dramatic and determining roles in human affairs and that their followers fulfill a complementary and equally important function.

Perhaps without being aware of it, most of us devote considerable amounts of time to activities that are concerned with leaders of one kind or another. Every family develops a leader, usually either the father or the mother. Occasionally, upon the death of a parent, one of the older children assumes leadership. In school, teachers provide leadership for their pupils. The teachers, in turn, defer to other leaders in the educational hierarchy — principals, supervisors, chairmen of boards of education. Every business organization has a system of leadership, which may be exceedingly elaborate in the case of a large corporation. On election day we vote for individuals to fill positions of political leadership at all levels of government. Service with the military establishment immerses one in a tightly organized system of leaders and followers.

General Theory

Leaders provide many of the discriminative stimuli to which others respond. They are usually also in a position to reward or punish the behavior of their followers. Performances of the followers, in turn, serve as potent sources of stimulus control over the leader's behavior. As in every social situation, the leader-follower relationship is a reciprocal one in which each party provides both discriminative stimuli and reinforcing stimuli for the other. This point of view has also been expressed in general terms by Bass (1961), who states that individuals form groups either for reward or to avoid punishment. The more their activities are rewarding, the more effective is the group and the more the members are attracted to it. In order to better achieve rewards and avoid punishment, some members attempt to change the behavior of others. Such efforts, according to Bass, represent *attempted* leadership. *Successful* leadership accomplishes behavior change in others, and *effective* leadership (a value judgment) provides reinforcement, or reward, for such induced changes.

A leader's control over his followers may depend upon coercion or persuasion. We might say, in more technical terms, that coercion involves the use of negative reinforcement; that is, the followers are reinforced not by reward but by the avoidance of the aversive consequences of failure or disobedience. Persuasion, on the other hand, frequently involves the use of incentives, or positive reinforcers, to evoke certain kinds of performances from the followers. It is important for us to recognize that in most social organizations leaders are also followers. That is, every leader except the one at the very apex of the hierarchy must defer to the authority of the leader immediately above him. Perhaps this is why individuals tend to choose as potential leaders the same persons they would also like to have as followers.

Authority in the family. We have emphasized the reciprocal control and reinforcement of behavior that occurs between leader and follower. The essential difference between a leader and a follower is that the former has a great many more reinforcers at his disposal than the latter. He also has access to a larger range of aversive stimuli. This does not mean that everyone who is able to control someone else's behavior by dispensing appropriate rewards and punishments automatically becomes a leader. Many husbands and wives unwittingly use such methods of behavioral control with one another without any clear-cut resolution of who is leader and who is follower.

The family, in fact, provides us with a situation in which certain elements basic to the leader-follower relationship can be elucidated. A common feature of social groups is the existence of a hierarchy of power or authority. Let us imagine that one's first exposure to such a hierarchical arrangement of authority is in one's immediate family. Let us further suppose that no disputation exists between the husband and wife as to who shall wear the pants and that the father is the acknowledged head of the household. The children, inevitably, occupy the lowest rung on the ladder of influence. In the normal course of events, control over the behavior of the children frequently is exercised by the father, with the mother as intermediary. That is, when the children are bad, the father may issue orders to the mother, and she passes these on to the unruly offspring in an attempt to restore a state of affairs that will be agreeable to the father. We may borrow and slightly modify a situation used by Adams and Romney (1959) to illustrate their functional analysis of authority relationships. The schematic diagram in Figure 7.1, using the devices now familiar to you, analyzes a chain of interactions that might be initiated when a child annoys his father by making excessive noise.

In this schematic, the occasion on which the father responds rather testily to the mother is a noisy child. Rather than chastise the child directly, however, the father issues a command to the mother, who in turn uses threat to bring about compliance from the child. Both the mother and the father are negatively reinforced, one by the avoidance of an argument and the other by the termination of an aversive stimulus. The child is positively reinforced by the mother's approval. A less submissive wife might have turned upon the husband with the remark, "Tell him yourself!" or a less obedient child might have ignored the mother's request. Obviously, the past history of interaction among the family members will determine which of these several alternatives occurs. Variants of this situation may be found in countless social organizations, with the chain of command feature being quite evident in the military establishment and scarcely concealed in most other social groupings.

Figure 7.1

Analysis of an authority hierarchy in terms of controlling and reinforcing stimuli. (Adapted from Adams and Romney, 1959)

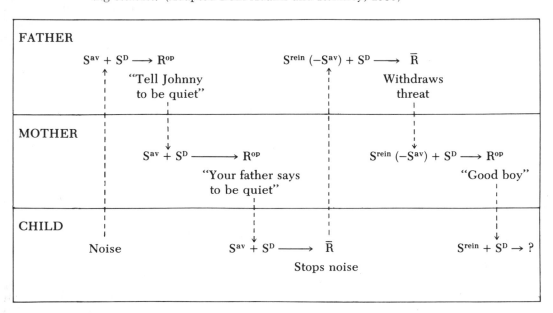

Peer nominations. A study of leader and follower preferences by Hollander and Webb (1955) required that aviation cadets at Pensacola complete three peer nomination forms at the conclusion of their preflight training. On the first of these forms, each cadet marked the three individuals from his section whom he considered best qualified to lead a "special military unit with an undisclosed mission." On a second form, each cadet was asked to assume that he was the leader of this special unit and to nominate three persons whom he would most want to serve under him. Finally, on the third form, each cadet selected three individuals from his unit whom he considered to be his best friends.

The investigators found that leader and follower nominations were highly correlated; that is, each cadet tended to nominate the same individuals, whether they were designated as potential leaders or as potential followers. Interestingly, friendship nominations overlapped very little with leader and follower nominations. These results support our general contention that a stable leader-follower interaction involves frequent mutual reinforcement and infrequent mutual aversiveness. When the leader's behavior for any reason becomes aversive to the group, one of the first results is a disturbance in productivity (Berrien, 1961). This decrease in the frequency of certain behaviors by the group members is aversive to the leader, who may attempt by coercion or persuasion to restore the group's former level of productivity. Whether or not the leader accomplishes this depends upon how the followers respond to the techniques he employs to modify their behavior. Herein lie many of the intriguing problems and the practical difficulties of understanding and manipulating leadership behavior.

Role Behavior

Different kinds of performances are reinforced when one is a leader and when one is a follower. Thus, a leader at any given level of a hierarchy except the very top may be domineering with respect to his subordinates but deferential when dealing with his superiors. The fact that individuals do exhibit consistently different behaviors in different situations has led Sarbin (1968) to develop a theory of role enactment. Not satisfied with a description of social behavior in terms of an interaction between individuals, Sarbin (1954) proposed that human conduct is the product of the *interaction of self and role.* Rephrasing Sarbin, we may say that the term role refers to an individual's behavior when he encounters other persons under particular circumstances, such as at home, in school, or on the street. A role, then, is seen as linked with a situation rather than with the person who momentarily enters that situation.

What would be some examples of roles, according to this definition? Because we have all been children, we have all played the roles of children. Even among children, however, there is *role differentiation.* A child may behave one way with his parents and quite differently when he is with his peers. Among other children, he may even be a leader, something he is unlikely to become with his parents. As adults, many of us become parents and thereby acquire certain responsibilities of leadership in the family, even though we may not be leaders in the other social groups to which we belong. As Gibb (1954) points out, leadership involves a complex pattern of roles, with the individual changing roles, or adapting his behaviors, to fit the requirements of the situation. Effective leaders are more adept at this than the average person. An example that comes to mind is the politician who, in seeking re-election, appears in suspenders before his rural constituents and in formal attire at Washington cocktail parties. His behavior in each case is appropriate to the circumstances and is designed to elicit supportive reactions from the individuals with whom he is interacting.

A significant feature of social interaction resides in the fact that we come to expect certain characteristic behaviors from other people. These expectations, says Sarbin, may be regarded as acquired anticipatory reactions. One learns that (a) he can expect or anticipate certain actions from other persons, and (b) others have expectations of him. A child learns to expect certain nurturant behaviors from adults. Adults, in turn, anticipate certain behaviors, such as respect and obedience, from children. When both child and parent behave in these predicted ways, they are fulfilling or reinforcing one another's role expectations.

The concept of role is a convenient shorthand for designating certain well practiced behaviors that are specific to situations in which particular individuals are involved. To "play a role" is simply to perform in a manner that has been reinforced in certain classes, or categories, of situations. Individuals who shift from one role to another, say from head of a family to apprentice in a construction firm, have learned to react differentially in these situations because of the different consequences generated by their behavior. Behavior that is reinforced by the members of one's family will not necessarily be reinforced by one's co-workers. As a result of early learning experiences, each individual comes to behave in those ways that are appropriate to a given set of circumstances. One responds differentially to the cues provided in various situations as a result of having experienced the social consequences of alternative modes of behaving. The expression "foot-in-mouth disease" comes to mind in this connection. All of us have committed gaucheries on certain occasions and, as a result of the aversive consequences, have learned more appropriate forms of response. The adolescent who is embarrassed at his first dinner party because he displays the same casual table manners that he uses at home is quick to learn more acceptable performances. We could say that he is learning a new *role*, that of a young adult. In countless other ways, his behaviors are modified according to the reactions they elicit from others. He may learn, as an accepted member of these new groups, to punish the performances of initiates, who are as inept as he was only a short time earlier. It is through this type of interaction in a variety of situations that individuals help shape each other's behavior and to establish what have been termed *social norms*.

The acquisition of these situation-specific patterns of behavior, sometimes called roles, is an essential process in the differentiation of leaders and followers. A leader may be adored or hated; he may be effective or ineffective; he may be democratic or authoritarian. Whatever the defining characteristics of his role as leader, however, we may be sure that his behavior is maintained through interaction with others who, in turn, are reinforced in their roles as followers. As leaders control certain behaviors of their followers, so do the followers react in ways that either maintain or modify the behavior of their leaders. When the behavior of either leader or follower becomes aversive to the other, a new mode of accommodation must be achieved. Sometimes the leader is deposed, and sometimes the dissident followers are punished. Only when leader and follower provide mutual reinforcement for one another's actions will the relationship be stable.

Styles of Leadership

Authoritarianism

Psychological interest in the phenomena of leadership was given a sharp impetus after 1940, when the fate of Europe seemed to lie in the hands of charismatic leaders like Hitler, Mussolini, and Stalin. Following the war, neither victors nor vanquished could seem to offer a rational explanation for the almost hypnotic power that Adolph Hitler had wielded, for example, over the German people. Writing in 1950, in the foreword to a volume dealing with the authoritarian leader and his followers, Horkheimer and Flowerman made this observation about Nazi Germany:

> Today the world scarcely remembers the mechanized persecution and extermination of millions of human beings only a short span of years away in what was once regarded as the citadel of Western civilization. Yet the conscience of many men was aroused. How could it be, they asked each other, that in a culture of law, order, and reason, there should have survived the irrational remnants of ancient racial and religious hatreds? How could they explain the willingness of great masses of people to tolerate the mass extermination of their fellow citizens? What tissues in the life of our modern society remain cancerous, and despite our assumed enlightenment show the incongruous atavism of ancient peoples? And what within the individual organism responds to certain stimuli in our culture with attitudes and acts of destructive aggression? (1950, p. v)

One of the investigations that stemmed from such questions as these dealt with the correlation between a number of deeply rooted personality traits and behavior indicative of prejudice toward ethnic and minority groups. The term *authoritarian personality* has been applied to the individual who, through his expressed sentiments, reveals both a susceptibility to antidemocratic ideas and a readiness to exhibit antidemocratic behavior (Adorno, Frenkel-Brunswik, Levinson, and Sanford, 1950). Based largely on their interrogations of men and women in California, Adorno and his coworkers developed two well known and widely used attitude scales. These are the E (Ethnocentrism) Scale and the F (Fascism) Scale. Scores on these two instruments are highly correlated, indicating that persons who tend to be prejudiced toward minority ethnic groups also tend to hold antidemocratic, or authoritarian, beliefs and attitudes. Extreme conventionality and submissiveness toward authority characterize the authoritarian individual, who presumably will support dictatorial forms of leadership. A great many persons, on the other hand, can be described as *equalitarians*. They exhibit some basic personality differences from the authoritarian type, and they tend to prefer democratic forms of leadership. The personal histories of individuals classified as equalitarians differ in consistent ways from those of authoritarians. Among other things, these persons have enjoyed more affectionate, democratic, and permissive relationships with their parents. As a result, they are capable of more flexible behavior as adults, and they enjoy a greater variety of experiences without guilt than the authoritarian.

An experiment designed to establish the typical reactions of a sample of Americans to authoritarian leadership was reported by Sanford (1952). He defends a position similar to the one we have taken, namely, that it is futile to search for traits of leadership as though they could be measured apart from the leader-follower relation. "If we want to learn about marriage," writes Sanford, "we do not study only husbands or wives. We have to study the relation that exists between them. The same thing holds for friendship or enmity, or partnership or leadership" (p. 329). In this particular experiment, Sanford focused his attention on the generally neglected follower and his role in the relationship.

Interviews were administered to 963 persons sampled randomly in the city of Philadelphia. Two of the items on the questionnaire are of particular interest here. One is a cartoon showing an individual addressing a small group as follows: "Since I'm head of this group, you'd better do as I say." The respondent is asked to imagine himself a member of the group and to provide a rejoinder to this authoritarian pronouncement. Nearly half of the persons to whom this "projective" device was administered gave answers indicating rejection of the leader: "You're nuts," or "You're too arbitrary." However, nearly a third of the respondents volunteered answers that indicated either complete or qualified acceptance of the leader's behavior: "Okay, tell us what you want," or "It depends on what you want." Only 10 per cent suggested that the majority should decide whether or not to obey the leader, a rejoinder that seems appropriately democratic.

A slightly different approach to the same question was made by asking the respondents to complete the following sentence: "Followers who disagree with the leader should. . . ." Analysis of the completions of this sentence fragment revealed that about 45 per cent added such predicates as ". . . resign, not follow; rebel." About one third completed the sentence with phrases that were categorized as "speaking out for the group when its welfare was threatened."

This report by Sanford is interesting because it drew upon a nonstudent population for data and utilized two projective-type items rather than the usual poll-type questions. The replies that were obtained suggested that directive leadership was not necessarily aversive to everyone interviewed, although a substantial proportion of the respondents displayed a "somewhat cantankerous rejection" of this type of leader.

Authoritarian versus Democratic Leadership

A compelling demonstration of the controlling effects of several different styles of leadership is provided in a classic experiment reported by Lippitt and White (1952). These investigators studied the effects on member behavior of three types of adult leadership in clubs of eleven-year-old boys. One group was assigned an *authoritarian* leader who (a) determined all policies regarding the club's activities, (b) dictated the steps to be undertaken in various projects one at a time, so that long-range goals were never disclosed, (c) made all assignments of activities and partners, and (d) remained aloof from the group, except for giving directions and demonstrations. Another group worked with a *democratic* leader who (a) resolved policies and procedures through group discussion, (b) gave the group a long-range perspective on the tasks to be completed, (c) allowed the group to decide on individual responsibilities as well as work partners, and (d) entered into the spirit, if not the actual work, of the group. Finally, a *laissez-faire* situation was provided in which the adult played a relatively passive role in the group, allowing complete individual freedom in regard to activities and procedures, and supplied aid or information only when asked. To control for possible differences between the groups of boys, who had been matched as closely as possible in terms of intelligence and other selected personality traits, each group was observed under all three leadership conditions. Records were then kept of the individual behaviors and group products that emerged from the groups under these three types of leadership.

The investigators found that "expressions of irritability and aggressiveness toward fellow members occurred more frequently in both the authoritarian atmosphere and the laissez-faire situation than in the democratic social climates" (p. 347). Under an authoritarian leader, the boys became dependent to the point of showing almost no initiative. Demands for attention from the adult in these conditions was also greater than in the other situations. "It seemed clear," the authors write, "that getting the attention of the adult represented one of the few paths to more satisfactory social status in the authoritarian situation . . ." (p. 347). We have already noted that the attention of someone else is a powerful conditioned reinforcer for most persons. It appears that attention from an authoritarian leader serves to reinforce deference, or submission, from the followers. To be other than submissive to an authoritarian figure may, of course, have aversive consequences, depending upon the amount of power wielded by the leader.

In contrast to the authoritarian social climate, the members of the democratically led groups made many more suggestions on matters of group policy. They were also able to work productively in the absence of the leader, as contrasted with the virtual standstill that occurred in the authoritarian groups when the leader was not present. In similar circumstances, the members of the laissez-faire groups were active but not productive. Even with the leader present they made fewer constructive suggestions than were observed in the democratic groups. This is attributed by Lippitt and White to the lack of cooperative working arrangement between group members and the adult leader.

Things were not all bad in the authoritarian groups. The level of "interpersonal friendliness" was as high as in the democratic and laissez-faire situations. It is not infrequently observed that individuals under an authoritarian leader are apt to ignore their own differences of opinion and to present a united front toward the autocrat. An underlying spirit of rebellion toward the leader coupled with aggressive reactions toward outgroups constitutes the cohesive force in aggressive autocracy, according to Lippitt and White. Although we cannot report all the details of this interesting experiment, it seems to have demonstrated adequately that different styles of leadership behavior have a measurable impact on the performances of the group members.

Directive versus Permissive Leadership

We should not confuse authoritarian with *directive* leadership. The latter provides guidance without being arbitrary or oppressive. Page and McGinnies (1959) arranged for adult groups to discuss a mental health film under either directive or nondirective leadership. In contrast to the directive situation, the nondirective leader refrained from making interpretations of points in the film, reflected questions back to the group instead of providing answers, and refrained from injecting his own viewpoint into the discussion. The leader, who played both roles in different groups, was rated significantly more favorably by the groups in which he was more directive. Further analysis of the data disclosed that this result could be attributed largely to the reactions of those members who had participated least in the discussion.

Why should this be so? We may presume that the nonparticipants in group discussion, through lack of sufficient prior reinforcement, have never developed a high level of activity in this type of situation. Perhaps they have been members of social groups in which other, more vocal individuals preempted the discussion periods. Such behavior might become aversive to those thus deprived of an opportunity to respond. As a result, these more reticent members prefer to listen to the remarks of an "expert" rather than to the opinions of their peers. Such an interpretation is further suggested by the fact that the less verbal members of college seminars frequently suggest that the professor take a more active, directive role in the group's discussions. Evidence confirming this supposition has been presented by Wispe (1951), who found that college students tended to prefer classes that were led directively to those that were led permissively.

Trait Theory

Millions of American males have had opportunities during recent years to experience directive leadership in various branches of the armed services. Data accumulated by psychologists in the Office of Strategic Services during World War II revealed that leadership performance in military field situations correlated fairly highly with leadership in discussion and debate (OSS Assessment Staff, 1948). This evidence for leadership as a "relatively general trait" was contrary to the conclusions of some investigators that leadership is specific to the particular situation under investigation (Jenkins, 1947). Perhaps, as suggested in the OSS report, a high degree of similarity existed among the situations in which the behavior of the leaders was evaluated. We are inclined to agree with this interpretation, at least to the extent of suggesting that a person who exhibits leadership qualities in one situation will doubtless generalize his behavior to other *situations that he perceives as similar.* The accomplished quarterback of a football team may be an equally effective leader on a basketball squad, but he may become tongue-tied in speech class.

The problem, in practical circumstances, is one of identifying the stimuli that control the leader's behavior and the reinforcers that maintain it. In team competition, for example, many functionally equivalent stimuli are present from one contest to another, i.e., crowds of people, referees or umpires, teammates, opponents. The effective reinforcers (applause, cheers, backslaps) are also similar from one situation to another. Performance in a classroom, however, is under the control of a very different set of stimuli (austere surroundings, a quiet audience, a critical professor), and the reinforcement for an effective performance is considerably less dramatic.

Much of the confusion that has been generated over attempts to classify leadership as a *general* or *specific* trait could be avoided if the discussions were couched in terms of the functional relationship between situations, behavior, and reinforcers. The effectiveness of the leader-follower relation as dependent upon a "special sensitivity between the individual and *specific* other persons" has been recognized by Jennings (1965, p. 517). This is another way of saying that leaders and followers control one another's behavior and that all leaders are not equivalent for all followers, or vice versa. "There may be very little overlap," Jennings points out, "between the individuals who support one leader and those who support another" (p. 517).

Predictors of Leadership

Despite the obvious importance of situational factors in leadership, psychologists have not ignored the possibility of a relationship between the traits or personality characteristics of a leader and the effectiveness with which the leader controls the performances of his followers. This has involved a search for *predictors,* that is, those leader characteristics that are correlated with effective group performance. Much of this research has been conducted in various branches of the military, where leadership is of critical importance, and where controlled investigations can be carried out with groups of various sizes.

Havron and McGrath (1961) used a battery of paper-and-pencil tests to measure leadership traits that might be related to the performance of military units in the field. They studied both Army rifle squads and Air Force crews. The *criteria* of group performance were developed both from combat situations and from ratings of the groups by trained umpires. Characteristics of the unit leader were then related to *unit* performance effectiveness. In a word, these investigations revealed that among Army squads the predictors that were most highly related to unit effectiveness were the *intelligence* of the leader and the *knowledge* that he had about his job. In a few cases where the leader scored low on the intelligence measures, satisfactory job knowledge was sufficient to yield a high unit score in the performance tests. In addition, significant correlations were found between unit performance scores and the accuracy with which the leader could estimate the intelligence, abilities, and attitudes of his men. The investigators concluded that apparently a good leader knows his men and a poor one does not.

We have already noted that leadership behavior is demonstrated more with respect to specific situations than it is with respect to specific individuals. Havron and McGrath produced further evidence for this generalization. Many of the relationships they found between predictors and criteria in Army units did not hold for Air Force crews. A basic difference in these two groups was that the task in which the air crews were observed involved survival training in the Sierra Nevada Mountains, considered by many of them to be thankless duty. Their performances seemed to be reinforced more by the extent to which they reduced their discomfort than by their acquisition of new skills. This meant that criterion measures were confounded with behaviors quite irrelevant to the task, so that no meaningful relationship of these indices to leader behavior was obtained. A leader can do little to shape the performance of a follower if the desired class of behaviors is not emitted.

On the other hand, in situations where the leader can control some of the behavior of his followers, it is important that he *do something* when the occasion demands action. When interviewed, many of the Army squad members indicated that they regarded as leaders the ones with a "willingness to act." It would seem that almost any behavior by a designated leader is more reinforcing than no behavior. It follows, then, that a leader who is judged as effective by his men is one who emits more leadership behavior in a variety of situations. Havron and McGrath describe an interesting test of this hypothesis:

> The experimenter seated the squad leaders of effective and ineffective squads one at a time in his interview room. During the interview he left the room on some pretext, walked to the next room and started ringing a field telephone, the other outlet of which was across the room from where the squad leader sat. Almost all of the effective squad leaders answered the phone, most of them after only a few rings. Most of the ineffective squad leaders did not answer it at all, even after ten rings (p. 173).

Perhaps the most significant finding to emerge from the program of research reported by Havron and McGrath is that those kinds of performances commonly designated as leadership can be learned by individuals who would otherwise be unlikely to show such behavior. The investigators devised a mission in which the leader of a unit and his assistant were both "killed." The problem of the unit was to complete its mission. Twenty-four squads that had previously been trained by the investigators in giving suggestions to their leaders were markedly superior in this test than twenty-four squads trained by traditional methods. In the latter groups, the members had learned to depend entirely upon the leader's initiative, and when he was removed, the men were unable to function effectively. But in those squads where some of the actions typical of leaders had been practiced and socially reinforced among the members, someone inevitably assumed leadership so that the group could complete its mission. Havron and McGrath concluded that, "A group can act effectively and in a co-ordinated way even with a leader of indifferent ability, or can reorganize quickly without leaders, if the *concept of leadership and how it is to be exercised operationally* is learned and appreciated by all group members" (p. 175).

In somewhat more behavioral terms, we might say that a group can continue to function effectively in the absence of its designated leaders if functionally equivalent behaviors have been acquired by other members of the group under conditions of reinforcement by their peers, so that the frequency of such behaviors will increase in situations where the leader is absent. Some of the specific behaviors that characterize leaders can with training be acquired by nonleaders. The practical problem is one of keeping such behaviors under narrow stimulus control so that they will not be emitted except in the absence of the designated leader. Under ordinary circumstances, the assumption of leadership by followers would amount to a usurpation of the leader's role. The training procedures successfully developed by Havron and McGrath, therefore, might constitute a two-edged sword in some circumstances.

Follower Reactions

In the military, of course, followers have little or no voice in the matter of selecting leaders. Perhaps for this very reason, the reactions of soldiers to their leaders have been a matter of interest to social scientists. Stouffer and his associates (1949) reached some interesting conclusions about attitudes toward leadership in the Army during World War II. Among other conclusions, they report the following: (a) New recruits had more favorable attitudes toward officers than did men with longer service. (b) As the war progressed, enlisted men in general tended to have less favorable attitudes toward officers. (c) At any given period during the war, the most favorable dispositions toward officers were found among combat troops, the least favorable were manifested by inactive overseas troops, and stateside troops were intermediate in their judgments. (d) With rank and longevity constant, the better educated men were less favorably inclined toward officers than those who were less well educated.

These findings are reminiscent, in some respects, of the Bennington College survey conducted by Newcomb that we discussed in Chapter 3. It may be recalled that the attitudes of the students became progressively more liberal as they advanced from the freshman through the senior years. In somewhat analogous fashion, the attitudes of enlisted men toward officers changed in a predictable direction as their time in service lengthened. In both instances, the effective reinforcers for the observed individuals changed with time. Officers represent, in a sense, the entire military establishment. Resentment toward the Army was found to increase as a function of length of service, and it is not surprising that officers, because of their identification with the aversive aspects of military life, received a share of this antipathy. New recruits, we may presume, had not yet experienced some of the less pleasant features of military service and, consequently, viewed both the Army and its leaders more favorably than did seasoned troops.

Sociometric Choices

Considerable research has been directed toward the reactions of followers to their leaders aside from questions dealing specifically with the matter of authoritarian leadership. The most straightforward method of ascertaining the personal relationships that exist among the members of a group is to ask them how they like one another and with whom they would prefer to associate. This procedure, called *sociometry*, was introduced by Moreno (1934) for the purpose of determining patterns of acceptance and rejection among individuals in a group. Both the popular members and the "isolates" can thus be identified.

Sociometric measures have also been used to determine which individuals in a group are perceived as leaders. Groups frequently give emergence to what Bales and Slater (1955) have termed a "task leader" and a "social-emotional leader". This distinction is similar to one made earlier by Gibb (1950) between the "social" leader and the "functional" leader of a group. The task or functional leader stimulates and reinforces behavior that is instrumental in reaching a group goal. In so doing, however, he must, occasionally at least, disturb other activities that the group members might prefer, and he presents a threat to the extent that he is capable of meting out punishment for inefficient performance. Thus, because he is the source of both reinforcing and aversive stimuli, the task leader is also the object of ambivalent feelings by the group members. For this reason, another person frequently emerges as the agent for expressing the group members' hostilities toward the task leader. Called the social-emotional leader, this individual, because he provides no aversive consequences to others, is well liked. He, in turn, generally likes the other group members strongly and about equally. The task leader, on the other hand, being concerned with effective performance, likes some members of the group better than others. It is not difficult in the groups that we encounter from day to day to identify individuals who seem to fit these two descriptions.

Actually, as Bales (1953) has indicated, the best-liked member of a group is not necessarily associated with any leadership functions. After obtaining sociometric ratings from the members of adult discussion groups, Lana, Vaughan, and McGinnies (1960) found that the discussants tended to direct their comments more toward those individuals whom they perceived as leaders than toward those whom they had designated as their friends. The social reinforcers in a task-oriented discussion situation, therefore, appear to be different from those in a casual, friendly conversation. In general, those who are perceived as leaders are in the best position to reinforce other members of the group, hence, they are more often the recipients of communications. Friends offer different kinds of reinforcement than leaders and are more sought after in situations that do not demand task-oriented performance.

Individuals having the status of leaders in task groups, then, are more effective agents of reinforcement than persons who are not perceived as leaders. A leader, in general, is defined as one who has influence within a group (Gibb, 1950). In the 1948 OSS Assessment Staff report alluded to earlier, it is suggested that leadership involves "a man's ability to take the initiative in social situations, to plan and organize action, and in doing so to evoke cooperation" (p. 301). However, a leader is to be distinguished from a head, in that a leader's authority is accorded him by his followers, whereas the authority of a head derives from some external source (Gibb, 1954). There is evidence that an elected supervisor, who is a leader rather than a head, is able to control work output more effectively than an assigned supervisor because his power is seen as having greater "legitimacy" (Raven and French, 1958). The distinction seems to involve the techniques of reinforcement that are used, with positive control being more characteristic of a leader and aversive control more frequent with a head. A follower might be friendly with an elected leader but rarely with an imposed head.

Ordinarily, friends and leaders do not overlap, and one interacts with them differently, depending upon the situation. Those whom we perceive as leaders are the ones who are able to control our fates in situations that are relevant to their leadership status. For this reason, we initiate more remarks to them in a formal discussion situation than to our friends. The behavior of our friends is also reinforcing to us but under different circumstances.

Stress

It is a matter of common observation that the dispositions of individuals toward their leaders are changeable and that these changes reflect in part an alteration of the total situation as well as the influence of new groups with which the person becomes involved. One rather dramatic set of circumstances that may radically enhance the status of a group leader is crisis. Sargent and Williamson (1966) point out that an open threat to the survival of the group is an important factor in bringing out leadership tendencies. They reason: "Undoubtedly the most devoted followers are attached to leaders who have effectively solved a major crisis" (p. 431). Although their personalities and their ideologies were strikingly different, Franklin D. Roosevelt and Adolph Hitler are cited as leaders who were essentially the products of crises in their respective countries. In one sense, a crisis establishes a deprivation state for a group, so that the consequences of effective leadership will be more reinforcing than otherwise. The circumstances are roughly analogous to those of depriving an experimental animal of food so that food becomes a more effective reinforcer.

A crisis affecting a group increases the probability that the group will react favorably to effective action by a leader. A leader who fails to provide solutions to the problems of a group, on the other hand, may take on aversive qualities and be rejected. Sargent and Williamson suggest that Herbert Hoover, who was president during the 1929 depression, and Neville Chamberlain, who capitulated to Hitler at Munich, were blamed by their countrymen either for lack of appropriate action or for action that led to calamity.

An attempt to test these two general propositions, namely, that leaders have more influence during periods of crisis than periods of noncrisis, and that groups tend to replace an old leader with a new leader when the old leader does not effectively meet the crisis, was conducted by Hamblin

(1958). Twenty-four three-person groups of college students were subjects in the experiment. Twelve of these groups were destined to experience a "crisis" situation, while the remaining twelve served as controls. All of the groups first learned to play a modified shuffleboard game in which they attempted to better the records previously made by teams of high school students. They had to discover the rules of the games themselves, the only indications of their correctness being flashing lights, red whenever a rule was violated and green whenever a score was made. During the first of two fifteen-minute periods, the subjects improved their performances to the point where their scores exceeded the posted scores of the high school students. After this, however, the experimenter arranged things in the crisis groups so that the rules changed frequently and arbitrarily. As a result, the players' scores rapidly deteriorated. Observations made by the experimenter enabled him to classify each team member as either high or low in influence, depending upon how frequently his suggestions for improvement were accepted both before and after development of the crisis. The initially most influential person was considered to be the "leader," and his fate throughout the game was noted.

In the crisis groups, the leader who had emerged during the first half of the game improved his influence score for a short time following the beginning of the crisis, thus confirming the hypothesis that he would have more influence during a time of crisis than of noncrisis. Such an enhancement of the leader's influence score did not occur in the control groups, where the rules of the game were not changed, and the group's performance continued to improve rather than deteriorate. In the crisis groups, as scores continued to plummet, the leader whose influence had momentarily increased was finally replaced during the last ten minutes by the individual who had initially scored second in number of suggestions accepted. Thus, the original leader, who could not by the very nature of the situation provide a solution to the problem, was replaced. This did not occur in the control groups. As an interesting sidelight, it was observed that in the control groups the leader often maintained his position of dominance through a coalition with the third-ranking member of the group. This is apparently a common tendency in three-person groups, as observed earlier by Mills (1953). Because two members of a triad can usually overpower the third member, however, this turns to be an unstable social configuration (Caplow, 1956; Vinacke and Arkoff, 1957).

Studies of panic. A considerable amount has been written about the behavior of individuals in groups under stress. Under these special circumstances, the performance of the leader may be critical to the fate of the group. One function that the leader can perform to prevent panic in a group under stress is to help maintain channels of communication among the members. A breakdown in communication among soldiers in combat, for example, can lead to panic. After investigating seven such incidents among American troops in World War II, Marshall (1947) concluded that a common feature was the unexplained flight of a few men to the rear. "In every case," writes Marshall, "the testimony of all the witnesses clearly developed the fact that those who started to run, and thereby spread the the fear which started the panic, had a legitimate, or at least a reasonable excuse, for the action. It was not the sudden motion which of itself did the damage, but the fact that others present were not kept informed" (p. 146).

It is also true, as Schultz (1964) points out, that history does not record a high incidence of panic among military troops. Either the designated leaders provide necessary direction for the behavior of the group, or certain performances occur spontaneously in the group to prevent disaster. Such a group might be said to have high *morale*. Torrance (1961) has suggested a framework in which some of the factors that generate stress in groups may be related to certain behavioral consequences. The duration and intensity of the stress-inducing variables as well as the reactions of leaders and group members combine to determine the final outcome. The conceptualization outlined by Torrance is presented in Figure 7.2.

Let us consider one feature of the behavioral consequences of group stress in more detail. Torrance suggests that "mutual support and self-sacrifice" of the members is a possible reaction to threat. Is this consistent with our general theory that individuals tend to behave in ways that are reinforcing? The best prediction from this point of view would seem to be "every man for himself," which, in fact, sometimes happens. But there are numerous recorded examples of selfless and self-sacrificing behavior in situations that threatened the destruction of an entire group. Such behavior is frequently exhibited by the formal or informal leaders of the imperiled groups. It is necessary here to recognize that those behaviors representing "self-interest" may eventually have aversive consequences to the group and, hence, ultimately to the individual himself. In instances where behavior commonly called "heroism" arises, it may be assumed that the self-sacrificing individual has a personal history in which this general class of behaviors has been reinforced. Perhaps this amounted to no more than being rewarded by one's parents for generosity or consideration to others. Individuals who have never acquired these behavioral dispositions can seldom be expected to exhibit them under stress, especially when the immediate consequences are aversive. It is also possible that some individuals have been punished for behaviors designated as selfish, and that self-sacrificing performances are negatively reinforced by their instrumentality in avoiding shame or guilt. It is noteworthy that persons who fail to exhibit altruistic behavior in times of stress may later experience overwhelming feelings of guilt. We say that such individuals are "conscience-stricken."

Obviously, the factors that impel either leaders or followers to act in ways detrimental to their own immediate welfare in order to achieve consequences of benefit to others are multiple and varied. These include the

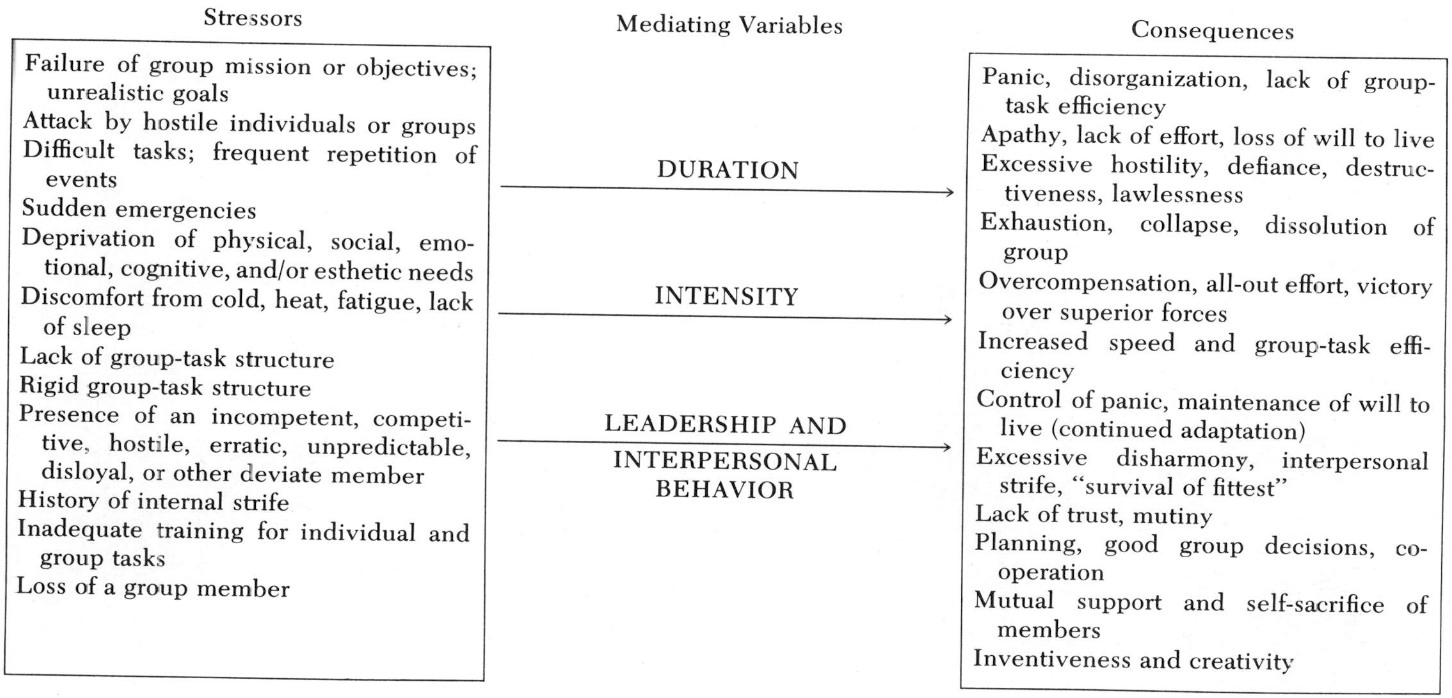

Stressors	Mediating Variables	Consequences
Failure of group mission or objectives; unrealistic goals		Panic, disorganization, lack of group-task efficiency
Attack by hostile individuals or groups		Apathy, lack of effort, loss of will to live
Difficult tasks; frequent repetition of events	DURATION	Excessive hostility, defiance, destructiveness, lawlessness
Sudden emergencies		Exhaustion, collapse, dissolution of group
Deprivation of physical, social, emotional, cognitive, and/or esthetic needs		Overcompensation, all-out effort, victory over superior forces
Discomfort from cold, heat, fatigue, lack of sleep	INTENSITY	Increased speed and group-task efficiency
Lack of group-task structure		Control of panic, maintenance of will to live (continued adaptation)
Rigid group-task structure		Excessive disharmony, interpersonal strife, "survival of fittest"
Presence of an incompetent, competitive, hostile, erratic, unpredictable, disloyal, or other deviate member	LEADERSHIP AND INTERPERSONAL BEHAVIOR	Lack of trust, mutiny
History of internal strife		Planning, good group decisions, co-operation
Inadequate training for individual and group tasks		Mutual support and self-sacrifice of members
Loss of a group member		Inventiveness and creativity

Figure 7.2

Typical group stressors and the mediation of their consequences. (From Torrance, 1961) acquisition of verbal repertoires organized around such concepts as duty and self-sacrifice, as well as emotional reactions such as fear and anger that might, respectively, inhibit or facilitate adaptive behavior under stress. Experience in stressful situations, for example, usually has the effect of decreasing the intensity of emotional reactions conditioned to these situations. Experience also provides the individual with an opportunity to acquire proficiency in those kinds of verbal and nonverbal performances that might be useful under stress. Leadership training is frequently designed with precisely these objectives in view.

The Concept of Power

Regardless of whether the consequences of their decisions are beneficial or detrimental to the group, leaders possess a distinctive characteristic that is described simply as *power*. Kaplan (1964) has defined power as the ability of one person or group of persons to influence the behavior of others. Although this statement can be applied to a broad range of social interactions, it is clearly intended in this context to imply that leaders are uniquely capable of acquiring stimulus control over the behavior of their followers. But, as we have seen, a stimulus normally gains control over a response only if the response is followed closely by a reinforcing state of affairs. It follows, therefore, that leaders must be in a position, or have the power, to determine the consequences that will follow from alternative courses of action by their followers. By thus controlling the reinforcements that are contingent on the behavior of the followers, they effectively maintain their leadership status. Of course, leaders may not always be able to control or even predict the outcome of decisions that affect the welfare of their followers. This is one of the hazards of leadership, namely, that the leader assumes responsibility for the consequences to others of actions that he has taken. Not infrequently, such consequences are disastrous, in which case the leader must either repair the damage or suffer a loss of influence.

Types of power. French and Raven (1959) have distinguished between *reward power* and *coercive power*. The difference is essentially one between the positive and the aversive control of behavior. A leader who rewards his followers utilizes such positive reinforcers as promotions, wage increases, or desirable work assignments. The leader who coerces his followers uses such aversive controls as wage cuts, delays in promotion, or assignment of undesirable tasks. Some data obtained by Brigante (1958) revealed that individuals whose power derived from their capacity to reward were more favorably rated by adolescents than persons whose power lay in their capacity to punish. This does not mean that effective leaders are necessarily those who have warm interpersonal relations with their subordinates. In fact, quite the opposite is often the case. We shall consider this matter in greater detail shortly.

An important transformation of reward power into *referent power* sometimes occurs. This means that the leader need no longer directly administer reinforcements in order to effectively control his followers. The followers, in this instance, are said to *identify* with the leader and to emulate his behavior even in his absence. Parental power, as suggested by Secord and Backman (1964), is largely referent power, whereas police power is based on coercion. This observation is consistent with findings that we discussed earlier demonstrating that children are more prone to imitate those with whom they have previously experienced a rewarding relationship.

A leader having referent power, that is, a leader with whom followers are able to identify, is more apt to influence behavior over the long run. Back (1961) argues that the application of coercive power by a leader may bring about only superficial changes in behavior. Under coercive leadership, in other words, certain undesirable behaviors of the followers may be temporarily depressed in frequency as a result of their having aversive consequences. When the aversive controls are removed, however, the behaviors often are reinstated in full strength. Thus, the punished child refrains from certain actions only in the presence of the parent, and the undisciplined motorist observes the traffic ordinances only if he is observed by others. A leader who shapes his followers' performances by using positive reinforcement instead of punishment will more often accomplish a relatively permanent modification of their behavior. This leader's position, in turn, will be more secure because he will be less likely to incur hostility. On the other hand, a leader who uses aversive control must be prepared to escalate his punitive measures in order to match the increasing resentment of his followers.

In general, we may assume that elected leaders, having less power, are not as likely as appointed leaders to use punishment as a means of behavioral control. They will, therefore, be more acceptable leaders and frequently will be more effective. Raven and French (1958) found, for example, that an elected supervisor exerted greater influence over his work group than a nonelected supervisor. Horwitz (1963) reported that students evaluated an instructor less favorably when he arbitrarily assigned more weight to his own vote in a group decision. A leader who falsely raises expectancies of democratic procedures among his followers is quite likely to be resented. On the other hand, an avowed authoritarian, who makes no pretense of being otherwise, may be fairly well received by his followers, provided his leadership is effective. He may even be regarded as a "benign autocrat," who rewards more than he punishes. In actuality, most leaders are probably the targets of ambivalence by their followers. They may be respected, as Homans (1961) points out, but they will not necessarily be liked. In Homan's terms, both rewards and costs are involved in performance under a leader. The rewards for compliance with the leader's directives are likely to be delayed, whereas the costs (in terms of effort or the foregoing of other activities) are immediate. Perhaps more important, a leader, in order to induce compliance, must use both positive and aversive controls; he rewards, but he also punishes. Thus, he incurs not only the positive feelings that attach to agents of positive reinforcement but also the negative feelings that are evoked by agents of punishment. It is a rare leader who will be loved by his followers all of the time. He should perhaps be content if he has earned their respect.

Leadership Effectiveness

Leaders may be viewed generally as effective or ineffective, depending upon both the degree to which they guide the group in the achievement of certain goals and the extent to which they enjoy support from the group. A large-scale investigation into the factors involved in leadership effectiveness has been reported by Fiedler (1967). Noting that concern with leadership has increased markedly during the past fifty years, Fiedler comments as follows:*

> An increasingly greater share of creative as well as routine tasks is being carried out by teams, panels, boards, crews, task groups, and corporate bodies of various sorts. Modern production methods and contemporary organizations have become more complex. These complex methods require greater coordination of effort and an increasingly high degree of specialization. One man can no longer master all the skills which may be required for the performance of various tasks. As a result, teams of highly trained specialists must, somehow, be made to work together toward a common goal. This requires competent leadership. Prima donnas, in business, in industry, in government, or in science, no less than in ballet and in opera, are a temperamental crowd whose peculiarities and sensibilities have to be respected. Highly skilled leadership is required to reconcile and utilize constructively different abilities, viewpoints, attitudes, and ideas in the performance of group tasks and organizational missions (p. 3).

Leader characteristics. Identification of potential leaders in terms of particular traits or capacities has not, as Fiedler observes, led to the assembling of effective groups. Indeed, attempts to identify traits that are consistently associated with leadership frequently have produced contradictory results (Stogdill, 1948). A major reason for this situation, according to Cartwright and Zander (1960), is that personality traits are both poorly conceived and unreliably measured. Should a time come when our techniques for assessing personality are more dependable, it may be possible to differentiate between leaders and nonleaders on the basis of selected personality variables. Even then, suggests Fiedler (1960), the events that

---

* From *A Theory of Leadership Effectiveness*, by F. E. Fiedler. Copyright © 1967 by McGraw-Hill, Incorporated. Used with permission of McGraw-Hill Book Company.

enable a person to become a leader may have little connection with the characteristics that make him an effective or ineffective leader. Ascent to leadership may depend upon age, family connections, financial windfalls, and other fortuitous events quite unrelated to relevant personality attributes. Becoming an *effective* leader, on the other hand, involves a complex interaction between the nature of the situation and the leader's use of power to influence his group's behavior.

Some groups, such as those found in military organizations, do not, by tradition, accept their leaders, so that only an unusual person would readily invite the adulation of his followers. A droll passage from the novel *Mr. Roberts,* by Thomas Heggen (1946), illustrates this point:

> The Captain of a naval vessel is a curious affair. Personally he may be short, scrawny, unprepossessing; but a Captain is not a person and cannot be viewed as such. He is an embodiment. He is given stature, substance, and sometimes a new dimension by the massive, cumulative authority of the Navy Department which looms behind him like a shadow. With some captains this shadow is a great, terrifying cloud; with others, it is scarcely apparent at all: but with none can it go unnoticed. Now to this the necessary exception: Captain Morton. With Captain Morton it could and does up to a point go unnoticed. The crew knows instinctively that the Captain is vulnerable, and he is unaware of the full dimensions of his authority; and, thus stripped of his substance, they find him detestable and not at all terrifying. He is not hated, for in hate there is something of fear and something of respect, neither of which is present here. And you could not say loathed, for loathing is passive and this is an active feeling. Best say detested; vigorously disliked. As the chosen enemy he is the object of an incessant guerrilla warfare, which is, for the Navy, a most irregular business (p. 12).

Yet another leader may be so revered by his followers that a successor is hard-pressed to take over the reins and gain acceptance by the group. For example, following the death of President John F. Kennedy, several of his close advisors resigned their positions rather than serve a new chief executive. In brief, the circumstances that propel an individual to a position of leadership are no guarantee that he will be either a popular leader or an effective leader, or even that he will remain a leader should new and unforeseen circumstances arise.

Fiedler (1967) has addressed himself to two essential questions: (a) How does a person get to be leader (b) What personality traits, attributes, or behaviors determine a leader's effectiveness? In responding to the first of these queries, he concludes that attainment of a position of leadership is often dependent less upon personality factors than upon the course of events. The answer to the second question involves the development of reliable predictors, and here Fiedler has made a major contribution. The criteria by which effective leadership might be measured, of course, have not escaped scrutiny by previous investigators. Stogdill and Coons (1957) and Bass (1960) have suggested that a leader's effectiveness is reflected in certain dimensions of the group's performance, namely, (a) output, (b) morale, and (c) satisfaction of the members. Fiedler points out, however, that many groups continue to exist only so long as they effectively perform the tasks for which they were formed in the first place. High morale and member satisfaction, although desirable by-products, are not necessarily essential to successful pursuit of the group's mission. Should the group fail in its task objectives, high morale will not justify its continued existence. For this reason, Fiedler proposes that leader effectiveness be evaluated in terms of group performance on its primary assigned task.

Group characteristics. Because of the great variety of tasks which individuals as members of groups may set themselves, it is useful to develop several categories that will differentiate among groups in terms of the kinds of member interactions that are required by different tasks. Fiedler proposes that groups be classified as *interacting, coacting,* or *counteracting.* He describes these three classes of task groups as follows:[*]

> *Interacting groups.* These groups ... require the close coordination of several team members in the performance of the primary task. The ability of one man to perform his job may depend upon the fact that another has first completed his share of the task. . . .
> *Coacting groups.* These groups also work together on a common task. However, each of the group members does his job relatively independently of the other team members. The characteristic pattern in such groups is that each group member is on his own, and his performance depends on his own ability, skill, and motivation. . . .
> *Counteracting groups.* The third category of groups consists of individuals who are working together for the purpose of negotiating and reconciling conflicting opinions and purposes. These groups are typically engaged in negotiative and bargaining processes, with some members representing one point of view, and others an opposing, or, at least, divergent point of view (pp. 18, 19, 20).

The importance of distinguishing among these three types of groups, Fiedler contends, lies in the different demands that they make upon leaders. The impact of these demands will, in turn, be tempered by such additional factors as the leader's personality and the types of situations that are involved. Fiedler has developed two measures of leadership style: The LPC (least-preferred co-worker) scale and the ASo (assumed similarity between opposites) score. These measures require the leader to rate the persons with whom he works best and least well on sixteen scales describing such personal dispositions as pleasant-unpleasant, cooperative-uncooperative, and boring-interesting. ASo scores are computed from the

[*] From *A Theory of Leadership Effectiveness*, by F. E. Fiedler. Copyright © 1967 by McGraw-Hill, Incorporated. Used with permission of McGraw-Hill Book Company.

difference between the leader's ratings of his *most* and *least* preferred co-workers. A high ASo (or high LPC) leader is one who gives reasonably favorable ratings on personality characteristics to those with whom he would prefer not to work. That is, he tends not to differentiate too strikingly in terms of personality between his most- and least-preferred co-workers. In short, according to Fiedler, the high ASo person distinguishes between work performance and personality, while the low ASo person attributes an individual's poor performance on a task to undesirable personality characteristics. High ASo leaders are more concerned with establishing good interpersonal relations and obtaining recognition and prominence, whereas low ASo leaders are more concerned with the task and are more punitive toward inefficient subordinates.

Contingency theory. Fiedler has found, in general, that leaders who can be described as permissive and considerate (high ASo) perform better under moderately stressful circumstances than leaders who are more managing and task-oriented (low ASo). However, task-oriented leaders perform better under highly stressful conditions. It is probably useful to make a distinction here, as several writers have done, between the therapeutic and the administrative functions of leadership. The behaviors typical of these two approaches are often incompatible, since concern by a leader with the personal problems of his subordinates subtracts from the time that both can devote to the task. Why, then, should the task-oriented leader be more effective under high stress, and the person-oriented leader more effective under moderate stress?

Although Fiedler interprets his findings in terms of the needs and motives of leaders, we shall use a slightly different set of explanatory terms. Let us assume that leaders do, in fact, have these two basically different orientations toward their followers. The ongoing behavior of the person-oriented leader is maintained more by how the group members act toward one another than by their performance on the assigned task. Specifically, he is more strongly reinforced by an atmosphere of cordiality in the group than by actual accomplishment. He responds effectively to moderate deteriorations in morale. However, when this social atmosphere breaks down under severe stress, the person-oriented leader lacks the resources to cope with the situation. It is so aversive to him that he reacts with irritability and withdrawal. On the other hand, a task-oriented leader, one whose behavior is maintained more by the productivity of the members than by their congeniality, is less likely to be disturbed by interpersonal frictions, unless these frictions cause a disruption of task performance. Such a mission-oriented leader may or may not be effective in re-establishing smooth interpersonal relationships among the group members. But he is able to continue reinforcing their task behavior even under severe stress because his own patterns of reaction to the group have not been disarrayed.

An insecure leader may bolster his position by encouraging (reinforcing) a certain amount of dissension among the members of a group over which he presides. In this case, we would say that he is able by certain manipulations to direct hostility from the group members away from himself and have it reflected in factional strife within the group. This, in turn, strengthens his own position as leader. Little if any research, however, has been done on this aspect of leadership.

One study reported by Fiedler illustrates the consistency that he has typically found between leadership effectiveness and the leader's judgments about his followers. Twenty-two surveying teams, each composed of three to four civil engineering students, were rated by an instructor on their efficiency and accuracy. Using a series of rating scales, the members of each team described themselves as well as their most-preferred and least-preferred co-workers. They then described on the same scales the two persons with whom they could work *best* and *least* well. These judgments were made in terms of all the individuals with whom the team members had ever worked, a method that yields more reliable results than judgments based on just the immediate situation.

Analysis of these several sets of ratings disclosed that ASo scores of the team leaders correlated negatively with team performances. In other words, the leaders of the more efficient teams rated their most- and least-preferred co-workers quite differently. Leaders of the less efficient teams, on the other hand, submitted rather similar sociometric ratings for their most- and least-preferred co-workers. Fiedler summarizes the findings as follows: "The picture of the effective informal task team as it emerges from our studies thus seems to be a rather tense, psychologically somewhat distant group which fares best under a directive, managing leader" (p. 71).

As we pointed out, however, the most effective pattern of leader behavior is a function of both the type of group and the task requirements with which the leader is engaged. Fiedler found that the leader of a successful board of directors performed better when he was relationship-oriented, whereas the foreman of an efficient open-hearth shift performed better when he was task-oriented.

The rather extensive data that Fiedler has collected on the relationships among the several dimensions of groups and leader-member relations has led him to propose a *contingency model* of leadership effectiveness. He states the essence of this model as follows: "*The appropriateness of the leadership style for maximizing group performance is contingent upon the favorableness of the group-task situations*" (p. 147). Specifically, task-oriented leaders may be expected to perform well in situations that are either highly favorable or relatively unfavorable to them. Relationship-oriented leaders will tend to perform best in situations where they have only moderate influence and which therefore are only moderately favorable.

It is implicit in the contingency model that group performance can be improved either by modifying the leader's style of behavior or by modifying the group's task requirements. Fiedler suggests that it is more feasible, generally, to change a man's work environment than to change his personality or his style of relating to others. This amounts to saying that matching a leader and a group so as to maximize the possibilities for mutual reinforcement is one way of attaining effective leadership. Where this is not possible, as within a family, it may be necessary through external intervention (such as psychotherapy) to modify individual behaviors in such a way as to generate better interpersonal relationships.

The Psychiatric Theory of Leadership

We should probably not conclude this discussion of leaders and followers without taking brief note of an approach to leadership that is based on clinical observation rather than experimentation. Bluemel (1950) asked the following question from the standpoint of a psychiatrist: "What urges a man into the political field, and what creates in him the desire to dominate the lives of other men? What are the distinguishing traits of personality that make this urge effective?" (p. 1).

We can recognize in this phraseology a commitment to the theory that leaders are distinguished by certain traits of personality that are not as conspicuous in their followers. Although this viewpoint has been seriously questioned (Stogdill, 1948), it has been suggested by Darley (1961) that the possibility of a relationship between certain general personality factors and leadership capability cannot easily be set aside. Bluemel argues that some of the traits that characterize mentally disturbed individuals are not infrequently found in leaders who have influenced the course of history. Human strife, according to Bluemel, results not so much from a conflict of interests as from a conflict of personalities. Personality clashes between leaders have far-reaching effects, including war. Bluemel describes, in brief, the relationships among *war, politics,* and *insanity:*

> One of the cardinal causes of war, in the opinion of the present writer, is the fact that national leadership frequently falls to men of abnormal mental makeup. There are ill-balanced men of history who have been directed by a star of destiny, an inner voice, or a guiding light. Other men, free from hallucinosis, have been motivated by hatred or suspicion having a paranoid quality. Still others have displayed delusions of grandeur in their political aspirations and wars of conquest. While some political leaders have been energized by a psychosis or mental illness, others have been afflicted with a less evident personality disorder but they have displayed pathological aggressiveness and obsessive-compulsive attitudes. These traits of personality may bring a man from obscurity to leadership and from leadership to dictatorship; they may at the same time bring a country from peace to war (p. 12).

If a certain class of behaviors appears so frequently in an individual's repertoire as virtually to dominate his activities, he is said to be obsessive or complusive. The social effects of such behavior, argues Bluemel, may be either beneficial or detrimental according to the pattern that the behavior assumes and the reactions that it elicits from others. Many famous explorers, for example, might be viewed in retrospect as having exhibited obsessive-compulsive behavior. Perhaps Columbus would never have reached America had he not obsessively persisted in his efforts to reach India by sailing westward. Robert Peary made several expeditions to Greenland and three unsuccessful attempts to reach the North Pole before he finally succeeded. Florence Nightingale's obsession with serving those who were in need of nursing care enabled her to surmount hardships and difficulties that would have discouraged most. With these persons, we must assume that certain early activities of an exploratory or a social service nature were reinforced so consistently as to make them characteristic modes of response. We can only speculate about the exact circumstances in which these persistent behavior patterns were acquired. But the fact that certain classes of activities were engaged in by these individuals with a relatively high frequency is what distinguished them as leaders in their particular fields of endeavor.

Other examples cited by Bluemel concern leaders whose influence on society in general was in many respects destructive and whose behavior was "pathological." Hindenberg was eighty-five years old and probably senile when he appointed Hitler as Chancellor of Germany. George III, against whom the authors of the Declaration of Independence leveled the charge of tyranny, probably suffered from manic-depressive psychosis. Manic, or hyperactive, behavior was displayed in milder form by Napoleon and Mussolini. Because hallucinations are common in the psychotic syndrome called schizophrenia, Bluemel concludes that both Joan of Arc and Mohammed experienced periods of psychosis. Adolph Hitler is alleged to have shown symptoms of paranoia, a personality disturbance characterized by delusions of grandeur and persecution. Stalin is described by Bluemel as "an aggressive obsessive-compulsive individual" and as "mildly paranoid" (p. 74).

Certainly not all of those who practice or do research in the area of behavior disturbances would necessarily agree with Bluemel's conclusions. But his observations are interesting, if only because they emphasize the point that the *relative frequency* of certain performances is essentially what distinguishes leaders from nonleaders. Their performances would scarcely be reinforcing to their followers if the followers did not have some of the same dispositions. That is, a follower tends to applaud a leader for doing what he himself can do only infrequently or ineffectively. The reinforcement in many instances is probably indirect, or vicarious. Frequently, the performances of a leader have instrumental value to his followers by helping them to achieve goals that they could not attain through their own efforts. We cannot here enter into an analysis of such psychiatric terms as obsessive-compulsive except to note that they have reference to performances that are conspicuous to an uncommon degree in an individual's behavior. The same performances are found to a lesser degree in persons not labeled neurotic or psychotic. Perhaps leaders simply display in exaggerated form and frequency those same dispositions that are found in their followers and that are instrumental in achieving certain goals valued by the followers.

Summary   The actions of certain individuals in any society serve as potent sources of both stimulus control and reinforcement for the behavior of other persons. Such individuals are called leaders. Followers also control the behavior of a leader to the extent that he perceives their performances as supportive or effective. Because the same individuals may be leaders in some situations and followers in others, they may be said to play different roles at different times. The term *role* refers to the class of behaviors that is maintained by social reinforcement in a particular set of circumstances.

A resurgence of interest in the various phenomena of leadership occurred after World War II, with considerable research being directed toward a comparison of authoritarian and democratic leaders. The term *authoritarian personality* has been coined to designate those individuals who reveal antidemocratic attitudes and who prefer strong, autocratic leaders. When randomly selected individuals are placed under authoritarian leadership in an experimental setting, they perform effectively when the leader is present but compare unfavorably in performance with democratically led groups when the leader is absent.

Some controversy has taken place on the matter of leadership traits. Although it is generally agreed that leaders tend to be effective only with specific groups and in certain kinds of situations, there is evidence that both intelligence and knowledge about the tasks confronting a group are predictors of a leader's effectiveness. Another general characteristic of effective leaders is the fact that they take the initiative in situations where some action is required.

The members of groups frequently may be observed to have designated certain individuals as *task* leaders and others as *social* leaders. The task leader generally exercises more power in the group; he reinforces behaviors relevant to the group's assigned tasks, whereas the social leader reinforces behaviors not necessarily relevant to these tasks. For example, in group discussion situations the members tend to distinguish between those they perceive as friends and those they perceive as leaders.

The leader of a group under stress will be positively reinforced by the members for actions that he takes to effectively meet the critical situation.

However, if his performance does not reduce the aversiveness of the situation to the members, he will lose control of the group and may even be replaced as leader. Some group members may react to stress in ways that are aversive to themselves but are instrumental over the long run in averting disaster to the group. Such selfless behavior may be considered the product of earlier experiences in which this class of performances has been socially reinforced. Training designed to generate group *morale* has the effect of increasing the frequency with which this type of behavior will occur.

Depending upon whether they tend to use positive or aversive control over their followers, leaders may be said to exercise *reward power* or *coercive power*. The former alternative is more likely to bring about persisting changes in behavior and is more characteristic of elected than of appointed leaders. Becoming an effective leader, however, involves a complex interaction between the situation and the leader's use of power over his subordinates. Fiedler's *contingency theory* of leadership asserts that the most effective pattern of leader behavior is a function of the type of group involved and the characteristics of the assigned task. A leader whose performance is directed primarily toward the group's productivity will be most effective in situations that are either very favorable or very unfavorable to him. On the other hand, a leader whose performance is concerned with interpersonal relations in the group will function best in situations that are only moderately favorable to him. We interpret this as evidencing the capacity of the situation to reinforce selected aspects of the leader's behavior. A leader who is on relatively close, intimate terms with his followers is rewarded when he can intervene effectively in moderately stressful situations. In completely favorable circumstances, his "therapeutic" talents are not needed, and under severe stress they may be inadequate. The more impersonal, or distant, leader, on the other hand, is effective in maintaining task-directed behavior under either very favorable or very unfavorable circumstances because his own performance is not disrupted by feedback from the group. But this lack of a personal touch, which protects him from a certain degree of anguish in very stressful circumstances, may detract from his effectiveness in only moderately difficult situations, where the more empathic leader is apt to take palliative measures.

Finally, we examined the suggestion that all leaders simply show exaggerations of behavioral tendencies that are common among their followers. When certain deviant behaviors characterize the leader, such as mania, depression, or paranoia, the results may be catastrophic for the group under their control. The psychiatric theory of leadership purports to explain the rise of powerful leaders, both benign and destructive, and emphasizes the place of leaders rather than their followers in human history.

References

ADAMS, J. S., and ROMNEY, A. K.   A functional analysis of authority. *Psychological Review*, 1959, *66*, 234–251.

ADORNO, T. W., FRENKEL-BRUNSWIK, ELSE, LEVINSON, D. J., and SANFORD, R. N. *The authoritarian personality.* New York: Harper and Row, 1950.

BACK, K. W.   Power, influence and pattern of communication. In L. Petrullo and B. M. Bass (Eds.), *Leadership and interpersonal behavior.* New York: Holt, Rinehart and Winston, 1961.

BALES, R. F.   The equilibrium problem in small groups. In T. Parsons, R. F. Bales, and E. A. Shils (Eds.), *Working papers in the theory of action.* New York: The Free Press of Glencoe, 1953.

BALES, R. F., and SLATER, P. E.   Role differentiation in small decision-making groups. In T. Parsons and R. F. Bales (Eds.), *Family socialization and interaction process.* New York: The Free Press of Glencoe, 1955.

BASS, B. M.   *Leadership, psychology, and organizational behavior.* New York: Harper and Row, 1960.

BASS, B. M.   Some observations about a general theory of leadership and interpersonal behavior. In L. Petrullo and B. M. Bass (Eds.), *Leadership and interpersonal behavior.* New York: Holt, Rinehart and Winston, 1961.

BERRIEN, F. K.   Homeostasis theory of groups: Implications for leadership. In L. Petrullo and B. M. Bass (Eds.), *Leadership and interpersonal behavior.* New York: Holt, Rinehart and Winston, 1961.

BLUEMEL, C. S.   *War, politics and insanity.* Denver: The World Press, 1950.

BRIGANTE, T. R.   Adolescent evaluations of rewarding, neutral, and punishing power figures. *Journal of Personality,* 1958, *26,* 435–450.

CAPLOW, T. A.   A theory of coalitions in the triad. *American Sociological Review,* 1956, *21,* 489–493.

CARTWRIGHT, D., and ZANDER, A.   Leadership and group performance: Introduction. In D. Cartwright and A. Zander (Eds.), *Group dynamics: Research and theory* (2nd ed.). New York: Harper and Row, 1960.

DARLEY, J. G.   Critique. In L. Petrullo and B. M. Bass (Eds.), *Leadership and interpersonal behavior.* New York: Holt, Rinehart and Winston, 1961.

FIEDLER, F. E.   The leader's psychological distance and group effectiveness. In D. Cartwright and A. Zander (Eds.), *Group dynamics: Research and theory* (2nd ed.). New York: Harper and Row, 1960.

FIEDLER, F. E.   *A theory of leadership effectiveness.* New York: McGraw-Hill, 1967.

FRENCH, J. R. P., JR., and RAVEN, B. H.   The bases of social power. In D. Cartwright (Ed.), *Studies in social power.* Ann Arbor, Mich.: University of Michigan Press, 1959.

GIBB, C. A.   The sociometry of leadership in temporary groups. *Sociometry,* 1950, *13,* 226–243.

GIBB, C. A.   Leadership. In G. Lindzey (Ed.), *Handbook of social psychology.* Vol. 2. Reading, Mass.: Addison-Wesley, 1954.

HAMBLIN, R. L.   Leadership and crisis. *Sociometry,* 1958, *21,* 222–235.

HAVRON, M. D., and McGRATH, J. E.   The contribution of the leader to the effectiveness of small military groups. In L. Petrullo and B. M. Bass (Eds.), *Leadership and interpersonal behavior.* New York: Holt, Rinehart and Winston, 1961.

HEGGEN, T.   *Mister Roberts.* Boston: Houghton Mifflin, 1946.

HOLLANDER, E. P., and WEBB, W. B.   Leadership, followership, and friendship: An analysis of peer nominations. *Journal of Abnormal and Social Psychology,* 1955, *50,* 163–167.

HOMANS, G. C.   *Social behavior: Its elementary forms.* New York: Harcourt, Brace and World, 1961.

HORKHEIMER, M., and FLOWERMAN, S. H.   Foreword. In T. W. Adorno, E. Frenkel-Brunswik, D. J. Levinson, and R. N. Sanford, *The authoritarian personality.* New York: Harper, 1950.

HORWITZ, M.   Hostility and its management in classroom groups. In W. W. Charters, Jr., and N. L. Gage (Eds.), *Readings in the social psychology of education.* Boston: Allyn and Bacon, 1963.

JENKINS, W. O.   A review of leadership studies with particular reference to military problems. *Psychological Bulletin,* 1947, *44,* 75.

JENNINGS, H. H.   Leadership and sociometric choice. In H. Proshansky and B. Seidenberg (Eds.), *Basic studies in social psychology.* New York: Holt, Rinehart and Winston, 1965, pp. 511–519.

KAPLAN, A.   Power in perspective. In R. L. Kahn and E. Boulding (Eds.), *Power and conflict in organizations.* New York: Basic Books, 1964.

LANA, R. E., VAUGHAN, W., and McGINNIES, E.   Leadership and friendship status as factors in discussion group interaction. *Journal of Social Psychology,* 1960, *52,* 127–134.

LIPPITT, R., and WHITE, R. K.   An experimental study of leadership and group life. In G. E. Swanson, T. M. Newcomb, and E. L. Hartley (Eds.), *Readings in social psychology.* New York: Henry Holt, 1952.

MARSHALL, S. L. A.   *Men under fire.* New York: Morrow, 1947.

MILLS, T. M.   Power relations in three person groups. *American Sociological Review,* 1953, *18,* 351–357.

MORENO, J. L.   *Who shall survive?* Washington, D.C.: Nervous and Mental Disorders Publishing Company, 1934.

OSS ASSESSMENT STAFF.   *Assessment of men.* New York: Holt, Rinehart and Winston, 1948.

PAGE, R. H., and McGINNIES, E.   Comparison of two styles of leadership in small group discussion. *Journal of Applied Psychology,* 1959, *43,* 240–245.

RAVEN, B. H., and FRENCH, J. R. P., JR.   Group support, legitimate power, and social influence. *Journal of Personality,* 1958, *26,* 400–409.

SANFORD, F. H.   The follower's role in leadership phenomena. In G. E. Swanson, T. M. Newcomb, and E. L. Hartley (Eds.), *Readings in social psychology.* New York: Henry Holt, 1952, pp. 328–340.

SARBIN, T. R. Role theory. In G. Lindzey (Ed.), *Handbook of social psychology.* Vol. 1. Reading, Mass.: Addison-Wesley, 1954.

SARBIN, T. R. Role theory. In G. Lindzey and E. Aronson (Eds.), *Handbook of social psychology,* Vol. 1. Reading, Mass.: Addison-Wesley, 1968.

SARGENT, S. S., and WILLIAMSON, R. C. *Social psychology* (3rd ed.). New York: Ronald Press, 1966.

SCHULTZ, D. P. *Panic behavior.* New York: Random House, 1964.

SECORD, P. F., and BACKMAN, C. W. *Social psychology.* New York: McGraw-Hill, 1964.

STOGDILL, R. Personal factors associated with leadership. *Journal of Psychology,* 1948, *25,* 35–71.

STOGDILL, R. M., and COONS, A. E. Leader behavior: Its description and measurement. Research Monograph No. 88, Ohio State University, Columbus, Ohio, 1957.

STOUFFER, S. A., SUCHMAN, E. A., DeVINNEY, L. C., STAR, S. A., and WILLIAMS, R. M., JR. *The American soldier.* Vol. I. Princeton, N.J.: Princeton University Press, 1949.

TORRANCE, E. P. A theory of leadership and interpersonal behavior under stress. In L. Petrullo and B. M. Bass (Eds.), *Leadership and interpersonal behavior.* New York: Holt, Rinehart and Winston, 1961.

VINACKE, W. E., and ARKOFF, A. An experimental study of coalitions in the triad. *American Sociological Review,* 1957, *22,* 406–414.

WISPE, L. G. Evaluating section teaching methods in the introductory course. *Journal of Educational Research,* 1951, *45,* 161–186.

8

Language and
Communication

Most of the behavioral exchanges we have discussed in the preceding chapters involve verbalization and language. Not all verbal utterances are examples of language, as for example shouts, cries, and exclamations. Nor is all language necessarily verbalized; it may consist of formalized gestures, as in the case of sign language. The vocal and written forms of language not only serve as vehicles for communication and behavior control, they also establish their authors as inhabitants of a particular locality, members of certain social groups, and possessors of varying degrees of formal education and training. Language obviously is one of the most significant of human characteristics, and we shall want to examine rather closely both its acquisition and its function in society.

We shall deal with language as a form of behavior that is acquired and maintained largely by its effects on other persons and the consequences of those effects for the user. The problem of meaning can be approached in the same general fashion; that is, words have meaning in the sense that they bear a functional relationship to other performances. We shall consider this problem in more detail later in the chapter. From a behavioral viewpoint, the verbal performance of a speaker or writer is maintained by the effects produced either on an audience or directly on the speaker himself. The exact nature of these effects can only be roughly estimated at our current state of knowledge, but an approach in terms of stimuli and reinforcers promises to advance our understanding of these complex processes.

"When we talk about the meaning or the use of a word," write Ferster and Perrott (1968), "we generally refer to the variables which generated it and which are currently maintaining it. The significance of a verbal performance is obviously not its form, topography, or articulation pattern, but its effect on the behavior of the listener and on the variables controlling the behavior of the speaker" (p. 513). If a listener is to respond appropriately, however, he must be influenced not only by the verbal performance of the speaker but also by the situational variables that have controlled the speaker's behavior. The word "boy," for example, might be emitted as a request for service in a hotel, as a derogatory way of referring to a Negro, or as an exclamation of delight. The "meaning" that the word conveys obviously is a function of the stimuli that prompted its use, and its effects upon a listener will be partially a function of these same variables.

Many nonverbal performances are maintained by the verbalizations that they evoke from an audience. In other words, one does many things because he is reinforced verbally by someone else. Words acquire conditioned reinforcing properties both by themselves and in conjunction with other words in sentences. These reinforcing properties are derived from the pairing of words with the nonverbal behavior of individuals who are in a position to reward or to punish the behavior of the listener. Parents, for example, reinforce their children by both words and gestures for correctly naming objects. The child learns to make requests as a result of having received the objects he requested. Nagging, expressions of profanity, and other verbalizations that are aversive to the parent are usually punished, hence the child learns to avoid the use of such expressions, at least in the parent's presence. Many behaviors, both verbal and nonverbal, are strengthened because of their instrumentality in avoiding aversive, or punishing, vocalizations from others. Such behaviors are said to be maintained by negative reinforcement. As Staats and Staats (1963) have argued, one of the most potent sources of reinforcement for shaping behavior is the application and withdrawal of words that have conditioned reinforcing properties, either positive or negative.

The Communication Process

A Systems Model

One useful model for placing the essentials of the communication process in a broad perspective has been provided by Shannon and Weaver (1949). According to these scientists, "The fundamental problem of communication is that of reproducing at one point either exactly or approximately a message selected at another point. Frequently the messages have *meaning;* that is, they refer to or are correlated according to some system with certain physical or conceptual entities" (p. 3). These writers consider the semantic aspects of communication as irrelevant to the engineering problems with which they are primarily concerned. We may also, for the moment, disregard the semantic problems of language and consider merely the formal elements that are involved. In so doing, let us examine the generalized communication system described by Shannon and Weaver, shown in Figure 8.1.

Figure 8.1
A generalized communication system.

Although this manner of representing the communication process was originally intended to describe such mechanical events as those involved in communication by telephone or television, it is also useful in outlining some of the events that occur in face-to-face vocal communication. The *information source* may be viewed as an individual whose behavior is under the control of stimuli that he is attempting to represent verbally. Thus, the sentry who picks up a field telephone and reports to headquarters that an enemy patrol is approaching is translating a perceptual experience into words. If he were not in possession of transmitting equipment, he might simply repeat the message to himself. This, however, would not represent communication.

Although the *transmitter* that one uses may be mechanical, such as signal lights or a telephone, the human vocal apparatus ordinarily represents the first link in the chain of transmission. The *channel* over which the message is carried will be determined by the method of transmission; a telephone requires wires, whereas the human voice is transmitted by air. The *receiver* consists of the auditory apparatus of a listener, aided in some instances by equipment that detects and amplifies a communicated signal. Finally, the *destination* of a message is a listener or viewer, whose accurate reception of it will depend upon how faithfully it has been reproduced at each stage of transmission. How accurately the original message is reproduced at the destination depends, therefore, upon how much *noise*, or *error*, characterizes the particular communication system.

Sources of error. Many of us have played the parlor game in which a whispered message is transmitted around a circle of participants and finally spoken aloud by the terminal recipient. Rarely does the terminal reproduction closely resemble the original message. Where did noise, or error, enter the communication system? One common source of error is the verbal representation, or *encoding*, of the communicated information. That is, the source does not invariably select those linguistic units that are conventionally accepted as representing the nonlinguistic entities that are the subject of the message. For example, if I am shown a visual display containing six objects and I report the presence of only five objects, then I have encoded the information available to me incorrectly according to the generally accepted rules for the verbal representation of number. A great many factors can influence the encoding process in the direction of either greater accuracy or distortion. Perhaps some of the individuals in the parlor game just described did not hear clearly what was whispered to them, or perhaps one or more of the words in the whispered message were unfamiliar to them. In encoding, or reproducing, the message, the recipient will tend to replace any missing elements and to substitute meaningful items for meaningless ones. Indeed, as Allport and Postman (1947) have pointed out, the original perception of an event is always fused from its beginning with relevant previous experience. This means that transmitted information is frequently contaminated by elements already within the verbal repertoires of both the speaker and the listener.

Decoding, or the extraction of the original information from the words or other units of a message, is susceptible to the same types of errors as the encoding process. In a variation of our parlor game, Jack Paar on his nightly television show used to have multilingual guests pass a humorous story from one to the other, each time in a different language. The final version, rendered in English, was often dramatically and amusingly different from the original. Apparently, the more times a message is encoded and decoded, the greater are the chances for it to be distorted. The inaccurate substitution of foreign words in translation, selection of the wrong combinations of dots and dashes in Morse code, and the misperception or misinterpretation of what someone says are all sources of error in communication.

Disturbances in the channel due to electrical, mechanical, or atmospheric conditions also introduce error, or noise, into systems of communication, but these are problems for the engineer rather than the psychologist.

Problems in communication may also occur because a host of social variables have influenced the behavior of both speaker and listener. All in all, the possibilities for error and misunderstanding in human communication are endless. In the pages that follow, we shall attempt to analyze the behavioral functions of language and, in so doing, perhaps throw some light on the practical problems of communication. After reviewing some speculations concerning the historical origins of language, we shall consider briefly the phylogenetic (comparative) and ontogenetic (developmental) approaches. Finally, we shall direct out attention to a behavioral analysis of language and meaning.

The Origins of Language

One cannot help but wonder how man learned to speak in the first place. A number of theories have been proposed to account for this momentous event in human history, but most are more entertaining than they are instructive. As Revesz (1956) has commented so picturesquely, "Language is the most wonderful creation of the mind of man. Its origin is hidden in the distant darkness of irrecoverable antiquity. Sheer lack of empirical evidence prevents our attaining any direct knowledge of the mental constitution of earliest man; we are similarly barred from any direct knowledge of the first beginnings of language" (p. 1).

Despite his pessimism about the prospects of acquiring any reliable knowledge about the origins of language, Revesz has outlined what seem to be the principal theories that have been devised to explain this problem. It may be instructive to examine and interpret these briefly.

The theory of expressive sounds. Probably the earliest sounds made by man were involuntary verbalizations associated with some event having the capacity to elicit an emotional reaction. Thus, for example, a painful injury would cause the individual to cry out, perhaps in the form of "Ow" or "Oh" or "Ugh." Any warnings that had immediately preceded such an unpleasant occurrence could become conditioned stimuli for these vocalizations. Positively reinforcing events, such as tasty foods or aesthetically pleasing sights or sounds, might also elicit certain involuntary expressions, such as "Ah" or "Mmm." These vocalizations could then be conditioned to the sight of food or to the recall of previously experienced gustatory delights. Communication of these essentially emotional expressions might have taken place when one individual responded to another in such a way as to reinforce the utterance and thus increase the probability of its recurrence. Having learned that certain experiences could be communicated vocally to someone else, the individuals involved might have generalized this type of performance to other, more complex reactions. Language, according to an interjectional theory, may have evolved from such humble beginnings as these.

The theory of imitation. Known to grammarians as onomatopoeia, another possible source of language in the dawn of man's history was his imitation of sounds that he heard in nature. Certain animals, principally birds and porpoises, are known to imitate human speech, and so we need not stretch our imaginations very far to suspect that early man also attempted to mimic nature in both voice and gesture. According to this theory, certain words in every language have phonetic characteristics similar to the sounds they represent. The comic strips make use of this device to communicate by printed word a variety of sounds, such as "bang," "crackle," "pop," "snap," "tinkle," and "crash." If two early humans happened to hear one another emit the same sound in imitation of a common stimulus, they must have been both startled and gratified by the discovery of this means of communicating a mutual experience. Such a social event could then have led to further experimentation with imitation as a means of communicating; this, in turn, might have led to the invention of words. Neither the theory of expressive sounds nor the imitation theory, however, can do more than suggest how primitive man might have come to use vocal utterance as a means of communication.

The theory of phonetic symbolism. This viewpoint holds that certain words convey something of their meaning by the nature of their sound, or phonemic structure. This is perhaps the most intriguing of the theories that we have mentioned, because it is susceptible to experimental verification. One of the earliest studies on this problem was done by Sapir (1929), who asked subjects to identify the nonsense syllables "mal" and "mil" as referring to a large or to a small table. About 80 per cent of his subjects, who ranged from children to adults, judged "mal" as being the larger. The notion here is that the broad *a* sound is more symbolic of large objects than the higher pitched *i* sound. Newman (1933) went even further than Sapir by demonstrating that when the vowels were ordered according to decreasing frequency of vocal resonance, they were judged as not only increasing in size but decreasing in "brightness"; for example, *e* as in feet, *a* as in ate, *i* as in kite, *o* as in dote, *u* as in flute. One could also cite examples of vowels used by both children and adults to express diminutiveness, such as "teensy-weensy" and "itsy-bitsy." High-fi enthusiasts refer to low frequency speakers as "woofers" and to high frequency units as "tweeters," the phonetic symbolism being obvious.

A host of investigators have been intrigued by this problem. Tsuru (1958) reported that Harvard and Radcliffe undergraduates were able to match Japanese antonyms with their English equivalents more frequently than would have been expected by chance. For example, given the information that the Japanese words *atsui* and *samui* meant either hot-cold or cold-hot, the students were able to make the correct choice more frequently than the 50 per cent chance expectancy. A similar experiment was performed later by Brown, Black, and Horowitz (1955) using English antonyms having reference to sensory qualities, such as warm-cool and light-heavy. Harvard and Radcliffe subjects were required to match these words with their equivalents in the Chinese, Czech, and Hindi languages, none of which were familiar. Again, the subjects' responses were correct beyond chance expectancy. Brown (1958), however, reports that he and a colleague enlisted the cooperation of nineteen members of the Chinese community in Boston in making the same judgments. Out of the twenty-one pairs of antonyms, only three pairs from the Hindi list and two pairs from the Czech list were correctly matched with their English equivalents by these English-speaking Chinese subjects. Brown concludes that the subjects did not share a conception of the most likely translations for unfamiliar phonetic sequences and that, consequently, the results cast doubt upon the existence of a universal human phonetic symbolism. This question may never be satisfactorily resolved, because, as Brown has pointed out, some associations of sound and meaning doubtless have a universal human basis while others are cultural products.

A similar conclusion was reached by Taylor and Taylor (1965), who reviewed the evidence on this problem and concluded that speakers of some languages are more susceptible to phonetic symbolism than speakers of other languages. Different communities, in others words, seem to differ in the extent to which they incorporate phonetic symbolism in their languages. This is an interesting problem because the existence of phonetic symbolism demands an explanation in terms of either (a) an innate proclivity on the part of individuals to favor certain sounds for attributes having no apparent acoustic referents, or (b) the acquisition of phonetic symbolism through learning. Taylor and Taylor favor the latter alternative and describe the generation of phonetic symbolism in terms of "feedback." Briefly, this theory suggests that in the development of a language certain sounds have occurred more often in connection with particular concepts than would be expected by chance. This overrepresentation of certain sounds in words symbolizing concepts would influence the speaker in his choice of additional words having the same or a similar connotation. That is, a speaker who happens to have used an initial R in words associated with *hot* will tend to develop other words beginning with R to designate this concept. In referring to *cold*, R words would seem inappropriate, and some other invariant sound would be adopted. A tendency to use "clang" associations (associating words having similar sounds) would facilitate the further development of phonetic symbolism. This is a provocative theory that provides a basis for understanding the acknowledged occurrence of phonetic symbolism in terms of stimulus and response without recourse to assumptions about innate linguistic dispositions.

We are forced to the conclusion that while each of the three theories briefly outlined here probably has some validity as an explanation of the origins of language, none begins to explain the acquisition of those complex forms that characterize human speech. We may make more headway with this problem by examining the comparative and developmental bases of speech, that is, the extent to which vocalizations are employed by the lower animals and the manner in which vocalization develops in children. If it is possible to train any species of animals to talk, then the process by which language is acquired can be studied under conditions of experimental control.

Comparative Approaches

The birds and the bees. As we noted earlier, most animal forms have the ability, quite remarkable in many instances, to communicate with one another. They do this, as do humans, either by gesture or by sound, and the integrity of their social organizations frequently depends upon these communicative acts. A brief glance at some examples of communication among animals will help us appreciate the manner in which communicative behavior develops according to the capacities of a particular species.

For example, we know that the honeybee, once it has discovered a source of food, returns to the hive and communicates both the direction and the distance of its find to the other bees in the colony. In 1923, a German scientist, Karl von Frisch, became interested in this curious ability of bees and made a series of ingenious and painstaking observations in order to describe the behavior more precisely. He constructed an artificial hive with glass walls so he could observe the behavior of the bees when they returned from a food-seeking flight. When the source of nectar was fairly close by, say under thirty meters, the finder bee would execute a "dance" consisting of a circular movement. When longer distances were involved, the bee would run in a straight line while moving its abdomen rapidly from side to side, then make a turn and repeat the maneuver. For distances greater than two hundred meters, the number of turns made by the bee decreased, so that a run followed by only two turns might indicate that the food was several miles away.

After observing this behavior, the other bees were able to fly directly to the food. It was apparent that they received cues to the location of the food from the direction of the "run" made by the finder bee. An upward vertical run in the hive indicated that the food source would be found by flying into the sun, whereas a downward vertical run indicated that the food source was away from the sun. Inbetween directions were signaled by runs that deviated in varying degree from the vertical. Von Frisch found that bees that were restricted to a horizontal surface and deprived of sunlight were unable to communicate the direction of their find. We can only marvel at the evolutionary process by which this simple but effective communicative behavior developed.

The famous Swiss naturalist, Konrad Lorenz, reported in 1952 some of his fascinating observations on the behavior of animals living in a free state. Lorenz's studies of the jackdaw, a bird whose lifespan approximates that of man, are particularly interesting. It was evident to Lorenz that certain responses by the jackdaws were associated with typical calls. The jackdaws possessed a courtship call, calls for flight either away from or toward the nesting area, and a rattling sound elicited by any fluttering black object. The last response appeared to express anger, since it was frequently followed by assault upon the offending stimulus. In each instance, we can identify a discriminative stimulus for the particular vocal response as well as consequences that might logically reinforce its occurrence. Courtship calls are eventually followed by mating behavior, flight calls by a movement of the flock in a given direction, and the rattle of anger by disappearance of the threatening object. The fact that reinforcement of these vocal responses is probably intermittent insures that they will be resistant to extinction.

Mowrer (1952), using birds such as the mynah and parakeet, which are able to imitate human speech, attempted systematically to train them to talk. By speaking himself while feeding and watering the birds, Mowrer succeeded in training a parrot and a mynah bird to vocalize a particular word before eating or drinking. These sounds became instrumental acts in that they were strengthened through reinforcement. However, the birds never developed any new combinations of sounds, so it is doubtful whether they possess any capacity for speech analogous to that of humans.

As Mowrer (1960) has further reported, there are many authentic instances of parrots, parakeets, and mynah birds that have learned to speak complete sentences. There are no grounds for believing that they comprehend the "meaning" of the words, and the vocalizations are apparently emitted in the presence of *releasing stimuli* that have no linguistic relationship to the responses. The vocal performances of these birds apparently are not reinforced by any effects that such performances have on a listener, which would be a prerequisite for any speculations about meaningful communication.

Vocalization in primates. Perhaps the animals of greatest interest to psychologists, because of their almost uncanny resemblance to humans, are the great apes. Chimpanzees, gibbons, orangutans, and gorillas have all been studied rather intensively. Two psychologists, Dr. and Mrs. Keith Hayes (1951), actually raised a chimpanzee in their home from the age of three days through four years. The chimp, named Viki, was treated as nearly as possible like a human child with respect to such activities as feeding, toilet training, play, and discipline. Viki not only learned to imitate much of the behavior of the adult humans with whom she lived, she also learned to respond to spoken commands. As Mrs. Hayes describes it, "It was not necessary to teach Viki to imitate; she had already done so in play. What we had to teach her was the meaning of the command 'Do this!' so that she would imitate our actions even when they seemed pointless" (p. 182).

Virtually all the sounds that Viki made, however, were the reflex vocalizations customary for chimpanzees. When she was ten months old, she succeeded with much effort in emitting a sound like "ahhh" just before reaching for milk. Mrs. Hayes describes this as her "asking sound." The only words that Viki ever learned to whisper were "papa," "mama," and "cup" when food was used as a reinforcement.

One must applaud the patience and ingenuity with which the Hayeses tested the proposition that a chimpanzee raised under special circumstances might display a greater capacity for acquiring human speech than had previously been suspected. From this point of view, however, their efforts must be judged as unsuccessful. As a matter of fact, chimpanzees in their natural environment manage to communicate with one another about as well as do chimps exposed to human tutors. A young Englishwoman, Jane Goodall (1963), lived for years among the great apes in Tanganyika. She reports that these animals have a tremendous variety of calls, many of which serve to control the behavior of other chimpanzees. "These calls," writes Miss Goodall, "while they are not a language in our sense of the word, are understood by other chimpanzees and certainly form a means of communication" (p. 290). The chimpanzee apparently lacks either the vocal apparatus or the central neural mechanisms necessary for the attainment of actual speech.

Ferster (1964), however, suggests that teaching animals a form of speech may be primarily a matter of choosing a set of stimuli and responses that are appropriate to their capacities. He has attempted to teach chimpanzees to use mathematical symbols as a type of language, employing the binary system containing two digits, 0 and 1. Whereas human vocal responses are reinforced by the reactions of a listener, the chimpanzees in this experiment were rewarded with food. In one of the problems devised by Ferster, the animals learned to press the appropriate buttons on a display panel to produce a binary number that would match the number of objects presented on that trial. Figure 8.2 gives a chart of numbers in the decimal system, their binary equivalents, and the pattern of lights that corresponded to each number for the chimpanzees.

When, for example, the chimpanzee was shown six objects, not necessarily similar nor arranged in any particular fashion, his task was to press

Figure 8.2

The binary system, in which numbers are represented by only two digits, 0 and 1, was used for chimpanzee arithmetic. The digits were presented as lights turned off (0) or on (1). (From "Arithmetic Behavior in Chimpanzees" by C. B. Ferster. Copyright © 1964 by Scientific American, Inc. All rights reserved.)

Decimal	Binary	Lights
0	000	● ● ●
1	001	● ● ○
2	010	● ○ ●
3	011	● ○ ○
4	100	○ ● ●
5	101	○ ● ○
6	110	○ ○ ●
7	111	○ ○ ○

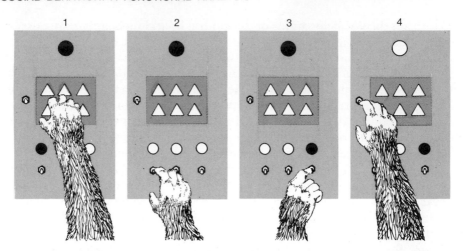

Figure 8.3

The animal touches the numerosity panel (1), which shows that he is paying attention. Then he operates the three switches at the bottom to produce a previously learned binary sequence in the lights just above (2 and 3) which corresponds to the number of objects (triangles, squares, or the like) in the numerosity panel. When the sequence of lights appears to the chimp to be correct, he presses the upper switch; if the binary number is correct, the reinforcement light at the top comes on (4). (From "Arithmetic Behavior in Chimpanzees" by C. B. Ferster. Copyright © 1964 by Scientific American, Inc. All rights reserved.)

the buttons that would produce a display of lights representing the binary number 110 (corresponding to decimal number 6). Figure 8.3 shows such an arrangement and the correct response of the subject.

Two chimpanzees, Dennis and Margie, learned to match the correct binary number to one through seven objects with better than 95 per cent accuracy. However, it took them two hundred sessions and five hundred thousand trials to develop this repertoire. Through such procedures as these, Ferster reports that he has developed in these animals "forms of behavior that bear a much more complex relation to the environment than chimpanzees normally show" (p. 105). He concludes that in a suitably organized environment, a chimpanzee can acquire many of the elements of a symbolic repertoire such as arithmetic. Experiments such as these may eventually shed light on the manner in which man's verbal performances are formed.

The dolphin. As we have seen thus far in our survey of comparative approaches to language, only a few investigators have ventured to suppose that animals actually might acquire the ability to speak. Certainly there have been few experimental results to support such a proposition. However, one scientist, Dr. John Lilly, has observed the behavior of the dolphin at some length and is convinced that they are capable not only of intelligent communication but of language as well. The dolphin, Lilly points out, has a first-class brain, of the same order of complexity as the human brain. Dolphin vocalizations, as perceived by man, consist of an odd assortment of "clicks, creakings, whistles, squaks, quacks, and blats" (Lilly, 1962, p. 111). Many of the sounds they produce are of such high frequency as to be well above the range of human pitch perception. Perhaps one of Dr. Lilly's most startling reports is that tape recordings of these dolphin noises revealed that one animal appeared to have been mimicking human speech. So far, however, Dr. Lilly has not succeeded in establishing the type of linguistic communication between himself and his aquatic subjects that would confirm even his more modest expectations of their vocal capacities.

Attempts to communicate with animals will probably continue, and one should keep an open mind with respect to the ultimate success of these ventures. It is clear that nearly every species that has been studied has revealed a capacity for communication and that this ability to communicate is a vital aspect of the forms of social organization that they have developed. The use of abstract language, however, seems to be a uniquely human accomplishment.

Developmental Approaches

Before we undertake a functional analysis of adult human language behavior, it will be instructive for us to consider some of the research that has been done on language development in the child. This developmental approach offers a foundation for understanding the general process by which language is acquired.

The research findings in this area were reviewed by Dorothea McCarthy (1954), who concluded that it was possible to sketch an adequate picture of the child's linguistic development. Methodologically, the problems here are formidable, involving as they do accurate recording and measurement of children's speech as well as precise definition of the units of speech that one is studying. McCarthy agrees with earlier investigators, such as F. H. Allport (1924), in stressing the importance of imitation in the earliest stages of language development. In fact, she states a position that embodies the essential elements of reinforcement theory:

> When the child accidentally, and later purposefully, reproduces sounds which he himself has made, the adults in the environment usually say a real sound which the child's sounds appear to approximate. This tends to give auditory reinforcement to the sounds the child has just made, at the same time making for more precise perception and rendition of the approved sound groups. Thus there occurs a progressive elimination of errors and a selection of movements which give the best approximation to the real word heard in the speech of adults. Continued practice thus results in the fixation of the sound groups, which come to be uttered habitually (p. 518).

This statement of the acquisition process, although it omits some obviously difficult details, provides an objective, behavioral account of the learning process involved when a child first begins to speak. Among the many vocalizations emitted by the child are some that resemble words. These responses are selectively reinforced by a parent or other adult in a shaping process which leads ultimately to the child's learning to pronounce words. All of the basic speech sounds from which those elements peculiar to the parents' language may be selected and reinforced are in the child's repertoire of vocal behavior. As Latif observed in 1934, children can make sounds resembling the German *umlaut* as well as French guttural *r*'s. The inflections that adults find so difficult to learn in a foreign tongue come easily to the child, whose speech apparatus is apparently more adaptive, and whose learning is less hampered by competing verbal habits. Many primary schools are currently making use of the plasticity of children's vocal capacities by introducing foreign language instruction into their curricula.

The ability of children to acquire the use of language is probably in large part an example of species-specific behavior. Miller (1965) suggests that:

> All human societies possess language, and all of these languages have features in common — features that are called "language universals," but are prelinguistic in character. It is difficult to imagine how children could acquire language so rapidly from parents who understand it so poorly unless they were already tuned by evolution to select just those aspects that are universally significant. There is, in short, a large biological component that shapes our human languages (p. 17).

What course does language development take in the child? Again, measurement difficulties compel us to make estimates rather than assertions, but we can indicate some of the major landmarks. McCarthy has listed ninety identifiable developments, of which we shall note only a few. Table 8.1 shows the approximate ages at which the appearances of selected aspects of language have been reported by different investigators.

Not all children achieve these capacities on the same schedule, but an orderly sequence generally seems to characterize language development during the first two years of life.

It is important that we appreciate the functional role that language serves for the child because this underlies the entire acquisition process. As Ferster (1963) points out, a verbal response can achieve many important consequences in the environment of a child that otherwise would be unavailable because of the child's limited physical and social development. The agent of direct control over the environment, of course, is the parent. The main function of a child's verbal response, argues Ferster, is to provide a discriminative stimulus which specifies a form of parental behavior that is reinforcing to the child. The child's verbalizations are also reinforcing

Table 8.1

Age in months at which different speech sounds occur in children.
(Taken from data by McCarthy, 1954)

Age in Months	Item of Language Development
1	Vocal grunt
2	Random vocalizations
4	Turns head at sound of voice
6	Several well defined syllables
8	Single consonants
10	Rudimentary imitation of sounds
12	Can say *bye-bye*
15	Expressive jargon
18	Names an object, asks with words, understands simple questions
24	Composes simple sentences and phrases

to the parent, hence certain behaviors of both parent and child are maintained by a shared vocal interaction. "The verbal response," says Ferster, "is maintained by its effect on the environment; it is shaped by differential contingencies; it comes under the control of relevant stimuli; and it may avoid aversive consequences" (p. 325). Approached from this point of view, verbalization is amenable to the same type of analysis as any other muscular activity. It will be useful, therefore, for us to pursue an understanding of verbal behavior in terms of stimulus, response, and reinforcement. In so doing, let us turn from the acquisition of language in children to its maintenance through social reinforcement in adults.

Maintenance of Verbal Behavior

A Reinforcement Model

A functional analysis of verbal behavior has been developed by B. F. Skinner (1957). Skinner's approach, as he himself concedes, de-emphasizes both experimental and statistical facts and is not even theoretical in the usual sense. His aim is the prediction and control of verbal responses. What is a verbal response? Or, more precisely, what unit of verbal behavior can we most conveniently examine? Linguists are apt to be concerned with speech sounds (phonology), rules for forming words (morphology), and rules for combining words (syntax). Linguistic analysis, then, provides one basis for defining the elementary units of language. These may be phonemes, loosely defined as the minimal number of distinguishable sounds in a language; or they may be words, phrases, or sentences. In practice, the unit that one studies is selected according to

the kinds of questions one is asking. For example, in studying free association, the unit is generally a single word. In content analysis, or the classification of particular kinds of references in a given sample of language,
one might take independent clauses or complete sentences as the units to
be categorized and counted.

Positive control. Skinner has used a single *utterance* as his unit of analysis. An utterance may be a word, a phrase, or a sentence. An exchange of
utterances between two or more individuals constitutes, in Skinner's terms,
a *total speech episode.* This verbal interaction can be explained by considering in appropriate temporal order all the relevant events in the behavior
of speaker and listener. In order to clarify this type of analysis, let us consider an example, slightly modified from that used by Skinner, of an episode in which one person asks another for bread. We may assume that the
speaker is hungry, and that the listener is already predisposed to reinforce
him with bread. The presence of the listener provides the occasion (S^D)
for the speaker's demand. The speaker's request ("Bread, please") provides an occasion (S^D) for the listener to respond, and he does so by acceding to the request and passing the bread (R^{op}). This behavior reinforces
(S^{rein}) the speaker's request and also provides a stimulus (S^D) for the speaker
to respond with "Thank you." A "courteous" reply of this sort serves to
reinforce the bread-passing behavior and to insure that it will occur again
when another request is made. Because the listener has learned that
"Thank you" must also be reinforced if it is to be maintained, he replies
with "You're welcome." This speech episode is shown diagrammatically
in Figure 8.4.

Figure 8.4

A speech episode analyzed in S-R terms. (Adapted from *Verbal Behavior,* by B. F. Skinner. Copyright, 1957, Meredith Corporation.
Reproduced by permission of Appleton-Century-Crofts.)

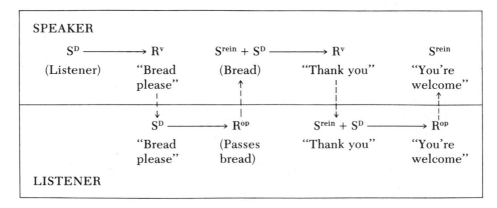

Aversive control. In the example just described, positive reinforcements are used by speaker and listener to support each other's behavior. Many verbal episodes, however, involve aversive stimuli, such as threats, which control behavior through negative reinforcement. Suppose, again following an example provided by Skinner, that the speaker adopts a threatening tone of voice in demanding that a listener "Step aside!" It must be assumed that the listener provides not only a discriminative stimulus but an aversive stimulus to the speaker. We may also assume that the speaker has successfully used threats in the past to control the behavior of others when their behavior is aversive to him. If the listener responds to the demand by stepping aside (R^{op}), he reinforces the speaker's belligerent behavior ($S^{neg\ rein}$). At the same time, the listener, by acceding to the demand, causes the speaker to terminate his threat ($\bar{R}$) and is himself reinforced ($S^{neg\ rein}$). In more general terms, a "dominant" performance has been strengthened in the speaker, and a "submissive" performance has been reinforced in the listener. The situation is shown symbolically in Figure 8.5.

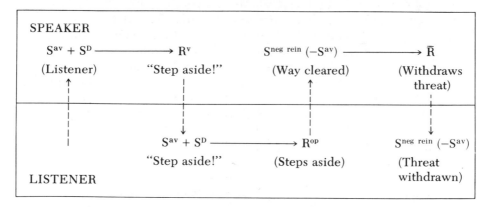

Figure 8.5
A speech episode involving aversive stimulation analyzed in S-R terms. (Adapted from *Verbal Behavior*, by B. F. Skinner. Copyright, 1957, Meredith Corporation. Reproduced by permission of Appleton-Century-Crofts.)

One might just as easily imagine a situation in which the listener does not acquiesce to the speaker's threatening demand. If the listener succeeds in resisting the threat, the speaker's belligerence is not reinforced, and the probability that he will behave this way in the future is reduced. More probably, the speaker will learn to discriminate between those individuals whom he can and cannot dominate; he may learn that he can threaten with impunity only individuals smaller or weaker than himself. There are, of course, many nonverbal behavioral elements that enter into situations such as this. The extent to which disputes are resolved through words or through physical violence depends upon the reinforcement contingencies that have become associated with each alternative. It is characteristic of social behavior that verbal episodes frequently precede nonverbal interaction, and many possibilities exist for exploring social situations in these terms.

Mands and tacts. The examples that we have just examined make use of what Skinner has termed the *mand.* A mand is a verbal operant, the controlling stimuli for which arise from conditions of deprivation or aversion. Like the more common term "demand," from which it is derived, a mand is reinforced by a stimulus relevant to the deprivation. Often, a mand specifies its own reinforcement, as in the request "Please pass the bread."

It is obvious that only a small segment of language consists of mands. Other verbal responses consist of naming or identifying things in the environment, such as "tree" or "doll." To these kinds of verbal operants, which make contact with the physical world, Skinner has assigned the word *tact.* A tact is defined by Skinner as "a verbal operant in which a response of given form is evoked (or at least strengthened) by a particular object or event or property of an object or event" (p. 81). The tact gains response strength by being characteristically reinforced in a given verbal community. Some of the earliest vocalizations learned by children are tacts, that is, names assigned by the adult members of a verbal community to common objects and events. We can diagram the temporal sequence of stimuli and responses that under conditions of social reinforcement maintain this class of verbal performance. Figure 8.6 illustrates a verbal episode involving the use of tacts. In this example, the speaker and listener are referring to an environmental event that is perceptible to both.

Figure 8.6

A speech episode involving the use of a "tact." (Adapted from *Verbal Behavior,* by B. F. Skinner. Copyright, 1957, Meredith Corporation. Reproduced by permission of Appleton-Century-Crofts.)

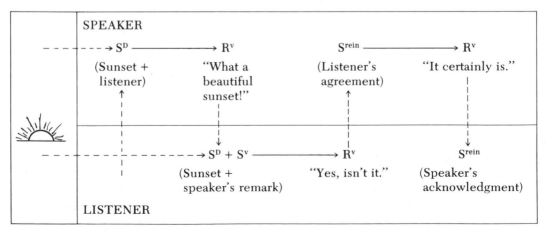

In Figure 8.6, neither speaker not listener is manipulating his environment; rather, the two are engaging in a common type of social interaction
that is largely under the control of a shared environment and that is maintained by reciprocation of response. The success of such an exchange presumes virtually identical verbal repertoires in both the speaker and the
listener. Even if the repertoires of speaker and listener are not identical,
however, the speaker may still partially influence the behavior of the listener. But rather than communicating his own experience or perception,
he may be simply strengthening, or increasing the frequency of, that part
of the listener's repertoire to which he has access by virtue of the verbal
stimuli he can emit. Perhaps this point will be made clear if one imagines
a Frenchman and an Englishman, each of whom knows a little of the other's
language, attempting to converse. The extent to which they could exchange platitudes about the weather and the scenery would be limited by
the degree to which they shared a verbal repertoire relevant to these
themes.

Other stimulus controls. Skinner also identifies verbal behaviors that he
calls *echoic, textual,* and *intraverbal.* Briefly, echoic behavior is repetition
of what someone else has said. Its reinforcement may consist of removing
an aversive stimulus or achieving clarification of a mand emitted by another
person. We have already considered the role of echoic behavior in the early
verbal training of children. Echoic behavior is not simply talking to oneself. A person may vocalize when he is alone, but this is more appropriately
explained in terms of the conditioned reinforcing quality of the words or
sounds. If one's performance, say on the golf course, has previously been
reinforced by the expression "Good shot" from someone else, one may say
this to himself when playing alone. Other expressions, some of them un-
printable, may be uttered following a hook or a slice or a missed putt.
    Textual behavior refers to verbal operants that have come under the con-
trol of visual, or textual, stimuli. A text may consist of any formalized set
of representations, such as pictures, alphabetical combinations, or mathematical symbols. Textual behavior usually consists of reading. What
Skinner calls intraverbal behavior is illustrated by exchanges in which the
verbal response is different in form from the stimulus that evokes it. Most
verbal behavior is of this variety, as when the expression *two plus two*
evokes the response *four.* To the query *How are you?* one responds *Fine,
thanks.*
    Intraverbal behavior resembles the tact insofar as the point-to-point
correspondence between stimulus and response seen in echoic and textual
behavior is lacking. But the reinforcing contingencies are less consistent
in intraverbal behavior than in tacts. This is because the referent, or denotation, of a tact can be more clearly specified than that for an intraverbal response. The word *red,* for example, has reference to a discriminable hue,
the optical specifications of which are a matter of common agreement. The

expression, "What a beautiful red rose," therefore, illustrates a tact. A tetrad (group of four objects), however, is a concept having no specific denotation. It involves the concept of *number*, which is acquired through experience with a variety of situations having in common the operation of counting. A statement of certain logical relationships, therefore, is classified as an example of intraverbal behavior.

Criticism of Skinner's position. Not all students of language behavior agree with Skinner's method of analysis. In a bitingly critical review of Skinner's position, Chomsky (1959) asserts: "We cannot predict verbal behavior in terms of the stimuli in the speaker's environment, since we do not know what the current stimuli are until he responds" (p. 32). Chomsky also questions the assumption that adults shape the verbal repertoires of children through careful differential reinforcement. "It is a common observation," he states, "that a young child of immigrant parents may learn a second language in the streets, from other children, with amazing rapidity, and that his speech may be completely fluent and correct to the last allophone, while the subtleties that become second nature to the child may elude his parents despite high motivation and continued practice" (p. 42). We will not delve further into Chomsky's detailed appraisal of Skinner's position, except to note that he poses some irrelevant problems. In response to just the two points that we have mentioned, it may be said that some reasonable prediction about an individual's response, say to a painting, might be made if we knew a great deal about the observer's past experience. On the basis of such information we might be able to guess rather closely what specific properties of the stimulus object would control his response. In any case, this particular question can be examined experimentally. With regard to the other point raised by Chomsky, it would seem relevant to point out that a child who learns a language "in the streets" is very much influenced by social reinforcement from his peers, who will actively shape his verbal repertoire to match their own in many respects. Whether or not all of his assumptions are sound, Skinner's approach has the considerable merit of placing verbal behavior within the scope of a set of psychological principles that are susceptible to empirical investigation.

The Problem of Meaning

We have now reached one of the most difficult areas in the analysis of language — that involving abstract meanings and conceptualizations. This is a problem that has also attracted the attention of the general semanticists, who are concerned with the adequacy of language as a "map" of the "territory" of experience being discussed (Hayakawa, 1962). We will confine ourselves here, however, to a theory of meaning that has proved fruitful in generating testable hypotheses.

Mediation Theory

One of the most promising approaches to meaning employs the notion of *mediational processes.* According to this theory, words are *signs* which substitute for or stand for other objects or events. Not all stimuli are signs. A blow on the patellar tendon, for example, elicits the kicking reflex directly and does not signify anything else. Signs, of course, are stimuli; but they are more appropriately seen as *surrogate stimuli* in the sense that they substitute for other stimulus events. A physical object, such as a chair, provides an immediate visual stimulus, but the word "chair" is a sign that evokes only some of the responses associated with the actual object. This is where the problem of meaning begins: What are the responses to signs and how do these differ from the responses made to the things signified? Osgood (1953, p. 691) has suggested that the following symbols be employed in this analysis:

$\dot{S}$ = object = any pattern of stimulation which evokes reactions on the part of an organism;

$\boxed{S}$ = sign = any pattern of stimulation which is not $\dot{S}$ and yet evokes reactions relevant to $\dot{S}$.

According to Osgood's reasoning, "the pattern of stimulation which is the sign is never identical with the pattern of stimulation which is the object — the word *hammer* is not the same stimulus as the object hammer, yet the sign does elicit behavior that is in some manner relevant to the object, a characteristic not shared by an infinite number of other stimulus patterns which are *not* signs of that object" (p. 691). Osgood, like Skinner, rejects the mentalistic conception of signs as giving rise to the same "ideas" that are evoked by objects. He also discredits the possibility that signs have become conditioned stimuli through repeated association with particular objects; signs almost never evoke the same responses as do the objects they represent. "Words," argues Osgood, "represent things because they produce some replica of the actual behavior toward these things" (p. 695).

This replica of actual behavior is called a mediating reaction. Let us consider an example of a typical mediational process. The word "hammer" is a denotative sign because it refers to an object that one grasps and uses to pound nails. Because the actual object designated by the term "hammer" has certain unique visual characteristics as well as reportable tactual and proprioceptive experiences when used, it constitutes a stable and unambiguous referent. Mediation theory assumes that certain anticipatory portions of the behavior associated with the sight, sound, and manipulation of a hammer occur as responses to the sign "hammer." This representational mediation process logically involves the effector system of muscles and glands, but it is not critical to the theory that any such peripheral mediators be identifiable. The mediating process might occur entirely within the central nervous system. Figure 8.7 illustrates the process by which a sign might come to evoke a characteristic mediation process and thereby ac- quire meaning.

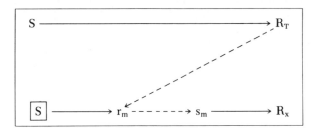

Figure 8.7
Development of a represen- tational mediation process. (From Osgood, 1953)

In Figure 8.7, R_T represents the behavior originally evoked by a stimulus object (S). The representational mediation process (r_m), which becomes conditioned to the sign of the object (S), causes self-stimulation (S_m) which in turn mediates certain instrumental responses (R_x). The mediation process (r_m) is the meaning of the sign. Obviously, many words acquire meanings without having been associated with the objects to which they refer. Osgood points out that a child can understand the word "zebra" without ever having seen the living animal. The child, has, however, come into contact with a number of other *signs* for zebra, including pictures of the beast and words such as "stripes," "wild," "horse," and "run." To a child who has acquired his knowledge of zebras indirectly — through signs rather than through objects — the word "zebra" is more properly called an *assign;* that is, its meaning has been assigned through association.

The significance of this type of theory may be underlined if we consider a word having emotional as well as abstract connotations, such as "Commu- nist." How many Americans have actually seen a "Communist"? Probably very few, yet the word evokes reactions in nearly everyone; it has all the characteristics of an assign, or in Skinner's terms, a tact. For many persons, the word "Communist" is an aversive stimulus that evokes negative affect as well as verbal expressions of hostility. These reactions have come about through the association of this word with other words having similar negative connotations, such as "undemocratic," "un-American," or "athe- istic." How these words have acquired their aversive qualities is a ques- tion that is difficult to answer. We will make an attempt to analyze the genesis of such reactions in considering the matter of attitudes and their development in the next chapter. For now, let us examine further the man- ner in which meaning, defined here as an implicit mediational response, is measured.

The Measurement of Meaning

Affective responses. Osgood takes the position that the representational mediation process that he postulates as a behavioral description of meaning should ideally be identifiable as a specific set of physiological events. If one could identify such events, then meaning would be as open to direct observation and measurement as, say, the pupillary response or the patellar reflex. Stated another way, mediation theory assumes that the mediating reaction (r_m), which includes a fractional part of the response made to an object or event, is essentially no different from any other detectable response of the organism. Like other implicit responses, the mediating reaction involves self-stimulation (S_m), and it is this response-produced stimulation that controls the instrumental behavior (R_x).

Let us be more specific. Imagine that a young man has never known a girl by the name of Alice. However, he meets a girl by this name and falls in love. His reaction to the word "Alice" is now quite different from what it was previously; the name has acquired new meaning. Theoretically, one might say that the mediating process that represented the meaning of the sign "Alice" before our hero ever knew a real Alice, probably was limited to certain muscle responses — perhaps in the vocal apparatus. "Falling in love" with an individual possessing this name, however, involves a new set of responses — roughly designated as emotional or affective — becoming conditioned to the name. The mediating, self-stimulating process is altered, and some new instrumental behaviors come under the control of this sign process.

One could also cite examples of positive affective responses associated with words such as "God" or "mother" and negative affective responses evoked by words such as "death" or "filth." We do, in fact, group many diverse things and events because they evoke a common affective response, as observed by Bruner, Goodnow, and Austin (1962). In this sense, many discriminably different objects or concepts may share a common core of meaning. Discriminatory behavior toward members of a minority racial or religious group, such as Negroes or Catholics, is supported in part by this tendency to "label" all members of these groups and to generalize one's response to them accordingly.

It is one thing, of course, to infer the operation of mediating responses, whether muscular or glandular, and something else to demonstrate their existence empirically. One of the classic studies in this connection was done by Razran (1936), who used himself as a subject and reported both his associations to the word "saliva" in different languages and the actual amounts of saliva that he secreted. Because Russian was Razran's native tongue, salivation was greatest to the Russian word for "saliva" and less to the English, French, Spanish, and Polish equivalents. The galvanic skin response, or increase in electrical conductivity of the skin, has also been used as a measure of meaning. For example, Bingham (1943) obtained GSR's from fifty subjects when they were presented with rather abstract words, such as "perfection," "knowledge," "individual," "possess," and "spiritual." The subjects rated the words in terms of meaningfulness, significance, and importance (yielding an MSI index). Those stimulus words having the highest MSI ratings were reported by Bingham as evoking the largest galvanic skin responses.

It now seems well established that words having reference to attitudes and beliefs are, in fact, capable of provoking an autonomic reaction. Recently, Dickson and McGinnies (1966) have shown that religious subjects respond with GSR's of greater magnitude to anti-church than to pro-church statements. In a related study, McGinnies and Aiba (1965) found that Japanese students who supported American foreign policy yielded higher GSR readings when listening to passages taken from a speech by Nikita Khrushchev than when listening to passages from a speech by Adlai Stevenson. We are dealing here, of course, with the meanings not of single words but of complex verbal materials. Analogous mediating processes, however, seem to be involved in both cases.

One may question whether the postulation of a mediational process necessarily increases our understanding of those verbal events that we are able to observe and measure. In a sense, mediation theory puts the problem back inside the organism, where it becomes less susceptible to examination. Actually, the reflex effect of a verbal stimulus is not necessarily its major consequence. More important are the related verbal behaviors that it increases or decreases in frequency as well as the nonverbal behavior to which it leads. The attractiveness of a mediation theory approach may derive from the fact that a lot of verbal behavior occurs privately, or implicitly, and a great many complex interactions occur within the individual's verbal repertoire before an overt verbal performance is emitted. Another way of looking at this is to say that a single verbal stimulus may control many verbal performances. If we know something about the individual's pre-existing repertoire, then we are in a better position to predict which of the components will be activated by any given verbal stimulus.

Association techniques. One approach to the measurement of meaning involves determination of the number and types of associations that an individual can produce in response to a stimulus word or group of stimulus words. The classic procedure was developed by Kent and Rosanoff (1910) as a method of studying insanity. As normative data, they obtained the associations of one thousand normal subjects to one hundred common English nouns and adjectives. Certain responses turn out to be very common — such as "thread" to "needle," or "home" to "house." Not all of the "free associations" to a word, of course, are controlled by a semantic relationship. As Osgood points out, the verbal response is not necessarily mediated by the *meaning* of the stimulus word. For example, one of the most frequent associations to a word is its opposite; other associations are rhyming or "clang" reactions. Thus, the stimulus word "man" may evoke the clang reaction "pan" or the opposite reaction "woman." Mediated associations, on the other hand, would include such responses as "strong," "male," and "boy." Associations, however, are not meanings, and they can provide only a limited approach to solving this problem.

A quantitative method for measuring meaningfulness (rather than meaning) has been proposed by Noble (1952), who counted the number of associations that individuals produced to a stimulus word during a sixty-second period. This research was an extension of work done earlier by Glaze (1928), who determined the association value of nonsense syllables. Noble found that the more frequently used English words, such as "kitchen," elicited more associations than did less frequently used words, such as "ferrule." It may be assumed that words differ in their instrumental utility and that the richness of meaning that attaches to a word is related to frequency of use. The correlations reported by Noble between meaningfulness and frequency do not reveal which is antecedent and which is consequent. Greater frequency of usage doubtless enhances meaningfulness by providing more occasions on which new associations can be formed to a given word. By the same reasoning, a word that becomes a useful operant will be emitted more frequently and will thereby become more "meaningful." Slang expressions illustrate this process; their meaning is assigned rather arbitrarily, and thereafter they gain rapidly in probability of usage and accretion of new associations.

The semantic differential. One of the more interesting approaches to the analysis of meaning is that of Osgood, Suci, and Tannenbaum (1957). Their method derives in part from the same assumption made by Skinner, namely, that it is not profitable to look for the origins of meaning in "ideas." "Thoughts" and "ideas," despite their conceptual usefulness in metaphysics and epistemology, are susceptible neither to operational definition nor to independent observation. Osgood, Suci, and Tannenbaum center their interest on the representational process and on a technique for making it public and measurable.

We defined *encoding* earlier as the process of translating meaning into language. Osgood, Suci, and Tannenbaum describe the encoding process more explicitly as "the selective evocation of overt instrumental acts (R_x) by the representational mediation process $(r_m \rightarrow S_m)$, presumably on the basis of differential reinforcement" (p. 18). They propose the use of linguistic encoding as an index of meaning. Their method involves (a) devising a set of alternative verbal responses standardized for all subjects, (b) eliciting these alternatives from subjects in a standard procedure, and (c) ordering the alternative responses along the major, generalized dimensions of meaning. The procedure, as the authors suggest, amounts to a game of Twenty Questions. In assessing the meaning of the abstract word "sophisticated," the experimenters might ask the subject: Is "sophisticated" pleasant or unpleasant? Is it hard or soft? Is it fast or slow? These three pairs of bipolar adjectives, in fact, represent three dimensions of meaning that have emerged from analysis of responses to many such terms: *evaluation, potency,* and *activity.* In practice, the subject is allowed to make his choice along a seven-point scale, where both direction and the intensity of his judgments can be measured. Following is an example of the manner in which the concept "father" might be subjected to semantic analysis:

FATHER

good |___|___|___|___|___|___|___| bad

hard |___|___|___|___|___|___|___| soft

slow |___|___|___|___|___|___|___| fast

The first of the three scales represents the *evaluation* dimension of meaning, the second represents the *potency* dimension, and the third represents the *activity* dimension. A larger number of scales may, of course, be used in connection with any given concept, but it turns out that three or four are usually adequate to account for each of these three dimensions of meaning.

Thirty-three student supporters of Lyndon Johnson and the same number of student adherents of Barry Goldwater responded to semantic differential scales during the 1964 presidential campaign (Rosenbaum and McGinnies, 1967). Six concepts were examined, one of these being "myself." It is evident in Figure 8.8 that the students perceived themselves in very similar terms, except on the dimension liberal-conservative. If one groups the responses according to the three dimensions of meaning represented by the different scales, it appears that, on the average, all of the students viewed themselves as *good, strong,* and *active.* Goldwater supporters, however, rated themselves as significantly more conservative than did Johnson supporters.

How did these same students perceive the office of the presidency, for which the two political candidates were contending? The word "presidency" is a concept for which connotative rather than denotative meaning must be sought. One approach to establishing the connotative meaning of this term is through semantic differential scales, where judgments can be made along more familiar dimensions. Figure 8.9 (page 282) shows the results when the same students who evaluated "myself" with the semantic differential also expressed their associations to "the presidency."

Although the students assigned approximately the same meanings to themselves (except on the dimension liberal-conservative) regardless of their political preference, they showed a number of significant differences in the meanings they ascribed to "the presidency." The supporters of

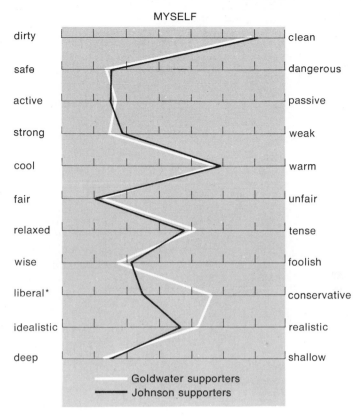

Figure 8.8

The semantic differential applied to the concept MYSELF *by pre-election supporters of Lyndon Johnson and Barry Goldwater. Results are averaged over the thirty-three students in each group. The starred item represents a significant difference.* (From Rosenbaum and Mc-Ginnies, 1967)

Lyndon Johnson saw the office of president as significantly *cleaner, stronger, wiser,* more *active,* more *fair,* and more *liberal* than did the supporters of Barry Goldwater. Apparently, one's political convictions may determine to some extent the meaning of a related concept, such as a political office. Self-concepts, in terms of the semantic differential at least, appear not to vary significantly as a function of political preference.

If one assumes that three general factors, evaluation, potency, and activity, do account for a substantial proportion of the meaning of concepts, then it is possible to locate a given concept within a *semantic space,* the dimensions of which are defined by these three factors. One can then see graphically the relationships or clusterings among different concepts and can tell which among a given set of concepts are similar and which are dissimilar in meaning. Meaning, it should be recalled, is defined here by a set of

THE PRESIDENCY

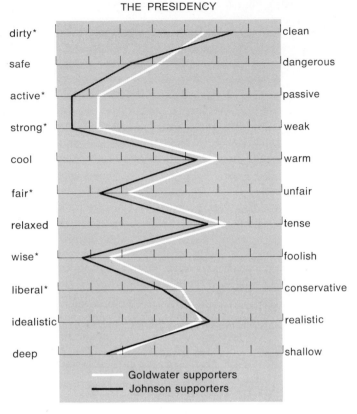

Figure 8.9

The semantic differential applied to the concept THE PRESIDENCY *by pre-election supporters of Lyndon Johnson and Barry Goldwater. The starred items are those where significant differences occurred.* (From Rosenbaum and McGinnies, 1967)

judgmental operations employing a number of rating scales, i.e., good-bad, hot-cold, smooth-rough, and the like.

The data in Figures 8.8 and 8.9 were analyzed together with similar ratings of four other concepts relevant to the 1964 presidential election to derive measures showing how these concepts would cluster in semantic space. Figure 8.10 shows how these six concepts related to one another in terms of meaning for the supporters of Lyndon Johnson. An identical analysis performed on the semantic differential ratings made by Barry Goldwater supporters yielded the clusters shown in Figure 8.11 (page 284). Remember that this type of analysis combines the values for the three meaning dimensions, evaluation, activity, and potency. It is not necessary to provide axes for these figures; they are to be viewed simply as three-dimensional representations of the extent to which the concepts share a common meaning.

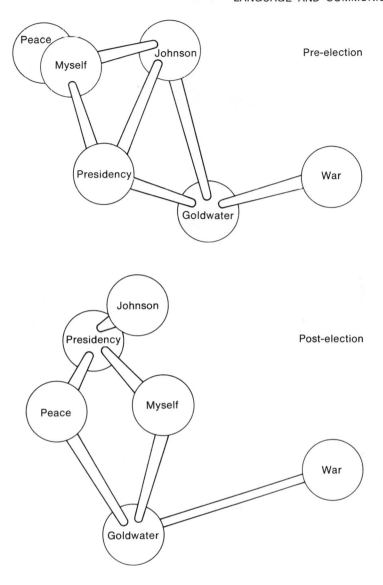

Figure 8.10
Semantic space of Johnson supporters before and after the election.
(After Rosenbaum and McGinnies, 1967)

In this theoretical structure, meaning (as inferred from an individual's responses to the semantic differential) is seen as coincident with a set of mediating reactions. The mediators are (a) those responses involved in judgments of opposing attributes (good-bad, strong-weak); and (b) those responses involved in intensity of judgment (position on the scale). In most social situations, the discriminative stimuli are extremely complex,

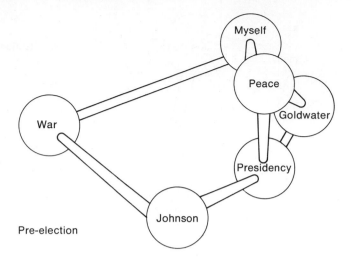

Pre-election

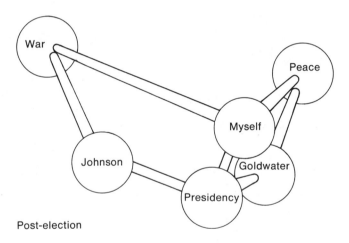

Post-election

Figure 8.11
Semantic space of Goldwater supporters before and after the election.
(After Rosenbaum and McGinnies, 1967)

and one's concept of himself may vary as a function of the occasion. Thus, "myself" may be courageous in one context, cowardly in another. To this extent, the theory of Osgood, Suci, and Tannenbaum, ingenious though it is, overlooks the specific situational factors that determine how one might respond to an evaluation or a potency item. Although admittedly complex, this analysis, as the authors point out, avoids the awkwardness of having a theory of meaning without a related procedure for measuring it.

Finally, we should note that the semantic differential represents only a partial approach to the study of meaning. Osgood, Suci, and Tannenbaum acknowledge the limitations of their method and indicate that semantic space for concepts in general has a large number of dimensions. For many words, however, the single dimension of evaluation seems to represent a large portion of the meaning. The authors recall the young lady from Brooklyn who, when asked if she would like to see the dinosaur in the museum, first wanted to know, "Is it good or is it bad?"

The Experimental Control of Verbal Behavior

The theory that verbal behavior is acquired and maintained by social reinforcement is susceptible to experimental test. During the past decade, a substantial volume of research has been done in an effort to study this area of behavior. Krasner (1958) reviewed thirty-one experiments concerned with the conditioning of verbal behavior, and many more have appeared since that time.

Before looking at some typical approaches that have been made to the experimental control of verbal behavior, let us review some of the theoretical assumptions that underlie this research. First, it should be noted that most verbal operants are the occasions for either reinforcing, neutral, or aversive rejoinders from others. Verbal performances are also related to states of deprivation or to aversive stimulation. Control over these performances, therefore, is exercised in part by stimulation from the environment, both social and nonsocial. Words, because they have been paired with various primary reinforcers (i.e., food, affection, pain), may become *generalized conditioned reinforcers*. Skinner (1957) describes such a process as follows:

> A common generalized conditioned reinforcer is "approval." It is often difficult to specify its physical dimensions. It may be little more than a nod or a smile on the part of someone who characteristically supplies a variety of reinforcements. Sometimes . . . it has a verbal form: *Right!* or *Good!* Because these "signs of approval" frequently precede specific reinforcements appropriate to many states of deprivation, the behavior they reinforce is likely to be in strength much of the time.
>
> Another common generalized reinforcement is escape from or avoidance of aversive stimulation. One man may stimulate another aversively in many ways — by beating him, restraining him, or depriving him of positive reinforcers, not to mention many sorts of "verbal damage." This stimulation can be used to strengthen behavior, verbal or otherwise, because its cessation is reinforcing. Conditioned aversive stimuli (stimuli which frequently precede or accompany aversive stimulation) are also reinforcing when their withdrawal is contingent upon behavior (p. 54).

One parent may control his child's behavior by the appropriate use of verbal approval as a generalized conditioned reinforcer. Another parent may place his child under aversive control by criticizing his faults instead of praising his accomplishments. Probably such verbalizations have on a number of occasions preceded physical punishment and, thus, have become preaversive or conditioned aversive stimuli. The child, in this case, accedes to the parents' demands in order to avoid or escape from this aversive stimulation. The actual situations in which certain verbalizations have acquired their reinforcing properties cannot always be identified, but we may assume that such learning did take place.

Verbal Conditioning

Although the origins of the reinforcing character of words may be obscure, we need not rely upon sheer speculation concerning the capacity of verbal reinforcement to control verbal behavior. One of the early experiments on this phenomenon was performed by Greenspoon (1955), who instructed seventy-five student subjects: "Say all the words that you can think of. Say them individually. Do not use any sentences or phrases. Do not count. Please continue until I say *stop*." Although his design was somewhat more complicated than will be considered here, Greenspoon's main independent variable was the experimenter's saying "Mm-hmm" whenever the subject voiced a plural noun. As compared with subjects in a control group, to whom the experimenter made no differential response, those subjects who were reinforced with "Mm-hmm" emitted a significantly greater number of plural nouns.

A somewhat different method was devised by Taffel (1955). He prepared a number of three-by-five index cards with the past tense of a verb printed in the center of each. Below the verb were printed the pronouns *I, we, you, he, she, they*. These six pronouns were arranged in ninety different orders on as many cards. The subjects' task was to use the verb in the center of the card in constructing a sentence and to start the sentence with one of the pronouns listed underneath it. The experimenter then proceeded to reinforce the subject, by saying "Good," for every sentence beginning with either *I* or *we*. By means of the Manifest Anxiety Scale, Taffel had previously determined which of his subjects were most anxious and which were least anxious. The results of the verbal conditioning procedure showed that the individuals characterized by high and medium anxiety were influenced by reinforcement, whereas those low in anxiety were not. This finding is consistent with the position that learning takes place most readily when the learner is somewhat deprived. Anxious persons, we may assume, have been insufficiently reinforced by others. Approval voiced by another person provides the kind of reinforcement of which they have been deprived and, thus, is more reinforcing than it would be to someone who has been satiated on social approval.

Reinforcement of continuous discourse. It seems to be fairly well established that the vocalizing of single words can be controlled to a certain extent by selective reinforcement. Is verbal reinforcement effective in the control of continuous discourse? Under the guise of an opinion survey, Adams and Hoffman (1960) had students discuss without interruption problems of "conformity and education in America." An experimental group and a control group, each consisting of thirty-one students, were studied. Each student was allowed to express his opinions on the topic for up to fifty minutes. During the first ten minutes, the experimenter kept his eyes on his notebook and recorded every self-reference statement made by the subject. Self-reference statements were those in which the subjects referred to "me, my, mine, myself." This first period of observation established the operant level for emission of self-references. During the next ten minutes, the experimenter lifted his head, looked at the subject, and said "Mm-hmm" every time a self-reference was uttered. This behavior constituted reinforcement of this class of responses. Two extinction periods then followed, the first lasting ten minutes and the second lasting up to twenty minutes, during which no further reinforcements were supplied. For each of these time periods, a ratio was computed between the number of self-references and total remarks of the subjects. The results of these reinforcement and extinction procedures are shown in Figure 8.12.

The control subjects, who were not differentially reinforced during the four time periods, showed little change in their rates of emitting self-references. Their self-reference remarks in general, however, were more numerous than among the experimental subjects, probably due to non-experimental factors. The effect of selective reinforcement upon the verbal behavior of subjects in the experimental group is evident from the Figure 8.12. The self-reference ratio increased during the period of reinforcement and declined nearly to the operant level during extinction. Observation of

Figure 8.12

The frequency of self-reference statements as a function of generalized reinforcement. (Adapted from Adams and Hoffman, 1960)

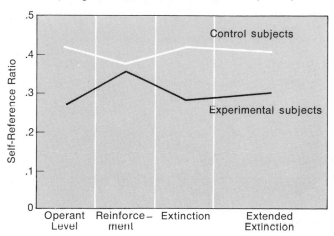

the subjects' behavior during extinction led the experimenters to comment that the subjects appeared to be emotionally disturbed, presumably because of the sudden termination of reinforcement. Verbal expressions of approval become powerful generalized reinforcers for most of us, and we display behavior which is indicative of deprivation when they are suddenly withdrawn.

Another instance in which continuous discourse was placed under the control of reinforcement has been provided by Kanfer (1964), who studied pairs of subjects, or dyads. The members of each dyad were seated in adjacent booths and communicated by means of an intercom unit. One member of each pair was a confederate of the experimenter and could speak only when the subject changed a control switch from "Talk" position to "Listen" position. The task of the subjects, who were student nurses, was to make up stories describing a series of pictures from the Thematic Apperception Test and discuss these stories with their partners. A light was flashed by the experimenter to indicate that either the subject or the confederate had made an insightful statement and had earned points, exchangeable for money, for the team. The experimenter was thus able to reinforce selectively either *talking* or *listening* by the subjects. For example, if the subject observed that her partner was being frequently awarded points for her interpretations of the pictures, it was expected that she would depress the "Listen" switch for a longer period of time than if she herself were being reinforced for her comments. The amount of time spent by the subjects either talking or listening under these two reinforcement contingencies was observed and recorded by the experimenter.

Kanfer reports that when the subjects were reinforced for talking, their verbal output increased sharply over time. When the subjects observed that their partners (the confederates) were being reinforced, however, their own verbal output also increased but at a significantly slower rate. The effect of differential reinforcement on the amount of time spent either listening or talking by one member of a dyad thus appears to have been demonstrated.

The conditioning of continuous speech in young children has been demonstrated by Salzinger and her colleagues (1962). Reinforcement was rather ingeniously provided by means of a *papier-mâché* clown's head, the nose of which was a red light bulb turned on and off by the experimenter. Following instructions to try to make the clown happy by talking to him, the children were reinforced according to several different contingencies and schedules. Speech rate was found to increase when it was accompanied by illumination of the clown's nose on either a fixed interval or variable ratio schedule. Resistance to extinction was stronger under the latter schedule. Production of first person pronouns increased with differential reinforcement, as did speech rate in general. A control group of children who were given no reinforcement showed no systematic changes in rate of speaking.

The control of conversation by differential reinforcement would seem to be most convincingly demonstrated by procedures that effectively shape and maintain continuous discourse in adults. Some success at this was achieved by Levin and Shapiro (1962), who asked subjects to discuss a problem and reach a unanimous conclusion. The experimenter reinforced certain sequences of interaction by announcing that the solution was "incorrect." For example, one group was reinforced only if Subject B always spoke after Subject A. The order in which the speakers participated was successfully brought under experimental control by this procedure, and this result was usually accomplished within about thirty minutes of selective reinforcement. These findings suggest that not only the content of conversation but the sequence in which individuals speak is under the control of social reinforcement. In everyday situations, of course, we are not always able to identify the specific reinforcers. And again it must be emphasized that social behavior is under multiple stimulus control, hence nonverbal as well as verbal cues can effectively direct both the rate and the content of an individual's conversation.

Reinforcement variables. Dependence upon social approval as a factor that might enhance the effectiveness of verbal reinforcement was studied by Crowne and Strickland (1961). These investigators developed a scale to measure the "need" for social approval and administered it to 145 students taking introductory psychology. Their experimental procedure was the familiar one of requiring the subjects to say single words (in this instance for a period of twenty-five minutes) and reinforcing with a nod and "Mm-hmm" all plural nouns. It was found that those subjects who had indicated a greater need for social approval were conditioned more readily to emit the class of words that was reinforced. We would interpret their results as indicating that subjects who identify social approval as being an important reinforcer do, in fact, acquire performances upon which this type of reinforcement is contingent.

Other social variables, needless to say, determine the effectiveness of the types of reinforcement procedures that have been described. For one thing, the personality and physique of the individual who supplies the reinforcement seem to be relevant variables in the success of the conditioning procedure. There is evidence that subjects do not emit as many hostile verbs when reinforcement is provided by a brawny male experimenter as when administered by an attractive, petite female (Binder, McConnell, and Sjoholm, 1957). Avoidance of potentially aversive consequences suggests itself as an explanation of this particular finding. The precise relationship of other factors of this nature to the conditionability of subjects remains to be determined. The effects of different schedules of verbal reinforcement also have been studied and seem, in general, to agree with the findings of infrahuman organisms with respect to nonverbal operant behavior. High reinforcement rates produce faster conditioning than lower rates (McNair, 1957), and partial reinforcement during conditioning favors resistance to extinction (Kanfer, 1954).

Manipulating opinions. Most of the verbal conditioning experiments have been done under laboratory conditions with reinforcement provided for a specified set of responses. Would the same type of procedure prove an effective means of controlling verbal behavior in a more naturalistic setting? Verplanck (1955) carried out a study in which some of his students, in the course of ordinary conversations with their friends, reinforced statements of opinion by saying "I agree." Individuals reinforced in this fashion volunteered significantly more opinions during the period of reinforcement than they had during a control period when their opinions were not reinforced.

Might a specific opinion be influenced by verbal reinforcement of statements relevant to a particular issue? This question was investigated by Insko (1965), who telephoned seventy-two students at the University of Hawaii to inquire whether they agreed or disagreed with a series of statements concerning creation of a Springtime Aloha Week. Half of the telephoned subjects were reinforced with "Good" if they responded in a way that indicated support of an Aloha Week, while the remaining half were reinforced for expressing disapproval of this project. Approximately one week later, questionnaires were passed out in class to determine opinions on a number of issues, including the subject of the telephone survey. Seventy of the students who had been interviewed by phone completed the classroom questionnaire and rated themselves on a fifteen point scale ranging from "definitely favor" (15) to "definitely oppose" (1) an Aloha Week. Those subjects who had previously been reinforced for agreeing with positive statements on the issue had a mean attitude score of 10.40; those who had been reinforced for agreeing with the opposite statements had a mean score of 8.20. On the fifteen-point scale these means, which differed significantly, corresponded to attitudes "somewhat in favor of" and "uncertain" about an Aloha Week, respectively. It was apparent that reinforcement of different viewpoints in the telephone situation had generated different patterns of response to a subsequently administered opinion questionnaire.

The role of awareness. One of the stickier problems in this area of research has been that of subject awareness. Is it essential to verbal conditioning that the subject be aware of the fact that certain of his verbalizations are being reinforced? Some investigators have reported that verbal conditioning of the type we have been discussing was successfully achieved only with subjects who later reported that they had been aware of the relationship between their verbal performance and the reinforcing event (Spielberger, 1962). If awareness is essential, then verbal conditioning might have to be viewed as a rather complex type of interaction between subject and experimenter. The essential problem here, as Green-spoon (1962) suggests, probably hinges on one's definition of awareness. Some subjects undoubtedly make various guesses about what the experimenter is up to. Those who discover the reinforcement contingency may voluntarily behave in accordance with their hypotheses; others may react quite differently. Prediction of alternative behaviors would require more knowledge than is usually available about the subject's disposition to co-operate with or to frustrate the experimenter. Verplanck (1962), of course, sees little difference between behaviors designated "voluntary" and those designated "operant," and he was able to condition subjects' responses to a simple task regardless of the types of hypotheses they devised about the experimental procedure. The control of verbal behavior through reinforcement is an area ripe for further research, and the implications for such diverse social situations as psychotherapy and group problem solving are considerable.

The Prediction of Verbal Behavior

Certainly not all of the long and complex verbalizations that individuals emit can be understood at present in the simple reinforcement terms that we have outlined here. But this theoretical framework, together with a growing body of supporting evidence, promises an opportunity for analysis of language behavior in terms that are subject to both operational defini-tion and experimental verification. It may be argued, as Miller (1965) has done, that language is too complex, arbitrary, improbable, and mentalistic to be studied as a set of instrumental acts. For example, how does one use the concepts of learning theory to explain the production of a philosoph-ical treatise or the composition of an epic poem? This task makes heavy demands on the meager store of empirical data provided by current behavior theory. Even so, an approach to the problems of complex linguis-tic structures should first exhaust the resources of lower-order behavioral principles before resorting to such abstractions as innate "linguistic com-petence," favored by such theorists as Chomsky (1968).

Statistical Properties of Language

We may ask: What factors operating within an individual speaker govern his production of sentences when the prospects for reinforcement are remote and potentially even aversive? Can we predict, even in part, what he will say next? Leaving aside for the moment problems of stimulus control and reinforcement, let us consider some of the statistical properties of speech that make it to some extent predictable. It is quite obvious that some words are uttered more frequently than others and that certain sequences of words have a greater probability of occurrence than other combinations. The word *table* is more commonly used than the word *prolix,* and even a statistician will more frequently say "What are we having for dinner?" than "These data require a multivariate analysis."

Language is partially predictable to the extent that we know something about the relative frequencies of usage of words and combinations of words.

Context. Language is also made predictable in part by various other constraints that operate within a given social group. One of these constraints is grammar. Conventions of usage dictate that certain rules of transition be followed in a given language, although the rules differ from one language to another. Children spend a great deal of time in school learning to order their words in a manner consistent with the grammar of their natural language. Still another constraint on word sequences is context. Once a speaker has begun a sentence "She looked around the. . . . ," he is not free to select the next word at random, at least not if he wants to make sense. If we asked a hundred students to supply the missing word in this sentence, we would doubtless exhaust all the meaningful and grammatical possibilities and would know which predicates were the most probable. The more words a person utters, the more his future utterances are constrained by what he has already said. We have all had the experience of beginning a sentence in such a way that it cannot be completed grammatically; the only remedy is to stop and begin again.

Grammar and common usage alone, however, do not control the production of speech. The *meanings* of the words that precede a given utterance are important contextual determinants of that utterance. Howes and Osgood (1954) studied this matter of associative probability by using a variation of the word association techniques. Instead of asking subjects to associate to a single stimulus word, they presented subjects with clusters of four words with instructions to respond only to the last word in the series. However, they varied the order of the stimulus words. Some subjects heard the words "skin, hour, utter, *rough*," while for others the sequence was changed to "utter, hour, skin, *rough*." It was hypothesized that the probability that *hands* would be given as an associate to *rough* would be determined in part by the position of *skin* among the preceding neutral contextual words, i.e., utter and hour. The experimenters report that a contextual word does, in fact, have its greatest effect upon the association when it occurs immediately before the test word. Similar determinations were made of associations to such sequences as "devil, eat, basic, *dark*" and "devil, fearful, sinister, *dark*." The association "hell," as predicted, occurred more frequently under the second contextual condition. Thus, the probability of a given association to a stimulus word is shown to be alterable by placing the stimulus word in context with other words. The particular contextual words used here have zero transitional probabilities; that is, they do not occur together in ordinary usage in these particular sequences. Imposing the additional constraint of frequency of occurrence of the four-word sequences would permit increased accuracy in predicting associations to the final word in the set; however, this information has not been tabulated.

In ordinary speech, contexts such as those manipulated by Howes and Osgood operate as subtle but little understood determinants of the sequences of words that we produce.

Dependent probability. An interesting demonstration of the effect of verbal context on recall has been provided by Miller and Selfridge (1953). By context they mean the extent to which choice of a particular word depends upon the words that precede it. One can refer to this as the *dependent probability* of a word. For example, given the word "white," it is more likely that the next word will be "house" than "before," although either could be grammatically correct in a sentence. Drawing words from a dictionary with no knowledge of their relative frequencies of occurrence in the language would result in a zero-order approximation to English; for example:"by way consequence handsomely financier bent flux cavalry swiftness weatherbeaten extent." We do, however, know the relative frequencies with which individual words appear in print (Thorndike and Lorge, 1944). If words are selected on the basis of their relative probabilities, the result might be: "abilities with that beside I for waltz you the sewing." When words are selected in terms of their actual frequency in the language system, the result is a first-order approximation to English. The same procedure may be repeated using pairs and then triplets of words, thereby achieving second- and third-order approximations. As the approximations become increasingly higher-order, the word sequences look more and more like meaningful prose. A seventh-order approximation might be: "recognize her abilities in music after he scolded him before."

These lists, and others, were read aloud to subjects, who were then required to reproduce as many of the words, in any order, as they could. Miller and Selfridge found that the higher-order approximations to English yielded better retention scores than the lower-order approximations. In fact, beyond a second-order approximation, individual words were as easily recalled as those appearing in actual prose passages. The investigators concluded that ". . . meaningful material is easy to learn, not because it is meaningful *per se*, but because it preserves the short range associations that are familiar to the subjects. Nonsense materials that retain these short range associations are also easy to learn" (p. 182).

This approach to the analysis of language stresses its *statistical* character and shifts the emphasis from the meaning of an utterance to the degree of contextual constraint imposed upon that utterance. Having emitted certain words, there is a greater probability that I will now emit certain additional words rather than others. This generality seems to hold regardless of what "meaning" I am attempting to communicate. It is not suggested that the prediction of language will be reduced to analysis of its statistical properties. Rather, we may hope that consideration of this aspect of language will provide an additional resource for experimental investigation of this most important of man's capacities.

Summary   In this all too brief examination of language and communication, we first considered several of the theories that have
been advanced to account for the development of language in humans.
Each of these theories possesses some credibility, but none by itself offers
more than a partial response to a question which is probably unanswerable.
Attempts have been made to produce vocalization in animals, but in
general these have not succeeded. The animals below man seem to lack
both the vocal apparatus and, more importantly, the neural capacity required for human speech. Animals, to be sure, communicate with one
another quite effectively in many instances, but they do so in ways that we
do not yet fully understand.

The human infant is biologically prepared to utter any of the large number of sounds that characterize human speech. In a given society, the
adults selectively reinforce certain of these sounds and their various
combinations. By the age of twenty-four months, the average child is thus
able to compose entire phrases and even sentences. This verbal repertoire
gives the child an important added measure of control over his environment, for he is now able to make his needs known more immediately and
more effectively to the adults about him. The reciprocal reinforcement of
verbal behavior emitted by both child and parent insures both the acquisition and the maintenance of interactions that will shape the lives of each.
This process has been formalized by Skinner, whose theory of verbal
behavior was discussed in some detail.

Although Skinner does not explicitly deal with the problem of meaning
in language, preferring instead a functional and descriptive approach,
other investigators, principally Osgood, have developed a theory of meaning based on implicit, or mediating, responses. This behavioral analysis
of meaning lends itself to experimental investigation, an advantage not
always enjoyed by more strictly linguistic approaches. One technique for
arriving at an operational definition of connotative meaning is the semantic
differential, which involves having individuals rate concepts along various
descriptive dimensions. Rather intensive experimentation with this procedure has led to the conclusion that many concepts can be located within
a "semantic space," the major dimensions of which are evaluation, potency,
and activity.

Some very interesting research within the past fifteen years has demonstrated that the verbal behavior of individuals can be controlled to a certain
extent by selective reinforcement. A common procedure in such experiments is to have a listener respond according to a prearranged schedule
of agreement or approval when a speaker emits a certain class of utterances.
Both acquisition and extinction can be shown to occur under controlled
conditions of this sort.

Although far from being a practical enterprise, the prediction of verbal
behavior is made possible in some degree by the statistical nature of
language. Word association has been shown to depend upon the context

in which the stimulus word appears. Verbal context, because it imposes a constraint upon the utterance of each word in a series, can be used for purposes of predicting the next response. Greater understanding of both the external and the internal variables that control verbal behavior as well as increased knowledge of the formal characteristics of language will be necessary before a comprehensive theory of language behavior can be developed.

References

ADAMS, J. STACY, and HOFFMAN, B.   The frequency of self-reference statements as a function of generalized reinforcement. *Journal of Abnormal and Social Psychology*, 1960, *60*, 384–389.

ALLPORT, F. H.   *Social psychology.* Boston: Houghton Mifflin, 1924.

ALLPORT G. W., and POSTMAN, L.   *The psychology of rumor.* New York: Henry Holt, 1947.

BINDER, A., McCONNELL, D., and SJOHELM, N. A.   Verbal conditioning as a function of experimenter characteristics. *Journal of Abnormal and Social Psychology,* 1957, *55*, 309–314.

BINGHAM, W. E., JR.   A study of the relations which galvanic skin response and sensory reference bear to judgments of the meaningfulness, significance, and importance of 72 words. *Journal of Psychology,* 1943, *16*, 21–34.

BROWN, R.   *Words and things.* Glencoe, Ill.: Free Press, 1958.

BROWN, R., BLACK, A. H., and HOROWITZ, A. E.   Phonetic symbolism in natural languages. *Journal of Abnormal and Social Psychology,* 1955, *50*, 388–398.

BRUNER, J. S., GOODNOW, JACQUELINE, and AUSTIN, G. A.   *A study of thinking.* New York: Science Editions, 1962.

CHOMSKY, N.   Review of B. F. Skinner, *Verbal behavior.* In *Language*, 1959, *35*, 26–58.

CHOMSKY, N.   *Language and mind.* New York: Harcourt, Brace and World, 1968.

CROWNE, D. P., and STRICKLAND, BONNIE R.   The conditioning of verbal behavior as a function of the need for social approval. *Journal of Abnormal and Social Psychology,* 1961, *63*, 395–401.

DICKSON, HOLLIDA, and McGINNIES, E.   Affectivity in the arousal of attitudes as measured by galvanic skin response. *American Journal of Psychology,* 1966, *79*, 584–589.

FERSTER, C. B.   Essentials of a science of behavior. In J. I. Nurnberger, C. B. Ferster, and J. P. Brady, *An introduction to the science of human behavior.* New York: Appleton-Century-Crofts, 1963.

FERSTER, C. B.   Arithmetic behavior in chimpanzees. *Scientific American,* 1964, *210*, 98–106.

FERSTER, C. B., and PERROTT, MARY C.   *Behavior principles.* New York: Appleton-Century-Crofts, 1968.

FRISCH, K. VON *Ueber die "Sprache" der Bienen: Eine tierpsychologische Untersuchung.* Jena, Germany: Fischer, 1923.

GLAZE, J. A. The association value of nonsense syllables. *Journal of Genetic Psychology,* 1928, *35,* 255–267.

GOODALL, JANE. My life among wild chimpanzees. *National Geographic Magazine,* 1963, *124*(2), 278–308.

GREENSPOON, J. The reinforcing effect of two spoken words on the frequency of two responses. *American Journal of Psychology,* 1955, *68,* 409–416.

GREENSPOON, J. Verbal conditioning and clinical psychology. In A. J. Bachrach (Ed.), *Experimental foundations of clinical psychology.* New York: Basic Books, 1962.

HAYAKAWA, S. I. *The use and misuse of language.* Greenwich, Conn.: Fawcett Publications, 1962.

HAYES, CATHY. *The ape in our house.* New York: Harper, 1951.

HOWES, D., and OSGOOD, C. E. On the combination of associative probabilities in linguistic contexts. *American Journal of Psychology,* 1954, *67,* 241–258.

INSKO, C. A. Verbal reinforcement of attitude. *Journal of Personality and Social Psychology,* 1965, *2,* 621–623.

KANFER, F. The effect of partial reinforcement on acquisition and extinction of a class of verbal responses. *Journal of Experimental Psychology,* 1954, *48,* 424–434.

KANFER, F. H. Control of communication in dyads by reinforcement. *Psychological Reports,* 1964, *15,* 131–138.

KENT, G. H., and ROSANOFF, A. J. A study of association in insanity. *American Journal of Insanity,* 1910, *67,* 37–96.

KRASNER, L. Studies of the conditioning of verbal behavior. *Psychological Bulletin,* 1958, *55,* 148–170.

LATIF, I. The physiological basis of linguistic development and of the ontogeny of meaning. I, II. *Psychological Review,* 1934, *41,* 55–85, 153–176.

LEVIN, G., and SHAPIRO, D. The operant conditioning of conversation. *Journal of the Experimental Analysis of Behavior,* 1962, *5,* 309–316.

LILLY, J. C. *Man and dolphin.* New York: Pyramid Publications, 1962.

LORENZ, K. *King Solomon's ring.* New York: Crowell, 1952.

MCCARTHY, DOROTHEA. Language development in children. In L. Carmichael (Ed.), *Manual of child psychology.* New York: Wiley, 1954.

MCGINNIES, E., and AIBA, F. H. Persuasion and emotional response: A cross-cultural study. *Psychological Reports,* 1965, *16,* 503–510.

MCNAIR, D. M. Reinforcement of verbal behavior. *Journal of Experimental Psychology,* 1957, *53,* 40–46.

MILLER, G. A. Some preliminaries to psycholinguistics. *American Psychologist,* 1965, *20,* 15–20.

MILLER, G. A., and SELFRIDGE, JENNIFER A. Verbal context and the recall of meaningful material. *American Journal of Psychology,* 1953, *63,* 176–185.

MOWRER, O. H. The autism theory of speech development and some clinical applications. *Journal of Speech and Hearing Disorders,* 1952, *17,* 263–268.

MOWRER, O. H.   *Learning theory and the symbolic processes.* New York: Wiley, 1960.

NEWMAN, S.   Further experiments in phonetic symbolism. *American Journal of Psychology,* 1933, *45,* 53–75.

NOBLE, C.   An analysis of meaning. *Psychological Review,* 1952, 59, 421–430.

OSGOOD, C. E.   *Method and theory in experimental psychology.* New York: Oxford University Press, 1953.

OSGOOD, C. E., SUCI, J. S., and TANNENBAUM, P. H.   *The measurement of meaning.* Urbana, Ill.: University of Illinois Press, 1957.

RAZRAN, G. H.   Salivating and thinking in different languages. *Journal of Psychology,* 1936, *1,* 145–151.

REVESZ, G.   *The origins and pre-history of language.* New York: Longmans, Green, 1956.

ROSENBAUM, L. L., and MCGINNIES, E.   A semantic differential analysis of concepts associated with a presidential election. Technical Report No. 11, Office of Naval Research, December, 1967.

SALZINGER, SUZANNE, SALZINGER, K., PORTNOY, STEPHANIE, ECKMAN, JUDITH, BACON, PAULINE M., DEUTSCH, M., and ZUBIN, J.   Operant conditioning of continuous speech in young children. *Child Development,* 1962, *33,* 683–695.

SAPIR, E.   A study in phonetic symbolism. *Journal of Experimental Psychology,* 1929, *12,* 225–239.

SHANNON, C. E., and WEAVER, W.   *The mathematical theory of communication.* Urbana, Ill.: University of Illinois Press, 1949.

SKINNER, B. F.   *Verbal behavior.* New York: Appleton-Century-Crofts, 1957.

SPIELBERGER, C. D.   The role of awareness in verbal conditioning. In C. W. Eriksen (Ed.), *Behavior and awareness: A symposium of research and interpretation.* Durham, N.C.: Duke University Press, 1962.

STAATS, A. W., and STAATS, CAROLYN K.   *Complex human behavior.* New York: Holt, Rinehart and Winston, 1963.

TAFFEL, C.   Anxiety and the conditioning of verbal behavior. *Journal of Abnormal and Social Psychology,* 1955, *51,* 496–501.

TAYLOR, INSUP K., and TAYLOR, M. M.   Another look at phonetic symbolism. *Psychological Bulletin,* 1965, *64,* 413–427.

THORNDIKE, E. L., and LORGE, I.   *The teacher's word book of 30,000 words.* New York: Columbia University Press, 1944.

TSURU, S.   Sound and meaning. Unpublished manuscript cited in R. Brown, *Words and things.* Glencoe, Ill.: The Free Press, 1958.

VERPLANCK, W. S.   The control of the content of conversation: Reinforcement of statements of opinion. *Journal of Abnormal and Social Psychology,* 1955, *51,* 668–676.

VERPLANCK, W. S.   Unaware of where's awareness: Some verbal operants-notates, moments, and notants. In C. W. Eriksen (Ed.), *Behavior and awareness,* Durham, N.C.: Duke University Press, 1962.

9   *Attitudes and Behavior*

Where is a performance when it is not being emitted? We handle this question quite simply by assuming that it becomes part of the individual's *latent repertoire*. A latent performance becomes manifest when prompted by some relevant stimulus. Thus, I brush my teeth every night just before retiring, prompted by the other activities that habitually precede going to bed. In the morning, I put water on the stove to boil for coffee as part of the ritual of preparing breakfast. We refer to such activities as *habits;* they are learned according to the principles of acquisition that we discussed earlier, and they are maintained as vital links in chains of behavior that are instrumental in achieving a variety of both primary and conditioned reinforcers. They are emitted in the presence of the discriminative stimuli that have come to control them.

Now, how do we explain the fact that when I read an account in the morning paper about the encroachment of one nation's military forces on the territory of its neighbor, I exclaim: "That's just what I expected from those blankety-blank so-and-so's. We ought to drop the Bomb on them!" I have expressed what is termed an *attitude,* and my comment is derived from my latent verbal repertoire. It was prompted by a printed stimulus, and it was expressed promptly and vociferously. Perhaps my partner at breakfast agreed with me, thus reinforcing the utterance. If he disagreed, then I may have responded in kind, and an argument may have ensued.

It should be clear from this brief example that an attitude is both a *response* and a *disposition* to respond. It may also be a *covert* or an *overt* response. My intemperate reaction to what I had read in the paper might have been merely subvocal, in which case there would have been no danger of my starting an argument. My attitude, in this case, would have been expressed covertly rather than overtly. Whether I spoke aloud or merely to myself might have been determined by how much I knew about the attitudes of those within earshot. If I suspected that their reactions would be similar to my own, I might have voiced my reaction aloud in the expectancy of prompting agreement. On the other hand, if I suspected that my attitude was that of a minority, I may well have responded covertly, in order to avoid an aversive rejoinder. I would probably have reacted in the same way had no listeners been present. A speaker who voices an attitude is probably reinforced automatically in his role of listener to his own verbal production (Skinner, 1957).

The term *attitude* is used to cover not just a single reaction but a wide range of behaviors under the control of stimuli of a particular class. A "religious attitude," for example, would be manifested in a certain pattern of church attendance, in the statements one makes about certain moral and ethical issues, and in the behaviors relevant to religion that one rewards or punishes in one's children. It is often said that someone has a "negative attitude" toward his job or his employer, or a "positive attitude" toward formal education, or "no attitude" on the question of war as an instrument of national policy. If we know what a person's attitudes are on a variety of matters, we feel we can better understand that person.

Theoretical Considerations

Let us try to orient this concept within the framework of the behavior principles that we have developed. From one standpoint, attitudes are viewed simply as response dispositions, essentially no different from those that are presumed to underlie any learned performance. From another point of view, they are conceived as "cognitions," or beliefs, having characteristic affective, or emotional, components. Psychologists who adhere to these contrasting viewpoints may be referred to as *behaviorists* or *quasi-phenomenologists*. Campbell (1963), who suggests this distinction, sees the difference as residing in the methods one uses; the behaviorist observes his subjects, while the phenomenologist interviews them.

However, it should be clear by now that an adequate description of someone's behavior is approached only when we record the verbal as well as the nonverbal components. Interviewing, then, may be viewed as another method of observation, although its product is a verbal statement of the respondent's perception of a situation, which is what Campbell means by "quasi-phenomenological." Because psychologists often think of attitudes as involving *cognitions* as well as *behavior,* the concept of attitude is seen by Campbell as being "...a valuable intermediary just because it has the multiple connotations of 'view of the world' and 'predisposition to respond'" (p. 96).

There is a tendency among psychologists to postulate mediating or intervening processes to account for a variety of observed behaviors. Many theorists are not satisfied to view attitudes as special classes of performances; rather, they feel that an attitude is represented by some latent, covert process that mediates between stimulus and response. One difficulty with this approach is that it fails to account adequately for the situational determination of attitudinal behavior. Perhaps a more serious criticism of the definition of attitude as an implicit response is that it puts attitudes back inside the organism, where we are forced to deal with essentially unreachable processes. In a science that stresses *observables*, the concept of a latent variable is awkward to deal with (DeFleur and Westie, 1963).

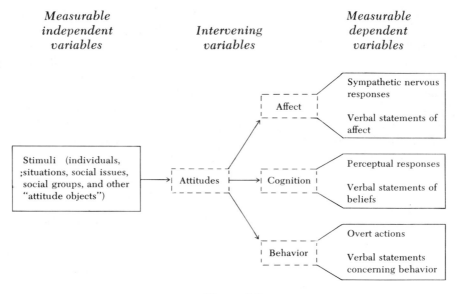

Figure 9.1

One conceptual schema for relating attitudes to stimuli and responses.
(From Rosenberg and Hovland, 1960)

One such approach to attitudes is typified by the scheme shown in Figure 9.1. Although this particular approach is useful in specifying the response components of those behaviors that we term attitudes, we may question whether it is necessary to view an attitude as an implicit or intervening process. It seems sufficient to propose, as Green (1954) has done, that an attitude is a disposition inferred from a large number of related acts or responses. He defines an attitude as ". . . a consistency among responses to a specified set of stimuli, or social objects" (p. 335). "This definition," Green adds, "does not divest attitudes of their affective and cognitive properties, which may be . . . correlates of the responses that comprise the attitude" (p. 336).

The term *attitude*, then, refers to a class of behaviors that are under the control of a single social variable, called the *referent* of the attitude. A common feature of attitudes is that they involve emotional reactions as well as overt performances. Attitudes also reveal a verbal as well as an action component in that a person may say one thing but do something different. It will be useful for us to examine briefly these correlated aspects of those behavioral dispositions that we call attitudes.

The Structure of Attitudes

Affective components. An emotional or affective reaction may be measured physiologically, through such reactions as the galvanic skin response (GSR), or verbally, through interview and questionnaire procedures. The emotional component of an attitude is presumed to have developed as a conditioned response to stimuli having either rewarding or punishing effects on behavior. Probably the earliest unconditioned stimuli for a positive affective response are expressions of warmth and affection from one's parents; the stimuli for a negative affective response probably are derived from parental disapproval or neglect. Any behavior by either parent or child that immediately precedes these rewarding or punishing stimuli gains some measure of control over the elicited reactions. Thus, the word "love," because it has tended to precede physical demonstrations of affection, becomes a conditioned stimulus to reactions that most persons would describe as pleasant. Threat words, such as "hate," elicit other reactions, generally reported as unpleasant because they have characteristically preceded some aversive event. These words thus become cues for emotional reactions, and we may assume that connected discourse in which they are used comes to serve the same function.

There is considerable evidence to support the contention that a consistency exists between certain items in an individual's verbal repertoire and his emotional reaction in the presence of these items. Cooper (1959) measured the galvanic skin response (GSR) in college students as they listened to statements that were either complimentary or derogatory to certain ethnic groups. While hearing statements that derogated ethnic groups which they favored, most of the subjects displayed GSR's of greater magnitude than when listening to derogatory statements about groups toward which they were neutral. In addition, the magnitude of the subjects' GSR's were greater to complimentary statements about disliked groups than to complimentary statements about neutral groups. Westie and DeFleur (1959) also examined the relationship of autonomic responses to racial attitudes. Students whose attitudes toward Negroes had already been determined were shown color slides depicting Negroes and whites in various situations. The subjects' GSR's as well as other physiological changes were recorded as they watched the slides. These measures showed that prejudiced subjects responded to the slides with more elevated GSR's than did nonprejudiced subjects.

Rankin and Campbell (1955) attached electrodes to the hands of white subjects for the purpose of measuring emotional reactivitiy and found that higher GSR's were recorded when adjustments to the apparatus were made by a Negro experimenter than when the same adjustments were made by a white experimenter. This effect, as later reported by Porier and Lott (1967), is greatly reduced when both a Negro and a white experimenter attend to the subject. In a cross-cultural study of the relationship between attitudes and GSR, McGinnies and Aiba (1965) presented Japanese college students with both pro-American and pro-Soviet viewpoints on the issue of American response to the discovery of missile bases in Cuba. They report that the subjects responded with GSR's of greater magnitude when they were listening to a communication with which they disagreed than when listening to one with which they agreed.

This general line of inquiry into the affective component of attitudes was pursued further by Dickson and McGinnies (1966), who first determined by means of a questionnaire the attitudes of a sample of university students toward the church. They then presented these students with tape-recorded statements that either praised or derogated the church, while simultaneously recording their GSR's. Both pro- and anti-church subjects responded with greater emotion (as revealed by elevations in GSR) to statements that contradicted their attitudes than to those that reflected their attitudes. These investigators suggest that an autonomic response, such as the GSR, is elicited more strongly when someone's attitudes are challenged than when they are confirmed.

These several investigations, corroborated by evidence from everyday observation, seem to have demonstrated that attitudes do have emotional support, and that the emotional component is more apparent when someone's attitudes are attacked than when they are supported. Negative attitudes, in other words, appear to have a greater degree of affect conditioned to them than do positive attitudes. Perhaps positive attitudes are maintained, in part, as a means of avoiding the aversive effects of exposure to a conflicting viewpoint.

Cognitive factors. The term "cognition" is a troublesome one in psychological theory because it refers to a postulated and unobservable set of events that are presumed sometimes to be independent of and sometimes to underlie overt performances. Each of us, of course, is convinced of the reality of his own mental processes, but the only evidence we have of someone else's thoughts and feelings is what we see him do or hear him say. For our purposes, it will be sufficient to define a cognition as what a person has thought or said to himself. These covert expressions of an attitude may be revealed in overt verbal behavior or translated into some nonverbal performance.

Someone to whom the concept "atheist" is aversive can be said to have a negative attitude toward atheists because he gives voice to certain propositions about atheists, becomes emotionally aroused if atheism is proposed to him as a viewpoint meriting acceptance, and may refuse to associate with persons designated by this label. Somewhere in this person's history he has acquired a set of avoidance reactions to the class of persons described as atheists. How does this particular attitudinal referent come to control someone's behavior in the manner that we have described?

This problem may be examined, in part, with reference to the concept of semantic generalization. Staats and Staats (1963) give an example of this, which we present in modified form. If a word is used as a CS, and a response is conditioned to it this new conditioned response will also be elicited by any referent of the word. For example, if the word BLUE is used as a CS, and some autonomic response is conditioned to it, this response will also be elicited, without further conditioning, by a blue light. "Since there is no physical similarity between a word and the object it denotes," they maintain, "one cannot explain this occurrence on the basis of primary stimulus generalization" (p. 147). These writers argue further that the

Figure 9.2

When the word BLUE *is paired a sufficient number of times with a blue light, a part of the sensory response to the light (R^s) becomes conditioned to the word* BLUE *(r^s). This also constitutes a portion of the meaning of the word, as suggested by Osgood (1963), and so is denoted r^s_m. If the word* BLUE *is later paired with an electric shock, the response r^s, which is common to both the word and the light, will also elicit the GSR. Because the mediating response can thus act as a conditioned stimulus, it is shown as r^s_m. (Adapted from Staats and Staats, 1963)*

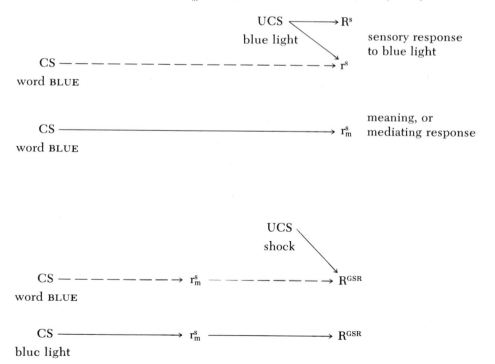

conditioning of an implicit meaning response is the basis for semantic generalization. That is, a child learns that the word BLUE is the appropriate designation for the blue light that may emanate from a variety of sources. Part of the sensory response to a blue light, according to this explanation, has become conditioned to the word BLUE. If the word BLUE is now used as the stimulus for some new response, this response (or some fractional component of it) will also be elicited by blue objects.

We might, for example, administer a mild electric shock to a person's hand just after showing him the word BLUE. The word by itself would soon come to elicit a conditioned galvanic skin response (GSR). We would probably also discover that a variety of blue objects also now elicited a GSR, although they had not previously done so. Probably what occurs is that a blue object elicits the implicit (mediating) verbal response BLUE, which in turn elicits some components of the reaction to an electric shock. The diagram in Figure 9.2 may clarify the several steps of this learning process.

In applying these general principles to the positive or negative aspects of an attitude, Staats and Staats suggest that once the word BAD has come, through classical conditioning, to be a conditioned aversive stimulus, it may serve to reinforce negative attitudinal responses (avoidance or escape) to other stimuli. By having learned to say, "Atheists are bad," for example, a child or adult would be expected to associate the negative meaning of the word BAD with the word ATHEIST. One aspect of this transfer of meaning would involve the attachment of similar patterns of autonomic reactivity to the word BAD and the word ATHEIST. Figure 9.3 illustrates this process.

Figure 9.3

As a result of prior learning, in which punishment probably was used as a reinforcer, the word BAD *has come to have aversive qualities. Because it has been the occasion for punishment, it will evoke an emotional reaction, including the GSR. It will now function as a conditioned aversive stimulus, and if it regularly follows some other word, such as* ATHEISTS, *that word will come to elicit similar reactions.* (Adapted from Staats and Staats, 1963)

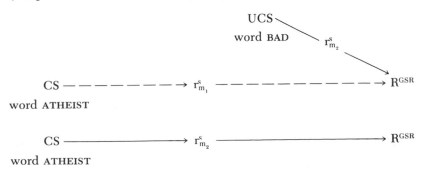

As indicated in the diagram, the words BAD and ATHEIST do not acquire identical meanings; rather, they act as mediators ($r^s_{m_1}$) and $r^s_{m_2}$) for other responses. But to the extent that they have been experienced or used contiguously, they will come to share certain meanings ($r^s_{m_2}$), as the diagram illustrates. Alternatively, we could say that these two words come to control similar behaviors in the appropriate circumstances. This view of attitudes as meaning responses that have either positive or aversive reinforcement histories has been advanced by several investigators, including Rhine (1958) and Staats, Staats, and Heard (1961).

Implicit and overt behaviors. An implicit response, as defined by Doob (1947), is ". . . a response occurring within the individual and not immediately observable to an outsider. . . . Such an implicit response may be conscious or unconscious, distinctly verbal or vaguely proprioceptive" (p. 136). In this mediational theory, the implicit response component of an attitude is assumed to be anticipatory to some overt response. An implicit, anticipatory response is one that has originally preceded some other reinforced response and is evoked by the S^Ds that have gained control of that response. Doob suggests that "If an individual . . . dislikes a fruit or a person, he tends to avoid eating the fruit or meeting the person. Originally, the avoidance occurred only after actual contact had been established and after that contact had proved to be punishing and the withdrawal to be rewarding" (p. 136). Doob argues further that attitudes frequently bring about behaviors which have the effect of increasing the likelihood of occurrence of reward rather than punishment. "Attitudes," he goes on to say, "can be evoked so easily because as mediating responses involving only language, imagery, or proprioceptive reactions they need not conflict with the overt behavior of the individual or with his environment" (p. 137). Thus, an individual might say and do things that would seem quite inconsistent; his actual behavior belies his verbally expressed attitudes.

To illustrate more concretely Doob's theory of an attitude as a mediating response, let us consider the following event. Each of eighteen children is shown three jar tops, colored green, yellow, and black, that they have never seen before. Each is told that if he chooses the correct one, he will receive a marble. Fourteen of the children unerringly make the correct selection and are rewarded. How did this statistically improbable event occur? We are less perplexed when we learn that the children had previously been taught that three rectangular wooden blocks, colored green, yellow, and black, were to be called "egg," "car," and "shoe," respectively. Prior to this, the children had played a game in which a marble was hidden under one of three white wooden blocks shaped as a triangle, circle, and square and called "egg," "car," and "shoe," respectively. A moment's consideration reveals to us that the one element that has consistently been paired with reinforcement in these various situations is the verbal label.

For example, the child who first found a marble under the white triangular wooden block called "egg" learned subsequently that a green rectangular block also was called "egg." When given a choice between green, yellow, and black jar covers, this child selected the cover with the same *name* as the block under which marbles had previously been found.

This experiment, which was conducted by Eisman (1955), might be summarized as one in which children learned that green rectangular blocks can be called "eggs" and that things called by this name may conceal marbles. Through stimulus generalization, other green objects, such as jar covers, then will tend to evoke a preferential response tendency (or attitude). Eisman suggests that, as a result of similar training, children might ". . . learn to prefer people called Englishmen over those called Poles or Italians, even though they have no differential reward or punishment experience with any of these three national groups" (p. 325). It is necessary only that they learn to attach the same labels to the word "Englishmen" as to stimuli that have been followed by reinforcement.

The possibility that attitudes might be either developed or changed through procedures analogous to those of classical conditioning was raised in several earlier experiments by Razran (1938, 1940). In one instance, Razran showed subjects who were eating lunch pictures of girls bearing different ethnic labels. Subsequent ratings of these pictures were more favorable than those made prior to pairing with the reinforcing act of eating. Razran also found that ratings of political slogans were less favorable after the slogans had been presented contiguous with unpleasant odors. More recently, Staats and Staats (1958) attempted to establish an attitudinal response by classical conditioning. Their procedure consisted of projecting a nationality designation such as *Dutch* onto a screen and following this immediately with auditory presentation of another word that was repeated aloud by the subject. Thus, *Dutch*, for one group of subjects, was followed by a positively valued word, such as *gift, sacred,* or *happy*. Another group of subjects saw *Swedish*, then heard a negatively valued word, such as *bitter, ugly,* or *failure*. (For different groups of subjects, these pairings were reversed; *Dutch* was followed by a negative stimulus word and *Swedish* by a positive stimulus word.) Other nationality names were included as "filler" items and were paired with nonevaluative words, such as *chair*.

When the nationality designations were later evaluated by the subjects on a seven-point rating scale, the names presented contiguous with the positive words were rated as more "pleasant" than those paired with aversive words. The authors interpret their findings in terms of an implicit attitudinal response that mediated scoring of the critical words on the rating scale. Whether attitudes toward the several nationalities were actually altered is seriously questioned. A modest conclusion would be that verbal behavior was effectively manipulated in a situation that allowed mediated generalization to occur. The mediators in this case were acquired experimentally and presumably overrode those that were already in the verbal repertoires of the subjects.

As Remmers (1954) has pointed out, the concept of attitude is closely related to a number of other psychological concepts, such as interests, motives, morals, ideals, values, prejudices, sentiments, and loyalties. We will not attempt to distinguish among these terms because they all have reference to classes of behaviors that are more appropriately analyzed in terms of their individual topographies and the stimuli that control them. Attitudes are studied almost exclusively as vocal or written responses, but they might also be inferred from nonverbal performances that are taken as "indicators." A person's attitude usually is determined by asking him to indicate the extent to which he agrees or disagrees with selected statements; it is assumed that a correspondence exists between his reactions to certain verbal propositions and the actions he will take on other occasions related to the subject matter of the attitude. Nonverbal behavior often is clearly indicative of an attitude when it involves applauding, cheering, booing, running, fighting, or other such dramatic performances. The stimuli that are characteristically the occasions for these verbal or nonverbal attitudinal manifestations are said to be the referents of the attitude. According to Kerlinger (1967), "... an attitudinal referent is a construct that stands for a set or category of objects, ideas, properties, or behaviors that can be the focus of an attitude" (p. 111). An attitude, as we have suggested, predisposes the individual to behave selectively with respect to these social referents.

The Shaping of Attitudes

Stimulus Control

We shall now examine more closely the proposition that attitudes represent classes of behaviors that have increased or decreased in frequency as a result of the positive or aversive social consequences that they have generated. We will assume that no one is born with complex social attitudes, but that most persons acquire a great many attitudes from the interactions they have with parents, teachers, friends, and acquaintances. Frequently, a particular constellation of attitudes is peculiar to a group or subculture. This is not surprising when we consider that the members of such groups influence one another and tend to reinforce common patterns of behavior. We discussed some of these group phenomena in earlier chapters.

In order to understand the acquisition of attitudes, we must first reexamine the process of behavior shaping as it applies to both verbal and nonverbal performances. Consider, for example, the various behaviors emitted by a child during his early encounters with those persons and occasions that will determine his later posture with reference to the church. It is important to remember that a wide range of situations and performances will be related to religious attitudes. As Green (1954) has observed, "The concept of attitude does not refer to any specific act or response of an individual, but is an abstraction from a large number of related acts or responses" (p. 335). Thus, a positive attitude toward some social institution, such as *war* or the *church*, would be inferred from those performances controlled by occasions relating to that institution.

What are some examples of the kinds of occasions and behaviors that might come to form the core of, say a religious attitude? Among the earliest that the child encounters are probably the saying of grace at the dining table and the reciting of prayers at bedtime. Later comes attendance at church or Sunday school. Conversations with family members and friends may provide almost daily occasions on which verbal references are made to the church, to specific religious practices, or to conduct that is either sanctioned or condemned in religious terms. Appropriate behaviors by the child in these various situations are positively reinforced by the other members of the particular family and community of which the child is a part. Performances that are aversive to the other members of this community either go unreinforced or are punished. The author recalls an occasion on which a neighbor asked her young daughter to say grace before eating a picnic lunch. The child replied that she "didn't want to," whereupon the mother became quite irate, slapped her, and told her never to "say a thing like that." We may assume that refusals by the child to attend Sunday school or to observe a host of other rituals, both verbal and nonverbal, would have incurred similarly aversive consequences. Instances of compliance with the religious practices and precepts of the mother, on the other hand, were undoubtedly rewarded with approval and affection. This gradual shaping of behavior by selective reinforcement underlies the acquisition of attitudes of many kinds.

By the same token, a single attitude may be under the control of a number of discriminative stimuli. The referents of the attitude, in this instance, are said to form a *concept*. A person may have generally positive attitudes toward such concepts as democracy, education, charity, peace, freedom, and so forth. Conceptual behavior, according to Millenson (1967), is demonstrated when the behavior of organisms comes under the discriminative control of a broad class of S^Ds. This occurs even when the stimulus members comprising a particular class are quite dissimilar. Many items of food, as Millenson points out, bear very little physical resemblance to one another, yet all are readily recognized as edibles and all have the joint capacity to control similar performances, namely, those involved in the acquisition and ingestion of food. The relationship of such heterogeneous S^D classes to attitudinal behavior is perhaps obvious. One may become indignant upon reading that Russian troops have occupied Czechoslovakia, that a Negro has been refused purchase of the home of his choice, or that a Congressional filibuster has prevented the majority from voting on a controversial issue. Someone else may take satisfaction in the fact that a group of campus demonstrators were subdued by the police, that an open housing measure was defeated in a state legislature, or that federal foreign aid funds have been cut. Because individuals tend to react rather consistently to issues such as these, and because we can often predict their reactions from their performances on attitude scales, we say that they have formed different attitudes with respect to such concepts as "democracy" and "liberalism." But neither the complexity of these verbal performances nor the fact that they are under multiple stimulus control need deter us from attempting to analyze them in the language of objective behavior theory. We may conveniently refer to them as expressions of attitudes, but at the same time we also recognize them as products of the particular reinforcement histories that have obtained for the individual in the groups among which he moves.

Selective Reinforcement

Similar performances are not necessarily reinforced in every situation the individual encounters. For this reason, it should not surprise us that individuals express what seem to be inconsistent attitudes at different times and in different places. For example, someone who dislikes Armenians will probably give verbal expression to this attitude only among those from whom he has reason to expect agreement. In other situations, where expression of ethnic or racial prejudice would be likely to have aversive consequences, he remains silent on the matter. Similarly, an avowed agnostic probably voices his skepticism only among others of similar persuasion, and he gets along well with devout churchgoers simply by avoiding religious discussions and by expressing only sentiments on which he anticipates agreement. Each of these individuals has learned to discriminate among situations in which the expression of an attitude will evoke expressions of approval and of disapproval from others.

There are notable cases, of course, where individuals appear to deliberately antagonize others. How can such instances be squared with reinforcement theory? One answer to this is deceptively simple. It is the obvious reminder that a reinforcer is defined in terms of changes in the frequency of the performance upon which its presentation is made contingent. Therefore, a stimulus event which increases the frequency of the behavior that produces it is said to be positively reinforcing; if the stimulus decreases the frequency of such behavior, it is said to be aversive. It follows from these definitions that any repeated performance is maintained by its consequences. Although the consequences may appear to an observer to be "aversive" or "punishing," these labels are both arbitrary and deceptive. The person who plays devil's advocate in a discussion, thereby eliciting expressions of antagonism from others, is being quite effectively reinforced for his performance. Perhaps he is both gaining attention and punishing those listeners who are aversive to him. The rebellious adolescent, whose behavior both infuriates his parents and generates aversive consequences for himself as well, is similarly reinforced. Perplexing instances such as these are the reason many psychologists have felt obliged to postulate such motivating forces as hostility and such descriptive concepts as rebelliousness. But the invention of motives and the use of pejorative labels for a class of behavior not only fail to explain it but add a new set of terms which themselves require definition and explication in terms of antecedents and consequences.

For example, when we say that a boy has a "bad attitude toward school," we are stating in effect that certain of his performances are aversive to us. He may characteristically: (a) use profane language, (b) play hooky, (c) neglect his homework, and (d) act up in class. All of these behaviors may, however, secure him a great deal of attention, and they may also be his way of avoiding or terminating situations that have become aversive to him, namely, those involving studying and learning. His behavior may be well described as hostile, but it is also under fairly specific situational control, and frequently it can be modified through appropriate alteration of the environment that is maintaining it. The teacher might, for example, ignore undesirable behavior and selectively reinforce those performances that she wishes to increase in frequency. Or the learning situation might be rearranged so as to provide more direct reinforcement, such as money or privileges, for desirable behaviors. If such procedures are effective, then we have effectively modified the boy's attitude toward school.

Aversive control. To put these several considerations into more concrete form, consider the case of a child who is told by a parent to do something that is related to attitudes held by the parent, for example, to "say grace," to study his lessons, or to stop associating with some other child. The instrumental learning paradigm, assuming aversive control, is as follows:

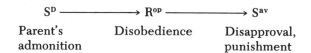

$$S^D \longrightarrow R^{op} \longrightarrow S^{av}$$

Parent's   Disobedience   Disapproval,
admonition   punishment

Because of the aversive consequences that it achieves, the response of disobeying the parent will tend to decrease in frequency. Other performances, such as conforming to certain religious rituals or spending more time studying, may be reinforced negatively by their instrumentality in simply avoiding punishment. However, the parent's use of punishment as a means of control may also have the effect of eliciting hostile behavior from the child. Hostility, in turn, is likely to be the occasion for further punishment from the parent, thus setting up a "vicious cycle" that may result in the acquisition of performances (attitudes) by the child that are

distinctly aversive to the parent. Lundin (1961) has observed that delinquents who have been reared under conditions of frequent punishment
commonly exhibit rebelliousness against authority. Of course, the aversive
stimuli that cause the resentment may arise not only from family relationships but also from such factors as economic distress or community dis-
organization.

Positive control. Let us assume for the moment that the use of punishment as a means of parental control is minimal, and that positive reinforcement is more commonly employed. The occurrence of positive reinforcement may be diagrammed as follows:

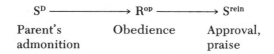

$$S^D \longrightarrow R^{op} \longrightarrow S^{rein}$$

Parent's   Obedience   Approval,
admonition   praise

Here it is clear that the frequency with which the child will obey the
parent's requests will increase in proportion to the extent that he is rewarded for so doing. Because parental approval comes to act as a generalized reinforcer, the incidence of behavior compliant with other parental
instructions will also increase. In the case of a favorable attitude toward,
say, the church or school, additional factors operate to shape the individual's conduct. Attendance at church or school, for example, provides
occasions on which other behaviors can be reinforced. The result is to
establish a class of S^Ds that will control the individual's behavior in a variety
of situations.

This analysis assumes that parental approval is positively reinforcing to
most children. This, in turn, is predicated on the assumption that such
approval makes possible other performances that are reinforcing, whereas
parental disapproval tends to limit the occasions on which other reinforcements might occur. It happens, of course, that disapproval sometimes
seems to increase the frequency with which children behave in a manner
designed to frustrate and antagonize their parents. That is, the child sometimes seems to be reinforced by any reaction of distress evident in the parent. As we have already suggested, it is probable that the parents have in
the past favored the use of aversive controls over the child. The resulting
emotional reactions in the child may interfere with compliant behavior,
thus increasing the probability that the child's behavior will come under
the control of extraparental stimuli. The net result is that the child may
well develop some attitudes that are inconsistent with those of the parents.
He learns that one kind of stimulus that is aversive to the parent is a
performance which is incompatible with important items in the parent's
verbal repertoire.

Even though the parents use positive rather than aversive control, the reinforcers provided by the child's peers may be prepotent and may have the effect of shaping the child's behavior along lines different from those intended by the parents. Perhaps the "generation gap" in attitudes, which seems to have been demonstrated so dramatically in recent years, can be partially accounted for in these terms. Drastic changes in the social order have so altered the structure of events that many young people are less influenced by the incentives that effectively controlled the behavior of their parents. Many of the aphorisms that rang so convincingly in their parent's ears strike upon the younger generation with a hollow sound.

Modeling

We described in Chapter 3 the process by which children often learn to model their behavior after that of others. This is a powerful concept in understanding the genesis of attitudes, because the operant learning model that we have described is not presumed to account for all the complex forms taken by social attitudes. There is now considerable evidence that children can learn a great deal simply by *observing* the behavior of others. Whether or not they then *perform* in a similar manner will depend upon the consequences that they themselves experience. But a sufficient condition for the learning of a performance seems to be the vicarious reinforcement that is experienced by an observer who witnesses the consequences to someone else of a particular course of action. Bandura (1962), as we noted earlier, found that differential vicarious reinforcement experienced by children who watched a film of an adult being either rewarded or punished for aggression produced different amounts of imitative behavior. Children who observed the model punished performed fewer imitative aggressive responses than those who saw the model rewarded.

The pervasiveness of modeling influences on attitude development in the individual is evidenced by the fact that the *consequences* of a particular class of behavior to the model need not actually be witnessed in order to be imitated. Bandura and Walters (1963) point out that an individual may be influenced by his knowledge that a model during his lifetime either has amassed reinforcers or has generally been punished for his behavior. These long-term rewarding and punishing consequences are frequently dealt with in such terms as prestige, competence, status, and power. Hence, an individual may, within the limits of his capabilities, tend to emulate those whom he perceives as powerful and successful and to avoid performing in ways that connote failure or social rejection. Because the adults to whom the child is exposed early in life represent powerful agents of reward and punishment, they are the ones he is most likely to imitate. Once a child has emitted some performance similar to that of a parent, he is generally rewarded, or reinforced. What began as modeling behavior now comes under the control of both discriminative and reinforcing stimuli. Most adults have already acquired fairly stable attitudes, and they tend to reinforce similar performances in their own children. This is why parents and children usually exhibit similar attitudes and beliefs.

Self-reinforcement. The fact that most individuals tend to exhibit these acquired attitudes long after they have become independent of parental controls suggests that reinforcement of the attitudes has become self-administered. In effect, a person rewards himself when he expresses a "proper" attitude and punishes himself when he demonstrates an "improper" attitude. Mischel and Liebert (1966) have described this state of affairs cogently: "Humans evaluate their own performance and frequently set standards which determine, in part, the conditions under which they self-administer or withhold numerous readily available gratifications and a multitude of self-punishments." They observe further that ". . . for humans self-administered reinforcers constitute powerful incentives for learning and powerful incentives for the maintenance of behavior patterns" (p. 45).

The transmission of criteria for self-reinforcement is an important aspect of attitude formation. It commonly observed, moreover, that adults may impose certain standards upon the behavior of their offspring but adopt either more lenient or more restrictive standards for themselves. How does a child respond when there is a discrepancy between the occasions for reinforcement that he observes in others and the occasions on which he is reinforced himself? An experiment performed by Mischel and Liebert provides some partial answers to this question. These investigators employed a situation in which a woman could serve as model for the performances of fourth-grade children. The adult began by instructing each of fifty-four children individually in a simple bowling game, with scores of 5, 10, 15, 20 announced by signal lights (not unlike a pinball machine). For some children the adult model imposed a more lenient reward criterion for them than for herself. She did this by helping herself to a reward token only for scores of 20 but encouraging the child to take a token whenever he achieved a score of 15 or 20. It was explained that the tokens could later be exchanged for valuable prizes.

For other children, the model set a more stringent performance criterion for them than for herself; that is, she allowed the child to reward himself only for a score of 20, but she helped herself to tokens for scores of 15 or 20. In a final condition, the model held both the child and herself to strict criteria, allowing a reward only for scores of 20 in each case.

In the next stage of the experiment, the children either played the game by themselves or demonstrated the game to a younger child. Thus, the children could be observed in the role of either performer or demonstrator subsequent to their different experiences with the adult model. (The sequence in which they took the roles of performer and demonstrator was found to be unimportant.) The results of the experiment confirmed the assumption that a model's behavior is more likely to be imitated when the consequences are the same for both model and observer. Those children for whom the observed as well as the imposed criteria were consistent demonstrated adherence to a higher standard of performance than children who had experienced inconsistent criteria. Specifically, the children who had been instructed by a model who rewarded both them and herself only for scores of 20 held to higher performance levels, either alone or with another child. When the model established different performance criteria for herself and the child, the more lenient alternative was later adopted by the child both alone and as demonstrator. One is reminded at this point of the classic parental admonition, "Do as I say, not as I do," which seems to be as ineffective in the laboratory as in the home.

Inconsistencies between the behavior of adult models and the performances that they require of their children and pupils may be an additional factor contributing to what we have already noted as the sometimes perplexing ecology of delinquency or even simple youthful rebellion. Related to this is the fact that the behavior of their offspring that is so frequently distressing to parents is under the control of immediate positive reinforcement, whereas the behavior they wish to encourage may have only delayed reward value. Attitudes are formed not only in the home but in the community as well. As the agents of immediate reinforcement shift progressively outside the family group, the attitudes of offspring are less likely to be modeled after those of their parents. Peer groups become important sources of both positive and negative reinforcement, and their influence will increase if the parents provide inconsistent behavior examples for their children to emulate. One result is that the teenager may learn to play one role with his family and a different role with his peers. To put it in more technical language, he learns to behave selectively in terms of the probable outcomes of his behavior in different situations. This, as we shall see in Chapter 10, complicates the problems of attitude measurement, which is generally undertaken in very restricted circumstances.

The Organization of Attitudes

Attitudes on different issues are interrelated in complex ways, and sometimes a person is seen as exhibiting attitudes that are apparently inconsistent with one another. Only a complete description of the reinforcement histories underlying the acquisition of each attitude can untangle these interwoven dispositions. In general, however, attitudes tend to form consistent patterns, or constellations. That is, a person who is best described as "conservative" will tend to behave predictably with regard to various political and economic issues, whereas one who is "liberal" will tend to reveal characteristically different sets of attitudes on these same issues. It would be inconsistent, for example, for someone who believed in states' rights and loose federal controls over the economy to hold a favorable attitude toward the Socialist party. To do this, the person would have to entertain simultaneously assertions that are logically incompatible. His cognitive structure, if one wishes to use this notion, would be unbalanced (Heider, 1958), and his cognitions, or ideas, would be under some internal stress to arrange themselves in the direction of greater "congruity" (Osgood and Tannenbaum, 1955). Only through the achievement of a more stable, or balanced, set of attitudes would this "cognitive dissonance" be reduced.

It is probably true, as McGuire (1960) has argued, that most of our beliefs tend to be logically related to other beliefs. And, as McGuire also suggests, individuals may tend to maintain logical consistency among their cognitions. However, it is important for us to recognize that the "laws" governing the degree of logic or illogic among propositions are imposed arbitrarily upon these particular verbal performances and do not reflect the manner in which they have been acquired. To be more explicit, if I recognize that the conclusion in a syllogism does not follow logically from the premises, it is because through my experiences in the educational system I have acquired a disposition to respond in this particular fashion to syllogisms. There is nothing intrinsic in the notations of symbolic logic to evoke a "balanced" or "unbalanced" set of cognitions in the user. To the extent that one is interested in the changes in verbal response that individuals will manifest when confronted with logical inconsistencies (or unbalanced structures), one is no longer concerned with either the acquisition or the maintenance of a particular response class. The focus of interest, rather, is on variations in the kind and frequency of specific verbal performances as a function of "rules" that the individual has learned for the manipulation of symbols. Such an endeavor consists mainly of "inventorying" the forms and contents of social behavior (to borrow a phrase from Schoenfeld, 1965), rather than analyzing the processes of acquisition and maintenance of the behavior. A great many experiments have been conducted in an attempt to verify the various predictions that can be made from cognitive theories of attitudes and attitude organization, and we shall examine several of these as examples of analysis in terms of consistency.

Consistency Theories

In somewhat droll fashion, Roger Brown (1965) has observed, "The human mind expects good things to cluster together and to be opposed to the cluster of bad things" (p. 553). He elaborates in terms of a congruity model of attitude organization, adding that ". . . positively valued objects should be linked by associative bonds and, similarly, negatively valued objects should be linked by associative bonds. Between positively valued objects and negatively valued objects there should be only dissociative bonds" (p. 553). Whenever these rules are violated, a state of disequilibrium is presumed to exist, and a tension is generated that is reduced only when equilibrium is restored. This restoration of balance or consistency is generally assumed to be accomplished by a reordering of several cognitive components that have come into imbalance.

To put these abstract principles into more concrete form, consider a lifelong Democrat who finds that in a particular election year he prefers the Republican candidate for public office. Democrats recently were faced with this situation in a case where the nominee of their party was unacceptable to many of them, and they had the choice of voting for him despite their misgivings, not voting, or voting for a Republican. One is accustomed to entertaining positive attitudes toward both his political party and its candidates. It is unsettling to find that one cannot in good conscience support the candidate of his party. In terms of consistency theory, there is a dissociative, or negative, bond between two things that ought to be associated positively. In other words, it is incongruous for one to be a Democrat and yet vote for a Republican. How is such a dilemma resolved?

There are two levels on which a situation like this can be analyzed. One involves dealing with "discrepant cognitions" and examining the alternatives that will resolve the discrepancies and restore balance or equilibrium to the stressed cognitive structure. Such an approach, in fact, has been worked out in detail by Festinger (1957), Brehm and Cohen (1962), and others of this persuasion. We will consider this approach in more detail in Chapter 11, Persuasion and Attitude Change. It is sufficient here to note that the analysis proceeds in terms of an assumed state of drive or tension that stems from dissonant cognitions and is resolved through some type of cognitive reorganization that results in either (a) the substitution of new propositions for those that cannot be reconciled with the dissonant elements, or (b) the distortion or rejection of the dissonant information.

Because the conceptual elements in balance, congruity, and dissonance theories are essentially similar, we may pursue this cognitive approach to attitude organization in terms of a convenient symbolic model suggested by Newcomb (1953). The basic elements in this system are two persons, A and B, and some object or concept of common regard, X. The attitudinal dispositions of the two persons toward one another as well as toward the object of their concern are represented by plus (+) or minus (−) signs. A positive (+) relationship implies acceptance, liking, or approach, whereas a negative (−) relationship implies rejection, dislike, or avoidance. These conceptual dispositions would each have their verbal and nonverbal counterparts, such as statements of approval or disapproval and actions indicative of a positive or a negative disposition.

Imbalance. Consider a situation that arose during 1968 with respect to the position taken by the Pope on birth control and the reactions of a number of Catholic clergymen and laymen who disagreed with this position. Borrowing Newcomb's model, let us represent a dissident priest, Father O'Donoghue, as A, Cardinal O'Boyle, a spokesman for the Pope, as B, and the Pope's encyclical on birth control as X, the referent of these two individuals' dispositions. The orientation of each party toward X is shown by plus and minus signs (see Figure 9.4, left).

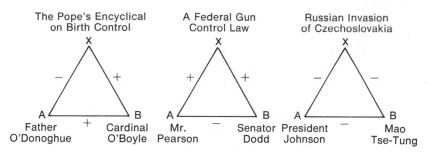

Figure 9.4
Unbalanced systems.

We may assume that Father O'Donoghue, although he believes that the use of contraceptives should be a matter of individual conscience for Catholics, nevertheless holds Cardinal O'Boyle in high esteem. The Cardinal, on the other hand, believes that he is committed to the defense of the Pope's encyclical. Hence, the situation with respect to these two individuals and this issue is in a state of imbalance. How can balance be restored? It is obvious that either Father O'Donoghue or Cardinal O'Boyle must come to agree with the same propositions with respect to artificial methods of birth control. Otherwise, each must live with the knowledge that an area of disagreement exists between two clergymen whose attitudes with respect to such an important issue should be congruent.

As another example of an unbalanced system (Figure 9.4, center) we may assume that columnist Drew Pearson probably was not a great admirer of Senator Thomas Dodd, whom he castigated at some length in his columns. At one time both Mr. Pearson and Senator Dodd advocated stricter federal controls over the sale and possession of firearms. It probably was difficult for the two to join forces in common advocacy of a gun control law because of their mutual antipathy. Again, the system is unbalanced.

Finally, we occasionally have a situation where two individuals who fail to agree on most issues and also dislike one another find themselves sharing objections to some event (Figure 9.4, right). For example, in August, 1968, Russian troops and those of certain of her satellites occupied Czechoslovakia on the pretext of forestalling a counterrevolution by pro-Western elements. Both Lyndon Johnson and Mao Tse-Tung condemned this action by Russia, becoming for the moment strange bedfellows on the international scene. Inasmuch as there were no pressures on Communist China and the United States to react jointly, the imbalance was of more heuristic than practical importance.

Balance. A balanced system, on the other hand, is one in which the two individuals involved have a positive relationship to one another as well as similar attitudes toward a common referent. While he was vice president, Hubert Humphrey, long-time friend and admirer of Lyndon Johnson, loyally supported the policies of the President with respect to American military involvement in Vietnam. This particular constellation of individuals and issues was balanced. However, when Mr. Humphrey became the Democratic nominee for president, he found his views at variance with those of many of the electorate. This constituted an unbalanced system, which he tried to restore to equilibrium by modifying his statements about Vietnam in a more "dovish" direction. That this maneuver tended to unbalance his relationship with Mr. Johnson simply demonstrates that one cannot have his cake and eat it too. Figure 9.5 illustrates several balanced systems.

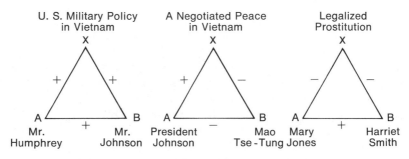

Figure 9.5
Balanced systems.

In the second balanced system in Figure 9.5, two individuals are antipathetic toward one another and also disagree about some issue or policy. President Johnson and Mao Tse-Tung probably had no great admiration for one another, and neither did they agree on many international issues, including, notably, procedures for securing a negotiated peace in Vietnam. This disagreement was consistent with their lack of mutual attraction. Finally, a common and quite obvious example of balance occurs when two individuals with positive dispositions toward one another are united in their opposition to some other person or concept. Chances are that any two housewife friends selected at random would be vigorously opposed to, not to mention horrified at, a proposal to legalize prostitution. Should one of them happen to favor such a proposal, we may be sure that the resulting imbalance would rapidly end the friendship, thus restoring balance to the system.

It should be clear by now that a determination of balance or imbalance in any of the relationships we have described is made simply by multiplying the signs. Two minuses and a plus always yield a plus, and two pluses and a minus always yield a minus. In general, we may suppose that unbalanced systems, those involving incompatible behaviors, are somehow aversive to the individuals involved. They frequently engage in behaviors that have the effect of restoring balance to the system. Balanced systems, on the other hand, provide positive reinforcement to both participants in the interaction and so tend to be maintained. The concepts employed in this type of formulation can readily be translated into behavioral language, and there would seem to be little difficulty in achieving a rapprochement between behavior theory and these essentially cognitive descriptions of attitude organization.

Attitudes and Beliefs

When we describe several methods that have been developed to measure attitudes, it will become apparent that many of the items on so-called attitude scales are actually statements of belief, to which the individual indicates either assent or dissent. The rather obvious relationship between attitudes and beliefs has captured the attention of a number of investigators. Almost any concept has, as Osgood, Suci, and Tannenbaum (1957) have shown, an evaluation dimension, a fact that places beliefs squarely in the domain of attitudes. A distinction between attitudes and beliefs has been made, however, by Fishbein and Raven (1962), who suggest that the term attitude refers to the evaluation dimension of a concept while the term belief refers to its probability or improbability. Thus, the concept "God" might be evaluated favorably by someone who disbelieved in the existence of God. In a later theoretical statement, however, Fishbein (1965) takes the position that all statements of belief have an evaluative aspect. He points out that most attitude scales are scored in terms of the extent to which a respondent indicates belief or disbelief in certain propositions. These beliefs, because they have evaluative aspects, are taken as indications of the person's attitude. It follows, therefore, that an individual's attitude toward some referent can be changed if we alter his beliefs about that referent. By the same token, we may induce a change in belief by changing a person's attitudes.

Consider the following statements, used by Fishbein to illustrate his argument:

1. *Negroes* are *good.*   4. *Negroes* are *superstitious.*
2. *Negroes* are *dirty.*   5. *Negroes* are *tall.*
3. *Negroes* are *musical.*   6. *Negroes* are *dark-skinned.*

Which of the foregoing statements represent beliefs, and which represent attitudes? Many persons would judge statements 1 and 2 as expressive of attitudes. Statements 5 and 6 would seem to represent beliefs. But considerable disagreement might arise as to whether Items 3 and 4 represent beliefs or attitudes. From Fishbein's viewpoint, all the statements represent beliefs, because each consists of an association between "Negro" and some other concept. But they also reflect attitudes, because each concept, such as "dirty," "musical," or "tall," has an evaluation dimension. Thus, if I evaluate the concept "musical" favorably, and I agree with Statement 3, then I probably also evaluate "Negroes" favorably. This general approach to the relationship between attitudes and beliefs seems to be shared by

Rokeach (1968), who defines an attitude simply as an organization of inter-related beliefs around a common object.

This view of the relationship between beliefs and attitudes is consistent with the behavioral position that we have adopted. We have analyzed the manner in which an affective response may become conditioned to a verbal performance. If the verbalization can be categorized as a belief statement, and if it has a conditioned emotional component, then it becomes one element in the behavior class comprising an attitude. If the belief has little or no affect associated with it, as in the affirmation, "Leaves are green," then it is essentially unrelated to an attitude. Dickson and McGinnies (1966) found, for example, that both religious and nonreligious subjects gave lower GSR's to statements unrelated to the church than they did to statements about the church. This view of attitudes as necessarily involving a polarization of affect in conjunction with certain expressions of belief has also been advanced by other theorists (Katz and Stotland, 1959).

Situational Control of Attitudes

Although we can sketch in broad strokes the manner in which attitudes probably have been acquired, many of the details of the acquisition process are still beyond our capacity to understand. Probably we are better equipped to assess the current status of a person's attitudes than we are to state specifically how they were learned.

Concepts in psychology, as we have noted previously, are useful only to the extent that they can be anchored to both antecedent (stimulus) and consequent (response) conditions. Even concepts which can be so defined are not of great scientific value unless they refer to entities that can be measured. Attitudes are no exception to this general principle, and techniques have been developed for locating an individual along a continuum presumed to represent varying stands on some issue. It is perhaps no surprise to learn that we rely almost exclusively upon measures of a person's verbal behavior as indicators of his attitudes. Whether or not the verbal behavior we are able to observe is a reliable predictor of other behavior, of course, is often debatable.

As Hyman (1949) has pointed out, the situations in which attitudes are measured usually differ rather dramatically from those social settings in which the attitude is expressed. One is disposed to respond in certain ways to questionnaire items and in other ways to situations requiring social interaction. Rokeach (1968) has commented that ". . . encountering a Negro on a bus in Montgomery, Alabama, will not necessarily activate the same predispositions as encountering a Negro on a bus in Paris, or in a restaurant, or in a dance hall, and consequently will not necessarily lead to the same response toward the attitude object" (p. 120).

Social situations, in other words, provide the controlling stimuli for attitudinal behavior. The verbal behaviors likely to be emitted are those prompted by stimuli relevant to these situations. The reinforcements that are contingent upon performance in the natural environment are different from those that follow expression of an attitude in the typical measurement situation. For example, someone might display verbal behavior indicative of tolerance toward ethnic minorities when being interrogated by a psychologist or sociologist; however, on those occasions when his friends provide both the controlling and reinforcing stimuli for his behavior, he may frequently volunteer expressions of prejudice toward minority racial and religious groups. Obviously, the individual has acquired performances differentially under the control of, or appropriate to, the two situations.

Direct and indirect control. How may we account for the frequently observed inconsistency between an individual's *stated* attitudes and his performance in situations related to that attitude? There is no mystery here if we remember that the stimuli controlling responses to an attitude scale are quite dissimilar to those that govern behavior in situations requiring social interaction. A response to an item on a questionnaire does not generally have the same reinforcement history as a reaction to another individual. LaPiere (1934) demonstrated this by traveling through the United States with a Chinese couple. In a total of 250 stops for food or lodging, they were refused service only once. However, when the same establishments were later contacted by mail concerning their policies with regard to accommodating Chinese, over 90 per cent of the 128 replies indicated that the proprietors were unwilling to serve them.

A similar difference in the expression of attitude-relevant behavior has been reported by Kutner, Wilkins, and Yarrow (1952). Two white women and one Negro woman arriving together were served without delay or unpleasantness by eleven restaurants in a northeastern city. When the same establishments were later asked by mail to hold reservations for a group containing both whites and Negroes, none replied. Telephone calls to these same restaurants were likewise unsuccessful in securing reservations, although five of the managers reluctantly agreed to accept the party on a nonreservation basis.

In both of these instances, it is clear that attitudes toward two minority groups would have been assessed differently from observation of direct and indirect contact between the holders and the objects of the attitudes. An unfavorable attitude was expressed in each instance only when remoteness from the objects of the attitude minimized the probability of an embarrassing or unpleasant outcome. Actual confrontation with the minority group members resulted in behavior that would have been difficult to identify with a prejudicial attitude.

Lohman and Reitzes (1954) interrogated 151 members of a property owners' association that had been organized for the purpose of resisting Negro penetration into an all-white neighborhood. Paradoxically, these individuals also belonged to a labor union that had a record of promoting

job equality for Negroes. Despite the apparent inconsistency of their attitudes in these two group situations, the persons interviewed were able to
justify their behavior in terms of the norms and beliefs that were appropriate to each setting. The situational control of behavior is again evident
in this account.

Attitudes as predictors. In a further investigation of this problem,
DeFleur and Westie (1958) devised a procedure for presenting individuals
with an "action opportunity," that is, an occasion on which they could give
public testimony of their acceptance or rejection of a Negro in a specific
context. College students were first given a questionnaire on which they
indicated by means of rating scales the degree to which they accepted
Negroes or whites in various social situations. Groups of subjects designated as relatively prejudiced or relatively unprejudiced toward Negroes
on the basis of their verbal responses were then shown colored slides depicting interracial pairs of Negroes and whites in ordinary social situations.
Following this procedure, during which the experimenters had made GSR
recordings, the subjects were asked whether or not they would be willing
to be photographed with a Negro person of the opposite sex. Their replies
could vary from willingness to have the photographs used only in laboratory experiments to willingness to have them used in a nationwide publicity
campaign advocating racial integration.

DeFleur and Westie found a significantly greater tendency for the prejudiced subjects than the unprejudiced to indicate unwillingness to being
photographed with a Negro. They argue that the results demonstrate a correspondence between attitudes measured by verbal scales and an act of
acceptance or avoidance toward the attitude object.

With respect to this experiment in particular, and attitude research in
general, we may seriously question whether asking a subject to indicate on
a printed form his intentions with regard to several alternative performances is a measure of action. If an individual responds to an attitude scale
in such a manner as to reveal prejudice, we should not be too surprised
when he responds similarly to another type of questionnaire. Both situations control approximately the same kinds of verbal behavior. In order to
really test the generalizations of their subjects' verbal reports to other
overt behavior, perhaps DeFleur and Westie should have brought the subjects into a room containing photographic equipment, a photographer, and
a Negro. Refusal by the prejudiced subjects to be photographed with the
Negro in these circumstances would have provided more compelling evidence of the power of attitude scales to predict nonverbal behavior.

After taking note of such discrepancies between verbal attitudes and
overt action as we have just reviewed, DeFleur and Westie (1963) suggest
that both of these universes of behavior are equally legitimate objects of
study; the question of when an attitude will be expressed verbally and
when in some other fashion is a matter for empirical investigation. The

emphasis that we have placed upon analyzing behavior in terms of stimulus control is also expressed by these writers. With respect to attitudes they state, "... there is ample evidence to suggest that as the normative system about the individual changes, as his group memberships change, or as he moves from one role to another, his behavior toward an attitude object will undergo corresponding alterations" (p. 27).

Green (1954) has commented on the fact that "... many investigations have found that specific acts or action attitudes often cannot be predicted very accurately from elicited verbal attitudes" (p. 340). Perhaps one reason for this rather frequent lack of correspondence among the several performances that relate to an attitude is the manner and circumstances in which these are measured. For example, we should not necessarily expect someone to behave in the same way in a psychological laboratory as he would on the street or in his own home. Yet psychologists have freely generalized about behavior in general from attitude measures taken in highly contrived and artificial circumstances.

In a critical review of this problem, Tittle and Hill (1967) point out that "... the degree of correspondence between measured attitude and other behaviors varies not only with the measure of attitude used, but also with the criterion which is taken as an indicator of behavior" (p. 202). In an empirical test of this proposition, they found that they were best able to predict behavior from a measured attitude when the behavioral criterion incorporated a wide range of activities. Specifically, student attitudes toward personal participation in campus political activity were less predictive of any single act than of a composite index of ten specific performances of a political nature. The most realistic statement we can make about attitude measures as predictors of behavior, then, is that they are useful to the extent that the testing and the criterion situations have a large number of stimulus elements in common.

Pathological Attitudes

Thus far we have not dealt with those kinds of performances that are judged as either harmful to the person himself or aversive to others. Nor will we devote much attention to this topic, which is more appropriately covered in books on personality. However, we may take note of the fact that certain behaviors expressive of attitudes may take forms that are clearly deviant from the modal patterns of a group or that are pathological in terms of their consequences to the group as a whole. Thorne (1949) has provided an instance of deviant behavior having an attitudinal basis, and he refers to "... attitudes which are so atypical, deviant, erroneous, or untenable as to constitute etiologic factors in maladjustment" (p. 2). The term *attitudinal pathosis* is suggested as a name for behavior of this type. "For example," Thorne states, "all degrees of religiosity may be ranged according to the 'normality' of the individual core attitudes from the most genuinely devout behavior to the religious fanatic, whose attitudes are completely pathological" (p. 11). He describes the behavior of a fifty-two-year-old spinster to illustrate an attitudinal pathosis of the religious type:

> Religious attitudes characterize her life. . . . She reads her Bible the first thing on arising and the last thing before retiring. She loses no opportunity to attend a religious meeting and spends most of her time in church work. The only deviation from piety occurs when someone persuades her to go to movies or do something else which makes her feel vaguely guilty. She is uneasy when in the presence of those who are not devoutly religious and has progressively limited her contacts to those whose piety she can trust. . . . In a convent, this lady would be an ideal citizen since her whole life has been dedicated to religious ideas. In a large Eastern city in 1948, she is less ideally adjusted, finding herself becoming more and more isolated from the main stream of events (p. 12).

Of course, not all attitudes involving intense emotional components need be characterized as morbid, and the case that Thorne cites represents the borderline. Some attitudes may however, lead to socially destructive consequences — as in the case of political attitudes involving militant fascism or communism. In fact, the concern of social scientists over the rise of anti-Semitism in Nazi Germany prior to World War II led to an extensive program of research by psychologists at the University of California into attitudes designated as ethnocentric and authoritarian. As described by Adorno, Frenkel-Brunswik, Levinson, and Sanford (1950), the *authoritarian personality* values obedience and respect for authority, believes in strict discipline for youth, has faith in supernatural agencies, is ultra-conservative and conventional, and feels that war and conflict are rooted in human nature. Closely allied to the authoritarian personality is the highly *ethnocentric* individual, whose prejudicial attitudes toward ethnic minorities may dispose him to acts of terrorism and violence. Scales for measuring both sets of attitudes have been found to be highly correlated.

An underlying unity seems to characterize attitudes of unyielding authoritarianism and intolerance. Rokeach (1960) takes the position that this unifying principle is to be found in the study of "belief systems," and he advances the concept of the "open and closed mind" to account for the correlations that are so frequently found among attitudes toward ideas, people, and authority. He argues that although a tolerant or egalitarian person may exhibit attitudes that are quite different from those of the authoritarian personality, he still can be described as having a "closed mind." That is, such a person may take a militant stand against segregation, he may advocate permissiveness in parent-child relationships, and he may oppose political demagogues of the "far right," yet still be authoritarian or intolerant in his own attitudes. Intolerance, or a "closed mind," therefore, is seen as a characteristic that can be applied to anyone holding intransigent attitudes; it is not necessarily peculiar to either authoritarians or bigots.

Prejudicial attitudes, whatever their nature, are generally instrumental in maintaining the individual's acceptance by a particular community. Buss (1961) has commented regarding prejudice: "It is acquired early in life and receives strong, repeated reinforcement. The normal individual acquires prejudiced behavior from those around him, and he rarely questions his own behavior, which in this instance is only right and proper and familiar — being similar to those around him" (p. 264).

Many cases of unreasonable fear or intense inhibition may be described as pathological attitudes. For example, when a child utters words or expressions that are offensive to the parents, he is usually punished. This aversive consequence has the effect both of reducing the frequency with which the utterance will occur in the presence of the parents and of generating in the child an emotional reaction to the utterance, or some variant of it, even when it is heard rather than used. Because learning of this sort frequently involves aversive control, the contribution of such experiences to the development of an attitude (say, toward sex) is readily apparent. However, the punishment of certain instrumental behaviors, such as those involved in sex or aggression, frequently occurs before the child is able to verbalize what is happening to him. The subsequent reduction in frequency of the punished performances and the increased frequency of alternative or substitute performances represent the beginning of an attitude. But the critical component in this instance is a conditioned emotional reaction rather than a relevant verbalization. It is through such early emotional conditioning that the person generates his own rewards and punishments for either avoiding or indulging in prohibited behaviors.

In simpler terms, what we are suggesting here is that an individual acquires the rudiments of certain positive or negative attitudes (approach or avoidance tendencies) early in life, before he is able to verbalize, or describe, adequately the relevant learning experiences. The entire basis of psychoanalysis rests on this assumption, and most psychotherapeutic strategies consist of attempts to assist the individual in recovering or reconstructing those early learning experiences that provided the bases for certain of his adult attitudes. When this has been accomplished, then the associated emotional reactions can be subjected to extinction procedures, if that is considered desirable. Or, certain inhibited reactions may be reinstated through reinforcement by the therapist or others. One could say that the patient has experienced a change in certain attitudes. We cannot explore this aspect of attitudes here, but an approach to psychotherapy in terms of learning principles similar to those that we have employed has been elaborated by Dollard and Miller (1950).

Manipulation by Reinforcement

Relatively little experimental work has been done on the control of attitudes by reinforcement, probably because it is difficult in the laboratory to provide contingencies that would be sufficiently powerful to either establish new attitudes or modify existing ones. When we attempt to measure attitudes by any of the techniques just described, we are, after all, merely tapping into a complex verbal repertoire that has been acquired and maintained by a host of social influences over which we have little or no control. It is probably somewhat presumptuous at the current stage of our knowledge to think that we can significantly modify these dispositions, although a considerable amount of research has been directed toward validating various theories of persuasion. We will review some of this work in Chapter 11. For now, let us consider briefly an experiment in which the investigator was successful, through selective reinforcement, in increasing the frequency with which subjects responded in a particular way to items on two related attitude scales.

Singer (1961) undertook to discover whether the responses of subjects to a scale measuring authoritarianism could be modified through verbal reinforcement, and whether this effect would generalize to performance on a scale measuring ethnocentrism. He selected sixty items from the California F Scale, which was devised as a measure of authoritarian, or antidemocratic, attitudes by Adorno, Frenkel-Brunswik, Levinson, and Sanford (1950). We have already described some of the characteristics of those who score high in authoritarianism. Table 9.1 lists a few items of the kind found in this scale. As a matter of additional interest, we have included some data obtained by Hyman and Sheatsley (1954) on the manner in which groups of college, high school, and grammar school students responded to these items.

Table 9.1
Responses of students to selected items from the California F Scale.

Item*	Per Cent Agreeing		
	College	High school	Grammar school
There are two kinds of people in the world: the weak and the strong.	30	53	71
The most important thing to teach children is obedience to their parents.	35	60	80
Any good leader would be strict with people under him in order to gain their respect.	36	51	66
No decent man can respect a woman who has had sex relations before marriage.	14	26	39

* From the F Scale, in *The Authoritarian Personality*, by T. W. Adorno *et al.* (New York: Harper, 1950). Copyright 1950 by The American Jewish Committee. Reprinted by permission of Harper and Row, Publishers.

Singer chose as subjects for his experiment only those subjects who, on the basis of their scores on the complete F Scale, displayed relatively non-authoritarian, or pro-democratic, attitudes. Specifically, he chose subjects who responded in a pro-democratic manner to between half and three quarters of the items on the scale. This meant that they would have a fairly high initial operant level for responses of this type and, thus, could effectively be reinforced for a pro-democratic performance. The subjects met a similar criterion on an ethnocentrism scale, the E Scale. This questionnaire was designed by the authors of the F Scale to detect the degree to which one is prejudiced toward minority ethnic groups. Two of the items on this scale are as follows:[*]

There may be a few exceptions, but in general Jews are pretty much alike.

Negroes have their rights, but it is best to keep them in their own districts and schools and to prevent too much contact with whites.

Subjects who attained the same scores (forty-eight in all) were paired, and one member of each pair was assigned to an experimental group; the other members of the pairs made up a control group. The experimenter met with the experimental subjects and read aloud each statement on the F Scale. Whenever the subjects responded in a pro-democratic manner, the experimenter said "Good" or "Right." He read the same statements to the control subjects and recorded their responses without comment. Following this procedure, the experimenter met with half of the experimental subjects and read aloud statements on the E Scale, merely recording their replies. The remaining half of this group filled out the scale by themselves with the experimenter not present. An identical procedure was followed with the control subjects.

Thus, all of the experimental subjects were reinforced for responding in a pro-democratic fashion to the items on the F Scale. Half of them later responded to the items on the E Scale read aloud by the experimenter, while the remaining half did so alone. Did the reinforcement operation increase the frequency of pro-democratic responses, and was there any transfer of this effect to performance on the E Scale, either with or without the experimenter present? Figure 9.6 shows the results obtained by Singer in both the learning and the transfer situations.

The experimental subjects were clearly influenced by the experimenter's selective reinforcement of pro-democratic responses, while no such effect was found in the control group. There was a transfer of the effects of reinforcement to those experimental subjects who responded to the E Scale in the presence of the experimenter. This effect was greatly reduced when

[*] From the E Scale, in *The Authoritarian Personality*, by T. W. Adorno *et al.* (New York: Harper, 1950). Copyright 1950 by The American Jewish Committee. Reprinted by permission of Harper and Row, Publishers.

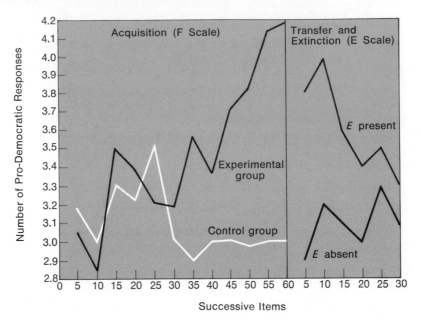

Figure 9.6

The acquisition of pro-democratic responses by reinforced subjects and the generalization of similar responses by these subjects to related items in the presence and in the absence of the experimenter. (After Singer, 1961)

the experimenter was absent during testing. These data demonstrate the complex situational control of attitudinal behavior. For example, the "acquisition" situation was such as to elicit the cooperation of the subjects in what they undoubtedly perceived as the "demand characteristics" of the situation. The author interrogated his subjects afterward about their awareness of the contingency between their responses and comments "Good" or "Right" by the experimenter. Although he reports that they had a "low level of awareness," he also states that the aware subjects were more subject to influence. That the subjects were responding in a manner designed to please the experimenter is further suggested by the fact that the transfer effect to the E Scale was not significant when the experimenter was not present. It is probable that certain similarities in the attitudinal referents of the items on the authoritarian and ethnocentrism scales became apparent to the subjects and that they therefore tended to react to the E Scale in the experimenter's presence according to the reinforcement contingencies that had obtained during their previous performance on the F Scale. No delayed measure of attitudes was taken, so we do not know whether the observed effect had any permanence. The behavior modification, in any case, appeared to be limited to the presence of the experimenter as an agent of reinforcement. There was evidence that the items on the two attitude scales were clues for verbal performances that belonged in part to the same response class. This, of course, is not surprising in view of the positive correlation known to exist between scores on the authoritarian and ethnocentrism scales.

Still another attempt to devise controlled conditions in which an attitude might be formed was conducted by Lott and Lott (1960). They tested the assumption that if a person is rewarded by his fellow group members, he will develop positive attitudes toward them. The subjects in this experiment were forty-eight children attending the third and fifth grades. Sixteen groups of three members each were formed for the purpose of playing a game called "Rocket Ship." It should be noted that each group of three contained children who had not previously chosen one another on a sociometric questionnaire. The object of the game was to land a cardboard rocket ship on a planetary objective by way of a "safe" or a "dangerous" path. The experimenter, of course, controlled this feature of the situation and could arbitrarily reward or punish the subjects, regardless of which choice they made. Half of the subjects were allowed to "land safely," while half were prevented from doing so by a signal from the experimenter that they had chosen an unsafe path and their ship had been blown up. Those who reached their objective had been promised rewards in the form of plastic car models.

Inasmuch as the children played the game in groups of three, it is obvious that either success or failure at the game was experienced by each child in the presence of two others. Later in the day, the teacher gave the children another sociometric questionnaire on which they could nominate two other children as companions on a trip with their parents to a "nearby star out in space." Lott and Lott report that the proportion of play-group members chosen by rewarded subjects was significantly greater than the proportion chosen by nonrewarded subjects. Thus, the prediction that positive attitudes toward other persons will be formed by one who experiences reward in their presence appears to have been confirmed. The findings not only follow readily from reinforcement principles but conform to what we can observe in everyday experience.

Summary   An attitude is defined broadly as a class of related performances that are controlled by the referent, or object, of the attitude. Attitudes are learned and seem to have identifiable emotional, cognitive, and behavioral components. Physiological measures as well as verbal expressions of affect are taken as indicators of the emotional component. Cognitive responses are considered here as consisting of implicit verbalizations that are prompted by occasions similar to those on which the attitude has been reinforced. Such covert reactions may serve as cues to an overt performance. One's performance in a social situation, however, does not necessarily correspond to one's responses on a questionnaire, or attitude scale. Situational factors are paramount in controlling attitudinal behavior, and a testing situation may not evoke the same kind of performance that occurs in direct confrontation with another person.

Attitudes are acquired and maintained by the social consequences that they have for the individual. When a certain class of performances either increases or decreases in frequency as a result of having been selectively reinforced or punished, and when these performances have verbal and emotional components indicative of acceptance or rejection of some social object, we say that the individual has acquired an attitude. Attitudes tend to be expressed only in those social groups where they are reinforced. Apparent inconsistencies in attitudinal behavior thus are explained in terms of specific agents of stimulus control.

Children may acquire attitudes from merely observing the behavior of someone else who is either rewarded or punished following certain actions or who has a known history of success or failure. Attitudes tend to be organized into consistent, or predictable, patterns. Various theories have been proposed to account for the manner of such organization as well as for the conditions in which inconsistency will be resolved. To the extent that an attitude involves beliefs about the attitude object, any change in the individual's beliefs will tend to bring about a corresponding change in related attitudes. Similarly, a change in the emotional reaction elicited by the object of an attitude will be reflected in those performances normally expressive of the attitude.

Relatively little research has been directed toward the experimental shaping of attitudes using reinforcement procedures. The few studies that have been reported seem to indicate that such shaping is possible, at least within the limitations of the laboratory setting. Deep-seated attitudes, however, are the products of extensive reinforcement histories in the natural environment, and it is unlikely that these learning experiences can be duplicated experimentally. However, it is possible to analyze attitude acquisition and maintenance within the framework of behavior theory and, thereby, arrive at a better understanding of much social behavior.

References

ADORNO, T. W., FRENKEL-BRUNSWIK, ELSE, LEVINSON, D. J., and SANFORD, R. N. *The authoritarian personality.* New York: Harper, 1950.

BANDURA, A.   Social learning through imitation. In M. R. Jones (Ed.), *Nebraska symposium on motivation.* Lincoln, Neb.; University of Nebraska Press, 1962.

BANDURA, A., and WALTERS, R. H.   *Social learning and personality development.* New York: Holt, Rinehart and Winston, 1963.

BREHM, J. W., and COHEN, A. R.   *Explorations in cognitive dissonance.* New York: Wiley, 1962.

BROWN, R.   *Social psychology.* New York: The Free Press, 1965.

BUSS, A. II.   *The psychology of aggression.* New York: Wiley, 1961.

CAMPBELL, D. T.   Social attitudes and other acquired behavioral dispositions. In S. Koch (Ed.), *Psychology: A study of a science.* Vol. 6. New York: McGraw-Hill, 1963.

COOPER, J. B.   Emotion in prejudice. *Science,* 1959, *130,* 314–318.

DEFLEUR, M. L., and WESTIE, F. R.   Verbal attitudes and overt acts: An experiment on the salience of attitudes. *American Journal of Sociology,* 1958, *23,* 667–673.

DEFLEUR, M. L., and WESTIE, F. R.   Attitude as a scientific concept. *Social Forces,* 1963, *42,* 17–31.

DICKSON, HOLLIDA W., and MCGINNIES, E.   Affectivity in the arousal of attitudes as measured by galvanic skin response. *American Journal of Psychology,* 1966, *79,* 584–589.

DOLLARD, J., and MILLER, N. E.   *Personality and psychotherapy.* New York: McGraw-Hill, 1950.

DOOB, L.   The behavior of attitudes. *Psychological Review,* 1947, *54,* 135–156.

EISMAN, BERNICE J. Attitude formation: The development of a color preference through mediated generalization. *Journal of Abnormal and Social Psychology,* 1955, *50,* 321–326.

FESTINGER, L.   *A theory of cognitive dissonance.* Evanston, Ill.: Row, Peterson, 1957.

FISHBEIN, M.   A consideration of beliefs, attitudes, and their relationship. In I. D. Steiner and M. Fishbein (Eds.), *Current studies in social psychology.* New York: Holt, Rinehart and Winston, 1965.

FISHBEIN, M., and RAVEN, B. H.   The AB scales: An operational definition of belief and attitude. *Human Relations,* 1962, *15,* 35–44.

GREEN, B. F.   Attitude measurement. Chapter 9 in G. Lindzey (Ed.), *Handbook of social psychology,* Reading, Mass.: Addison-Wesley, 1954.

HEIDER, F.   *The psychology of interpersonal relations.* New York: Wiley, 1958.

HYMAN, H.   Inconsistencies as a problem in attitude measurement. *Journal of Social Issues,* 1949, *5,* 38–42.

HYMAN, H. H., and SHEATSLEY, P. B.   The authoritarian personality: A methodological critique. In R. Christie and Marie Jahoda (Eds.), *Studies in the scope and method of "the authoritarian personality."* New York: The Free Press, 1954.

KATZ, D., and STOTLAND, E.   A preliminary statement to a theory of attitude structure and change. In S. Koch (Ed.), *Psychology: A study of a science.* Vol. 3. New York: McGraw-Hill, 1959.

KERLINGER, F. N.   Social attitudes and their criterial referents: A structural theory. *Psychological Review,* 1967, *74,* 110–122.

KUTNER, B., WILKINS, C., and YARROW, P. R.   Verbal attitudes and overt behavior involving racial prejudice. *Journal of Abnormal and Social Psychology,* 1952, *47,* 649–652.

LAPIERE, R. T.   Attitudes vs. actions. *Social Forces,* 1934, *13,* 230–237.

LOHMAN, J. D., and REITZES, D. C.   Deliberately organized groups and racial behavior. *American Sociological Review,* 1954, *19,* 342–348.

LOTT, BERNICE E., and LOTT, A. J.   The formation of positive attitudes toward group members. *Journal of Abnormal and Social Psychology*, 1960, *61*, 297–300.

LUNDIN, R. W.   *Personality: An experimental approach*. New York: Macmillan, 1961.

McGINNIES, E., and AIBA, H.   Persuasion and emotional response: A cross-cultural study. *Psychological Reports*, 1965, *16*, 503–510.

McGUIRE, W. S.   A syllogistic analysis of cognitive relationships. In M. J. Rosenberg, C. I. Hovland, W. J. McGuire, R. P. Abelson, and J. W. Brehm, *Attitude organization and change*. New Haven: Yale University Press, 1960.

MILLENSON, J. R.   *Principles of behavioral analysis*. New York: Macmillan, 1967.

MISCHEL, W., and LIEBERT, R. M.   Effects of discrepancies between observed and imposed reward criteria on their acquisition and transmission. *Journal of Personality and Social Psychology*, 1966, *3*, 45–53.

NEWCOMB, T. M.   An approach to the study of communicative acts. *Psychological Review*, 1953, *60*, 393–404.

OSGOOD, C. E., and TANNENBAUM, P. H.   The principle of congruity in the prediction of attitude change. *Psychological Review*, 1955, *62*, 42–55.

OSGOOD, C. E., SUCI, G. J., and TANNENBAUM, P. H.   *The measurement of meaning*. Urbana, Ill.: University of Illinois Press, 1957.

PORIER, G. W., and LOTT, A. J.   Galvanic skin responses and prejudice. *Journal of Personality and Social Psychology*, 1967, *5*, 253–259.

RANKIN, R. E., and CAMPBELL, D. T.   Galvanic skin response to Negro and white experimenters. *Journal of Abnormal and Social Psychology*, 1955, *51*, 30–33.

RAZRAN, G. H. S.   Conditioning away social bias by the luncheon technique. *Psychological Bulletin*, 1938, *35*, 693.

RAZRAN, G. H. S.   Conditioned response changes in rating and appraising sociopolitical slogans. *Psychological Bulletin*, 1940, *37*, 481.

REMMERS, H. H.   *Introduction to opinion and attitude measurement*. New York: Harper, 1954.

RHINE, R. J.   A concept-formation approach to attitude acquisition. *Psychological Review*, 1958, *65*, 362–370.

ROKEACH, M.   *The open and closed mind*. New York: Basic Books, 1960.

ROKEACH, M.   *Beliefs, attitudes, and values*. San Francisco: Jossey-Bass, 1968.

ROSENBERG, M. J., and HOVLAND, C. I.   Cognitive, affective, and behavioral components of attitudes. Chapter 1 in Rosenberg *et al.*, *Attitude organization and change*. New Haven: Yale University Press, 1960.

SCHOENFELD, W. N.   Learning theory and social psychology. In O. Klineberg and R. Christie (Eds.), *Perspectives in social psychology*. New York: Holt, Rinehart and Winston, 1965.

SINGER, R. D.   Verbal conditioning and generalization of pro-democratic responses. *Journal of Abnormal and Social Psychology*, 1961, *63*, 43–46.

SKINNER, B. F.   *Verbal behavior*. New York: Appleton-Century-Crofts, 1957.

STAATS, A. W., and STAATS, CAROLYN K.   Attitudes established by classical conditioning. *Journal of Abnormal and Social Psychology*, 1958, *57*, 37–40.

STAATS, A. W., and STAATS, CAROLYN K. *Complex human behavior.* New York: Holt, Rinehart and Winston, 1963.

STAATS, A. W., STAATS, CAROLYN K., and HEARD, W. G.   Denotative meaning established by classical conditioning. *Journal of Experimental Psychology,* 1961, *61,* 300–303.

THORNE, F. C.   The attitudinal pathoses. *Journal of Clinical Psychology,* 1949, 5,   1–21.

TITTLE, C. R., and HILL, R. J.   Attitude measurement and prediction of behavior: An evaluation of conditions and measurement techniques. *Sociometry,* 1967, *30,* 199–213.

WESTIE, F. R., and DEFLEUR, M. L.   Autonomic responses and their relationship to race attitudes. *Journal of Abnormal and Social Psychology,* 1959, 58, 340–347.

10

Attitude and
Opinion Measurement

In the previous chapter we alluded to the use of attitude scales, but we did not elaborate on the several methods by which attitudes are measured. Because the terms attitude and opinion are often used interchangeably, we will consider jointly the methodologies that have been developed for their study. In general terms, it may be said that attitudes and opinions both represent dispositions involving approval or disapproval, approach or avoidance with regard to controversial matters. One does not ordinarily have an attitude toward trees or an opinion about the multiplication table, even though one may decline to climb trees or may dislike mathematics. Many persons do, however, have attitudes toward *apartheid* in South Africa, and others have opinions about the wearing of beards by public figures.

Why do we speak of an *attitude* in one instance and an *opinion* in the other? One answer to this question is provided in the distinction between these terms made by Sargent and Williamson (1966):

> The two concepts, attitude and opinion, are often used synonymously, although psychologists sometimes make a distinction between them. Attitudes are treated as fairly consistent and lasting tendencies to behave in certain ways — primarily positively or negatively — toward persons, activities, events, and objects. Some would say they reflect the deeper, inner core of personality. Opinions are considered closer to the conscious level, more transient, and more likely to be verbalized than are attitudes. Some, indeed, consider opinions the verbal expressions of attitudes (p. 473).

If any useful distinction can be made between attitudes and opinions, it is probably one that emphasizes (a) the extent of their generality, and (b) their degrees of affective involvement. Attitudes, as we have noted, are reflected in a number of related performances, as in the case of religiosity, patriotism, or prejudice. An opinion, on the other hand, is revealed by verbal expressions of belief or intent with respect to specific people, issues, or events. Operationally, the expression of an opinion is generally prompted by a single question, whereas an attitude is revealed in one's performance on a series of related items comprising a scale. Not only is a wider range of performances mediated by an attitude than by an opinion, but such performances tend more often to have a pronounced emotional component. One may, for example, have an attitude toward the church, but one is said to have an opinion about using public funds for busing children to private schools. The two are not unrelated, but the attitude represents a wider range of predictable activities than does the opinion.

It might even be suggested that attitudes, since they are dispositions to respond predictably in a number of different situations, are the bases from which opinions relevant to particular issues are generated. Someone with a generally "conservative" political outlook can be expected to express a more favorable opinion about the Republican candidate for a public office than for the Democratic or Socialist party candidates. He will also react predictably to new legislation dealing with corporation tax benefits or protective tariffs. Opinions on specific issues such as these represent components of that broader spectrum of response dispositions that we call attitudes.

Occasionally, individuals will express opinions on issues about which they have little or no information and in which their emotional involvement is minimal. This happens, probably, because people are expected to have opinions on public issues, and one is reinforced more frequently for expressing partisanship on controversial matters than for professing either ignorance or disinterest. Even so, public opinion polls frequently report a substantial proportion of the persons interviewed as having "no opinion" on an issue; whether such persons display the same diffidence in conversation with their friends is questionable. In any case, opinions are often communicated without the degree of affect that is evident with strong attitudes. Albig (1956) mentions the drama critic who when rebuked for having slept through the last act of a play about which he was to write an opinion replied, "Sir, sleep is an opinion" (p. 2).

Opinion Formation

Opinions may be adopted and discarded with a fair degree of abandon, depending upon the circumstances. Unlike attitudes, which are usually acquired early in life and have a long history of social support, opinions frequently follow public events. As events change, so do opinions. Thus, the American public expressed strong support for military intervention in the Vietnam conflict until it became apparent that the enemy was likely to continue the struggle indefinitely. Then public opinion began to swing in favor of a negotiated settlement. We do not know the extent to which other factors, such as the public utterances of a number of distinguished citizens who opposed the war, contributed to this opinion change. We may be reasonably certain, however, that most opinions are expressed with deference to the reactions they are likely to elicit from other persons. "In middle-class American society," Albig (1956) observes, "one does not ordinarily sympathetically discuss the theories of Karl Marx in the meeting of the local Chamber of Commerce, engage in excessive profanity and obscenity before one's grandmother and her associates, or address the Catholic Women's League on birth control" (p. 245).

Opinion formation may be viewed as a special case of social influence. The influence may be direct, as in face-to-face interaction, or indirect through contact with the mass media of radio, press, and television. Attitudes and opinions have functional utility in that they serve as vehicles both for prompting and for reinforcing a variety of communicative acts. As such, they make up a substantial part of ordinary conversation. A number of social scientists have recognized a distinction between "public" and "private" attitudes and opinions. These terms refer to the frequency with which a particular disposition is expressed openly or covertly. We could imagine, for example, a situation in which a person delivers himself of an opinion that he expects will be favorably received by a high status listener but mutters something quite the contrary to himself as soon as he is out of earshot. It is probably not meaningful to ask what a person's *real* opinion is on an issue. Rather, we should ask what kind of an opinion he is likely to express in a given set of circumstances.

Kelman (1961) has suggested three processes of social influence which he relates to the formation and change of opinions. He refers to these as compliance, identification, and internalization. In *compliance* an individual is under direct positive or aversive control by others. One might, for example, come to express certain opinions as a means of being accepted into a particular social group or to avoid being fired from a job in which certain opinions are expected of the employees. "Opinions adopted through compliance," says Kelman, "should be expressed only when the person's behavior is observable by the influencing agent" (p. 64).

Identification is said to occur when the individual adopts the attitudes and beliefs of others as part of a reciprocal role relationship. The behavior is manifested both publicly and privately and does not depend upon observation by the influencing agent. But opinions adopted through identification are not necessarily integrated with other attitudes that the individual holds, and they depend upon social support. Thus, the radicalism that many college students display both in the United States and abroad could be said to incorporate opinions adopted temporarily as a result of identification with a peer group in which such opinions are valued. After graduation, when the individual acquires new affiliations and adopts a different role, the radicalism of the college years is often quite suddenly replaced with more conservative behaviors.

Finally, using the term *internalization*, Kelman refers to the acquisition or modification of an opinion because it is congruent with other opinions that the individual holds. The content of the induced behavior is intrinsically reinforcing, quite apart from the reactions it induces in others. Internalized opinions may thus compete with socially more acceptable responses simply because they are more self-rewarding. For example, a visitor to a foreign country might discover certain patterns of behavior — say Zen Buddhism — that are more in keeping with certain of his attitudes than are the patterns of his home country. He might retain them for this reason and not because they are either externally reinforced or prerequisite to any role relationships that he enjoys in his own country.

Attitude Scaling Procedures

In the case of attitude scales, we are limited to sampling from a verbal repertoire rather than from nonverbal performances that might be more meaningful expressions of an attitude. Green (1954) has commented on this situation as follows: "From a sample of verbal responses to questions about opinions, one should not make inferences about behavior other than verbal responses to similar verbal questions. It may be that responses to these verbal questions are correlated with responses in nonverbal situations, but this must be determined experimentally" (p. 336). Green suggests that we distinguish among three different indicators of attitudes. When we sample from an individual's verbal repertoire, we are studying his *elicited verbal attitudes.* In normal conversation with his friends, an individual is apt to express *spontaneous verbal attitudes.* Finally, behavior directed by someone toward the actual referent of his attitudes is called an *action attitude.* Performances in these three catagories may or may not be highly correlated with one another.

So far as most psychological research is concerned, attention has been focused on elicited verbal attitudes. The vehicle for eliciting the verbal expression of an attitude is called an attitude questionnaire, or scale. A number of techniques are available to elicit and to quantify attitudes as they are expressed verbally. We will examine briefly the manner in which several instruments for attitude measurement have been developed and applied.

Thurstone-Type Scales

One of the more interesting techniques for measuring attitudes is that described over forty years ago by Thurstone and Chave (1929). The procedures for selecting items, as well as the actual steps followed in building the scale, are fairly simple. First, the objectives of constructing the scale must be kept in mind. Our goal is to present the respondent with an occasion on which he can respond to a number of statements that represent different facets of an attitude on some subject. His responses to the items on the scale are then presumed to be indicative of the class of performances that constitute his attitude. In short, we assume that his responses to the scale items will be a direct function of what Lazarsfeld (1950) has called his "latent attitude."

Item selection. How are items for the scale selected? We cannot arbitrarily designate any particular group of statements as being representative samples of the attitude universe under investigation. The selection of appropriate items must be done empirically. An initial step in constructing a Thurstone-type scale, therefore, is to select a large number of statements that seem to sample the broad range of all possible attitudinal positions. Let us represent certain of the assumptions underlying this approach with a simple diagram. It is assumed that the scale items can be ordered along a continuum, the opposite poles of which represent extremely favorable and extremely unfavorable attitudes on the issue under consideration.

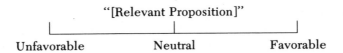

"[Relevant Proposition]"

Unfavorable   Neutral   Favorable

If the referent of the attitude scale is the church, then it is assumed that all possible attitudes toward the church can be ordered along this continuum. How are we to determine the point, or position, or value, on this scale that a particular statement should be assigned? According to Thurstone's procedure, a large number of judges are assigned the task of placing the collected statements into *eleven* piles, assumed to be equidistant from one another, and identified only by the letters A through K. Those statements which a judge deems least favorable toward the church are placed in pile A; those which he considers most favorable are sorted into pile K. Statements representing intermediate positions he assigns, as seems appropriate, to the intervening categories. Only the extremes and the center, or neutral point, on the continuum are identified as such to the judges.

The judges will not all agree concerning the exact positioning of each item to be scaled, and it is necessary to eliminate those statements that are ambiguous, that is, that were assigned by different judges to widely discrepant positions. Statement 41, for example, may have been assigned as follows by three judges:

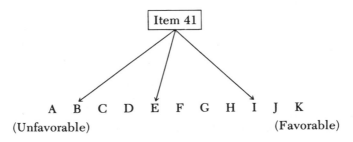

Item 41

A   B   C   D   E   F   G   H   I   J   K
(Unfavorable)   (Favorable)

Because this statement is considered by the judges to vary all the way from "very unfavorable" to "moderately favorable," it obviously is the occasion for a variety of judgmental responses and does not merit inclusion among the final scale items. Item 56, on the other hand, may have been assigned as follows:

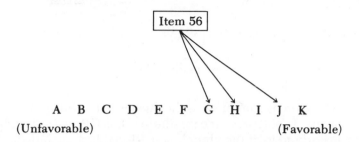

$$\boxed{\text{Item 56}}$$

A B C D E F G H I J K
(Unfavorable)   (Favorable)

Although agreement among the judges is not perfect on this item, it is considerably closer than on Item 41. This statement should probably be retained for the final scale. It seems to represent a moderately favorable attitude. By following this procedure, we select for the attitude scale only those items which show a relatively small degree of dispersion among the judges' ratings (see Figure 10.1).

From the statements that meet this criterion of interjudge agreement an arbitrary number are then selected so that their positions along the continuum are approximately equidistant from one another. The exact scale value of each statement is computed as the *median* value of the positions assigned to it by the judges when the lettered positions A through K are given values 1 through 11. The items are then arranged in random order, and the respondent has only to place checkmarks beside those statements with which he is in agreement. (The scale values are not, of course, shown

Figure 10.1

Cumulative proportions of judges who assigned attitude statements to different scale positions for a "good" item and a "bad" item. (Adapted from Thurstone and Chave, 1929)

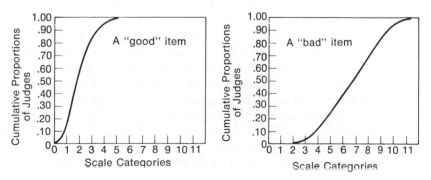

to the respondent.) To make this perfectly clear, let us assume that Individual X has endorsed the following statements concerning the church, and that each statement has the scale value indicated in parentheses:

> I believe that the church is losing ground as education advances. (3.8)

> I am slightly prejudiced against the church and attend only on special occasions. (4.2)

> I feel that the church is pretty easily disturbed by matters of little importance. (3.0)

> I believe that the church is nonscientific, depending for its influence upon fear of God and hell. (2.0)

The subject's score is computed as the mean scale value of the statements he has endorsed. In the present case, the score is 3.3, indicating that Individual X's attitude toward the church is moderately antagonistic. We may represent his position on the attitude continuum as follows:

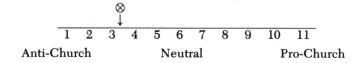

We should take note of one potential drawback to Thurstone's scaling method, namely, the assumption that the attitudes of the judges do not influence the manner in which they assign scale positions to items from the original pool. It was found by Hovland and Sherif (1952) that judges holding extreme positions and having a high degree of personal involvement with respect to some issue made finer distinctions among items that fell near their own position on the scale. They tended to lump together items representing a position that they themselves rejected. Ward (1965) has cautioned further that extremity of attitude as a factor influencing the position to which a judge assigns an item along a scale should not be confused with personal *involvement* in the issue. He contacted sixty students, all of whom held extremely favorable attitudes toward Negroes. Forty of these students had actually picketed a movie theater in North Carolina to protest racial segregation. Before they judged the favorability of a number of items relating to Negroes, half of the pickets were reminded of their demonstration, and half were not so reminded. Degree of involvement in the issue of racial tolerance was thus made to have maximum salience for one group of pickets, somewhat less salience for a second group of pickets, and minimal salience for a third group, who had never picketed.

Ward reports that the greater the degree of involvement of the subjects, the more negatively the Negro statements were judged. Thus, both extremity of attitude and personal involvement in the issue predisposed the judges to assign statements along a scale differently than if they had held more moderate positions. Problems such as these in developing a set of equally spaced statements relative to some attitudinal referent have probably discouraged many researchers from attempting to develop Thurstone-type scales.

Reliability and validity. Two additional problems that must be faced concern the *reliability* and the *validity* of our conclusion about X's attitude toward the church. By reliability is meant the extent to which the measuring instrument will yield consistent results. Validity refers to the accuracy with which the instrument measures what it purports to measure.

Reliability of a test or an attitude scale is determined generally in one of three ways: (a) by determining the correlation between test and retest scores on a sample of respondents; (b) by correlating scores on the first half of the test with those on the second half; and (c) by correlating scores on even-numbered items with those on odd-numbered items. In assessing the reliability of their original scale of attitudes toward the church, Thurstone and Chave used a modification of the third method, being careful that the average scale values of the two alternate forms were nearly identical. Using two hundred college freshmen as subjects, the investigators determined the reliability of their scale to be 0.92, which is very high indeed. A scatter plot representing a correlation of this magnitude might look like the one shown in Figure 10.2.

The question of the validity of any scale is a much thornier one to answer. Here we face the problem of determining whether an individual's endorsements of certain statements about the church are actually indicative of his behavior in general toward the church and its symbols. If the score that an individual obtains on the scale is viewed as having *predictive validity*, then it is assumed that certain *criterion* measures exist from which the predictive power of the scale can be determined. What might such criterion behavior consist of in this instance? Thurstone and Chave assumed,

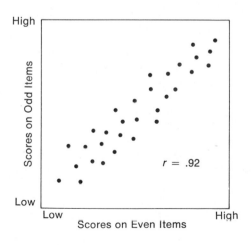

$r = .92$

Figure 10.2
Scatter plot representing a correlation coefficient of .92.

for one thing, that divinity students should attain scores indicating more favorable attitudes toward the church than nondivinity students. Divinity students did, in fact, endorse on the average more of the favorable statements than did members of any of the other groups tested. It was also found that Catholics, Protestants, and Jews ranked in that order with respect to acceptance of the church. Finally, active church members as well as individuals who attended church more frequently obtained scores indicating more favorable attitudes than both nonchurch members and those who attended church infrequently. This particular relationship is shown in Figure 10.3. These findings provided convincing evidence that the verbal behavior tapped by the scale is consistent with a variety of performances exhibited on other occasions where the church, or its conceptual representations, provide the controlling stimuli.

Likert-Type Scales

In responding to items on scales of the type just described the individual is given no opportunity to indicate the extent of his agreement with the items that he checks. Each statement must be either accepted or rejected *in toto.* In 1932, Likert described an alternative method of attitude scale construction whereby the respondent expressed the *degree* of his agreement or disagreement with the scale items. Since this basic technique — known as the method of *summated ratings* — is widely used today, we shall consider it in some detail.

Item selection. The initial step in constructing a Likert scale is similar to that employed by Thurstone, namely, the collection of a large number of

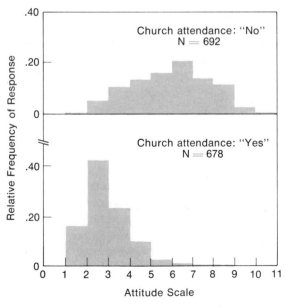

Distributions of attitude scores among active church members and among those who do not attend church. (After Thurstone and Chave, 1929)

assertions dealing with the issue in question. These are then presented to a group of respondents, generally not less than one hundred, whose task is to indicate the extent of their agreement or disagreement with each statement. This is generally accomplished by providing each statement with a rating scale containing five or more choices. Here is an example of such a statement with five categories of acceptance or rejection:

I believe church membership is almost essential to living life at its best.

    Strongly   Disagree   Undecided   Agree   Strongly
    disagree   agree

The respondent is instructed to place a checkmark (✔) over the position that best describes his reaction to the statement. It should be emphasized that the person responding to the statements is supposed to make a choice for *every* statement. He does not simply mark those items with which he agrees, as in the case of a Thurstone-type scale.

The experimenter has determined in advance how he will score each item. For example, if the statement above is one of many comprising a scale of attitudes toward the church, then a score of 5 might be assigned to the "Strongly agree" position and a score of 1 to "Strongly disagree." An assumption is made that *agreement* with the statement indicates a positive attitude toward the church and that disagreement represents a negative attitude. Other items on the scale would be worded so that disagreement is scored as 5 and agreement as 1. For example:

I believe the church is full of hypocrites, and I have no use for it.

    Strongly   Disagree   Undecided   Agree   Strongly
    disagree   agree

In this case, *disagreement* would indicate a favorable disposition toward the church. By scoring each statement in this manner, we have determined that a high total score will indicate a favorable attitude toward the church and a low score an unfavorable attitude. Of course, some items on the scale may appear not to be measuring the same disposition that most of the other items are measuring. Such a statement might be: "I do not think the church is essential to Christianity."

Most persons who achieved a low score on the total scale, indicating a negative attitude toward the church, probably agreed with this item, since it reflects their antipathy toward the church as an institution. But many of the persons who scored high on the scale, indicating a positive attitude toward the church, may also have indicated agreement with this statement.

That is, they are favorably disposed toward the church, perhaps for social or political reasons, and do not actually identify it with religious conviction. This statement, in brief, lacks *discriminating power*. It may be agreed to equally often by individuals whose total scores place them on opposite sides of the attitude continuum. Such statements can be eliminated by an *item analysis* of the scores from a sample of respondents to the items. This procedure consists, in essence, of determining the correlation between the score for each item on the scale and the total score. Items having low correlations with the total score are discarded as being nondiscriminating. An offending item of the type just described might reveal the following scatter plot:

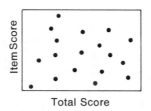

Total Score

We can see from inspecting the scatter diagram that individuals whose overall scores reveal positive attitudes toward the church are no less likely to agree with this item than individuals whose total scores reflect negative attitudes. Since the item does not differentiate between those who support and those who oppose the church, it is eliminated from the item pool. In general, those items that show the highest correlations with total score are retained for use in the final scale.

In some cases, it is desirable to allow more response categories for each statement on the scale, say seven, nine, or eleven. If the investigator wants to force a division of subjects into those who are favorable and those who are unfavorable with regard to the attitudinal referent, he may elect to use a scale with an even number of categories. This type of scale dichotomizes readily and eliminates the problem of what to do with persons who score in the exact center of the scale. Individuals whose scores place them at the center of the attitude continuum are a problem anyway, since we do not know whether their scores reflect neutrality, uncertainty, or confusion. The same is true, of course, in the case of a Thurstone scale, where an individual might achieve a "neutral" score by endorsing an equivalent number of positive and negative statements.

Reliability and validity. These characteristics of rating scales, as instruments for measuring attitudes, are determined in essentially the same way as for a Thustone-type scale. Internal reliability, assessed in terms of the correlation between odd- and even-numbered items, is probably more widely used than test-retest reliability. The trouble with the latter method is that individuals tend to remember how they answered the items on the initial testing occasion, so that their scores on retesting may be more indicative of their tendencies to behave consistently than of the reliability of the test items.

Validity refers, as before, to a correspondence between the person's responses to the test items and his behavior in other relevant situations. A great variety of situational variables are capable of prompting attitudinal behavior, and often these variables, according to Scott (1968), can be accepted with greater confidence than the attitude scale itself as typical instances in which the behavior will occur. For example, the author has some unpublished data obtained from Japanese university students in which it was found that students who expressed themselves as opposed to American participation in the conflict in Vietnam were more often numbered among those who actually demonstrated in the streets about this issue. A high correlation between performance on any attitude scale and other behavior more dramatically related to the attitude is evidence for the validity of the scale.

Guttman's Scaling Procedure

A general problem with both Thurstone and Likert scales is that individuals who achieve approximately the same scores could have done so through many different patterns of response to the individual items. Interpretation of a score, therefore, raises serious problems.

Scaleability of items. An alternative procedure that has the merit of greatly reducing the ambiguity in the meaning of a total score was developed in 1941 for the Information and Education Division of the Army. An important feature of this procedure, as described by Guttman (1950), is that it provides information pertaining to the question of whether a true scale can actually be derived from a pool of items. Is there any doubt that the Thurstone and Likert techniques just described yield scales? Unfortunately, a serious doubt does exist, for this reason: The statements that make up the final scale may not actually demarcate intervals along an assumed latent attitudinal dimension. That is, if we assume that an attitude represents a class of related response tendencies, the verbal components of which vary along a continuum from favorable to unfavorable, then we must be able to identify a series of statements that define positions along this latent continuum. Consider the following example:

Unfavorable   Favorable

I strongly dislike labor unions.	I dislike labor unions.	I tolerate labor unions.	I support labor unions.	I strongly support labor unions.

In actual practice, we would want to use more than just one statement about labor unions in order to determine where a given individual falls along this dimension. It is unlikely that a single statement would sample enough of the verbal behavior that the respondent has acquired with respect to unions. However, when we add additional items to our questionnaire, we run the danger of branching off into other attitudinal dimensions. The statement, "The government should exert more control than at present over the affairs of labor unions," may belong not only to a group of propositions relevant to labor unions, but also to a universe of verbalizations concerning the acceptability of a strong federal government. Persons with negative attitudes toward unions might respond to this statement in different ways, depending upon whether or not they also favored federal intervention in labor and management affairs.

Remmers (1954) provides us with an interesting illustration of the problem of the meaning of a score derived from a presumed attitude scale.

> Suppose, now, that we had been foolish enough to include items designed to measure prejudice against some racial group and items to test knowledge of algebra in the same test, and that by some means we derived a single total "score" for each individual to whom we gave this test. These "scores" would now be ambiguous. . . . A's score might be higher than B's either because he is more prejudiced than B, and knows the same amount, or less algebra, or because he knows more algebra than B, but is equally, or less prejudiced. And though C and D have equal scores, one may be more prejudiced than the other, and know less algebra, or vice versa (p. 97).

The problem is basically one of whether we can establish a set of verbalizations that will be *unidimensional* with reference to the attitude under consideration. That is, do the statements progress in ordinal fashion from one end of the attitude continuum to the other, such that a person who endorses an item representing one position on the dimension will accept all items representing less extreme positions? Let us borrow an example from Guttman and work it through to a conclusion about the scaleability of the statements involved. Consider the following three items:

1. I would marry a Negro.   ( ) Yes   ( ) No
2. I would invite a Negro to dinner.   ( ) Yes   ( ) No
3. I would permit a Negro to vote.   ( ) Yes   ( ) No

Since it is not necessary, when following Guttman's procedure, to assume that a given statement represents a more favorable attitude toward Negroes than any other statement, there are 2^3, or 8, possible response patterns, as shown on the next page:

	Statements	
1	2	3
Y	Y	Y
Y	Y	N
Y	N	N
N	Y	Y
N	N	N
N	N	Y
N	Y	N
Y	N	N

Obviously, if eight respondents gave us these eight patterns of responses, we would have to conclude that the statements certainly do not lie along a single dimension. An attitude toward Negroes, if one exists for these respondents, is not scaleable in terms of these items.

Let us assume, however, that our eight respondents actually answer as follows:

		Statements	
Respondents	1	2	3
1	Y	Y	Y
2	N	Y	Y
3	N	Y	Y
4	N	Y	Y
5	N	N	Y
6	N	N	Y
7	N	N	N
8	N	N	N

In this instance, the subjects have grouped themselves into four patterns, and it is clear that the statements can be ranked unambiguously according to their degree of favorableness toward, or acceptance of, Negroes. The scores when grouped this way make up a *scalogram*. The respondents can also be ranked in terms of their attitudes, with the person at the top being most favorably inclined toward Negroes, those in the two middle groups less favorably inclined, and those at the bottom least favorably inclined. The items apparently elicit responses which lie along a single dimension, and the scale that they define is said to be *unidimensional*.

Reproduceability. If we had included the statement, "I would lend money to a Negro," we might have found that this item was responded to favorably as frequently by the persons in the bottom group as by those in the top. That is, individuals who express an unwillingness to associate with Negroes might be willing to lend money to a Negro, either for profit or perhaps out of regard for an old employee. This type of behavior, money-lending, is not a good predictor of other behavior with respect to Negroes and probably lies on some other attitude dimension. Guttman's method of scale analysis permits such items to be identified and removed from the scale.

Of course, individuals do not always fall into the neat groupings that we have just pictured. But if only a few deviate from this, then the attitude is considered to be scalable. A measure called the *coefficient of reproducibility* tells how well a person's answers to each item are revealed by his total score. If this correlation is .90 or above, the scale is considered to be acceptably unidimensional. As an example of a minor departure from a "perfect" scale pattern, the bottom person in the previous example might have answered the questions with Yes, No, Yes. If only a few individuals out of a large sample of respondents behave in this fashion, then the scalogram can be closely approximated from their scores, and the scale is considered adequately unidimensional.

The Semantic Differential

As described by Osgood, Suci, and Tannenbaum (1957), the evaluative dimension of the semantic differential can be used as a measure of attitude toward persons or concepts. This technique is based on the assumption that concepts can be assigned evaluative meaning such as "good" or "bad" along a linear scale. A concept that received more positive ratings would be taken as reflecting a positive attitudinal orientation. Concepts with negative evaluations would be presumed to be the referents of negative attitudes. Because the procedure of setting up rating scales for the attitudinal referents in which one is interested is a relatively simple procedure, this method is finding increased usage in research. We discussed the semantic differential in some detail in Chapter 8 and so need not elaborate the method further here.

An interesting use of the semantic differential procedure to measure attitudes in an experiment on prejudice has been reported by Triandis, Loh, and Levin (1966). As they summarize their methods, ninety-four subjects were shown slides of either a young Negro or a young white man, who was either well dressed or poorly dressed. Simultaneously the subjects heard a tape-recorded statement which either favored or opposed integrated housing and which was spoken either in excellent or in ungrammatical English. The reactions of the subjects to these stimulus persons were thus influenced by race, dress, spoken English, and opinion.

Following this experience, the subjects responded to several behavioral differential scales developed previously by Triandis (1964). Three of these scales involved judgments reflecting *admiration, social distance,* and *friendship*. For example, each subject rated the extent to which he "admired the character of this person," "would exclude this person from the neighborhood," or "would accept this person as an intimate friend." In addition, the subjects responded to two semantic differential scales for each slide, in which they rated the Negro or white youth along dimensions good-bad and wise-foolish. Finally, the subjects completed a questionnaire in which they indicated, by means of semantic differential scales, their dispositions toward a number of civil rights issues, such as integrated housing, interracial marriage, and integrated schools. Thus, the attitudes of the subjects on matters of racial equality could be compared with their reactions to the stimulus persons in the several roles assigned to them.

A scalogram analysis of the responses of the subjects to the civil rights items revealed them as grouped into five categories. Type I subjects favored interracial marriages, sit-ins, freedom marches, integrated housing, and integrated schools, and opposed segregated schools. Type II expressed only the last four of these, Type III agreed with the last three, and Type IV favored only integrated schools. Type V agreed with none of the first four items and, in addition, favored segregated schools. (If the last two items seem confusing, it may help to point out that someone who favors integrated schools might not necessarily oppose *de facto* segregation. In this case, however, those subjects who favored integration also opposed segregation.) These particular items apparently fall along a single dimension.

The results of the experiment may be summarized briefly. Race and proficiency in English were the most important determinants of social distance. Friendship was judged mainly by the quality of the English, then by race, and least by the dress of the stimulus person. In the case of both social distance and friendship, prejudiced individuals gave more weight to race than did tolerant persons. Correct English was the critical determinant of admiration for all of the subjects. The authors note that ". . . while most of our subjects are willing to admire the ideas of a qualified Negro, many of the same subjects are not willing to accept him in their neighborhood" (p. 471).

Perhaps the most significant finding was that prejudice has many dimensions and that an individual's response to the object of his prejudice, in this instance a minority group member, varies according to the situation. Exclusion of a Negro from one's neighborhood is apparently a matter of race, whereas admiration is primarily determined by status cues, such as language. Social distance, as reported in other studies, for Americans is a function of race, for Greeks a function of religion, and for Japanese and Germans a function of occupation (Triandis and Triandis, 1960, 1962).

Opinion Surveys

Unlike attitude measurement, which usually is carried out with accidental samples of no more than a few hundred individuals, opinion surveys may involve thousands of carefully selected respondents. Although surveys may be conducted by mail or telephone, we shall be concerned here only with those techniques that involve face-to-face interviews with samples of individuals drawn from some larger population. As such, a survey provides social scientists with a quantitative method for establishing relationships among social variables and for generalizing about known populations. Dean, Eichorn, and Dean (1967) describe the standardized data collection procedure of a survey as follows:

> A systematically selected sample of individuals is exposed to a fixed set of questions; then their reactions to those questions are systematically classified so that quantitative comparisons can be made. The survey analyst can then establish whether a larger proportion of the clergy or of the legal profession favors participation in the civil rights marches; whether a higher proportion of respondents who said they had happy childhoods or of those who said they had an unhappy childhood agrees that, "Communists are taking over the country" (p. 247).

These authors also point out one of the survey method's greatest shortcomings, namely, "It exposes each respondent to identical questions and classifies his responses into a few simple types regardless of the distinctive qualities of each response" (p. 247). The reason for this procedure, of course, is that a survey is designed to obtain information from a sufficiently large sample of respondents to justify generalizations to some larger population. Experimentation with groups of this size ordinarily is not feasible. Surveys and experiments, therefore, are used to answer different kinds of questions, although both methods may yield data that provide a basis for making predictions about future behavior. In both instances, the investigator usually expects to generalize beyond the specific individuals he has observed. The extent to which he can legitimately do this depends upon the representativeness of the individuals on whom he has based his limited observations. Surveys, which generally employ sampling procedures designed to ensure such representativeness, offer more secure grounds for drawing conclusions about a population than do experiments, in which college students frequently are used as subjects.

Measurement and Prediction

The operational distinction between opinions and attitudes, we have suggested, lies in the respective procedures by which they are made public. For example, an opinion can be elicited by a single question, such as: "Do you think that the United States should exercise its veto power more frequently in the United Nations?" The response alternatives allowed to the respondent may include Yes, No, and Undecided. Any one of these replies is probably related to attitudes on wider issues such as democracy, economic policy, and power politics. But the opinion in question relates to a specific issue and is responsive to a single probe. The strength of the opinion may be determined, as in the case of attitudes, by allowing the respondent to use a rating scale. For example:

The United States should exercise its veto power in the United Nations more frequently.

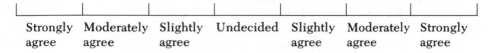

| Strongly agree | Moderately agree | Slightly agree | Undecided | Slightly agree | Moderately agree | Strongly agree |

Usually it is not necessary to approach an opinion such as this through a number of different statements in order to make sure that we have sampled a sufficient number of the response dispositions that it represents. Actually, the opinion may have little predictive value so far as any other performance of the respondent is concerned. Many persons who have opinions on this subject have nothing directly to do with the official posture of the United States in the United Nations, and their opinions will never be translated into other relevant actions. Such opinions, therefore, may or may not have value in predicting other behavior. Whether they are useful in this respect depends to a large extent upon whether the individual has an opportunity to act on his opinion. In the case of elections, a person's expressed preference for one candidate may be used to predict which lever he will depress in the voting booth. Where international affairs are concerned, however, the individual's opinions may have predictive value only with regard to his future utterances on the same issues.

Opinions which tend increasingly to be accompanied by emotional reactions, and which are prompted by an ever-widening range of cues, can readily develop into attitudes. Generally, such a process involves the accretion of a number of opinions which relate to the same dimension of behavior. Such would be the case where opinions about political candidates, government spending, foreign aid, and the like are interrelated in such a way as to suggest a latent attitudinal continuum of, say, liberalism-conservatism. Statements relating to any one of these matters may, through stimulus generalization, come to elicit a characteristic response. An opinion about the President of the United States, for example, probably is predictive of an individual's responses to a host of other social issues, such as labor legislation, governmental spending, and national defense. When a number of opinions coalesce in this fashion to form a coherent pattern, we may say that an attitudinal structure has developed. One might even argue that most attitudes have their origins in the opinions that one learns early in life.

In most instances, a person responding to items on an attitude scale must be able to read and understand twenty or more statements and be willing to spend the time necessary for responding to them. In opinion polling, we recognize that the respondents may have neither the time nor the inclination nor the degree of literacy required to answer the number and type of items used in attitude scales. Indeed, in view of the simpler structure of an opinion, we need not apply the elaborate techniques of attitude measurement to opinion polling. By asking six different questions we may, in fact, obtain answers expressing opinions on six different issues. Six related questions, on the other hand, would seldom be adequate to determine the nature of a person's attitude.

It should be remembered that one goal of opinion measurement is to predict later behavior on occasions when relevant issues are concerned. As in the case of attitudes, opinions expressed in an interview are not always consistent with behavior in other situations. In many instances, however, opinion measurement at the level of verbal response does reliably predict other, related performances. Marketing surveys, for example, are often useful in predicting the purchasing habits of consumers. Pre-election polls are able to predict the outcome of a presidential contest within several percentage points. Both the reliability and the validity of any polling procedure depend, of course, upon care in developing the various stages of the investigation. These are: (a) questionnaire construction, (b) sample selection, (c) interviewing, and (d) data analysis. Suppose we examine each of these briefly.

Questionnaire construction. In attitude measurement, a number of statements or questions must be devised which relate not only to the assumed attitudinal disposition but also to one another in consistent fashion. To insure that the items actually have these characteristics, investigators employ such procedures as item scaling, item analysis, and scalogram analysis. These methods of securing reliable items are neither feasible nor, in fact, necessary in constructing the questions for an opinion survey, since no assumptions are made about an underlying attitude dimension. Each item must stand by itself, and its reliability can be insured only by careful wording, pretesting with a sample of respondents, and appropriate revision. The questions in an opinion survey, ideally, should be concise, simply stated, and relevant to the issue at hand.

Two basic types of questions are generally employed in opinion surveys: the open-end question and the poll, or multiple-choice, question. In the open-end question, the respondent is allowed to frame his own answer, which is recorded verbatim (if possible) by the interviewer. An example of this type of question might be: "What do you think about admitting Red China to the United Nations?"

If, on the other hand, the purpose of the survey is to obtain an estimate of the number of individuals favoring and opposing the admission of Red China to the U.N., then the question might be asked so as to obtain a more exact indication of the respondent's opinion. This would put it in the form of a poll question, as follows:

Do you think that Red China should be admitted to the United Nations?

Yes _____   No _____   Don't know _____

Typically, some of the persons interviewed will have no opinion about this matter, and they are classified in the "Don't know" category. Regardless of how simple the question or how well publicized the issue, some individuals inevitably fall into this indeterminate group.

If the pollster wishes to obtain information about the basis for the respondent's reply, an open-end query may be used following the poll question, such as: "For what reasons do you feel this way?" Clearly, a great deal more work is involved in classifying replies to open-end items than in tabulating responses to multiple-choice items. Few individuals will give exactly the same answer, and because succinct reporting of the results is generally desired, the many different replies received must be reassigned into a few descriptive categories. This involves a process known as *content analysis*. The investigator examines each response and groups it with others which despite differences in wording seem to imply the same general opinion. Probably no more than six or eight categories should result if the poll results are to lend themselves to concise summarizing and reporting. The exact number of categories depends upon both the purpose of the study and the variety of responses that are obtained.

A more efficient procedure than merely asking Why? after the respondent has said Yes or No to a poll question is to present him with a number of alternative reasons for his answer and allow him to choose one or more that are applicable. How are these alternatives to be devised? This is where a *pilot study* is useful. Rather than determining arbitrarily the kinds of reasons that might be offered for admitting or not admitting Red China to the United Nations, the investigator might interrogate a relatively small sample of individuals using the open-end technique. He analyzes the content of these replies to determine what kinds of reasons people have for favoring or opposing such action. The resulting categories are then used as multiple-choice alternatives with the larger sample of individuals for whom the questionnaire is being designed. Analysis of open-end replies in the pilot study is made less tedious by the small number of individuals who are queried, and a great deal of time and effort is saved by using this information in devising a poll question for the survey proper. A special category termed "other reasons" may be included for respondents who fail to find any of the stated alternatives applicable.

An example of this approach to survey question construction is provided in a study by Dahmer and McGinnies (1949). Their survey dealt with student opinion at the University of Alabama on the issue of admitting Negroes to the University. A pilot study was first conducted to determine what reasons might be advanced by undergraduates for either granting or denying entrance to Negro students. The various replies obtained were then classified into five general categories, to be used in the actual poll. Following are the questions* as they appeared in the final questionnaire, together with the per cent Yes replies that were recorded:

Which of the following statements best expresses your opinions concerning the admission of qualified Negroes at the present time to the undergraduate college of the University?

(a) I would favor their admission without any segregation what-
     ever within the classroom.   (18%)

(b) I would favor their admission if they were segregated within
     the regular classes.   (4%)

(c) I would favor their admission if they attended special segre-
     gated classes.   (21%)

(d) I would favor their admission under certain other conditions.   (7%)

(e) I would favor their admission under no circumstances at the
     present time.   (50%)

Of some additional interest in this example is the fact that a question asked immediately prior to this yielded the following results:

Would you be willing to admit Negroes to the University of Alabama if this step were necessary in order to receive funds under a federal educational aid program?

Yes, 33%   No, 62%   No opinion, 5%

When presented only with Yes or No alternatives, just 30 per cent of those interviewed indicated a willingness to admit Negroes to the University. However, 50 per cent of the interviewees at that time actually were willing to accept Negro students under some conditions, when these conditions were specified by the interviewer. This difference illustrates the manner in which formulation of the questions in a survey can influence the replies that are obtained.

The survey questionnaire generally contains a few final items intended to elicit certain additional information about the respondent, such as age, sex, occupation, income level, and religion. These data are used for purposes of *cross-tabulation* when analyzing the results of the poll and will be discussed later.

* From C. Dahmer and E. McGinnies, "Shifting sentiments toward civil rights in a southern university," *Public Opinion Quarterly*, 1949, 2, 241–251. Reprinted by permission of the authors and the copyright holder.

Sampling theory. Of critical importance in opinion polling is the manner in which individuals are to be interviewed. In order to understand the various kinds of sampling procedures that are employed, we shall have to consider briefly the theoretical basis of sampling in general. Sampling design, according to Kish (1967), has two aspects. One is a *selection process,* which defines the rules and operations by which some members of the population are included in the sample. The other is an *estimation process,* in which certain characteristics of the sample are treated statistically in order to yield estimates of corresponding characteristics of the population.

In practically all psychological research, it is impossible for the investigator to study all the members of the species or class in which he is interested. His generalizations about behavior are necessarily based on data obtained from those individuals who can be observed either in the laboratory or under natural conditions. The generalizability of predictions made from these data to individuals as yet unobserved depends, in part, upon the representativeness of the individuals that were originally studied. It has been charged, for example, that psychologists have based too many of their generalizations on data obtained from college sophomores. The basis for this allegation, which has considerable merit, lies in the relative availability of this particular group for laboratory experimentation. However, the dangers of improper generalization to other groups is probably fairly small in experiments where the concern of the experimenter is behavior related to sensory processes or simple motor skills. The behavior of people in general tends to be fairly predictable with respect to these particular variables. However, where attitudes and opinions are concerned, it would be unjustified for one to conclude that a sample selected from some unique population is necessarily typical of any other population.

Let us amplify more specifically the concepts of "sample" and "population." A population is any aggregate or group subject to statistical study. Populations are either *finite* or *infinite.* A finite population is bounded by both space and time, as would be the case if we were interested in some behavioral characteristic of all males in the United States born between 1945 and 1950. Generalizations made from a sample of this population would not necessarily apply to males of other nations or to males born in different periods.

An infinite population is one which has no definable limits, generally with respect to time, but theoretically also with respect to space. Much of our knowledge about the basic principles of learning, for example, has been obtained from experiments with inbred albino rats and pigeons. We assume that the behavior of the animals that have been used in these experiments is not essentially different from that of generations of laboratory animals as yet unborn. It is our conviction that data from the samples of animals already studied can be generalized to this theoretically infinite population. Similarly, we assume that theories about human behavior derived from psychological research over the past sixty years will be applicable to the behavior of individuals born in the next century. This is probably a safe assumption so long as we limit ourselves to behavioral processes that are common to people of specific ages and cultures.

Populations may also be classified as *homogeneous* or *heterogeneous*. A homogeneous population is one in which all the members, or units, are alike in some specifiable manner. If one were to mix a pitcher of iced martinis and then take a sip to determine whether the correct proportions of gin and vermouth had been used, it might be assumed that the sample sip would be the same as any additional sips that might be tasted. This would be true, of course, only if the mixture had been well stirred. A product taken at random from a production line for purposes of quality control is presumed to be identical with any other unit that might have been selected. So far as behavior is concerned, however, we base our observations upon individuals selected from heterogeneous populations. No two humans are ever completely alike; the closest approximation to this is provided by identical twins, and even here we could not with confidence predict the behavior of one by observing the other.

A sample is composed of those members or units drawn from a population for observation or experimentation. We study samples because the populations in which we are interested are generally too large to make practical the study of each member. As Parten (1950) puts it, "The process of sampling, or the selection of part of a population from which the characteristics of the whole are inferred, has long been accepted as a legitimate and expeditious method of research procedure" (p. 106).

Two types of errors are to be avoided in sampling for opinion surveys. These are *biased* sampling error and *chance* sampling error. Biased sampling errors occur when certain members of the population have a greater probability of being included in the sample than other members. In the now classic example of the presidential election poll conducted by the *Literary Digest* in 1936, described by Fenton (1960), respondents' names were drawn from telephone directories and lists of automobile owners. This obviously eliminated from possible inclusion in the sample those individuals who were less favored economically. In the 1930's, workers with low incomes had swung heavily behind Franklin D. Roosevelt, while the more affluent citizens tended to back Landon and the Republican party. Since its sample excluded a major portion of the less economically secure voters, the *Literary Digest* understandably predicted that Landon would win the election, with 57 per cent of the vote. Landon actually received 37.5 per cent of the vote, embarrassing the *Digest*'s editors with a prediction error of some nineteen percentage points. That poll, incidentally, contained other serious errors, but the most grievous was the sampling procedure. Since that time, the presidential election polls, with the exception of the 1948 Truman versus Dewey campaign, have been remarkably accurate in predicting actual voting behavior. When estimates of the support for opposing candidates have been so close as to fall within the margin of error, as in the 1968 contest between Nixon and Humphrey, the major pollsters simply declined to predict the outcome.

Chance sampling errors occur when the sample is too small to provide a reliable estimate of characteristics of the population from which it was drawn. Suppose that the object of a poll is to determine which of two candidates, Smedley or Finster, is more likely to win an election. Assuming that everyone in the population of voters has a preference for one candidate or the other, we can divide them into two groups according to which candidate they support. The exact proportion of individuals falling into each of these groups, of course, is unknown. Since it is impractical to interrogate every member of the voting population, we hope to obtain an estimate of these proportions by polling a representative sample of respondents.

The sampling problem here is analogous to that of drawing black and white marbles, well mixed, from a large urn containing equal numbers of each. We know that in a large number of draws, black marbles should be drawn as often as white marbles. If we concern ourselves only with the probability of obtaining a black marble on each draw, we know that there is one chance in two that this event will occur. The probability of obtaining a black marble on the first draw is $\frac{1}{2}$. If we replace the marble drawn, then the probability of again drawing a black marble is still $\frac{1}{2}$. But the probability of two black marbles being drawn twice in succession is $\frac{1}{2}$ times $\frac{1}{2}$, or $\frac{1}{4}$. A moment's reflection will reveal that the event in which we are interested, two identical events occurring in succession, is one of four possible events, namely, BB, BW, WB, WW.

If the marbles are evenly mixed, and there are equal numbers of black and white in the urn, the probability of obtaining successive black marbles becomes increasingly smaller with each draw. For example, the chance of obtaining five black marbles in succession would be only $\frac{1}{32}(\frac{1}{2}\times\frac{1}{2}\times\frac{1}{2}\times\frac{1}{2}\times\frac{1}{2})$. Now what are the implications of these elementary principles of probability for opinion sampling? Suppose that in two selections, with replacement, from the urn black marbles had turned up each time. Would we have been willing to conclude that the urn contained more black marbles than white? Probably not, since this event could very well have occurred by chance. Now suppose that the first two people randomly polled with respect to the two election candidates both favor Smedley. Would we conclude that Smedley will probably win the election? This prediction would scarcely be justified, since by mere chance we might have picked two of Smedley's supporters, even though an equal number of people favor Finster. Our sample is too small to be reliable.

If the numbers of individuals favoring Smedley and Finster are, in fact, nearly equal in the population, then the probability of continuing to select at random only the constituents of one of them becomes increasingly smaller. We must, as in the case of drawing from an urn, sample enough individuals, or events, so that deviations from chance will average out. We might actually pick three or even four respondents in succession all favoring Smedley, but if we continue to increase the size of our sample we shall inevitably begin to include those who support Finster, thus eventually giving us a reliable estimate of the probable vote for each candidate.

In actual practice, the members of the population will seldom be equally divided in their allegiance to one or another candidate (although this nearly happened in the 1968 presidential contest). Let us assume that in our fictitious example 55 per cent prefer Smedley and 45 per cent prefer Finster. Sampling at random from this population is analogous to drawing marbles from an urn containing 55 per cent black marbles and 45 per cent white marbles. If we remove (sample) 100 marbles at random, there is a strong probability that we will have 55 black marbles and 45 white ones. However, it is unlikely that we would obtain these proportions with a sample of only 10 marbles. Similarly, if we sample enough voters, we would expect to find 55 per cent of our sample favoring Smedley and 45 per cent favoring Finster. As in the previous example, however, we would not expect to obtain these proportions with a small sample, since chance variations could easily throw us off the correct estimates.

Armed with these basic facts about predicting from samples, we are ready to consider some of the sampling problems that are encountered in opinion polling. The voting population, for example, is composed of individuals with many differing characteristics, including sex, age, religion, political affiliation, education, and occupation, to mention only a few. These various factors frequently are related in systematic fashion to opinions on certain issues. Religion and age, for example, are related to opinions about birth control. Occupation probably influences opinions concerning labor unions. Income and education are two variables controlling voting behavior. Because persons of different ages, different occupations, and varying degrees of educational attainment are systematically biased with respect to certain issues, a reliable sample must give proportional representation to each of these subgroups. For example, when religion may be involved in an issue, each religious group should contribute to the sample according to the proportion of the population that it represents. With other issues, appropriate weight in the sample should be allotted to educational and occupational groupings according to their numerical representation in the population. A sample of voters, for example, should not contain as many college graduates as grade school graduates, since there are many more of the latter. Nor should the sample contain equal numbers of farmers and physicians. A small but representative sample, by careful design, can be relatively free of both biased and chance sampling errors.

Sampling procedures. A procedure known as *quota control* is commonly employed to insure that the composition of a sample mirrors accurately the composition of the population from which it is drawn. This is necessary, as we have noted, when certain population variables may be systematically related to the opinions under investigation. In quota sampling, the interviewers are required to locate respondents who satisfy certain specifications as to age, socioeconomic status, or other factors determined in advance by the survey director. These quotas are derived from statistics describing the demographic composition of the population and, if properly filled, insure that the specified groups are proportionately represented. Because of the freedom allowed the interviewer in selecting respondents who fit the specifications, the opportunities for bias are numerous. The interviewer may be tempted to interview those who are more available or more attractive instead of those who meet the quota requirements.

A more precise, but more expensive, method of guaranteeing a representative, or proportional, sample is provided by *area probability sampling.* This procedure does not leave the final choice of respondents to the discretion of the interviewer but, rather, specifies in advance which persons shall be interviewed. Although the details of this method are rather complex, we can outline the general steps that might be followed. Let us imagine that a survey is to be undertaken within a state to determine opinions about enactment of a state sales tax. A representative sample of persons within the state are to be interviewed on this issue. It is important that the sample accurately reflect the variables of population density and income level, since rural-urban location as well as income may be related to opinion on this issue. If the state contains thirty counties, a first step might be to divide these into three groups according to population density. Within each group of ten counties, three are then selected at random. In each of these counties, a further division is made in terms of cities and towns of differing size. Perhaps three such groupings result, each containing ten cities or towns. Three cities are selected randomly from each group, and each of these is further subdivided by selecting block and dwelling according to income level of the inhabitants. The interviewer then can be instructed to go to a specific address in a particular city or town and interview one or more of the adults living there.

Many variations in area sampling procedures are possible. As Stephan and McCarthy (1958) point out, different criteria may be used for defining the areas and for sampling individuals or households within the selected areas. It is obvious that while this method greatly reduces the interviewer bias commonly found in quota samples (interviewing better educated people or favoring more elegant residential sections), it entails more detailed planning and greater expense, since call-backs may be necessary when a particular respondent is not at home.

Interviewing. The behaviors required of the interviewer depend to a large extent upon the type of questionnaire that is used. Open-end questions require greater skill, and consequently more interviewer training, than do poll questions. In either case, it is essential that the interviewer be able to approach people in a manner that will elicit their cooperation and establish the rapport necessary for a successful interview. Various studies have shown that a strong opinion bias on the part of the interviewer may influence the kinds of answers that he obtains from respondents. In such instances, it is likely that the interviewer has inadvertently revealed his own inclinations to the respondent and thereby influenced the respondent's behavior. If the questionnaire deals with issues involving minority groups, any obvious relationship between the interviewer and the minority group under consideration may also influence the respondent. Ideally, the interviewer should maintain a perfectly impartial demeanor and should provide the respondent with no cues that would systematically bias the respondent's replies.

When the interviewer is assigned the additional task of making judgments concerning the respondent's age, education, or income level, he must exercise considerable skill in both observation and judgment. Some of the persons interviewed may be reluctant to reveal information of this nature, and the interviewer must then make estimates based on the respondent's appearance, his behavior, and his home and possessions. The highest degree of skill on the part of the interviewer is probably required in so-called *depth interviews.* Here he must try to disclose the reasons underlying a respondent's opinions by further questioning or probing along lines suggested by the answers first given. Reliable interviewing of this type can be done only after considerable training and practice.

Finally, it is assumed that interviewers will faithfully carry out their assignments and will not falsify or fabricate data. Most large polling organizations conduct a certain number of check-backs with respondents selected at random to ascertain whether the interview was actually conducted and whether it was done according to the instructions. It is partly for this purpose that respondent's names and addresses are generally recorded on their questionnaires.

Analysis of the Findings

Summarizing the results of a survey involves basically no more than counting the number of responses in the various categories. If one wants to describe the population rather than just the sample, percentages and estimates of their reliability must be obtained. Some of the most interesting information to be gained from a survey is found in the relationships between the patterns of response and certain background characteristics of the respondents. Nearly every questionnaire contains items designed to obtain some biographical information about the person interviewed. The exact nature of the items included depends, of course, upon what factors the survey director thinks might conceivably be related to opinions on the issue under investigation. Age, sex, and occupation are frequently included here. Other factors, such as income and education, may also be relevant to the respondent's opinions on certain matters. These, however, are sometimes more difficult to ascertain, since many individuals are reluctant to reveal their incomes and may tend to overstate their educational attainments. Some, in fact, may even hesitate to give their correct age. If difficulty is foreseen in obtaining this kind of information, the interviewer may be instructed to make the best estimates he can. These data, obviously, can also be used as a check on the accuracy of the particular sampling methods that were employed.

Having obtained biographical information about the sample members through either direct interrogation or estimates by the interviewer, a process of *cross-tabulation* frequently is used to discover whether any systematic relationships exist between this information and responses to the survey questions. If the questionnaire, for example, deals with preference for one of two political candidates, those individuals favoring each candidate might be subdivided according to religious affiliation, income, and education. The purpose would be to see whether either candidate is drawing support more heavily from certain segments of the population than from others.

In the previously cited study concerned with student attitudes in 1949 toward admission of Negroes to the University of Alabama, a breakdown of the responses to one of the questions was done by divisions of the University and by the religion of the respondent. The results of cross-tabulating answers by divisions and by religious preferences were as follows[*]:

Do you believe that Negroes who meet the entrance requirements should now be admitted to the Medical School of the University of Alabama?

	Graduate School	Law School	Arts and Sciences	Other Undergraduate Colleges
Yes	69%	41%	46%	32%
No	28	57	50	64
No opinion	3	2	4	4

	Protestant	Catholic	Jewish	Other Religions (including none)
Yes	36%	40%	80%	54%
No	60	51	18	42
No opinion	4	9	2	4

The purpose of cross-tabulation is to reveal relationships between opinions and background variables that would otherwise be concealed in the

[*] From C. Dahmer and E. McGinnies, "Shifting sentiments toward civil rights in a southern university," *Public Opinion Quarterly*, 1949, 2, 241–251. Reprinted by permission of the authors and the copyright holder.

reporting of percentage totals. Certain conjectures about the determinants of public opinion can also be tested by analysis of these breakdowns. For example, we may suspect that prejudice toward minority groups decreases with increasing edcuation. The fact that graduate students indicated significantly greater acceptance of desegregation than undergraduate students supports this notion. Why law students should have been less liberal on this matter, of course, is unexplained, unless we postulate certain selection factors that operated at that time in the choice of law as a profession by students at this university. It is also apparent that Jewish students were more willing to admit Negroes to the University than either Protestants or Catholics, even though 80 per cent of the Jewish students identified themselves as "Southerners." Perhaps membership in the Jewish faith involves experiences as a minority group member that lead the individual to adopt more sympathetic attitudes toward other minority groups.

We might also expect that greater egalitarianism, as expressed in dislike of autocratic political figures, would be related to occupational identification. In 1953, Gallup reported a breakdown of prominent citizens (selected from *Who's Who in America*) who expressed opinions concerning Senator Joseph McCarthy. Although a majority in all of the occupational groups interviewed held unfavorable opinions of the Senator, some interesting differences appeared among them:

	Opinion of McCarthy		
	Favorable	Unfavorable	No opinion
Business	41%	52%	7%
Journalism, Law, Medicine	39	56	5
Government	30	64	6
Science	26	66	8
Religion	23	75	2
Education	15	80	5

Since both clergymen and educators had been objects of some of Senator McCarthy's inquisitorial zeal, it is not surprising that these individuals reported the greatest disapproval. Businessmen traditionally have demonstrated greater conservatism than other occupational groups, and they revealed this disposition by showing the least disapproval of Senator McCarthy.

Breakdowns of this general type are necessary if one is to obtain the kinds of information that will be useful in the analysis and prediction of behavior. Of course, not all of the obtained differences will be meaningful. Statistical procedures are employed to determine which of the differences could have resulted from chance and which reveal functional dependencies between opinions and other biographical and demographic factors.

Determinants of Public Opinion

To be consistent with the position that we have taken regarding the acquisition of attitudes, we shall assume that opinions are also formed largely as a result of social learning. The fact that individuals in the same society may hold many different opinions about the same matters simply indicates that they have had different reinforcement histories in this respect. Opinions, like attitudes, are derived from a varied and complex set of social learning situations. Some opinions seem to be formed quickly, perhaps on the basis of a first impression or a single experience. Others result from repeated exposure to a particular class of reinforcing events. Since opinions and attitudes, as we have suggested, are often functionally equivalent, the individual's existing attitude structure provides a substrate upon which new opinions as well as new attitudes are based. For example, a staunch conservative is less likely to acquire a favorable opinion toward a new program of increased government spending than is a political liberal. Knowledge of the basic attitude framework of a person enables us, in many cases, to predict the opinions he will form with respect to evolving social issues. The total behavior of an individual, including his opinions, as Smith, Bruner, and White (1956) have pointed out, reflects certain underlying regularities that are to some extent predictable.

Such variables as sex, socioeconomic status, religion, skin color, and marital status frequently are related in predictable fashion to the opinions that people have. In discussing some of the problems of analyzing poll data, we noted the way in which such variables as religion and educational level were related to opinions about desegregation in the 1940's among students in a Southern university. Another example of demographic analysis is provided by Lazarsfeld, Berelson, and Gaudet (1948) in their study of the 1940 presidential election, in which Franklin D. Roosevelt defeated Wendell Willkie. They found that three variables were efficient predictors of voting behavior, namely, socioeconomic status, religious preference, and place of residence. More specifically, they suggest that Catholics, urban residents, and individuals having a lower socioeconomic status are more likely to vote Democratic, whereas Republican votes are more apt to come from the non-Catholic, rural, and economically more favored segments of the electorate.

Evidence that these traditional alignments are giving way to new patterns of political preference has been reported by Miller (1968). Citing some of the findings of pollster Louis Harris, he suggests that the old divisions along economic lines are being abandoned in favor of divisions over social issues, such as race relations. Data obtained by Harris indicates that two new political coalitions were evident in 1968, one advocating social change and one resisting such change. The no-change coalition seems to be represented by Deep South whites, low-income whites in Northern industrial cities, conservative suburbanites, and older people. The advocates of social change include Negroes, Spanish-speaking and Jewish people, the young, the affluent, and the college-educated. Until these realignments show evidence of really shaping up, however, the traditional support given the Democratic party by union members and by Catholics, Jewish, and Negro voters in the big cities probably will continue (Harris, 1968).

It is, of course, easier to discover relationships between demographic variables and opinions than to reach an understanding of their psychological significance. Certainly the mere fact of living in a large city or in a rural community does not automatically predispose one to a preference for a particular political party. Nor do religion and socioeconomic status by themselves determine opinion and attitude formation. However, each of these factors set the stage, so to speak, for the learning situations in which each of us acquires his opinions. One tends to assume membership in social groups composed of individuals having comparable age, income, and educational levels. The group members tend to reinforce those performances, including attitudes and opinions, that are supportive rather than disruptive to the group. An individual living in a small Southern community, or perhaps in a Northern industrial suburb, is reinforced only when he expresses certain opinions about Negroes. He may even be punished for voicing opinions that are contrary to the group norm. Similarly, an individual living in a Catholic or a Jewish family will elicit characteristic reactions from parents and friends when expressing opinions on issues important to the group. As a result, each person comes to express more frequently opinions that have been positively reinforced and to either abandon or suppress those that have prompted aversive reactions from others.

The situation is not always this simple, of course, and there are many exceptions to this basic conception. But even where an individual's opinions are apparently out of step with those of other persons with whom most of his social interactions occur, we may still assume that his behavior is under some form of stimulus control. Perhaps the reinforcing contingencies that effectively maintain his behavior are not obvious. If he is rebellious or resentful toward his family, for example, then he may be positively reinforced for voicing opinions that cause them displeasure and distress. Perhaps this is the most effective way in which he can gain their attention.

Because opinions are more varied and fragmented than attitudes, we cannot look for their origins entirely within the individual's range of close social contacts. Constant exposure to the mass media — press, radio, television, and motion pictures — provides a host of situations in which people can form new opinions and modify old ones. It will be sufficient for us to suggest here that these mass media are mainly effective in prompting existing behavior. One result of such prompting may be opinion change, that is, a rearrangement of certain items within the repertoire.

A great deal of research is currently being done to determine the conditions in which attitude and opinion change occur. We shall consider some problems of persuasion and attitude change in the next chapter.

Summary   To the extent that each has reference to an evaluative disposition, the terms attitude and opinion are often used interchangeably. Nevertheless, a distinction can be made between the two. Opinions are conceived as being more specific, more transient, and less emotionally toned than attitudes. In addition, whereas attitudes tend to be learned and maintained largely as a consequence of the reinforcement contingencies associated with one's parents and peer groups, opinions are influenced to a large extent by the mass media of radio, press, and television. Opinions are relatively easier to assess than attitudes, and indices of public opinion are used as a basis for predicting voting behavior, consumer purchasing, and other performances at the level of mass behavior.

Attitudes may be expressed "spontaneously" (meaning that the controlling stimuli are unknown), or they may be prompted by direct interrogation. Attitudes are also inferred from certain nonverbal behaviors that may or may not be consistently correlated with the individual's verbal performances. The measurement of verbal attitudes, as differentiated from action attitudes, may be accomplished in several ways. Four techniques discussed in the chapter were (a) Thurstone scaling, (b) Likert scaling, (c) Guttman scaling, and (d) Osgood's semantic differential. Attitude scales are considered reliable if they are internally consistent and if they yield similar scores on consecutive administrations to the same persons. Validity, which is more difficult to determine, is reflected by the extent to which an attitude score is predictive of other relevant behavior.

Opinion measurement involves four basic steps: (a) questionnaire construction, (b) sample selection, (c) interviewing, and (d) data interpretation. Some opinions are revealed in response to a single item or "poll question." Others are approached more circuitously, using a series of "funneled" items or sometimes open-end questions, the answers to which must be categorized and evaluated for their content. Scientific opinion polling makes use of representative samples from which generalizations can be made about the characteristics of some larger population. Representative samples can be selected in several ways, the more common of these being the methods of quota control and area probability sampling. Bias can enter into opinion polling either through the method of sample selection or as a result of improper interviewing procedures.

The results of opinion polls become more meaningful when the results are considered in the light of relevant background characteristics of the respondents. These include age, education, sex, religious preference, and socioeconomic level. Variables such as these define the social context in which attitudes and opinions are acquired and maintained and in which they are often subjected to modification and change.

References

ALBIG, W.   *Modern public opinion.* New York: McGraw-Hill, 1956.

DAHMER, C., and McGINNIES, E.   Shifting sentiments toward civil rights in a southern university. *Public Opinion Quarterly,* 1949, *2,* 241–251.

DEAN, J. P., EICHHORN, R. L., and DEAN, LOIS R.   The survey. In J. T. Doby (Ed.), *An introduction to social research.* New York: Appleton-Century-Crofts, 1967.

FENTON, J.   *In your opinion.* Boston: Little, Brown, 1960.

GREEN, B. F.   Attitude measurement. Chapter 9 in G. Lindzey (Ed.), *Handbook of social psychology.* Reading, Mass.: Addison-Wesley, 1954.

GUTTMAN, L.   The basis for scalogram analysis. In S. A. Stouffer *et al., Measurement and prediction.* Princeton, N.J.: Princeton University, 1950.

HARRIS, L.   As reported in *The Washington Post,* November 4, 1968, p. 1.

HOVLAND, C. I., and SHERIF, M.   Judgmental phenomena and scales of attitude measurement: Item displacement in Thurstone scales. *Journal of Abnormal and Social Psychology,* 1952, *47,* 822–832.

KELMAN, H. C.   Processes of opinion change. *Public Opinion Quarterly,* 1961, *25,* 57–78.

KISH, L.   *Survey sampling.* New York: Wiley, 1967.

LAZARSFELD, P. F.   The logic and mathematical foundation of latent structure analysis. In S. A. Stouffer *et al., Measurement and prediction.* Princeton, N.J.: Princeton University Press, 1950.

LAZARSFELD, P. F., BERELSON, B., and GAUDET, H.   *The people's choice* (2nd ed.). New York: Columbia University Press, 1948.

LIKERT, R.   A technique for the measurement of attitudes. *Archives of Psychology,* 1932, No. 140, 1–55.

MILLER, N. C.   Who are the voters? *The Wall Street Journal,* November 5, 1968, p. 1.

OSGOOD, C. E., SUCI, G. J., and TANNENBAUM, P. H.   *The measurement of meaning.* Urbana, Ill.: University of Illinois Press, 1957.

PARTEN, MILDRED.   *Surveys, polls, and samples.* New York: Harper, 1950.

REMMERS, H. H.   *Introduction to opinion and attitude measurement.* New York: Harper, 1954.

SARGENT, S. S., and WILLIAMSON, R. C.   *Social psychology* (3rd ed.). New York: Ronald Press, 1966.

SCOTT, W. A.   Attitude measurement. In G. Lindzey and E. Aronson (Eds.), *Handbook of social psychology.* Vol. 2. Reading, Mass.: Addison-Wesley, 1968.

SMITH, M. B., BRUNER, J. S., and WHITE, R. W.   *Opinions and personality.* New York: Wiley, 1956.

STEPHAN, F. F., and McCARTHY, P. J.   *Sampling opinions: An analysis of survey procedures.* New York: Wiley, 1958.

THURSTONE, L. L., and CHAVE, E. J.   *The measurement of attitude toward the church.* Chicago: University of Chicago Press, 1929.

TRIANDIS, H. C.   Exploratory factor analysis of the behavioral component of social attitudes. *Journal of Abnormal and Social Psychology,* 1964, 68, 420–430.

TRIANDIS, H. C., LOH, W. D., and LEVIN, LESLIE ANN.   Race, status, quality of spoken English, and opinions about civil rights as determinants of interpersonal attitudes. *Journal of Personality and Social Psychology,* 1966, 3, 468–472.

TRIANDIS, H. C., and TRIANDIS, LEIGH M.   Race, social class, religion, and nationality as determinants of social distance. *Journal of Abnormal and Social Psychology,* 1960, 61, 110–118.

TRIANDIS, H. C., and TRIANDIS, LEIGH M.   A cross-cultural study of social distance. *Psychological Monographs,* 1962, 76, Whole No. 540.

WARD, C. D.   Ego involvement and the absolute judgment of attitude statements. *Journal of Personality and Social Psychology,* 1965, 2, 202–208.

Persuasion and Attitude Change

Perhaps one of the most common phenomena to be observed in any society is the time that individuals spend attempting to manipulate one another's behavior. These efforts range all the way from a mother's attempts to toilet-train her children to the largely ineffectual measures adopted by most penal systems to reform criminals. Some types of behavior modification involve what we may call *persuasion,* where a change is contemplated not just in some specific habit but in some long-term disposition, or attitude. Unlike the type of social influence that is revealed in many studies of imitation and conformity, the critical element in persuasion is that it be accomplished as an *instrumental act* by someone who stands to benefit in some manner by achieving a modification in the attitudes and behavior of another. Thus, I may urge you to see a movie in which I am interested rather than one that appeals to you. Or I may try to convince you that our foreign policy in Southeast Asia is faulty or that Catholics should be allowed to exercise individual freedom of conscience with regard to birth control. In the first instance, choosing a movie, I am merely attempting to influence your current behavior, whereas in the latter two situations I am endeavoring to bring about changes in your attitudes.

The Mass Media

The significant role of communication in persuasion becomes apparent as we consider the importance of radio, print, television, and the motion picture in our daily lives. Social scientists have for some time been concerned with the effects of these mass media on the behavior of viewers and listeners. Regulatory agencies have generally assumed that the mass media have a profound influence upon attitudes and opinions, with the result that self-imposed censorship has restricted both the scope and the treatment of controversial topics in radio, television, and the movies. Books and magazines have characteristically been allowed more freedom from formal regulation of their content, presumably on the theory that they reach a smaller, more discriminating audience and are less likely to be disruptive of morals or manners. Recently, of course, court decisions have cleared the way for the expression in print of all but "hard-core pornography," and even the television and motion picture industries have abandoned their timorous approach to deal with topics and issues formerly considered too controversial for programing.

What effects do the mass media actually have upon opinions and attitudes? We cannot answer this question until we understand more about the variables that are involved in persuasion in general. In a naturalistic setting, such as that involving the reactions of a vast television audience, so many unknown and uncontrolled factors are involved in the reactions of the viewers that it is difficult for an investigator to reach any valid conclusions about the impact of a program alone. The persuasive power of a speech, a motion picture, or a printed tract can be determined with precision only under conditions in which the attitudes of the recipients can be evaluated following exposure, and where control can be exerted over such variables as the source of the material, its organization and manner of presentation, and the extent of its discrepancy from the position of the recipient.

Experiments may be designed not only to disclose something about the ways in which audiences react to persuasion but also to develop more effective procedures for communicating a point of view. At the present time, various federal agencies are vitally concerned with more effective methods of presenting the philosophy and practices of democratic government to peoples around the world who may have little or no conception of Western political thinking. Although such efforts are generally represented as programs of education and information, the goals frequently are opinion and attitude change. We now realize that many of the methods employed in this direction have been based on either common sense or sheer rule of thumb; as a result, they not only lack practical utility but may even produce the opposite of the intended results.

Because of the pervasiveness as well as the practical significance of persuasion and attitude change, social psychologists during recent years have devoted a great deal of attention to this topic. We will review some of this research and will analyze a few of the more dependable findings as they relate to behavior theory in general. There are several ways in which we might organize our discussion. One strategy would be to examine the variables that seem to determine whether or not people are persuaded by communication. Thus, we might consider source credibility, personal involvement, and initial disposition of the recipients in relation to attitude change. Alternatively, we might review experiments relevant to several major theories of persuasion. Or, again, we could survey the available data as it relates to the four principal elements in a persuasive encounter: the communicator, the message, the medium, and the recipient. However, these turn out to be highly interrelated; for example, the message has a particular impact depending upon the credibility of the communicator, the medium of transmission, and the degree of the recipient's involvement in the issue.

Perhaps the most effective approach to the research in this area for our purposes will be, first, to outline some of the theoretical problems in persuasion, next, to review several of the variables that have received fairly intensive study, and finally, to reconsider the state of theory in view of the available experimental data.

Theoretical Considerations

A number of theories have been propounded to account for the various aspects of persuasion. Insko (1967) identifies at least fourteen theoretical orientations, each of which can be supported to some extent by empirical data. We will find it more convenient, however, to consider all of these various approaches as belonging essentially to two camps: (a) reinforcement, or behavior, theory, and (b) cognitive, or balance, theory. Suppose we look at cognitive theory for a moment, inasmuch as a great many testable hypotheses have been derived from its assumptions.

Cognitive Theory

This viewpoint has derived largely from the research and writings of Festinger (1957) and his associates. Cognitive theory, however, has its roots in the earlier work of Heider (1946, 1958) and Newcomb (1953, 1959). The major emphasis for each of these theorists has been the *perception* of the situation by the individual whose attitudes are subjected to influence. Thus, the investigator's attention is focused on implicit or cognitive events rather than on the discriminative and reinforcing stimuli that control behavior.

We reviewed in Chapter 9 some aspects of balance theory as developed independently by Heider and by Newcomb. A basic assumption of balance theory is that a state of psychological imbalance, caused perhaps by the individual's perception of a discrepancy between his attitudes and those of someone he respects, sets in motion processes designed to change attitudes and, thus, to restore balance. Unfortunately, such processes are not susceptible to direct observation; they must be inferred from responses that the individual makes to attitude items, rating scales, adjective checklists, and other psychometric probes.

Those theoretical positions that describe attitude change as a restoration of balance or a reinstatement of congruity or consistency among beliefs, therefore, are most simply referred to as cognitive theories. What is the precise nature of the psychological variables that are presumed to have come into imbalance or disequilibrium? Operationally, these consist of evaluative judgments made by an individual about some aspect of his environment. According to Osgood and Tannenbaum (1955), "Predictions about attitude change are assumed to hold for *any* situation in which one object of judgment is associated with another by an assertion" (p. 50). Attitudes are described as favorable (+), neutral (0), or unfavorable (–). Assertions may be positive (+) or negative (–). The nature of the assertion connecting two objects of judgment determines congruence or incongruence. For example, the statement "Nixon favors freedom of the press" is congruent with the existing frame of reference of most persons. However, the assertion that "Pravda favors freedom of the press" is attitudinally incongruent. Suppose that attitudes toward the concepts "Pravda" and "freedom of the press" are found to be polarized on a seven-point scale such that "Pravda" is given a –2 rating and "freedom of the press" is rated +3.

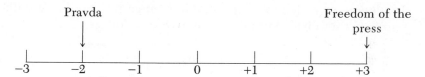

Following the steps outlined by Osgood and Tannenbaum, we can determine the change in attitude toward these two concepts, or objects of judgment, that should occur when they are connected by an associative link, such as "favors." The pressure toward congruence for each concept is given by the equations:

$$P_{oj_1} = d_{oj_2} - d_{oj_1}$$
$$P_{oj_2} = d_{oj_1} - d_{oj_2}$$

Here, P_{oj_1} is the pressure toward congruity for the first object of judgment, "Pravda," and P_{oj_2} is the pressure toward congruity for the second object of judgment, "freedom of the press." The evaluative scale positions for these two concepts are given as d_{oj_1} and d_{oj_2}, respectively. If these two concepts are not equally polarized, as in the present instance, then the less polarized of the two absorbs more of the pressure toward congruity. In other words, the concept which is the object of the less extreme attitude will change more than the one that is the object of a more extreme attitude. The relative attitude change (AC) that will occur with respect to each of the concepts is determined by the following formulas:

$$AC_{oj_1} = \frac{|d_{oj_2}|}{|d_{oj_1}| + |d_{oj_2}|} P_{oj_1}$$

$$AC_{oj_2} = \frac{|d_{oj_1}|}{|d_{oj_1}| + |d_{oj_2}|} P_{oj_2}$$

where d_{oj_1} and d_{oj_2} are taken at their absolute value, regardless of sign.

The particular example that we have chosen can then be solved as follows with respect to the pressures toward congruity for each concept:

$$oj_1 = \text{Pravda}$$

$$oj_2 = \text{Freedom of the press}$$

$$P_{oj_1} = d_{oj_2} - d_{oj_1}$$

$$= +3 - (-2)$$

$$= +5$$

$$P_{oj_2} = d_{oj_1} - d_{oj_2}$$

$$= -2 - (+3)$$

$$= -5$$

The degree to which attitudes should change in accordance with these pressures to establish congruity is computed as follows:

$$AC_{oj_1} = \frac{|d_{oj_2}|}{|d_{oj_1}| + |d_{oj_2}|} P_{oj_1}$$

$$= \frac{3}{2 + 3} (+5)$$

$$= +3$$

$$AC_{oj_2} = \frac{|d_{oj_1}|}{|d_{oj_1}| + |d_{oj_2}|} P_{oj_2}$$

$$= \frac{2}{2 + 3} (-5)$$

$$= -2$$

Referring now to our attitude scale, we can see that the point of equilibrium is +1. "Pravda" should improve its position on the scale, and "freedom of the press" should suffer somewhat as a result of being tied to this originally negative source.

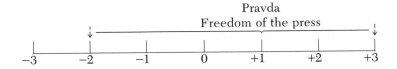

Although Osgood and Tannenbaum have buttressed their position with some rather sophisticated concepts and techniques derived from the semantic differential, earlier investigators had hit upon this same general problem. Farnsworth and Misumi (1931) found that individuals tended to judge a painting more favorably if told that it was by a well-known artist than if told it was by an unknown artist. Saadi and Farnsworth (1934) reported that students tended more often to agree with statements attributed to admired sources (i.e., Edison, Aristotle) than to less admired sources (i.e., Al Capone, the Hearst papers). Presumably, in both of these instances, the subjects perceived some discrepancy between the object of evaluation and the attributed source. The result was that they evaluated the object either more positively or more negatively, according to whether they held the source in high or low regard. Their ratings, in other words, were compromises between their judgments of the source and of the object.

A similar effect has been reported by Sherif (1935), who attributed sixteen short prose passages from the writings of Robert Louis Stevenson to sixteen different authors, whose relative popularity with a group of students had previously been determined. The students tended to rank the passages in accordance with their ranked preferences for the authors to whom the passages were attributed. Again, we may assume that the passages, by any objective standard, did not vary greatly in attractiveness, since they were all written by one person. But to have a balanced set of judgments requires that prose attributed to a highly favored author be ranked higher than prose attributed to a little favored author.

A more dramatic instance of imbalance resulting from a course of events that directly contravened the attitudes of a group of individuals was studied by Festinger, Riecken, and Schachter (1956). These investigators devoted three months to observing a group whose members believed that the continent would soon be engulfed in a cataclysmic flood. The leader of the group, a woman who claimed to have received news of the impending disaster from Guardians living in outer space, assured her followers that they would be whisked to safety in a flying saucer. Although the believers waited outdoors for three hours one cold, wintry night and indoors from midnight to 5 A.M. another night, no rescuers from outer space appeared. Fortunately, the flood did not occur either. Were the followers made skeptical by the failure of their prediction and the doubt that this should have cast upon the validity of their beliefs and attitudes? On the contrary, those members who had remained together through the period of disillusionment decided that their faith and adherence to "instructions" had prevented the flood and saved the world. They renewed their proselyting efforts by giving extended interviews to the press, summoning photographers, and inviting the public at large to attend their gatherings.

These "true believers" can be said to have experienced not just an imbalance between beliefs and reality but also a severe state of what Festinger (1957) has called *cognitive dissonance*. This term, which has attracted wide attention in the research literature, refers to a psychological state resulting from confrontation with information that is inconsistent with some attitude or opinion held by the individual. The role of cognitive dissonance in attitude change is stated by Festinger as follows: "The existence of dissonance, being psychologically uncomfortable, will motivate the person to try to reduce the dissonance and achieve consonance" (p. 3). Consonance refers to a state in which the cognitive components of an attitude are logically consistent and noncontradictory. Festinger argues further that the concept of dissonance is motivationally equivalent to the more familiar terms hunger, frustration, and disequilibrium. "Cognitive dissonance," he writes, "can be seen as an antecedent condition which leads to activity oriented toward dissonance reduction just as hunger leads to activity oriented toward hunger reduction" (p. 3). This particular theoretical approach has stimulated a great deal of research. However, more emphasis is placed on assumed cognitive states than on the stimulus variables of which a particular performance is a function. For this reason, we will treat the results of dissonance experiments in terms different from those used by Festinger and his collaborators.

Reinforcement Theory

The basic concepts and vocabulary of behavior theory, developed, as they have been, largely from research done with lower animals, are often neither immediately nor obviously perceived as applicable to the more complex forms of human social behavior. Nevertheless, as we have tried to demonstrate in the previous chapters, a great deal is gained both in parsimony and in uniformity of terminology by using reinforcement language whenever possible. Fortunately for our purposes, a giant stride in studying the phenomena of persuasion from a reinforcement standpoint has been made by Hovland, Janis, and Kelley (1953) and their associates at Yale University. They have taken the position that attitudes and opinions, like other habits, tend to persist unless the individual undergoes some new learning experience. For example, they state: "Exposure to a persuasive communication which successfully induces the individual to accept a new opinion constitutes a learning experience in which a new verbal habit is acquired" (p. 10). Hovland, Janis, and Kelley explicitly mention the role of *inducement* in attitude change, thus implying that attitude change in the face of persuasion is contingent upon some incentive that either is provided by the communicator or is implied as a consequence of accepting the communicator's message.

In one sense, what is induced by a persuasive communication is a form of *imitative behavior,* in which the recipient adopts some of the verbalizations contained in the communication. As we noted with regard to the research on imitation by Bandura and his colleagues, an imitative performance can be demonstrated to occur in an individual who has merely observed another person's performance reinforced. It follows, then, that observing a verbal performance by another person might cause one to incorporate certain elements of it into his own behavior, provided that these elements are perceived as the occasions for reinforcement.

Several possible sources of reinforcement for yielding to persuasion have been identified by Hovland, Janis, and Kelley. These include (a) the expectation of being right rather than wrong, especially if the communicator is perceived as expert or credible, and (b) the expectation of social approval for adopting a position that emanates from a prestigeful source or that already enjoys a high degree of acceptance by others. In other words, the recipient of a persuasive communication will be influenced to the extent that his acceptance of the position advocated will be instrumental in either achieving positive reinforcement or avoiding aversive consequences. We understand "expectation" as deriving from a history of having been reinforced for adopting the position advocated by an expert or a prestigeful source.

Unfortunately, as Lazarsfeld (1949) has pointed out with reference to persuasion, the incentives for a change in attitude or opinion are often minimal, and the potential rewards, or reinforcements, may not be obvious either to the experimenter or to the subject. This is certainly the case with most laboratory experimentation. Subjects often give evidence of having been persuaded on some issue where no incentive for change had been offered and no reinforcement received. Simple exposure to a persuasive argument often appears to be sufficient to induce attitude change. Why should this be so, and how do such results square with reinforcement theory?

There are a number of possible explanations for the positive results reported from persuasion experiments. Perhaps the subjects were performing according to what they perceived as the "demand characteristics" of the situation (Orne, 1962), that is, the experimental manipulations were transparent to the subjects, who simply responded to the post-treatment attitude scales in a manner they considered to be consistent with the experimenter's purposes. The incentive for such behavior might be the anticipated approval of the experimenter, who is generally a prestigeful figure, such as an instructor or a graduate assistant. Or, the experimenter may quite unwittingly have provided cues to which the subject responded in the predicted fashion (Rosenthal, 1967). These cues might have been implicit in the experimenter's posture or manner of speaking and may have served either as incentives for the subjects to respond in a certain way or as reinforcers that aided the subject in learning performances consistent with the experimenter's hypotheses. We are reminded of Clever Hans, the horse that was able to solve arithmetic problems, tell time, and answer questions, all by tapping his forefoot. It turned out, as described by Pfungst (1911), that Hans could perform these feats only if someone in his field of vision knew the answers. His master as well as others were unknowingly providing facial and body cues that signaled Hans when to stop tapping. If the questions were whispered in his ear, or if he was prevented from seeing his audience, Hans was no more clever than any plowhorse.

A third possibility is that the subjects in a great many experimental situations have actually been persuaded to change their opinions or attitudes. We know from everyday experience that individuals do modify their behavior as circumstances change, and most laboratory studies are designed to simulate the kinds of conditions under which attitudes tend to be influenced. How can an attitude be brought partially under experimental control? For one thing, we may assume that a counter-attitudinal communication arouses some verbal processes in the recipient that are aversive. Perhaps he perceives some inconsistency between his beliefs or attitudes and those voiced by a highly regarded source. It is then necessary only to make the further assumption that such perceived inconsistency is a noxious state and that any verbal reactions that have the effect of reducing or eliminating this condition will be negatively reinforced. The organism, according to Cofer and Appley (1964), ". . . tends to resist changes in its environment that are of a magnitude large enough to upset its equilibrium or threaten its survival as a stable system" (p. 364). It is not necessary, in their view, that a disturbed system return to its previous state of equilibrium. Indeed, as a great deal of data seem to indicate, attitude change can be viewed as the expression of a new equilibrium between the previous dispositions of the individual and the immediate situation in which he finds himself.

Approached in this manner, some instances of attitude change appear as behavior modifications that are negatively reinforced through the reduction or the avoidance of aversive stimulation. The aversive state results from whatever inconsistency or logical incongruency the individual perceives between certain attitudes he holds and those that are offered to him either as more tenable or as representative of someone he holds in high esteem. Alternatively, of course, attitude change might be seen to occur as the result of incentive or reward and to be maintained through positive reinforcement.

Because of the number of elements involved, it is difficult to represent a persuasive encounter in simple S-R terms. However, the following diagram outlines some of the now familiar components of such an interaction in a very limited situation.

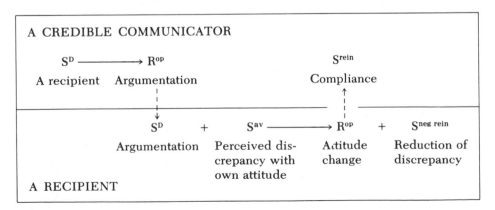

The foregoing model could, of course, be complicated in various ways. For one thing, the communicator might combine his presentation with the offer of an incentive for compliant behavior. Attitude change can be measured before or after monetary payment has been made for some performance by the subject that is inconsistent with his attitudes. This particular type of situation, involving *induced compliance*, will be examined more closely in a later section of this chapter. But however one chooses to complicate the situation by introducing additional variables suspected of playing a role in persuasion, it is useful to analyze the total behavioral exchange in terms of the antecedent or "setting" operations of the experimenter and the consequent performance of the subject.

In the diagram above, the persuasive behavior emitted by the communicator, whether in writing or by voice or picture, is indicated by R^{op}. His behavior is not only an occasion on which the recipient will tend to respond in some fashion, it is also an aversive stimulus, since it involves presentation of a viewpoint with which the recipient disagrees. (If the recipient agrees with the viewpoint advocated, of course, no aversive stimulation is involved.) When the recipient disagrees but modifies his attitude so as to bring it more in line with the communicator's point of view, then he has effectively reduced the aversiveness of the situation, and his behavior is reinforced. Any evidence of his agreement with the communicator will positively reinforce the communicator's efforts. It is characteristic of some individuals that failure in their efforts to convert others to their point of view does not dissuade them from future attempts. Perhaps their behavior is maintained by the attention they receive. The important point is that this set of interactive events is not resistant to a functional analysis. Although vastly simplified, this symbolic representation of events is intended to illustrate the manner in which the behavior of two individuals — a communicator and a recipient — might interact to maintain the persuasive efforts of one and modify the attitudes of the other. We can draw a broad picture of the stimulus-response components, even though the details are still beyond our grasp.

Determinants of Persuasibility

Persuasion, when it occurs, results from a complex interaction of variables associated with the source, the medium, the persuasive argument, and the recipient. We are just at the threshold of understanding the manner in which these factors determine the outcome of a social interaction involving persuasion. We cannot hope within the scope of this chapter to do more than touch upon the voluminous research that has accumulated on this topic over the past fifteen years, a period during which an increasing sophistication in research design has become evident. We will, therefore, focus our attention on the following variables: (a) the communicator, (b) the argument, (c) the recipient, (d) resistance to persuasion. Despite some inconsistent findings, particularly as they relate to predictions from theory, a number of conclusions can be reached concerning the relative effectiveness of various persuasive devices as well as the means by which they might be resisted.

Communicator Credibility

The stimulus value of a communicator is determined not only by what he says but also by how the recipient perceives him in terms of his established identity, his mannerisms, and his appearance. Since we considered the problem of person perception in a previous chapter, we shall limit ourselves here to those characteristics of a communicator that might be said to establish his credibility as a source of information and opinion.

Hovland and Weiss (1951) conducted a study comparing the effectiveness of written communications attributed to trustworthy communicators with those attributed to untrustworthy sources. They first devised arguments representing pro and con positions on the sale of antihistamine drugs without prescription, the practicability of atomic submarines, blame for the steel shortage, and the future of movie theaters. For half of the subjects in the experiment, whose opinions had previously been ascertained on these issues, the communications were attributed to trustworthy sources and for the remaining half to untrustworthy sources. When opinions were tested again immediately following exposure to the communications, it was found that on the average 23 per cent of the subjects who had been told that the sources were trustworthy changed in the direction advocated. Fewer than 7 per cent of the subjects who thought they were reading from untrustworthy sources showed evidence of persuasion. Table 11.1 summarizes the data.

When the opinions of the subjects were determined again after an interval of four weeks, it was found that agreement with the untrustworthy source had increased, while agreement with the trustworthy source had

Table 11.1*

Net percentages of cases in which subjects changed opinion in direction of communication.† (From Hovland and Weiss, 1951)

Topic	Trustworthy Source N	Trustworthy Source Per cent	Untrustworthy Source N	Untrustworthy Source Per cent
Antihistamines	31	22.6	30	13.3
Atomic submarines	25	36.0	36	0.0
Steel shortage	35	22.9	26	−3.8
Future of movies	31	12.9	30	16.7

* C. I. Hovland and W. Weiss, "The influence of source credibility on communicative effectiveness," *Public Opinion Quarterly*, 1951, *15*, 635–650. Reprinted by permission of author and copyright holder.

† Net changes = positive changes *minus* negative changes.

decreased. The investigators suggest that over time there is a tendency to dissociate the source from the content. Apparently the stimulus value of the source is maximized at the time of presentation. The implication is that individuals may reject a message from an untrustworthy source at the time they are first exposed to it but may show a delayed acceptance of the communication when its source has been forgotten. Gossips, rumormongers, and propagandists may in this way have a pernicious influence that survives long after they themselves have been discredited as sources of information.

A similar experiment was conducted by Kelman and Hovland (1953), using treatment of juvenile delinquents as the topic of persuasion. Three different groups of summer high school students listened to the recorded voice of a speaker variously identified as (a) a judge in a juvenile court, (b) an interested layman, or (c) a dope peddler out on bail. The speaker, who was actually the same person in every case, gave a talk favoring extreme leniency in the treatment of juvenile delinquents. A scale measuring attitudes on the treatment of criminals, with a high score favoring leniency, was administered to the student subjects immediately after the communication and again three weeks later. The scores obtained by the subjects on the immediate post-test are shown in Table 11.2.

Table 11.2

Mean post-treatment scores on attitudes toward treatment of delinquents. (Based on Kelman and Hovland, 1953, Table 3, p. 331)

Group	N	Mean
Positive communicator (judge)	97	46.7
Neutral communicator (layman)	56	45.7
Negative communicator (dope peddler)	91	42.8

The students who heard either the positive or the neutral communicator achieved approximately the same scores on the attitude scale. Both of these groups, however, scored significantly higher, indicating agreement with the communication, than the students who heard the negative communicator. Three weeks after the experiment, when attitudes were again measured, these differences had disappeared, thus confirming the previous finding that over time a source tends to become dissociated from communication content.

An experiment by Fine (1957), however, failed to reveal any advantage of a highly credible source over a less credible source in influencing opinions. This was a complex study, in which other variables, such as initial position of the audience and subject anxiety, were also examined. The communication was a printed article on biological warfare. Some of the subjects were told that the article was taken from *The New York Times* (high credibility) while others were told that the article was from *The Daily Worker* (low credibility). When opinions on the issue were measured immediately following presentation of the communications, all of the subjects were found to have moved in the direction advocated. However, the presumed high credibility source had stimulated no more attitude change than the presumed low credibility source. Although these findings might be interpreted as casting doubt upon the general efficacy of high source credibility in modifying opinions as compared with low source credibility, it should be pointed out that not all of the subjects necessarily perceived *The New York Times* as more trustworthy than *The Daily Worker*. A danger exists in arbitrarily attributing credibility to the source of a communication unless there is overwhelming reason for believing that the average person would agree with this designation.

Reversal effects. A "boomerang effect" apparently can also take place in a situation where the recipient of a communication perceives the communicator as lacking expertise. Aronson, Turner, and Carlsmith (1963) studied 112 female college students who met in small groups for the purpose of rank-ordering nine stanzas from obscure modern poems. The criterion for ranking was "the way the poet uses form to aid in expressing his meaning." After she had ranked the stanzas, each subject read a critical essay on poetry which, by way of example, contained an evaluation of one of the stanzas that she had read. The experimenters arranged the materials so that this evaluation was always about the stanza that a given subject had ranked eighth. For one third of the subjects there was a mild discrepancy between the subject's opinion and that of the communicator, for one third a moderate discrepancy, and for one third an extreme discrepancy. In the latter instance, for example, the critic would have rated the stanza as very good, when it had been rated next to last by the student. The same procedure was followed for two groups of subjects, but the critical essay was attributed to different sources for each group. Half of the girls thought the essay, including the rating of one of the stanzas, was by T. S. Eliot, while the remaining half were told that the essay had been written by a student at a teachers' college. Following this experimental procedure, the girls again rated the stanzas.

The results of the experiment are summarized in Figure 11.1, where it can be seen that opinion change following exposure to a highly credible source increased as a direct function of distance between the subjects' opinions and the position advocated by the communicator. For the less credible source, however, opinion change first increased with discrepancy between subject and communicator and then decreased. The investigators explain this finding by suggesting that the subjects found it easier to reject the opinion of the less credible source, particularly when the position advocated was widely discrepant from their own. The highly credible source, on the other hand, could not easily be discredited, even under the extreme discrepancy condition.

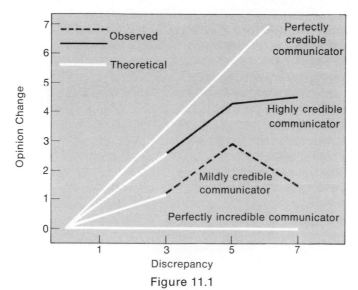

Figure 11.1

Opinion change as a function of communicator credibility and amount of discrepancy between the recipient's view and that of the communicator. (After Aronson, Turner, and Carlsmith, 1963)

If a communicator is not even mildly credible, then he may have even less impact as his own position becomes increasingly discrepant from that held by the recipient. Such an effect was demonstrated by Bergin (1962). Two groups of college students filled out self-rating forms as well as several tests that included the trait of masculinity-femininity. Several days later, the members of both groups were shown spurious records of their test results that differed in varying degrees from their self-ratings. In one group, however, the discrepant information was delivered by the director of the project, while in the other group the discrepant ratings were attributed to a confederate of the experimenter who posed as a high school student. Following these disclosures, the subjects again rated themselves on the personality traits. Their self-ratings changed as a function of the credibility of the source of the contrived ratings as well as the amount of discrepancy between these and the original ratings. The results are shown in Figure 11.2.

Individuals may, of course, comply with suggestions made by a disliked communicator and may even change their opinions in the direction of greater consistency with their actual behavior. Zimbardo and his colleagues (1965) used both "positive" and "negative" communicators in inducing Army reservists to eat fried grasshoppers. Although the communicator was presented in both instances as capable and conscientious, he assumed a negative role for some of the groups by appearing "snobbish, demanding, tactless, bossy, cold, and hostile." Interestingly, about 50 per cent of the subjects ate the grasshoppers regardless of which role the communicator had adopted with them. However, in their response to an

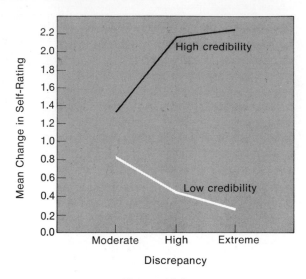

Figure 11.2
*Mean change in self-rating as a function of discrepancy of information
and credibility of the source.* (After Bergin, 1962)

adjective checklist, the subjects revealed significantly more favorable impressions of the communicator in his positive role. Finally, many of those
who complied with the request to eat the grasshoppers expressed a greater
liking for them following this experience. This finding is consistent with
others that have shown attitude change to accompany compliant behavior.

Involvement. In a series of cross-cultural investigations, McGinnies
(1966a, 1968) found that communicator credibility was a primary factor in
inducing attitude change among Oriental students on such current vital
issues as the Cold War and the conflict in Vietnam. Even when confronted
with evidence from a highly credible source that American military participation in Vietnam was justified, only those Japanese college students who
professed little personal involvement in this issue were influenced to adopt
a less antagonistic attitude toward U.S. policy. A similar effect of involvement was observed among students in Taiwan, where initial attitudes
strongly supported military intervention by the United States and where a
communication advocating American withdrawal from Vietnam was used.
Only the less involved recipients responded to persuasion with a significant change in attitude.

Source credibility emerges, then, as a potent variable determining the
responsiveness of individuals to a persuasive communication. However,
it interacts with such additional factors as involvement in the issue and discrepancy between the initial attitudes of the subjects and the position advocated by the communicator. We will consider the matter of initial attitude
and discrepancy in somewhat more detail later in this chapter.

The Communication

Order effects. Not all arguments are equally effective, even when they
deal with the same subject matter. They may differ in wording as well as
in the placement of various contentions within the general framework of the
communication. There are certain features of organization that seem to
have a significant bearing upon the effectiveness of persuasive material.
One of the most widely investigated of these involves order of presentation
of opposing arguments. The problem may be posed as follows. If two different sides of an issue are to be presented, will the side presented first
or that presented second have a greater influence on opinion? A typical
experiment dealing with this problem was performed some years ago by
Lund (1925). He presented subjects with arguments both proposing and
attacking such concepts as higher protective tariffs for the United States
and the future of monogamous marriage. Half of his subjects heard the
affirmative argument on each issue first, and the remaining half heard the
negative argument first. Opinion questionnaires were administered to
all of the subjects initially and again after each of the two opposing communications. Lund found that opinion change measured following the first
communication was significantly greater than that measured following
the second communication, suggesting the operation of a "law of primacy"
in persuasion. Cromwell (1950), on the other hand, found that the second
of two conflicting communications was more effective in influencing opinion, and thus obtained a "recency" rather than a "primacy" effect. However, the procedure in Cromwell's experiment differed from Lund's in that
post-testing took place only after both communications had been presented.
As in many psychological experiments, such variations in procedure can
easily produce differences in results. The conflicting results of these and
similar experiments have led to a primacy-recency problem in persuasion.
Hovland and Mandell (1952), who also failed to replicate Lund's findings,
suggested that primacy may operate under some conditions and recency
under others. Among the several conditions that seem to influence order
effects in persuasion are familiarity and controversiality of the topic, subject awareness of the communicator's intentions, and subject interest in
and knowledge of the topic.

Lana (1961) examined the influence of order of presentation of both pro
and con communications about vivisection on subjects who had been differentially familiarized with this topic. He found that increasing familiarity
with the issue facilitated a primacy effect, whereas lack of familiarity was
associated with a recency effect. It is possible that greater familiarity with
an issue enhances the stimulus value of the first communication and induces a degree of attitude change in the recipient that is refractory to further influence. Consistent with this interpretation are some findings by
Hovland, Campbell, and Brock (1957), who reported that the public expression of opinion following persuasion tended to "freeze" the subjects' views

and to make them resistant to influence by opposing arguments on the issue. It is conceivable, then, that any kind of initial interest, familiarity, or commitment on an issue tends to favor the impact of the first of two opposing arguments.

In his early statement of the law of effect, which was the precursor of modern reinforcement theory, Thorndike (1933) presented data to show that behavior occurring either before or after presentation of a reward would be strengthened. This so-called *spread of effect* has been investigated in relation to persuasion by Rosnow (1968), who argues that rewarding and punishing events can have both a forward (proactive) and a backward (retroactive) influence on a persuasive communication. If true, such an effect might help to account for some of the findings concerning argument organization as a factor in persuasion. For example, Corrozi and Rosnow (1968) tested the hypothesis that subjects' opinions would change in the direction of whichever of two arguments was closer in time to a reinforcing stimulus or farther from an aversive stimulus. Borrowing from a technique developed by Golightly and Byrne (1964), they used as reinforcers statements with which the subjects agreed (consonant statements) or disagreed (dissonant statements). These had been found to be effective reinforcers in discrimination learning, and it seemed likely that they would also influence performance on an opinion questionnaire.

Corrozi and Rosnow developed positive and negative commentaries about the noted artist Pablo Picasso. These were read to eight groups of high school students, each of whom also heard either an agreeable or a disagreeable communication preceding or following the persuasive arguments. The various orders of presentation of these materials were counterbalanced according to the following design:

Consonant after	Consonant before	Dissonant after	Dissonant before
Pro Con	Pro Con	Pro Con	Pro Con
first first	first first	first first	first first
(Recency predicted)	(Primacy predicted)	(Primacy predicted)	(Recency predicted)

As shown above, both pro and con arguments appeared in each position, and the rewarding and punishing events (statements favoring a longer or shorter school week) also occurred both before and after each of these argument sequences. The predictions, as noted above, were based on the assumption that a "spread of effect" would take place from the consonant (positive) and dissonant (aversive) materials to the persuasive arguments about the merits of Picasso. When the results of the before and after opinion scores about Picasso were analyzed, it was found that all of the changes were in the predicted directions, and only one failed to reach statistical significance. A primacy effect was evident when the persuasive arguments either followed a consonant communication or preceded a dissonant communication. Recency occurred when the persuasive arguments either preceded a consonant communication or followed a dissonant communication. Inasmuch as similar findings have been obtained in other experiments, summarized by Rosnow (1968), it seems safe to conclude that the persuasive effects of opposing communications presented one after the other can be predicted to some extent from their temporal relationships with other reinforcing events.

One-sided and two-sided arguments. Perhaps an even more interesting problem involving the organization of persuasive arguments concerns the relative effectiveness of one-sided versus two-sided presentations. As stated by Hovland, Janis, and Kelley (1953), "Two patterns are usually open to the communicator: concentration on the points supporting the position he advocates, or presentation of these *plus* discussion of the opposed arguments" (p. 105). In everyday situations in which persuasion is attempted, one generally has the option of stressing only one side of an issue or of acknowledging, and refutating, opposing arguments. The recipient is correspondingly either exposed to a point of view that is totally uncongenial or confronted with argumentation with which he can at least partially agree. Which of these stimulus situations will generate greater attitude change consistent with the position advocated by the communicator?

In an early study, Hovland, Lumsdaine, and Sheffield (1949) determined the beliefs of over four hundred soldiers on the single question of whether or not the war with Japan would come to an early end following Germany's surrender. An experimental group composed of about two hundred soldiers was then presented with a fifteen-minute talk consisting only of arguments suggesting that the war with Japan would be a long one. A second experimental group of the same size heard a communication which contained these same arguments but also included certain considerations of Japan's weaknesses that might support prediction of an early end to the war. Following this procedure, the subjects were again asked to estimate the probable length of the war with Japan. Both types of arguments were found to be extremely effective with both experimental groups. A control group, which had not been exposed to persuasion, showed no shifts in opinion on the issue. However, the critical prediction had been that the two-sided argument would be more effective with those individuals who were initially in disagreement with the communicator's opinion that the war would continue for at least two years after VE Day. Figure 11.3 shows the results.

Since the men who initially tended to agree with the position advocated could not take a position very discrepant from the stand of the communicator, there was no reason for them to be more influenced by the two-sided argument. In fact, the one-sided argument was more effective with these individuals, perhaps because it more strongly reinforced their opinions

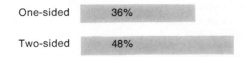

A. Among men initially opposed to communicator's position.

One-sided   36%

Two-sided   48%

B. Among men initially favorable to communicator's position.

One-sided   52%

Two-sided   23%

Figure 11.3

*Per cent of individuals changing opinion in direction of position advo-
cated by communicator.* (Adapted from Hovland, Lumsdaine, and
Sheffield, 1949)

than did the two-sided argument, which introduced some discordant elements.

The apparent superiority of two-sided over one-sided communications
has received more recent documentation in an experiment by Insko (1962),
who presented subjects with tape-recorded summaries for both the prose-
cution and the defense in a fictitious trial. Some subjects heard the prosecutor's argument first, while other subjects listened first to the defense
argument. Each position was presented in both one-sided and two-sided
versions. Insko found the two-sided argument to be more effective in
influencing opinion whether it occurred before or after the one-sided
presentation.

In a different cultural context, McGinnies (1966b) studied the reactions
of Japanese college students to both one-sided and two-sided arguments
supporting (a) the actions taken by the United States during the Cuban
missile crisis (which the students supported), and (b) visits by American
nuclear-powered submarines to Japanese ports (which they opposed).
Those students who were antagonistic to the proposed submarine visits
took a less belligerent stand following exposure to the two-sided communication but did not change following a one-sided presentation. Conversely, those students who initially favored the policies adopted by the
United States in the Cuban crisis were somewhat negatively influenced by
the two-sided communication and were moved slightly in a more pro-U.S.
direction by the one-sided argument. The two-sided communication on
the submarine issue was judged as more convincing than the one-sided
version, and the communicator was evaluated more favorably when he
read the two-sided argument. On the Cuban situation, where the recipients were already sympathetically disposed toward the viewpoint advocated, the communicator was judged more favorably when he presented a
two-sided argument, but the argument itself was rated as less convincing
than the one-sided argument.

Theoretically, the addition of positively reinforcing elements to a communication should provide some incentive for its acceptance, assuming that the source is credible. Attitude change should be greater than in the case of communications having only dissonant, or aversive, content. In addition, a two-sided argument, by presenting elements of both contending positions, appears to many recipients as fairer and therefore more credible. The available data suggest that a two-sided communication does, in fact, elicit more attitude change among those individuals opposed to it than a one-sided argument. Probably a two-sided appeal has no advantage with sympathetic recipients because it incorporates aversive elements in addition to those with which they already agree.

Emotional appeals. In Chapter 9 it was suggested that attitudes have behavioral, cognitive, and affective components. Changing the cognitive component of an attitude, that is, altering the implicit verbalizations that define the individual's position on an attitude continuum, might be expected to bring about corresponding adjustments in both the affective and the behavioral systems. A person whose verbal attitude becomes less extreme as a result of persuasion should be less emotional about his position as well as less inclined to former actions in situations where the attitude is elicited. But what about the effects of arousing an emotional response during the persuasion process? Should affective arousal facilitate or inhibit attitude change? Several experiments have been concerned with these questions, and we can reach some tentative conclusions about this problem.

Perhaps the classic study on the problem of emotional versus rational appeals in persuasion was done some years ago by Hartmann (1936). It is well known that politicians frequently lard their orations rather heavily with references to concepts having strongly reinforcing affective connotations, such as "duty," "honor," "morality," and so forth. In fact, one is inclined to suspect that many political appeals contain more emotion than logic. To determine the relative influence on voting behavior of emotional and rational approaches, Hartmann distributed two leaflets in different sections of a community just before a local election. Both leaflets urged the voters to support the Socialist party, but one was emotionally worded and described the election outcome in terms of extreme alternatives, such as war or peace, depression or prosperity. The other leaflet presented the more immediate and practical outcomes of the election in the form of an "intelligence test" and urged voters who agreed with the items to support the Socialist party's candidates. A third set of wards received no leaflets and were used as a control group to see how the voters would act in the absence of either type of appeal. After the election, the vote was analyzed to determine which type of appeal had been more effective in increasing the Socialist vote over that recorded in a previous year's election. In the wards receiving the "emotional" appeal, the Socialist vote increased 50 per cent, in the wards exposed to the "rational" appeal it increased by

35 per cent, and in the control wards it increased by only 24 per cent. Hartmann concluded that the emotional political appeal was a better vote-getting instrument than the rational approach. Parenthetically, we might note that the emotional appeal probably tapped the voter's real concerns (war and peace, depression and prosperity). Its effectiveness may have derived more from this fact than from any affect that it aroused.

It is possible to manipulate the degree of affective arousal engendered by a communication more precisely in the laboratory, although the salutary effects of such appeals are often assumed by Madison Avenue ad men in the absence of any hard data. Many advertisements utilize the arousal of fear or anxiety as a means of influencing purchasing behavior. For example individuals are reminded of the aversive social consequences of having bad breath, body odor, loose dentures, a dirty collar, or an irascible disposition as a means of inducing them to buy products that will prevent or overcome these various deficiencies. Political campaigns frequently emphasize the potentially disastrous results of voting for an opposing candidate rather than stressing the gains associated with a vote for the advocated candidate. Perhaps because of this emphasis in the mass media on the aversive consequences of doing or not doing certain things, attention in several laboratory studies has been directed toward the capacity of a fear-arousing communication to effect attitude change.

An experiment by Janis and Feshbach (1953) throws some light upon this problem. They divided two hundred high school students into four groups and presented them with lectures on dental hygiene. Fifty of the students listened to a communication designed for minimum fear arousal, fifty listened to one with moderate capacity for fear arousal, fifty heard a talk having strong fear arousal capacities, and fifty served as control subjects. Strength of fear arousal was defined by the amount of emphasis placed on the deleterious effects of improper care of the teeth and mouth. Before exposure to the communication, all of the experimental groups, as well as the control group, had replied to a questionnaire designed to determine the extent to which they conformed to a set of dental hygiene recommendations. All of the groups were initially low in conformity to good dental hygiene practices. One week following exposure to the different lectures, the groups were again queried on their adherence to the recommended dental hygiene procedures. The results in terms of per cent of the subjects whose answers changed are shown in Table 11.3.

Quite clearly, the group exposed to the most threatening communication showed the least influence effect, and the group subjected to minimum fear arousal revealed the greatest effect of persuasion. The experimenters were careful to point out, however, that the results indicated only verbal adherence to a set of recommended practices. As in most attitude change studies, we have no way of knowing to what extent changes in verbal behavior on an attitude scale or questionnaire are carried over into other behaviors. As a theoretical explanation for their findings the experimenters suggest that the strong fear appeal left the audience in a state of emotional

Table 11.3

Attitude change as a function of fear arousal. (Based on Janis and Feshbach, 1953, Table 6, p. 84)

Type of Change	Strong Fear	Moderate Fear	Minimal Fear	Control
Increased conformity	28%	44%	50%	22%
Decreased conformity	20	22	14	22
No change	52	34	36	56
Net change	8%	22%	36%	0%

tension that was not fully relieved by rehearsing the reassuring recommendations contained in the communication. Consequently, the recipients
were inclined to either ignore or minimize the importance of the threat.
Attitude change in the other groups could be interpreted as having been
negatively reinforced by its instrumentality in reducing anxiety aroused by
the moderate and slight fear appeals.

The arousal of a strong emotional response, then, does seem to interfere
with an individual's acceptance of a persuasive argument. Why should this
be so? You may recall the experimental evidence we presented earlier
showing that emotional arousal serves to disrupt ongoing behaviors. If one
effect of a persuasive communication is to prompt rehearsal of the argument, then clearly it is detrimental for the material to arouse emotional
reactions that would interfere with this process. In fact, an emotional response may even trigger verbal reactions that are incompatible with those
that would normally be evoked by the communication. We would expect
this to occur, however, only when the communication is counter-attitudinal
in content. Material that is agreeable to the recipient should not be disruptive but, rather, should prompt additional verbalizations consistent
with the communication.

Janis (1967) has reported several unpublished studies in which it was
found that communications designed to provoke feelings of guilt merely
induced resistance in the recipients. In one instance, students who were
reminded of the dreadful fatalities resulting from the A-bomb attacks on
Hiroshima and Nagasaki were actually less receptive to arguments proposing an international ban on H-bomb testing. In the other instance, a
high guilt-inducing communication was less effective than a medium
guild-inducing communication in enlisting student support for civil rights
activites. Appeals that arouse feelings of guilt, fear, or anxiety are un-
questionably aversive. Direct evidence for this contention was adduced by
Nunnaly and Bobren (1959), who found that adult subjects were actually
unwilling to read accounts of the treatment of mental illness when these
were worded so as to arouse fear.

One might wonder about the apparent failure of information concerning
the established relationship between cigarette smoking and lung cancer
to alter markedly the smoking habits of the nation. Since the threat of can-

cer is certainly capable of producing anxiety, it is probable that heavy smokers handle the potential anxiety by discounting, ignoring, or rationalizing the threatening information. Research by Janis and Terwilliger (1962) has shown that a strong threat appeal on the subject of smoking and lung cancer does in fact elicit more antagonism to the communication in post-experimental discussion than does a mild threat.

In considering these and similar results, however, Leventhal and Niles (1964) suggest that fear may be an effective inducement to some immediately available response but may interfere with acceptance of a long-range decision. They conducted an experiment in which adults attending the New York Health Exposition of August, 1961, were assigned to low, mild, and high fear conditions with regard to smoking. The low-fear group read a pamphlet giving data on the relationship of smoking to lung cancer. Subjects in the mild- and high-fear conditions not only read the booklets but also were exposed to a film on smoking and cancer. The film shown to the mild-fear group portrayed the diagnosis, hospitalization, and preparation for surgery of a young man suffering from lung cancer. The high-fear group saw both this film and an additional ten-minute sequence showing portions of the surgical procedure in color. It was recommended to all subjects that they have an X-ray taken immediately following the information session and that they embark on a program to stop smoking.

The investigators found no difference in the numbers of individuals in the mild- and high-fear groups taking advantage of the opportunity for an X-ray examination, but fewer of those in the low-fear condition had X-rays taken. Data from questionnaires administered after the meetings did suggest a positive relationship between the intensity of induced fear and expressed intention to pursue one or both of the two recommended preventive measures. Leventhal and Watts (1966) report a similar experiment in which a majority of the recipients of a highly threatening communication declined to have X-rays taken but, at the same time, reported more success in quitting smoking than the subjects exposed to less threatening material. A possible explanation for these results, according to Leventhal (1965), is that an X-ray taken as a necessary precursor to surgery is very threatening, hence is likely to be avoided. Giving up smoking, although it entails aversive deprivation effects, is not as threatening as surgery.

In other words, the immediately aversive aspects of an X-ray, such as the possible disclosure of cancer, were made salient by the high-fear communication, so that having an X-ray became an unattractive course of action. The mild-fear appeal, by playing down the threat feature of an X-ray, made having an X-ray an effective means of reducing anxiety. The incentive value of an X-ray examination was enhanced by a mildly threatening appeal, whereas the incentive value of giving up smoking altogether was enhanced by severe threats.

In a detailed theoretical analysis of this area of research, Janis (1967) has suggested that "... whenever a strong fear-arousing communication is found to be less effective than a milder version, the outcome is always potentially reversible" (p. 216). The problem, he suggests, is one of discovering a technique that will ". . . enable people to tolerate a relatively high level of fear arousal without becoming so resistant that they would reject the message" (p. 218). Janis argues for more research directed toward determining the optimal levels of emotional arousal to induce attitude change in the direction advocated. We have suggested that a major factor in persuasion is the extent to which the communication controls some behavior by the recipient that can be immediately reinforced. Such an approach promises to be more fruitful than a search for "motives" to accept or to reject the communicator's recommendations.

The Recipient

Initial attitude. It would seem logical that an extreme attitude — one representing either pole of an attitude continuum — would be more resistant to change than a neutral, or uncommitted, stance. Such, indeed, seems to be the case, as an experiment by Tannenbaum (1956) has demonstrated. In his experiment, subjects showed wide differences in initial attitude toward such topics as legalized gambling and abstract art. They were then exposed to persuasive communications designed to move them in either direction on these issues. Figure 11.4 shows that subjects falling at the extremes of the continuum changed less than those in the middle, although the dip in the curve at the neutral point of the scale suggests that neutrality may represent a committed position to some individuals.

Two recent experiments by McGinnies, Donelson, and Haaf (1964) have confirmed the assumption that, in general, those individuals who are neu-

Figure 11.4

Initial attitude as a factor in attitude change. (From Tannenbaum, 1956)

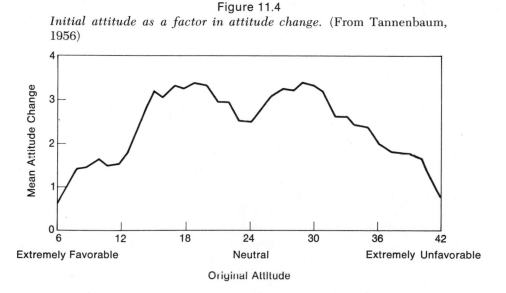

tral on an issue are persuaded more readily than those holding extreme viewpoints. These investigators asked students whose attitudes were either neutral, moderately favorable, or extremely favorable toward the church to read a strongly anti-church essay to six acquaintances outside the laboratory. This procedure was designed to provide a mildly aversive experience for the subjects, who were required to voice opinions with which they did not agree. The extent of disagreement, of course, was greater for the moderately and extremely pro-church subjects than for the neutral subjects. When their attitudes were measured again following this compliance experience, the moderately pro-church subjects were found to have shifted toward a less favorable position, although they were still on the favorable side of neutral. The neutral subjects had actually moved to the anti-church side of the scale. Those subjects who were strongly pro-church to begin with, however, were uninfluenced by the repeated readings of the critical essay. Apparently they had resolved any discomfort that they experienced in this situation by a strategy other than that of modifying their own attitudes. Perhaps they simply rejected the arguments as unfair and unconvincing. Hovland and Pritzker (1957) have also found that a marked discrepancy between the positions of the communicator and the recipients may actually bring about a smaller amount of attitude change than would be produced were the discrepancy not so great.

In many situations, it appears that increasing the attitude discrepancy between the source and the recipient results in first an increase, then a decrease in attitude change. Hovland, Harvey, and Sherif (1957) found that with increasing discrepancy between the position of the subject and the position advocated by a communicator, any initially favorable reaction is lessened, and the communication may be perceived as propagandistic and unfair. They further report that the most frequent reaction by subjects whose own stands diverged widely from that advocated by a communicator was to remain unchanged in their initial attitudes. As we have noted, however, this effect may also depend upon the degree of credibility of the communicator.

Although several experiments conducted with American college students have found neutral individuals to be more persuasible than those holding well-defined attitudes, the author found exactly the opposite to be the case with Japanese college students. During the spring of 1963, the reactions of Japanese students at several large universities were observed in response to pro-American and pro-Soviet arguments dealing with responsibility for the Cold War. The attitudes of several groups of students were measured before and after they had listened to tape-recorded statements borrowed from speeches by Adlai Stevenson and Nikita Khrushchev and translated into Japanese. Somewhat surprisingly, those students who had expressed neutralist sentiments — and these were a majority — showed no significant attitude change in response to either persuasive communication. Further consideration of the results led to the hypothesis that neutrality on the issue of the Cold War represented a firmly entrenched attitude to many Japanese students, one from which they were not readily moved by persuasion. Evidently, the significance of the neutral position on an attitude continuum must be evaluated before one can predict how the individual displaying such a stand will respond to persuasion. In the case of the Japanese subjects, we had obviously not provided sufficient incentive to induce a change in attitude consistent with either of the positions advocated. The fact that the subjects rated the arguments as "slightly unconvincing" suggests that they reacted by discrediting the communication. This seems to be a common response of persons who are firmly committed to a position under attack.

The relationship between initial attitude and communicator credibility was further examined by March and McGinnies (1968). A sample of college students listened to a tape-recorded argument advocating unilateral withdrawal of American military forces from Vietnam. The recipients were classified on the basis of initial attitude as "doves," "moderates," or "hawks." One finding was that a highly credible source produced a significant amount of attitude change in the direction advocated, whereas an incredible source induced an opposite reaction. Those subjects holding initially moderate attitudes showed the greatest amount of attitude change in the direction advocated by the highly credible source. Why was the low credibility source so ineffective? Analysis of the reactions of the recipients to the two communicators revealed that both derogation of the communicator and devaluation of the message were greater in the case of the less credible speaker. Furthermore, unfavorable ratings of both the source and the message content increased as the initial attitudes of the subjects became more discrepant from the position advocated. The general finding that an optimal amount of attitude change seems to be reached when there is a moderate degree of discrepancy between initial attitude and position advocated has also been reported by Whittaker (1963, 1965).

Personality factors. In addition to data showing that initial attitude is a determiner of susceptibility or resistance to persuasion, there is evidence that personality variables may predispose some individuals to greater persuasibility than others. Unfortunately, information on this is tentative, and a number of experiments have yielded contradictory findings. Hovland and Janis (1959) have summarized some of the more reliable conclusions. It seems fairly well established, for example, that individuals with relatively low self-esteem, defined as feelings of social inadequacy, inability to express aggression, and emotional depression, are more susceptible to persuasion than individuals with high self-esteem. In addition, when persons high in self-esteem interact with persons low in self-esteem, the former are more apt to influence the latter than vice versa. High-esteem individuals are also more *active* in trying to influence others.

We might conjecture that low self-esteem and high persuasibility stem from the same type of previous experience, namely, negatively reinforced instances of agreement with other persons. That is, individuals who have systematically been punished for disagreeing with or being different from others may come to agree or to comply with greater frequency. Lowered self-esteem, meaning a reduction in the frequency with which a person emits socially assertive performances, would tend to accompany learning of this sort. The individual with high self-esteem, on the other hand, is not as strongly reinforced for yielding to persuasion. Perhaps he is more inclined to self-reinforcement and so is more impervious to social influence.

One conclusion does seem to be well documented, namely, that females are more persuasible than males. Hovland and Janis suggest that this is due to the fact that our culture demands greater acquiescence from females. Females, in other words, seem to be more often reinforced for conformity behavior and more often censured for nonconformity behavior than males. A female lacking in self-confidence, however, may not necessarily be more persuasible than one with high self-confidence. Cox and Bauer (1964) found that among middle-class housewives, those whose opinions about the quality of nylon stockings changed least in the direction of the judgments of a salesgirl had obtained middle rather than extreme scores on a questionnaire measuring self-confidence. They suggest that females with strong feelings of inadequacy may react defensively to attempts at persuasion. Whether this is also true of men we do not know.

Personal commitment. Inducing someone to commit himself publicly to an opinion after he is exposed to a persuasive communication has been shown to increase his resistance to further change. This effect seems to occur for several reasons. First, a public declaration on an issue creates a situation in which the individual invites reactions from others to his behavior. If these reactions are supportive, or reinforcing, then his stand is strengthened. If he is not reinforced, or is punished, he is likely to modify his behavior. In the absence of any social consequences, commitment may still exercise a consolidating influence on an attitude, perhaps because the explicit statement of one's position serves as a conditioned reinforcer.

Hovland, Campbell, and Brock (1957) studied the effects of commitment on resistance to counterpropaganda by presenting two groups of high school students with communications advocating either no change in the legal voting age or reducing the legal voting age from twenty-one to eighteen. Following this procedure each of the subjects was asked to write a short paragraph stating his position on the issue. Half of the subjects were told that their statements would be printed in the school paper and identified with their names. The other half were permitted to remain anonymous and were told that their answers would be kept secret. Finally, each group of subjects listened to a lecture that advocated the position opposite to the one they had heard earlier. Determination of opinions following this counterpropaganda effort revealed that significantly fewer of the students who had written out their opinions in the expectation that these would be made public were influenced by the second argument. The results are shown in Table 11.4.

Table 11.4
The effects of commitment on reaction to counterpropaganda. (Adapted from Hovland, Campbell, and Brock, 1957, p. 30)

	Public Commitment	Private Commitment
Influenced positively by counterargument	14%	41%
Influenced negatively by counterargument	11%	9%
Not influenced either way	75%	50%

Worthy of note is the fact that half to two thirds of the subjects were not influenced in either direction by the communication. Possibly a greater number would have changed their opinions had they not been required to state their initial position. These results are very similar to those reported by Deutsch and Gerard (1955), who had subjects commit themselves in varying degrees to judgments in the Asch-type situation before they were exposed to majority opinion. Some wrote their responses on a sheet of paper, some used a "magic writing pad" (where erasure was accomplished by merely lifting the top sheet), and others made no commitment at all. Independence of response in the face of majority opinion was greatest among the subjects who had previously written their judgments and least for those who had made no prior commitment.

Induced social interaction. There are relatively few situations in which the experimenter can introduce social consequences of sufficient potency to alter the frequency of an attitude-related performance. Occasionally, however, the social milieu provides circumstances that can be adapted to the purpose. Deutsch and Collins (1958) conducted such a field study in interracial housing projects in Newark and New York City. They obtained most of their data from interviews with one hundred white and twenty-five Negro housewives living in four interracial housing projects. The interviews, which were conducted in the respondents' homes, elicited information concerning the housewife's attitude toward living in the project, her attitudes toward members of the other group (white or Negro, as appropriate), the amount and intimacy of her contact with other women in the project, the attitudes of other people toward her, and her own personal characteristics. In Newark, the white housewives who were studied lived in the same project as Negroes but in different buildings. In New York, on the other hand, families were assigned to apartments in the same building regardless of race. Although both projects were biracial, one was essentially integrated and the other segregated.

Deutsch and Collins discovered, first, that the likelihood of white tenants getting to know and associate with Negro tenants was considerably greater in the integrated than in the segregated projects. The same was true of the

Negro tenants, who came to know more white persons in the integrated buildings. Interestingly, most of the white housewives in the integrated projects did not originally like the idea of living in the same building with Negroes. However, such friendly activities as "visiting back and forth" and "helping one another out" were decidedly more frequent in the integrated developments than they were in the segregated units. Interviews with women in the integrated projects revealed that their attitudes toward Negroes were distinctly more favorable than those of the housewives in the segregated projects. Interracial contact, therefore, was shown to be related to attitude differences between the residents in the two types of projects. The results of the study are summarized by Deutsch and Collins as follows: "It is evident that from the point of view of reducing prejudice and of creating harmonious, democratic intergroup relations, the net gain resulting from the integrated projects is considerable; from the same point of view, the gain created by the segregated biracial projects is slight" (p. 592).

From our own theoretical viewpoint, we would say that encouraging physical contact between members of the two racial groups afforded them a situation in which nonprejudicial responses could be emitted and positively reinforced. Had such encounters been aversive, as through insults or violence, the results might have been quite different. The latter situation, unfortunately, does develop in circumstances where the social pressures promoting amicable relations are weak or nonexistent. In the situation that Deutsch and Collins studied, however, friction and unpleasantness would have resulted only in increasing discomfort and tension for all involved, whether white or Negro. It may be assumed that some incidents did occur but did not increase in frequency for this reason. Inevitable and continued contact with members of the other racial group allowed time and opportunity for the acquisition of amicable forms of behavior. Open conflict, on the other hand, typically follows relatively superficial interaction between the antagonistic factions, and there is little opportunity for the selective acquisition of positively reinforced performances.

Another example of the importance of arranging an opportunity for nonprejudiced responses to occur so that they can be reinforced is provided by a report of Negro infantry platoons that were introduced into white companies during World War II. As the authors of this report (Star, Williams, and Stouffer, 1949) point out, the Negro platoons were volunteers for combat and contained a higher proportion of high school graduates having higher classification test scores than Negro infantrymen in general. Nevertheless, when a survey of attitudes was conducted among the white troops shortly after VE Day, it was found that 93 per cent of the white officers and 63 per cent of the white enlisted men thought the arrangement had worked out "very well." About two thirds of the respondents reported that they remembered having had initially unfavorable attitudes toward serving in a racially mixed company. It is interesting that favorable attitudes toward the integrated companies varied among troops, in general, as a function of their proximity to them. Figure 11.5 shows this relationship.

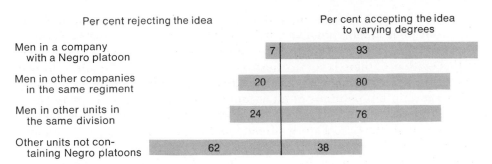

Figure 11.5

Attitudes among white infantrymen toward serving in a company containing Negro and white platoons in Europe in June 1945. (Adapted from Star, Williams, and Stouffer, 1949)

Since the conditions under which attitudes were effectively modified involved the shared experience of combat, the authors concluded that efforts at integration of white and colored troops into the same units were more successful when attention was focused on concrete tasks or goals rather than on abstract considerations of justice or desirable policy. The latter approach tended to emphasize the "race issue" and arouse traditional prejudices. Attitudes seem to be modified more effectively when the situation is such as to encourage performances that are incompatible with an individual's initial dispositions. Behavior modification occurs most readily in circumstances that permit new responses to be emitted and to be reinforced.

Active rehearsal. A more direct way of increasing the frequency of a verbal performance is to instruct the individual to repeat a particular assertion one or more times. It has been observed that debaters will come to believe in the side of an issue that they have argued, provided they have been reinforced by winning (Scott, 1957). In cases where specific reinforcement is absent, the findings are not entirely unambiguous. Janis and King (1954) had students improvise arguments that favored an extreme position differing from their initial beliefs on three mildly controversial issues, namely, the future of motion picture theaters, the probable meat supply for civilian consumers during the year 1953, and the chances of a cure being discovered for the common cold. In each experimental group, one student actively defended the point of view assigned to him on one of these topics while two others listened. Each of the other two then was called upon to take an active role in arguing a position on one of the remaining topics. The results of the experiment showed that the active participants were more influenced than the passive controls by two of the communications. For the third communication (the common cold), there was no difference in opinion change between active and passive participants. Thus, it would appear that voicing a point of view influences the individual's opinion more than simply listening to the same arguments. King and Janis (1956), however, failed to find a consistent change of opinion in subjects who read orally a persuasive communication. On the basis of this evidence, there is some question as to whether a single unreinforced repetition of an argument is sufficient to substantially modify an attitude.

That multiple repetitions of an argument before an audience may effectively influence an individual's attitude was shown by McGinnies, Donelson, and Haaf (1964), in a study already mentioned. Students with demonstrably favorable attitudes toward the church were asked to read a strongly worded, anti-church essay to six acquaintances outside the laboratory and to ask for a rating of the convincingness of the essay from each listener. Half of the subjects were told that their own attitudes would subsequently be re-evaluated while the other half were deceived into thinking that they were coexperimenters helping to study the effectiveness of a persuasive communication. It was found that the extremely pro-church subjects were uninfluenced by this experience. Both the neutral and the moderately pro-church subjects, however, whether they were informed about the purpose of the experiment or not, became significantly less pro-church following this procedure. Other experimenters (Walster and Festinger, 1962; Kerrick and McMillan, 1961) have reported that being aware of an attempt to influence him renders the recipient of a communication less susceptible to attitude change. Merely overhearing a persuasive argument, however, may result in attitude change when the advocated position is not too discrepant from that of the subject; but overhearing is not more effective than direct confrontation for unacceptable arguments (Brock and Becker, 1965). It appears that repeated utterance of a viewpoint that is only moderately antagonistic to the reader will induce him to change his attitude in the direction of the communication, even if he is aware of the influence attempt. Mere passive exposure to argumentation, however, fails to achieve this effect. As we have noted previously, those individuals who are committed to an extreme position seem relatively impervious to persuasion under any circumstances.

Inoculation

There are procedures by which people can be forearmed against persuasion. One theory of the manner in which such resistance is acquired is based on the medical analogy of inoculation as a means of conferring immunity to disease. In the biological sense, an individual who is exposed to a weakened form of a virus develops immunity to any subsequent attack by the same virus. By analogy, a person who is exposed to a weak attack on his attitudes or beliefs should develop resistance to a later, massive attack.

A test of this theoretical approach was made by McGuire and Papageorgis (1961). As topics of persuasion they used the following four truisms: (a) Everyone should brush his teeth after every meal if at all possible.

(b) Mental illness is not contagious. (c) The effects of penicillin have been, almost without exception, of great benefit to mankind. (d) Everyone should get a yearly chest X-ray to detect signs of TB at an early stage. These are assertions that enjoy nearly universal acceptance and, therefore, have not been subjected to prior attack. They represent, according to McGuire, a "germ-free" ideological environment.

The purpose of the experiment was to determine whether a supportive or refutational type of prior defense would be more effective in rendering these truisms less vulnerable to subsequent assault. A *supportive* defense consists simply of bolstering the individual's position with additional arguments, whereas a *refutational* defense involves the presentation and refutation of counterarguments. Student subjects, numbering 130, were divided into two groups, each of which experienced a different type of defense preparation. Half the subjects read arguments of the supportive type while the other half were exposed to the attack-refutation procedure. When later tested for the extent to which they subscribed to the truisms, the subjects displayed differential behavior according to these two treatments. The refutational type of prior defense was clearly superior to the supportive type of defense. On a fifteen-point scale where 1 represented rejection of the truism and 15 represented complete acceptance, the subjects in the refutation condition showed a mean score of 10.33, whereas those in the supportive condition gave the statements a mean rating of only 7.39. Thus, while the truisms still enjoyed credibility in both groups, those subjects exposed to counterarguments preceded only by a supportive defense changed more in comparison with those upon whom "immunity" had been conferred through prior refuted attack.

McGuire and his coworkers have conducted a number of experiments designed to examine additional parameters in this type of immunization procedure. Some of the major findings have been summarized by McGuire (1964) as follows: (a) "A refutational defense is almost as effective when it refutes arguments against the truism which are different from those to be used in the later attack as when it refutes the very same arguments used in the attack" (b) "When combined with the threatening refutational defense, the supporting defense gains an efficacy that it lacks when used alone" (c) "An extrinsic threat (forewarning) of the impending attack prior to the defenses enhances their immunizing effectiveness, especially that of the otherwise not-threatening supportive defense" (p. 205).

McGuire cautions that these conclusions have reference only to a special type of belief, namely, cultural truisms. Whether the same effects would be found in the case of controverted attitudes, where the recipient may already have been exposed to alternative viewpoints, is a matter of conjecture. An attempt to cast McGuire's findings into reinforcement language, therefore, is probably premature. One point may be made, however. Any threatening stimulus complex, such as an attack on one's beliefs, probably stimulates that person to rehearse arguments that serve both to refute the attack and to provide additional support for his own position. Exposure to additional supportive material, however, does not stimulate this type of refutational practice, so that the recipient of a later persuasive argument is not prepared with a set of counterarguments. Perhaps a truism even older than those used by McGuire is relevant at this point, namely: *Forewarned is forearmed.*

Manipulated Contingencies

Reinforcement Effects

Relatively little of the research done on persuasion has focused upon reinforcement effects in the natural social milieu that would help account for attitude change following persuasion. The principal consequence of most experimentally induced changes in attitude has been some reduction in the discrepancy that the individual perceives between his own dispositions and those expressed by a credible communicator. To the extent that a discrepancy of this sort is aversive, the attitude change is negatively reinforced. In some studies we are able to identify more tangible social consequences that have followed the exposure of subjects to a persuasive communication. In one such experiment, Mitnick and Mc-Ginnies (1958) obtained scores on the California Ethnocentrism (E) Scale from a large number of high school students. Eighteen nine-member groups were then formed from both the extremes and the middle of the resulting distribution. The groups could be characterized as containing individuals who harbored slight, moderate, or extreme prejudice toward minority groups. Twelve of these attitudinally homogeneous groups then viewed a sound film, the content of which was designed to induce greater tolerance of ethnic minorities. The remaining six groups served as controls. A critical manipulation in the experiment was giving six of the groups an opportunity to discuss the film after they had seen it.

Among the highly prejudiced subjects, those who did *not* discuss the film showed a reduction in ethnocentrism when retested. Those prejudiced subjects who engaged in discussion following the film presentation, however, displayed very little change of attitude. A reverse effect was found among the tolerant subjects, with those who discussed the film achieving even lower ethnocentrism scores than those who had no opportunity for discussion. Analysis of the tape-recorded discussions disclosed that the prejudiced subjects had used this occasion to reiterate their original biases, thereby undoing any liberalizing effect that the film may have had on them. On the other hand, not only did the tolerant subjects experience reinforcement of their attitudes from the film, but those who engaged in discussion found additional support for their sentiments in the views expressed by the other group members.

A similar effect of group discussion in both maintaining and modifying attitudes was reported by Goldstein and McGinnies (1964). Twelve college students, whose scores on a Thurstone scale had shown them to have highly favorable attitudes toward the church, were asked to read a lengthy statement critical of the church before three-person audiences. Unknown to any of them, four of the speakers addressed audiences composed of pro-church individuals, four talked to persons who were neutral on this matter, and four spoke before audiences of individuals antagonistic to the church. Each group then entered into a twelve-minute discussion of the anti-church tract. The stage was thus set for the speakers to be positively reinforced for their performances in some of the groups but not in others.

Only those speakers who discussed the persuasive argument with either neutral or anti-church audiences changed to a significant extent in the direction advocated. These audiences tended to agree with the content of the communication, and they voiced comments that supported what the speaker had *said* rather than what he actually *believed*. Faced with pro-church audiences, on the other hand, the speakers encountered disagreement with the content of the speech, a reaction which they could share since they themselves were pro-church. Their own attitudes were thus reinforced in the group discussion, whereas those of the speakers addressing anti-church subjects were subjected to attack.

The use of verbal conditioning procedure to bring about a modification in the attitudes of undergraduates toward television has been reported by Buckhout and Rosenberg (1966). In brief, their method involved having a graduate student provide positive reinforcement by saying "Good" in response to anti-television statements made by each subject during a structured interview. A mildly aversive rejoinder in the form of "Really?" was made to statements by the subjects favoring television. Subsequent evaluation of the attitude of the subjects, who initially had tended to favor television, showed them to have shifted in a less positive direction as a result of this experience. The authors suggest that individuals frequently test attitude statements in anticipation of the approval or disapproval of other persons. Reactions by others serve then to alter the frequency with which particular attitudes are expressed. Whether a private shift in attitude accompanies such changes in public performance is of course more difficult to determine.

Incentive Effects

A series of experiments, beginning with one reported by Festinger and Carlsmith (1959), have dealt with the role of incentives in persuasion. A number of these studies have been designed to test predictions from cognitive dissonance theory. It has become apparent, however, that the results are also susceptible to interpretation in reinforcement terms and that inferences about cognitive processes have probably served to muddy the theoretical waters rather than to clarify them.

Festinger and Carlsmith thought there was reason to believe that the cognitive dissonance induced by engaging in a performance inconsistent with one's attitudes would be greater for a small reward than for a large reward. They argued that a small reward provides little justification for engaging in counter-attitudinal behavior, thereby creating greater dissonance and more pressure toward attitude change. A large reward enables the individual to justify his compliant behavior on rational grounds, thereby reducing dissonance and resulting in relatively little attitude change. To test these assumptions, these investigators first had subjects engage in the very dull task of turning small pegs in a pegboard. On the pretext that they would be filling in for an absent assistant, the subjects were then persuaded to tell other students that the task had been interesting. They were promised and given either a small ($1) or a large ($20) sum of money for doing this. There was a small but statistically significant difference on subsequent ratings of the task by the two groups of subjects, with the low-reward group rating the task as more interesting than the high-reward group. (At the conclusion of the procedure, the experimenters asked the subjects to return the money.)

Some objections have been raised to the interpretation of these results in terms of cognitive dissonance and its resolution. For one thing, as Chapanis and Chapanis (1964) have pointed out, the $20 reward may have seemed implausible to the subjects in the high-reward condition, thus accounting for their ratings of the task as only neutral in interest. Other possibilities include the operation of what Rosenberg (1965) has termed "evaluation apprehension," that is, the tendency of subjects to think that they were being evaluated by the experimenter and, as a result, to behave in a manner designed to enhance this evaluation. To be offered a large sum of money for conveying a false impression of a task might impress the subject as being in the nature of a "bribe," and he might strive to avoid the appearance of having been susceptible to this type of influence.

An obvious source of confusion in experiments of this type is the exact timing of either the reward or the offer of an incentive. It might be suggested, for example, that the payment of $1 or $20 in the Festinger and Carlsmith study served more to reinforce the subject's impression of the task he had just completed than as an incentive to change his impression of that task. Such a coincidence of events makes it possible to conclude that $20 was more effective than $1 in reinforcing the subject's perception of the just completed task as dull. This sort of *ad hoc* explanation, of course, can best serve as a stimulus to research in which the temporal placement of a monetary reinforcer is varied systematically among the several behavioral events in a compliance episode.

An *incentive*, according to Logan (1960), refers to what might be described as the subject's expectation of a reward. As such, it acts as a controlling stimulus for some subsequent behavior. A *reinforcement*, on the other hand, is a stimulus occurring after a performance that bears some functional relationship to its frequency. If we imagine a situation in which the individual is induced to engage in behavior that is inconsistent with an attitude, opinion, or belief that he holds, then it is apparent that incentives and reinforcers may be introduced singly or in combination according to four different schedules.

A: Setting operations — Incentive — Compliance — Reinforcement — Attitude measurement
B: Setting operations ——————— Compliance — Reinforcement — Attitude measurement
C: Setting operations — Incentive — Compliance ——————— Attitude measurement
D: Setting operations — Reinforcement — Compliance ——————— Attitude measurement

In the schedule of events shown above, the *setting operations* include instructions from the experimenter as well as performance on some task that is to be evaluated following the compliance experience. Compliance represents a performance, usually verbal, that is inconsistent with some known disposition of the subject. The incentive is a promise of reward to the subject for engaging in the counter-attitudinal behavior. Reinforcement is some tangible consequence of the behavior, such as money, and it may be presented either before or after compliance. As indicated, an incentive may be offered without reinforcement, and reinforcement may replace an incentive. We do no employ notions of commitment or choice, as these are basically mentalistic concepts that do not enlarge our understanding of the several behaviors involved. Offering the subject a choice of performing or not performing a task would be part of the setting operations, but we would still face the task of identifying the factors controlling his so-called choice.

After reviewing some of the research in which the timing of rewards and incentives has followed one or more of these schedules, Rossomando and Weiss (1968) conclude that (a) incentive alone results in an inverse relationship between the magnitude of incentive and attitude change, and (b) reinforcement after compliance and incentive-plus-reinforcement result in a direct relationship. Experiments where the reinforcement is given prior to compliance have yielded conflicting results. In other words, a direct relationship between attitude change and magnitude of both incentive and reinforcement is predicted for conditions A and B, whereas an inverse relationship is predicted for condition C. A test of the relationships described in A, C, and D was conducted by Rossomando and Weiss, using as compliant behavior the writing by students of an essay favoring establishment of a tuition charge at the City University of New York. Virtually all of the students opposed such a charge, and they were offered either $1.50 or $5.00 for engaging in this counter-attitudinal performance. Some were merely promised payment (incentive only), others were given payment before they wrote the essay (reinforcement before compliance), and still others were offered the incentive before compliance and were rewarded after compliance. Attitudes toward the proposed tuition charge were measured following the treatments. Table 11.5 gives the results of this experiment.

Table 11.5

Mean ratings of the tuition proposal. A score of 11 represents maximum opposition. (Data from Rossomando and Weiss, 1968)

Groups	Amount of Reward	
	$1.50	$5.00
Incentive only	8.4	10.2
Reward before compliance	9.0	7.2
Reward after compliance	10.6	8.5

In general, the data in Table 11.5 show a direct relationship between amount of money actually paid the subjects, whether before or after compliance, and magnitude of attitude change. (Remember that a lower rating of the tuition proposal showed less opposition to it.) There is an inverse relationship, however, between the amount of money promised as an incentive and extent of attitude change. Although this latter finding follows from dissonance theory predictions, it can also be interpreted in other terms. For example, Bem (1967) argues that the individual takes into account whether the stimuli controlling his behavior derive primarily from the attitude object or from some extrinsic reward. If the individual sees himself as responding to a large monetary reward, then he will not view himself as a credible communicator. Under these circumstances, his attitudes will not change as much as if he were reacting to a smaller incentive. Weiss (1968), on the basis of some experimental data, has called both Bem's findings and his theoretical interpretation into question. Many of the results in this area of research, as Insko (1967) points out, are highly inconsistent, so we are left without an entirely satisfactory solution to the problem of why a weak incentive for engaging in some types of counter-attitudinal behavior appears to generate more change than does a stronger incentive.

A Reconsideration of Theory

Early in this chapter, we suggested that the several theories of persuasion could be reduced to essentially either *behavioral* or *cognitive* interpretations. By now, it should be clear that we favor a behavioral, or reinforcement, theory of attitude change following persuasion. This preference is based on the fact that behavior theory involves fewer assumptions about unobservable and unmeasurable events than does cognitive theory. Cognitive dissonance theory, in particular, is shakily erected on what Insko (1967) has termed "... two poorly conceptualized constructs, dissonance and cognitive elements" (p. 283). It is true that this viewpoint has stimulated a great deal of research and that it leads to certain nonobvious predictions that occasionally find empirical support. But it must also be conceded that much of the data obtained by dissonance theorists cannot be replicated and that predictions from the theory often are not confirmed. Arguments to the effect that "choosing" to engage in counter-attitudinal behavior increases dissonance are difficult to evaluate because of the imprecise manner in which choice, or volition, is defined. One could argue that individuals only have an illusion of choice. Whatever they do is a joint function of their learning histories and current circumstances. Choice, then, reduces to a matter of stimulus control, and a subject will expose himself to a persuasive communication if there are sufficient social pressures for him to do so. Our problem is to determine the nature of the stimuli that control the individual's behavior and to describe the functional relationships between the behavior and its consequences. Inferences about cognitive and/or motivational events are neither required nor made in this type of analysis. This approach does not, however, prevent us from viewing certain inconsistencies that may be generated within the individual's verbal repertoire as aversive. Indeed, behavior theory and balance theory strike common ground if we view restoration of consistency as reinforcing.

A functional analysis of persuasion does require that we be able to specify the critical stimuli to which the individual is responding. In an experimental setting, these will include instructions from the experimenter, the presence or absence of other persons, and any verbal behavior that the subject is required to emit before he is exposed to the persuasive manipulation. These are the setting operations that determine what S^Ds will effectively control the individual's subsequent performance. Adequate assessment of the subject's post-experimental expression of attitude is equally important. Too many experiments have relied upon simple rating scales or upon questionnaires of unknown reliability to measure attitude change. And, too often, the issues used as topics of persuasion have been so trivial as to raise doubts concerning the generalizability of the findings to nonlaboratory situations. It is probably safe to say that a reasonably complete statement of the conditions in which attitudes may be modified through persuasion cannot be made at present. However, the rapid rate at which research in this area is being generated promises answers to at least some of the more perplexing questions that have been raised.

Summary   A persuasive encounter has several essential ingredients: a communicator, a message, and one or more recipients. These interact in complex fashion to determine a behavioral outcome. The major theoretical positions from which empirical studies of persuasion and attitude change have stemmed are cognitive theory and behavior theory. Cognitive approaches stress the individual's *perception* of the situation and emphasize the states of balance or imbalance that obtain among opinions, beliefs, attitudes, and feelings. According to this point of view, one effect of persuasion is to introduce discordant elements and thus induce a state of imbalance among the recipient's cognitions. This imbalance is presumed then to initiate a series of events that have the effect of restoring equilibrium, one by-product of which may be a change in attitude. The imbalanced state, because it is considered to be psychologically uncomfortable, is referred to as cognitive dissonance.

Behavior theory, on the other hand, stresses the role of incentives and reinforcements in persuasion. In some respects, persuasibility resembles imitative behavior, in which the communicator serves as a model for the recipient's performance. When a persuasive communication presents views that are discrepant from the recipient's beliefs and attitudes, and when it emanates from an unimpeachable source, the recipient may be influenced to move in the direction advocated. To the extent that this perceived discrepancy is aversive to the individual, any behavior change that reduces or eliminates it is reinforced (negatively). This type of explanation, to be sure, is not dissimilar to that advanced by dissonance theory, but it has the advantage of preserving an emphasis on the external variables of which the individual's behavior is a function. Attitude change may also occur when appropriate incentives are offered to the recipient of an argument as well as when a performance indicative of attitude change is reinforced.

A number of factors have been shown to determine the effectiveness of persuasion. Source credibility is one of these, with the evidence strongly supporting the conclusion that a more credible communicator exerts greater immediate influence than one who is less credible. Over time, however, the influence of a less credible source may become more evident, as the recipients dissociate the message from its origin. Although the findings with respect to order effects in persuasion are not altogether consistent, it appears that the more effective of two opposing arguments will be the one that is closer in time to a reinforcing stimulus.

Two-sided presentations are generally more effective with those recipients who oppose the position advocated, whereas one-sided arguments are better received by those who already support the viewpoint of the communicator. In some situations, emotional appeals seem to exert more influence than rational arguments. Threatening communications, on the other hand, such as those stressing the deleterious effects of smoking on health, may have delayed rather than immediate effects on behavior.

Subjects who fall in the middle, or indeterminate, range of an attitude scale are often found to be the most persuasible. However, if a neutral stance on an issue represents a position of great conviction, the individual may be quite resistant to persuasion. Both high self-esteem and restatement of one's position in public tend to reduce susceptibility to persuasion.

Social interaction between the members of antagonistic groups may be an effective means of bringing about great mutual tolerance and understanding. Theoretically, this is explained as the result of a third party having introduced occasions on which new performances can be emitted and reinforced. Obviously, this situation must be arranged to insure that a greater proportion of mutually rewarding rather than mutually aversive behaviors occur. Otherwise, the result could well be increased antagonism.

Resistance to persuasion can be developed by providing the target individual with prior experience in refuting the arguments to which he will later be exposed. This procedure seems superior to that of merely adding supportive arguments to the individual's repertoire.

References

ARONSON, E., TURNER, J. A., and CARLSMITH, J. M. Communicator credibility and communication discrepancy as determinants of opinion change. *Journal of Abnormal and Social Psychology*, 1963, *67*, 31–36.

BEM, D. J. Self-perception: An alternative interpretation of cognitive dissonance phenomena. *Psychological Review*, 1967, *74*, 183–200.

BERGIN, A. The effect of dissonant persuasive communications upon changes in a self-referring attitude. *Journal of Personality*, 1962, *30*, 423–438.

BROCK, T. C., and BECKER, L. A. Ineffectiveness of "overheard" counterpropaganda. *Journal of Personality and Social Psychology*, 1965, *2*, 654–660.

BUCKHOUT, R., and ROSENBERG, M. J. Verbal reinforcement and attitude change. *Psychological Reports*, 1966, *18*, 691–694.

CHAPANIS, NATALIA, and CHAPANIS, A. Cognitive dissonance: Five years later. *Psychological Bulletin*, 1964, *61*, 1–22.

COFER, C. N., and APPLEY, M. H. *Motivation: Theory and research.* New York: Wiley, 1964.

CORROZI, J. F., and ROSNOW, R. L. Consonant and dissonant communications as positive and negative reinforcers in opinion change. *Journal of Personality and Social Psychology*, 1968, *8*, 27–30.

COX, D. F., and BAUER, R. A. Self-confidence and persuasibility in women. *Public Opinion Quarterly*, 1964, *28*, 453–466.

CROMWELL, H. The relative effect on audience attitude of the first versus the second argumentative speech of a series. *Speech Monographs*, 1950, *17*, 105–122.

DEUTSCH, M., and COLLINS, MARY E. The effect of public policy in housing projects upon interracial attitudes. In E. E. Maccoby, T. M. Newcomb, and E. L. Hartley (Eds.), *Readings in social psychology.* New York: Henry Holt, 1958, pp. 612–623.

DEUTSCH, M., and GERARD, H. G. A study of normative and informational social influence upon individual judgment. *Journal of Abnormal and Social Psychology*, 1955, *51*, 629–636.

FARNSWORTH, P., and MISUMI, I. Further data on suggestion in pictures. *Journal of Abnormal and Social Psychology*, 1931, *43*, 632.

FESTINGER, L. *A theory of cognitive dissonance.* Evanston, Ill.: Row, Peterson, 1957.

FESTINGER, L., and CARLSMITH, J.   Cognitive consequences of forced compliance. *Journal of Abnormal and Social Psychology*, 1959, 58, 203–210.

FESTINGER, L., RIECKEN, H., and SCHACHTER, S.   *When prophecy fails*. Minneapolis: University of Minnesota Press, 1956.

FINE, B. J.   Conclusion-drawing, communicator credibility, and anxiety as factors in opinion change. *Journal of Abnormal and Social Psychology*, 1957, 54, 369–374.

GOLDSTEIN, I., and McGINNIES, E.   Compliance and attitude changes under conditions of differential social reinforcement. *Journal of Abnormal and Social Psychology*, 1964, 68, 567–570.

GOLIGHTLY, CAROL, and BYRNE, D.   Attitude statements as positive and negative reinforcements. *Science*, 1964, 146, 798–799.

HARTMANN, G. W.   A field experiment on the comparative effectiveness of "emotional" and "rational" political leaflets in determining election results. *Journal of Abnormal and Social Psychology*, 1936, 31, 99–114.

HEIDER, F.   Attitudes and cognitive organization. *Journal of Psychology*, 1946, 21, 107–112.

HEIDER, F.   *The psychology of interpersonal relations*. New York: Wiley, 1958.

HOVLAND, C. I., CAMPBELL, ENID H., and BROCK, T.   The effects of commitment on opinion change following communication. In C. I. Hovland *et al.*, *The order of presentation in persuasion*. New Haven: Yale University Press, 1957.

HOVLAND, C. I., HARVEY, O. J., and SHERIF, M.   Assimilation and contract effects in reactions to communication and attitude change. *Journal of Abnormal and Social Psychology*, 1957, 55, 244–252.

HOVLAND, C. I., and JANIS, I. L.   Summary and implications for future research. Chapter 11 in I. L. Janis, C. I. Hovland, P. B. Field, H. Linton, E. Graham, A. R. Cohen, D. Rife, R. P. Abelson, G. S. Lesser, and B. T. King, *Personality and persuasability*. New Haven: Yale University Press, 1959.

HOVLAND, C. I., JANIS, I. L., and KELLEY, H. H.   *Communication and persuasion*. New Haven: Yale University Press, 1953.

HOVLAND, C. I., LUMSDAINE, A. A., and SHEFFIELD, F. D.   *Experiments on mass communication*. Princeton, N.J.: Princeton University Press, 1949.

HOVLAND, C. I., and MANDELL, W.   An experimental comparison of conclusion drawing by the communicator and by the audience. *Journal of Abnormal and Social Psychology*, 1952, 47, 581–588.

HOVLAND, C. I., and PRITZKER, H. A.   Extent of opinion change as a function of amount of change advocated. *Journal of Abnormal and Social Psychology*, 1957, 54, 257–261.

HOVLAND, C. I., and WEISS, W.   The influence of source credibility on communication effectiveness. *Public Opinion Quarterly*, 1951, 15, 635–650.

INSKO, C. A.   One-sided versus two-sided communications and counter communications. *Journal of Abnormal and Social Psychology*, 1962, 65, 203–206.

INSKO, C. A.   *Theories of attitude change*. New York: Appleton-Century-Crofts, 1967.

JANIS, I. L.   Effects of fear arousal on attitude change; Recent developments in theory and experimental research. In L. Berkowitz (Ed.), *Advances in experimental social psychology*. Vol. 3. New York: Academic Press, 1967.

JANIS, I. L., and FESHBACH, S. Effects of fear-arousing communications. *Journal of Abnormal and Social Psychology*, 1953, *48*, 78–92. Copyright 1953 by the American Psychological Association. Data in Table 11.3 of this book reprinted by permission.

JANIS, I., and KING, B. The influence of role playing on opinion change. *Journal of Abnormal and Social Psychology*, 1954, *49*, 211–218.

JANIS, I. L., and TERWILLIGER, R. F. An experimental study of psychological resistance to fear arousing communications. *Journal of Abnormal and Social Psychology*, 1962, *65*, 403–410.

KELMAN, H. C., and HOVLAND, C. I. "Reinstatement" of the communicator in delayed measurement of opinion change. *Journal of Abnormal and Social Psychology*, 1953, *6*, 185–214. Copyright 1953 by the American Psychological Association. Data in Table 11.2 of this book reprinted by permission.

KERRICK, JEAN S., and McMILLAN, D. A. The effects of instructional set on the measurement of attitude change through communications. *Journal of Social Psychology*, 1961, *53*, 113–120.

KING, B. T., and JANIS, I. L. Comparison of the effectiveness of improvised versus nonimprovised role-playing in producing opinion change. *Human Relations*, 1956, *9*, 177–186.

LANA, R. E. Familiarity and the order of presentation of persuasive communications. *Journal of Abnormal and Social Psychology*, 1961, *62*, 573–577.

LAZARSFELD, P. F. Foreword. In J. T. Klapper (Ed.), *The effects of mass media*. New York: Bureau of Applied Social Research, Columbia University, 1949.

LEVENTHAL, H. Fear communications in the acceptance of preventive health practices. *Bulletin of the New York Academy of Medicine*, 1965, *41*, 1144–1168.

LEVENTHAL, H., and NILES, P. A field experiment on fear arousal with data on the validity of questionnaire measures. *Journal of Personality*, 1964, *32*, 459–479.

LEVENTHAL, H., and WATTS, JEAN C. Sources of resistance to fear-arousing communications on smoking and lung cancer. *Journal of Personality*, 1966, *34*, 155–175.

LOGAN, F. A. *Incentive*. New Haven: Yale University Press, 1960.

LUND, F. H. The psychology of belief: IV. The law of primacy in persuasion. *Journal of Abnormal and Social Psychology*, 1925, *20*, 183–191.

MARCH, B. A., and McGINNIES, E. Communicator credibility and initial attitude as variables in persuasion. Technical Report 13, Office of Naval Research, November 1968.

McGINNIES, E. Involvement and source credibility as variables in persuasion with Japanese students. Technical Report 9, Office of Naval Research, May 1966a.

McGINNIES, E. Studies in persuasion: III. Reactions of Japanese students to one-sided and two-sided communications. *Journal of Social Psychology*, 1966b, *70*, 87–93.

McGINNIES, E. Studies in persuasion: IV. Source credibility and involvement as factors in persuasion with students in Taiwan. *Journal of Social Psychology*, 1968, *74*, 171–180.

McGINNIES, E., DONELSON, ELAINE, and HAAF, R. Level of initial attitude, active rehearsal, and instructional set as factors in attitude change. *Journal of Abnormal and Social Psychology*, 1964, *69*, 437–440.

McGuire, W. J.   Inducing resistance to persuasion. In L. Berkowitz (Ed.), *Advances in experimental social psychology.* New York: Academic Press, 1964.

McGuire, W. J., and Papageorgis, D.   The relative efficacy of various types of prior belief-defense in producing immunity against persuasion. *Journal of Abnormal and Social Psychology,* 1961, 62, 327–337.

Mitnick, L. L., and McGinnies, E.   Influencing ethnocentrism in social discussion groups through a film communication. *Journal of Abnormal and Social Psychology,* 1958.

Newcomb, T.   An approach to the study of communicative acts. *Psychological Review,* 1953, 60, 393–404.

Newcomb, T.   Individual systems of orientation. In S. Koch (Ed.), *Psychology: A study of a science.* Vol. 3. New York: McGraw-Hill, 1959.

Nunnally, J. D., and Bobren, H. M.   Variables governing the willingness to receive communications on mental health. *Journal of Personality,* 1959, 27, 38–46.

Orne, M.   On the social psychology of the psychological experiment: With particular reference to demand characteristics and their implications. *American Psychologist,* 1962, 17, 776–783.

Osgood, C., and Tannenbaum, P.   The principle of congruity in the prediction of attitude change. *Psychological Review,* 1955, 62, 42–55.

Pfungst, O.   *Clever Hans, The horse of Mr. Van Osten.* New York: Holt, 1911.

Rosenberg, M.   When dissonance fails: On eliminating evaluation apprehension from attitude measurement. *Journal of Personality and Social Psychology,* 1965, 1, 28–42.

Rosenthal, R.   Covert communication in the psychological experiment. *Psychological Bulletin,* 1967, 67, 356–367.

Rosnow, R. L.   A "spread of effect" in attitude formation. In A. G. Greenwald, T. C. Brock, and T. M. Ostrom (Eds.), *Psychological foundations of attitudes.* New York: Academic Press, 1968.

Rossomando, Nina P., and Weiss, W.   Effect of timing of payment of money on the relationship between magnitude of incentive for counterattitudinal behavior and magnitude of consequent attitude change. Paper read at Eastern Psychological Association meetings, April 1968.

Saadi, M., and Farnsworth, P.   The degree of acceptance of dogmatic statements and preferences for their supposed makers. *Journal of Abnormal and Social Psychology,* 1934, 29, 143–150.

Scott, W. A.   Attitude change through reward of verbal behavior. *Journal of Abnormal and Social Psychology,* 1957, 55, 72–75.

Sherif, M.   An experimental study of stereotypes. *Journal of Abnormal and Social Psychology,* 1935, 29, 371–375.

Star, Shirley, Williams, R. M., and Stouffer, S. A.   Negro infantry platoons in white companies. Chapter 10 in S. A. Stouffer *et al., The American Soldier,* Vol. I in *Studies in social psychology in World War II.* Princeton, N.J.: Princeton University Press, 1949.

Tannenbaum, P. H.   Initial attitude toward source and concept as factors in attitude change through communication. *Public Opinion Quarterly,* 1956, 20, 413–425.

THORNDIKE, E. L.   An experimental study of rewards. *Teachers College Contributions to Education*, 1933, No. 580.

WALSTER, ELAINE, and FESTINGER, L.   The effectiveness of "overheard" persuasive communications. *Journal of Abnormal and Social Psychology*, 1962, 65, 395–402.

WEISS, W.   The effects of persuasive communications on attitudes. Annual Report, Office of Naval Research, October 1968.

WHITTAKER, J. O.   Opinion change as a function of communication-attitude discrepancy. *Psychological Reports*, 1963, 13, 763–772.

WHITTAKER, J. O.   Attitude change and communication-attitude discrepancy. *Journal of Social Psychology*, 1965, 65, 141–147.

ZIMBARDO, P. G., WEISENBERG, M., FIRESTONE, I., and LEVY, B.   Communicator effectiveness in producing public conformity and private attitude change. *Journal of Personality*, 1965, 33, 233–255.

Games, Strategies, and Decisions

One fairly recent development in the field of mathematics is known as *game theory*. First elaborated by von Neumann and Morgenstern (1944), this application of mathematical principles, particularly set theory, to the strategies that people employ in their various interactions has attracted the attention of social psychologists. In a number of respects, the basic postulates of game theory are similar to the objective principles of social behavior that we have tried to develop in this book. A game, in its broadest sense, is any situation in which individuals make decisions in accordance with rules. The patterning of these decisions determines the outcomes for the participants. In order to improve their outcomes, the participants may try different strategies. A strategy can be defined as "a complete plan of behavior which specifies the player's behavior, that is, his decisions for all possible circumstances that may arise during the course of play" (Burger, 1963, p. 2).

Implicit in most discussions of strategies and decision making is the assumption that the players or participants, are at cross-purposes, in short, that they have a conflict of interests. However, the competitive aspects of many social interactions stem not from any inherent demands of the situation but, rather, from the joint performances of the participants. Their performances, in turn, are functions both of the incentives held out to them and of one another's choices. Each person's behavior is controlled in part by what the other does. If this is not immediately clear, just think of the behavior of individuals playing bridge, checkers, or chess. Many everyday social interactions take on some of the aspects of a game, in which each person attempts to maximize his own gains, whether these are tangible, like money and goods, or intangible, like status, prestige, or "winning."

Making a decision requires choosing among a set of alternative actions. Moreover, choices, as Rapoport (1966) points out, must have known consequences in order for this to be a meaningful problem. Finally, a choice implies that the chooser has preferences. Behaviorally, a preference means that for a given individual certain behavioral outcomes have greater incentive value than others. The origins of individual differences in preferences must be referred to the reinforcement histories of the persons concerned. These are frequently assessed indirectly through the use of various personality inventories, in which the respondent's answers are used as a basis for predicting how he will react in specific situations.

The situational determinants of choice behavior include recent past behavior. Other things being equal, I might prefer to attend a movie rather than watch television. However, if I have seen a movie the previous evening, then I may be satiated on this particular activity and will elect television viewing. Similarly, I may choose one food instead of another, even though I like both, simply because I have recently eaten one of them. Relevant prior experiences combine with contemporary stimulus factors to determine the decisions that one makes. In this chapter we will examine how these variables relate functionally to alternative performances in decision making.

In many situations, what I choose to do is controlled in part by what someone else does. That is, certain alternatives may have been preempted by others so that I must choose among those that remain. My decisions may be further limited by certain *rules* that govern the situation. Driving an automobile involves a chain of performances requiring a great many rapid decisions made in accordance with a set of rules, varying road conditions, and the behavior of other motorists. Many of the decisions made in the course of this demanding performance result from the strategies that one employs in order to maintain one's "right of way," to "beat the lights," or to stay in the fastest-moving lane. Everyday conversations often involve an element of game playing to the extent that the participants engage in "one-up-manship," each endeavoring to display his superior knowledge or wit.

Individuals may compete individually or collectively. A poker table with five players ordinarily presents a situation in which all of the participants are in competition. However, if two of the players form a *coalition* in which they agree to pool their winnings as well as their losses, then the situation represents a four-person rather than a five-person game. In this sense, bridge is a two-person game. The effective number of participants in a game, therefore, is the number of distinct sets of interest that are represented. Most theoreticians have concerned themselves with two-person games, because the mathematical computations become immensely difficult when more than two interests are involved. Of course, one way of simplifying a situation that involves n persons is simply to consider it as a game involving oneself against everyone else.

The result of most games is a *payoff* to the participants. In a two-person game, there are two general types of payoff contingencies. If one person's winnings equal the other's losses, we speak of a *zero-sum game*. In situations where the payoffs (both positive and negative) do not add up to zero, we refer to a *nonzero-sum game*. Like games involving more than two persons, nonzero-sum games present mathematical complexities that are only gradually yielding to investigation. Let us first consider some examples of two-person zero-sum games as illustrative of one approach to strategy and decision making.

Zero-Sum Games

One of the simplest examples of this type of game is that of matching pennies. It may be described as follows: Each player, A and B, puts down a penny covered by his hand so that his opponent cannot see whether heads or tails is up. If A is matching B, then A wins both coins whenever two heads or two tails appear; if the coins differ, then B wins. Unlike games such as chess or checkers, where each player knows exactly what his opponent has done, matching pennies is not a game of *perfect information* (Venttsel, 1963). As a result, there is no "best way" to play, as there is in games where the moves of one's opponent are always visible. It is convenient to represent the players and the payoffs in a two-person zero-sum game in the form of a matrix, as shown below.

		B	
		Heads	Tails
A	Heads	1	−1
	Tails	−1	1

Each player has only two strategies open to him; he can place the penny down either heads or tails. Thus, the columns of the matrix represent B's strategies and the rows represent the strategies available to A. When A wins, his payoff is plus one cent; when he loses, his payoff is minus one cent. The same holds for B. Suppose we are rooting for A to win. What strategy should he employ? If the game is played only once, there is no way to determine which of the two strategies is better. Let us assume, however, that A and B continue to play, and that A adopts the strategy of playing heads each time. This will soon become apparent to B, who will counter by playing tails, so that A is guaranteed to lose. If A adopts a different strategy, say, of playing heads and tails alternately, this also will soon become apparent to B, who will again win every time. Clearly, the best strategy for A is one in which even he himself does not know what he will

do next. He might, for example, flip the coin to determine whether to play
it as heads or tails. Since there is no system or pattern to his plays, his
opponent will be unable to anticipate and thereby counter them.

There is something vaguely unsatisfying about this solution, because it
relies on chance rather than on "rational" strategy. Here, in fact, lies one
of the critical problems of game theory so far as the psychologist is concerned. An adequate theory of decision making rests upon three assumptions: (a) Both alternative actions and alternative outcomes can be defined
unambiguously. (b) The consequences of joint choices can be specified
precisely. (c) The participants have distinct preferences among the outcomes (Rapoport, 1966). Assumptions (a) and (b) are formal requirements
that present no particular problems to the psychologist. The matter of
preferences, however, involves us in predictions about which of several
outcomes will have greater incentive value for a given individual. This, in
turn, directs our attention to those kinds of outcomes that are generally
either positive or aversive in a given situation. When someone chooses to
act in a manner that maximizes positive reinforcement, we tend to say that
he is behaving "rationally." When he behaves otherwise, so as to generate
either a less rewarding or perhaps a punishing outcome for himself, we feel
that he is behaving "irrationally." Looked at in this fashion, much of human behavior would appear irrational. As even von Neumann and Morgenstern (1944) have acknowledged, however, there exists, at present, no satisfactory treatment of the question of rational behavior, so we may direct our
attention for the moment to some of the formal aspects of decision making.

The minimax principle. Military commanders frequently engage in
"war games," played about a table, in which the outcomes of various
strategies are estimated. Two factors must be taken into account in any
strategic decision. One involves the enemy's *capabilities*, the other concerns his *intentions*. Although appraisal of both of these variables is dependent upon effective intelligence, it is generally easier to guess what an
opponent *can do* than it is to guess what he is *going to do*. The general rule
under which a military command operates is explained by Haywood (1954):
"The doctrine of decision of the armed forces of the United States is a doctrine based on enemy capabilities. A commander is enjoined to select the
course of action which offers the greatest promise of success in view of the
enemy capabilities" (p. 365).

Luce and Raiffa (1957) have summarized the application of this line of
reasoning to a decision made by the American command during the Battle
of the Bismarck Sea in World War II:

>   In the critical stages of the struggle for New Guinea, intelligence reports
> indicated that the Japanese would move a troop and supply convoy from the
> port of Rabaul at the eastern tip of New Britain to Lae, which lies just west
> of New Britain on New Guinea. It could travel either north of New Britain,

where poor visibility was almost certain, or south of the island, where the weather would be clear. General Kenney had the choice of concentrating the bulk of his reconnaisance aircraft on one route or the other. Once sighted, the convoy could be bombed until its arrival at Lae (p. 64).

If the American command predicted incorrectly, precious bombing time would be lost. The following outcomes, in terms of days of bombing time, were estimated:

		Japanese Strategies	
		Northern route	Southern route
Kenney's Strategies	Northern route	2	2
	Southern route	1	3

A cardinal rule in game theory, when B is bound to lose to A, is for A to act in such a manner that the least advantage he can gain is as great as possible. B, on the other hand, wants to make the disadvantage that he must sustain as small as possible. If A departs from this optimum strategy, he risks gaining less than he might have received; if B departs from it, he may lose more than he could have settled for. There is a way to play every two-person game that will satisfy this criterion (Williams, 1966). Let us imagine that General Kenney is in the role of A and the Japanese commander has the role of B. The Japanese leaders envisage certain loss in moving their convoy, but they want to minimize it. The American forces hope to strike a telling blow, and they want to maximize it. There is, in fact, an *equilibrium point* in the above situation, namely, the northern route for both forces. As a point of history, the Japanese force was sighted after one day and was subjected to severe losses. Although, as Haywood (1954) has observed, the Battle of the Bismarck Sea ended in a disastrous defeat for the Japanese, one could not say that the Japanese commander erred in his decision. The total strategic situation was not favorable to him, and he made as good a decision as he could have under the circumstances.

A matrix such as the one shown above is said to have a *saddle point*. In order to discover it, we inspect each row for a minimum value and select the largest of these, examine the columns for a maximum value and select the least of these, and then compare the two numbers. If they are equal, there is a saddle point which provides the solution to the game. The corresponding strategies are based on the best outcome that each side could anticipate if the other side were to make its most clever move. This *minimax* strategy is essentially a conservative one. But it is also unstable, because if the game continues, each side gains information concerning the strategy of the other and will be tempted to change its own strategy to one yielding a larger payoff. However, if the game has a true solution — that is, if the saddle point corresponds to a pair of minimax strategies — then the player who departs from his optimal strategy can never gain by doing so.

Nonzero-Sum Games

In a classic example of the two-person nonzero-sum game, called the Prisoner's Dilemma, two suspects have been taken into custody by the police. They are interviewed separately by the district attorney, who tries to convince each one to turn state's evidence in order to obtain a lighter sentence. Both prisoners know that if neither confesses the worst that will happen to them is a light sentence for vagrancy. If one confesses and the other does not, the one who confesses will be given lenient treatment while the one who refuses to confess will have the book thrown at him. On the other hand, if both confess, then both will be punished with moderate rather than severe sentences. Each prisoner thus has two strategies — to confess or not to confess — and different payoffs, or consequences, are associated with each course of action.

Suppose that the payoff matrix shown in Figure 12.1 obtains for the parties to this dilemma. The dilemma for each suspect is obvious. If neither knows what choice the other has made, and if each chooses the alternative most advantageous to himself with no consideration for the other, then both will receive sentences of eight years. A moment's consideration will reveal why this is so. The rules of the game, it should be recalled, specify the outcome for each combination of choices. The strategy elected by A determines the row in which the outcome will fall and that chosen by B determines the column. The joint outcome is designated by the point of intersection.

Prisoner B

		Does not confess	Confesses
Prisoner A	Does not confess	1 year for A; 1 year for B	20 years for A; 6 months for B
	Confesses	6 months for A; 20 years for B	8 years for A; 8 years for B

Figure 12.1
Payoff matrix for the Prisoner's Dilemma. (Adapted from Brown, 1965)

From A's point of view, the verbal problem-solving process probably goes something like this: "If I do not confess, I may get only one year. But if B turns state's evidence, then I will get twenty years. On the other hand, if I confess, I may get only six months, and the worst I can get is eight years. I had better confess and avoid the possibility of a twenty-year sentence." If B reasons the same way, then the outcome is a moderate penalty for both.

If A and B can trust one another, then each is better off not confessing, since the maximum sentence that each can receive is one year. In the absence of mutual trust, the best they can achieve is a compromise eight-year sentence. They have then arrived at what can be called a *noncooperative equilibrium point* (Shubik, 1964). If the suspects were to cooperate, in effect, to form a *coalition* against the prosecutor, then they could achieve a better mutual outcome by escaping with only one-year sentences. Effectively, what each has done is to envision the worst thing that could happen to him for either confessing or not confessing. He then selects the lesser of these two evils, thus fixing his strategy. In A's case, this means selection of the row, and in B's case selection of the column, corresponding to "confess."

It should be apparent that a great many social and political problems take on aspects of the Prisoner's Dilemma. In a sense, the student's moral dilemma of cheating or not cheating on an examination has elements of this type of situation. If he does not cheat, he must depend upon the honesty of his classmates in order that the grade distribution not be unfairly tipped in favor of those who have used illicit tactics. If the basically honest student does not have this much faith in the integrity of his fellows, then he may compromise by cheating "a little" in order to maintain his own standing in the grade distribution. Whether or not he cheats, of course, depends also upon the probability of his being detected, the magnitude of the anticipated punishment should he be caught, and, most important, his conscience.

What happens if a game such as the Prisoner's Dilemma is repeated? Luce and Raiffa (1957) discuss a situation in which the players make their choices simultaneously and are payed off after each trial. The matrix below shows the strategies and payoffs for each player.

Player B

		1	2
Player A	1	(5, 5)	(−4, 6)
	2	(6, −4)	(−3, −3)

Perhaps this example will be more meaningful if we think of the payoffs in terms of either money of points. Each player starts the game with a fixed number of assets, which can be either augmented or diminished according to the strategies that he selects. The most attractive solution from the point of view of both participants is that involving the choices A1, and B1. Suppose that after some experience at the game each arrives at this pattern. Now suppose further that Player A, assuming that Player B will adhere to Strategy 1 on the next trial as well, tries to squeeze a little more profit out of the game by switching to Strategy 2. A little foresight should warn him that such a maneuver will result in Player B changing to Strategy 2 on the following trial, in which event he is committed to follow-ing Strategy 2 also in order to minimize his loss. The advantage of receiv-ing 6 units instead of 5 on one trial will not offset the loss of 3 units that he will suffer on the following trial. This line of reasoning, assuming that it occurs to him, will tend to keep Player A "honest." Should he defect, the resulting aversive consequences should soon restore his original pattern of performance. Thus, although the nonconforming strategy is profitable in the short run, it is not to the continuing advantage of either player to deviate from a common strategy that assures a modest profit to each. As Luce and Raiffa point out, this situation represents an unstable equilib-rium, because any loss of "faith" in one's opponent sets up a chain of events that is disastrous for both.

Over the long run, it is possible for individuals to learn that A1, B1 strat-egies are more desirable. These, of course, are immediately reinforced, and deviations from them are eventually punished. But the deviations may also be reinforced to the extent that they protect the victim from con-tinued losses of the order that he receives when his opponent defects. Frequently, a degree of cooperative collusion will develop, even without communication between the players, so that A_1 and B_1 strategies will dominate the play. Unfortunately, in both military and political spheres, as Luce and Raiffa observe, the participants frequently seem to have a single-play orientation, which means that they each adopt the essentially self-defeating but also most self-protective strategy.

The Concept of Utility

You may be wondering what relevance these theoretical models have for real-life behavior. If so, you will be relieved to learn that a great deal of experimental research has been done with human subjects in situations having the essential elements of a "game." At the same time, it should be kept in mind that there is no necessary relation between the predictions made from formal, mathematical models and the behavior of individuals in interpersonal situations. We would, of course, be happy to discover that a formal model is actually useful in predicting behavior, but we should not be surprised to discover that certain assumptions contained in the model have no exact psychological counterparts. For example, the *utility* of an outcome is not identical with the *payoff*. A payoff is expressed in quantitative terms, such as money, points, years in prison, and so on. Utility is a far more subjective concept, since it refers to satisfaction or value. It is difficult, for example, to equate prestige with money; for one person prestige has greater utility, for another money has more utility. Thus, the several payoffs associated with a matrix may not necessarily reflect the utilities these payoffs have for the participants.

Consider another problem in military strategy, one described by Dresher (1961). It is the mission of the Blue forces to capture an objective held by the Red forces. The Blue commander has certain information about the capabilities of the Red commander to defend his position. There seem to be three ways for Blue to capture the objective, B1, B2, B3, and three possible countermoves by the Red defenders, R1, R2, R3. These nine possible outcomes to Blue can be represented in a three-by-three matrix:

Red Courses of Action

		1	2	3
Blue Courses of Action	1	Fail	Succeed	Succeed
	2	Draw	Succeed	Draw
	3	Succeed	Draw	Fail

This is a problem in competitive behavior in which Blue wishes to maximize the outcome of a proper choice of strategy, and Red wishes to minimize this same outcome. The actual outcome, of course, depends jointly on the choices made by both Blue and Red. Game theory predicts that Blue will elect strategy B2, which yields either a successful outcome or at worst a draw. If the Blue commander uses strategies B1 or B3, he may fail to accomplish the mission. To be sure he may, as Dresher suggests, alter the outcomes by taking chances or by bluffing; but a conservative course of action would require the choice of strategy B2.

Now consider the behavior of a football coach in a similar situation. He is behind 21 to 20, but his team has just scored and is within one point of a tie and within two points of winning. Should he kick the extra point and gain a tie, or should he gamble on a running or pass play that may score two points and win the game? (Of course, should this play fail, he will lose.) A strictly utilitarian approach to this problem would suggest that the options are, in decreasing order of desirability, win, tie, lose. However, the probabilities of occurrence may be in the order tie, lose, win. That is, perhaps the place kicker almost never misses, but the team has a habit of becoming stalled on its opponent's goal line.

One strategy is better than another, according to Marschak (1964), if it brings the player more. But more of what? The criterion of "utility" refers to something that is being maximized. Even if the player could clearly rank-order the utilities of the several options open to him, he would still face the fact that these options differ in probability of occurrence. The mathematical solution to the problem of scaling utilities in terms of both desirability and subjective probability is beyond the scope of this chapter. The general point is simply that the utility, or incentive value, of a particular outcome in a game situation is not as easily specified as one might think. It depends upon a great many variables, including the personality of the person faced with the decision and any antecedent and current situational factors that he perceives as relevant.

For instance, our football coach, whom we left impaled on the horns of a dilemma a short paragraph back, may consider a tie no better than a loss. Therefore, he will gamble on a play that, if successful, will win the game. Another coach, or even the same coach with a different win-loss record for the season, might be delighted to settle for a tie. It is obvious that game theory can do no more than specify the optimal outcome in such a competitive situation when the values of both preference and subjective probability are known. The problem for the psychologist is to provide behavioral definitions for these terms and to determine the manner in which they control performance in a given situation.

The Eumax model. In a concise and fascinating discussion of some aspects of decision making, Edwards, Lindman, and Phillips (1965) summarize the problem of strategy in situations where one must choose among several alternative performances. This is an alternative to the *minimax* principle that we discussed earlier, and it suggests that one should choose the act with the largest expected utility. In short, one should *maximize expected utility*. To apply this model, one first assigns a numerical utility to each outcome in a decision-making situation. Next, one determines, if possible, the numerical probability for each of the outcomes. Multiplying the utility associated with the outcome of an act by its probability of occurrence and summing these over the various states that may result gives one

STATES

		Windy, no rain	No wind, no rain	Windy, rainy	No wind, rainy
	Go sailing	Good sailing	Becalmed	Uncomfortable sailing	Uncomfortable and becalmed
		100	20	−20	−50
ACTS					
	Go golfing	Poor golfing	Good golfing	Stop golfing, take shelter	Stop golfing, take shelter
		30	90	−35	−35

Figure 12.2

Acts, states, outcomes, and the payoffs assigned to outcomes. (From Edwards, Lindman, and Phillips, 1965)

an index for making a decision. To maximize utility, one would do this for each available act and choose the one for which the sum was largest.

As an application of this strategy, which calls for *maximizing expected utility*, Edwards, Lindman, and Phillips ask us to imagine that we are faced with a decision to go sailing or to play golf. The satisfaction to be derived from each of these activities will depend largely upon the weather, and the several contingencies may be summarized by the matrix in Figure 12.2.

Observe that in the matrix shown in Figure 12.2, numerical values have been assigned to the various outcomes. Thus, "good sailing" is valued at 100, whereas "good golfing" is valued at 90; this implies that, other things being equal, one would have a slight preference for sailing over golfing. The least satisfactory contingency is to go sailing and find oneself becalmed in the rain (−50). If the same type of weather occurs during a round of golf, however, one can always retreat to the clubhouse (−35). How can probabilities be assigned to the various weather outlooks? One way of doing this is to call the weather bureau for the relevant information. Suppose that the following values are obtained:

Windy, no rain	0.3
No wind, no rain	0.4
Windy, rainy	0.1
No wind, rain	0.2

Since it is certain that the weather will resemble one of these states, the sum of the probabilities is 1.00. The sums of the expected utilities for each course of action can then be computed as follows:

$$\text{For sailing}$$
$$0.3\ (100) + 0.4\ (20) + 0.1\ (-20) + 0.2\ (-50) = 26$$

$$\text{For golfing}$$
$$0.3\ (30) + 0.4\ (90)\ + 0.1\ (-35) + 0.2\ (-35) = 34.5$$

If we believe in maximizing our expected utility, we will decide to play golf.

We may summarize the discussion to this point by saying that decisions are made in terms of both their utility, or subjective value, and their probability, or subjective expectancy. If we attempt to rephrase this terminology in behavioral language, we would say that an individual in a situation that requires one of n courses of action is under the control of stimuli in the presence of which certain performances have been reinforced. What he does will reflect those past occasions on which a given type of performance was either rewarded or punished. Manipulation of the controlling stimuli should lead to predictable outcomes in decision making, and we turn next to a review of such attempts at experimental control of strategy.

Experimental Tests of the Game Model

The Prisoner's Dilemma

Because it provides the type of situation in which such factors as trust and suspicion can be investigated, the Prisoner's Dilemma has been employed most frequently in experimental tests of the game theory model of decision making. A study reported by Scodel and Minas (1960) illustrates the procedures and some typical outcomes in this particular experimental setting. In their version of the Prisoner's Dilemma, either money or cigarettes were assigned to the outcomes, and the game was repeated for fifty trials. One interesting feature was that their subjects were actual prisoners from the Federal Reformatory at Chillicothe, Ohio.

Eighteen pairs of prisoners were treated in the following manner. The members of each pair were seated on opposite sides of a partition facing a panel containing a red button and a black button. They were instructed as follows:

> On each trial you will press either the black button or the red button. If you press the black button, two things can happen. If you press the black button and the other person also presses the black button, you get three cigarettes and he gets three cigarettes. If you press the black button and he presses the red button, you get nothing and he gets five cigarettes. Suppose you push the red button. Again two things can happen. If you push the red button and the other person presses the black button, you get five cigarettes and he gets nothing. If you push red and the other person also pushes red, you get one cigarette and the other person gets one cigarette (p. 134).

These various combinations of events can be summarized in matrix form:

		Player B	
		Black	Red
Player A	Black	3, 3	0, 5
	Red	5, 0	1, 1

It should be noted that the matrix shown above was posted on the partition in front of each subject, so that the various options and their consequences to both parties were clearly evident. The results were compared with data obtained previously from college students who had been paid off with pennies (Scodel, Minas, Ratoosh, and Lipetz, 1959). The cooperative solution to this problem is obviously for each player to choose Black, since each will then receive a payoff of three units. By defecting from this cooperative strategy and playing Red while his opponent is still playing Black, Player B can increase his winnings. Player A can do likewise by switching his play to Red. However, a defensive move made by one player in response to defection by the other will result in both receiving a payoff on one unit. How did the performances of college students in this situation compare with those of actual prisoners?

Among twenty-two pairs of college subjects, a collaborative choice (Black, Black) was made most frequently by only two pairs. In the remaining cases, the subjects behaved as though suspicious of one another and settled for the minimum reward associated with plays of Red, Red. In the group of prison subjects a very similar result was obtained. None of the pairs of actual prisoners displayed collaboration. Among both the college subjects and the prison subjects, the number of competitive (Red, Red) choices increased during the last twenty-five trials as compared with the earlier trials. The investigators concluded that any attempts at collaboration in an effort to maximize joint return were quickly abandoned.

The results obtained in this experiment are consistent with a "rational" solution to the problem, since one cannot really lose by playing Red on a single trial. However, in repeated play, a more reasonable solution would be for both players to switch to Black, inasmuch as this would result in their mutual benefit. Do these results square with what one might predict from behavior theory? It seems at first blush that a collaborative strategy would be more strongly reinforced than a competitive strategy and would, therefore, eventually dominate play. But game theory must be construed within a context of other social variables, and one of these is the prevalent tendency among individuals in our society to compete with one another. The rewards for successful competition, including success at avoiding defeat, are probably more potent in some situations than the reward that one might receive for employing a cooperative strategy that has an outcome of dubious utility.

Without any systematic intervention on the part of the experimenter, as we have already noted, players in the Prisoner's Dilemma tend to become even more competitive as the trials progress (Minas, Scodel, Marlowe, and Rawson, 1960). Although this is true of games involving up to fifty trials, there is some evidence that prolonging the interaction will bring about an increase in cooperative play. Some investigators have found that in games involving three hundred to seven hundred trials the frequency of collaborative choices decreases during the first fifty trials but then increases to an asymptotic value of 65 per cent by Trial 100 (Rapoport, 1963; Rapoport and Chammah, 1965). Even this, however, is not as high a proportion of mutually advantageous choices as one might expect if the players were seeking to maximize their gains. One difficulty in escaping from the competitive equilibrium is that bilaterally cooperative responses are required, and these will not occur consistently if either player finds that his attempts to cooperate are not reciprocated.

Matrix and nonmatrix formats. It is possible to trace the determinants of cooperative and competitive strategies further by employing a confederate of the experimenter in game situations. The performances of the confederate can be manipulated so as to simulate cooperative, competitive, or reciprocative behavior. Might a subject show cooperative game behavior more frequently if he were exposed to consistently collaborative reactions from his partner in the Prisoner's Dilemma setting? Minas and his coworkers (1960) found that even when a confederate was instructed to "match" the responses of naive subjects, only about 36 per cent of the subjects' choices over fifty trials were cooperative. The incentive of "winning" apparently was prepotent over that represented by a cooperative payoff.

The low level of cooperation frequently displayed by the participants in this game might be due, in part, to the fact that they are constantly confronted with the game matrix. This might have the effect of suggesting to them more forcefully the temporary advantage to be gained by defecting from a collaborative style of play. Evans and Crumbaugh (1966) found that the amount of cooperation manifested by subjects playing the Prisoner's Dilemma game without seeing the matrix was significantly higher than that of subjects playing the game with a matrix format, even though the two situations were strategically and mathematically identical.

Contingent strategies. There is some evidence that an initially hostile confederate, that is, one who plays competitively at first and then switches to a cooperative choice, produces more cooperation from naive subjects than a confederate who plays cooperatively from the beginning (Bixenstine and Wilson, 1963). This finding, however, was not confirmed by Sermat (1964), thus making the point inconclusive. On the question of the effect of reciprocal responses made by a confederate, there is evidence that a confederate who makes all cooperative responses affects the play of a naive subject no more than a confederate who simply matches the naive subject's previous response (Oskamp and Perlman, 1965). An attempt to manipulate both the format of the Prisoner's Dilemma and the pattern of play by a confederate was made by Crumbaugh and Evans (1967). They report an experiment in which subjects were confronted by (a) a matrix or a no-matrix format, (b) an initially hostile or an initially neutral confederate, and (c) contingent cooperation or noncontingent cooperation by the confederate.

The subjects in this experiment were eighty college students who could earn up to $1.00 for their participation. In the no-matrix condition, the subjects chose between two alternatives presented in a formboard.

Give me 1	Give him 3

This no-matrix format was accompanied by a complete explanation of the payoff possibilities; thus, each subject knew that if he pressed the button corresponding to "Give him 3," he himself might receive either 3 or nothing. By indicating "Give me 1," he would assure that his opponent also received one. The confederate, of course, could play either cooperatively or competitively or could change strategies part way through the game. A cooperative choice would be one in which the other player is awarded three points, thus permitting him the opportunity either to reciprocate with the same choice or to award himself four points at the expense of the first player. The matrix format makes this clear.

Player B

	1	2
1	3, 3	0, 4
2	4, 0	1, 1

Player A

Several findings from this experiment are of interest. For one thing, more cooperation was exhibited by the subjects under the no-matrix condition. This confirms previous findings and leads us to suspect that when the situation is arranged so as to make the competitive possibilities obvious the players will behave more competitively. A no-matrix game format de-emphasizes competition and thus results in more cooperative performances. Similar findings when the alternatives are "decomposed" in this manner have been reported by Pruitt (1967).

The findings by Crumbaugh and Evans (1967) with regard to the effects of early competitive responses by the confederate on later reactions of the subject to cooperative choices were inconclusive. However, the subject behaved more cooperatively when the confederate employed the strategy of matching the subject's responses than when the confederate's choices were not contingent upon his own. In other words, when a cooperative choice by a subject was followed by a cooperative response from the confederate, the subject continued to perform cooperatively with greater frequency than he did when the confederate's reaction was variable. We might generalize this finding by suggesting that in a bargaining situation the individual tends to emit those kinds of performances that elicit positively reinforcing reactions from others in preference to performances that elicit either aversive or unpredictable reactions. If a cooperative response is followed by a similar response from someone else, it is reinforced; if it is followed by a noncooperative response, it is punished. A noncooperative response that elicits a like reaction from another person is punished and, under some circumstances, will give way to more cooperative behavior.

As plausible as this interpretation might seem, the experimental evidence indicates that there are many exceptions, at least so far as the Prisoner's Dilemma game is concerned. Komorita (1965) varied the percentage of trials on which a confederate matched cooperative responses by a naive subject. Regardless of whether such matched reactions occurred 25, 50, or 75 per cent of the time, cooperative choices by the confederate were not reciprocated to a significant degree by the subjects. An additional finding of interest was that the female subjects were more apt to reciprocate cooperative behavior than were the males, who reacted competitively under all conditions. Post-experimental interviews with the male subjects revealed that many of them felt that their partners (simulated by the experimenter) "didn't understand the game or used poor strategy." Those who admitted that they thought the other person was attempting to cooperate took advantage of these attempts nevertheless. Komorita suggests that the females may have been "more sociable, sympathetic, and sensitive to the responses of others" (p. 743), thereby reacting more often in kind to cooperative choices.

Prior affiliation. Why have so many experimenters failed to obtain more than token levels of cooperative behavior from subjects in the Prisoner's Dilemma? Is it characteristic of individuals to compete in this situation rather than to enhance their winnings through collaboration? Several possible explanations have been suggested to explain the typical finding of a high level of competitive behavior in experiments where the subjects are strangers to one another. Perhaps existing friendships or peer group relationships among the participants in an experiment might lead to a higher frequency of cooperative choices. Such an effect was, in fact, found by Oskamp and Perlman (1965), who conducted their research at Pomona College, a relatively small institution where nearly all of the students have some contact with one another. Pomona students yielded a significantly higher proportion of cooperative responses than did students from UCLA. In a further study of the "friendship effect," Oskamp and Perlman (1966) found that subjects cooperated more often with partners whom they identified as friends or acquaintances than with persons they disliked. It appears, then, that personal relationships existing among the participants in a game determine, in part, the extent to which cooperative or competitive choices are made.

Magnitude of payoff. Another factor that seems to bear upon the degree of competitiveness exhibited by players in this type of game is the absolute value of the payoffs. If competitive choices are reinforced proportionately more strongly than cooperative choices, then we would expect them to predominate. Cooperative behavior, on the other hand, should increase in frequency when the payoff matrix is such as to provide relatively more reinforcement for this type of play. To be more specific, we would expect a higher level of cooperation in a game where the payoffs are high simply because the incentive for cooperating is stronger than that for competition.

In a game where the payoffs are low, on the other hand, there is little absolute difference between winning and losing, and so the incentive of competing successfully will outweigh the relatively small gain to be achieved
by cooperating.

These alternatives are made clear in an experiment reported by Mc-
Clintock and McNeel (1966). They modified the Prisoner's Dilemma game
so that the payoff matrices were as follows:

I.   Player B   II.   Player B

                    1   2   1   2

	1	1, 1	−2, 2
Player A			
	2	2, −2	−1, −1

	1	6, 6	0, 5
Player A			
	2	5, 0	0, 0

Remember that each player really has three alternative strategies available
to him: For example, in these two situations Player A can play to (a) maximize his own gain (A2, A1); (b) maximize the joint gains of himself and his
partner (A1, A1); or (c) maximize the difference between his own gains and
those of his partner (A2, A2). These three approaches have been termed
individualistic, cooperative, and *competitive* (Deutsch, 1958). In their
experiment, McClintock and McNeel varied not only the magnitude of the
rewards available to the players but also the information about their scores
that was fed back to the participants. They hypothesized that both higher
rewards and limited information feedback would increase the frequency
of cooperative choices. Competitive behavior was expected to increase in
games where the rewards were higher and where the opponents were kept
informed of both their own and the other's cumulative scores.

The subjects in this experiment were 120 male undergraduates at the
University of Louvain in Belgium. The members of each pair were strangers to one another, and the game matrix was clearly displayed to each.
Payoffs were in francs, with the low reward group being able to earn up to
the equivalent of 66 cents and the high reward group up to $13.20. Half of
the subjects in each reward condition were shown only their own cumulative scores, whereas the other subjects were shown their opponents'
cumulative scores as well. The results for each of the experimental conditions in terms of percentage of cooperative responses are summarized
in Table 12.1 for all one hundred trials.

The data show quite convincingly that cooperative play was enhanced
under conditions of high reward and minimal feedback about the performance of one's opponent. Competitiveness was increased between those
players who were confronted with low payoff possibilities and were kept
informed of the cumulative scores attained by their opponents.

Table 12.1

Mean percentages of cooperative responses in a modified Prisoner's Dilemma game involving two conditions of payoff and two conditions of score feedback. (Data taken from McClintock and NcNeel, 1966)

Joint feedback, low reward	24%
Joint feedback, high reward	36%
Individual feedback, low reward	52%
Individual feedback, high reward	66%

The effect of a low monetary payoff is probably to cause the participants to become more interested in competing with one another instead of maximizing their own returns. In other words, as the payoff incentive decreases, the incentive of winning increases. This possibility may account for the high level of competitiveness found in most experiments, where the monetary incentives have generally been quite low.

Radlow (1965) also attempted to determine the role of a more substantial monetary payoff in bringing about either cooperative or competitive strategies by participants in a Prisoner's Dilemma game. Fourteen pairs of male university students served as subjects. The customary procedure was followed, with the subjects separated by a partition and the complete play-off matrix displayed before each player. The matrix was as follows:

Player B

		1	2
		1	2
Player A	1	$4, $4	$2, $5
	2	$5, $2	$3, $3

The subjects were told that they would receive the amounts resulting from their joint choice of Strategies 1 or 2 on a single trial, chosen at random from a total of ninety-eight trials. In this way it was hoped that the subjects would perform on each trial in a manner designed to produce a favorable outcome. It was apparent from the game matrix that cooperative behavior would result in a joint return of $4.00, whereas competitive play would yield each participant only $3.00. The subjects simply pressed one of two buttons corresponding to the two strategies, and the outcome was indicated by a light that appeared in the appropriate cell of the matrix. A cooperative choice by each subject, therefore, would illuminate a light in the upper-left cell, whereas a competitive, or defensive, choice by each would be indicated by a light in the lower-right cell. A cooperative choice by one paired with a competitive choice by the other would be signaled by a light in either the upper-right or the lower-left corner of the matrix.

Before looking at the results obtained by Radlow in this experiment, we had better describe briefly a second study that he did because of certain problems he detected in the subjects' interpretations of the instructions. It appeared that many of them did not really understand the payoff matrix. Frequently, one player would adopt Strategy 2 in the vague hope that he would get five dollars rather than three. He usually accomplished this for a few trials until the other player became annoyed at receiving only two dollars and switched to Strategy 2 also. "When it became clear that each would receive three dollars instead of four," Radlow reports, "the first player innocently tried to switch to the cooperative choice, but the other player often was so angry at this point that he would not return to his cooperative strategy. The result was that both players were stuck with a competitive strategy that neither wanted" (p. 225).

In a second experiment, therefore, the instructions emphasized the correlations between the payments that each subject would receive. For instance, it was made clear that if one player received five dollars, the other would receive only two dollars. Eight dollar bills were also displayed openly as incentives for the subjects to strive for the most favorable joint payoff. The results of the two experiments are shown in Figure 12.3.

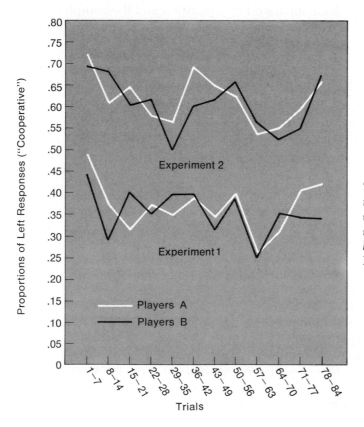

Figure 12.3
The effects of instructions and payoff utility upon cooperative play in the Prisoner's Dilemma game. (From Radlow, 1965)

The overall increase in the proportion of cooperative choices made in the second experiment as compared with the first experiment demonstrates quite pointedly the importance of the setting operations in a situation of this type. While the results do not imply that *any* Prisoner's Dilemma game can be played with the degree of cooperation evidenced in the upper set of curves in Figure 12.3, they do suggest that cooperation will occur to the extent that the utility structure of the game approaches the nominal payoff matrix. Four dollars, in short, has more utility value than four "points" or even four cents. Why both sets of curves appear U-shaped is not entirely clear, although it is likely, as evidenced from post-experimental interviews with the subjects, that the dips in the center are attributable to transitory attempts by both subjects to maximize their own scores. The consequences of such a maneuver, of course, were aversive to the extent that they brought about retaliation from the other person, thereby reducing the joint payoff. A cooperative pattern of choices was more often mutually reinforcing and tended eventually to predominate.

Bargaining and Risk Taking

Trust and Threat

It has probably occurred to you that an important element of everyday social interaction is missing in most of the experiments on game playing, namely, verbal communication between the participants. When allowed to develop simply as a consequence of the choices made by two players, cooperation has been shown to be a function of such variables as the manner in which the situation is presented to the subjects (matrix or no-matrix format), the strategy employed by an accomplice of the experimenter, and magnitude of the payoffs. However, as Deutsch (1958) has shown, allowing the players to communicate by means of notes can greatly increase the proportion of cooperative choices. "Trust" in a situation like this becomes operationally defined in terms of the extent to which one party, through the control he exercises over the other party's outcome, can reduce any incentive that the other person has to cheat. If he can do this by direct verbal communication, then a great deal of time is saved. For example, one of Deutsch's subjects was able to send the other the following note: "I will cooperate, and I would like you to cooperate. That way we can both win. If you don't cooperate, then I will choose so that you can't win. If you decide to cooperate and make a cooperative choice after first not doing so, then I will cooperate" (p. 274).

The dialogue just cited suggests that *threat* is an effective device in a bargaining situation. The effect of a threat is to make clear to one's opponent that an undesirable performance on his part will have aversive consequences for him. He is thereby provided with an incentive for performing in a manner acceptable to the one who poses the threat. If both parties

possess means of threatening one another, of course, an impasse may develop. Two parties to a transaction reach a bargain when each decides that
what he is required to give and what he will receive are not disadvanta-
geous to him; if the results are advantageous, so much the better. However,
in many bargaining situations where cooperation would be mutually rewarding, agreement may never be reached. Cooperation seems to be
achieved only when the incentives for cooperating are perceived as clearly
outweighing those for competing. Arriving at a cooperative agreement is
facilitated when the participants are able to communicate verbally. Communication that can only take place by means of the moves and countermoves that each makes is usually slow and uncertain. Direct communication that outlines in advance the consequences to each person of the other's
course of action is more likely to bring about a mutually favorable outcome.
Threat is often a vital element in such communication.

The trucking game. Deutsch and Krauss (1960) have reported an interesting simulation of a real-life bargaining situation in which the effects of the
availability of threat to each party were experimentally investigated.
Threat was defined as the expression of one person's intention to do something detrimental to the interests of the other. Sixteen pairs of adult female
subjects were asked to imagine that they were in charge of rival trucking
companies engaged in carrying merchandise over a road to a destination.
For each completed trip they earned sixty cents less operating expenses,
which were calculated in terms of the number of seconds it took them to
make the trip, at the rate of one cent per second. Thus, if a player consumed forty seconds in reaching her destination, her net profit was twenty
cents. The two companies were named Acme and Bolt, and each subject
was given a map showing the available routes from starting point to destination (see Figure 12.4).

It can be seen in the map that the shortest route for each player to her
destination was over a one-lane stretch of road. If the two should chance
to meet in the center of this stretch, one would have to back up in order for
the other to pass. Each player also controlled a gate at her entrance to this
one-lane segment, and by closing it she could prevent the other party
from reaching her destination. The experimenter determined whether
neither party, one party, or both parties had access to the gates. Each subject had a control panel with toggle switches which allowed her to select
either route to the destination, to open or close her gate, and to go forward
or in reverse. Her total mileage was recorded on a counter. The subjects
understood that the monetary winnings and losses were imaginary and that
no money would change hands.

This situation is obviously one in which some sort of mutual accommodation is essential if both subjects are to maximize their payoffs. Furthermore, the type of agreement reached will be a function of whether the
gates can be used by neither party, by one party, or by both. Psychologi-

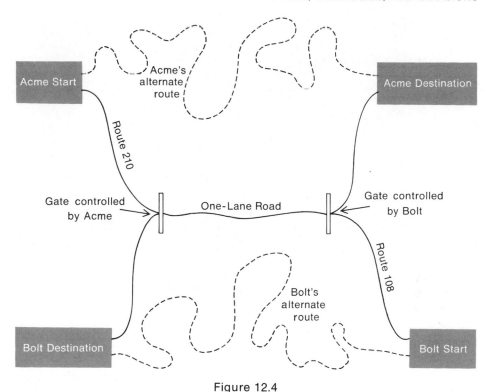

Figure 12.4

Subject's road map in the Trucking Game. (From Deutsch and Krauss, 1962)

cally, the alternatives are no threat, unilateral threat, or bilateral threat. How did the subjects perform under each of these conditions?

The results are summarized in Figure 12.5, which shows the sum of the payoffs to both players on any given trial over a total of twenty trials. A high payoff means that the players arrived at a procedure for sharing the one-lane stretch of the most direct route.

In the no-gate (no threat) condition, the subjects arrived most quickly at a solution to the problem. An accommodation was reached somewhat more slowly in the unilateral threat condition, but in the end unilateral threat proved as effective as no threat. Virtually no agreement was reached when both subjects had threat available, so that both were losing money at the end of twenty trials. Deutsch and Krauss found the following solutions to by typical of those that were achieved in each of these three situations:

(a) *No threat.* Acme and Bolt fall into a pattern of alternating who is to go first on the one-way section. This follows some trials on which the players either were deadlocked or both chose to take the alternate, longer route.

(b) *Unilateral threat.* Both players take the main route and meet in the center of the one-way stretch. Bolt waits a few seconds, then reverses to the end of this section, allowing Acme (who controls the gate) to go through.

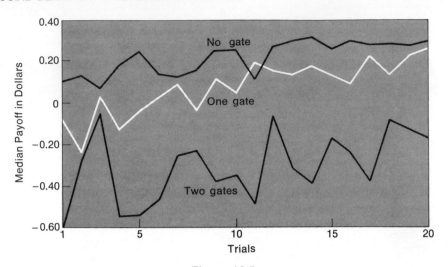

Figure 12.5

Median joint payoff over trials in the Acme-Bolt Trucking Game. (After Deutsch and Krauss, 1962)

Then Bolt proceeds forward to her destination. This follows some trials in which Acme simply closes the gate and takes the alternate route, opening the gate after she has reached her destination.

(c) *Bilateral threat.* Both players start out on the short route, immediately close their gates, reverse themselves, and take the alternate route to their destinations. This follows some period of jockeying for position and eventual selection of the alternate route by both subjects.

The investigators concluded that the availability of threat makes it more difficult for bargainers to reach agreement. Conflict is further intensified when both competitors possess a threat capability. Post-experimental interrogation of the subjects revealed that the several outcomes also had differential reinforcing value. Money was the most potent incentive, doing better than one's opponent was next, followed by simply "having fun." Helping the other person was the least attractive incentive. There is a familiar ring to this rank-ordering of reinforcers when one thinks of how people behave in everyday, nonlaboratory situations.

What would have happened in the Bolt-Acme trucking game had the participants been allowed to communicate verbally with one another? To find out, Deutsch and Krauss (1962) conducted another experiment in which the subjects could talk to one another over an intercom. This innovation, rather surprisingly, produced no greater degree of cooperation under the three threat conditions than had occurred in the previous experiment. The reason for this was that most of the subjects simply did not use the opportunity for communication that was afforded them. They may have been exhibiting something analogous to what Newcomb (1947) has termed *autistic hostility,* in which mutual antagonism inhibits communication between two individuals and thus precludes use of the single most effective means of resolving the hostility.

As a consequence of this finding, Deutsch and Krauss designed a further study in which communication between the subjects was compulsory; the players were required to say something to each other on every trip. This, however, had an effect only in the unilateral threat condition. Under no-threat conditions, the solution of alternating in use of the short route was apparently so obvious that it was acquired with or without communication. In the bilateral threat condition, the opportunities for competitive responses apparently were prepotent over those cooperative performances that might have been achieved through communication. Communication, then, is not necessarily the solution to every bargaining problem, especially where each of the protagonists has a threat capability. But compulsory communication seems to be better than none.

Even more effective than compulsory communication, however, is communication that results from pre-experimental "tutoring" of the subjects. Krauss and Deutsch (1966) found a significant difference between the performances of subjects who were allowed to communicate without specific instructions before the start of the game and the performances of subjects who were tutored in "how" to communicate. These instructed subjects were told to make proposals that each would be willing to accept if she were in the other person's shoes. The effect of training some of the subjects to communicate fair proposals was to greatly increase their joint payoffs.

Additional research has disclosed that simply increasing the utility of the payoffs will bring about greater cooperation in the trucking game. Gallo (1966) allowed his subjects to earn up to $16 in a replication of the original Deutsch and Krauss study. He found that even under bilateral threat conditions, the players earned as much money as those observed by Deutsch and Krauss who had played for imaginary money but had no mutual threat capabilities. This is consistent with findings in the Prisoner's Dilemma game and leads us to conclude that the relative incentive values of earning money or of simply winning the game are important determinants of the frequency with which cooperative responses are made. If cooperative behavior is more strongly reinforced by making the acquisition of money contingent upon it, cooperation occurs more frequently than competition. When successful competition is the most tangible reinforcer in a situation, then this is the type of performance that can be expected. One important point should be reiterated in passing, namely, that the absolute value of a payoff is not necessarily a measure of its utility. A payoff is valued in comparison to what the other person is receiving. As Becker and McClintock (1967) observe, "Anyone who has doubts of this ought to be readily persuaded by observing the behavior of two siblings on Christmas morning" (p. 278).

Coalition Formation

In situations where more than two persons are involved, and where possibilities exist for both competitive and cooperative behavior, it is observed that certain of the participants frequently will pool their resources in order to achieve a joint outcome more favorable than might be obtained through individual action. Defined by Gamson (1964) as *the joint use of resources to determine the outcome of a decision* (p. 82), coalition formation has been receiving increasing attention from social scientists. We will not attempt to review here the large number of studies that have been published in this area but will be satisfied with mentioning a few of the more general findings.

Minimum resource theory. A number of investigators have attempted to test what is known as the *minimum resource theory.* Based essentially on common sense, this theory states that a coalition tends to have the smallest number of resources that are sufficient to win. Gamson (1964) provides the following example of how this theory should predict the outcome in a political situation. Imagine that three candidates are in the lead at a nominating convention. Candidate A controls 48 per cent of the votes, Candidate B controls 30 per cent, and Candidate C controls 22 per cent. A simple majority is needed for nomination. Three coalitions are possible: A and B, with 78 per cent of the votes; A and C, with 70 per cent of the votes; B and C, with 52 per cent of the votes. The coalition that can win with the smallest total resources is B and C, and this is the coalition predicted by the theory. Candidate A will then discover his 48 per cent of the votes to be a liability. Strength, in such instances, may turn out to be weakness.

The basis for minimum resource theory is the *parity norm,* that is, the belief that a person should derive from a coalition an amount proportional to what he contributes to it. Thus, in the above example, Candidate C would expect to gain more from collaborating with B than with A, since his share of the total initial resources is greater. Distributive justice requires that Candidate B receive 30/52 of any rewards stemming from a coalition with C, who in turn should receive 22/52 of the rewards. This assumption obviously is vulnerable to experimental test. Unfortunately, the prediction is not quite this simple. As Thibaut and Kelley (1959) point out, A can share in the rewards only if B and C do not form a coalition. One way that A can prevent this from occurring is to enter into a coalition with one of them himself. If he is successful in doing this, he might feel justified in demanding a lion's share of the jointly acquired assets. Actually, he may be in no position to make such a demand, since his participation in a coalition is no more valuable to B than the participation of C. Indeed, as we have already indicated, B stands to gain more with less disputation regarding an equitable division of the spoils from an alliance with C.

Vinacke and Arkoff (1957) adapted the game of pachisi to an experimental situation in which the minimum resource principle could be evaluated. In their version of this parlor game, each player's single counter was moved a certain number of spaces along a path to a goal according to the values that appeared on a die rolled by the experimenter. Each player was permitted to multiply the number shown on the die by a weight that had been assigned him at the beginning of the experiment. Furthermore, the players could form coalitions if they wished and move a single counter according to their combined weights. Thus, in one situation, Player A had a weight of three, Player B a weight of one, and Player C a weight of one. Under these conditions, needless to say, no coalition was formed, since Player A could win by himself regardless of whether or not Players B and C formed a coalition. But when A had a weight of four, B a weight of three, and C a weight of two, the most frequently formed coalition was between B and C, exactly as predicted by the theory. Finally, when A had a weight of one, B a weight of two, and C a weight of two, A was greatly sought after as the partner for a coalition. This result again fitted the requirement of the theory that a coalition represent the smallest aggregation of resources sufficient to win.

It is scarcely necessary to rephrase these predictions and results in reinforcement language, since the positive and aversive consequences of the several types of coalitions envisaged by the theory are implicit in the outcomes. It is not illogical that an individual should anticipate a reward that is proportional to the assets that he brings to a coalition. Nor does it surprise us to learn that he forms the type of coalition in which he can expect maximum reinforcement in terms of this parity norm. However, the past histories of the individuals in competitive situations may have been such that the achievement of tangible rewards as a result of coalition formation is less reinforcing than the attainment of some sort of social accommodation. In short, there may be persons for whom an altruistic solution is more reinforcing than either a monetary reward or just "winning."

Anticompetitive behavior has actually been observed in a number of experiments. Uesugi and Vinacke (1963) found that females tended to behave more altruistically than males in the pachisi game, using such devices as forming alliances that included all the players. Unlike the males, who behaved competitively, as expected, the females seemed to approach the situation as one that offered opportunities for social interaction. Similar reactions by their female subjects were recorded by Bond and Vinacke (1961), who concluded that feminine strategy is oriented toward achieving an equitable or fair outcome for all concerned. Because these differences in behavior between males and females arise in competitive as well as cooperative settings, it has been suggested that the male approach be termed *exploitative* and the female approach *accommodative* (Vinacke, 1968). We can only speculate about the origins of this behavioral difference between the sexes. Perhaps it is due in part to genetic factors and in part to the acquisition by females of strategic approaches to problems that are consistent with their muscular limitations. The "weaker" sex may simply have learned that maximum utility in a competitive situation is not always realized through the exercise of power, confrontation, and aggression.

International Affairs

Utter Confusion Theory

The fact that individuals in everyday situations are faced with problems for which they seem to find no logical solutions leads us to wonder to what extent formal theories of decision making can predict actual behavior. Gamson (1964), in suggesting an "utter confusion theory," summarizes this state of affairs rather nicely:

> Most coalition situations are conducted under conditions which are not at all conducive to rational calculations and analysis. It is well known that political conventions, for example, are frequently scenes of bedlam. Thus, according to this theory, coalition formation is best understood as an essentially random choice process. The coalition which forms will be the result of such fortuitous events as a chance encounter or a missed telephone call (p. 92).

Some of the principles that appear to govern coalition formation in triads do not seem to apply in larger groups. Although the weaker members of a large coalition do have an advantage that exceeds their actual contribution in terms of power, the coalitions tend to form around the stronger individuals (Vinacke, 1968). Anyone who observes even casually the operations of the United Nations can see evidence of this. The powerful nations form the hubs of coalitions, but the smaller and weaker nations frequently wield an influence out of proportion to their actual strength.

When important decisions are in the balance, the relative utilities of different outcomes for different cultures must also be taken into account. Those cultural variables that determine the incentive value of different outcomes in the decision-making process are as yet poorly understood. For example, "face saving" for an Oriental may be more important than either money or power. We are just beginning to understand something about the relative values of incentives and reinforcers in different nations and different cultures.

Political Strategies

The roots of conflict. One of the major impediments to the achievement of more amicable relations between nations is simply that, like so many of the competitors in the Prisoner's Dilemma game, they do not trust one another. In addition, the rewards for competition often seem to outweigh those for cooperation. The participants in international conflict behave as though they were engaged in a zero-sum game, in which one party's gains are necessarily the other's losses. The possibility that all of those concerned might increase their outcomes through collaborative effort seems not to have been as widely accepted as might be hoped. And since all of the major participants to the more serious disputes possess approximately equal threat capabilities, they, like the players in the trucking games, are often forced to take the longest rather than the shortest routes to their respective destinations. You are invited to draw further analogies between those games that have been studied in the laboratory and the more serious confrontations that seem to occur constantly and inevitably between nations.

In fact, nearly all of the principles that we have discussed in this book have relevance for understanding the problems of international conflict and misunderstanding. Many of these bitter fruits undoubtedly have their roots in the socialization process, whereby individuals are taught that "We" are better than "They" or that in-group qualities are invariably superior to out-group qualities. Attitudes that are learned in the home and the neighborhood have a way of permeating the international scene as well.

Nor can the role of perception and judgment be discounted in any analysis of this problem. In a penetrating analysis of the conflict in Vietnam, White (1966) shows how *misperception* or cognitive distortion pervades even "normal" psychological processes, thus providing a basis for the behaviors that lead ultimately to war. White identifies six key misperceptions that underlie the inability of antagonists in the international arena either to understand or to communicate effectively with one another. These are:

(a) A *diabolical enemy image*. The enemy is always perceived as the criminal and the aggressor.

(b) A *virile self-image*. Each party is concerned more with status and prestige than with moral values and views taking the initiative in conciliatory action as a sign of cowardice or weakness.

(c) A *moral self-image*. Each side ignores evidence of its own culpability and perceives itself as noble and peace loving.

(d) *Selective inattention*. Each side ignores its own weaknesses and shortcomings and fails to foresee certain tragic consequences of its own actions.

(e) *Absence of empathy*. Neither side is able to visualize the situation as it appears to the opponent or to understand what factors are controlling the opponent's behavior.

(f) *Military overconfidence*. Both sides exaggerate their own military strength and underestimate either the determination or the capacity of the enemy to resist.

These factors undoubtedly play important roles in determining the courses of action taken by both individuals and nations in conflict. They do not, of course, tell the whole story. The vast network of communications in the world today, as well as the greater freedom with which information can be dispensed and obtained in many countries, makes it difficult for an entire population to indulge itself in the kinds of cognitive distortions that White discusses. Although these factors may account for a large measure of the misunderstanding that so frequently characterizes negotiation, a sizable group of people in those countries where accurate information is available are able to avoid these misperceptions. One result, as we have seen in the case of Vietnam, can be considerable conflict within the body politic about the policies to be adopted and the actions to be taken.

The roles that leaders play as determining factors in international conflict are difficult to assess. As we noted earlier, there are two schools of thought on this matter. One holds that the Great Men of history have given direction to human affairs, whereas the other maintains that leaders are themselves the products of unfolding events over which they have little, if any, control. We should not go far wrong, however, in suggesting that leaders with obvious psychopathic tendencies can wreak havoc on the international scene, given a situation that is sufficiently unstable and followers who are momentarily susceptible. Certainly the occurrence of an Adolf Hitler in our century is sufficient evidence of this possibility.

The vagaries of the countless language systems in use throughout the world also provide fertile ground for misunderstanding and a general failure of communication. Words like "democracy," "freedom," and "human rights" often translate differently in different tongues, although they are used indiscriminately by political leaders who have little in common ideologically. Misunderstandings that occur through failures of language, however, are only a small part of those conflicts that are generated by a simple failure of different national and cultural groups to understand the bases for differences in their attitudes and value systems.

Despite the appearance of the "utter confusion" that often seems to characterize coalition formation and decision making on the international scene, we do have some well established psychological principles which, if applied, might bring about more orderly and rational interactions among sovereign states. Let us consider one psychologically based approach that has received serious attention.

Conflict Resolution

Reciprocal de-escalation. A competitive response by one's partner in the Prisoner's Dilemma situation is a stimulus for one to retaliate in kind. The result of a series of such episodes is that the players become trapped in a competitive situation from which there is no exit. Nations often present a similar picture of entrapment, and they exascerbate the situation further by escalating the threats that each possesses for the other. Is there any way out of this dilemma?

Osgood (1962) has suggested that by adopting a different type of strategy nations could reduce and control threats and tensions rather than create additional ones. Such a joint strategy would have to be introduced unilaterally by one of the antagonists, and the success of the venture would depend upon the other following suit. The technical name for this policy is *graduated reciprocation in tension reduction*. Appropriately nicknamed GRIT, this policy is proposed by Osgood as a means of reversing the current trend toward escalation of the arms race, with all of the attendant conflicts and tensions that this involves. It is an application of the Golden Rule, with built-in safeguards. In its essentials, GRIT requires that one of two disputants do the following: (a) Unilaterally take some conciliatory action, such as closing down a military base to which the other side objects. The step that is taken should not be of such magnitude as to reduce the initiator's capacity for retaliation should his opponent take it as a sign of weakness and attack. (b) The action should be announced prior to its execution, and its role in a planned program of tension reduction should be made clear. (c) The unilateral step should be accompanied by an explicit invitation for the other side to reciprocate in some manner. (d) Once it has been announced, the action should be taken on schedule regardless of whether the other power has indicated an intention to reciprocate. (e) These unilateral initiatives should be continued for a period of time, even if they are not reciprocated, in order to convince the opponent that they are reflections of a sincere and genuine policy of gradual tension reduction.

Osgood makes clear that the opponent must eventually learn the following rules of the game: (a) If he tries to change the status quo by force, we will resist forceably. (b) If he takes unfair advantage of our initiatives, we will shift to firm resistance. (c) If he reciprocates our moves by taking steps to reduce tensions, we will reward him by taking even larger steps in this direction. This, as Osgood (1967) points out, amounts to the familiar process of *shaping behavior* on an international scale. A combination of positive and aversive control is used, because an opponent faces the possibility of nuclear retaliation should he misinterpret the unilateral steps toward de-escalation as signs of weakness. "The kind of de-escalation embodied in GRIT," says Osgood, "includes firm resistance to aggressive attempts by an opponent to change the status quo, but it also includes the persistent applications of initiative designed to decrease tensions and increase the prospects for non-violent resolution of conflict" (1967, p. 15).

Risk taking. There is a certain element of risk in this proposed method of reducing the level of conflict in international affairs, insofar as one of the parties in a dispute must unilaterally take actions that slightly weaken its own position. The situation is not entirely unlike the moment in a Prisoner's Dilemma game when one player must make a choice that exposes him to loss but at the same time sets the occasion for his opponent to reciprocate with a move that would maximize the joint outcome.

Under what conditions are individuals willing to take risks? Considerable research has been done on this question, but we still do not have all the answers. It seems logical that risk taking should be influenced by the kinds of consequences that follow from one's choice of action. In one experimental examination of this problem, Edwards (1953) found that subjects gambling on the outcome of scores on a pinball machine took greater risks when gambling with their own money than with either "points" or chips. That is, they showed a preference for bets having a large monetary payoff but a low probability of winning over bets with a small payoff but a high probability of winning. On the other hand, a number of studies have shown that as the monetary incentives are increased, college student subjects behave more conservatively in risk-taking situations (Kogan and Wallach, 1967).

There seem to be wide individual differences in risk taking. Intensive investigation of the role of such personality variables as "defensiveness" and "anxiety" led Kogan and Wallach (1964) to conclude that the traits of rigidity and flexibility in decision making determine how one responds to failure in pursuit of a risky strategy. Persons having apparently fewer emotional problems were more inclined toward conservative choices following failure of a risky strategy. Disturbed individuals, on the other hand, often showed extremes of reaction, some inclining toward even greater risk and others toward greater conservatism. A *risky shift* effect is found not only in certain individuals who may have emotional problems but also in groups where the decision-making process allows a diffusion of responsibility. Greater risk taking, in other words, may tend to occur not only in some types of persons but also in instances where individual responsibility for the consequences can be concealed in a group decision (Kogan and Wallach, 1967).

It is difficult enough to measure personality in the laboratory, let alone in the outside world, where the knowledge gained would be invaluable. In the chapter on leaders and followers we raised some speculations about the extent to which the course of world events has been altered because of an unusually prominent trait of personality possessed by a powerful leader. Although we are seldom in a position to obtain professional diagnostic appraisals of the personalities of politicians and statesmen, there can be little doubt that personality factors play an important, perhaps critical, role in decision making at high levels of government. One method of estimating certain salient personality features of a leader is to scrutinize his utterances. Robinson and Snyder (1965) report the results of a content analysis of the legislative speeches of a number of congressmen done by Margaret Hermann. An effort was made to relate their support for nationalism or internationalism to such manifest traits as security or insecurity, tolerance or intolerance of ambiguity, and a positive or negative valuation of people. Those congressmen who voted nationalistically revealed greater insecurity, intolerance of ambiguity, and a negative orientation toward people — performances characteristic of the "authoritarian personality." Support for internationalism was related to manifestations of personal security, tolerance of ambiguity, and a positive valuation of people. In negotiations in general, individuals who score high in "authoritarianism" usually have been found less willing to compromise and to change their own position; for example, they should fail to reach a collaborative solution to the Prisoner's Dilemma (Sawyer and Guetzkow, 1965). Under some circumstances, of course, rigid or authoritarian persons might be very successful negotiators. The personality characteristics of their opponents as well as the exact nature of the bargaining situation would determine whether their particular dispositions were functional or dysfunctional.

At the present time, we can only speculate about the role of personality in bargaining and decision making. To the extent that measures of personality reveal something about the individual's more stable behavioral dispositions, they are useful in predicting what he is likely to do in certain kinds of situations. And to the extent that social stimulation exercises a large measure of control over what a person does, studies of social interaction will provide us with general principles from which predictions about individual behavior can be made.

Summary   Many aspects of social interaction can be approached from the point of view of *game theory*. In order to achieve more favorable outcomes in game situations, individuals employ different strategies. If only two persons are involved, and the gains of one are equal to the losses of the other, we speak of a zero-sum game. The most conservative strategy in such a situation follows the minimax principle, in which one acts so as to minimize losses and maximize gains.

The most frequently studied nonzero-sum game is the Prisoner's Dilemma, in which a choice by each player to maximize his own gain will result in a less than optimal solution for both. When they have engaged in this struggle over a long period of time, however, a form of cooperative collusion frequently develops between the opponents. This is more likely to occur when the utility of the payoffs is greater, that is, when the payoffs are more potent reinforcers of the decision-making behavior. Ten dollars, in this sense, has greater utility than one dollar. But the subjective expectancy of an outcome — its anticipated probability — also affects what an individual will do, and this combines with subjective utility to determine choice behavior.

Because of the relative ease with which the outcomes can be manipulated and behavior can be recorded, the Prisoner's Dilemma has served as a major research vehicle in the study of decision making using a game theory model. Several factors have been identified that seem to favor either cooperative or competitive strategies in this type of situation. Control over certain of the variables that determine the participant's performances is gained by instructing confederates of the experimenter to employ certain strategies. The results of a number of experiments confirm the general principle that cooperative behavior becomes more frequent when it is reciprocated, that is, when it is reinforced. Situational features that emphasize the competitive aspects of the situation or that minimize the utilities of the outcomes tend to encourage competitive performances.

When the participants to a gaming situation are allowed to communicate verbally with one another, a bargaining process develops that is characterized by the use of threat, the presence or absence of trust, and varying degrees of risk taking. Experiments using a "trucking game" have demonstrated that either unilateral or bilateral use of threat tends to increase the frequency of competitive behavior in situations where there are no tangible reinforcers, that is, payoffs to both parties. The most effective incentive in this situation seems to be money, and a real rather than an imaginary monetary payoff leads to cooperation even under conditions of bilateral threat.

When more than two individuals are involved in a potentially competitive interaction, the formation of a *coalition* is commonly observed. In triads, or groups of three, the two "weaker" individuals frequently unite against the strongest. A plausible explanation for this pooling of minimum resources is that each member of the coalition can anticipate a proportionately greater share of a payoff than if he had aligned himself with the most powerful individual. There is some evidence that females are more prone to achieving accommodative solutions to competitive situations, whereas males behave in a more exploitative manner.

Decision making in international affairs sometimes appears to be best described in terms of an "utter confusion theory." We are still a long way from understanding all of the factors that control strategy, coalition formation, and decision making in large groups or in groups that function at the level of international politics. Cross-cultural studies of the socialization process and developments in personality theory promise to yield information that will increase our ability to predict behavior in the sphere of international events. Even now, some reduction in international conflict might be achieved through the systematic employment of those behavior principles that have been established both experimentally and through field research.

References

BECKER, G. M., and MCCLINTOCK, C. G. Value: Behavioral decision theory. In P. R. Farnsworth, O. McNemar, and Q. McNemar (Eds.), *Annual Review of Psychology.* Palo Alto, Calif.: Annual Reviews, Inc., 1967.

BIXENSTINE, V. E., and WILSON, K. V. Effects of level of cooperative choice by the other player on choices in a Prisoner's Dilemma game. *Journal of Abnormal and Social Psychology,* 1963, 67, 139–147.

BOND, J. R., and VINACKE, W. E. Coalitions in mixed-sex triads. *Sociometry,* 1961, *24,* 61–75.

BROWN, R. *Social psychology.* New York: The Free Press, 1965.

BURGER, E. *Introduction to the theory of games.* Englewood Cliffs, N.J.: Prentice-Hall, 1963.

CRUMBAUGH, C. M., and EVANS, G. W. Presentation format, other-person strategies, and cooperative behavior in the Prisoner's Dilemma. *Psychological Reports,* 1967, *20,* 895–902.

DEUTSCH, M. Trust and suspicion. *Journal of Conflict Resolution,* 1958, 2, 265–279.

DEUTSCH, M., and KRAUSS, R. M. The effect of threat upon interpersonal bargaining. *Journal of Abnormal and Social Psychology,* 1960, *2,* 181–189.

DEUTSCH, M., and KRAUSS, R. M. Studies of interpersonal bargaining. *Journal of Conflict Resolution,* 1962, 6, 52–76.

DRESHER, M. *Games of strategy: Theory and applications.* Englewood Cliffs, N.J.: Prentice-Hall, 1961.

EDWARDS, W. Probability preferences in gambling. *American Journal of Psychology,* 1953, *66,* 349–364.

EDWARDS, W., LINDMAN, H., and PHILLIPS, L. D. Emerging techniques for making decisions. In T. Newcomb (Ed.), *New directions in psychology, II.* New York: Holt, Rinehart and Winston, 1965.

EVANS, G. W., and CRUMBAUGH, C. M. Effects of presentation format on cooperative behavior in a Prisoner's Dilemma. *Journal of Personality and Social Psychology,* 1966, *3,* 486–488.

GALLO, P. S. Effects of increased incentive upon the use of threat in bargaining. *Journal of Personality and Social Psychology,* 1966, *4,* 14–20.

GAMSON, W. A. Experimental studies of coalition formation. In L. Berkowitz (Ed.), *Advances in experimental social psychology.* Vol. I. New York: Academic Press, 1964.

HAYWOOD, O. G., JR. Military decision and game theory. *Journal of the Operations Society of America,* 1954, 2, 365–385.

KOGAN, N., and WALLACH, M. A. *Risk taking: A study in cognition and personality.* New York: Holt, Rinehart and Winston, 1964.

KOGAN, N., and WALLACH, M. A. Risk taking as a function of the situation, the person, and the group. In T. M. Newcomb (Ed.), *New directions in psychology, III.* New York: Holt, Rinehart and Winston, 1967.

KOMORITA, S. S. Cooperative choice in a prisoner's dilemma game. *Journal of Personality and Social Psychology,* 1965, *2,* 741–745.

KRAUSS, R. M., and DEUTSCH, M. Communication in interpersonal bargaining. *Journal of Personality and Social Psychology,* 1966, *4,* 572–577.

LUCE, R. D., and RAIFFA, H. *Games and decisions.* New York: Wiley, 1957.

MARSCHAK, J. Scaling of utilities and probability. In M. Shubik (Ed.), *Game theory and related approaches to social behavior.* New York: Wiley, 1964.

McCLINTOCK, C. G., and McNEEL, S. P. Reward level and game playing behavior. *Journal of Conflict Resolution,* 1966, *10,* 98–102.

MINAS, J. S., SCODEL, A., MARLOWE, D., and RAWSON, H. Some descriptive aspects of two-person, non-zero-sum games. II. *Journal of Conflict Resolution,* 1960, *4,* 193–197.

NEUMANN, J. VON, and MORGENSTERN, O. *Theory of games and economic behavior.* Princeton, N.J.: Princeton University Press, 1944.

NEWCOMB, T. M. Autistic hostility and social reality. *Human Relations,* 1947, *1,* 69–86.

OSGOOD, C. E. *An alternative to war or surrender.* Urbana, Ill.: University of Illinois Press, 1962.

OSGOOD, C. E. Escalation and de-escalation as political strategies. *Phi Kappa Phi Journal,* 1967, *47,* 3–18.

OSKAMP, S., and PERLMAN, D. Factors affecting cooperation in a prisoner's dilemma game. *Journal of Conflict Resolution,* 1965, 9, 358–374.

OSKAMP, S., and PERLMAN, D. Effects of friendship and disliking on cooperation in a mixed motive game. *Journal of Conflict Resolution,* 1966, *10,* 220–226.

PRUITT, D. G. Reward structure and cooperation: The decomposed Prisoner's Dilemma game. *Journal of Personality and Social Psychology,* 1967, 7, 21–27.

RADLOW, R. An experimental study of "cooperation" in the Prisoner's Dilemma game. *Journal of Conflict Resolution,* 1965, 9, 221–227.

RAPOPORT, A. Formal games as probing tools for investigating behavior motivated by trust and suspicion. *Journal of Conflict Resolution,* 1963, 7, 571–579.

RAPOPORT, A. *Two-person game theory.* Ann Arbor, Mich.: University of Michigan Press, 1966.

RAPOPORT, A., and CHAMMAH, A. M. *Prisoner's dilemma.* Ann Arbor, Mich.: University of Michigan Press, 1965.

ROBINSON, J. A., and SNYDER, R. C. Decision-making in international politics. In H. Kelman (Ed.), *International behavior.* New York: Holt, Rinehart and Winston, 1965.

SAWYER, J., and GUETZKOW, H. Bargaining and negotiation in international relations. In H. Kelman (Ed.), *International behavior.* New York: Rinehart and Winston, 1965.

SCODEL, A., and MINAS, J. S. The behavior of prisoners in a "Prisoner's Dilemma" game. *Journal of Psychology,* 1960, *50,* 133–138.

SCODEL, A., MINAS, J. S., RATOOSH, P., and LIPETZ, M. Some descriptive aspects of two-person non-zero-sum games. *Journal of Conflict Resolution,* 1959, 3, 114–119.

SERMAT, V. Cooperative behavior in a mixed motive game. *Journal of Social Psychology,* 1964, *62,* 217–239.

SHUBIK, M. (Ed.) *Game theory and related approaches to social behavior.* New York: Wiley, 1964.

THIBAUT, J. W., and KELLEY, H. H. *The social psychology of groups.* New York: Wiley, 1959.

UESUGI, T. K., and VINACKE, W. E. Strategy in a feminine game. *Sociometry,* 1963, *26,* 75–88.

VINACKE, W. E. *Negotiations and decisions in a politics game.* Technical Report No. 13, Office of Naval Research, September, 1968.

VINACKE, W. E., and ARKOFF, A. An experimental study of coalitions in the triad. *American Sociological Review,* 1957, *22,* 406–414.

WHITE, R. K. Misperception and the Vietnam war. *Journal of Social Issues,* 1966, *22,* 1–164.

WILLIAMS, J. D. *The compleat strategyst.* New York: McGraw-Hill, 1966.

VENTTSEL, E. S. *An introduction to the theory of games.* Boston: D. C. Heath, 1963.

Author Index

Full references to an author's work may be found on the italicized pages.

Subject Index

Academic performance, reinforcement of, 44
Accidental reinforcement, *see* Noncontingent reinforcement
Acquired behaviors, 61
Action attitude, 323, 337
Action research, 192
Affiliative behavior, 36
Aggressive behavior, 20–21, 78, 84, 107
Anticipation of reinforcement, 79–81
Anxiety, 30
Area probability sampling, 359
Argument organization, in persuasion, 385–387
Aristotle, 4
Assumed similarity (ASo) score, 167–169, 246
Attitude:
    action, 323, 337
    verbal, 323, 337
Attitudes:
    acquisition and shaping of, 307–314
    affective components of, 301–302
    cognitive components of, 302–305
    definition of, 300
    implicit and overt, 305–307
    organization of, 314–320
    pathological, 323–325
    and persuasibility, 391–393
    political, 180
    as predictors, 322–323
    referents of, 300, 307
    situational control of, 320–323
Attitude scaling, 337–349
Authoritarianism, 165–166, 229–231, 326
Authoritarian personality, 162, 230, 324, 442–443; *see also* F Scale
Autokinetic movement:
    group influence on, 140–143
    reinforcement of, 143
Autonomic nervous system, 18, 31
Aversive control of behavior:
    with children, 89–92
    and conformity, 109–110
    in group discussion, 213
Aversive stimulation, 35
Avoidance behavior, 40, 41–45
Awareness, and verbal conditioning, 290–291

Bacon, Sir Francis, 6
Bales interaction categories, 201
Bandwagon effect, 112
Bargaining, 431–438
Basic personality type, *see* Modal personality
Beliefs, 319–321

Bennington College study, 180, 236
Biased sampling error, 356
Boomerang effect, 380
Brain stimulation, 38

Causality, 2
Chaining, 38, 41, 48–50
Chance sampling error, 357
Child behavior, 74–93
Child-rearing practices, 71–74
Classical conditioning, 28–30, 301, 303–306
Coalition formation, 413, 436–438
Coercive power, of leader, 242–243
Cognitive dissonance, 373
Cognitive theory, 54–56
    in persuasion, 370–374, 404–405
Commitment:
    and conformity, 111–112
    and persuasibility, 394
Communication, in animals, 21–22, 262–267
Communication, in humans:
    reinforcement model, 269–274
    sources of error in, 258–259
    systems model, 257–258
Communication networks:
    durability of, 195–197
    efficiency of, 194–195
    manipulation of, 193
    and participant satisfaction, 197–199
    and reinforcement, 199–200
Communicator credibility, 378–382
Comparative psychology, 19–23
Competence, and status, 118–121
Competition, 208–215
    in game playing, 424–431, 432–435
Compliance, forced, 127–128
Comte, Auguste, 5
Concept formation, 274
Conditioned aversive stimuli, 40–42
Conditioned emotional reaction, 29–31
Conditioned reinforcement:
    and language, 257
    theory of, 36–39
Conditioned response, *see* Classical conditioning
Conflict, 40, 104
Conformity behavior:
    definition of, 102
    following commitment, 112
    generalization of, 112
    and group cohesiveness, 115–116
    and imitation, 104–105
    personality factors in, 121–124